LEGAL ASPECTS
OF THE MUSIC INDUSTRY

LEGAL ASPECTS OF THE MUSIC INDUSTRY

An Insider's View

RICHARD SCHULENBERG

BILLBOARD BOOKS
An imprint of Watson-Guptill Publications / New York

Executive Editor: Robert Nirkind
Editor: Sylvia Warren
Senior Production manager: Hector Campbell
Designer: Jay Anning, Thumb Print

ISBN: 0-8230-8364-0

First published in 2005 by Watson-Guptill Publications,
Nielsen Business Media, a division of The Nielsen Company
770 Broadway, New York, NY 10003
www.watsonguptill.com

Library of Congress Control Number: 2005920216

Printed in the United States
First printing, 2005

2 3 4 5 6 7 8 9 / 10 09 08

CONTENTS

List of Sample Contract Provisions   xi
Foreword   xxiii

INTRODUCTION   1

CHAPTER 1
FORMATION AND OPERATION OF GROUPS   3
Corporation or LLC?   4
Ground Rules   6
    Decision Making   6
    Who Owns the Group Name?   7
    Profits and Losses   8
    Songwriting/Publishing   9
Concert Riders   10
    Billing   11
    Advertising   12
    Recording the Performance   12
    Merchandising   13
    Tickets   14
    Let's Eat   17

CHAPTER 2
THE ANATOMY OF A RECORD COMPANY   20
A&R   21
Business Affairs and Legal   22
Sales, Merchandising, and Distribution   22
Art and Editorial   24
Promotion   24
Publicity   25
Artist Relations   25
Licensing, Accounting, and Royalties   25
Special Products and Merchandising   25
International   26
Publishing   26

CHAPTER 3
ARTIST RECORDING AGREEMENTS   27
Term of the Agreement   28
Exercise of Options   35
    Advance on Exercise of Option   38
    Advance Payable When Option Period Commences   39
    Advance Payable on Delivery   40
    Notice of Option   40
    Timely Exercise of Option   41
The Recording Commitment   44
    Negotiating a Maximum   47
    Delivery   50
    A Cautionary Tale of Nondelivery   52
Suspension and Termination   54
    The Impact of Suspension on Term of the Agreement   55
    Alternatives to Suspension   56
Force Majeure   59
Royalties   62
Wholesale or Retail   63
Percentage of Sales   65
Royalty Acceleration   68
Returns and Reserves   71
Freebies   75
Record Clubs   77
Foreign Sales   82
Compact Discs   87
Electronic Transmission   90
Premium Records   92
Budget and Mid-Line Records   94
    Budget Records   95
    Mid-Line Records   96
Container Charges   98
Cross-Collateralization   101

To Katie and Amy, the best daughters a Dad could have—
who have tolerated 'ol Dad all these years and who have
the good sense not to follow directly in his footsteps.

To the next generation, Kalan, Connor, and Harper—the future.

To my brother Bob, who first taught me to love music.

To my parents, who never could quite figure out
just exactly what it was I was doing—but let me do it anyway.

To Arlene, for her infinite patience and support.

Special thanks to my editor, Sylvia Warren,
for being able to survive this twice.

The manuscript was edited with a pen from
"The Law Offices of Daniel I. Simon"; thanks for the ink, Dan.

And, finally, to whoever in his or her infinite wisdom first said:

Non Aequus Est
IT AIN'T FAIR

The Recoupment of Advances   103
    Recording Costs   106
    Master Purchases   108
    The Recording Fund   108
MPTF and Special Payments Funds   116
Promotion Costs   117
Artist/Production Company Royalties   119
Accounting   121
    Audits   122
Coupling   125
Joint Recording   129
Unrecorded Masters   130
Release of Recordings   135
Equitable Relief   137
Sampling   145
Grant of Rights   148
Warranties and Representations   153
Rerecording Restrictions   158
Key Man Clause   165
The Morals Clause   163
Label   165
Name   167
Publicity   173
Merchandising   177
Artwork and Photographs   181
Notice Provisions   184
Sideman   186
Group Provisions   188
Ownership of Musical Compositions   191
Rate   196
Inducement   202

CHAPTER 4
INDEPENDENT
PRODUCER AGREEMENTS   206
Duties of the Producer   206
Term of the Agreement   210
Production Fee   211
Recording Costs   213
Producer's Royalty   215
Record One   217
Publicity and Advertising   219

CHAPTER 5
MASTER PURCHASE   222
Master Purchase Agreements   222
Purchase Price   223
Incorporation by Reference   225
Transfer of Ownership   226
Delivery   226
Warranties and Representations   227
Transfer of Copyright   229
Lease of Masters   230

CHAPTER 6
PRODUCTION
AGREEMENTS   233
Royalties   235
Production Company–Producer   240
Injunctive Relief   243

CHAPTER 7
OPTION AGREEMENTS   246
Term of the Option   247
Exercise of the Option   248
The Recording Commitment   249
Incorporation by Reference   250
Rights on Nonexercise   251

CHAPTER 8
VIDEO AND DVD   255
What Is Video?   255
Video Rights   257
Guaranteed Video   259
Production Costs   261
Video Royalties   263
Music Rights   265

CHAPTER 9
SONGWRITERS'
AGREEMENTS   269
Term of the Agreement   270
Writer As Recording Artist   274
The Songwriting Commitment   277
Songwriter Compensation   280

Purchase Price   280

Exclusive Agreements
and Songwriter's Guaranteed Advance   282

Songwriter's Share of
Mechanical License Fees   287

Public Performance Fees   288

Print Rights   292

Synchronization Licenses   294

Miscellaneous Income   296

Songwriter's Share of Foreign Receipts   296

Nonshared Advances   298

Demonstration Costs   299

Cowriters   300

Songwriter Warranties
and Representations   301

Grant of Rights by the Songwriter   304

Equitable Relief   307

CHAPTER 10
COPUBLISHING
AGREEMENTS   310

Which Compositions?   311

Term of the Agreement   312

Territory   313

Ownership   314

ADMINISTRATION   316

Costs   318

Performing Rights   322

Arm's Length   324

Right of First Refusal   325

CHAPTER 11
ADMINISTRATION
AGREEMENTS   328

Duties of the Administrator   330

Term of the Agreement   334

Territory   336

Compensation   337

Costs   339

Obtaining Information
from the Copyright Owner   340

CHAPTER 12
FOREIGN SUBPUBLISHING
AGREEMENTS   342

Term of the Agreement   343

Territory   344

Advances   345

Fees   347

Costs   348

Payment   349

Duties of the Subpublisher   353

The Black Box and
Other Evil Companions   355

CHAPTER 13
MERCHANDISING   358

Term of the Agreement   358

Territory   360

Rights Licensed   361

Royalty   362

Advances   364

Trademarks   364

CHAPTER 14
SOUNDTRACKS   367

Duties of the Music Supervisor   368

Duties of the Composer   370

Duties of the Film Producer   374

Employment Status   375

Certificate of Authorship   377

Loan-Out Agreements   378

Exclusivity   381

Grant of Rights   381

Retention of Rights   385

Credit   387

Sources of Income   390

  Creating the Soundtrack   390

  Source Music   393

  Soundtrack Albums   394

  Synchronization Licenses   396

  Master Use License   398

  Performing Fees   399

  Mechanical Fees   401

  Miscellaneous Income   405

CHAPTER 15
PERFORMANCE,
PERFORMING, AND
NEIGHBORING RIGHTS   406
American Performing Rights Societies   407
ASCAP   408
BMI   411
SESAC   412
International Copyright Overview   412
Foreign Societies   413
Neighboring Rights   416
The Rome Convention of 1961   419
    Performers' Rights   420
    Producers' Rights   421
Broadcasting Organizations   422
National Laws on Neighboring Rights   423
    China   424
    France   424
    Germany   425
    Italy   426
    Japan   426
    Latin America   426
    Russian Federation   426
    Sweden, Denmark, Norway,
    Finland, and Iceland   427
    Spain   427
    United Kingdom   428

CHAPTER 16
DISTRIBUTION AGREEMENTS   429
Term of the Distribution Agreement   430
Territory   431
Distributor's Obligations   433
Company's Obligations   435
Exclusivity   438
Product   439
Conversion of Artists   440
Representations and Warranties   443
Distribution Fees   446
Free Goods   447
Reserves   449
Inventory   451
Termination   453

CHAPTER 17
MANUFACTURING AND
SECURITY AGREEMENTS   456
Manufacturing   456
Security   459

CHAPTER 18
FOREIGN DISTRIBUTION
AGREEMENTS   463
Territory   464
Product   465
Rights Granted to Licensee   466
Royalties, Advances, and Costs   468
Guaranteed Release   471
Payment   474
Supplying of Materials and Product   475
Trademarks   477
Cover Records   479
Rights on Termination   480

CHAPTER 19
DIGITAL TRANSMISSION   484
Rights Licensed   484
Territory   486
Compositions   487
Royalty   489

CHAPTER 20
COPYRIGHT   493
Copyright Definitions   494
Copyright Infringement   498
Subject Matter of Copyright   499
Exclusive Rights in the Copyright   502
Section 107—Fair Use   504
Section 109—Limitations on
Exclusive Use: Effect of Transfer of
Particular Copy or Phonorecord   507
Section 110—Limitations on
Exclusive Use: Exemption of Certain
Performances and Displays   509
Section 112—Limitations on
Exclusive Use: Ephemeral Recordings   509
Section 114—Scope of Exclusive
Rights in Sound Recordings   510

Section 115—The Compulsory License   512

Determination of the Statutory Rate   519

Section 116—The Jukebox Exempion   521

Section 118—Noncommercial
Broadcasting   522

Fairness in Music Licensing Act   522

Term of the Copyright   526

Audio Home Recording Act   527

Work for Hire   530

Sampling   532

Transfer of Copyright   533

CHAPTER 21

THE DIGITAL MILLENNIUM
COPYRIGHT ACT   535

Getting into the Act   536

*Section 1201: Circumvention of
Copyright Protection Provisions*   536

*Section 1202: Integrity of Copyright
Management Information*   537

Section 1203: Civil Remedies   539

*Section 1204: Criminal Offenses
and Penalties*   540

File Sharing   541

CHAPTER 22

PERSONAL MANAGERS   544

Manager Acting As Agent   546

Personal Management Agreements   551

Commission   551

Term of the Agreement   553

Escape   553

Obligations of the Manager   554

Disclaimer   555

Review of Employment   555

Exclusivity for Artist   556

Nonexclusivity for Personal Manager   556

Closing Thoughts   556

CHAPTER 23

TURN OFF THE LIGHTS
WHEN YOU LEAVE   558

LIST OF SAMPLE
CONTRACT PROVISIONS

Administration Agreements

Administrator Has Exclusive Rights 328

Administrator Has Right to License
Subpublishing 329

Administrator to Make "Best
Efforts to Exploit" Compositions 332

Administrator's Duties 330

Administrator's Duties: Short Form List 331

Coadministration 333

Compensation: 20% Fee 338

Compensation: Higher Fee
Due to Advance 338

Compensation: Higher Fee
for Cover Records 338

Exclusive Grant of Rights 329

Information to Be Supplied
by Copyright Owner 341

Lists of Expenses to Be
Charged Back to Owner 339

Net Receipts Paid to Publisher 340

Term of the Agreement: Administrator's
Decision to Extend Term 335

Term of the Agreement: Decision
to Extend Term Must Be Mutual 335

Term of the Agreement: Five-Year Term 335

Term of the Agreement: Minimum
$300,000 in Initial Term Before Admin-
istrator Can Exercise First Option 335

Term of the Agreement: Term
Tied to Individual Compositions 336

Term of the Agreement: Term
Tied to Recoupment of Advance 336

Territory 337

Worldwide Exclusive Right
to Administer 332

Artwork and Photographs

Artist May Submit Photographs
for Covers 183

Artist's Approval in 5 Business Days 182

Artist's Right of Consultation 183

Only Photographs and Biographies
Submitted by Artist 183

Overbudget Costs Charged to Artist 183

Budget Records (*See* Reduced Royalty Rate Record Categories)

Copublishing Agreements

10% Administration Fee Off the Top 320

15% Administration Fee Off the Top 319

50%–50% Split 316

Administration Fee Higher
for Cover Records 320

Administrator's Duties and Rights 317

Arm's-Length Rates 324, 325

Conditional Copublishing Agreement 315

Copublisher As Administrator 317

Copublisher's Share Increases
with Each Option Period 315

Copublishing Agreement Tied
to Recording Agreement 311

Copyrights Owned Jointly 311

Exclusive Administrator 316

Life of the Copyrights
As Implied Term 313

Life of the Copyrights
As Specified Term 313

No Administration Fee 320

Ownership and Income Split Differently 312

Performing Rights: Administrator
Receives Full Payment 323

Performing Rights: Direct Payment
After Recoupment of Advances 323

Performing Rights: Direct Payment,
Including Administration Fee 323

Right of Refusal: Mutual No First
Refusal for Entire Catalogue 325

Right of Refusal: One-Sided No First

Refusal If Entire Catalogue Is to Be Sold   326
Right of Refusal: Time Limit On   326
Schedule of Compositions "Added
to From Time to Time"   311
Territory Is the U. S. and Canada   314
Territory Is the Universe   314
Territory Is the World   314

Delivery

Delivery Requirements   52, 53
Delivery and Form I-9   53

Digital Transmission

Controlled Composition   488
Licensee's Responsibility for
Mechanicals and Performance Royalties   487
Licensor Responsible for Payments   488
Licensor's Responsibility for Obtaining
Licenses for Compositions   487
Limitation of Rights Licensed   485
Publishing Information   487
Rights Licensed   485
Rights Licensed: Short Form   485
Royalties: The Miniseries—A Percentage   490
Royalties: The Sequel Miniseries—
Dollars and Cents   491
Similar to a Traditional
Distribution Agreement   489
Technical Terms, Digital Agreement   486
Territory Is the World   486
Territory, Restricted   487

Distribution Agreements

Conversion: Incorporation by Reference
of Distribution Agreement   443
Conversion: Production Agreement
Attached   442
Conversion: Separate Production
Agreement in Case of Conversion   443
Distributed Label's Obligations   436, 437
Distribution Fees: Company's
Share After Deducting Distribution Fee   446
Distribution Fees: Example   446
Distributor's Contractual Obligations   433
Distributor's Obligations as Basic

Services   433
Exclusive to Specified Market   438
Exclusivity: Distributor's Right Not to
Distribute Rejected Product   439
Exclusivity: Record Club Sales Excluded   439
Free Goods: Value of Free Goods Shipped
Incorporated in Invoice Price   447
Inventory: Distributor Entitled to Scrap
Excess Product   452
Inventory: Risk of Loss Borne by
Company   452
Liquidation of Reserve at One-Sixth
Per Month   451
Minimum Sales Requirement   430
Product: All Recordings Released on
Specified Labels   440
Product: Distributor Has Right to
Distribute "Each and Every Master"   440
Product: Distributor to Accept "Every
Master"   440
Product: The Right to Cherry-Pick   440
Representations and Warranties:
Distributor Indemnified   445
Representations and Warranties: Scope   444
Reserves: Higher Reserve for Singles   450
Reserves: Liquidation Begins in
Seventh Month   451
Reserves: Liquidation of Reserve
at One-Sixth Per Month   451
Term: 14 Months Plus Three 1-Year
Options   431
Term: 3 Years Plus Two 1-Year Options   431
Term: Minimum Sales Requirement   430
Termination: Company Financially
Responsible for Returns   453
Termination: Optional Cutout
Notice; Special Reserve   454
Territory Is the United States   432
Territory: North America Is Territory   432
Territory: Ships, Aircraft, Oil Rigs, and
Marine Installations Count   432

Equitable Relief

Annual Minimum
Compensation Guaranteed   144
Incorporate Code Provisions   143

Minimum Compensation for Entire Group 143
Superstar Method   144
Unique and Extraordinary Services   144

Exercise of Options

Automatic Exercise—
10 Days' Notice of Nonexercise   44
Automatic Exercise—30 Days'
Notice of Nonexercise   43
Classic 10-Day Notification   42
Negate Exercise of Option   44
Notification Prior to Expiration   43
Option with Conditional Advance   43
Record Company/Production Company   44

Force Majeure

Basic Force Majeure   60
Force Majeure, 6 Month/30 Day   61
Force Majeure, 12 Month/10 Day   61

Foreign Distribution Agreements

Cost of Materials Borne by Distributor   476
Cover Records: 10-Week Hold-Back
on Cover Records   480
Cover Records: 2-Month Hold-Back on Cover
Records   480
Grant of Rights: Example   267
Grant of Rights: Export Provision and
Limited Configuration   267
Guaranteed Release: Guaranteed
Release of All Top 100 Records   472
Guaranteed Release: Top 100 Singles
and Albums/Minimum of 50%/
Soundtrack Albums   474
Guaranteed Release: Top 100/Minimum
of 20%/Soundtrack Albums   473
Payment: All Taxes Paid by Distributor   475
Payment: Paid in Dollars   474
Product: All Product Not Excluded
from the Territory   466
Product: All Product on Licensor's
Three Labels   465
Product: All Product Released in
the United States   466
Royalties, Advances, and Costs: Advance
As Guaranteed Minimum Royalty   470

Royalties, Advances, and Costs:
Costs Borne by Distributor   469
Termination: Parties' Rights   481
Termination: Product to Be Destroyed
After 180 Days   483
Territory: Colombia and Venezuela   464
Territory: Germany, France, Italy, Spain 464
Trademark License   478
Trademark Protection: Quality
Control Essential   479

Foreign Subpublishing Agreements

Copyright to Remain in
Publisher's Name   354
Exclusive Right to Administer
in Territory   342
Fees: 20% of Gross Receipts   347
Fees: 20% of Net Publisher's Share   348
Fees: 25% of Gross Receipts   348
Fees: Subpublisher's Share 50%
for Cover Records   348
Gross Receipts   349
Net Income   349
Payment Defined   349
Payment Procedures   350
Rolling Advance   346
Signing Advance   346
Subpublisher As Exclusive
Administrator   343
Subpublisher's Duties   353
Subpublisher's Right to Administer   353
Term of 5 Years or Expiration
of Rights   343
Term: 3-Year Term; Option for
Second 3-Year Term on Payment
of Additional Advance   344
Term: 5-Year Term   344
Term: 6-Month Extension
for Recoupment   344
Territory: France and Belgium   345
Territory: Italy   345
Territory: U.K. and PRS Territories   345
Waiving New Advance Upon
Recoupment Lowers
Subpublisher's Fee   346

Freebies and Record Clubs (*See* Reduced Royalty Rate Record Categories)

Grant of Rights

Artist Grants Rights   153
List of Rights Granted   156

Group Provisions

Access to the Box Office   16
Approval over Advertising   12
Artist's Control of Tickets   16
Artist's Control Over
Advertising Content   12
Artists'Rooms: Not So Simple   18
Artists'Rooms: Relatively Simple   17
By-Laws Provision and
Corporate Resolution   7
Complimentary Tickets   17
Copyrights Jointly Owned   10
Counterfeit Tickets   15
Designated Member Can Make Decisions   6
Each Member Owns Their Own Songs   10
An Exhaustive (and Exhausting)
Listing of a Label's Rights   151
Group Contract Provisions—Recording
Contract [Chapter 3]   189
Group/Label Contract Provisions   189
Informal Agreement of Form Corporation   5
Intention to Form Corporation   5
Leaving Member Has No Right
to Use Name   7
Misuse May Cancel Concert
and Forfeiture of Deposit   12
Name Owned by Founding Member   7
New Member Bound by
Name Restrictions   7
No Bottom Left Behind   15
No Recording Equipment or Cameras   13
Penalty for Miscount   16
Profits and Losses Divided Equally   8
Profits Shared in Different Portions   8
Promoter Provides Merchandising Stall   14
Promoter Responsible for [All?]
Recording Costs   13

Pro-Rata Royalty   9
Royalties of a Member Who Left Can't
be Used for Subsequent Recordings   9
Sole and Exclusive Right to
Sell Merchandise   14
Sole Headline Billing   11
Sole Star Billing   11

Independent Producer Agreements

Checklist of Duties   207
Company May Replace Producer   211
Conditional Option to Continue   211
Credit Obligations Detailed   219
Credit on Half-Page or Larger Ads   219
Credit: Producer Shall Be Given
Credit in All Paid Advertising   219
Credit: Producer Shall Be Given Credit   219
Excess Recording Costs Producer's
Responsibility   214
Fee Amount Per Selection   212
Fee as an Advance   212
Fee Not an Advance   212
Fee Payment Schedule   213
Nonexclusive Producer   211
Producer's Creative Duties   207
Producer's Responsibility for Form I-9s   208
Recording Costs Charged to Artist   214
Recording Fund: Over 110%   214
Recoupment of Production Fee   218
Retroactive to First Record Sold   218
Royalty: 3% with Escalation   215
Royalty: 3%; Paid as Production
Company Is Paid   216
Royalty: Credited from Record One   218
Royalty: Direct Payment/Same
Calculation as Artist   216
Session Discontinued for
Exceeding Budget   214

Inducement

Artist–Independent Entity:
Inducement Clause   203
Artist's Inducement Letter and
Acknowledgment   203
Sample Inducement Letter   203

Key Man clause

Delayed Termination   162

Dual Key Man   162

Label

Any Label   166

Any Label Plus Coupling   167

List of Acceptable Labels   167

Same as Best-Selling Artists   167

Same Label as Major Artists   167

Manufacturing and Security Agreements

Manufacturing: Delivery
Requirements for Manufacturing   457

Manufacturing: Distributor to Be
Manufacturer   456

Manufacturing: Payment Deferred   458

Manufacturing: Payment Prior to
Manufacture   458

Manufacturing: Record Label
Responsible for Manufacturing   457

Manufacturing: Record Label to Use
Distributor's Designated Manufacturer   456

Security: Everything You Can
Think of Is Collateral   460

Security: Grant of Security Interest   459

Security: Post Bond and
Personal Guarantee   461

Security: What Does Collateral Cover?   461

Master Purchase

Copyright: Instruments of Transfer   230

Copyright: Sell, Transfer,
and Assign Copyright   230

Delivery Checklist   227

Delivery: When and Where   227

Incorporation by Reference:
"Deemed to Have Been Made"   225

Incorporation by Reference: Exhibit
Incorporated by Reference   225

Lease of Masters: 10-Year Lease   231

Lease of Masters: Rights
Granted to Record Company   231

Purchase Price Cross-Collateralized   224

Purchase Price: Cost of Recording   224

Royalty Adjusted After Recoupment   224

Transfer of "All Right, Title, and Interest"   226

Warranties and Representations   228, 229

Merchandising

Advance Recoupable   364

Merchandising Rights Granted   179

Rights Licensed: Clothing   361

Rights Licensed: Just About Everything   362

Rights Licensed: Perfume   361

Rights Licensed: Video Games   362

Royalty: 20% of Gross Receipts   363

Royalty: 35% of Net Income   363

Royalty: 50% of Net Receipts   363

Royalty: 50%of Net Monies   363

Signing Advance and Option Advances   364

Standalone Agreement   359

Term Coterminous with Distribution
Agreement   359

Term Coterminous with Production
Company/Record Company Agreement   359

Territory: Entire World   360

Territory: Limited Territory   361

Territory: United States and
Canada Only   361

Types of Products   180

Mid-Line Records (*See* Reduced Royalty Rate Record Categories)

The Morals Clause

Morals Clause—Felony   165

Morals Clause—
"Substantially Brings . . ."   164

Morals Clause—"Tending to . . ."   164

Morals Clause—Violation of the Law   165

Name

Company Must Approve Name Change   172

Company's Right to Use Name   173

Federal Trademark Registration   173

Group Name   171

Leaving Member Has No Right to Use Name   7

Name Owned by Founding Member   7
New Member Bound by
Name Restrictions   7

Notice Provisions
Change of Address   185
Classic Notice Provision   185
Courtesy Copy   185
Personal Service Permitted   185

Option Agreements
Demo Minimum of Four   250
Exercise: 7 Months Within
Which to Give Notice   248
Exercise: Distributor Agreement with
Major Label Prerequisite for Exercise   248
Exercise: Exhibit A Incorporated
As the Agreement   250
Exercise: Good-Faith Negotiations
May Extend Period   249
Exercise: Option May Be Exercised
up to Last Moment   248
Four Demos, One Album, And. . .   250
Masters: Four—No More No Less   250
Masters: Two—No More No Less   250
Nonexercise: Override (Long Form)   252
Nonexercise: Payback and Override for
Contract Based upon Demos   252
Nonexercise: Payback and Override   252
Nonexercise: Producer's Right to
Use Masters If Option Not Exercised   252
Term: 1 Year; Start Recording
within 60 Days   00
Term: 10 Months from Signing or
6 Months from Recording   248
Term: 6 Months from
Delivery of Demos   247

Ownership of Musical Compositions
Separate Songwriter's Agreement/All
Compositions   194
Only Compositions Written
During Term   198
Owned or Controlled by
Production Company or Artist   199
Copublishing   195

**Premium Records (*See* Reduced
Royalty Rate Record Categories)**

Production Agreements
All-Inclusive Royalty   236
Cap on Royalty Paid to New Producer   242
Conversion of Artist   234
Injunctive Relief: Production Company
Guarantees Injunction Provision   245
Injunctive Relief: Production Company
Guarantees Payment   244
Injunctive Relief: Superstar Insurance   244
Mutual Approval of Producer   242
Producer Paid Directly   242
Producer's Future Right Subject
to Meeting Shipping Criteria   242
Production Company
Furnishes the Artist   234
Production Company Responsible for
Direct Payment of Royalties to Artist   236
Production Company's Right to
Change Artist's Royalty Computation   240
Pro-Rata Royalty for Artist   236
Pro-Rata with Double Dipping   239
Responsible for Royalties to Artist
and Producer   234

Publicity
Any and All Products or Services   176
Artist to Appear for Publicity Purposes   175
Basic Right of Publicity—Artist   174
Basic Right of Publicity—Group   174
For Purpose of Trade   175
Promotional Merchandise   175

Rate
Controlled Compositions/Excess
Charged to Artist   199
Earlier Date to Determine Rate   200
Production Company and Rate   201
Three-Quarters Rate   198
Variable Rates   198

Record Clubs (*See* Reduced Royalty Rate Record Categories)

Recording Commitment

Adjusted Minimum Commitment	49
Duration Extended by Overcall	49
Limit on Additional Masters	49
Minimum or More	48
Minimum Recording Obligation Tied to Sales	48
Minimum Recording Obligation	48
Studio Masters Specified	49

Reduced Royalty Rate Record Categories

1-year Restriction on Release of Premiums	94
75% of Rate Escalating to 80% of Rate	89
Artist's Right to Approve Premium Offers	94
Broad-Based Freebie Policy—Share Net Receipts	81
Budget and Mid-Line Royalty Three-Fourths	97
CDs at One-Half Royalty Rate	89
CDs at Three-Fourths Rate on 80% of Sales	89
CDs at Vinyl Royalty Rate	89
Consent Required After 1 year	97
Definition and Royalty Rate (50% of Otherwise Applicable) for Budget Records	96
Definition of Budget Record	96
Definition of Mid-Price Record	97
Definition of Premium 93	
Electronic Transmission 91	
Freebies and Record Clubs	77
Higher Packaging Deduction for CDs	89
Limitation on When Budget Records Released	96
Mid-Line Royalty Five-Eighths	97
Mid-Line Royalty Two-Thirds	97
No-Royalty Premium Clause94	
One-Half Royalty; Product/Moral Conflict	94
Record Clubs: One-Half Royalty	77
Tape or Analog Rate on 85% Plus Packaging Reduction	91
Telemarketing, Club, Paid on Excess	80

Release of Recordings

Artist's Option to Terminate	137
"Commercial Release" Defined	137
Contingent Release	137
No Obligation to Record or Release	136
Right to "Refrain" from Sale	136

Rerecording Restrictions

Cap of 6 Years	160
5-Year/2-Year Formula	160
Flawed Formula	160
Possible Further Extension	160
Special Provision for Unreleased Masters	160

Returns and Reserves

Pro-Rata Credit on Returns	77
"Reasonable" Reserve	74
"Reasonable" Reserve, 30% Limit	74
"Reasonable" Reserve," 35% Limit	74
"Reasonable Reserve," Liquidation Schedule	75

Royalties

A Laundry List of No-Royalty Deductions	76
Acceleration Based on Recordings and Sales	69
Acceleration Based on Sales Only	69
Accounting: 2 Years Plus 2 Years	124
Accounting: Biannual Royalty Accounting Periods; 90-Day Time Limit on Objection	124
Accounting: Manufacturing Records Excluded	124
Accounting: Quarterly Accounting Periods	124
Adjusted Base Rate	70
Advances and Recoupment: Advance Reduced by Unrecouped Balance	111
Advances and Recoupment: Advances for Injunction	112
Advances and Recoupment: Advances—General	110
Advances and Recoupment: All Monies (Except Royalties) Advances	110

Advances and Recoupment: Minimum/
Maximum after Second Album   115

Advances and Recoupment:
Minimum/Maximum Based on Royalty   114

Advances and Recoupment: Production
Company and Artist Share Advances   113

Advances and Recoupment: Recording
Costs Shared by Artist and Production
Company   113

Advances and Recoupment:
Recording Fund Payment Schedule   111

Albums 85%, Singles 80%   67

Artist's Right to Approve Premium Offers 94

Audit   124

Broad-Based Freebie Policy—
Share Net Receipts   81

Budget and Mid-Line Royalty
Three-Fourths   97

Calculation of Wholesale Price   64

CDs at One-Half Royalty Rate   89

CDs at Three-Fourths Rate on
80% of Sales   89

CDs at Vinyl Royalty Rate   89

Change Wholesale to Retail   64

Consent Required After 1 year   99

Container Charges: Analog 20%,
Other 25%   100

Container Charges: Special Packaging 100

Container Charges: Vinyl 15%,
Tape 20%, CDs 25%   100

Container Charges: Vinyl 15%,
Tape 25%   99

Coupling Rights "In Perpetuity,
Throughout the Universe"   128

Coupling: Limit on Number of Coupled
Albums   128

Coupling: Proportionate Royalty/
Prior Consent   127

Coupling: Royalty Rate Based on
Cuts and Time   128

Coupling: Tip-Offs to Coupling Rights

Cross-Collateralization:
". . . and/or affiliates"   103

Cross-Collateralization: ". . . This
and/or Any Other Agreement"   103

Cross-Collateralization: All
Agreements as One Accounting Unit   103

Cross-Collateralization: Limit
on Cross-Collateralization   103

Definition and Royalty Rate
(50% of Otherwise Applicable)
for Budget Records   96

Definition of Budget Record   96

Definition of Mid-Price Record   97

Definition of Premium   93

Electronic Transmission   91

Excess Free Records Based on Formula 81

Flow-Through   120, 121

Foreign Sales: Blocked Funds   86

Foreign Sales: One-Fourth Reduction 86

Foreign Sales: Same Rate of Exchange;
Blocked Funds   86

Foreign Sales: Traditional
One-Half Foreign Royalty   85

Foreign Sales: Variable
Reduction by Territory   86

Freebies and Record Clubs   77

Higher Packaging Deduction for CDs   89

Joint Recording Definition
and Royalty Formula   130

Joint Recording Formula   130

Joint Recordings and Recording Costs 130

Limitation on When Budget Records
Released   96

Mid-Line Royalty Five-Eighths   94

Mid-Line Royalty Two-Thirds   94

Moral Conflict/Product:
One-Half Royalty   94

MPTF Payments Not Charged to Artist 117

MPTF Payments Not Recording Costs   113

MPTF Payments Not Recoupable   117

Ninety Percent of Net Sales   66

Normal Retail Channels
in the United States   70

No-Royalty Premium Clause   94

One Hundred Percent or 90 Percent—
Conditional   66

One Hundred Percent—Record Club 85% 66

One Hundred Percent—Modified by
Licensees   67

Premiums: 1-year Restriction on Release 94

Production Company/Artist: Royalties
and Advances Shared Pro-Rata   121

Promotion Costs: 50% Charged to Artist 118
Promotion Costs: Minimum Dollar
Amount Specified 119
Pro-Rata Credit on Returns 77
Rate: 75% Escalating to 80% 89
"Reasonable Reserve," Liquidation
Schedule 75
"Reasonable" Reserve 74
"Reasonable" Reserve, 30% Limit 74
"Reasonable" Reserve," 35% Limit 74
Record Clubs: One-Half Royalty 77
Royalty on the Basis of
Constructed Price 65
Same Percentage of Net Sales 67
Suggested Retail List Price 64
Tape or Analog Rate on 85%
Plus Packaging Reduction 91
Telemarketing, Club, Paid on Excess 80
Union Costs Limited to Those
Based on Payroll 117

Sampling

Artist Indemnification for Samples 147
Permission Delivery Requirements 146
Royalty Payments for
Sampled Material 147
Sample Clearance as Delivery
Requirement 144

Sideman

Artist Exclusivity 187
Group Members as Sidemen 187
Three Conditions 187

Songwriters' Agreements

Advance $500/"Purchase Price" 281
Advances Not Shared 298
Advances Paid in Three Installments 00
Advances Tied to Record Contract 285
Advances Yearly and Weekly 283
Commitment Equals
Controlled Compositions 279
Company's Right to Change
Music and Words 301
Division of Royalties to Cowriters 300

Equitable Relief: Company Has Right
to Make Up Minimum for Equitable
Relief under California Law 308
Equitable Relief: Loan-Out Company
to Make Minimum Payment 308
Equitable Relief: Minimum under
California Law Guaranteed 308
Foreign Print Royalties 298
Grant-of-Rights Shopping List 306
Grant of Rights: Single-Song Agreement 305
Half of Demo Costs As Advance;
Cross-Collateralization 299
Half of Demo Costs Recoupable 299
Independent of Record Contract:
1 Year Plus Four 1-Year Options 272
Independent of Record Contract:
2 Plus 2 Plus 2 Years 273
Independent of Record Contract:
3 Years Plus Two 1-Year Options 273
Independent of Record Contract:
Later of 1 Year from Commencement
or Delivery 274
Miscellaneous Income 296
Minimum Commitment of
15 Compositions per Year 278
No Commercial Use of Demos 300
No Separate Recording Agreement,
No Advances 276
Periods Extended for Nondelivery 280
Periods Tied into Delivery
under Separate Record Contract 275
Print Royalties 293–294
Publisher's Right to Add New
Music or Lyrics 301
Purchase of Preexisting Works 282
Song Writer Paid Directly; Writer
Has No Claim to Publisher's Share 292
Songwriter's Share of Mechanical
License Fees 288
Songwriter Paid Directly 291
Songwriting Commitment and
Advances Tied to Record Contract 275
Submissions Must Be "Satisfactory" 279
Synchronization Royalties 295
Tied to Record Contract: Artist to
Make "Reasonable" Effort to Acquire
Compositions Not Written by Artist 272

Tied to Record Contract: Copublishing (Company Affiliate and Company Designated by Artist)   272

Tied to Record Contract: Coterminous Period   272

Tied to Record Contract: Grant of Rights   271

Tied to Record Contract: Single-Song Agreement Attached   271

Warranties, Representations, and Indemnification   302

Weekly Advances   284

Writer Designates Payment Schedule   284

Writer Has No Claim to Publisher's Share   291

Writer Is Not to "Unreasonably" Withhold Consent to Settlement   303

Writer Represents That He Has Not Elsewhere Agreed to a Controlled Composition Clause   303

Soundtracks

Composer Duties: Composer and Record Producer   373

Composer Duties: Length of Score   372

Composer Duties: Score and Soundtrack   371

Composer Duties: Score and Title Song   373

Composer as Music Supervisor   370

Copyright: Copyright Retained by Composer   387

Copyright: Music Supervisor Retains 50% of Copyright   385

Copyright: Producer Assigns Copyright to Composer   386

Copyright: Supervisor Assigned Copyright   387

Credit: "Composed and Performed By"   388

Credit: Conditional Credit   388

Credit: Credit Provisions   387

Credit: Individual Screen Credit   387

Credit: Single Card Credit on the Same Card   387

Employment Status: Copyright in Producer's Name   376

Employment Status: Definition of Work for Hire   376

Employment Status: Loan-Out Work for Hire   377

Employment Status: Moral Rights— Certificate of Authorship   377

Exclusive During Employment   381

Exclusivity Period Specified   381

Film Producer's Duties: Responsible for Licenses   375

Film Producer's Duties: What Costs Will Not Be Charged to Composer   375

Film Producer's Duties: Changes and Travel Expenses Film Producer's Responsibility   374

Film Producer's Duties: What Company Will Provide   375

Grant of Rights   382

Grant of Rights: Lender and Composer   383

Grant of Rights: Producer's Right to Composer's Name and Likeness   382

Inducement Letter   379

Lender's Warranties and Representations   379

Lending Company Agrees to "Cause Composer to Comply"   378

Lending Company Agrees to Exclusivity   379

Master Use License: Credits   399

Master Use License: Nonexclusive Assignable Rights   399

Master Use License: Simple Grant to Use Master Recording   398

Mechanical Fees: Broadcast Mechanicals   404

Mechanical Fees: Writer Paid 50% of Mechanical License Fees   404

Miscellaneous Income: 50% of Miscellaneous Income   405

Miscellaneous Income: Composer Gets Percentage of Net   405

Music Supervisor/Recording Session Producer   370

Music Supervisor's Duties   369

Nonexclusive; First Position Rights   381

Performance Fee Not Paid by Producer   400

Performance Fees Not Paid by Publisher   400

Performance Fees Paid by Writer Directly   400

Soundtrack Albums: "Usual and Standard Recording Costs" Recouped   395

Soundtrack Albums: Composer
Royalty from Soundtrack Album   395
Soundtrack Albums: Supervisor's and
Producer's Cut of Album Deal   395
Source Music as Separate Budget Item   393
Source Music Distinguished
from "Scores and Recordings"   394
Source Music: Artist's Share   394
Sources of Income: Flat Fee   392
Sources of Income: Flat Fee—
Songwriter's Agreement   390
Sources of Income: Net of Budget—50%
of Net Proceeds from Record Royalties   392
Synchronization License Included in
Agreement   396
Synchronization License: Composer's
Share of Synchronization
License Fees 50%   396
Synchronization License:
Grant of Rights   397
Synchronization License: Television   397

Suspension and Termination

Extension of Term or Increase in Next
Term's Minimum Commitment   57
Extension of Term or Reduction of
Minimum Number of Masters   57
Suspend, Terminate, and/or Repay   59
Suspension or Termination   57
Suspension with Conditional
Limit on Time   58
Termination   58

Term of Artist Recording Agreements

18 Months Plus Four 1-Year Options   33
18 Months Plus Three 18-Month Options   33
Flat 5-Year Term   33
1 Year Plus Four 1-Year Options   32
Open-Ended   34
Term Adjusted With Limitations   33
Term Based on Delivery—Open Ended   33

Unrecorded Masters

Artist to Notify Company   133
Monetary Payment for
Unrecorded Masters   133

Notice Required; Reduce
Number of Masters   134
One-Half of Recording Fund   134
Union Scale Payment for
Unrecorded Sides   133

Video and DVD

Artist Agrees to Issue
Synchronization Licenses   259
Artist May Appear in Films   259
Artist's Consent to Video   258
Company's Exclusive Rights
to Artist for Videos   258
Definitions: "Audiovisual Work"   256
Definitions: "Sight and Sound Device"   257
Definitions: "Sound Synchronized with
Visual Images"   256
Guarantees: Company to
Produce One Video Per Album   260
Guarantees: Good-Faith Negotiation
Regarding Video Production   260
Guarantees: Minimum Budget
Guaranteed   261
Music Rights: $100 Synchronization Fee   266
Music Rights: Free Licenses or Fees
Deducted from Artist's Royalties   267
Music Rights: Synchronization License
Fees Waived for Owned Compositions   266
Production Cost Recoupment   262
Production Costs: Definition   261
Royalties: 50% Recoupment from
Record Royalties   262
Royalties: Definition   263
Video Grant of Rights   258
Video Royalties   264

Warranties and Representations

Artist Warrants, Represents,
and Indemnifies   156
Basic Warranties, Representations,
and Indemnification   155
Detailed Indemnification   157
Production Company   156

FOREWORD

I have spent over thirty years in the music business and there is one area which still baffles and frightens me—the "legal" end of the industry. Those of us who have survived and prospered learned early on the importance of relying on professionals to protect our interests. Those who didn't learn this lesson didn't survive. I know better than to try to do my own legal work—if we accept the old saying that "a lawyer who represents himself has a fool for a client," what can we call artists, producers, or writers who try to represent themselves? My advice: Writers should write, artists should perform, managers should manage. You get the point. Still, a strong working knowledge of the law of the music business is essential, if for no other reason than to recognize that problems exist and that help is often a necessity. This book, *Legal Aspects of the Music Industry*, is an invaluable resource for music industry professionals and nonprofessionals alike. Reading it not only answered many questions and cleared up many mysteries for me, it also alerted me to dangers I hadn't even known were there. If there is anything important about the music business that Richard missed in writing the book, I sure didn't find it.

The amazing thing about *Legal Aspects of the Music Industry* is that while it looks like a textbook, it is actually fun to read. To illustrate points—and sometimes just because it's a good story—Richard has filled the book with personal anecdotes and experiences from his many years in the business.

I used to think the film *Spinal Tap* was the only place where you could get insights into the music business and laugh at the same time. Now I know better.

I don't know a more comprehensive and more important book for anyone who wishes to become a part of the music industry. From now on, if anyone asks me about how the music business works or how to get started in the business, the first thing I'm going to say is: "There's this book. It's called *Legal Aspects of the Music Industry*. Get it. Read it. Then come back to me."

—DENNY DIANTE
September 1999

FOREWORD TO THE SECOND EDITION

A little over five years has gone by since I wrote the Foreword to the first edition of *Legal Aspects of the Music Industry.* If anyone had told me then that the music industry would have changed as much as it has during those years, I would have told them they were out of their minds.

Thank God that in the last Foreword I praised the book (which I still do) but didn't go into details about the technicalities of the content. If I had, I wouldn't have been able to recycle my earlier praise and build on it. It's still the best damn book around about the music business! Reading this new edition was for me like getting a *Best of* CD of my favorite artist and finding a whole new bunch of tracks on it, all great.

The industry may have changed radically, but my boy Richard is still on top of it. If you want to know where the music business has been, where it's at now, and where it's going, you've cracked open the right book.

—DENNY DIANTE
January 2005

INTRODUCTION[1]

*For without music, life is a journey through a desert
that has not ever heard the rumor of God.*

—PAT CONROY, *Beach Music*

This book is a study of both the legal and practical aspects of the music industry, written not only through an analysis of representative contract provisions in music industry agreements, but also on the basis of my own experiences in the trenches. Don't be intimidated by the legal stuff. That it's hard to understand is a myth that we lawyers like to perpetuate to keep ourselves in business. If you run across something that's really hard to understand, it's probably not your fault. More likely than not, it's bad drafting. There's something about a lawyer and a blank piece of paper or a computer screen that seems to breed turgid writing.

We lawyers love to rewrite other people's work—think of a dog marking his territory. In my first job out of law school, the head of Legal said he wanted to review everything I wrote. Several times a day I would bring a pile of documents to his office for review. Shaking his head in disapproval, he would cross out words, add new ones, and circle phrases, indicating with an arrow where they should be moved. When he was done, most sheets looked like a chalkboard from an advanced physics class. I became depressed. Was I really that bad a writer? In a moment of divine inspiration I had my secretary retype one of his memos with that day's date and my name on it, then shoved the memo into the middle of the daily pile. When he got to the memo, he shook his head, rolled his eyes, and marked it up as usual. I had learned a valuable lesson. Give a lawyer a document and if it hasn't already gone out, he will change it.

The longest chapter in this book, Chapter 3, deals with artist recording agreements and the provisions which make up those agreements. These provisions are the basic building blocks of contracts in the music industry—the DNA. They represent the fundamental concepts also used in other music industry agreements, such as production agreements, producer's agreements, songwriter's agreements, publishing agreements, and even label distribution agreements.

The contract examples are all from my own files. Some are cited as originally submitted, before negotiations; some were modified, reflecting negotiated changes. Usually, more than one example of each type of provision is included, illustrating the truism that there is more than one way to skin an artist.

The voluminous examples also illustrate how deadly dull contract provisions can be. But beware!—you skip them at your own risk, because buried in those boring provisions are veins of gold and veins of fool's gold.

---

[1] To quote Orson Welles: I have the terrible feeling that, because I am wearing a white beard and am sitting in the back of the theatre, you expect me to tell you the truth about something. These are the cheap seats, not Mt. Sinai.

The trick is learning the difference.

One of the first tricks to learn is the nasty secret about "standard contracts." The secret is, There is no such thing. There just aren't any one-size-fits-all contracts. Sure, I have my standard contract, but so does the guy next door—and they are probably entirely different. *Never* fall for the line: "Oh, just sign it. It's a standard contract."

My hope is that a firm understanding of these agreements will give the reader a base from which to expand his or her knowledge of the music industry. Hope does spring eternal—but please never forget that the music business is, like all industries, profit-driven. This particular industry finds it profitable to exploit an art form. Most record companies are shoving containers of whatever the current configuration of recording is out the door, not art. Let's face it, they are in the business of selling stuff—and you are responsible for creating the art. Mind you, when we say business, we mean BUSINESS. Ultimately, we are not talking about some mom-and-pop operation. We are talking about a multinational multi-billion-dollar industry (albeit that the record end of the business has begun to shrink, we are, still, talking billions).

One thing which is not included in this work (apart from the occasional war story thrown in by way of illustration)—but which should be an essential field of study for anyone who wishes to be a part of this strange and wonderful industry—is history. Please learn as much of the history of our business as you can cram into the corners of your brain.

If you want to succeed in the music industry (or any industry) you need a working knowledge of what went before. It wasn't just the invention of word processors that increased the size of recording agreements from the one page of the earliest days to pushing 100 pages today. As new technology developed, new provisions were created. As new markets opened up, so did still more new provisions. Sometimes to understand the "why" of a provision you have to know where it came from.

If you are serious about becoming a professional in the music business, the most important thing for you to understand is that it is made up of relationships. All of the entertainment industry runs on nepotism—but not the form of nepotism most people think. Sure, there are sons and daughters and nephews and nieces who get breaks, but the real nepotism involves the extended family, not the blood family. As time passes you gather a family of friends about you whom you know you can depend upon. If I need somebody to do something, I reach out to someone I've worked with before. If I don't already know someone who fits the particular requirements, I call someone in my "family" and ask for a recommendation.

Build that family. These are the people with whom you will be spending your professional life.

Oh yeah, finally, there's that Latin phrase you might have noticed on the dedication page:

Non Aequus Est

This was not meant as a cheap way of trying to display a little learning but to distill the essence of this work. Memorize it, burn it into your brain, and it will help maintain your grip on the reality of the music industry—and on sanity. Translated (freely), *Non Aequus Est* means:

IT AIN'T FAIR

or, as someone informed me: "The only fair is the county fair."

Don't ever say I didn't warn you.

CHAPTER 1

FORMATION AND OPERATION OF GROUPS

HENRY:

From this day to the ending of the world,
But we in it shall be remember'd;
We few, we happy few, we band of brothers;

—WILLIAM SHAKESPEARE
Henry V, Act IV, Scene 1

So you wanna be in a group? Getting together. Banging away on your instruments. Can fame and fortune be far away? The road to fame and fortune has many major potholes cratering the gold bricks. Next to lack of talent, perhaps even tied for first, one of the biggest obstacles to success for a group is self-destruction. Drummers in the band Spinal Tap may have been prone to spontaneous human combustion, but *all* musical groups are prime candidates for spontaneous group implosion, another term for self-destruction.

The first step down the slippery slope of self-destruction for a group is not to formalize the relationship between the members. Sort of a musical prenup. Memory is both fleeting and selective. Get your understanding down in writing before minds wander. Early on in the relationship, when everyone's memory is still fresh and everyone is still in agreement, put it in writing! Until things get serious, you don't need a lawyer to do this for you. Just write out your understanding in your own language and have everyone sign off.

Having "formalized" your relationship, there's good news and there's bad news. The good news is that you've taken the first step toward vaccinating yourself against group implosion. The bad news (which probably isn't that bad unless, of course, something bad happens;—see below) is that you have formed a "general partnership." Now there's nothing inherently bad about a general partnership except for one important detail: Each individual partner is personally liable for the debts of the partnership and for the acts of the other partners in the business of the partnership.

Here are the sort of liabilities that can pop up in a partnership:

Example

Buster, your bass player, driving the van with the equipment to a gig, is distracted by the blonde in the Jaguar and crashes into a school bus, triggering a string of accidents culminating with the destruction of the local nuclear power plant, resulting in ... well, you get the idea. Buster, a free spirit, neglected to get automobile insurance. All the individual members of the partnership are now responsible for the resulting hundreds of millions of dollars in damages.

Example

Snake, the vocalist, in a moment of inspiration block-books this wonderful recording studio on a private ranch in Montana for the month of February at a mere $20,000 per week, neglecting to do three things: (1) to take into consideration that the ranch is isolated under 15 feet of snow in February; (2) take his medication; and, as a result, (3) not only neglects to tell anyone else that he booked the studio, but forgets doing it himself. *All* the partners are individually responsible for the $80,000 studio bill.

Now that you've had the b'geebers scared out of you, what do you do about it?

CORPORATION OR LLC?

> FLAVIUS:
>
> **They answer in a joint and corporate voice,**
>
> —WILLIAM SHAKESPEARE
> *Timon of Athens*, Act II, Scene 2

To avoid the potential problems of a partnership, a group should organize itself into either a corporation or a limited liability company (LLC). There are two basic reasons for any group to organize itself as either a corporation or an LLC. The primary reason is, of course, to avoid liability. Especially if you have a potential Buster or Snake in your group. The second reason is tax planning.

The choice between forming a corporation or an LLC is based upon a given group's needs, but to be frank, there's not that much practical difference between the two. There are *some* differences between the two types of organizations, differences which may vary from state to state. Both types will protect individuals as shareholders (corporation) or members (LLC) from personal liability from debts of the organization. Note, however, that, depending on the jurisdiction, directors and/or officers of a corporation may still be held liable and managing managers of an LLC may be held liable.

One of the pitfalls of general partnerships is that any general partner can incur an obligation or liability on behalf of the partnership (see Buster and Snake, above). With a corporation, only officers and directors can obligate the corporation. Individuals, as shareholders, are not responsible for the acts of the directors, officers, or the corporation itself. In the Buster and Snake examples, if they had been officers or directors of the corporation, the corporation, but not the individual shareholders, could be held liable for the damages and the costs. With LLCs, the question of liability gets a little tricky. In organizing the LLC, there are two ways of handling it:

1. All the individuals making up the LLC are "members" and, as with a general partnership, their acts can obligate the LLC to debts and liabilities.

2. Under the other method, certain "members" can be made "managing members" and only they have the ability to obligate the LLC.

In the Buster and Snake examples, under the "members can obligate" method, the LLC would be responsible. Under the "managing members" method, if Buster was not a manager but Snake was, the LLC would not be liable for contaminating a large portion of North America, but the LLC would be liable for booking the snowbound studio in Montana. The bottom line: Corporation or LLC, serious thought should be given to taking out insurance.

The other main reason for forming a corporation or an LLC is that both provide various forms of tax relief generally unavailable to individuals. Corporations and LLCs can choose between different methods of taxation. The reasons behind choosing a corporation or an LLC and choosing the method of taxation will vary from case to case and, sometimes, depending on location (some laws vary from state to state). When the times comes to make this move, it is best to rely on the advice of professionals. The prevention of problems is always cheaper than scrambling to clean up the problem after the fact.

A method I like to suggest for groups "in transition" (not quite ready to invest in a corporation or LLC) is a "preincorporation agreement" setting out the group's intention to incorporate and specifying the current understanding of the members as to how the corporation will operate when it is formed.

SAMPLE CONTRACT PROVISIONS

EXAMPLE 1: Intention to Form Corporation

12. CORPORATION. The Members agree that the Corporation will be formed as a corporation and shall be entitled ["NAME"] or other mutually agreeable name.

(a) The Members agree that of the shares of stock to be initially issued by Corporation, such stock shall be distributed as follows:

Member 1: Twenty Five (25%) Percent;

Member 2: Twenty Five (25%) Percent;

Member 3: Twenty Five (25%) Percent; and

Member 4: Twenty Five (25%) Percent;

(b) Each of the Members shall initially serve as a member of the Board of Directors of the Corporation.

(c) The Members acknowledge that the above pre-incorporation provisions are a memorandum of the understanding and agreement of the Members, and that more details will be provided in the Minutes of the Board of Directors and in the By-Laws of the Corporation when formed.

☛ This paragraph sets forth the intention of the parties to form a corporation; that each
   member shall own 25% of the stock of the corporation; each member will serve on the
   board of directors; and the details of the operation will be worked out when the
   corporation's directors hold their organizational meeting.

EXAMPLE 2: Informal Agreement to Form Corporation

The undersigned members of "[Group]" have agreed to form a corporation when there is either the unanimous agreement of the undersigned to form the corporation or for the signing of a record contract. Until that time, the undersigned have agreed to perform together under the following rules and understanding. . . .

☛ A self-penned agreement between members of a group setting forth their intention to
   incorporate.

GROUND RULES

> ULYSSES:
>
> **The specialty of rule hath been neglected,**
>
> —WILLIAM SHAKESPEARE
>
> *Troilus and Cressida*, Act I, Scene 3

Whatever the form of the organization—partnership, corporation, or LLC—it is important to lay out the group's own intentions as to the ground rules for the group. There is no "one way" for any of these rules, nor is there necessarily a "right" or "wrong" way to do any of these (until, of course, it is too late). Each group has its own needs and expectations. Different groups may approach the same question and come up with totally different solutions, which may succeed brilliantly or fail miserably. What follows are different issues, in no particular order, which members of a group should consider, reaching their own solutions.

Decision Making

Who is going make the decisions for the group? Does one individual make the business decisions? Or does the group collectively make the decisions? Is unanimous agreement required? Or a majority? Who chooses which songs to record? Is there a designated spokesperson for the group? Is there a "point" person for contact?

When a corporation or an LLC is formed, at least some of these questions will usually be taken care of and documented in the organizational meeting.

SAMPLE CONTRACT PROVISIONS

EXAMPLE 1: Designated Member Can Make Decisions

14. GROUP: In connection with the operation of the Group, [the designated individual member] shall be deemed to be the "business manager" of the group when time specific decisions must be made and the Group as a whole cannot be consulted in a timely manner.

> ☞ This agreement requires the unanimous agreement of the members for any decision. It does, however, recognize that circumstances may arise where time is of the essence and the members may be scattered hither and yon (wherever those two places may be).

EXAMPLE 2: By-Laws Provision and Corporate Resolution

[By-Laws Provision] Section 2. DAY TO DAY OPERATIONS. The Board of Directors may delegate the management of the day to day operations of the Corporation to a management company or other person, provided that the business and affairs of the Corporation shall be managed and all corporate powers shall be exercised under the ultimate direction of the Board of Directors.

[Corporate Resolution] WHEREAS, the Board of Directors of this corporation deems it to be in the best interests of this corporation and its employees that [Member 1] be designated as the President of the corporation with full power to conduct business on behalf of the corporation based upon directions received from the Board of Directors;

NOW THEREFORE, BE IT RESOLVED, that the President of this corporation be and hereby is authorized and directed to conduct business on behalf of the corporation under the direction of the Board of Directors.

Who Owns the Group Name?

By the time a group has gone through even the most rudimentary organization, a name will probably have been chosen. There are a number of contractual issues involving group names (see, e.g., "Name," pages 167–173, in Chapter 3, "Artist Recording Agreements"). The issue addressed here is entirely internal to the group: who owns the name and who can use it?

This is not as simple as it seems. The name may not even be owned by the group as a whole or by the corporation or LLC (Example 1). It also goes beyond "simple" ownership; it includes who may or may not use the name now or in the future. Some thought should go into what happens if (and when) members leave the group and/or new members join the group (Examples 2 and 3). For a group that becomes successful, there is obvious value in having rights of exploitation of the name. Recent history is filed with legal cases involving name disputes and stories of clashes between former members of groups such as the Beach Boys, the Doors, etc. Better to get it in writing now and avoid grief and expense later.

SAMPLE CONTRACT PROVISIONS

EXAMPLE 1: Name Owned by Founding Member

4. The name [Group Name] shall be owned individually by [Founding Member] and shall be licensed to the Corporation by [Founding Member] at no cost to the Corporation. In the case of any dissolution of the Corporation prior to entering into a record contract, the name shall automatically revert to [Founding Member] without any claims or rights remaining in the name to the Corporation or other members of the Group.

> ☞ A different provision provides for the name to be assigned to the group's corporation if the group signs a recording agreement with a record company. If the group breaks up prior to signing with a record company, the founding member keeps the name and the other members have no rights to the name.

EXAMPLE 2: Leaving Member Has No Right to Use Name

12. Any leaving member of the Group shall have no right to use the name "[Name]" in connection with any commercial endeavor other than the factual statement that such leaving member is a "former member of [Name]" in biographies, resumes, etc. There shall be no reference to such fact in advertising, on album covers, etc., without the prior written approval of the remaining members of the Group.

> ☞ Any member leaving the group may use the name only in connection with bios, resumes, etc. stating that the leaving member is a "former member" of the group, but even this may not be used for advertising, album covers, or any other commercial use.

EXAMPLE 3: New Member Bound by Name Restrictions

7. If any member leaves [Group], either voluntarily or otherwise, the leaving member waives all interest in and to the Name and any right to use the name commercially. Any party joining [Group] shall agree to be bound by the terms and conditions of this agreement. No joining party may be a "member," as defined herein, unless accepted as a member by the unanimous consent of all existing members.

Profits and Losses

There is another important issue which, ideally, should be dealt with in writing up front while everyone is still in a good mood. It's called dividing up the boodle. Most starting groups choose to divide the group's income and losses equally (Example 1). Others choose not to (Example 2).

More complicated is figuring out the best way to divide future royalties for leaving members and/or new members. (See also, the Section on "Group Provisions" in Chapter 3, "Artist Recording Agreements," pages 188–191. Arguably, it should be fairly easy to segregate royalties on an album-to-album basis, but what happens when sales of a new album (minus a leaving member, but with a new member) are used to recoup the recording cost of a prior album (with the leaving member, but not the new member)? Or vice versa, royalties from the old album are used to recover recording costs of the new album?

An example might be a leaving member who is in the black (owed royalties), but his or her money is used to help pay recording costs on a new album from which the leaving member will receive no economic benefit. Or suppose a new member *would be* in the black except sales of the new album are being used to recoup recording costs on the old album. How about this: A "Greatest Hits" album couples recordings with a member who left with those containing a new member. Without the cooperation of the record company, it ain't easy. (See Examples 3 and 4, below.)

SAMPLE CONTRACT PROVISIONS

EXAMPLE 1: Profits and Losses Divided Equally

9. PROFITS AND LOSSES: Any net profits or losses, if any, that may accrue to the Band shall be distributed to or borne by the Band Members in the following proportions:

> Band Member 1: Twenty Five (25%) Percent;

> Band Member 2: Twenty Five (25%) Percent;

> Band Member 3: Twenty Five (25%) Percent; and

> Band Member 4: Twenty Five (25%) Percent;

The terms "net profits" and "net losses" as used in this Agreement shall mean the net profits and net losses of the Band as determined by generally accepted accounting principles for each accounting period provided for in this Agreement.

EXAMPLE 2: Profits Shared in Different Portions

5. The profits, if any, from all sources, including, but not limited to, live performances, royalties of any nature, publishing, licensing, etc., including advances, shall be shared as follows:

> Leader: Thirty-Five (35%) Percent

> Member 2: Twelve and One-Half (12.5%) Percent

> Member 3: Twelve and One-Half (12.5%) Percent

> Member 4: Ten (10%) Percent

> Member 5: Ten (10%) Percent

Member 6: Ten (10%) Percent

Member 7: Ten (10%) Percent

☛ This division reflects a founding member (Leader), senior add-ons (Members 2 and 3), and the newest members (Members 4–7).

EXAMPLE 3: The Royalties of a Member Who Left Can't Be Used for Subsequent Recordings

15. If any member leaves the Group, no royalties shall be due such member on any recording made after such member's departure; provided, however, that such member's share of royalties for recordings made prior to such departure shall not be used for recouping costs for any subsequent recording.

☛ Good luck. Easier said than done without the cooperation of the record company.

EXAMPLE 4: Pro Rata Royalty

(h) In the case of any recording in which my performances are contained are included in a compilation or with recordings by the Group in which my performances do not appear because I was not a member of Group at the time of recording, my applicable percent royalty shall be applied against that portion (to the nearest cent) of the royalty computation price of a given record which the selection(s) performed by me thereon bears to the aggregate of all selections on the said record.

☛ Note that this formula applies only to recordings coupled with recording made after the artist has left the group.

Songwriting/Publishing

A particularly sensitive subject between group members is whose songs will be recorded and who will own the publishing on those songs. The mix of ego and income can become pretty volatile, if not at inception, certainly with success. There is no one *right* answer to the potential problems in this area. This is one of those unique situations where you probably would be wrong even in hindsight. How do you reward the successful writer/composer(s) in a group without ticking off the unsuccessful writer/composer(s)?

Obviously, there are numerous possible variations on how to share (or not share) the songwriters' share and/or ownership of the copyrights. Any or all of the variations, no matter how well intentioned and well thought out, have the potential to breed dissension. Nonetheless, trying to come to an understanding is better than not trying.

One solution I frequently suggest, which gives every member at least a taste of the income from songs even if they do not write, is that the group do one of the following:

1. Each member becomes his or her own publisher (or enters into a separate publishing agreement).

2. (This is more practical.) The group forms a collective publishing entity, owned equally by the members.

Then all of the group's original songs (or, perhaps, original songs recorded by the group) are put either in (a) the individual publishing entities in equal shares or (b) into the publishing company owned by the group. Either way, the group shares collectively in the publishing share of income and each writer keeps the writer's share of the income for songs he or she has written. (See Example 1.)

SAMPLE CONTRACT PROVISIONS

EXAMPLE 1: Copyrights Jointly Owned

13. PUBLISHER: In connection with the operation of the Publisher(s) and the rights and obligations of the Members in connection therein, the Members agree as follows:

(a) A publishing company or companies will be formed with a name mutually acceptable to the Members and with a performing rights society (ASCAP and/or BMI), based upon the individual affiliations of the Members as songwriters.

(b) The Publisher(s) shall be the copyright owner of all musical compositions written and/or controlled by the Members individually which are also recorded by the Group.

(c) The individual Member(s) who compose each such musical composition shall receive the writer's share of income from such composition.

(d) The individual Members shall enter into a songwriter's agreement with the Publisher(s).

☛ The reason for having the possibility of multiple publishers is because the members of the group may not all belong to the same performing rights society (ASCAP or BMI) and the rules are that the publisher, which can affiliate with only one performing rights society, and the writer both belong to the same society. Accordingly, an ASCAP writer can only be affiliated with an ASCAP publisher and a BMI writer can only be affiliated with a BMI manager.

EXAMPLE 2: Each Member Owns Their Own Songs

6. Each Artist hereunder shall retain the copyright in songs written by such Artist; provided, however, for any song co-written with another Artist hereunder the Artists shall share ownership of the copyrights in the same proportion as they share the writers' share, to be determined between them.

☛ This is sort of like an old World War II movie where the soldiers roll up to a sign that reads: "Warning! Land Mines Ahead."

Concert Riders

Getting out and performing before a live audience is important to an artist or group for innumerable reasons, all of which are probably self-evident. The reasons range from everything to "getting your chops together" to building a fan base to attracting a record company to making money. Mind you, making money from live performances is only one of that great triumvirate of money makers: live performance; publishing and songwriting; and merchandising, none of which actually generate money unless the artist is successful. What follows presumes some level of success touring. Down on the first rung of the ladder of success, unfortunately, it's usually "take it or leave it."

Once the artist, an individual or group, reaches some level of notoriety and doesn't need to do self-booking, the artist will probably take on an agent to do the booking. (Note that in some jurisdictions personal managers may not book artists. See the section "Manager Acting As Agent" in

Chapter 22, "Personal Managers," page 546.) Generally, most successful artists use agents for booking. Agency agreements with licensed agents are pretty standard since they are based on union requirements and state regulations.

The one area of the booking contract that can be controlled by the successful artist is what is known as the artist's rider. An artist's rider sets forth the specific needs—personal and professional—of the artist for the concert. The more important the artist, the greater the likelihood that some of the demands will be, to put it politely, bizarre. Yes, it's true about only certain color M&Ms and other dietary peculiarities.

The following examples, which are all from the agreements of headliner artists, provide a general idea of some of the items that are usually included in a rider.

Billing

In the entertainment industry, billing (an artist's credit, including placement, order with other artists, size, prominence, etc.) is what makes the world go round. While ego certainly plays a part, there are important business aspects to billing. Past credits determine future earnings.

SAMPLE CONTRACT PROVISIONS

EXAMPLE 1: Sole Star Billing

1. BILLING. In all headline situations, Artist shall receive one hundred percent (100%) sole "star" billing in any and all publicity releases and paid advertisements, including but not limited to, programs, fliers, signs, lobby boards and marquees. No other name or photograph shall appear in the same type, size, thickness, boldness, and prominence as that accorded to Artist and no other name or photograph shall appear on the same line as that of Artist, or above Artist's name. When not headlining, Artist shall always receive one hundred percent (100%) "special guest star" billing.

EXAMPLE 2: Sole Headline Billing

1. HEADLINE ACT. Unless otherwise stated in the Contract, Artist shall receive one hundred percent (100%) sole headline billing in any and all press releases, advertisements and other publicity including, but not limited to, radio, television, ad mats, tickets, newspapers, programs, fliers, signs, lobby boards, and marquees. Artist shall have approval over each of the foregoing. No other name or photograph shall (i) appear in equal or larger type with respect to size, thickness, boldness or prominence than the type afforded Artist; nor (ii) shall appear on the same line or above the name or likeness of Artist.

2. SUPPORT ACT. If the Contract calls for Artist to perform as a support act, then Artist shall receive one hundred percent (100%) special guest star billing in any and all press releases, advertisements and other publicity including, but not limited to, radio, television, ad mats, tickets, newspapers, programs, fliers, signs, lobby boards, and marquees. Artist shall have approval over each of the foregoing. No other name or photograph of any other support act shall (i) appear in equal or larger type with respect to size, thickness, boldness or prominence than the type afforded Artist; nor (ii) shall appear on the same line or above the name or likeness of Artist.

☛ Hmmm. . . . "Size, thickness, boldness or prominence"; it sounds like unsolicited email spam. Apparently, size does mean something.

Advertising

In addition to protecting the artist's position as King or Queen of the billing mountain, most head-liner riders will provide for strict control over what and how advertising goes out to the public for the engagement. Indeed, usually the artist will insist that materials supplied by the artist (e.g., photographs, radio and television spots, advertising mats, etc.), frequently at a price, will be the only materials used for advertising and promoting the concert.

SAMPLE CONTRACT PROVISIONS

EXAMPLE 1: Approval Over Advertising

f. Artist shall have approval over all advertising and promotions. If requested, Promoter agrees to use all ad mats, photographs and other material provided by Artist. Upon a sell-out of an Engagement, Promoter shall promptly stop all advertising in connection therewith.

☞ This seems pretty mellow; however, as the Promoter in question, I can attest that the "request" was more of a flat statement: "You *will* use our materials." Note the last sentence, which is a smart PR move on the part of the artist's management. You don't want fans blaming the artist if they are urged to buy tickets when all the tickets are already gone.

EXAMPLE 2: Misuse May Cancel Concert and Forfeiture of Deposit

6. Company [furnishing the group] shall supply all advertising materials for use in promoting and advertising the Concert, including, without limitation radio spots, television spots, advertising mats for print, photographs and/or other likenesses used in connection with the Concert. Any variance in use from the materials supplied by Company hereunder by Producer shall be deemed to be a material breach of this Agreement and Company may, in Company's sole discretion cancel the Concert and retain any deposits previously made by Producer.

☞ OK. Now we're getting harsh. The promoter must use Company's materials, but *any* variance in the use of those materials or the use of any other nonapproved materials can mean the cancellation of the concert and forfeiture of any deposits.

EXAMPLE 3: Artist's Control Over Advertising Content

8. In all advertising and publicity, Artist shall be billed as: [Artist's chosen name].

a. When headlining, the Purchaser agrees to use *only* the ad mats supplied by the Artist to promote the Engagement. Promoter also agrees to use *only* the preproduced radio and television spots, the cost of which will be a show expense.

b. When not headlining, the Purchaser agrees to check with Artist's management for any specified artwork *before* printing any posters and/or advertising for this Engagement. The Artist's logo(s), as provided, must be used at all times and a copy of the poster/advertising *must* be sent to Artist's Manager for approval *before* going to print.

☞ Riders are the perfect canvases for a control freaks to paint their personal masterpiece.

Recording the Performance

Artists—and their management, agents, and record companies—do not take kindly to unauthorized recording of performances. Riders invariably have provisions about unauthorized recording, broadcasting, filming, etc., always laying down strict guidelines. Most of the guidelines are blithely ignored by the audience.

SAMPLE CONTRACT PROVISIONS

EXAMPLE 1: No Recording Equipment or Cameras

7. REPRODUCTION OF PERFORMANCE. No portion of the performance rendered hereunder may be broadcast, photographed, recorded, filmed, taped or embodied in any form for any purpose of reproducing such performance without Artist's prior written consent. Purchaser agrees to deny entrance to any persons carrying audio or video recording devices. Without limiting in any way generality of the foregoing prohibition, it is understood to include members of the audience, press and Purchaser's staff.

Purchaser shall provide, at his sole cost, signs at each entrance to the venue saying "SORRY, NO RECORDING EQUIPMENT OR CAMERAS ALLOWED," in large, bold, visible letters. Also, the Purchaser shall provide security at each entrance to check that recorders or cameras are not allowed into the performance or backstage areas.

☛ I have personal knowledge of a concert which was subject to this rider (just call me Mr. Purchaser) and I sure remember hundreds of flashbulbs continually going off all over that stadium. (By coincidence, the evening of the day I wrote this, I attended a charity event at a film studio. On the way out, stopping at the "goody bag" table—bags of gifts from sponsors of the event—I saw several plastic baggies with cameras and driver's licenses in them. Security was holding them for the owners. The event had a "no camera" restriction attached to it and the cameras had been confiscated to be returned to the guests as they left.)

EXAMPLE 2: Promoter Responsible for [All?] Recording Costs

7. Notwithstanding the foregoing [provisions similar to Example 1] Artist shall have the sole and exclusive right to record (audio and/or visual) Artist's performances at no cost to Artist. Purchaser shall secure at no cost to Artist, all approvals, consents and the like required by any third parties in connection therewith including, without limitation, those required by the Venue, and any unions or guilds.

☛ This provision would scare the b'geebers out of me if I were promoting this concert. I'm sure (I think) that this provision is overwritten—requiring more of the promoter than was intended. As drafted, if the Artist decides to record his own concert, the promoter is responsible for paying all recording costs (probably what is intended is no fee for use of the venue); promoter is responsible for obtaining all approvals and consents, such as mechanical licenses, consents to use artists who are under contract to other record companies, etc.; and promoter is responsible for paying union and guild fees (not only musicians and vocalists, but stagehands, lighting crew, etc.). Clearly, the intent of the scope of the promoter's responsibilities is not that all-encompassing. And, then again. . . .

Merchandising

The selling of merchandise at concerts is one of the cash cows for performers. It is generally accepted that major artists can probably make more from the sale of merchandise at concerts than they can from the concerts themselves. The control over sale of merchandise is very important and can be contentious. A promoter renting a venue for a concert may find him or herself in a squeeze between the venue that insists on exclusive control over the sale of merchandise and/or a cut of any sales and the artist who insists that only the artist can sell merchandise at the concert and they ain't splittin' with anybody.

SAMPLE CONTRACT PROVISIONS

EXAMPLE 1: Promoter Provides Merchandising Stall

18. *Merchandising.* The Promoter shall provide a well lit, secure place to erect a merchandising stall. The stall shall be in such a position as to be easily visible to the public using the main entrance. This is to be at no cost to the Artist. Promoter agrees that its arrangement for presenting the Engagement provided for herein shall prohibit the sale of souvenir or similar merchandise on the premises in connection with this Engagement other than Artist's official merchandise furnished by Artist and the receipts shall belong exclusively to Artist. Whether or not the Artist is headlining, Artist shall not be restricted as to the price, number of pieces or types of merchandise that Artist can sell.

☞ Anyone surprised that the Promoter has to pay for the building of Artist's merchandising stall?

EXAMPLE 2: Sole and Exclusive Right to Sell Merchandise

8. Producer [the company providing the services of Artist], or its designee, shall have the sole and exclusive right, without obligation to any party, to sell and distribute merchandise of any kind at the Engagement including, without limitation, merchandise containing the name, voice, likeness and logo of Artist and any member thereof (collectively "Artist's Merchandise"). Unless otherwise agreed to in writing, Producer shall retain one hundred percent (100%) of the gross receipts resulting from the sale of Artist's Merchandise. Promoter shall provide, at its sole cost, well lit, secure, prime locations for merchandising. Artist shall have sole approval over any vendors selling Artist's Merchandise. Promoter shall, at its sole cost, prohibit the sale or distribution of all unauthorized or so-called "bootleg" merchandise on or adjacent to the Venue.

☞ Where to start? Producer has the sole and exclusive right to sell "merchandise of any kind" at the concert, including, I suppose, armaments and drugs. Producer retains 100% of "gross receipts," leaving, presumably, things like sales taxes to be paid by Promoter, even though Promoter has no share of the sale. And how about the provision that says Promoter has to supply, at Promoter's cost, of course, "prime locations"? (Note that's plural.) Finally, not only does Promoter seem to have an obligation to check all merchandising items (including armaments and drugs) to see if they are "unauthorized," the Promoter is also responsible for "adjacent" properties, for example, the guy who lives next door to the stadium and is selling unauthorized armament and drugs from his front lawn.

Tickets

Putting bottoms on seats is the aim of every promoter of concerts. Short of counterfeit tickets or people sneaking in for free, selling tickets to concerts is one of the few areas of endeavor in the music industry that is not subject to piracy. For the artist able to get a percentage of "the door," the sale and other disbursement of tickets is, naturally, immensely important. Remember, the money from live performances is generally free from any recoupment by record companies. There is, however, a gradual drift toward the concept that if the record company contributes to tour support, it is entitled to share in the proceeds.

Presently some promoters and artist representatives are toying with the concept of having a portion of tickets for concerts available by auction on the Internet. Initial experiments all dealt with concerts for charitable organizations—presumably to avoid criticism for scalping. Some of the concerts found that unsold seats could be auctioned off at prices which were a significant multiple of the original price. One can easily imagine the Internet auction prices that could be charged for good tickets for superstar concerts. To the best of my knowledge, riders that address the complexity of determining the artist's share of the gate under these circumstances have yet to be developed.

A review of the following examples will show an understandable if rather obsessive preoccupation with tickets on the part of the artist. Example 4, for example, pretty much dictates to the concert promoter how the promoter is to run the concert, as do various other provisions in many riders. Without some negotiation on the part of the promoter, the promoter may be in the position of "I'll pay you a lot of money so I can have the pleasure of being bossed around by you."

It's reminiscent of something that happened to me in my meager career as a film producer. I was in Rome and was offered the opportunity to produce a Federico Fellini film. It was a great honor to produce a film for this legendary Italian director—until I was told the terms. My job was to provide the money and disappear. In addition, not only could I not see the script, they wouldn't even discuss what it was about. I thought of a story that Abraham Lincoln liked to tell about a man who was tarred and feathered and ridden out of town on a rail and who, when asked about the experience, replied, "If it wasn't for the honor, I would rather have walked"—and I walked.

SAMPLE CONTRACT PROVISIONS

EXAMPLE 1: Counterfeit Tickets

24. With respect to counterfeit tickets, the Promoter is liable for any and all such tickets and under no circumstances should the Artist assume any loss on these tickets.

☛ When the artist is receiving a percentage of the gate, the promoter takes a double hit on counterfeit tickets—the promoter doesn't receive any payment on the seats taken, but must pay the artist's percentage as if the counterfeit ticket was a full-price ticket.

EXAMPLE 2: No Bottom Left Behind

8. Promoter shall deliver to Artist's agent at least two (2) weeks prior to the Concert, a plot plan and printer's manifest of the Venue (including a notarized, signed statement from the ticket printer, listing the amount of tickets printed at each price); provided that Artist or Artist's agent's failure to request, review or comment on the same shall not be deemed a waiver of Promoter's obligations or Artist's rights herein.

a. If a computerized system, such as Ticketmaster, is not used, Promoter agrees to provide Artist, at the Concert, with all unsold tickets for Artist to count and verify.

b. Promoter shall also deliver to Artist, during the Concert, all reports, of any kind, available to

Promoter from any ticket agency (e.g., Ticketmaster) which describe seats at the Venue whether or not such seats are available for sale (collectively "Manifests"). These Manifests shall include, without limitation, box seats, corporate seats, luxury seats, standing-room seats, and subscription seats.

c. Artist shall be compensated for all tickets listed on the Manifests as being sold (at the price stated on the face of the Contract) less (i) approved complimentary tickets (pursuant to this Rider); and (ii) any unsold tickets presented to Artist at the Concert. In addition, Artist shall be compensated for all seats located in the Venue which are occupied during the Concert but not listed on the Manifests (including, without limitation, corporate box seats and permitted standing room): such seats shall be deemed sold for not less than the highest price for which the Venue is scaled.

☞ As you can see, no stone is left unturned to take credit for every seat in the house, including the oxymoron "standing-room seats."

EXAMPLE 3: Penalty for Miscount

21. BOX OFFICE PROVISIONS. Purchaser agrees to have on hand at the place of performance [on] the night of the show, for counting and verification by [a] representative of the Artist, all unsold tickets. Artist shall be compensated for the difference between the number of unsold tickets on hand and shown to its representative and the number of tickets printed as shown by the ticket manifest (a notarized, signed statement from the printer of tickets setting forth the number of tickets sold in each price category). If Purchaser shall violate any of the preceding provisions of [this] paragraph, it shall be deemed that Purchaser has sold a ticket for each seat in the house (and any permitted standing room) at the highest ticket price for which the house is scaled.

☞ Let's see. . . . The ticket count is off by one ticket and the Artist now has the right to be paid on every seat in the house, including permitted standing room, "at the highest ticket price for which the house is scaled." Wow!

EXAMPLE 4: Artist's Control of Tickets

6. [Artist] shall have approval of the sales of tickets including, without limitation, ticket price (including any discounts and premiums), facility fee (if any) and on sale date. [Promoter] shall not sell tickets to the Engagement as part of a subscription or other type of series of other contracts, without [Artist's] written consent. All tickets printed under the manifests shall be on the one stub, one price variety. No tickets shall be sold for seats located to the rear of the stage where the stage and equipment on stage is obstructing normal eye-level viewing of [Artist's] performance, unless the location is clearly indicated as "impaired vision" or "behind stage." [Promoter] shall be solely responsible for counterfeit tickets and [Artist] shall be deemed to be paid on said tickets. If [Promoter] requests or causes tickets to be "pulled," [Promoter] shall be solely responsible for same as if said tickets were purchased, even if [Promoter] attempts to return said tickets.

☞ Note the artist's control over the issuance of tickets, price, kind of tickets, and even the cost of the venue. The "impaired vision" provision is, presumably, to avoid the artist being blamed for ripping off customers with bad seats.

EXAMPLE 5: Access to the Box Office

9. Artist shall have the right to enter the box office at any time (before, during and after performance) to examine and make extracts from the box office records of Promoter relating to gross re-

ceipts of the performance. Promoter shall provide Artist with a written box office statement (certified and signed by the Promoter) within two (2) hours following the performance.

EXAMPLE 6: Complimentary Tickets

25. COMPLIMENTARY TICKETS. Promoter agrees to provide Artist with the following tickets:

(a) Fifty (50) complimentary tickets in a good location for Artist's personal use. Any unused tickets will be released for sale to the public prior to the performance.

(b) Artist reserves the right to request additional complimentary tickets in the following markets: [4 states listed].

(c) Six (6) complimentary tickets in the front row to be held for promotional use. . . .

(d) A minimum of twenty (20) tickets in a good location are to be held for [Record Company] for purchase. . . .

(e) Support artist will be permitted to use twenty (20) complimentary tickets in a good location.

(f) When Artist is not headlining, Promoter must provide Artist with up to thirty (30) complimentary tickets per performance in rows 10–20 directly in front of the stage.

Let's Eat

One of the legendary aspects of riders concerns artists' demands for special amenities. Yes, indeed, the story that M&Ms of a certain color are to be picked out of the mix and banished from a star's dressing room is true. Sometimes pages of information containing intricate menus are attached as exhibits. I have seen riders which dictate the types and even dimensions of furniture for the artist's dressing room. As an artist's success grows, the demands provided for in the artist's riders are likely to become increasingly detailed.

Anytime I read a rider mentioning "Coke," such as Example 2, below, I flash back to earlier, more innocent times. When I first went into private practice, I convinced my old roommate from law school that we should form a law firm. Early on, one of my music clients came to us and asked us to handle his money for him. He explained, "I'm spending too much money on coke."

"Coke?" my partner asked. "Why don't you just drink Pepsi like I do?"

It took a few moments to explain to my partner why the client was lying flat on the floor laughing.

The two examples below are both from riders of headliner stars. Note the curious coincidence that both stars want different bottled water from what the rest of the band receives.

SAMPLE CONTRACT PROVISIONS

EXAMPLE 1: Relatively Simple

STAR ROOM 1: [Star]

Assorted sodas, hot coffee (please include sugar and milk)

Tea (please include lemon and honey)

Gatorade (must be green gatorade), orange juice, ocean spray cranberry juice

One case of Peligrini [sic] water (water cool and at room temperature)

Fresh fruit tray (must include pineapple) veggie tray, potato chips, salsa and chips, 6 hand towels

STAR ROOM 2: BAND'S ROOM

Assorted sodas

Hot coffee (please include sugar and milk)

Tea (please include lemon and honey)

Gatorade, orange juice

One case of Evian water (water cool and at room temperature)

Potato chips, pretzels, salsa and chips,

12 hand towels

☛ By headliner standards this is very basic. Do note, the star gets Pellegrini water while the band gets Evian water.

EXAMPLE 2: Not So Simple

5. BAND DRESSING ROOM:

To be set up by 3:30 PM. Please provide the following items. All drinks to be served on ice with cups and proper openers. Please ensure that all dressing room beverages are iced down throughout the day and ice is replenished as needed. For food items, please provide china or stoneware plates and bowls, and stainless steel forks, knives, and spoons. . . .

a. Twelve (12) liter bottles of spring water

b. Twelve (12) bottles of Budweiser Beer

c. Twelve (12) bottles of Clausthaler nonalcoholic beer

d. Two (2) large bottles of unflavored Perrier

e. Twenty four (24) cans assorted sodas, include Coke Classic and Diet Coke

f. One (1) gallon of fresh-squeezed orange juice

g. One (1) gallon fresh whole milk

h. Six (6) assorted yogurts

i. Fifty (50) 16 oz. Solo cups

j. Six (6) bars of chocolate candy (Hersheys, Nestle Crunch, Snickers). . . . [and so forth with another half-dozen detailed entries]

6. [STAR] DRESSING ROOM:

a. One (1) fresh cheese board with knife

b. One (1) fresh fruit platter

c. One (1) raw vegetable platter

d. One (1) basket of Carrs Tablewater [sic] crackers

e. Three (3) small bags of dry roasted cashew nuts (no added sugar)

f. Twelve (12) small bottles of spring water (Evian, Vittel or similar)

g. Twelve (12) small bottles of sparkling water with lemon, preferably Calistoga or other "Napa" brand.

h. Twelve (12) cans of assorted sodas, including diet sodas

i. Six (6) small bottles of unsweetened apple juice

    j. Hot water setup for tea

    k. English breakfast tea bags

    l. Three (3) packages of dry miso soup mix from a health food store

    m. Honey, lemons, knife, and cutting board. Lemon squeezer and cayenne pepper. . . . [and so forth with more items]

7. PRODUCTION OFFICE:

    a. Six (6) cans Coke Classic on ice

    b. Twelve (12) small bottles of spring water

    c. Twelve (12) bottles of Budweiser Beer on ice

    d. Eight bars of Ivory soap

    e. Eighty-four (84) clean white towels. If towels are new, they must be washed prior to use.

☛ Subparagraph 6.m ("Honey, lemons . . . "), above, is the "road cure" for singers' laryngitis. Chop up cayenne pepper as hot as you can stand it, mix it with honey, and dribble it down your throat. Any singer I've ever mentioned this to has always sworn by it.

CHAPTER 2

THE ANATOMY OF A RECORD COMPANY

Dealing with record companies is like being nibbled to death by ducks.

—WOODY HERMAN

There is no universal structure for record companies. Indeed, there are record companies which exist, figuratively and literally, totally in the back pocket of their founder and sole employee. In small companies—and even some larger ones—many of the departments described in this chapter may not even exist; their functions may be farmed out or ignored; or several people may double, triple, or more in various capacities in order to get the jobs done.

Today, with many record companies, both large and small, finding themselves in dire straits financially, and cutting back on staff, and with the so-called "majors" buying, absorbing, and/or joint venturing with each other, it's hard to say what model structure record companies will take in the future. (Samuel Goldwyn said: "Never make forecasts, especially about the future," and I won't.)

The fictional record company model used here is based upon the structure found in most of the larger record companies. Indeed, as more and more power is centralized within the hands of what's left of the majors, it is becoming harder to find an actually functioning record company, other than independent labels or production companies which have attached themselves to majors, that does not now resemble this model.

A discussion of what makes a record company "major" seems in order. Size of the company and the volume of sales, while important, are not the defining factors. If size were the yardstick, the term "majors" would be better replaced by "bloateds." As to sales volume, from time to time one of the nonmajors will outsell one or more of the majors. Within the music industry, the royal title "major" is not necessarily bestowed for success, but for owning a national network.

In these discussions it seems unnecessary to describe executive functions and departments which are common to any large company, such as mail rooms, payroll departments, human resources, etc. Do, however, realize that they exist and perform a very important function. Also be aware that some executive officers who oversee the operation of an entire company may also oversee the day-to-day operations of specific departments, such as a president who personally oversees A&R or a comptroller who also oversees accounting, royalties, copyright and licensing, and corporate finance. In some companies there is a chairman of the board or chief executive officer who outranks the president; in others, there is a vice chair or deputy chair position under the chair or CEO. CBS Records, for example, once had both a president and a deputy president. Some top-heavy companies have executive vice presidents, administrative vice presidents, and/or vice president/general managers.

Companies with more than one label may have parallel positions at each label report to one or more executives who function for both labels. For example, Sony Music Entertainment, Inc. (the United States–based subsidiary of Sony, which is Japanese-owned) has a number of labels, including Columbia and Epic; some corporate departments (e.g., Legal) function for both these labels and some departments (e.g., A&R) function for only one.

It should be noted that the record industry is dominated by a small number of entertainment/communications conglomerates. At one time there were six companies that could qualify as majors; now we are functionally down to four: the Universal Music Group, the Sony/BMG joint venture, the EMI Group, and the Warner Bros. Group. Considering that the Warner Bros. Group was purchased by investors headed by a Canadian, none of the majors are presently United States–owned. So much for "buy America," unless, of course, selling majors to foreigners counts.

Finally, keep in mind that no matter what the corporate structure, the various departments discussed below are all part of one large organism which is controlled from the top and the different parts of which interact for the general purpose of assuring the survival, and prosperous growth, of the whole.

A&R

One thing about the people at Atlantic, they can snap their fingers on the two-and-four beat. Which is something else you hardly ever see today. Record executives control all the money, but they can't keep time.
—RAY CHARLES

First in general interest and alphabetically is the A&R (Artist and Repertoire) Department, the department which traditionally chose the material to be recorded by the artist, developed the artists, and actually produced the recordings. The scope of A&R varies from company to company and has changed over time. Although some companies still have in-house producers, the general trend has been toward going outside, to independent producers, for many of the functions once handled by A&R executives. The A&R Department is still responsible for finding new talent or at least making the decision on which acts are to be signed. The department will probably have some hand in choosing the songs to be recorded and which producer to use for the recording session.

Arguably, the major function of today's A&R Department is the discovery of new talent, usually through reviewing recordings submitted to the company by outside sources—music attorneys, personal managers, producers, publishers, and relatives and friends of company executives. Please note that "unsolicited submissions"—recordings sent in by artists or individuals unknown to the company—have virtually no chance of making it through the screening process and obtaining any sort of offer from the company. The number of unsolicited submissions can run to hundreds per week, and most companies do not even listen to them.

An A&R department may be broken down into subdivisions based upon type of music—pop, hip-hop, rap, country, classical, R&B, etc. If the company is large enough, there may also be a geographic division: West Coast, East Coast, and, sometimes, Nashville. Usually when there is an acquisition of a label, a merger, or even an internal restructuring under a corporate umbrella having two or more separate labels, each of the labels will retain its own A&R department.

In some companies, the person responsible for seeing that session reports, label copy, bills, etc., are all handled efficiently is called an A&R administrator and is part of the A&R Department. In others, these functions are handled by someone in the Accounting Department. Some A&R administrators float uncomfortably in a kind of corporate limbo between Accounting and A&R.

The primary functions of the A&R Department are to determine which new artists are to be signed and to see that the recordings are produced, either internally or with the talents of outside producers.

BUSINESS AFFAIRS AND LEGAL

Assassins!

—ARTURO TOSCANNI (to his orchestra)

In some companies all legal matters are handled by one department; in others the Business Affairs and Legal departments, although closely aligned, are separate entities. Both departments are peopled mainly by attorneys, which probably accounts for the suspicion with which these departments are regarded by the company as a whole.

Business Affairs, when separate from Legal, is responsible for deal making and contract negotiations. After the A&R Department informs Business Affairs of its interest in a particular artist, the negotiations leading to signing the artist then proceed between the Business Affairs representative and the artist or artist's representative, who may be an attorney, manager, or "interested friend." Most formal negotiations take place between Business Affairs and the artist's attorney. Business Affairs is also responsible for the negotiations and deal making for the entire company; and distribution agreements, publishing agreements, international agreements, or whatever, flow through this department.

If a company has a separate Legal Department, Business Affairs will convey all negotiation-related information to the Legal Department via a "deal memo," and the contracts will then be prepared by the Legal Department. Further negotiation on the prepared and submitted contracts may be the responsibility of either Business Affairs or Legal.

Whether a single department or two are responsible for a company's legal affairs, the responsibility involves not only the preparation of contracts, but also the administration of the various agreements, copyrights, and trademarks controlled by the company, as well as leases, lawsuits, collections, and other mundane activities that are handled by attorneys. Lawyers may be responsible for various advertising-related matters—for example, is the copy included on the labels legally correct, are the trademarks used properly, does the company have the right to use that artist's likeness? And album covers and liners must all be checked for potential legal problems and for contractual obligations. Business Affairs and/or Legal are also frequently responsible for disseminating legal information to other departments—royalty information to the Royalty Department, up-to-date data on which artists are no longer with the label to the Promotion Department, etc.

SALES, MERCHANDISING, AND DISTRIBUTION

The salesman knows nothing of what he is selling
save that he is charging a great deal too much for it.

—OSCAR WILDE

The department which handles record sales and distribution is variously called Sales,

Merchandising, or, sometimes, just Distribution. As is true with every other department in a record company, there is really more to this department than its title suggests.

Companies with more than one label may handle sales and distribution of all their labels through a wholly owned subsidiary rather than a Sales Department. For example, WEA, a subsidiary of Time Warner, handles sales for Warner Bros. Records, Elektra, and Atlantic, among others, and EMD (EMI Music Distribution) handles sales for the EMI/Capitol group of labels.

In some companies, a number of distinct departments, each performing a specialized function, are under the direction of a sales executive—Sales; Special Products; Premiums; Manufacturing; Advertising and Promotion; and sometimes even the various "creative services" departments such as the Art Department and the Editorial Department. Different companies will have different organizational structures for carrying out these functions.

All major record companies employ both local and national sales representatives, who actually sell the records. The major entertainment conglomerates have their own national (and international) distribution system, whereby sales reps, usually under a regional executive, operate out of local branch offices, which are often tied into regional warehouses. Most companies divide the sales territory into "regions," sometimes bending the points of the compass into a curious collection: East, South, West, and Midwest.

Companies that do not qualify as "major" either distribute through another record company or through what are known as *independents*, or *indies*. A simple definition of an independent distributor is "any person or company, other than one of the remaining majors, who distributes recordings." Some independents, for example, Navarre, do have a national distribution network (but, perversely, are not regarded as majors); others may have territories as small as a single city.

Record companies having independent distribution generally have Sales Departments. However, these departments do not usually deal directly with the actual sales of product to the public or to retail dealers; rather, they deal with planning, marketing, and coordination with the independent distributor.

Some record companies have their records distributed through a distribution agreement with another record company. The distributing company may have its own branch system or may be part of an independent distributor's network. The company producing the *distributed labels*, as they are called, may have its own sales unit, which coordinates with the Sales Department of the distributing company. (See Chapter 16, "Distribution Agreements.")

In companies that have their own manufacturing plants, the Manufacturing Department may be a part of, or report to, the Sales Department. Some companies "share" manufacturing of certain products. At one time, Capitol Records manufactured cassettes for WEA companies (Warner Bros., Elektra, Atlantic, etc.) and, in turn, WEA manufactured discs for Capitol. (Prerecorded cassettes have been phased out by most record labels.) If demand exceeds capacity, all companies will outsource some of their manufacturing load, either to other record companies' manufacturing units or to independent manufacturers.

Some large record companies have a separate Advertising Department which functions as an internal advertising agency. The costs associated with using outside advertising agencies are high. In addition to creative fees and costs, plus a percentage markup, advertising agencies charge a commission for placing advertising—usually 15%—companies can save substantial amounts of money by creating and placing their own advertising.

ART AND EDITORIAL

Art is why I get up in the morning but my definition ends there.
You know I don't think it's fair that I'm living for something
I can't even define.

—ANI DIFRANCO

The Art Department is responsible for designing and creating—or hiring outside talent to design and create—artwork in the form of illustrations, photography, sculpture, or whatever, for the covers of the company's albums, for promotional pieces, and, if called on, a handmade birthday card for the CEO. Some companies have an Editorial Department to write or commission the writing of liner notes—the text appearing in the CD booklet. Editorial and Art, and sometimes Advertising, may also be part of a division known as Creative Services.

PROMOTION

Promotion is an extremely important department. It is responsible for obtaining radio airplay of that company's product. One of the unique aspects of the record industry is the incredible amount of "free" advertising the record companies receive. Every time a record plays on the radio or a music video airs on TV, it is being advertised. Records must have airplay in order to sell. Without airplay, there is virtually no chance of any substantial sales.

Formerly often part of Sales, today's Promotion Department is much more likely to be a separate department operating under its own vice president. Frequently, the structure of the Promotion Department will be parallel to that of the Sales Department: national promotion, with a series of regional executives overseeing the work of the local promotional personnel. And, just as Sales is organized by territory, the Promotion Department has subdivisions based on the type of music being promoted—country, pop, rock, etc. There may be further divisions, based upon market size, into primary or major markets, secondary markets, and, yes, even tertiary markets.

Primary markets are the *big* markets: New York, Los Angeles, Chicago, etc. Secondary markets are those areas which fall between the big markets and the small markets. Frequently, companies will introduce recordings in secondary markets and, if they are successful there, will promote them in the primary markets. One only slightly facetious definition of "tertiary market" was given to me by a promotion man, who said, "It's all the towns that end in 'berg and 'boro."

Sometimes, depending upon the current status of criminal indictments and payola scandals, independent promotion companies are used either to supplement the work of the Promotion Department or even do an entire promotional campaign. These independents may work on individual records, specific markets—by geographic location or type—or all products released by the company.

The costs of promotion may very well (and usually do) actually exceed the cost of producing the record. But it is a rare recording indeed that succeeds without an extensive—and expensive—promotion. This in and of itself is a good reason for the faint of heart or the light of pocketbook to avoid trying to promote a recording into that very rare species of animal: a profitable record. I have yet to be convinced that Internet promotion can, of itself, consistently produce meaningful record sales.

PUBLICITY

Don't pay any attention to what they write about you.
Just measure it in inches.

—ANDY WARHOL

It is important to understand the difference between advertising and publicity. Advertising is bought and paid for. Publicity, at least in theory, is free. The responsibility of the Publicity Department is to obtain free press for the company's product and artists. This includes arranging reviews of product by critics and interviews with the artists, preparing press kits, supplying publicity photos, and coming up with any other act, scheme, or scam which will have the desired effect.

ARTIST RELATIONS

The responsibility for artist relations—loosely defined as that of holding the hands of the label's important artists and making them happy—is frequently done by people in the A&R Department, or sometimes Publicity. Some companies have a separate Artist Relations Department. In either case, the person who becomes the company liaison for a particular artist sometimes ends up as an in-house manager for that artist, often being the sole conduit of information flow between artist and company. The Artist Relations Department is sometimes a social director for the artist on tour, the corporate equivalent of "for a good time, call. . . ." Artist Relations makes sure the limo is there to meet the artist at the airport, the right bottle of wine is sent backstage, and the hotel suites are waiting in all the strange towns, and tries to anticipate the artist's every whim.

LICENSING, ACCOUNTING, AND ROYALTIES

The accounting functions of the record company may be grouped under one banner or spread out through several departments. There are, of course, the standard accounting functions which must be performed for any company—payroll, preparation of financial statements, etc. In addition to these standard functions, the record company Accounting Department, or a subdivision, will also be responsible for the preparation and payments of royalty statements to artists, producers, production companies, other labels, publishers, songwriters, the American Federation of Musicians, and any other party who may receive a royalty payment from the company.

The function of obtaining the licenses from music publishers, the copyright owners of musical compositions, which allow the record company to record and sell the songs owned by the publishers, may be handled within the Accounting Department, the A&R Department, or Business Affairs.

Sometimes, the job of licensing to others and/or collecting from others when the record company is the licensor is also part of the Accounting Department's job.

SPECIAL PRODUCTS AND MERCHANDISING

Often a record company will have one or more departments with the responsibility of finding ways to further exploit the product—sometimes known as "getting the squeal out of the pig." These activities may vary from repackaging albums into low-priced product, licensing recordings for soundtracks, licensing to television for direct sales, creating premium records, and creating and selling T-shirts, posters, buttons, etc.

In a conversation with the head of Special Products for one of the remaining majors, I was told by him that the break-even "nut" for his department was $1 million per day. Even for record companies, ancillary rights are an important cash cow.

If a record company is actually marketing its own merchandise in-house, instead of licensing the merchandising rights out to third parties, it is more likely than not that the merchandising will be handled by the Special Products department.

INTERNATIONAL

As already pointed out, the closest any of the major records companies comes to being domestically owned is the one whose owner—although Canadian—lives in the United States. Most of the large domestically owned record companies have a separate International Department, which is responsible for obtaining foreign outlets for domestic product and, if appropriate, licensing foreign product for domestic release. Increasingly, the joint ownership of many of the domestic licensor/licensees and the foreign licensor/licensees makes the operation of the International Department an internal matter.

PUBLISHING

Publishing is the cash cow of the music industry. Record companies do not, technically, have publishing departments. What they do have are wholly owned affiliated companies, which acquire and create copyright ownership in musical compositions and, in turn, are paid fees for the use of the compositions. This legal distinction is based upon the rules of the three performing rights societies in the United States—American Society of Composers, Authors, and Publishers (ASCAP), Broadcast Music, Inc. (BMI), and the Society of European Stage Authors and Composers (SESAC)—which require that no publishing company may simultaneously belong to more than one performing rights society. As a result record companies usually have two or more separate publishing companies, each individually affiliated with one of the three societies.

Example

Record Company forms two separate wholly owned corporations, A Music and B Music, both of which it owns and runs. A Music affiliates with ASCAP. B Music affiliates with BMI. All copyrights created by ASCAP-affiliated writers are placed in A Music. All copyrights created by BMI-affiliated writers are placed in B Music.

It is essential that a publishing company be associated with *one* of the societies, as the societies are the entities that collect public performance royalties (the monies collected from radio stations and others for playing music) for the use of the publishing company's copyrighted music works.

While there is a legal fiction that the publishing companies associated with a given record company are independent and separate, more likely than not they will have the same officers and personnel.

CHAPTER 3

ARTIST RECORDING AGREEMENTS

We in the music industry depend on our contracts. They are the one thing that gives our industry some order. We need that (contractual) guarantee so the artists that are successful will continue making records for us, and we can reinvest those profits in new artists. It's important that everyone respect the sanctity of the contracts, otherwise there would be chaos.

—TERRY ELLIS, Imago Records,
suing DreamWorks Records for $40 million
Quoted in *Daily Variety*, June 12, 1996

We are about to embark on a safari into the untamed jungle of the music industry, where horrible monsters, such as Mr. Cross-collateralization, lurk in the deep underbrush awaiting an opportunity to spring out and devour us. Fortunately, we also have a guidebook to help us avoid stepping on venomous serpents and to tell us which fruits can be eaten and which are forbidden and poisonous. There will even be an occasional scary or funny story around the campfire.

We will begin with the *recording agreement* (or *recording contract* or *record agreement* or *record contract*—the terms are interchangeable), the generic term for the written document between a recording artist and a record company or production company which lays out the obligations and promises of each party. Depending upon your outlook, you may see the recording agreement as the pot of gold at the end of the rainbow or the rainbow itself. Unfortunately, it can also be like the pretty apple the wicked Queen fed to Snow White. I have had many artists come into my office looking for a recording agreement. Obscure and famous, talented and untalented, their goal is always the same: a recording agreement, the collection of rights, obligations, rules, and restrictions for both parties. It can be an artist's best friend or worst enemy. Sometimes it is both.

I want to state at the outset that the economics of the recording industry are such that the odds are overwhelmingly against making great sums of money through a recording agreement. Consideration should be given to the recording agreement as a tool, perhaps a loss leader, to enhance the artist's career in other areas, such as live performance, writing, acting, and merchandising. I truly believe that a new and/or unestablished artist should pay more attention to those provisions of the recording agreement which will create a career than those provisions which will not generate any income unless a career is created. The best royalty provisions in the world are meaningless if records are not sold. If enough records are sold, the opportunity will arise to go back in and renegotiate the royalty provisions.

Each of the provisions in a recording agreement has a specific purpose. All of them may conceal potential pitfalls for the artist and should be studied individually. Once the individual provisions have been understood, they must be studied again to see how they interact with each other. The provisions discussed here generally deal with an artist or artists signing directly with a record company. However, the same provisions are also used when an artist signs with a producer or a production company, and when a producer or production company signs with a record company and "furnishes" the artist to them.

Also, these discussions are purposely germane to the garden-variety recording agreements, not the superstar agreements—those agreements have a life and a logic of their own that is well beyond the scope of this work. Agreements like the (probably inflated) $1 billion Michael Jackson/Sony recording deal of yore and lore, while fascinating, are best left to the tabloids and read about in supermarket lines.

TERM OF THE AGREEMENT

> *A burglar who respects his art always takes*
> *his time before taking anything else.*
>
> —O. Henry

In the collection of sample contract provisions at the end of this and other sections, you will frequently find several examples that are saying basically the same thing, but with vastly different language. The fact is, there is no universal or standard language for these provisions. When a record company offers what it calls a "standard contract," what it really means is, "This is *my* standard contract." Also note that many of the samples are in their "prenegotiated" form; that is, one (or even both) of the parties would find the language unacceptable. Once the parties have read the preliminary document, each negotiation takes on a life of its own.

In the past, most recording artist agreements in the music industry ran for a period of 1 year followed by four 1-year options, for a total of 5 years (see Examples 1 through 4). (For a complete discussion of options, see the next section, "Exercise of Options.") Today, although the term of many agreements is still written as a total (if all options are exercised) of 5 years, more and more agreements are being written for total periods of longer than 5 years. In fact, even so-called 5-year agreements will probably run longer than 5 years (again, if all options are exercised) because of extensions and/or suspensions caused by the late delivery of recordings by the artist (see Examples 5 and 6).

In general, the total contract period will not run more than 7 years. This 7-year restriction can be directly traced to a provision of the California Labor Code, Section 2855, which reads, in part:

> A contract to render personal services . . . may not be enforced against the employee beyond 7 years from the commencement of services under it. Any contract, otherwise valid, to perform or render services of a special, unique, unusual, extraordinary, or intellectual character, which gives it a peculiar value and the loss of which can not be reasonably or adequately compensated in damages in an action at law, may nevertheless be

enforced against the person contracting to render such service, for a term not to exceed 7 years from the commencement of service under it. . . .

The "personal service contracts" referred to in Section 2855 are those where one party performs services for another. In our discussions, the services, the recording of musical compositions for the record company, are to be performed by the recording artist. The practical effect of this particular section of the California Labor Code is that few artist contracts are written for a period of more than 7 years. Those that are, are usually written with the understanding that no services are to be performed in the State of California.

Note that Section 2855 provides that the contract is not *enforceable* beyond 7 years, not that the entire contract is void if the term exceeds that time. The first 7 years can be enforced whatever the length of the contract, even in California.

Example
Subject to California law or jurisdiction, Artist A enters into a contract with Record Company B for a period of 10 years. After 5 years, A attempts to break the contract because it exceeds a period of 7 years. A is unsuccessful. The contract is enforceable for the next 2 years. It would, however, be unenforceable for years 8 through 10.

The same contract in New York, which does not have a 7-year restriction and which is not subject to California law or jurisdiction, would be enforceable for the entire 10 years. However, since so much of the record industry sooner or later passes through California and since it is relatively easy for a disgruntled artist to apply for California jurisdiction in an action, the 7-year restriction is always lurking in the background like an unwanted guest. (In 1987 an amendment to Section 2855 was passed which deals only with recording agreements; for a discussion of the amendment see pages 130–137, "Unrecorded Masters" and "Release of Recordings.")

Contracts can be enforced in California beyond 7 years with the agreement of the artist (see Example 8). If the artist is willing to renew the agreement, the 7-year period starts all over again as a new contract. This renewal is often accomplished by an agreement to extend the contract. Unfortunately, artists are not always aware that they have agreed to an extension. CBS Records used to send an option-exercise letter which requested the artist to acknowledge its receipt by returning an enclosed form. This voluntary acknowledgment by the artist resulted in a 1-year extension magically appearing in the artist's contract. The magician responsible for pulling this extension out of the hat was the carefully crafted language contained in the receipt acknowledgment providing that by returning the acknowledgment the artist was agreeing to an additional year being added to the contract. An astounding number of artists signed this letter unaware (until their contract turned into a pumpkin) that they had given their record company additional time on their agreement. The most innocent-looking document can be dangerous!

The California courts look at and question the specific circumstances surrounding any extensions of personal service agreements beyond the 7-year limit. At present, it seems that the earlier in the contract period the artist agrees to an extension, the less likely it is to be enforceable. Conversely, the later the artist agrees to the extension, the more likely it is that the courts will rule that it is enforceable. While hardly a clear-cut precedent (and not very helpful in the gray middle of the contract period), it is an indication that the courts continue to struggle with this issue.

You might wonder how the traditional "1 year plus four 1-year options = 5 years" agreement term was arrived at. This particular tradition began with the musicians' union, the American Federation of Musicians (AFM). The AFM requires record companies to become signatories to what is known as the AFM Basic Agreement, which is a list of rules and regulations. One former stipulation of this agreement was that the record company must obtain the AFM's approval of an agreement between the record company and a musician, and another was that no AFM member could enter into a recording agreement for a term exceeding 5 years. As a result, a recording agreement with a period exceeding 5 years simply would not be approved by the union and the record company could not enforce the agreement.

Accordingly, record companies limited their contracts with AFM artists to 5 years. However, the American Federation of Television and Recording Artists (AFTRA)—the union for singers and television and radio actors—had no similar time restriction. So some record companies made a distinction between an artist-musician and an artist-vocalist when determining the length of a recording contract. Indeed, in the old days it was not uncommon for a recording artist to sign two separate agreements with the record company—one as an AFM musician for 5 years and one as an AFTRA vocalist for 7 years.

The record companies began to chafe under the 5-year limitation. After all, wasn't it their God-given right to sign artists for as long as a period as *they* wanted? In early 1981 the industry movement away from 5-year contract periods accelerated because of a court ruling in a case entitled *Hagar v. Capitol Records, Inc.*[1] The artist Sammy Hagar's 5-year recording agreement with Capitol Records was about to run out. Capitol, however, claimed that Hagar still owed two albums under that agreement. Hagar, in turn, claimed that Capitol had breached the contract and he was not required to deliver the two albums. Pursuant to provisions in the agreement (see "Suspension and Termination," pages 54–59), Capitol tried to use what may be any record company's most powerful weapon against a nonperforming artist—suspension for nondelivery of product. Needless to say, both Hagar and Capitol took a trip to the courthouse.

Capitol argued that the countdown toward the 5-year anniversary expiration date was stopped by suspension and could not be resumed until Hagar had fulfilled all his contractual obligations, specifically delivery of the two new albums. (Note that no one argued that the suspension could stop the countdown to the 7-year limitation. That had been settled back in the 1930s.) The court, however, took the position that the 5 years meant 5 years—suspension or no suspension—and would not allow Capitol to suspend (and continue) the contract past the original expiration date.

Whether or not the *Hagar* decision would be binding in the State of California in similar cases remains in doubt—as the decision was never appealed—but it did cause everyone to reexamine their then-current contract forms, and many new contract forms were created to sidestep the question of whether or not the agreement could be extended beyond the original contract period as the result of a suspension.

Now, while there is still a tendency to structure agreements on the basis of a 5-year total, what passes for a "year" would startle anyone counting on their fingers or looking at a calendar. Instead of just stating that the initial period of the agreement, and the subsequent option periods, will be 1 year, the wording may be something like this: "1 year, or a period of 8 months after the delivery

---

[1]Marin County Sup. Ct., State of CA (index no. 100486, 12-22-80) unreported.

[of a specified number of recordings], *whichever is later.*" Human and artist natures being what they are, each of these periods is more than likely to be greater than 1 year. This type of agreement might be called "open-ended" (my terminology) because no one knows up front what the actual length of the contract will be, no matter what "set" number of years has been specified in the contract. For example, each option date may have a different anniversary date due to late delivery of committed recordings (see Example 10). Actually, determining the true length of any open-ended agreement is a nightmare.

Notwithstanding the time-expanding properties of the open-ended agreement, even the cleverest Machiavellian drafting by lawyers cannot extend the *enforceable* life of an agreement beyond the 7-year mandate of California Labor Code Section 2855, unless by mutual agreement of the parties or by change in the law itself—which, as a result of intensive lobbying by the record industry, did happen (take another look at the section "Suspension and Termination," pages 54–59).

There is, however, a difference between legality and being able to enforce something. Open-ended agreements, as drafted by most record companies and production companies, will, if all options are exercised, certainly exceed 7 years. If this, understandably, is getting confusing, just keep in mind that Section 2855 does not make it illegal to draft a contract that may extend beyond 7 years; it simply makes anything beyond the seventh year of such a contract unenforceable. Even open-ended agreements often specify a 7-year limit (see Example 10). It is not unusual to find these agreements calling for an initial period of a minimum of 1 year with six additional 1-year options, each period running no less than 1 year in length or, if longer, a set period from either delivery of the masters or even the release of the product. These additional periods usually run 8 or 9 months from the delivery or the release of the product. So, unless the product is delivered and/or released within the first 3 or 4 months of the agreement in each "year" of the agreement, the total term *must* exceed 7 years.

As a case in point, see Example 9. If I read that example correctly (and be assured that I do), even if there is on-time or early delivery in each period (and how likely is that?), the period is going to run at least 7 years. To make matters worse, the periods run not from the commencement of the current period, but from the "initial commercial release" of the *last* [emphasis added] "Commitment Album recorded by Artist and Delivered by Productions in fulfillment of the Recording Commitment for the Present Artist Contract Period." How likely is it that the record company is going to release all the required albums on or before the first day of each or any of the 9-month periods?

Not bloody likely is my answer!

The whole problem of indeterminate periods and the exercise of options for additional periods can be avoided by providing for a set period of time, without options (see Example 4). These agreements are sometimes referred to as "flat," or as having a "flat period." Such an agreement might provide for a flat 5 years or a flat 3-year period. Another form of flat agreement, one which is uncommon but does occasionally rear its head, involves a term based not upon the passage of time, but upon the delivery of product, for example, the delivery of a specified number of albums. If the product commitment to be delivered by the artist is small enough, say only one or two albums, flat delivery-based term agreements present few problems. If, on the other hand, the delivery requirement is extensive, the potential complications and danger to the artist are great (see Example 7). The timing of the delivery requirements must be looked at carefully, as must the possibility that the artist may be held responsible for unrecorded product (see the discussion of the 1987 amendment to California Labor Code 2855 referred to above, pages 28–29).

There may also be provisions within an agreement, open-ended or otherwise, which call for a flexible term of the agreement based upon matters other than delivery or performance. When an artist is being signed to a production company which in turn will be signing with a record company, there may be a need for the term of the agreement to be altered without a formal amendment (see Example 8).

SAMPLE CONTRACT PROVISIONS

EXAMPLE 1: 1 Year Plus Four 1-Year Options

1. Company engages my personal endeavors in connection with the production of records as a vocalist and musician for an initial period of one (1) year, as the same may be extended or renewed, commencing upon the date hereof. . . . I grant Company four (4) options, each to renew this agreement for a period of 1 year, said options to run consecutively beginning at the expiration of the initial period.

☛ You can't get much more basic than this.

EXAMPLE 2: 1 Year Plus Four 1-Year Options

1. a. Company hereby engages your exclusive personal services as a recording artist to perform in connection with the production of records for an initial period of one (1) year, as the same may be extended or renewed, commencing upon the date hereof.

• • •

19. You grant us the option to extend the term of this agreement for a first additional period of 1 year upon all the terms and conditions herein contained.

20. If we have exercised the option granted in paragraph 19 hereof, we shall have another option to extend the term of this agreement for a second additional period of 1 year upon all the terms and conditions herein contained.

21. If we have exercised the option granted in paragraph 20 hereof, we shall have another option to extend the term of this agreement for a third additional period of 1 year upon all the terms and conditions herein contained.

22. If we have exercised the option granted in paragraph 21 hereof, we shall have another option to extend the term of this agreement for a fourth additional period of 1 year upon all the terms and conditions herein contained.

☛ This is the same as Example 1, except for the language. Different words for different folks.

EXAMPLE 3: 1 Year Plus Four 1-Year Options

2. Term:

(a) The initial term of this Agreement shall commence as of the date hereof and shall continue for one (1) year.

(b) You hereby grant to us four (4) separate options, each to extend the term of this Agreement for a one (1) year term, such renewal terms to run consecutively, beginning at the expiration of the initial term, all upon the same terms and conditions applicable to the initial term except as otherwise specified herein. . . .

☛ Yup! Same as the first two, except for language. See what I mean about "standard" contracts?

EXAMPLE 4: Flat 5-Year Term

1. The term of Artist's services, pursuant to the terms and conditions of this Agreement, shall be for a period of five (5) years commencing upon the date hereof, as the same may be extended as provided for herein.

EXAMPLE 5: 18 Months Plus Four 1-Year Options

1. This contract shall commence as of the date hereof and shall continue for a term consisting of an initial term which shall expire eighteen (18) months from the date hereof and for the additional renewal term or terms hereinafter provided for.

• • •

19. You hereby grant us four (4) separate options, each to extend the term of the contract for a one (1) year term, such renewal terms to run consecutively beginning at the expiration of the initial term, all upon the same terms and conditions applicable to the initial term except as otherwise specified herein or in the schedule herein below set forth. . . .

☛ Presumably this variation from the 1 year + four 1-year options is to give the record company an extra 6 months in the initial period to decide whether to exercise the option on this new artist.

EXAMPLE 6: 18 Months Plus Three 18-Month Options

1. "Term." This Agreement shall commence as of the date hereof and shall continue in force for an additional period of eighteen (18) months (unless otherwise suspended, extended or terminated as herein provided). Artist grants Company three (3) irrevocable options, each option to renew this Agreement for eighteen (18) months upon all the terms and conditions herein contained. Each such option period shall run consecutively beginning upon the expiration of the prior contract period. . . . The initial period, and the option periods exercised, as such periods may be suspended, extended or terminated as herein provided, are hereinafter collectively referred to as the "term."

EXAMPLE 7: Term Based on Delivery—Open Ended

2. TERM

2.01 The term of this Agreement will commence on the date hereof and continue, unless extended as provided for herein, for a first Contract Period (sometimes referred to as the "Initial Contract Period") ending nine (9) months after the date of completion of ARTIST's services for the first album hereunder.

2.02 Additionally, you hereby grant [Company] seven (7) separate options to extend the term of this Agreement for additional Contract Periods ("Option Periods") on the same terms and conditions applicable to the initial Contract Period except as otherwise provided herein.

EXAMPLE 8: Term Adjusted with Limitations

(b) If Company enters into an agreement with a company which is, or is distributed by, one of the "six majors" (e.g., Sony, WEA, etc.) the period of this Agreement and the minimum recording commitment shall, in good faith, be adjusted accordingly; provided, however, that without my express consent the period of this Agreement shall not extend beyond seven (7) years from the commencement hereof nor shall the minimum recording commitment, in toto, be greater than six (6) albums.

☛ An old agreement (there were still 6 majors) between an artist and a production company allowing for an adjustment of terms to match the agreement between the production company and the record label.

EXAMPLE 9: Open-Ended

(i) The Artist Term for the Artist Agreement shall commence as of the date of the execution of the Artist Agreement and continue for a first Artist Contract Period (sometimes referred to as the "Artist Initial Period") ending on the date which is nine (9) months after Company's initial United States release of the Artist's Commitment Album Delivered by Productions in fulfillment of the Recording Commitment for the Artist Initial Period, but in no event earlier than twelve (12) months after the date of the commencement of the Artist Initial Period for the Artist.

(ii) The Artist Agreement shall provide that:

(A) Productions shall have six (6) separate, irrevocable and consecutive options ("Artist Option"), each to renew the Artist Term of the Artist Agreement for additional Artist Contract Periods (sometimes referred to as "Artist Option Periods").

(B) Each Artist Contract Period shall continue until the date ending no earlier than nine (9) months after the initial commercial release by Company in the United States of the last Commitment Album recorded by Artist and Delivered by Productions in fulfillment of the Recording Commitment for the Present Artist Contract Period, but in no event earlier than twelve (12) months after the date of the commencement of the current Artist Option Period for the Artist.

☛ This contract is flawed for the artist (not the record company—it's all relative), since the period can be extended almost indefinitely at the choice of the record company. All the company has to do is not "release" the "last Commitment Album" until the artist gives in to whatever the company demands.

EXAMPLE 10: Open-Ended Agreement

PAYMENT AND MASTER SCHEDULE

Period This Agreement	Duration	Min. No. of Masters	Amount per Master	Royalty
Initial Period	1 Year; or 8 Months following delivery of the minimum recording obligation (whichever is later)	1 LP	Scale	7%
1st Option Period	1 Year; or 8 Months following delivery of the minimum recording obligation (whichever is later)	1 LP	Scale	7%
2nd Option Period	1 Year; or 8 Months following delivery of the minimum recording obligation (whichever is later)	1 LP	Scale	7%

Period This Agreement	Duration	Min. No. of Masters	Amount per Master	Royalty
3rd Option Period	1 Year; or 8 Months following delivery of the minimum recording obligation (whichever is later)	1 LP	Scale	7%
4th Option Period	1 Year; or 8 Months following delivery of the minimum recording obligation (whichever is later)	1 LP	Scale	7%

Nothing contained in this Payment and Master Schedule shall result in this Agreement extending beyond seven (7) years from the commencement hereof.

EXERCISE OF OPTIONS

> *An honest man can feel no pleasure in the exercise of power over his fellow citizens.*
> —THOMAS JEFFERSON

As discussed in the last section, most artist agreements provide that the term is to be divided into separate periods, most commonly a year, but sometimes longer. However, even more common these days are "1-year periods" which have an "or" clause which can cause the period to be much longer than a year, as in Example 10 above, which uses the language "1 Year; or 8 Months following delivery of the minimum recording obligation (whichever is later)."

There may sometimes be an arrangement for a shorter period, usually a "testing" or "prove your worth" initial period, of less than 1 year. These shorter periods, usually 6 months, are almost always the initial period of the agreement. Sometimes the short period is not even a "prove your worth" period, since that implies that the record company will at least release a single. Instead of releasing product, the record company may just "hold" the artist, usually by way of an option, until the company makes up its mind whether or not to record the artist. (See Chapter 7, "Option Agreements," pages 240–250.) Generally, the record company wants to hold on to the artist for the longest possible period of time with the least obligation on the part of the company. This tug of war between length of time and obligation can be an important area of negotiation. In the best of all worlds for an artist, the artist gets a short term marked by quick success and an opportunity to negotiate for a better contract as a free agent. Conversely, in the best of all worlds for a record company, the company holds on to the artist as long as possible, with the least financial outlay; that way, if lightning should strike and the company finds it has a superstar, it can hang onto the new star for a bargain-basement price.

Record companies are not always smart in signing or, indeed, keeping artists under contract. Any record company that has been around for any length of time has either passed on or dropped artists who went on to great success elsewhere. Capitol Records first passed on the Beatles; when I was Director of Business Affairs at CBS Records, several artists I brought in who were passed on by the Columbia Records label A&R staff went on to be multi-gold and multi-platinum album artists. (Of course, I brought many more in who turned out to be—putting it politely—"less than commercially successful.") I discovered what is my favorite story on the subject while working as a just-out-of-law-school wet-behind-the-ears lawyer for Capitol Records. I was given the research task of going through every artist contract Capitol Records had signed from its inception. Somewhere in the first 40 or 50 contracts I ran across an agreement which had been entered into with Sammy Davis, Jr. Davis was to be paid, if I recollect correctly, something like $45 per master, and there was *no royalty* due for the sales of the records. Not only was there *no royalty* due—they chose *not to exercise the first option!*

After the initial period, the subsequent periods are usually referred to as *option periods*. By definition, an option is a privilege existing for the benefit of one party to an agreement. Three guesses which party benefits here—our old friend, the record company. It is very common, and *very* naive, for new artists to ask if the exercise of options can be made their choice, or at least a "mutual" decision. Alas, one of the facts of music industry life which must be faced is that the decision to exercise an option is almost always under the sole control of the record company. In other words, if the record company wishes to continue with the artist (the last album went gold!), it "exercises" the option and the agreement continues for one or more additional periods. If, however, the record company does not wish to continue with the artist (the last album bombed), it simply does not exercise its option and the agreement lapses. It's like joining the French Foreign Legion, you have signed on for the duration. The record company determines the duration for you.

Except for those agreements written for a flat period of time, all artist agreements must have a provision or provisions for the exercise or nonexercise of options. How the record company uses, or abuses, those provisions is another matter. My goal when representing the artist is to keep the abuse—what I call the "free ride"—to an absolute minimum. Here's what I mean. If the record company has no tangible obligation to the artist, such as a commitment to advance money or to actually record product, and it is isn't costing the company anything to hang on to the artist (the "free ride"), why not do it?

If the record company takes the free ride, the artist has big problems. It is difficult enough to become successful under the best of conditions, and a situation in which the record company is not expending any money or effort on the artist's behalf can hardly be described as "the best of conditions." In fact, the record company is holding the artist (for free) on the off chance that something might happen. And who knows? Something might. Meanwhile, the artist's career is in limbo. The philosophical question is, Is it better to have a "bad" contract with an uncommitted record company or to have no contract? One can certainly argue that if the record company lets the artist go, something better may come along—maybe even the "big break" with another record company.

There are many stories of dropped artists going on to fame and fortune with a different label. For example, Columbia Records signed Aretha Franklin in 1960 and then dropped her in 1965. She, of course, then signed to Atlantic Records and went on to fame and fortune. A true story of bad corporate internal communications, told to me by one of the participants, involves Aretha Franklin. Shortly after being dropped by Columbia Records, Aretha was appearing in San Francisco. The local Columbia Records sales office blew their entire year's discretionary budget throwing a party for the opening. She was extremely appreciative, she told the local boys, "especially since you went to all this trouble and I'm not even on the label anymore." They, of course, had never been told.

The best approach to signing a contract, of course, is to see that the contract is not "bad" in the first place. There are several ways to reduce the record company's potential for abusing artists in connection with the exercise of options. For example, there might be a provision requiring that a specific condition be met (a particular "fact" must exist, or "event" must take place) before the record company can exercise an option. It is essential that both parties be able to determine independently that the "fact" or "event" has indeed taken place. The usual choice is some quantitative criterion, such as a certain number of records being sold; or a chart position being reached; or a specific amount of money being spent to finance a tour. Nothing open to interpretation should be used. Imagine, for example, what would happen if the "event" was "commercial success"?

Example

Artist's contract with Record Company provides that the first option cannot be exercised unless Artist's first album sells 100,000 copies during the first year of the agreement. The album only sells 85,000 copies. Record Company cannot exercise the first option and the contract automatically terminates at the end of the initial period.

In most cases involving contracts like the one in the example, the record company would have the option to "make up" the number of albums to reach the agreed-upon figure. This is usually done by a credit being given to the artist's royalty account, although sometimes an actual payment is made to the artist for the difference. The difference can be considerable: A "credit" results in figures being transferred on paper somewhere in the record company's files, while "payment" results in real money in the artist's pocket.

Example

Artist's contract with Record Company provides that the first option cannot be exercised unless Artist's first album sells 100,000 copies during the first year of the agreement. If the 100,000 mark is not reached, Record Company has the option to make up the difference. The album sells 85,000 copies. Record Company credits Artist's royalty account with an additional 15,000 copies and then exercises the first option.

When faced with a record company's insistence that it be allowed to make up a difference, presuming the sales criteria are important to the artist, it is best to place some limitation on its ability to do so, for example, by inserting a provision that no more than 10,000 units may be credited by the record company. In this example, the record company would fall 5,000 short and could not exercise the first option.

In negotiating the exercise-of-options sections of contracts, whether representing the artist or the record company, I prefer to use an arrangement which gives the artist the opportunity to negate automatic termination in the case of a failure to meet a condition necessary for exercise of an option. Even if a condition is *not* met, the artist may have good reason for wishing to stay under contract to the record company.

Example

Artist's contract with Record Company provides that the first option may be exercised by the Record Company if Artist's first album does not sell 100,000 copies, *but* Artist has the right to negate the exercise if the 100,000 mark is not reached. The album sells 85,000 and the Record Company exercises the first option. Artist, painfully aware that no other record company wants Artist, wisely chooses not to negate the exercise of the option and the agreement proceeds into the first option period. (See Example 7 below.)

Another way to keep the record company from taking a free ride at the artist's expense is to require advances to be paid either "with" the exercise of options or "because of" the exercise of options. The distinction between "with" and "because of" depends upon the "when" and the "why" of the advance payment. "With" implies a payment triggered by the exercise of an option, while "because of" implies some fact which takes place after the option is exercised, such as the delivery of an album. For example, as a condition of exercising the second option of an artist's contract, a record company might be required to pay the artist a $25,000 advance—at the time of the exercise of the option ("with") or, perhaps, upon the delivery of the first album of the option period ("because of"). From a career standpoint, an advance is an important sign to the artist. It shows that the record company is interested and has at least some level of belief in the artist. Unfortunately for the artist, contractually mandated advances are not easy to come by these days. At perhaps no other time in the history of the music industry have there been so many artists and so few contracts for recording. It is a "buyer's market," with the record company being the buyer.

For the sake of discussion, let us presume that an artist has been able to get the record company to agree to an advance (other than a signing advance) in connection with option periods. This required advance may be paid

1. Upon the exercise of the option [*with*],

2. Upon the commencement of the option period [*with*], and/or

3. Upon the occurrence of some event, such as the delivery of the first album to be recorded during that option period [*because of*].

Advance on Exercise of Option

Because an advance payable to the artist upon exercise of option can create serious problems for the record company, this type of advance is rare. With this type of arrangement, the advance must be mailed out concurrently with the notice of exercise of option. If it does not accompany the notice, the exercise of option is not in effect. The inevitable lack of coordination between the department sending the notice and the department preparing the check can try the patience of even the most serene of record executives. Think of it. A check must be prepared and signed at the last minute; the check must be included with the option notice, which also has to be prepared and signed; both check and notice have to be mailed and postmarked that same day. Then some bozo in the accounting department informs you that the wrong requisition form has been used. Or that two signatures are required for a check that size and Mr. Crimby doesn't seem to have returned from lunch. It gets better.

What if the artist is under suspension at the time the exercise is due? Suppose the record contract has not been drafted properly (not an unusual circumstance). The record company now wishes to keep the artist under contract, and, according to the recording agreement, the option must be exercised in a timely manner, suspension or not. Now imagine that an advance is due with the exercise of option. This *forces* the record company to pay an artist on whom they would much rather be putting economic pressure. Maybe economic pressure is the only leverage the record company has over the artist, but the record company itself must come to his rescue. If they don't exercise, and pay the advance, they will lose the artist.

You think this is far-fetched? Read on.

I was once able to get an artist released from his contract under circumstances very much like those described above. Because of a court ruling (the artist had been a minor when originally signed, and in approving the form of this minor's agreement, the judge inserted some unusual special provisions), the contract specified that an advance was due concurrently with exercise of option, and that the option had to be exercised on a certain date if the company wanted to keep the artist. On the date that the exercise was due, the artist was under suspension for nondelivery of product. (The artist owed the record company one album, which was not forthcoming in spite of begging, bribing, and excessive threats from the company—indeed, from everyone connected with this artist.) Naturally, the record company did not want to pay the artist. Unfortunately for the company, the option-exercise due date was enforceable, suspension or no suspension. After deciding to keep the artist, the record company did four things, in this order:

1. Made a decision not to pay the advance while the artist was under suspension.

2. Decided to rely upon the suspension it had declared.

3. Neglected to review the contract (a fatal oversight).

4. Lost the artist.

The record company still wanted the artist and we negotiated a new contract. The artist's advance was enough for him to build his own recording studio. Over 30 years later his undelivered album turned up on another label and became a cult hit.

Before considering the second option, payment on commencement of the option period, it is worth emphasizing the inherent risk for a record company whenever *any* "nonreturnable advance against royalties" is made. The only source from which the company may recoup such an advance is earned royalties. It cannot go to the artist and demand payment. But if no royalties are earned, no advances are recouped. Generally, an advance is not returnable for nonperformance. An artist can be killed coming from the bank where he has just deposited the $1 million cash advance from the record company; a group can break up without recording, having each spent their shares of the advance on custom sports cars; an artist can lose his voice; and on goes the parade of horrible possibilities. Under these circumstances, the money is as good as lost for the record company.

Advance Payable When Option Period Commences

Making the advance payable when the option period commences, rather than on exercise, is preferable to the record company. If, for example, the artist is under suspension and money is payable upon commencement, the artist need not be paid until the suspension is lifted and the option period actually begins. As discussed above, if the advance payable with the exercise is late, it is probable that the option exercise itself is void. In contrast, chances are that a late payment in connection with advance payable on commencement will be treated simply as a late payment and not a breach of contract or a failure to properly exercise the option.

Advance Payable on Delivery

Far and away the wisest choice for the record company is to tie the payment of advances in option periods into actual delivery of product. For example, the record company might agree to pay the artist a specific sum of money for each album the artist delivers to the record company. If the artist does not produce, the artist does not get the money. In effect, the record company gets what it is paying for, a state of affairs not necessarily true if the advance must be paid upon the exercise of the option or upon the commencement of the option period. Options may also have what might be called a "conditional advance"—an advance during the period of an option which is triggered by some fact, usually some level of sales or, perhaps, reaching a specified chart position (see Example 3).

One record company, when forced to pay advances in option periods, often insisted that the advance be paid over the entire term of the period in equal biweekly payments. While ostensibly this is to "protect" the artist from throwing away the money, my suspicions are that the company is hedging its bets. If the relationship does not work out, the company can stop paying the advance and negotiate a termination, thereby losing less money than they would have had the advance been paid all at once.

Notice of Option

An important aspect of negotiations involving the exercise of options, and one which is frequently overlooked, is the notice period. How long before the expiration of the period must the notice of exercise (or, in the case of automatic exercise, the notice of nonexercise) be given? The record company wants the notice to be given as late as possible, usually 10 days prior to the expiration of the previous period, or even up to and including the last day of the period. The more time to make up its mind, the better. (I was once offered—and rejected—a contract which allowed the company the right to exercise its options up to 30 days *after* the expiration of any period.)

Not surprisingly, while the record company wants as long a period as possible before having to make a decision whether or not to exercise an option, most artists prefer to have that decision made as early as possible in case they need to shop for a new company. In cases in which a production company rather than a record company is signing the artist, and will subsequently "supply" the artist to the record company (see the introduction to Chapter 6, "Production Agreements"), the production company would like the best of both worlds, for example, a 30-day notice of exercise, or nonexercise, of option from the record company to the production company and a 10-day notice from the production company to the artist. That way, the production company will know whether or not the record company is going to exercise its option well before the production company has to make a decision.

Suppose the production company has an exercise date which is earlier than that of the record company and, deciding nobody really wants the artist, does not exercise its option for the artist, and then the record company surprises everyone by exercising. What then? The production company will find itself in the uncomfortable position of being in breach of its agreement with the record company. Conversely, the production company may find itself saddled with an advance commitment or an expensive recording commitment if it exercises the option and the record company does not. The production company's quandary with respect to timely exercise of options is frequently solved as follows: The record company insists on a clause whereby if the record company exercises its option, that's good enough for the artist. Under these circumstances, however, a failure by the record company to exercise might leave the production company out of luck if the production company wished to continue independently with the artist, *without* the record company (see Example 6). The issue can be very troublesome.

There may even be a problem when the production company has an exercise period which is later than that of the record company, as the following example shows.

Example

The agreement between Production Company in Los Angeles and Record Company in New York calls for the Record Company to give notice to Production Company of Record Company's election to exercise the Artist Option at any time before 15 days before the expiration of the present contract period. The agreement between Artist and Production Company calls for a 10-day notice. The option by Record Company is exercised when the notice is put in the mail. If the delivery of the notice is held up a day or two, Production Company may not learn of the exercise in time to exercise its own option with Artist, thereby breaching its contract with Record Company and losing Artist.

Timely Exercise of Option

Making sure that options are actually picked up on or before the right date is, in theory, an easy enough thing to do. In reality, determining the "right date" is not so simple, and even under the best of circumstances, mistakes are made and options are not exercised in time. This often makes no difference and the parties have a good laugh about it and move on to more important things. Sometimes, however, the "more important thing" which gets moved on to is another record company.

I know one story regarding a now-defunct record label and a major group. Option-exercise time came around, but the group failed to receive the expected exercise-of-option notice. The group, feeling rejected after what they thought had been a long and successful relationship, signed with another label. A few months later, while recording their first album for the new label, they were contacted by their old label to discuss their next album. The old label was genuinely horrified to learn that the group was no longer under contract—they had let the exercise date slip past them.

If horror stories exist where the contracts have been fairly definite in their periods—1 year plus four 1-year options, for example—think of the difficulty of determining the proper option-exercise date for what I have called the open-ended agreement, where every option period can, and probably does, have a different "anniversary" date.

Example

The agreement dated January 1 between Artist and Record Company calls for a term of 1 year plus four 1-year options; however, the agreement also provides that each period of the agreement shall expire on the anniversary date 1 year from the commencement of the current period or 6 months after delivery of the second album, whichever is later. The agreement calls for a 30-day notice of exercise. Thus if delivery of the second album is made by June 30, notice must be given no later than December 1 of each subsequent year. (First year = January 1 though December 31. December 31 minus 30 days = December 1.) Easy enough.

In the first "year," Artist doesn't deliver the second album until August 15. The first "year" now expires 46 days later than December 31 (delivery date August 15 plus 6 months = February 15) and notice must be given 30 days prior to the expiration (February 15 minus 30 days = January 16).

In the second "year" (February 16 through February 15), Artist delivers his second album October 12, extending this option period to an expiration date 6 months after delivery (April 12), an additional 59 days. Notice now must be given no later than March 16 (April 12 minus 30 days = March 16). And on it goes in subsequent years.

Obviously, in each of the subsequent periods there are likely to be different expiration dates and option notice dates. And if this administrative nightmare is not bad enough by itself, Artist and Record Company may each start counting on their fingers from a different day when figuring when an album is actually "delivered." (See "Delivery," pages 50–54.)

Many companies try to avoid the exercise-of-option problem by having a new option period commence automatically upon the expiration of the preceding period (see Examples 4 and 5). This can be trouble for the artist. Unless the company having the automatic exercise has some very serious obligations in the option periods, such as an automatic advance or release of product, the artist may find the contract automatically renewed year after year until the contract runs out of its contractual period. In effect, the artist is trapped.

The automatic exercise of options is particularly problematic for the artist when the agreement is with an independent producer because even if the producer vanishes (which they do with alarming frequency—it may be some form of spontaneous human combustion), the contract continues to run year after year until the end of the contract unless the producer sends a notice of nonexercise of the option. Now, the likelihood of an independent producer reappearing, once vanished, to give notice of nonexercise is somewhere between slim and zero.

At this point, with the producer no more than a bad memory (or, in the case of spontaneous human combustion, ash), the artist theoretically has the opportunity of signing elsewhere. But the first contract is still in effect. If the artist tells the new record company the situation, he will probably be told, "Clear it up, and then come back to us." If the artist does *not* tell the record company of the other contract's existence, there is always the risk that when the artist hits the big time, the independent producer will magically reappear to reap his undeserved reward.

In summary, because of open-ended periods, "floating" expiration dates, disputes over delivery dates, etc., there are many situations in which *no one* is sure just when any contract period actually ends. An automatic option may only add to the frustration. And, if there is a disagreement over the expiration date of a contract, future repercussions range from disputes over when (or whether) an artist is free to sign a new contract to disputes over when rerecording restrictions are no longer in force (see "Rerecording Restrictions," pages 158–161). Accordingly, option periods and exercise-of-option clauses are crucial points and should not be ignored or made light of during negotiations. If they are not taken seriously, they usually will come back and haunt you in one form or another (or, more likely, bite you on some southern part of your anatomy).

SAMPLE CONTRACT PROVISIONS

EXAMPLE 1: Classic 10-Day Notification
2. I grant Company four (4) options each to renew this agreement for the period set forth below, said options to run consecutively beginning at the expiration of the initial period. Each option may

be exercised by notifying me in writing at least ten (10) days prior to the expiration of then current period.

☛ Simple and straightforward, right? Unless, of course, you count wrong or simply forget.

EXAMPLE 2: Notification Prior to Expiration

21. You hereby grant us four (4) separate options, each to renew this contract for a one (1) year term, such renewal terms to run consecutively beginning at the expiration of the initial term. . . . Each option may be exercised only by giving you written notice prior to the commencement of the renewal term for which the option is exercised.

☛ This provision allows for the exercise of an option up until, and including, the last day of the current period.

EXAMPLE 3: Option with Conditional Advance

18. (a) Any option to extend the term of this agreement, as hereinafter in this agreement granted to us, may be exercised by us giving you notice in writing at least thirty (30) days prior to the expiration of such term. Such notice to you may be given by delivery to you by certified or registered mail to you at your address last known to us. Such notice by mail shall be deemed to have been given on the date on which it is mailed.

19. You grant us the option to extend the term of this agreement for a first additional period of 1 year upon all the terms and conditions herein contained except that . . . in the event that the aggregate net disc sales through normal retail channels in the United States, of a pop single produced hereunder during the first additional period, consisting entirely of Artist's performances and no other royalty artist, shall exceed 500,000 units of such specific pop single, we shall make a nonreturnable advance to you, promptly upon the commencement of the new period, in the amount of $50,000. [Subsequent conditional options advances in later periods are for an increasingly higher dollar amount.]

☛ With a predetermined number of sales and the exercise of an option for an additional period, an advance is due concurrently with the commencement of the new period.

EXAMPLE 4: Automatic Exercise—30 Days' Notice of Nonexercise

1. b. You grant Company the number of options as set forth in Item II of the schedule attached hereto, each to renew this Agreement for a period of one (1) year, said option periods to run consecutively, upon all the terms applicable to the initial period. Each option period shall commence automatically upon the expiration of the initial period (or the preceding exercised option period) and shall be deemed exercised by Company unless Company shall send you a written notice terminating this Agreement not later than the 30th day prior to the end of the initial period (or the preceding option period), as the same may have been extended pursuant to the provisions of Paragraph 14 and/or 19 of this Agreement.

☛ Paragraph 14 deals with delivery and/or extension of the period for nondelivery. Paragraph 19 deals with suspension for reasons of naughty behavior or force majeure.

EXAMPLE 5: Automatic Exercise—10 Days' Notice of Nonexercise

2. Term:

(a) The initial term of this Agreement shall commence as of the date hereof and shall continue for one (1) year.

(b) You hereby grant to us four (4) separate options, each to extend the term of this Agreement for a one (1) year term, such renewal terms to run consecutively, beginning at the expiration of the initial term, all upon the same terms and conditions applicable to the initial term except as otherwise specified herein. Each option shall be deemed automatically exercised unless we give you written notice to the contrary at least ten (10) days prior to the commencement of the renewal term for which such option is exercised.

> ☛ This and the prior example both provide for an automatic exercise of the option unless the record company gives timely notice that it is *not* exercising the option.

EXAMPLE 6: Record Company/Production Company

Company may direct Production Company to allow the Artist Term for the Artist to be renewed for an additional Artist Contract Period by giving Production Company notice of Company's election to exercise the Artist Option at any time prior to fifteen (15) days before the expiration of the Present Artist Contract Period. If Company elects not to exercise the Artist Option, then, as between Company and Production Company, the term of the Artist Agreement shall expire at the termination of the Present Artist Contract and the Artist shall be informed of such, provided, however, that Production Company may exercise the option for Production Company's own behalf.

EXAMPLE 7: Negate Exercise of Option

5. You hereby grant Company Four (4) Options, each to renew this Agreement for One (1) Year or Eight (8) Months following delivery of the minimum recording commitment hereunder (whichever is greater), to run consecutively beginning at the expiration of the Initial Period.

A. Each Option hereunder may be exercised by Company giving you written notice of Company's exercise of such Option no later than Ten (10) Days prior to the expiration of the then current Period.

B. Notwithstanding anything to the contrary contained herein, if in the then current Period aggregate sales of your Albums recorded hereunder have not sold the minimum amounts set forth below for such Period, you may negate any exercise of the Option for the subsequent Period by giving Company written notice of such negation within Thirty (30) Days of Company's notice to you of the exercise:

Initial Period	100,000 Units
First Option Period	200,000 Units
Second Option Period	400,000 Units
Third Option Period	750,000 Units

THE RECORDING COMMITMENT

The *recording commitment* is the obligation of the artist to record and deliver a specified number of "masters" (or "sides," "singles," "albums," "CDs"), or "the equivalent thereof" to the record company on the record company's demand. The record company usually prefers that the contract be worded in terms of a "minimum" recording commitment, leaving the way open for the company to demand additional product from the artist if it is to the company's advantage to do so.

The term "master" or "masters," when used without any modifying language, usually means the recording of one selection. For example, a contract calling for a "minimum of four (4) masters" to be recorded in the first year generally means that a minimum of four recordings, each of one selection, is contemplated by the parties over a 12-month period. One common definition of "master" found in recording agreements is as follows:

> The word "master" means any original recording which has been accepted by Company as commercially satisfactory for the production of records and which embodies performances by me of a selection chosen by Company. If said selection has a playing time not exceeding 5 minutes 30 seconds, it shall be deemed to be one master; if it has a playing time exceeding 5 minutes 30 seconds, but not exceeding 10 minutes 30 seconds, it shall be deemed to be two masters; and so forth.

By the terms of this definition, a recording of the "Minute Waltz" would be one master and a recording of the "Six-Minute Waltz" would be two masters, even though both are recordings of one selection.

This seemingly straightforward definition hides a couple of nasty twists. Who on earth, for example, is really qualified before the fact (and, perhaps, even after the fact) to determine what is "commercially satisfactory?" Is top 100 on the national charts good enough? Or does a record have to go top 10? Or top 5? Number one? (A friend of mine suggests that "commercially satisfactory" means "contains obscenity, violence, and gratuitous sex." He should know. He owns a record label.) Some contracts substitute "technically satisfactory" for "commercially satisfactory," a slightly more quantifiable criterion; some use both.

And what about those words "chosen by Company" at the end of the first sentence? Unless there is something else in the contract to counterbalance the legal effects of these words, they can, in effect, negate an artist's control over his or her own artistic life. Buried in a definition of "master," the record company has sneaked in language granting it artistic control over the artist.

It's insidious.

The term "side" (or "sides"), when used without any modifying language, usually has the same meaning as "master" and is used in the sense of "one side of a record" or "both sides of a record." However, in today's world of CDs, DATs, DVDs, and whatever new configuration is foisted off on the public, it is as important as it ever was, if not more so, to properly define terms such as "single" and "album."

The number of cuts (is this now an anachronism?) on an album is also a factor to be considered. At one time vinyl albums generally consisted of 12 individual masters, each made up of a single selection. Then there was some slippage, and the number of individual masters included in albums that were released was generally reduced to 10. The last time I was able to find newly released vinyl albums in general release, the number of cuts had been reduced to eight. The reason for this creeping deflation had nothing to do with art or quality. It was something much more basic and close to the heart of the record company: economics. Up until December 31, 1977, record companies paid a maximum of 2 cents per selection as a mechanical license fee, the fee paid to the publisher (the copyright owner) of musical compositions for the right to manufacture and sell copies of recordings of the composition. On January 1, 1978, the Copyright Act of 1976 went into effect, and the minimum mechanical license fee went up to 2½ cents, a 25 percent increase, overnight. As a result, in the last days before CDs relegated the vinyl LP to the endangered species list, record companies cut back on the number of selections which were released on each album. With the advent of pricing structures specifically for CDs, and the practice of charging "excess costs" against the artist, the number of selections normally released on albums began to creep back upward. (See "Rate," pages 196–201.)

The number of actual recordings required to fulfill the recording commitment pursuant to any recording agreement will vary from artist to artist and from record company to record company. The vast majority of all minimum recording commitments for, say, 1 year, call for at least two masters, the equivalent of one single, up to a maximum of two albums, but the number of masters may be as high as 20 to 24, or even more. Again, these commitments are usually only a minimum, and the record company has the option to demand additional masters. (See Example 1 below, where not only is there no limit on the number of excess masters—an open invitation for stockpiling—but no credit against future minimums. For a definition of excess masters see the next section, "Negotiating a Maximum.") The recording commitment is usually stated in terms of the requirement for each period of the recording agreement, usually 1 "year" (as extended). If the period is shorter or longer, chances are the recording commitment is going to be adjusted accordingly. Some agreements will specify the minimum number of recordings to be made over the entire term of the agreement.

In cases where an artist is signing with a production company, it may be necessary to build into the agreement an automatic increase or adjustment to the minimum recording commitment if a subsequent agreement between the production company and a distributing company makes this necessary (see Example 7).

It is a common provision in recording agreements that live recordings (for example, concerts) do not count toward an artist fulfilling the recording commitment, unless expressly agreed to by the record company. The prejudice against "live" (dead is better?) performances seems to stem from a belief that live performances are less "technically acceptable" and that live performances, presumably in concerts, will feature previously recorded material which normally does not count against minimums. Also, so-called multiple albums, such as two-disc sets or boxed sets with two or more discs, usually only count as one album. (See Examples 4 and 6.)

What is the ideal recording commitment for a new artist? Beats me. It depends upon the artist. In the early days of rock 'n' roll, the commitment was likely to be a new album every 8 months or so—the thought being that the commercial life span of any rock artist was, on average, about 18 months, so it was necessary to crank out the product *before* the artist suffered the inevitable slide into obscurity. With some artists now approaching and passing eligibility for social security and still recording, it appears that these early projections of commercial life span were unduly pessimistic.

Record companies have adjusted their "minimum" requirements from what they were in the earlier days of rock 'n' roll—now perhaps waiting more than a year for the delivery of just one album. These days a requirement to deliver two or more albums in 1-year period would probably be met with looks of astonishment from the artist. The average time between releases of albums by current artists is closer to 18 months, and I don't mean on the short side of 18. Indeed, at the time of this writing, I have personal knowledge of an artist who, after 6 years, has yet to deliver the initial album and is still carried on the company's roster. So far, the only punishment from the company has been a refusal for the last 2 years to advance further funds.

The minimum-commitment number is very important in open-ended agreements, where the period of the agreement may be extended by late delivery of product. Thus a commitment which requires more recordings than the artist is likely to be able to complete will probably serve to extend the term of the agreement past acceptable limits for the artist. In negotiating such agreements it is extremely important to strike a balance between the artist's desire to record and the negative consequences of entering into an overly ambitious recording agreement. Of course, no matter what the period of the original agreement is, a recording commitment which has been set too high will almost invariably lead to late deliveries of masters, suspensions, and, for the artist, potentially undesirable extensions of the term of the agreement.

It is important not to confuse "recording" with "releasing." A master recorded during a specific period of the agreement may not be released in that same period. It may in fact never be released! Later we will explore some of the horrors and pitfalls of so-called "guaranteed releases" (see "Release of Recordings," pages 135–137).

Artists negotiating the recording commitment with a record company must consider not only their abilities to deliver, but also their other activities and commitments. If, for example, the artist writes all the selections to be recorded and has a heavy schedule of live appearances, even one album a year may be an unacceptable burden. On the other hand, a vocalist who sings other artists' hits ("covers" them), may be able to record three albums a year without any hassle at all. (When I was with CBS Records, we had a very successful artist who just recorded cover records. The A&R Department would pick recordings which were currently working their way up the charts and put arrangers to work. Musicians would be brought in to lay down all the instrumental tracks. At this point the artist would arrive for two nights of vocals. The Art Department already had photographs for the cover art. At the last possible moment, the song that was highest on the charts would be slapped on the cover as the title of the album. This particular artist could have recorded and released an album every week of the year.)

Negotiating a Maximum

Be very careful of agreements which call for "a minimum" of so many masters, or some number "or more," and nothing is said about a maximum (see Example 2). Unless some contractual restriction is placed upon the record company, the company can nickel-and-dime (more accurately, $50,000-and-$100,000) the artist to death with requests or demands for what are sometimes known as "overcall masters" or "excess recordings," masters which are to be recorded in addition to the required minimum number set forth in the agreement. Not only does this put the artist at a disadvantage in terms of product delivery requirements, it gives the record company the opportunity to stockpile the overcall masters for future use, with or without the cooperation of the artist. Artists should always view contracts referring to overcall recordings with care, if not outright suspicion.

My preference is to provide that any recording commitment using the terminology "minimum" be restricted to one album, and anything in excess of one album in any one period be subject to the mutual approval of both parties, especially if an artist may have a problem delivering product. If there is *not* an upward limit on the amount of masters to be recorded, a record company can continue to demand additional product from the artist. And, since the artist pays the costs of recording masters as an advance against royalties (see "Recording Costs," pages 106–108), the result is that a successful artist may find herself or himself building up the company's supply of recordings, at the artist's own expense, at the same time reducing the artist's bargaining position with the company and, incidentally, creating problems for any new record company. The more unreleased recordings the company has on the shelf, the more power the company has over the artist.

Years ago I was investigating the background of a certain supergroup CBS was considering "purchasing" from its current label. The group had experienced phenomenal success from its very first release—a steady stream of number one records. However, as I dug into the files and the background, I discovered a very curious fact: Every time the group reached a credit position with its royalties, the record company threw them back in the studio to record more masters. In spite of a string of gold singles and albums, it was *3 years* before the group received its first royalty payment.

SAMPLE CONTRACT PROVISIONS

EXAMPLE 1: Minimum or More

1. Company engages my personal endeavors . . . to record during the initial period a minimum of one (1) album, or the equivalent number of masters, or more, at Company's election.

• • •

(c) During each option period, I will perform for and Company will record such master recordings in excess of the minimum recording obligation as Company may request in writing. Unless Company specifically consents in writing to the contrary, no master recorded hereunder as part of the minimum recording obligation for any option period or as a part of additional master recordings requested by Company shall count toward the satisfaction of any other recording obligation hereunder, nor shall the recording of material already contained on any master recorded hereunder count toward the satisfaction of any such recording obligation.

☛ The artist, who has no choice here contractually but to record as many additional masters as Company requests, has no right to apply the "extra" masters against any future minimum requirement.

EXAMPLE 2: Minimum Recording Obligation

3. MINIMUM RECORDING OBLIGATION. Artist's minimum recording obligation in respect to each contract period of the term hereof shall be as follows:

Initial Period	Sufficient masters to comprise one (1) Album.
First Option Period	Sufficient masters to comprise two (2) Albums.
Second Option Period	Sufficient masters to comprise two (2) Albums.
Third Option Period	Sufficient masters to comprise two (2) Albums.

EXAMPLE 3: Minimum Recording Obligation Tied to Sales

[From Attachment] I. Minimum masters: Initial term six (6) sides, however, if any single reaches

100,000 units in domestic sales, additional sides to complete one (1) Album. All option periods: one (1) Album per period.

☛ Presumably, if some single doesn't reach 100,000 sales, there *won't* be any additional periods.

EXAMPLE 4: Limit on Additional Masters

3. 1. During each contract period, Artist shall record and deliver to Company a minimum number of Masters embodying the performances of Artist sufficient to comprise one (1) Album (the "Minimum Recording Commitment") and, upon Company's written request, additional Masters sufficient in number to comprise one (1) additional Album ("Additional Product"). So-called "multiple albums" [i.e., a single package containing two (2) or more Albums or their tape equivalent which is sold as a single unit] shall, for purposes of calculating the number of Masters delivered hereunder, be deemed to be the equivalent of only one (1) Album. Multiple albums shall neither be recorded nor delivered hereunder without Company's prior written consent.

EXAMPLE 5: Duration Extended by Overcall

2. b. Company may give written notice to me within the earlier of nine (9) months following delivery of the Minimum Number of Masters in the Initial Period or five (5) months after the initial U.S.A. release of the Minimum Number of Masters in the Initial period to increase the Minimum Number of Masters in the Initial period of this agreement by one (1) Album-master ("Overcall Album") in which event the duration of the Initial Period shall be increased to the later of eighteen (18) months or until one hundred and twenty (120) days after delivery to Company of the Overcall Album. In no event shall the maximum number of masters to be recorded hereunder during the entire term of this agreement exceed seven (7) Album-masters

☛ The Good Company taketh and giveth—but mostly taketh. Not only does Company have the right to require an additional album in the initial period, the additional album automatically increases the length of the initial period by at least a year and a half. The only "giveth" here is that the maximum number of albums for "the entire term of" the agreement will not exceed seven.

EXAMPLE 6: Studio Masters Specified

(ii) Each Album to be delivered hereunder shall be a "studio" Album (as such term is commonly understood in the recording industry) unless otherwise agreed to by Company in writing. Neither "live" performances, instrumental master recordings nor multiple Albums shall be recorded and accepted as part of the minimum recording obligation without Company's prior written consent, and Company agrees that it shall not require Artist to record any multiple Album hereunder. Without limitation of the generality of the foregoing, any multiple Album recorded hereunder shall be deemed a single Album for the purposes of the recording obligations hereunder and payment therefor unless Company explicitly in writing by an authorized officer agrees otherwise.

EXAMPLE 7: Adjusted Minimum Commitment

(b) If Company enters into an agreement with a company which is, or is distributed by, one of the "six" majors (e.g. Sony, WEA, etc.) the period of this Agreement and the minimum recording commitment shall, in good faith, be adjusted accordingly; provided, however, that without my express consent the period of this Agreement shall not extend beyond seven (7) years from the commencement hereof nor shall the minimum recording commitment, in toto, be greater than six (6) albums.

Delivery

Delivery, both as a concept and as a point in time, now more and more determines the anniversary dates of the agreement, option dates, expiration dates, and payment of advances. Failure to deliver may trigger any number of other events, such as suspension. (The next section covers suspension issues in more detail.) As the following definition from an actual contract shows, "delivery" refers to much more than a mere arrival of tapes; in this case the delivery requirements include not only master tapes, but "all original session tapes," as well as licenses, artwork, etc. (See Examples 1 and 2.)

> The terms "deliver to Company," "delivered to Company," or "delivery to Company," or words of similar connotation, when used in connection with master recordings or Masters, shall mean (i) delivery for mastering, to a studio or other facility designated or approved by Company, of fully mixed, leaded, sequenced and equalized 15 i.p.s. stereo-phonic (and, at Company's request, monophonic) master tapes, or other materials approved by Company, technically satisfactory to Company, in proper form for the production of the parts necessary to manufacture records of first-class quality therefrom; (ii) delivery to Company at its offices in Los Angeles, California, of all licenses, consents, approvals, artwork, other than completed album artwork, label and jacket copy information, credits and other material reasonably required by Company to release recordings embodying such master recordings and to manufacture album covers or other packaging therefor; and (iii) delivery of all original session tapes and any derivatives, duplicates or reproductions thereof to Company or any other location designated by Company.

In fact, there are numerous very good reasons for the artist to pay careful attention to all the language in a recording agreement that applies to the requirements of delivery. For example, with an open-ended agreement, where the anniversary dates and the term of the agreement may run for a period of some months after the delivery date of a specific album, does an artist really want to be responsible for "delivery to Company at its offices in Los Angeles, California, of all licenses, consents, approvals, artwork, label and jacket copy information, credits and *other material* [emphasis mine] required by Company to release recordings. . ."?

I wouldn't want to be guilty of failure to comply with delivery requirements because some publisher hadn't returned a license form, or some record company's legal department hadn't gotten around to preparing and sending a confirming letter that a guest artist's name could be used on the liner notes with a "courtesy credit." Let's face it, if you are an overworked lawyer at, for example, Warner Bros., and have a pile of rush contracts sitting on your desk, what priority are you going to give to a letter granting some artist permission to make a guest appearance?

Even if the agreement is not an open-ended one, the clauses pertaining to date of delivery can be very important. Failure to "deliver" by a specified date can result in automatic suspension. Accordingly, even if everything was recorded, mixed, and mastered, and in the company's hands, on schedule, an artist who had failed to confirm that a courtesy credit was to be used would be technically subject to suspension. Note that there is no automatic suspension for late delivery in open-ended agreements—indeed, open-ended agreements were created to avoid suspensions for nondelivery—and what takes the place of suspension is extension.

Many artist recording agreements include a schedule for the completion and delivery of the minimum recording commitment. This built-in delivery schedule usually states that the masters must be recorded and delivered in finished form to the record company within a specified time, for example, "no later than 120 days" after the commencement of the then-current period. Some agreements even give individual delivery dates for specific masters. Some—but not many—agreements provide that delivery may take place in steps. In that type of agreement, the date of delivery is the delivery of the masters, but there is a built-in grace period to deliver such elements as licenses, permissions, etc. For example, a contract might contain the following clause:

> The date of Delivery of each Album shall be the date Company approves the reference disk for each and every Master delivered in fulfillment of Artist's recording commitment hereunder, which shall be deemed to have occurred on Company's receipt of the fully-mixed and edited stereo tape of the Masters concerned, provided, however, that Company is in receipt of all the items described in subparagraph (a) below, within forty-five (45) days of Company's receipt of the fully-mixed and edited stereo tape of the Masters concerned.

There are a number of factors that may complicate the requirements for delivery. For example, among the laundry list of items specified in Example 1 below that are part of the delivery requirement are "all clearances required in connection with the use of Samples." Depending on the artist, providing the necessary documentation for samples may be a time-consuming task, as possible sources include "musical and spoken-word recordings derived from motion pictures, television programs, political speeches, commercials, newscasts and Masters by musical recording artists." Examples 1, 2, and (especially) 3 in the section "Sampling," pages 145–148, show just how complex the requirements governing samples can be.

Since 1986, even the requirements of the immigration laws of the United States have become a delivery issue. Thanks to a high level of xenophobia in our corridors of power, it is now necessary for a U.S. employer to prove that any employee—permanent, temporary, or independent contractor—is a U.S. citizen, a foreigner with a green card, or a foreigner with a visa which allows the foreigner to work in the United States. Each individual involved in a recording session (artist, sidemen, engineers, producers, copyists, whatever) must fill out the U.S. Immigration and Naturalization Service Employment Eligibility Certificate (Form I-9). Although ignored by many companies, the Form I-9s are now a legally required delivery element. (See Example 3.)

Delivery requirements are not limited to physical objects. (See Example 2.) Because delivery requirements are so complex, and because the consequences of failure to meet these requirements may be so detrimental to the artist, I always insist that provisions dealing with suspension (or extension) as a result of nondelivery specify that these penalties apply *only* if nondelivery is the fault of the artist. (See Examples 1 and 2 in the following section, "Suspension and Termination," page 57.) This prevents a company from suspending an artist for nondelivery when the company *itself* has refused to let the artist record. To illustrate, I will end this section with a true story of how CBS Records was prevented from doing just that.

A Cautionary Tale of Nondelivery

After several years of only moderate success, a group I represented that was under contract to CBS finally made a successful single. To everyone's surprise and delight, the single went gold, going to #1 on the charts. The album containing the single had already been released and sales began to pick up.

The contract called for the group to record a second album in that contract year. This was just fine with the group and they began to write new songs for the second album. We contacted CBS and informed them we were prepared to record the second album. CBS was not quite as enthusiastic about the project as we were. They wanted to wait and see how the present album fared. They said something to the effect that "perhaps some new direction would appear for the group and it would be a shame to rush new material while the jury was still out." We had to admit that there was some logic to this approach. Since we had nearly 10 months still to go in that contract year, we waited for the verdict.

After several months had passed without a go-ahead from CBS, we began to get a little nervous. We submitted a budget for the new album. It was rejected. It was still too early, we were told. By now, we all had a nervous feeling in the pits of our stomachs. I suggested we run a new album project by CBS, using a different direction. Rejection again. Paranoia set in. We huddled. What to do? I said, "Submit a third proposal for the new album." The group protested they were "written out"— they couldn't possibly pull together a new album's worth of material. I didn't see that as a problem, since I knew that whatever they submitted would be rejected. "Make up 10 titles and a budget," I instructed them. "Doesn't matter."

With a certain gleeful attention to detail, we slapped together a budget, along with a list of 10 "new songs," and submitted it for approval. Of course it was immediately rejected. With this rejection, however, came word that the group was about to be put on suspension for nondelivery of the second album. (In my poker-playing days this was referred to as "up jumped the devil!")

Naturally enough, we protested, and asked on what possible basis could we be suspended for nondelivery when they wouldn't let us record? The logic of our position did not at first move them. They said we were being unreasonable. They still wanted the second album, just not at that time. It seemed perfectly logical to them that they could suspend the group until they felt it was time to request the second album.

Harsh words were exchanged. Finally, it was mutually agreed to waive the recording requirement for the second album and move into the next contract year. To this day, one of my major disappointments is that our bluff was not called on the third proposal. It would have been a magnificent album. (A cautionary footnote to the cautionary tale: I not only got stiffed for my fees by the group, but they also never gave me the gold album I was promised.)

SAMPLE CONTRACT PROVISIONS

EXAMPLE 1: Delivery Requirements

5. (a) "Delivery" shall consist of the actual receipt and acceptance by Company of the Masters as well as the submission, in written form, of all necessary information, consents, licenses and permissions required by Company in connection with the manufacture, distribution and release of Records embodying the Masters concerned, including, without limitation, all label copy (including the names of all producers, engineers, musicians and other third parties who participated in the recording ses-

sions of the Masters concerned), publishing and songwriting information (including, without limitation, names of songwriters, applicable music performance rights organizations and the names, addresses, and telephone numbers of publishers), Album credits, the timing of and lyrics to each Composition contained on a Record, ancillary materials prepared by or for Artist which are required hereunder, first use mechanical licenses, all necessary clearances, consents and releases required for any Materials used in connection with the release of the Masters concerned, all clearances required in connection with the use of Samples embodied on the Masters, side artist permissions or any other information required to be delivered to unions, guilds or other third parties.

EXAMPLE 2: Delivery Requirements

14.19. "Delivery," when used with respect to Master Recordings, means the actual receipt and acceptance by Company of the Master Recordings concerned and all documents and other materials required to be furnished to Company in connection with them. Without limiting the generality of the preceding sentence, no Master Recordings will be deemed Delivered and accepted until Company has received all of the related documentation required under subparagraphs 4.01(c), 4.01(e) and 4.01(g) and all other materials referred to in subparagraph 4.01(f). Company will have the right to disapprove and reject any Master Recordings which in Company's reasonable, good faith opinion, is patently offensive, constitutes an obscenity, violates any law, or infringes or violates the rights of any Person, or which might subject Company to liability or unfavorable regulatory action. A Master Recording will be considered technically and commercially satisfactory under this agreement if (a) it is technically satisfactory to Company for Company's manufacture and sale of Phonograph Records; (b) the Performance recorded in it is "first class" (as that term is understood in the record industry); (c) that Performance is at least the quality of your prior recorded Performances; (d) your Performance in the Recording concerned is in the same style as your prior recorded Performances; and (e) otherwise conforms with all of the other requirements set forth in this agreement. In addition to the foregoing, an Album will be considered technically and commercially satisfactory if the proportionate number and playing time of the Compositions in it written by you is at least substantially equivalent to the proportionate number and playing time of such Compositions in each of your previous Albums.

> ☛ This is a fascinating provision—great for the company, a nightmare for the artist. Among the words and phrases open to interpretation (with "interpretation" being, in reality, the Company's opinion) are "commercial," "first class," "at least the quality," and "in the same style."

EXAMPLE 3: Delivery and Form I-9

3. During each Artist Contract Period; Productions shall Deliver to Company technically and commercially satisfactory Masters the equivalent in playing time of one (1) album in digital format, fully edited and equalized (and fully leadered in the case of an analog recording), together with at least one (1) non-equalized master tape of the same. Productions will concurrently Deliver any and all multi-track tapes recorded in connection with the recording project, including, without limitation, all multi-track master tapes and any and all outtakes. Productions will Deliver all such Masters and tapes to the Senior Vice President of A&R at Company's offices.

4. Productions will, in a timely manner, supply Company with all information it requires in order to comply with other obligations Company may have in connection with the making of such

Masters and to prepare and release Records derived from such Masters. Without limiting the generality of the foregoing, Productions will furnish to Company all information it requires in order to comply with its obligations under its union agreements, including, without limitation, the following:

(a) If a session is held to record new tracks intended to be mixed with existing tracks (and if such information is requested by the American Federation of Musicians [AFM]), the dates and places of the prior sessions at which the existing tracks were made, and the AFM Phonograph Recording Contract (Form "B") number(s) covering such sessions;

(b) Each change of title of any Composition listed in a Form "B";

(c) A listing of all musical selections contained in Masters Delivered to Company hereunder; and

(d) Productions will furnish Company with the immigration control documentation required hereinbelow (the "INS Forms"), all applicable AFM and/or AFTRA session reports ("Session Reports"), tax withholding forms (W-4s) for all recording personnel engaged by productions, Form "B"s and other documentation required by Company.

5. In connection with each recording session conducted hereunder, Productions will comply with the following procedures required by United States immigration laws:

(a) Before any individual renders services in connection with the recording of any master hereunder (including, without limitation, each background instrumentalist, background vocalist, producer and engineer):

(i) Productions will require each such individual to complete and sign the EMPLOYEE INFORMATION AND VERIFICATION ("Employee Section") of a U.S. Immigration and Naturalization Service ("INS") Employment Eligibility Certificate ("Form I-9"), unless Productions has already obtained (and retained) such certificate from that individual within the past three (3) years;

(ii) Productions will complete and sign the EMPLOYER REVIEW AND VERIFICATION ("Employer Section") of each such certificate.

(iii) Productions will attach copies of the documents establishing identity and employment eligibility which Productions examined in accordance with the instructions of the Employer Section.

☛ Here are three separate paragraphs, all dealing with delivery requirements, including extensive language regarding Form I-9 procedures. Also note that masters must be delivered in both digital and analog configuration.

SUSPENSION AND TERMINATION

Inside of a ring or out, ain't nothing wrong with going down.
It's staying down that's wrong.

—Muhammad Ali

Generally, there are three types of acts or occurrences which will lead to the suspension or termination (as opposed to expiration) of an agreement: (1) acts of the artist, such as, but not limited to, the failure to deliver masters in a timely manner; (2) acts of the record company; and (3) so-called acts of God. The provisions in agreements covering acts of God are usually referred to as force majeure, and are covered in a separate section.

Suspension, or the threat of suspension, can be a very effective weapon for the record company to use in manipulating the artist. Suspension carries with it the possibility that the artist will be kept from recording for an extended period, the possible stoppage of income to the artist, and—the ultimate threat—destruction of the artist's career. As melodramatic as this sounds, it is quite true.

An artist who has been suspended not only does not record product for the suspending company for the duration of the suspension but may not record for any other company. This is a powerful threat indeed. Timing is very important in the music industry. An artist's failure to release new product can lead to oblivion. Record companies, not having all their eggs in one basket, are better able to withstand a period of time without product from the artist than the artist can withstand the lack of public exposure. The threat of suspension may be used against an artist who, for whatever reason, does not wish to produce product for the record company. The threat gives the artist the opportunity to "reconsider" his or her decision. Although suspension can be a two-edged sword, with neither party really gaining when it is used, generally the record company has less to lose from the suspension than does the artist.

It should be noted that suspension has to do only with the *recording* services of the artist. The artist's falling out with a record company does not contractually affect the artist's right to perform live, on television, or in films; to produce or compose; or to follow any other livelihood, as long as it does *not* include recording as a performer.

On what grounds can a company suspend an artist? There are various grounds for suspension, all arguably "breaches" of the contract provisions, such as an inability to perform (due to anything from sickness through unavailability [perhaps incarceration for attacking a company executive] to downright refusal), failure to "actively pursue a career," or any number of other transgressions, real or imagined (see Example 5). The most common ground is the failure to deliver product in a timely manner (see Example 2).

The simple explanation of the operation and desired end result of suspension is that the record company suspends (or halts) the operation of the agreement until the artist cures the alleged breach by, in most cases, delivery of the previously undelivered masters (see Example 2). Remember that suspension also halts the running of the clock for the agreement. Some contracts contain provisions that go on to state that such suspension will continue for 90 or 120 days *after* the delivery and acceptance of the masters. Others provide that the term of the agreement is automatically suspended if the masters are not completed and delivered by a date somewhat in advance of the end of the term. (The record company's rationale for this is that it needs time to package and market the record before making a decision as to whether or not to exercise subsequent options. In effect, the record company argues they need to "run it up the flagpole to see who salutes it." Obviously, if nobody salutes, or even stands at attention, the chances of an option being picked up are slim indeed.) Such provisions, and others like them, should be examined carefully, as they may be very unfavorable for the artist.

The Impact of Suspension on Term of the Agreement

In traditional recording agreements the period of suspension is usually added to the then current period of the term of the agreement (see Example 3). Now if an agreement is subject to the 7-year limit mandated by Section 2855 of the California Labor Code (see pages 28–29), the period of the agreement plus the period of suspension cannot be enforced beyond 7 years (but see the section "Unrecorded Masters," pages 130–134). However, this is small comfort to an artist who is, say, still in the first 3 years of a 5-year agreement. If suspension occurs early during the term of a traditional contract, it may not be practical for the artist to sit out the suspension, run the contract out, and still have a viable recording career. Indeed, in the absence of law similar to Section 2855 limiting the length of an agreement, it may very well be impossible for an artist to sit out a suspension.

Note that in California suspension may not be an adequate remedy for the record company near the end of the agreed-upon term of the recording agreement if the ruling in the Sammy Hagar case (see page 30) continues to be upheld. Under that ruling, suspension cannot extend beyond the end of the original term of the agreement, and so suspension in the last year of an agreement might have no effect upon the artist. This would also be true, of course, if the agreement were approaching the end of the 7-year period. The operation of a suspension, or in the case of an open-ended agreement, an extension, can easily turn a nominally 5-year contract into a longer contract.

Alternatives to Suspension

In the open-ended agreement there is no suspension for nondelivery or late delivery; instead, the period of the agreement is automatically *extended* to some point in time after the delivery of the required masters. This keeps the artist under the record company's control as effectively as an enforced suspension (always keeping in mind the 7-year limit).

Most recording agreements provide the record company with an option—"in addition to" or "in lieu of" suspension—if the artist fails to or cannot meet the minimum commitment; that option is termination. (See Examples 4, 5, and 6.) As a practical matter, under most circumstances, a company that has any interest at all in an artist will chose suspension over termination. In addition, a record company may reap short-term financial benefits by keeping an artist under suspension. After all, there may be advances due, which will not then have to be paid, and there almost certainly will be recording costs which, if not saved, will be deferred to a later date. Sometimes, of course, it will be less expensive, both in terms of economics and aggravation, to simply cut an artist loose. Why should a record company spend what may be a considerable amount of money recording an artist it no longer believes will generate revenue?

Some recording agreements also give the record company additional options: such as (1) the right to pay the artist union scale for unrecorded masters and move on to the next period without recording in the current period, or (2) the right to reduce the recording commitment for that period to the actual number of masters already recorded, as long as the minimum number of masters is not less than one. In the second option, the reason for the record company placing the floor for the minimum commitment at one master is to avoid any possibility, in case of a dispute between the company and the artist, that a court of law would determine that there was no "consideration" for the agreement if either no recordings at all were made or no payment for recordings were made (see Examples 1 and 3). *Consideration* is one of the three elements usually required to prove that there is a valid contract. Basically, "consideration" is the thing, or act, of value given by one party to the other. The other two elements are the "offer" of the agreement and the "acceptance" of the agreement.

EXAMPLE 1: Extension of Term or Reduction of Minimum Number of Masters

(b) If, during any period of this Agreement, I fail, except for Company's refusal without cause to allow me to perform, to complete the recording of a sufficient number of satisfactory masters to fulfill my recording obligation, as set forth in Paragraph 2 above, and to deliver to Company any required approval or consent in connection therewith, then, without limiting Company's rights in any such event, Company, by giving me written notice, shall have the option without liability to either extend the expiration date of then current period of the term hereof until sixty (60) days following the completion and delivery to Company of such number of satisfactory masters and delivery to Company of any required approval and consent in connection therewith; or to reduce the minimum number of masters to that number which had been recorded as of the date when such failure began, but in no event less than one (1) master.

EXAMPLE 2: Extension of Term or Increase in Next Terms Minimum Commitment

15. If at any time you fail, except solely for Company's refusal without cause to allow you to perform, to fulfill your Minimum Recording Commitment within the times set forth herein, then, without limiting Company's rights, Company shall have the option, exercisable by notice to you, to:

(a) extend the expiration date of then current period of the term hereof, and/or suspend Company's obligation to make payments to you hereunder, for the period of the default plus such additional time as is necessary so that Company shall have no less than sixty (60) days after completion of your Minimum Recording Commitment within which to exercise its option, if any, for the next following contract period, or

(b) increase the Minimum Recording Commitment in any subsequent Contract Period by the number of uncompleted Master Recordings, in addition to the otherwise applicable Minimum Recording Commitment under Paragraph 3 above. The payments due for such Recordings shall be the payments that would have been due had the Recordings been Delivered during the Contract Period in which such Recordings were originally required to be Delivered.

> ☛ Note the suspension of the "obligation to make payments" to the artist in subparagraph (a). See also the similar language in Examples 3 and 6. This, of course, adds to the pressure on artists to mend their errant ways.

EXAMPLE 3: Suspension or Termination

14. Company reserves the right at its election to suspend the operation of this Agreement if for any reason whatsoever you refuse or are unavailable to perform hereunder in accordance with the provisions hereof. Such suspension shall be upon written notice to you and shall last for the duration of any such refusal or unavailability. At Company's election, a period of time equal to the duration of such suspension shall be added to the end of then current term or option period, such term or option period shall be accordingly extended and specific dates, periods and time requirements referred to herein shall be postponed or extended accordingly.

15. In addition to any of Company's other remedies, Company shall be relieved of the obligation to make payments or accountings hereunder if you commit a breach of any material provision of this Agreement. . . .

16. If your voice should be materially and permanently impaired, or if your performances should cease to be of the high artistic quality which induced Company to engage you; or if you should cease to work seriously at and pursue your career as a singer and entertainer in the entertainment field, or if you should fail, refuse or neglect to comply with any of your other obligations hereunder, Company, in addition to the other rights or remedies it may have, may elect to terminate your engagement hereunder by notice in writing and thereby be relieved of any liability in connection with unrecorded masters.

17. If you should be unavailable, as that term is defined in this Agreement, for any recording session, the minimum number of masters required for then current period of this Agreement may be reduced to that number which have been recorded as of the date which such unavailability began, but in no event to less than one.

> ☛ Take a look at paragraph 16 of this example. I wouldn't want my career hanging on the Company's interpretation of "high artistic quality" or "cease to work seriously at"!

EXAMPLE 4: Suspension with Conditional Limit on Time

(c) We shall have the right, at our election, to suspend the running of the term of this contract and our obligations hereunder upon written notice to you if for any reason whatsoever your voice or your ability to perform as an instrumentalist shall become impaired or if you shall refuse, neglect, or be unable to comply with any of your obligations hereunder. . . . Such suspension shall be for the duration of any such event or contingency, and, unless we notify you to the contrary in writing, the term hereof (whether the initial term or any renewal term hereof) during which such event or contingency commenced shall be automatically extended by such number of days as equal the total number of days of any such suspension. During any such suspension you shall not render your services as a recording artist to any other person, firm, or corporation. Notwithstanding the foregoing, no such single period of suspension shall exceed six (6) months unless due to your inability, negligence or refusal to comply with any of your obligations hereunder or due to a condition which affects a substantial portion of the United States recording industry.

(d) In the event your voice or your ability to perform as an instrumentalist shall become impaired or if you shall refuse, neglect, or be unable to comply with any of your obligations hereunder, then we shall have the right, at our election, in addition to any other rights or remedies which we may have in such event, to terminate this contract upon written notice to you and shall thereby be relieved of any and all obligations hereunder except our obligations with respect to Masters recorded hereunder prior to such termination.

> ☛ For an explanation of the last sentence in paragraph (c), see the next section, "Force Majeure," which deals with so-called acts of God.

EXAMPLE 5: Termination

16. *Termination.* If Artist's voice becomes impaired, or if Artist ceases to pursue Artist's career as an entertainer, or if Artist does any act or is charged with the violation of any law which subjects Artist or Company to any hatred, ridicule, contempt or scandal, or if Artist fails, refuses or neglects to comply with any of Artist's material obligations hereunder, Company, in addition to any other rights or remedies which it may have hereunder or otherwise, may elect to terminate the engagement of Artist hereunder by notice to Artist in writing at any time during the contract peri-

od in which the event occurs giving rise to such right of termination, and Company shall thereby be relieved of any liability for the executory provisions of this Agreement, except for the payment of royalties with respect to Masters which were theretofore delivered to and accepted by Company.

☛ Well, lookee here, our first run-in with "morality." The Company can terminate Artist for anything that "subjects Artist or Company to any hatred, ridicule, contempt or scandal." For a more detailed discussion of this issue, see the section "The Morals Clause," pages 163–165.

EXAMPLE 6: Suspend, Terminate, and/or Repay

15.01. If you do not fulfill any portion of your Recording Commitment within the time prescribed in Article 3, Company will have the following options:

(a) to suspend Company's obligations to make payments to you under this agreement until you have cured the default;

(b) to terminate the term of this agreement at any time, whether or not you have commenced curing the default before such termination occurs; and

(c) to require to repay to Company the amount, not then recouped, of any Advance previously paid to you by Company and not specifically attributable under Article 6 to an Album which has actually been fully Delivered.

☛ Notice that this provision allows Company to (1) suspend payments, (2) terminate (even if Artist is curing the problem), *and* (3) make Artist repay unrecouped advances. Let's see now, suppose Company terminates prior to the cure and then never pays royalties, or anything else, because the default was never cured—after all, if the agreement is terminated, how can the artist cure or, for that matter, recoup advances?!

FORCE MAJEURE

A calamity that affects everyone is only half a calamity.
—ITALIAN PROVERB

Force majeure applies to those circumstances that cannot be controlled by the parties to an agreement, including natural disasters ("acts of God" such as earthquake, fire, flood, and plague) and other visitations, such as strikes and "labor occurrences," that would not be considered acts of God unless one accepts the American Federation of Musicians as an engine of God's will.

Note that force majeure stipulations are, in general, applicable even if the artist's company is the only one affected (see Example 1). However, I always try to modify any such provisions so that if the problem affects only the company that is party to the agreement, or perhaps a handful of companies, the suspension may continue for only a limited period of time. If the problem is industrywide, limiting the enforceable period of the suspension serves no practical purpose for the artist because the artist has nowhere else to go. If, on the other hand, the problem exists only for the artist's company and the artist can be freed from the contract with the company, there is, at least, a chance to find a new agreement elsewhere (see Examples 2 and 3). For the artist, the point of these modifications is to either be freed from an obligation to a company which cannot function or, at least, not lose what may be precious time in trying to create and maintain a career. With this sort of modification, at least the clock restarts, and the artist, if not actually freed from the contract, moves closer to being free of his or her obligations to the company. Note, however, that frequently the company need only remove the suspension, not cure the problem, in order to keep the artist under contract. (Again, Examples 2 and 3 are relevant.)

If the artist is able to get such a modification, the shorter the period, the better it is for the artist. Most of these modifications give the company a period from 90 days to 6 months to get their act together. Some of these modifications (a surprising number, in fact) will cause the agreement to terminate if the problem continues beyond the specified period; some just reinstate the operation of the agreement.

Force majeure clauses have become more and more detailed over the years. I can only speculate that this phenomenon is the result of some unconscious "doomsday" thinking on the part of the record companies that has led them to put more thought and worry into these provisions. The three examples following this section are roughly in chronological order, and in light of current marketing practices, probably should be titled "Large," "Tall," and "Grande."

SAMPLE CONTRACT PROVISIONS

EXAMPLE 1: Basic Force Majeure

(c) If the performance of Company's obligation hereunder is delayed or becomes impossible or impracticable by reason of any act of God, fire, earthquake, strike, labor disturbance, civil commotion, acts of government, its agencies or officers, any order, regulation, ruling or action of any labor union or association of artist musicians, composers or employees affecting Company or the industry in which it is engaged, or delays in the delivery of materials and supplies, Company may, upon notice to me, suspend its obligations hereunder for the duration of such delay, impossibility or impracticability, as the case may be. A number of days equal to the total of such days of suspension shall be added to then current period.

☞ This provision is fairly straightforward: If the problem affects Company and/or the industry, Company may suspend for the length of such problem. There is no language allowing artist to either terminate or halt the suspension if the problem affects only Company.

EXAMPLE 2: Force Majeure, 6 Month/30 Day

15. *Force Majeure; Suspension.* Company shall not be deemed in default hereunder if performance of its obligations hereunder is delayed or becomes impossible or commercially impractical, or if Company (or its distributor) is hampered in the recording, manufacture, distribution or sale of phonograph records or Company's (or its distributor's) normal business operations become commercially impractical, by reason of any force majeure event not reasonably within Company's (or its distributor's) control or which Company (or its distributor) could not by reasonable diligence have avoided. Company, in addition to any other rights or remedies it may have hereunder or otherwise, may elect, by notice to Artist, to suspend the term of and Company's obligations under this Agreement for the period of time that (a) any such force majeure conditions continue. . . . In the event of any suspension under this Agreement . . . the contract period hereof in which suspension began shall be automatically extended by adding thereto a period of time equal to the total number of days of such suspension. In the event of any such extension, specific dates, periods and time requirements referred to herein (including but not limited to the dates by which options hereunder must be exercised) shall be postponed or extended accordingly. During any such suspension, all

agreements, covenants and obligations of Artist hereunder shall continue in full force and effect. Without limiting the generality of the preceding sentence, during any such suspension, Artist shall not render Artist's services as a recording artist to any person other than Company. If any such suspension resulting from a force majeure event affecting only Company continues for more than six (6) consecutive months, Artist shall have the right to notify Company in writing of Artist's desire that this Agreement be terminated and, unless Company ends such suspension within thirty (30) days after its receipt of Artist's notice, the term of this Agreement shall terminate at the end of such thirty (30) day period. If Company ends such suspension within such period, then this Agreement shall continue in full force and effect.

☛ The range of force majeure events has now expanded to include commercial impracticality and being "hampered" (sort of the equivalent of grouping mass extinction and a hangnail together). There is a provision that if the event affects only Company and continues for 6 consecutive months, Artist may give a 30-day notice of Artist's "desire" to terminate. If Company does not end the suspension within 30 days of receipt of the notice, the agreement terminates. Note that Company is not required to "cure" to keep Artist from terminating, just to remove the suspension. Nothing stops the Company from then reinstating the suspension.

EXAMPLE 3: Force Majeure, 12 Month/10 Day

16.a. If at any time during the term hereof by reason of any act of God, fire, earthquake, flood, explosion, strike, labor disturbance, civil commotion, act of Government, its agencies or officers, any order, regulation, ruling or action of any labor union or association of artists, musicians, composers or employees affecting Company, its subsidiaries or affiliates or the industry in which it is or they are engaged or any shortage of or failure or delays in the delivery of materials, supplies, labor or equipment or any other cause or causes beyond the control of Company, any affiliate or subsidiary, whether of the same or any other nature;

(i) The enjoyment by Company, its subsidiaries or affiliates of any material rights, privileges or benefits hereunder, including, without limitation, the recording of masters or the manufacture, sale or distribution of records is materially delayed, hampered, interrupted or interfered with, or otherwise becomes impossible or impracticable; or

(ii) The performance of Company's obligations hereunder is materially delayed, hampered, interrupted or interfered with, or otherwise becomes impossible or impracticable, then Company may, upon notice to me, suspend the term of this agreement for the duration of any such contingency. The duration of the suspension shall be equal to the total of all such days of suspension and the delivery of masters shall be postponed accordingly.

b. Notwithstanding anything to the contrary contained in Paragraph 16.a. above, if any suspension hereunder:

(i) does not affect most of the major companies in the industry in which Company is engaged, and

(ii) continues for more than twelve (12) consecutive months;

then I may elect to terminate this agreement by notice to Company which termination shall be effective on midnight on the tenth (10th) day after such notice is given, if during such ten (10) day period, said suspension is not discontinued by Company.

☛ Force majeure has now evolved to include "shortages" and "delays" affecting not only Company but "its subsidiaries or affiliates" apparently whether or not they are in the music industry.

ROYALTIES

I've been rich and I've been poor. Rich is better.
—SOPHIE TUCKER

Royalties are, quite simply, the monies due for the sale or use of a product or a right. In the case of the recording industry, royalties are the money due to an artist for the sale of that artist's record-ings. Since the type of "record" affects the royalty to be paid, a definition is called for, and the fol-lowing is representative of terminology commonly used in record contracts:

> The nouns "records," "phonograph records," and "recordings" mean and include all forms of recording and reproductions, now known or which hereafter become known, manufac-tured or sold primarily for home use and/or school use and/or juke box and/or use on or in means of transportation whether embodying sound alone or sound synchronized with visual images.

This definition includes "all forms of recording and reproductions," you name it: tapes, discs (ana-log and digital), and so-called "sight and sound" devices, and any other type of recording "which [may] hereafter become known." The royalty rates specified in a single contract, however, may vary from one type of recording to another type of recording. For example, the royalty rate was differ-ent for vinyl disc sales, tape sales, CD sales, and, indeed, for analog and digital even in the same physical configuration—cassette vs. DAT. In addition, the royalty rate may vary according to the following factors:

• How they are sold, e.g., mail order, record club, discount labels, telemarketing

• Where they are sold, e.g., domestic or foreign

• The price at which they are sold, e.g., full, budget, or premium

• To whom they are sold, e.g., libraries, military PXs, or mass transportation companies

Royalty rate refers to the percentage of the monies paid to a company for a recording that will ultimately be paid to the artist: 5%, 10%, etc. Sometimes royalty figures are given in terms of *points*—but the term "point" is interchangeable with "percent." A 10-point royalty is the same as a 10% royalty. Rarely, contracts may specify a dollar figure instead of a percentage, such as $1 per album sold.

The royalty computation provisions of recording agreements tell how the dollar figure to be paid to an artist will be calculated using the royalty rates specified in the contract. The process of royalty computation ultimately consists of chipping away at a gross amount to come up with a net amount. What is left, if indeed anything is left, is the basis for the artist's royalty. Because the over-all formula for this calculation is so complex, I will analyze the relevant provisions one at a time. Do note, however, that the determination of the dollar amount that is actually to be paid to the artist per album (or tape, or side) is based on *all* of these provisions. That is, royalty rate ultimately depends not just on wholesale or retail price per album but on the computation price (wholesale or retail) *multiplied* by a royalty set forth as a percentage and then *minus* all the reductions and deductions provided for in the agreement.

WHOLESALE OR RETAIL

When a man tells you that he got rich
through hard work, ask him whose?
—Don Marquis

One of the first things to determine in analyzing a royalty rate is whether the royalty rate is based upon a wholesale price, the price charged to the seller of the record, or a retail price, the price paid by the consumer who buys the record. In either case, the "price" is basically artificial. For example, the term "retail list price" is usually preceded by the word "suggested," and a $17.98 "suggested retail list price" CD will probably sell for considerably less. Similarly, the term "wholesale price" is generally preceded by "applicable." The wholesale price set by the record company may vary from time to time, either because of sales programs, discounts, price changes, or whatever; the *suggested* retail list price is not necessarily affected by a change in the wholesale price, although the *actual* retail price, which is set by the retailers, may vary.

In reviewing contract provisions regarding calculation of royalty rate, *always* find out at the outset whether it will be based upon wholesale or retail price; otherwise, any discussion is meaningless. It is amazing the number of negotiations which have bogged down after considerable efforts because one side thought the figure was based on wholesale price and the other thought it was based on retail price. In practice, the majority of major record labels compute artists' royalties on the basis of the suggested retail list price. However, artists should not, as part of a negotiation, expect a record company to change from retail to wholesale, or vice versa, to suit their needs.

Because the suggested retail list price is usually about double the wholesale price (after distribution fees; see Example 1 below), the rule of thumb for determining the basic royalty rate is that royalty rate based on wholesale price is approximately double the royalty rate based on the retail price, and vice versa. For example:

5% retail	= 10% wholesale
12% wholesale	= 6% retail
10% retail	= 20% wholesale
15% wholesale	= 7½% retail

These prices—retail and wholesale—vary from product to product within a company's catalogue based not only on configuration (e.g., CD, cassette, etc.), amount of product (e.g., single, album, box set, etc.), but also, sometimes, on type of music. This is sometimes called *variable pricing*. Records within the various categories are identified with a code designating the price for the particular product. (See Example 1.) At record company conventions, inebriated sales reps inevitably throw letters and numbers of individual recordings back and forth in marathon games of *Name That Record*.

Sometimes, especially in foreign markets, there is no suggested retail list price and no wholesale price for the sale of recordings. Then it is necessary to determine what is known as a *constructed price* (sometimes expressed as *published price to dealers*, or *PPD*) on which the computation of royalty will be based. Constructed prices are frequently set by local copyright societies, performing or performance (there's a difference) rights societies, or industry organizations within the appropriate territorial boundaries. (Example 4 below contains a clause covering the situation in which it is not possible to use a retail or wholesale price as the basis of royalty calculation. Also see "Foreign Sales," page 82.)

SAMPLE CONTRACT PROVISIONS

EXAMPLE 1: Calculation of Wholesale Price

14.06. *Wholesale Price*

(a) With respect to Records sold for distribution in the United States: (1) the average net price received by Company from independent distributors for Phonograph Records during the six-month period immediately preceding the applicable accounting period pursuant to paragraph 11.01 hereof, which average net price shall be calculated separately for each price category of Records manufactured and sold by Company (e.g., PC, C, KC, E, KE, H, M, CG, CT, CA); and (2) if there are no applicable independent distributors, Company's published subdistributor price in effect as of the commencement of the applicable accounting period, less ten percent (10%).

(b) With respect to records sold for distribution outside of the United States, one-half of the suggested or applicable retail list price of such records in the country of sale.

☛ The wholesale price is determined by what is "received" from independent distributors or the subdistributor less 10%. The deduction of distribution fees from the actual wholesale price (usually around two-thirds of the suggested retail price) allows the "retail royalty equals one-half wholesale royalty" formula to work. Also note the reference to "price category" (the "variable pricing" referred to above). The letter prefixes listed are also known as stock keeping units (SKUs).

EXAMPLE 2: Change Wholesale to Retail

(h) As used in this paragraph, the term "royalty price" shall be deemed to be the applicable wholesale price of records manufactured and sold pursuant to this Agreement. If Company should alter the basis of its royalty computation to the applicable suggested retail list price of records manufactured and sold pursuant to this Agreement, or if Company's assignee or licensee bases its royalty computation upon the applicable suggested retail list price of records instead of the applicable wholesale price, Company shall have the right to change its accounting to me hereunder by reducing the applicable royalty rate by fifty (50%) percent and basing said reduced rate on the applicable suggested list price and such applicable retail list price shall thereafter be deemed to be the "royalty price" as defined in this subparagraph 3 (h).

EXAMPLE 3: Suggested Retail List Price

(f) The term "suggested retail list price" or similar terms means, with respect to records sold hereunder for distribution in the United States, the average suggested retail list price for Company's records during the six (6) month period for the computation of royalties to be made hereunder, it being understood that a separate calculation of the average suggested retail list price shall be made for each configuration of records manufactured and sold by Company.

☛ Note the reference to "separate calculation . . . for each configuration of records"; this is another example of variable pricing.

EXAMPLE 4: Royalty on the Basis of Constructed Price

6. (b) (xii) In any instance when the "suggested retail list price" or "list category" of records (less container deductions and any taxes) is to be utilized in computing any royalty hereunder, and, with respect to particular records sold, there exists no such "suggested retail list price" or "list category," and royalties are received by Company with respect to such particular records on the basis of a "constructed price" (such as a price agreed upon, or based on a formula agreed upon, between the copyright society of the particular country involved and recording industry of such country, for the purpose of computing such royalty hereunder with respect to such particular records sold, such "constructed price" (less container deductions and any taxes) shall be utilized hereunder in lieu of the "suggested retail list price" or "list category" (less container deductions and any taxes).

PERCENTAGE OF SALES

Ninety percent of the game is half mental.
—Yogi Berra

After determining whether the royalty rate is based upon wholesale or retail price, the next step is to determine what percentage of sales the royalty will be computed upon: 100%, 90%, 85%—or less.

Example

Assume an artist is being paid 10 cents ($0.10) per record sold. One hundred (100) records are sold. The computation of the royalties due will depend on what percentage of sales the calculation is based on:

1. Computation on 100% of sales: $0.10 x 100 records = $10.00. See Example 1.

2. Computation on 90% of sales: $0.10 x (.90 × 100) records = $9.00. See Example 2.

3. Computation on 85% of sales: $0.10 x (.85 × 100) records = $8.50. See Example 5.

In practical terms, this means that with royalties calculated on the basis of (2) above, only 9 out of every 10 records sold are used to determine the dollar figure to be paid as a royalty; with (3), only 8.5 of every 10 records sold.

The obvious question is, "Why accept 90% or 85% when you can be paid on 100%?" Usually the answer, while not particularly logical, is persuasive: "Take it or no contract." This is especially true in today's buyers' market, where recording agreements favorable to new artists are harder and harder to come by as the ability to sign artists is held in fewer and fewer hands.

Historically, the 90% figure was arrived at in the days of 78s, when companies claimed they needed to recoup their 10% losses due to broken records. The fact that this rationale is no longer valid does not deter some record companies from insisting on 90% or 85% (or less) as a basis of computation.

Companies can be very imaginative when concocting justifications for the 90% rate. Once, after looking over a draft of an agreement which indicated that royalties were to be computed on 90%, I protested, asking for 100%. I was told it had to be 90%. "Why 90%?" I asked.

"Pirates," I was told. "Bootleggers. The 10% covers the bootleg product out there."

"Pirates," I repeated. "You're not paying us for bootleg sales?" An affirmative nod. "So you're deducting a credit from actual sales to cover bootleg sales which you didn't have to pay us for in the first place."

"Uhhhh . . . I guess so."

"Seems a bit illogical to me."

"Right. Take it or leave it."

Like I said, they can be very persuasive.

Some companies are very self-righteous about computing on 100% and claim to look with disdain at their comrades who compute on a lower percentage. Some companies who start with a lower figure will, when pushed, agree to 100%; most will not. Besides, as you have already seen, there is more than one way to reduce royalty payments, and companies who compute on 100% can usually increase deductions in another area. For example, as you read through the contract provisions at the end of the section, note the references to "net sales," that is, gross sales less one or more specific deductions, such as returns, credits, and "reserves against anticipated returns, credits, and exchanges." (See Examples 2, 4, and 5.)

Note that the royalties for the sale of compact discs are commonly computed on the basis of 85%, 80%, or even 75%(!) of sales and that record club royalties are almost always calculated on the basis of 85% of sales. And, as you read through the contract provisions, also note the frequency of language specifying that the percentage of sales may be modified by an outside source, such as the record company's distributor and/or licensees (specifically, Examples 3, 4, and 6).

SAMPLE CONTRACT PROVISIONS

EXAMPLE 1: 100%, Record Club 85%

(iii) Royalties shall be computed and paid upon one hundred percent (100%) of sales (less returns) for which payment has been received, except that royalties with respect to record club sales shall be computed and paid upon eighty-five percent (85%) of sales (less returns) for which payment has been received.

EXAMPLE 2: 90% of Net Sales

3. In further consideration of and conditioned upon the full and faithful performance of all of your obligations hereunder, as to records manufactured solely from the masters recorded hereunder and sold by Company for distribution in the United States through normal retail channels, Company shall pay you a royalty of eight percent (8%) of the suggested retail list price of such records computed upon ninety percent (90%) of the net sales of such records.

EXAMPLE 3: 100% or 90%—Conditional

3. . . . As to records manufactured under this Agreement and sold for distribution in the United States, Company shall pay you . . . a royalty, during the initial period, of five and one-half (5½%) percent of the suggested retail list price of ninety (90%) percent, or one hundred (100%), of records sold, as Company is paid by its record company distributor. . . .

☞ In this example, the percentage of sales used for calculation (100% or 90%) is dependent upon the company's agreement with its distributor. If the distributor pays the company on the basis of 100% of sales, the artist's royalty is calculated on 100%; if the company is paid on 90%, so is the artist.

EXAMPLE 4: 100%—Modified by Licensees

11. Net sales of any record shall be determined cumulatively on the aggregate number of such records sold, for which Company has been paid, after deducting all returns, rebates, credits, cancellations, and exchanges. Royalties shall be computed and paid upon one hundred percent (100%) of net sales for which payment has been received by Company or credited to its account; provided, as to records sold by Company's licensees, if Company's royalties are computed with respect to such records on less than one hundred percent (100%) of net sales, royalties hereunder with respect to such records shall be computed and paid on the same percentage of sales as such licensee utilizes in computing and paying Company's royalties. Company may withhold from payments otherwise due from time to time reasonable reserves against anticipated returns, rebates, credits, cancellations and exchanges.

☞ The artist's royalties are calculated on the basis of 100% of sales. But if the company sells or licenses through a third party, e.g., a record club, the artist's percentage of sales for royalty calculation is automatically adjusted to match that of the company's. For record club sales, the percentage would probably go from 100% to 85%.

EXAMPLE 5: Albums 85%, Singles 80%

7. Net sales of any record shall be determined cumulatively on the aggregate number of such records shipped for sale hereunder after deducting all returns, credits, and exchanges. Royalties shall be computed and paid upon eighty-five (85%) percent of net sales of LP's and eighty (80%) percent of sales of singles for which payment has been received by Company or credited to its account. Company may withhold from payments otherwise due from time to time reasonable reserves against anticipated returns, credits and exchanges.

☞ There are different percentages of sales based upon the type of recording. Singles are more and more treated as a promotional item—a way to sell albums—rather than a way to generate profits. It is quite common to also see a ceiling placed upon royalties for singles. For example, a contract specifying that an artist will receive a 15% royalty for the sales of albums may also provide that the royalty for singles will not exceed 10%.

EXAMPLE 6: Same Percentage of Net Sales

(v) Royalties hereunder shall be computed and paid upon one hundred percent (100%) of net sales for which payment has been received by us; provided, however, that if any of our licensees (including Distributor) distributing records hereunder shall compute and pay royalties to us on less than one hundred percent (100%) of net sales, your royalties hereunder shall be computed and paid on the same percentage of net sales as such licensee or Distributor shall utilize in computing and paying to us royalties in respect of such records.

☞ Most royalty provisions, like this one, provide that royalties shall only be computed on "net sales [which have been] received by" the company. If the company has not received it, the artist is not going to get paid for it.

ROYALTY ACCELERATION

*There comes a time in every rightly constructed boy's life when he
has a raging desire to go somewhere and dig for hidden treasure.*

—MARK TWAIN

The difference between receiving a high royalty and a low royalty is the level of risk. The higher the risk, the lower the royalty. The lower the risk, the higher the royalty. Obviously, an unknown artist is a greater risk than an artist who has already achieved success. The concept behind *royalty acceleration* is that artists who are forced to accept a low royalty rate because they are unknown quantities may be given a reward (or "just due"), in the form of a higher royalty rate, for proving themselves. The "proof of low risk" may be record sales, or simply the fact that a company considers an artist valuable enough to pick up the next option.

The royalty which an artist receives may vary with success, with the passage of time, or with both. For example, a contract may specify that the "base royalty" (the starting royalty for "regular full-price sales") will increase upon the product reaching certain sales plateaus and/or for subsequent recordings. Thus an artist's base royalty of, say, 7% may increase to 8% for sales in excess of 250,000 units and to 9% for sales in excess of 500,000 units. The base royalty for the next album may start at 8% and increase to 9% and 10%.

The following ground rules usually apply to royalty acceleration as a result of reaching specified sales levels:

1. Only full-royalty sales apply toward the various plateaus.

2. Only domestic sales apply.

3. Only sales in excess of each stated plateau will apply to the higher royalty rate.

Of these three rules, only the third may occasionally be waived, and what is known as a *retroactive royalty* is used. When a retroactive royalty applies, the higher rate is awarded, retroactively, to earlier sales.

Royalties may also accelerate when, with the passage of time, the artist continues to record product for the company. For example, the artist may receive a royalty of 7% on the first album, 8% on the second album, and 9% on each album recorded thereafter (see Example 1).

As the contract provisions at the end of this section show, there may be a number of limitations pertaining to royalty acceleration. For example:

1. It usually applies only to sales of albums, not to singles. Today it is the norm that royalties for singles top out at a specified level, usually at about 10% of retail, even when the album royalty rate starts higher and/or is affected by acceleration clauses (see Example 4).

2. It usually applies to what is known as full-royalty sales, "sales of albums through normal retail channels in the United States" (USNRC sales), which by definition excludes record club sales, foreign sales, premium sales, etc., which are usually some percentage of the base royalty.

From the artist's point of view, the most favorable royalty acceleration provision (and the one least likely to be negotiated) is one in which acceleration is retroactive, is based upon low sales plateaus, increases with each subsequent album, and, for each subsequent album, begins at the royalty level where the last album ended. That, my children, is acceleration heaven!

EXAMPLE 1: Acceleration Based on Recordings and Sales

6. Royalties

(a) With respect to records sold which embody master recordings recorded hereunder, Company shall accrue to your credit a royalty at the rate (herein sometimes referred to as the "Base Rate") of eleven (11%) percent with respect to records embodying master recordings recorded prior to the Fourth LP [except ten (10%) percent with respect to singles records] and twelve (12%) percent with respect to records embodying master recordings recorded after the Third LP [except ten (10%) percent with respect to singles records], computed on a royalty base of the "suggested retail list price" or "list category" of records (less container deductions and any taxes) in the country of manufacture or the country of sale, as Company is paid.

(b)(i) In lieu of anything to the contrary contained in subparagraph 6(a) above, if Company's "sales through normal trade channels" (which term, as used in this agreement, shall exclude sales or uses set forth in subparagraph 6(c) [foreign, record club, freebies, etc.] except for subparagraph 6(c)(iii) [compact disc] on its top popular label in the United States of any album consisting entirely of master recordings recorded hereunder exceed three hundred thousand (300,000) units (as determined in accordance with Company's standard accounting procedures and as reflected on statements rendered hereunder), the royalties which shall accrue to your credit on any such excess shall be at the applicable Base Rate set forth in subparagraph 6(a) above plus one (1%) percent.

(ii) In lieu of anything to the contrary contained in subparagraphs 6(a) or 6(b)(i) above, if Company's sales through normal trade channels on its top popular label in the United States of any album consisting entirely of master recordings recorded hereunder exceed six hundred thousand (600,000) units (determined as aforesaid), the royalty which shall accrue to your credit on any such excess shall be at the applicable Base Rate set forth in subparagraph 6(a) above plus two (2%) percent.

(iii) Attainment of the respective sales figures set forth in subparagraphs 6(b)(i) and 6(b)(ii) above respecting any applicable album hereunder shall not obligate Company to accrue royalties under subparagraphs 6(c)(i), (ii), (iv), (v), (vi), (viii) or (ix) at rates greater than those accruable prior to such attainment.

☞ This rather convoluted provision starts with a base rate of 11% (10% for singles) and goes to 12% for masters recorded "after" the third LP [is recorded? or released?]. (Singles remain at 10%.) Since the acceleration depends upon when the masters are recorded, not when they are released, anything recorded *before* the third LP [we still don't know if that means recorded or released] remains at the lower rate, even if first released after the third LP. In addition, at designated sales plateaus, 1% and then 2% are added to the base rate.

EXAMPLE 2: Acceleration Based on Sales Only

(m) Notwithstanding anything to the contrary contained above, for each album which attains full royalty sales of 100,000 units, the base royalty shall increase by one-half (.5%) percent for such sales in excess of 100,000, and for any such album which attains full royalty sales of 200,000 units the base royalty shall increase by an additional one-half (.5%) percent for such sales in excess of 200,000.

☛ This acceleration applies to each album individually and neither previous success nor the passage of time raises the base royalty for subsequent albums. This is in contrast to Example 4 below, where the highest prior rate is applied.

EXAMPLE 3: Normal Retail Channels in the United States

(a) Subject to the other provisions of this Paragraph 8, in respect of Sales of Albums through Normal Retail Channels in the United States ("USNRC Sales"):

(i) Sixteen percent (16%) (the "Basic Rate"). In respect of Commitment Albums Delivered in fulfillment of each Artist Recording Commitment, the Basic Rate will apply to the first five hundred thousand (500,000) units of USNRC Sales of each Album. The royalty rate will be seventeen percent (17%) rather than sixteen percent (16%) on the next five hundred thousand (500,000) units of USNRC Sales of any such Commitment Album (i.e., USNRC Sales from five hundred thousand one [500,001] units through one million [1,000,000] units); and eighteen percent (18%) on USNRC Sales on any such Commitment Album in excess of one million (1,000,000) units.

(b) Subject to the other provisions of this Paragraph 8, in respect of USNRC Sales of Singles:

(i) ten percent (10%) (the "Basic Rate").

(ii) Subject to the other provisions of this Paragraph 8, in respect of USNRC Sales of Long Play Singles and EPs: eleven percent (11%) (the "Basic Rate").

EXAMPLE 4: Adjusted Base Rate

5. Subject to the other provisions of this Agreement, in respect of sales by Company on its top popular label in the United States of any album consisting entirely of masters through Normal Retail Channels in the United States ("USNRC Sales") the royalty payable hereunder for such sales (as determined in accordance with Company's standard accounting procedures and as reflected on statements rendered hereunder) shall be as follows:

USNRC Sales (Units)	Basic Rate
0–250,000	10%
250,001–500,000	11%
500,001–750,000	12%
750,001–1,000,000	13%
1,000,001+	14%

(a) Notwithstanding anything to the contrary contained herein, the starting Basic Rate for any album after the initial album hereunder shall be the highest Basic Rate attained by the immediately preceding album at the time of the release of the new album. The Basic Rate for such new album shall increase by One (1%) Percent for each block of USNRC Sales of 250,000 units (for example, if the initial album has a Basic Rate of Twelve (12%) Percent at the time of the release of the second album, the second album's Basic Rate would start at Twelve (12%) Percent and increase to

Thirteen (13%) Percent for USNRC Sales in excess of 250,000 units and would increase to Fourteen (14%) Percent for USNRC Sales in excess of 500,000 units) up to a maximum Basic Rate of Fourteen (14%) Percent.

(b) Notwithstanding anything to the contrary contained herein, the Basic Rate for USNRC of singles shall not exceed a maximum of Ten (10%) Percent.

☛ In this provision, the artist gets the benefit of the highest basic rate previously attained as the new starting rate.

RETURNS AND RESERVES

As many of the example contract provisions in the previous sections make clear, no matter what a contract specifies regarding wholesale or retail, percentage of sales, and royalty acceleration, the figure on which ultimate net royalty will be based is not reached until a number of items have been deducted. Two items—returns and reserves—are considered in some detail in this section, as are reserve provisions, which spell out the company's legal right to withhold royalty payments on the basis of these deductions. Hold on to your wallets, kids—from here on in, it's all downhill.

Royalties are computed upon net sales, always less "returns." Most record companies allow retail outlets to order records, but give them what is known as a "return privilege" allowing the retailer to return all or a portion of those which have not sold.

Example

Record Company ships 1,000 records. After 6 months, 700 have sold; 200 are returned to the Record Company. Another 6 months pass. Of the remaining 100 records, 10 have sold: the remaining 90 are then returned to the Record Company. The total number of returns is 290.

The allowable return may vary from time to time and from company to company. For many years, a 100% return privilege was common. In effect, the records were being given to the stores on a consignment basis—they paid only for those records they actually sold. Stores could afford to be optimistic in estimating the number of records they could sell. After all, if the records didn't sell, the retailer could just ship them back.

One by-product of this practice was that sales figures were frequently based on records shipped, which might have little to do with records actually sold. This was a great system for certain record companies (usually public stock corporations or companies about to be sold) because they could ship huge quantities of records out, citing the numbers as evidence of "growth" and inflating the paper value of the company beyond its actual worth. I know of one company that shipped the same records back and forth between its various warehouses, and then reported each shipment as "activity" in the field.

There was, however, a major financial problem for record companies that offered a 100% return privilege: Records which had been sold at a reduced rate were sometimes returned for a full-price refund, creating a deficit that no "we'll make it up in volume" campaign could offset. The death knell for 100% returns was sounded in 1979, when CBS instituted a 20%-only return policy, and today most major companies limit returns to 20 to 22% of most records shipped. The 100% return privilege still exists as a pump primer to encourage stores to stock certain special products and recordings by new artists, and for sales of singles.

Today, in the traditional bricks-and-mortar market, singles are really loss leaders; they are produced only to sell albums, mainly by generating airplay on radio and television, so continued use of the 100% return privilege for singles makes no real difference to the bottom line. Indeed, you can see that some of the provisions at the end of this section that put a cap on the amount of reserves which may be withheld specify that the cap applies only to albums (see Examples 3 and 4 below), which means there is *not* a cap on reserves for singles.

Singles, however, may have found a second life with some commercial viability on the Internet. They still serve a promotional purpose by promoting the sales of complete albums, either through retail record stores or as downloads. The real revival for singles is the retro idea that singles can commercially exist on their own, with or without an album to back them up. Not since the heyday of the 45-rpm record could anyone claim that singles fell into the money-making column in a company's books. Now it appears that the vast majority of downloads are single tracks, not complete albums. This is a mixed bag for both record labels and artists. No one really makes money off of single sales, especially record labels. It is unlikely that even the most successful single will generate enough money to recoup the cost of recording an album, not to mention promotion and advertising.

For artists signed to labels, the emphasis on singles may make the possibility of having a successful recording career even less likely than in the past. With an album an artist at least has a couple of shots at having a cut break out and drive sales. If the emphasis switches to singles, artists may be playing in a game where it's "one strike and you're out"!

Royalties are only paid on records which are sold. Since a record returned is not a record sold, no royalty payments are due artists for returned goods. Clearly, it is not in the company's best interest to calculate royalty payments on the basis of "records sold" when some—but no one knows how many—of these records are going to be returned. (And you may be sure that with few, if any, exceptions, there are going to be returns on any record shipped by a record company. Returns are practically a law of nature.) For example, suppose a record company has shipped out 1,000 units of a particular recording. If the record company paid the artist a royalty on all 1,000 copies and then, later, 250 of the recordings came back as returns, the record company would find itself in the position of having overpaid the artist royalties on those 250 copies. What is the poor record company to do to protect itself against the (heaven forbid!) overpayment of royalties?

It can either pay royalties on records sold, assuming future sales volume will allow the company to offset future earnings against returns, or it can hold back a certain portion of the royalties payable to the artist until the returns are accounted for. The second method—holding back royalty payments to the artist by maintaining what is known as a *reserve* against future returns—entails less risk and, not surprisingly, is the one used by the record companies. [Of course, the use of the money (the "float") to earn interest which is not shared with the artist has nothing to do with this choice (and pigs can fly if they try hard enough).]

Example: How a Reserve Works

First Accounting Period. Artist's contract calls for a royalty based on net sales of $1.00 per album. Record Company releases Album and has "net sales" of 100,000 units during the first accounting period. Artist's contract has a provision allowing Record Company to hold back a "reasonable" reserve. (See Example 1.)

Second Accounting Period: Record Company is now required to account to Artist and pay royalties for sales in the First Accounting Period. The "gross" royalty due would be $100,000 (100,000 units x $1.00 = $100,000). Record Company, however, determines a 50% reserve is "reasonable" and pays Artist $50,000 ($100,000 x 0.50 = $50,000), leaving a reserve of $50,000, based on 50,000 units held back. During the Second Accounting Period, 20,000 units are returned and debited against the reserve. The reserve is now reduced to $30,000 ($50,000 − $20,000) based upon the reduction to 30,000 units from 50,000.

Third Accounting Period: In this accounting period, Record Company decides to liquidate one-half (½) of the remaining reserve (30,000 units x 0.50 = 15,000 units x $1.00 − $15,000). Record Company pays Artist $15,000 from the reserve. During this period an additional 5,000 units are returned. This reduces the remaining reserve to $10,000 (15,000 units − 5,000 units x $1.00 = $10,000).

Fourth Accounting Period: In this accounting period, Record Company again decides to liquidate one-half (½) of the remaining reserve (10,000 units x 0.50 = 5,000 units x $1.00 = $5,000) and pays Artist $5,000. No more units are returned.

Fifth Accounting Period: Since there are no more returns, Record Company liquidates the remaining reserve and pays Artist the remaining $5,000 on the remaining 5,000 units sold.

In this example, Artist received a total royalty payment of $75,000, rather than the $100,000 that the company would have paid if they had not withheld a reserve. Of course the company would have had the right to recoup the $25,000 overpayment from future royalties. Nevertheless, by holding the reserve, the record company was not in the iffy position of relying on future sales, which very well might never have materialized.

The percentage held back as a reserve may differ from company to company and from artist to artist, even within the same company. In negotiating an agreement, it is important to try to limit the percentage of sales which is being held back as a reserve. Now that record companies are generally limiting the number of returns permitted to around 22% of records shipped, it would seem reasonable for them not to hold more than 22% in reserve against returns. As in the above example, however, they will often try to set up a much larger reserve. If pressed in negotiation, most record companies will move from the "reasonable reserve" language to a specified limit in the size of the reserve to 25% to 35%. Remember, no company in its right mind will agree to limit the reserve on singles. (See Examples 3 and 4, where the limitation is restricted to albums.)

It is important to negotiate some sort of limit on the length of time that the reserve can be held by the company. Most companies are willing to agree to a provision of some sort which requires the company to liquidate the reserve it is holding within a specified period, usually within three to four accounting periods. Sometimes the liquidation of the reserve is based upon a negotiated sliding scale, for example, 20% of the reserve liquidated in the next accounting period, 35% of the reserve liquidated in the following accounting period, and the remaining 45% of the reserve liquidated in the third accounting period.

All actual returns are taken out of the reserve as they come in. Accordingly, the amount liquidated will be reduced by the actual returns. Also, a new reserve is created for each accounting period. Until a recording is dropped from the catalogue and the record company will no longer accept returns for that product, or any other product by the artist, there will always be some reserve in existence being held by the record company. How free records are shipped, sold, and given away also affects the negotiations regarding reserves. (See the following section, "Freebies.")

SAMPLE CONTRACT PROVISIONS

EXAMPLE 1: "Reasonable" Reserve

11. Net sales of any record shall be determined cumulatively on the aggregate number of such records sold, for which Company has been paid, after deducting all returns, rebates, credits, cancellations, and exchanges. Royalties shall be computed and paid upon one hundred percent (100%) of net sales for which payment has been received by Company or credited to its account; provided, as to records sold by Company's licensees, if Company's royalties are computed with respect to such records on less than one hundred percent (100%) of net sales, royalties hereunder with respect to such records shall be computed and paid upon the same percentage of sales as such licensee utilizes in computing and paying Company's royalties. Company may withhold from payments otherwise due from time to time reasonable reserves against anticipated returns, rebates, credits, cancellations and exchanges.

☛ The company's right to withhold payments is based upon the company's own determination of what is "reasonable." Beware. I once convinced a party in a negotiation that 100% was "reasonable."

EXAMPLE 2: "Reasonable" Reserve, 30% Limit

9. ROYALTY ACCOUNTINGS

(a) . . . In computing the number of Records sold, only Records for which Company has been paid or credited will be deemed sold, and Company will have the right to deduct returns and credits of any nature and to withhold reasonable reserves therefor from payments otherwise due to Artist; provided, however, that such reserves shall not exceed thirty percent (30%) and shall be substantially liquidated over a period of four (4) full accounting periods from which the reserves were originally established. If Company makes any overpayments to Artist (e.g., by reason of an accounting error or by paying royalties on Records which are later returned), Artist will reimburse Company to the extent that Company does not deduct such sums from monies otherwise due Artist hereunder.

☛ In this Example there is a 30% cap on the reserve. While there is a provision for liquidation over four accounting periods, the language is modified by the word "substantially," which means not only that the company gets to set the rate of liquidation, but also that at least some part of the reserve may be held past four accounting periods.

EXAMPLE 3: "Reasonable" Reserve, 35% Limit

(b) In computing the number of Records sold, only Records for which Company has been paid shall be deemed sold, and Company shall have the right to deduct returns and credits of every nature and to withhold reasonable reserves therefor from payments otherwise due you. Each royalty reserve against anticipated returns and credits will be liquidated not later than the end of the fourth semi-annual accounting period following the accounting period during which it is established. A royalty reserve will not be established for any Album hereunder during any semi-annual accounting period in excess of thirty-five percent (35%) of the aggregate number of units of that Album hereunder shipped to Company's customers. (The preceding sentence will not apply to any Album hereunder sold subject to return privileges more liberal than Company's normal return policies.) If Company makes any overpayment to you, you will reimburse Company for it; Company may also deduct it from any payments due or becoming due to you. If Company pays you any royalties on Records which are returned later, those royalties will be considered overpayments. Company may at any time elect to utilize a different method of computing royalties so long as such method does not decrease the net monies received by or credited to you hereunder.

☞ This provision has a 35% cap on the reserve. But note that the 35% limitation does not extend to "return privileges more liberal than Company's normal return policies."

EXAMPLE 4: "Reasonable Reserve," Liquidation Schedule

8. In computing the number of records manufactured and sold hereunder, net sales shall be determined cumulatively on the basis of such records for which Company has been paid, after deducting returns and credits of any nature and to withhold reasonable reserves therefrom. Notwithstanding the foregoing, a royalty reserve will not be established for any Album recorded hereunder for any accounting period in excess of thirty-five (35%) percent of the aggregate number of units of that Album shipped to Company's customers and, furthermore, any such reserve shall be liquidated, in its entirety, over the following three (3) accounting periods as follows: (i) 25% in the first accounting period following the accounting period in which Company shipped such Album; (ii) 35% in the second accounting period; and (iii) 40% in the third accounting period.

☞ This example provides for a scheduled liquidation—25%, 35%, and 40%—over three accounting periods, as well as a 35% cap on reserves. But note that that applies only to albums, not to singles.

FREEBIES

I know but one freedom and that is the freedom of the mind.
—Antoine de Saint-Exupéry

The record company's distribution of free records, or, as they are sometimes called, *freebies*, both as a sales tool and a promotional tool, is a very important element in the record company's efforts to successfully sell its product. Freebies are just what they sound like—free records. They are also sometimes known as "frees," "free goods," and a variety of other terms, none of which has the lyric quality of "freebies." Freebies are important to the artist because first, they can help establish the artist; second, they help sell records; and third, the artist does not receive a royalty for them. Two out of three isn't too bad.

Because of the positive aspects of freebies, and the fact that record companies will rarely waive their rights to them, they remain in the agreements. However, it is possible to restrict the number of freebies a record company can give out. Most companies will agree to a freebie clause allowing 3 free records for each 10 bought. Some will agree to limit freebies in the same manner as they are restricted for "the majority of Company's major artists" (whatever *that* means, since we must now rely upon the record company's interpretation of its own very vague language).

While freebies are a wonderful sales and promotion tool, since the artist does not get paid for them, the practice of distributing freebies does have an affect upon the royalty received by the artist. In negotiating freebie provisions, the artist (or the artist's representative) has to consider that the consequences of maximizing royalties by limiting freebies may well be detrimental to promotional efforts. Certainly it would be counterproductive for a new artist to place too many restrictions on freebies. In fact, strictly speaking, *no* artist will succeed without freebies, as the important radio stations simply will not pay money to get copies of records. Word of mouth may sell some albums, but nowhere near the numbers generated from the airplay of a hit single.

Freebies also have an effect upon the royalties paid for record club sales. Short of not offering the records at all, it is impossible to restrict the number of royalty-free records distributed through record clubs. Other than subliminal manipulation, how can the record club make its subscriber pick or not pick one record over another? What the artist *can* do is insist on a formula that provides that royalties are calculated on a number which is the *greater* of the actual records sold or a specified percentage (e.g., 50%) of the total records *distributed*, which includes freebies. (See Example 4 at the end of the following section, "Record Clubs.")

If freebies are a problem when they are shipped out, they are a double problem when they are returned. Inasmuch as returns are deducted from sales to determine net sales, it is important to the artist that freebies not be deducted twice in determining net sales—once as not being a sale in the first place and once by being subtracted from sales when returned (see the following example).

Example: Freebies and Returns—Pro-Rata Credits

Company with a "3 free records for 10 purchased" policy sells 1,000 albums to Store and ships 1,300 (1,000 purchased plus 300 freebies). Accordingly, 23% of the albums shipped to Store are freebies. Store eventually pays for 650 albums and returns 650 albums. If the record company counted the entire return shipment as consisting of full-priced recordings, it would calculate Artist's royalties on 350 albums sold ($1,000 – 650 = 350). (Assume for the purpose of this example that artist is being paid on the basis of 100% of sales.) But 149.5 of the returned albums were, arguably, freebies (23% of 650 is 149.5); and if the freebies were credited on a pro-rata basis, Artist's royalty would be calculated on the basis of 500.5 albums (1,000 minus 77% of 650 albums returned = 500.5 albums) rather than 350. The difference to the Artist is significant—about 150 albums.

Another form of freebie, one that is harder to control for the artist, is the reduction or discount in price which is sometimes offered as a sales inducement. The argument can be made, and frequently is, that a discount or reduction is not the same as a freebie. I suppose that it really isn't, but does it make any difference if 25 records are given away with every 75 sold at full price, or if 100 records are sold at a price discounted by 25% so that 100 records are sold for the price of 75?

SAMPLE CONTRACT PROVISIONS

EXAMPLE 1: A Laundry List of No-Royalty Deductions

12. Royalties shall not be payable with respect to the following:

(a) records given away, invoiced on a "no charge" basis, or furnished at a substantially reduced price to any customary recipient of free or discounted promotional records, including, but not limited to, Artist, a disc jockey, a program director, a record reviewer, a radio or television station or network, a motion picture company, a music publisher, Company's employees, an individual producer, any performer on the record, an educational institution, a library, or for charitable purposes;

(b) records distributed under a sales program that are given away "free" or invoiced on a "no charge" basis as a bonus and/or as a sales inducement to a customary participant in such sales programs, including, but not limited to, a distributor, a sub-distributor, a dealer, or any other person, and regardless whether such records are sold by such participant or any other person;

(c) records cut out of Company's catalogue and sold as discontinued merchandise;

(d) records sold as scrap or at a price fifty percent (50%) or more below the regular price then in effect to subdistributors;

(e) records sold below cost;

(f) so-called "sampler" records sold for one-half (½) of or less than one-half (½) of then-current price normally charged by Company with respect to samplers; and

(g) records licensed or distributed or sold at a substantially reduced price for use by any transportation carrier or transportation facility or for in-store background music.

EXAMPLE 2: Pro-Rata Credit on Returns

(d) In computing the number of records manufactured and sold hereunder, Company shall have the right to deduct returns and credits. . . . Returns and credits shall be prorated as between records shipped as sold and records shipped as "free goods" as a sales inducement in the same proportion as when originally shipped.

> ☞ This example provision could easily have been included at the end of the last section, "Returns and Reserves," but is cited here because of the language relating the credit for free goods shipped to the determination of deductions for returns.

EXAMPLE 3: Freebies and Record Clubs

(e) No royalties shall be payable on records furnished as free or bonus records to members, applicants or other participants in any record club or as free or bonus records to purchasers through any direct mail distribution method, on records shipped on a no-charge basis or on records sold for scrap or as "cut-outs" or at less than fifty percent (50%) of the regular price (as established by us or any manufacturer and/or distributor with whom we have an agreement) for such records or as records sold to educational institutions or libraries. . . .

> ☞ See Examples 2 and 4 at the end of the next section, "Record Clubs."

RECORD CLUBS

As used in record contracts, a "record club" has traditionally been defined as a mail-order operation which sells records through the mail directly to the buying public.

Before the advent of the retail record megachains, record clubs were enormously popular, especially outside large metropolitan areas, where the record club might be the only source for a wide choice of records. Now, with national retail chains and relatively easy access around most corners, it is quite possible that the record club may be traveling the route of the woolly mammoth. Why wait for delivery of albums through the mail? Why pay the full suggested retail list price for an album when you can go down to the corner and purchase it for several dollars less at a discount chain?

Gone are the days when there were three separate and distinct major record clubs—the Columbia Record Club, the Capitol Record Club, and the RCA Record Club—in fierce competition for subscribers and exclusive licensing agreements. Now the fortunes of a traditional record club seem to wax and wane with the introduction and availability of new configurations. During the transition period between vinyl and CDs, record club sales picked up until CDs became the norm. Of course, whatever "new" format comes down the pike in the future may allow traditional record clubs to "reconfigure" and, at least temporarily, prosper. Many observers believe that downloading of digital music files from Internet-based record clubs is the wave of the future—although it is likely that any Internet-based record clubs will turn out to be controlled by individual record companies. (See "Electronic Transmission," pages 90–91.)

One growth area for traditional record club configuration was the specialty record club. Specialty record clubs are really mail-order operations aimed at niche marketing of different types of recordings which may be hard to come by in the regular retail market because of the narrow demand for this particular type of music or configuration. Potential specialty record clubs could range from those offering vinyl recordings (for those people who can tell the difference—I can't) to those offering a type of music or recordings of instruments not generally in demand (e.g., accordians, bagpipes, etc.). These specialty record clubs follow the same model, on a much smaller scale, that the major record clubs used in their formative years: supplying recordings often not available in the neighborhood record store. Not having the deeper pockets of the major record clubs, most of the traditional specialty record clubs will undoubtedly either switch to online stores or dwindle away.

Whether record clubs are on the endangered list or just reconfiguring, record club provisions still remain prominent in record contracts. As is true for every area where the record company licenses an artist's recordings to a third party (and yes, the record club is treated as a third party even if owned by or affiliated with the record company), there is going to be a reduction in the royalty paid to the artist. In the case of record clubs, the reduction is 50% of the otherwise applicable royalty (see Example 1 below) and is generally based upon 85% of sales. Accordingly, an artist having a royalty of, for example, 12% of 100% of net sales would, for record club sales, have a royalty of 6% of 85% of net sales.

Over the years the basic terms of the royalty clauses concerning record club sales have remained fairly constant; the language, however, has been refined to reflect the growth of television marketing of records. Currently, these provisions include terms such as "TV/key outlet merchandising," and "K-Tel" and "Ronco" type sales (see Examples 1 and 2 below), which generally refer to the late-night offers of oodles of recordings—either cassette or CDs—for a wonderfully low price and, by the way, where else can you get all these fine recordings in one place? Most telemarketing sales are through third-party licensees and, accordingly, call for a reduction in the royalty to the artist. The royalty provision included will usually provide that the royalty due the artist is 50% of the net receipts or net royalty received by the record company from the telemarketing licensee. (See Examples 2, 3, and 4.)

Also included in the record club clauses of recording agreements are provisions dealing with "bonus" and/or "free" records, those records offered without charge to members of the record clubs as perks for joining the club or for buying a set number of records. These, like the free records sent to retailers, are not included in royalty calculations. As discussed in the "Freebies" section, there is not much a given record company or artist can do to limit the number of an artist's recordings that are chosen as free or bonus records by club members; the only practical recourse for the artist is to restrict the number of freebies which may be distributed without paying a royalty (see Example 2). Given these circumstances, it is common to include a provision specifying that the number of royalty-free records will not exceed the number of records sold, as in the following extract from a contract:

> [N]o royalty shall be payable to you with respect to (i) phonograph records which are distributed to members of any such club operation; either as a result of joining such club operation, recommending that another join such club operation and/or as a result of the purchase of a required number of records distributed as "bonus" and/or "free" records; provided, however, that if on a cumulative basis the aggregate number of club "free" or "bonus" records exceeds the number of club sold records, Company shall pay the otherwise applicable royalty rate for such excess free records; or (ii) phonograph records for which such club operation is not paid.

The following story illustrates the sort of thing that happened before this simple solution was invented. Many years ago Frank Sinatra was one of the best-selling artists on Capitol Records, which at the time had its own record club. Naturally, the club had the record club rights to Sinatra's product. Defying all the rules of statistics and chance, whenever people chose to "join the club and get five free records," "buy three records and get one free," etc., the requests came down improbably heavy on the "free"—rather than the "buy"—side for Sinatra's albums. Understandably, Mr. Sinatra was not happy about this turn of events and when Capitol was unable to cure the problem ("Frank, Frank, how do we know which records people are gonna choose?"), he decided to take future matters into his own hands. Sinatra left Capitol and started his own record label, Reprise, which he later sold to Warner Bros., where it became the foundation of its pop catalogue. And so it was that a simple little royalty provision may have led to the establishment of Warner Bros. Records as a music giant.

To show you just how extreme the reduction of a royalty can be, I offer the following example from an agreement in my files, which illustrates how an artist's royalty on a suggested retail $15.98 list price CD was whittled down to 12 cents. First, the record club provision:

> 9.02. The royalty rate under paragraph 9.01 on Records sold through any Club Operation shall be five percent (5%) and such royalties shall be computed on the basis of ninety percent (90%) of Net Sales of such Records. No royalty shall be payable with respect to:
> (a) Records received by members of any such Club Operation in an introductory offer in connection with joining it or upon recommending that another join it or as a result of the purchase of a required number of Records including, without limitation, Records distributed as "bonus" or "free" Records, or
> (b) Records for which such Club Operation is not paid.

In this particular contract, the artist's base royalty was 12% of wholesale (the equivalent to a 6% retail royalty). The royalty for record club is reduced to 5% of wholesale (the equivalent of 2.5% of retail), which translates to nearly a 60% reduction in royalty. In addition, record club royalties were based upon 90% of net sales. Net sales were defined elsewhere in the agreement as "85% of gross sales, less returns, credits, and reserves"—an additional 15% reduction on top of the 60%.

To save you the bother of working the above numbers out, the net result is a 3.825% wholesale royalty or, if you prefer, a 1.9125% retail royalty. That, of course, is before the container deduction, which in this particular case was 25%, giving us a net royalty of 2.8688% wholesale and 1.4344% retail. Now 1.4344% works out to about 23 cents per album. But we're not done yet. In that agreement, the royalty for CDs was reduced by a further 50%. So, on a CD sold through a record club, the royalty was less than 12 cents per unit—for an actual royalty rate of about seven-tenths of 1%!

Before you begin reading the sample contract provisions, I would like to single out for comment Example 4, a particularly horrible example of law-school-driven gibberish. Subparagraph (b) seems to provide for the artist to share in the company's credit for free and bonus records in excess of the numbers of records actually sold. The formula calls for the artist to receive a "portion" of the company's payment for "excess" records distributed, as follows: Company retains 50%; the remaining 50% is then multiplied by a fraction, which can be set forth as: aggregate of "Excess Club Artist Records" distributed over "Aggregate Qualifying Excess Club Records" distributed. Contract drafting of this nature has given rise to the common belief that lawyers charge by the word.

SAMPLE CONTRACT PROVISIONS

EXAMPLE 1: One-Half Royalty

(b) As to records sold through any direct mail order operation or through any direct sales to consumer operation carried on by Company, its subsidiaries, affiliates, or licensees, including without limitation, any record clubs (herein collectively referred to as "record clubs") as well as any sales operation of the type known as "TV/key-outlet merchandising" the royalty rate shall be one-half (½) of the otherwise applicable royalty rate. Notwithstanding anything set forth in this Agreement, no royalties shall be payable to me with respect to (i) records which are received by members of any record club, either in an introductory offer in connection with joining such record club and/or as a result of the purchase of the required number of records including, without limitation, records distributed as "bonus" and/or "free" records or (ii) records for which the record club is not paid; provided, however, that if the sum of the royalties so payable to me under this subparagraph 3(b) shall exceed one-half (½) of the net royalty which Company shall receive from Company's licensee distributing such records, my said royalty under this subparagraph 3(b) shall be proportionately reduced so that the sum thereof shall be equal to one-half (½) of said net royalty received by Company.

> ☛ Did you catch the provision at the end of this example that there may be a further reduction of the royalty due the artist if the artist's royalty exceeds one-half of the company's net royalty?

EXAMPLE 2: Telemarketing, Club, Paid on Excess

(b) In respect of phonograph records sold primarily by means of advertisement in broadcast media, including, but not limited to, "K-Tel" or "Ronco" type records, in lieu of any royalty to which you might otherwise be entitled hereunder in respect of such use, Company shall credit your royalty account with fifty percent (50%) of the net amount received by Company. . . .

(d) In respect to phonograph records sold through any direct mail order operation or through any direct sales to consumer operation carried on by the Company, its subsidiaries, affiliates or licensees, including, without limitation, any record clubs (hereinafter collectively referred to as "club operations") and auto tape outlets, the royalty rate payable to you shall be one-half (½) of the otherwise applicable royalty rate which would have been payable to you with respect to such phonograph records; provided, however, that if on a cumulative basis the aggregate number of club "free" or "bonus" records exceeds the number of club sold records, Company shall pay the otherwise applicable royalty rate for such excess free records, or (ii) phonograph records for which such club operation is not paid.

EXAMPLE 3: Broad-Based Freebie Policy—Share Net Receipts

5. With respect to records sold by Company through a Direct Consumer Plan, the royalty rate shall be fifty percent (50%) of the otherwise applicable royalty rate and the Base Price shall be the actual selling price of such records charged to the consumer, not including any taxes or charges for handling, packaging, shipping and insurance. Unless Company is paid thereon, no royalties shall be payable with respect to (a) records sold through a Direct Consumer Plan at a substantially reduced price, (b) records received by members of a Direct Consumer Plan as part of an introductory offer in connection with joining such Plan or upon recommending that another person join such Plan, (c) records distributed to members of a Direct Consumer Plan as a result of the purchase of a required number of records, and (d) records distributed through a Direct Consumer Plan as "free," "bonus" or "dividend" records. Notwithstanding the foregoing or anything else contained in this Agreement, with respect to records sold through a Direct Consumer Plan by a licensee of Company, in lieu of any other royalty or royalty rate specified in this Agreement, Company shall pay to Artist an amount equal to Artist's Proportionate Share of fifty percent (50%) of Company's Net Receipts actually received from such licensee that are directly attributable to the sale of records manufactured from Masters hereunder.

☛ Note that the list of nonroyalty records includes records sold at a "substantially reduced price."

EXAMPLE 4: Excess Free Records Based on Formula

9.03 (a) The royalty rate on Phonograph Records sold through so-called "record clubs" shall be one-half (½) of the otherwise applicable royalty rate if manufactured and sold by Company, and an amount equal to one-half (½) of the Net Royalty from the sale of those Phonograph Records if manufactured and sold by Company's licensees.

(b) If, pursuant to Company's agreement with any record club licensee distributing Records hereunder through a direct mail or mail order operation ("Club Agreement") (1) the aggregate number of our Records (including Records hereunder) distributed thereunder during any particular period of time as "free" or "bonus" records shall exceed the aggregate number of our Records (including Records hereunder) sold thereunder during that period (hereunder such excess Records are referred to as "Excess Club Records"); and (2) the number of Records hereunder distributed thereunder during that time period by such licensee as "free" or "bonus" Records shall exceed the number of records hereunder sold during that time period by such licensee (hereunder such excess Records are referred to as "Excess Club Artist Records") then Company shall credit your royalty account hereunder with a portion of the adjusting royalty payment, if any, made by such licensee to Company in respect of the Excess Club Records distributed by that licensee during that time period which portion shall be determined by multiplying fifty (50%) percent of such adjusting royalty payment by a fraction, the numerator of which shall be the aggregate numerator of Excess Club Artist Records distributed by that licensee during that time period and the denominator of which shall be the Aggregate

Qualifying Excess Club Records (as defined in the following sentence), including Excess Club Artist Records, distributed by that licensee during that time period. As used in the preceding sentence, "Aggregate Qualifying Excess Club Records" shall mean the aggregate number of "free" or "bonus" records in the excess of records sold with respect to each artist signed to Company (or other royalty participant) whose "free" or "bonus" records distributed pursuant to a Club Agreement exceed the number of their records which are sold thereunder during the applicable time period.

FOREIGN SALES

The royalty provisions dealing with sales of records outside of the United States are usually lumped under the general heading "foreign." In negotiations, the term is used as a noun, as in: "What are you doing about foreign?" meaning: "What is the royalty for sales of the record outside of the United States?" The royalty for foreign sales for any artist other than a superstar and/or an artist who is able to make a deal on a territory-to-territory basis (see below), will be on a reduced basis. In the past, the foreign royalty percentage was one-half the domestic rate (e.g., an artist receiving a 5% retail base royalty in the United States would get 2.5% on foreign sales; see Example 1 below). Today, there still is a reduction in the royalty, but usually the reduction is less than 50%. Normally, the reduction in royalty is a third or a quarter, so the royalty would be two-thirds or three-fourths of the applicable domestic royalty. So, for example, an artist having a domestic royalty of 10% on a full-priced CD sold in the United States, with a 25% reduction for foreign, would have a 7.5% royalty for the same full-priced CD sold outside the United States. (See Example 2.) Note that it is also common for companies to write foreign royalty provisions on an "either/or," generally "lesser of," basis. For example, the foreign royalty rate might be "the lesser of seventy-five (75%) percent of the otherwise applicable royalty or fifty (50%) percent of company's net royalty." In these provisions and elsewhere, the reduction of the "applicable royalty" can lead to a multiple reduction of the royalty rate when a royalty rate already reduced becomes the "applicable royalty" subject to further reduction.

Example: Foreign Record Club Sales

A company has a base domestic royalty rate of 5% of the retail price, a record club royalty of 50% of the base royalty, and a foreign royalty of 50% of the "otherwise applicable" royalty. Thus the royalty for foreign record club sales becomes one-fourth of the base rate: base rate = 5%, applicable royalty for record club = 2½%, royalty for foreign record club sales = 1¼%.

The two basic factors in determining what the foreign royalty reduction will be are:

1. The record company's royalty arrangement with its foreign licensee (independent, affiliated, owned by, or whatever).

2. The royalty rate paid to the artist in question.

The starting point is always: What does the record company receive from its foreign licensees? It is a matter of basic arithmetic that a record company cannot give a foreign royalty to an artist that is more, or the same as, what the company itself receives and still make a profit. A general rule of thumb is that an artist's royalty will not exceed one-half of the gross amount received by the record company from its licensee. Therefore, a record company receiving the equivalent of 20%

from a licensee may be willing, if pushed, to provide for a foreign royalty as high as 10%. However, in most cases involving foreign sales the record company will usually have to make royalty payments to a producer also, and unless this is taken into account, if the artist takes too much, the producer's share will have to come out of the company's share. (See Chapter 4, "Independent Producer Agreements," pages 206–221.)

Record company agreements frequently provide that the royalty for foreign sales will be computed upon a price, retail or wholesale, "from time to time of such records in the country of manufacture, the country of sale, the country of import, or the country of export *as the company may elect*" [emphasis mine]. If this sounds a bit suspicious to you, you're right. It allows the company to pick the method of computation which is most favorable to the company. Suppose these different prices are as follows:

1. Country of manufacture $6.00

2. Country of sale $7.50

3. Country of import $8.50

4. Country of export $10.00

Which price do you suppose the record company will "elect" to compute the royalty on? If you chose anything other than (1), I suggest that you stop reading at this point and consider a career outside of the music business.

There are two approaches to making foreign royalty computation more equitable from the artist's point of view. The first, which I find too inflexible, is to insist that the record sales figures be computed using the price of the country of sale; this approach assumes that the price in the country of sale will be the highest of the choices. I prefer a different approach. Relying on the greed of the record company (and presuming that the company has already looked out for number one), I allow the language to stay as stated above, but add the words "as Company is paid" to the sentence. (See Example 4 below.) I believe you can't go too far in the wrong direction taking the same ride the record company is taking.

In some countries, by law or by custom, no suggested retail list price or set wholesale price for recordings exists. In such cases a fiction known as a "constructed" list price is used. In effect, we are saying that although no such thing as a "suggested retail list price" or "wholesale price" exists here, if there *were* such a thing, by golly, this is what it would be. And, as long as we are playing make-believe, we will compute your royalty as if these things really existed, although we all know they don't.

The construction of the constructed price is usually done either by some local government authority, such as a government copyright office, or some quasi-governmental organization, such as a performing or performance rights society, local trade group, or the like. (For an example of a contract provision specifying the use of a constructed price, refer back to Example 4 in "Wholesale or Retail," page 63.) Sometimes, for the purposes of royalty calculation, reference will be made to a published price to dealers (PPD; see page 64), which is, in reality, another form of wholesale price.

Exchange rates between U.S. dollars and foreign currency vary constantly. The exchange rate used at the time of accounting for foreign sales needs to be determined with some certainty. For the artist, unless the artist is fortunate enough to be paid at the source (see below), the exchange rate used will be determined by the record company's agreements with its foreign licensees (see Examples 1, 3, 4, and 5). (For more information on how the companies determine the exchange rate, see Example 2 in the section "Costs" in Chapter 12, "Foreign Subpublishing Agreements," pages 342–357.)

Some companies have a different rate of royalty reduction for different territories, for example, 25% for Europe and 33⅓% for South America. (See Example 4.) The strangest experience I had with the "variable royalty by territory" problem was when one major company told me to choose and list countries either in column A or column B; the A column countries would have a higher foreign royalty. After I noted that this method was like making choices on a menu, my first suggestion—that the Cayman Islands go into the B column and the rest of the world go into the A column—was rejected, and I was faced with the extremely difficult chore of determining which territories would pay little and which would pay even less.

Artists in a position to negotiate and receive payment for record sales *at the source*, that is, in the foreign country itself and at the same time that the record company receives payment from the licensee in that country, may reap significant benefits. The obvious advantage is timely payment: artists don't have to wait the minimum of 6 to 8 months it would otherwise take for the money to get to them. And if the artist is paid in the currency of the foreign country and has the nerve and expertise to engage in currency arbitrage—that is, buying and selling currency in different markets to take advantage of favorable exchange rates—he or she has a wonderful opportunity either to make a great deal of money or, more likely, to lose a great deal of money. It is not a game to be played by the faint of heart.

While not exactly about currency arbitrage, there is a story about an interesting way to make money. A successful European group did a concert in Russia and elected to take payment in grain rather than cash (yes, at the time it was American grain). The grain was shipped to another country and traded, at a profit, for another commodity, which, in turn, was shipped to still another country and traded, again at a profit, for another commodity. This was done several times until the end commodity reached the group's home country, where it was again sold, this time for an enormous profit. The end payoff for the group was several times what they would have received had they taken just plain old cash. (I told this story to a Russian friend and he exclaimed, "Hey! I was at that concert.")

In order to boost local economies, some foreign countries will not allow money to leave the country. This forces the recipients either to leave the payments in local banks or to spend the money in the local economy by, for example, purchasing local goods or raw materials for export. (For those desiring a different type of gratification, some of these countries present excellent vacation possibilities, which the artist can pay for with the local currency being held for spending only in that territory.) This situation is known as "blocked currency" or "blocked funds." In anticipation of blocked funds situations, most royalty provisions for foreign sales contain language stating that if there is a blocked funds situation, the record company may deposit the artist's royalty in a depository in that country. (See Examples 1, 3, 4, and 5.)

Under these circumstances the language in Example 3 is slightly more favorable to the artist than the language in the others because the artist, rather than the company, has to right to select the local depository. Some provisions sidestep the blocked funds issue by stating that royalties are not due the artist until payment is actually received in the United States. If this language is used, the artist should make sure there is also language that stipulates that the money should be deposited in the artist's name if payment is received in the foreign country. (See Example 3.)

Better than having money deposited in a local depository is having the record company pay the artist for monies credited to the record company. In addition to having credited royalties deposited locally, there are several other types of credits which may be applied when there are blocked funds, such as a noncurrency credit in the form of some commodity (in India, for example, major film companies often take their blocked funds credits in the form of airline tickets) or a credit against a prepayment or advance made by the licensee to the company. With regard to credit against advances, any record company worth its salt is going to demand, and get, a cash advance from a foreign subdistributor. Depending upon the amount of the advance and how long ago it was received, there may be some monies left from which the artist can be paid.

Sometimes (although not often), other countries, usually Canada, are miraculously transformed into domestic territories. Generally, this is not something the artist can bargain for: Either the language is in the contract or it isn't. (If it hadn't been for a stray musket ball hitting an American general by the name of Benedict Arnold in the knee before the walls of Montreal, this would probably not even be a question—but that's another story.) Examples 2 and 4 below both provide that the same royalty rate applies to the United States and Canada, but not to records sold outside these two countries.

Artists with enough clout may be able to negotiate a record contract with a company for the United States only, negotiating a separate agreement (or agreements) with a foreign record company (or record companies). If an artist is able to negotiate recording agreements on a territory-by-territory basis, with each territory standing on its own, by definition there is no "foreign" royalty and no need for any separate provision dealing with foreign royalty—each territory being, arguably, a "domestic" territory. Negotiating separate agreements would have several obvious advantages for the artist. One, of course, would be increased control over whatever situations might arise, as the artist would not have to go through the domestic company. Another would be the ability to avoid cross-collateralization on foreign sales. (Cross-collateralization is covered in detail in pages 101–102.) An example would be a case in which an artist was signed to one company for the entire world with a clause granting the company the right to cross-collateralize. In that case, the royalties for a hit in, say, France could be used to offset losses in the United States. On the other hand, if the artist was under different contracts with different companies on a territory-to-territory basis, the royalties from the hit in France could not be used to offset losses in any other territory.) Finally, the artist would have the very important ability to obtain separate advances (free from cross-collateralization) from the various foreign countries.

SAMPLE CONTRACT PROVISIONS

EXAMPLE 1: Traditional One-Half Foreign Royalty

(a) As to records manufactured, sold or licensed for distribution or manufacture outside of the United States of America, the royalty rate payable to me shall be one-half (½) of the applicable royalty rate which would have been payable to me therefor if such records had been manufactured or sold for distribution in the United States. The royalty for such records shall be computed in the national currency, at Company's election, of the country of manufacture, the country of sale, or the United States, and shall be paid at the same rate of exchange as Company is paid; provided, however, that royalties on records sold for distribution outside of the United States shall not be due and payable until payment therefor has been received by Company in the United States and, provided further, that if Company does not receive payment in United States dollars and elects to accept payment in a foreign currency, Company may deposit to my credit (and at my expense) in a depository selected by Company all payments so received as royalties applicable to this Agreement and shall notify me thereof promptly. Such deposits as above stated shall fulfill Company's obligations hereunder as to the record sales to which such royalty payments are applicable. All royalties applicable to this Agreement received from foreign sources shall be subject to any applicable taxes.

☛ This older provision (the 50% reduction reveals its age) contains all the basic elements of a foreign royalty provision: reduced royalty; reduction based upon "applicable royalty rate"; variable calculation price by territory; same exchange rate; and provision for blocked funds.

EXAMPLE 2: One-Fourth Reduction

(b) As to records manufactured, sold or licensed by Company for distribution or manufacture outside of the United States of America and Canada, the royalty rate payable to me shall be three-quarters (¾) of the applicable royalty rate which would have been payable to me therefor if such records had been manufactured or sold for distribution in the United States and Canada.

☛ Canada, presumably smuggled across the border into the United States, is included in domestic sales.

EXAMPLE 3: Blocked Funds

6. (b) ... Such royalties shall be computed in the national currency of the country of manufacture or the country of sale, as Company is paid, at the rate of exchange in effect at the time of payment to Company for such records, and shall not accrue until payment for the record sales to which such royalties are attributable has been received by Company in the United States, but, if at the time such sales are reported to Company in the United States such payment is instead applied to recoup an earlier advance received from such a third party by Company in the United States, then such royalties shall accrue when such sales are so reported and such payment is so applied. If Company is paid for records sold outside the United States but Company cannot receive such payment in the United States, then Company shall, at your election and expense, deposit the royalties payable to you with respect to such record sales in the currency in which Company receives payment therefor, and such deposit shall be made to your account in a depository selected by you and located in the country in which payment to Company is made for such record sales. Deposit and notice to you shall discharge Company of the royalty obligation for record sales to which such royalties are applicable.

☛ The artist is paid at the same rate of exchange as the company and will not be paid until payment is received by the company. If, however, the payment is not made because it is retained to recoup against an advance to the company, the artist is then credited for the sales.

EXAMPLE 4: Variable Reduction by Territory

(b) Royalties for the sales of records (in any configuration) outside of the USA and Canada, which embody only the masters delivered hereunder shall be paid at the following designated rates; which rates shall be computed on the basis of the retail list price (less all applicable taxes on the sale and/or transfer of such records) in either the country of manufacture, the country of sale or the USA, as Company is paid, on one hundred percent (100%) of the net retail sales of such records, except as hereinafter provided:

(i) Records sold in the United Kingdom, West Germany, Holland, France, Italy, Japan and Australia: Eight percent (8%);

(ii) Records sold in Austria, Switzerland, South Africa, Belgium, Spain, Scandinavia, Greece, Mexico and New Zealand: Seven percent (7%);

(iii) Records sold throughout the world except those territories set forth in Paragraphs (a) and (b) (i) and (b) (ii) above: Five percent (5%);

(iv) Foreign royalties shall be computed in the currency of the country involved, and shall be paid, only after receipt by or final credit to Company, at the same rate of exchange as Company was paid, less any and all foreign taxes on payments made to Company and not otherwise deducted hereunder. If Company is unable to receive payment in the USA and in USA currency due to currency control restrictions and elects to accept payment in a foreign currency, Company may deposit (at my expense) in such currency in a depository selected by Company, all payments so received as royalties applicable to this agreement and shall notify me thereof promptly. Such deposit as above stated shall fulfill Company's obligations hereunder as to record sales hereunder to which such royalty payments are applicable.

☛ This hodgepodge of royalty rates reflects the varying royalty rates for the domestic label in those territories.

EXAMPLE 5: Same Rate of Exchange; Blocked Funds

10.3 (a) Royalties on Phonograph Record sales outside of the United States shall be computed in the national currency in which Company's licensees pay to Company, shall be credited to your royalty account hereunder at the same rate of exchange at which Company's licensees pay to Company, and shall be proportionately subject to any withholding or comparable taxes which may be imposed upon Company's receipts.

(b) If Company shall not receive payment in United States dollars in the United States for any sales of Phonograph Records outside of the United States, royalties on those sales shall not be credited to your royalty account hereunder. Company shall, however, at your written request and if Company is reasonably able to do so, accept payment for those sales in foreign currency and shall deposit in a foreign bank or other depository, at your expense, in that foreign currency, that portion thereof, if any, as shall equal the royalties which would have been payable to you hereunder on those sales had payment for those sales been made to Company in United States dollars in the United States. Deposit as aforesaid shall fulfill Company's royalty obligations hereunder as to those sales. If any law, ruling or other governmental restriction limits the amount a licensee can remit to Company, Company may reduce your royalties hereunder by an amount proportionate to the reduction in Company's licensee's remittance to Company.

COMPACT DISCS

The advent of the compact disc affected not only record industry technology and economics, but also the underlying artist agreements. New provisions were required to define, deal with, and account for CDs. The following three definitions, which are in chronological order, show the evolution of contractual language dealing with CDs. The first definition, while slightly inaccurate—CDs aren't "pressed"—appeared during the early transition period from vinyl to compact disc (which, in the evolutionary sense might be deemed the "up from the primordial ooze" stage). Although it isn't very scientific, it does what it was designed to do—that is, reduce the artist's royalty payment on nonvinyl formats. (See Example 1 below.)

- In respect to records sold . . . [which are] disc records pressed on any material other than plain black vinyl as customarily used in the music industry . . . , the royalty rate payable shall be one-half of the royalty rate which would otherwise have been payable. . . .

- *Compact Disc*: The words "Compact Disc" mean one (1) twelve-centimeter (12-cm) [approximately four and three-fourths inches (4¾ in)] variable rpm digital LP.

- The words "compact disc" shall mean a 120-mm-diameter (or such other size) disc-type record primarily reproducing sound (whether or not synchronized with or accompanied by visual images), the signals of which are read and transmitted from such record by means of a laser, such record being commercially suitable in the opinion of Company for release to the public.

Some agreements even included compact discs in the category of "audiophile" recordings. Whatever the language, however, all these provisions were talking about a new record configuration, and all attested to the birth of a new species. As you read the examples below, you can see how the sections of agreements dealing with "compact discs" evolved and developed into different, more complex, provisions. At first, the plan was to compute the royalties "as if" the CDs were regular LPs and then, when the dust settled, negotiate for what was "fair" for both sides, working toward parity for CD royalty computation. Companies followed the same type of reasoning when 33⅓-rpm albums and 45-rpm singles appeared, and when tapes first came into being. The early tape provisions called for a one-half royalty on tapes of albums; it gradually moved up to a three-quarters and, finally, a full royalty.

The evolution of the CD royalty rate, however, has been different from that of tapes. In most instances, tapes, in the form of cassettes, came to be treated the same as vinyl records when it came to the computation of royalty (except for the container charge [see pages 98–100], which was normally higher, and suggested retail price, which was lower). In contrast, language regarding CDs usually stipulates an "extra" reduction in the form of lowering the percentage of net sales for which the artist is paid. For example, most record companies compute the royalty for sales of CDs on the basis of less than 100% of sales; 90% is common, as are 85% and 80%, and some go as low as 75% (see Example 5). In addition, in most instances, the percentage deducted for packaging charges for CDs is higher than it was for the equivalent vinyl LP (see Example 4).

Accordingly, in the same contract, an artist may have, for example, a royalty for the sales of cassettes based on 8% of retail on 100% of sales with a packaging deduction of 20%, while the royalty for CDs will be 8% of retail on 80% of sales with a packaging deduction of 25% (see Examples 3 and 4). My personal theory is that the royalty computation on CDs was manipulated so that the end dollar result of the calculation would come out to be pretty much the same as it would have been for the equivalent LP. Although I have no hard facts to prove my theory, if you take the relative prices of the different configurations at the time the language evolved into its then-final form, the math seems to support my hypothesis:

- \$12.98 LP. Artist has 10% royalty on 100% of sales and a 20% packaging reduction: $0.10 \times 1.00 \times 0.80 \times \$12.98 = \$1.0384$ royalty per LP.

- \$15.98 CD. Artist has 10% royalty on 85% of sales and a 25% packaging reduction: $0.10 \times 0.85 \times 0.75 \times \$15.98 = \$1.018725$ royalty per CD.

Kinda spooky, huh? Especially when you consider that the CD probably had four or more cuts on it than the LP did.

SAMPLE CONTRACT PROVISIONS

EXAMPLE 1: CDs at Vinyl Royalty Rate

(d) Notwithstanding any other provisions of this Agreement, with respect to compact discs, the price upon which the royalty rate hereunder shall be calculated shall be based upon the price of the equivalent vinyl disc and such sales shall be treated accordingly.

EXAMPLE 2: CDs at One-Half Royalty Rate

(n) Notwithstanding any other provision of this Agreement, with respect to "compact discs and twelve inch single records" the royalty rate hereunder shall be one-half (½) of the Basic Royalty Rate.

EXAMPLE 3: CDs at Three-Fourths Rate on 80% of Sales

(4) Notwithstanding any other provision of this Agreement, with respect to "compact discs and twelve inch single records" the royalty rate hereunder for twelve inch single records shall be three-fourths the otherwise applicable rate and for compact discs it shall be the otherwise applicable royalty rate but computed upon eighty percent (80%) of net sales.

EXAMPLE 4: Higher Packaging Deduction for CDs

(7) With respect to all records sold hereunder, royalties on records included in albums, jackets, cartridges, boxes or any other type of package or container (herein collectively referred to as "containers") shall be based solely on the applicable "royalty price" [as defined in subparagraph (9) below] of such records and containers less all taxes and also less a container charge equal to fifteen (15%) percent of the applicable royalty price; provided, however, that the container charges in respect of records not in disc form shall be twenty (20%) percent of the applicable royalty price and compact discs shall be twenty-five (25%) percent of the applicable royalty price. In addition, if Company uses a so-called "PPD" basis for the calculation for foreign royalties in any foreign territory, then the foreign container deduction shall be used for such territory rather than the deductions set forth herein.

☛ Note the higher deduction for CD packaging than for LPs (25% and 15%, respectively).

EXAMPLE 5: 75% of Rate Escalating to 80% of Rate

9.05 (a) The royalty rate on any Budget Record, any Mid-Priced Record, any Multiple Record Set, any Record sold for distribution through military exchange channels, any soundtrack Record, or any "picture disc" (i.e., a disc Record with artwork reproduced on the surface of the Record itself) will be one-half (½) of the applicable royalty rate prescribed in paragraph 9.01. The royalty rate of any Record which is not an Album, Single or a Long-Play Single will be one-half (½) of the applicable basic Album royalty rate prescribed in paragraph 9.01. The royalty rate on any compact disc Record will be seventy-five (75%) percent of the rate which would otherwise be applicable under this Agreement, subject to 9.05(b) below. The royalty on any digital compact cassette ("DDC") or any Mini-disc Record will be sixty (60%) percent of the rate which would otherwise be applicable under this Agreement. The royalty rate for any Record in a New Configuration will be one-half (½) the rate which would otherwise be applicable hereunder.

(b) The royalty rate on any compact disc Record shall escalate prospectively from seventy-five (75%) percent to eighty (80%) percent after USNRC Net Sales of top-line Albums in compact disc format of two hundred fifty thousand (250,000) units.

☞ The royalty escalation in this provision is the result not of raising the base royalty but of lowering the reduction.

ELECTRONIC TRANSMISSION

The digital revolution is taking the recording industry into relatively uncharted territory—the world of video, CDs, hypertext, e-mail, the information highway, and, of particular interest to the music industry, a world in which recorded product can be transmitted electronically. How does the "record company"(is this becoming an obsolete phrase, like "telephone dial"?) pay an artist for a product which has been sold by electronic transmission? First of all, it is important to make a clear distinction here between recordings which are sold electronically and recordings which are sold *and* transmitted electronically. By "sold electronically," I mean recordings which are sold through the Internet and then physically shipped to the buyer. This becomes a form of direct sales similar to record clubs and other mail-order operations in that the recording is shipped to the customer using traditional shipping methods, e.g., the mail, UPS, etc.

With electronic sale and transmission not only is the ordering done electronically, but so is the "shipping" to the customer. The consumer orders a recording via computer, and the company (or intermediary) transmits a digital signal to the consumer containing the recording. The transmission may be an individual cut or cuts, or perhaps an entire album. (See Chapter 19, "Digital Transmission," pages 484–492.)

How are these sales treated for purposes of royalty computation? With regard to electronic sale (but not electronic transmission), if the record company itself is doing the selling, the company has two choices: either treat it as a record club sale or as a regular sale. Since most record club royalty provisions already include "direct to consumer sales" (see Example 2 in the section "Record Clubs," page 80), it seems likely that, unless negotiated otherwise in the future, record companies will rely on record club provisions—and, of course, the usual reduction in royalty—for these "shipped" recordings. Think Amazon.

With regard to sale and transmission electronically, on the other hand, some companies seem to be leaning toward treating such sales as "regular" sales (see Example 2), albeit with the possibility, sometimes rather convoluted, that there will be some reduction in the royalty [see subparagraph (ii) in Example 1].

Those companies without electronic transmission provisions will probably rely upon record club provisions.

Even though recordings both sold and transmitted electronically exist only in electronic form, and have no traditional physical packaging, it appears that record companies will continue to specify a packaging deduction.

Once the record industry gets past paranoia and piracy, electronic transmission, in one form or another, will eventually become an important avenue for music sales. Why travel to a store if you can surf and shop the Internet and "instantaneously" (theoretically—transmission time is still an issue) download the recordings you want?

In one of my classes, I postulated that sale of recordings by electronic transmission may be the first sign of the eventual extinction of the retail record store (which, I also suggested, would be greeted with crocodile tears by the record companies as they finally found a way to cut out the middleman). A student disagreed vigorously. I asked her why she thought the retail stores would survive.

"It's a gathering place. Kids will always go there to get together and meet their friends."

I asked her: "When was the last time you went down to the drugstore for a chocolate malted and to meet your friends?"

Obviously not a fan of old Mickey Rooney films, her reply, I think, proved my point: "Huh?"

SAMPLE CONTRACT PROVISIONS

EXAMPLE 1: Electronic Transmission

1. (i) If Company sells or licenses third parties to sell Records via Electronic Transmission, Artist shall be paid royalties with respect thereto at the lesser of (A) the otherwise applicable royalty rate payable in respect of Net Sales of the particular Records, or (B) fifty percent (50%) of the net royalties actually received by Company from such third parties.

(ii) For the purpose of calculating royalties in connection with subparagraph 8(l)(i)(A) above, the Royalty Base Price of such Record shall be deemed to be the lesser of: (A) the then current Royalty Base Price of analog tape copies of such Record; or (B) the Royalty Base Price of the configuration concerned based on the Retail Selling Price of such Record and a twenty-five percent (25%) Container Charge.

➦ The royalty price is the lesser of (1) the applicable royalty rate, which includes a packaging reduction, on the base price for analog tape copies (which is already lower than the CD price), or (2) the retail price less a 25% packaging reduction. Any way you look at it, a reduced royalty. Plus the record company not only has no actual packaging costs, but also no manufacturing costs. Not bad at all for the company!

EXAMPLE 2: Tape or Analog Rate on 85% Plus Packaging Reduction

19. If Company licenses third parties to sell Records via telephone, satellite, cable or other direct transmission to the consumer over wire or through the air, the royalty rate will be the otherwise applicable royalty rate prescribed in Paragraph 4 but, for purposes of calculating royalties payable in connection with such sales, the retail list price of such Records shall be deemed to be the then-current retail list price of analog tape copies of such Records and in the case of Records which no longer have analog tape equivalent, the corresponding price of the vinyl disc (but in the United States, eighty-five percent [85%] of the then-current retail list price of such tape copies or corresponding vinyl disc), less the Container Charge which applies to analog tape copies; provided, however, with respect to Records sold by Company's Licensees, in no event shall your royalty exceed one-half (½) of Company's net receipts after deduction from Company's gross receipts of union and all other applicable third party payments actually made or incurred by Company.

☛ This example computes royalty on the basis of the tape or vinyl equivalent (already lower), based upon 85% of sales (shades of record club computations!), plus the packaging reduction.

PREMIUM RECORDS

No one should drive a hard bargain with an artist.
—LUDWIG VAN BEETHOVEN

The term *premium record* refers to a record which is sold at a substantial discount, or given away, to a customer for buying (or trying) another product being offered for sale. (See Examples 1 and 4 below for language defining "premium.") Premium record sales are really a kind of merchandising effort, although provisions regarding premium records have been in recording agreements much longer than those regarding merchandising. Some examples of premium records might be the following (all of which fit quite nicely into the definition of "premium" contained in Example 1 below):

• A Christmas album sold for $1 for visiting a tire store to check their selection of all-weather radials.

• A CD given away free for test-driving an automobile.

• A recording sent when a customer fills out a coupon attached to a product he or she has bought.

• A greatest-hits album sold to a customer, for a fraction of what the individual recordings would cost, when the customer buys a certain kind of soap, car, tire, etc.

• A compilation given away or sold for the sole purpose of enhancing the public's image of or feeling for a company's services or corporate image.

• A special compilation album created for a chain of clothing stores, both for in-store play and for sale to customers.

Although the royalty on premium records is always computed at a reduced rate, the sheer volume of premium sales may be so large (hundreds of thousand, even millions, of units may be sold which probably would not have been sold through regular retail channels) that premium merchandising can be profitable for both company and artist.

Generally, the royalty rate for premium sales is one-half of the otherwise applicable royalty based upon the price "received by the record company" for the sale of the records (that is, the price paid to the record company by the company giving away or discounting the records). (See Example 3.) If, for example, an automobile company pays $2 per record to the record company for albums to be used in a premium promotion but sells them for $3, the royalty computation is based on the $2 price; or, conversely, if the automobile company sells them for $1, the royalty is still based on the $2 price. So, if the base royalty is 10% of the suggested retail list price, the royalty for the premium sales is (not taking into account other deductions, such as container charges) 5% (half of 10%) of $2. Note that when computing royalties on premium sales, the difference between royalty computed on wholesale price and that computed on retail price can be substantial. The following examples illustrate why (again, for the purpose of simplicity, other deductions are not taken into account).

Example

The "price received by the Company" is $2.50 per album. The artist has a base royalty of 12% of wholesale, which is cut in half for premium sales to 6%. The royalty equals 15 cents per premium sold (12% × 0.5 = 6% × $2.50 = 15 cents).

Example

The "price received by the Company" is $2.50 per album. The artist has a base royalty of 6% of retail (the equivalent of 12% of wholesale), which is cut in half for premium sales to 3%. The royalty equals 7½ cents per premium sold (6% × 0.5 = 3% × $2.50 = 7½ cents).

Artists should be on the lookout for premium provisions written in such a manner that they should be totally unacceptable. For example, provisions calling for premiums to be royalty-free (Example 2 below) should be rejected. The record company should pay a royalty on any records for which they receive payment. Other than freebies, about the only instance where a royalty-free sale is justifiable is where there has been a scrap or close-out sale at a loss.

Artists should also try to impose some level of control on the record company's unrestricted right to issue an artist's records as part of a premium. I believe the artist's consent to the potential release of premiums is very important, as most premium offerings result in a link between the artist's name and a commercial product. The artist may have a personal or moral objection to being connected with a particular product (e.g., alcohol or cigarettes) or perhaps a particular brand (e.g., Ford automobiles when the artist is hosting a television series for General Motors). (Example 3 below has language that specifically addresses these issues of product control and moral conflict.)

One way to exercise some form of control with respect to whether or not recordings may be used for the purpose of premium recordings involves the practice of *coupling* an artist's work with the work of other artists. Since coupling is frequently used in compiling the greatest-hits albums that are often used in premium offers, restrictions on coupling may effectively restrict the company's release of premium records. (For more information on coupling, see pages 125–129.) Another form of control over the release of recordings as premiums is to specify in the agreement that records must be released on the record company's "top-priced label," or words to that effect, since traditionally, and by definition, a premium record will *not* be released on the top-priced label. This approach, however, is more effective in restricting the company's right to sell budget records. Examples 4 and 5 below show two other ways of limiting the release of premium records. In Example 4, release of a recording as a premium record is subject to the approval of the artist (but note the approval is "not to be unreasonably withheld"). In Example 5, the company must wait at least 1 year after the initial release before recordings may be included in premium records.

SAMPLE CONTRACT PROVISIONS

EXAMPLE 1: Definition of Premium

(c) ... As used herein, "premium" shall be defined as including, but not necessarily limited to, combination sales, free or self-liquidating items offered to the public in conjunction with the sale or promotion of a product or service, the primary intent of which is to use the records in such a way to promote, publicize and/or sell the products, services or business image of the user of such item.

EXAMPLE 2: No-Royalty Premium Clause

(i) No royalties shall be due or payable on records which embody performances hereunder when, as part of a promotional program, such records are distributed as premiums or in connection with the sale of any other product, commodity or service.

> ☞ Look how easily the language moves from royalty-free premiums attached to a "promotional program" (whose? the record company's or some other company's?) to any type of premium. Why bother with the first part other than to mask the fact to the casual reader that no royalties are going to be paid to the artist for any premium sales? Isn't this also a license to attach the artist's name to any product?

EXAMPLE 3: One-Half Royalty; Product/Moral Conflict

(ix) With respect to records sold to a commercial purchaser for use as a premium, promotional item, sales incentive or for a similar purpose ["premium record(s)"], royalties shall be at one-half (½) the rate otherwise applicable and the royalty base shall be Company's actual selling price of such record (less container deductions and any taxes). Notwithstanding the aforesaid, if, at any time, you advise Company in writing that you have a bona fide association with a particular product or service, Company will not sell a premium record during the term of such association which is intended for use in connection with a product or service which is competitive with the product or service with which you are associated. Furthermore, if you advise Company in writing of your objection to a type of product or service to which you have a strong and deeply held moral objection, Company will not thereafter sell a premium record associated with such type of product or service.

EXAMPLE 4: Artist's Right to Approve Premium Offers

(ee) "Premium Record"—a Record used to promote the sale of any product or service other than Phonograph Records. Premium Records shall be used subject to Artist's approval, not to be unreasonably withheld.

> ☞ Ah! This provision uses one of those words which causes lawyers to scream either in terror or in delight—depending, of course, on whose side the lawyer is taking. The word is "unreasonably." And who, pray tell, is to judge what is or is not unreasonable or reasonable? It is similar to Supreme Court Justice Potter Stewart's language regarding obscenity: "I can't define it, but I know it when I see it." As long as the "I" is "me," it is acceptable, but as soon as the "I" is "you," I have a problem with it.

EXAMPLE 5: 1-year Restriction on Release of Premiums

(e) With respect to records sold as premiums or in connection with the sale of any other product, commodity, or service, the royalty rate shall be fifty (50%) percent of Company's actual net receipts. . . . Notwithstanding anything to the contrary contained in this Agreement, during the term hereof, no records shall be sold as premiums until one (1) year after the initial U.S. release of the applicable records, without my prior consent, not to be unreasonably withheld.

BUDGET AND MID-LINE RECORDS

Budget (or *economy,* or, less elegantly, *low-price*) records are, as the name suggests, records which sell for a low price, usually after the active life of the master is over. *Mid-line* (or *mid-price*) records are those sold at a price approximately halfway between the full suggested retail price and the budget price. Record contracts usually have provisions dealing with the record company's right to release budget and mid-price records, and often the two are treated in the same clauses. The two financial goals that the record company keeps in mind when deciding whether to release recordings as budget or mid-line records are:

1. To make sure that full-price sales will not be affected by the release of a lower-priced version.

2. To get the last bit of possible profit out of the recordings.

The purpose of both, of course, is to maximize profits.

Budget Records

If possible, in negotiating the artist's recording agreement certain restrictions should be placed upon the record company's right to release budget records. Artists may have reasons—financial or personal, logical or illogical—not to have their records released as budget records. One reason is the possibility that the release of budget records may cut into the sale of the artist's full-price recordings, especially if the recordings by the artist to be released as budget records are also still in regular distribution at full price. While this is unlikely, since it would generally cut into the record company's profits also, it does not take much imagination to envision a situation where a current cut or two might be used to beef up a budget release. An obvious financial consideration is the fact that there is a considerable reduction in the royalty to be paid to the artist on budget records: 50% of the regular royalty based on the price of the budget record, which will probably be at least 50% less than the full-price record—for a whopping total reduction of at least 75% per unit sold. (See Examples 2 and 4.) Finally, a personal reason may have to do with an artist's discomfort at being "discounted"—that is, psychologically diminished in value.

One approach, which is usually acceptable to the record company, is to provide that a master cannot be used for a budget release until such time as the full-price version is deleted from the record company's catalogue (see Example 2). Presumably, the record company will be comfortable with this sort of restriction because the company, like the artist, wants to obtain the maximum profit from the sale of the recording. Sort of midway between this approach and a downright refusal by the company to grant any concession to the artist is a provision that the company may not use a recording in a budget record without the artist's consent within a specified period after the initial commercial release of the recording (see Example 3). Another is to require that the record company first obtain the artist's consent prior to releasing any records as budget records. For all the obvious reasons, such as the artist's right to say no, this method is less likely to be acceptable to the record company, and unless the artist in question is very important, one should not hold one's breath waiting for a record company to give this much up.

As mentioned above, the royalty for budget records is almost always at a reduced rate, usually one-half of the otherwise applicable rate, although I have had some agreements which provided for a rate of two-thirds of the otherwise applicable royalty rate. The reason for this lower royalty is a combination of history and economics. The history is that the early budget releases were all license agreements with third parties and, as noted in the section "Record Clubs," when there is a license to a third party, there is usually a reduction of royalties. When these provisions start with a reduction, it is very hard to move record companies away from that language. The economic reasons are more rational: Budget records sell for roughly half of what full-price records go for, but the cost of manufacturing, as well as many other costs (e.g., mechanical license fees), is virtually the same for both products.

Mid-Line Records

In the past, mid-line records did not exist. The price difference between full-price records and budget records was so small that there was no room for a practical and profitable middle ground. However, once the average suggested retail list price of vinyl LPs had doubled (from, say, $4.98 to $9.98), a middle ground, wide and enticing, opened. And when CDs appeared, and *their* suggested retail list price moved steadily upward (in spite of industry promises that prices would soon drop), a veritable gold mine beckoned. The music business, like nature, abhors a vacuum. When a niche opens, something—in this case, mid-line records—will fill it up.

"Mid-line" is sort of a catch-all modifier for any downwardly mobile recording, but there are no clear lines of demarcation between "mid-line," "full-price," and "budget." Compare Example 7 (80% to 60% of "top priced" as the boundary lines for mid-line) to Example 8 (85% to 67%). Sometimes records become mid-line because the lower price will stimulate sales. Sometimes records are repackaged as a "new" product and re-released at a lower price; these, too, are mid-line records.

The royalty rate for mid-line records is usually reduced by one-third, rather than the 50% reduction that is usual for budget records (see Example 7). The royalty rate, however, may be reduced by less (see Example 5 for a 25% reduction) or more (see Example 6 for 37.5%).

SAMPLE CONTRACT PROVISIONS

EXAMPLE 1: Definition of Budget Record

(a) "Budget Record"—a Record, whether or not previously released, bearing a Suggested Retail List Price which is sixty-seven percent (67%) or less of the Suggested Retail List Price in the country concerned applicable to the Top-line Record in the same configuration (e.g., long-playing Album, two-disc long-playing Album, Twelve-Inch Single, analog tape cassette, compact disc, etc.) released by Company or its Licensees in the territory concerned.

EXAMPLE 2: Definition and Royalty Rate (50% of Otherwise Applicable) for Budget Records

(d) As to records sold as part of a "budget" or "economy" line, as those terms are generally understood in the recording industry for records sold at a substantially lower suggested retail list price than the standard full price, the royalty rate payable to me shall be one-half (½) of the otherwise applicable royalty rate, but in no event more than fifty (50%) percent of the net amount received by Company therefrom. Company shall not, without my prior consent, release any record recorded hereunder as part of a "budget" or "economy" line until at least one (1) year after such record has been deleted from Company's catalogue.

> ☛ How's that for a loosey-goosey definition of "budget": records sold at a "substantially lower" price. What's next—how high is high and how low is low?

EXAMPLE 3: Limitation on When Released

(f) In the event that we, our subsidiaries, affiliates or licensees reissue, on phonograph records, a record originally released bearing such label which carries a suggested retail list price substantially lower than the suggested retail list price for records bearing the standard label or labels used by us, our subsidiaries, affiliates and/or licensees. It is specifically understood that no phonograph record made hereunder will be re-issued under such a special label in the United States prior to whichever of the following dates shall be earlier: (i) the date two years subsequent to the initial release date in the United States of such phonograph record, or (ii) the date two years subsequent to the expiration of the term of this agreement, without your consent.

☛ The artist has a period of "protection" before company may release budget records without the artist's consent: no budget version may be sold within the *earlier* of either 1 year after the initial U.S. release or 2 years after the expiration of the agreement. Be aware the company may release a budget version *anytime* with the consent of the artist.

EXAMPLE 4: Consent Required After 1 year

(d) With respect to records sold as budget-line records, the royalty shall be fifty percent (50%) of my otherwise applicable royalty rate calculated in the manner set forth in this agreement. Notwithstanding the foregoing, it is understood and agreed that such budget line records shall not be sold within one (1) year after the initial U.S. release of the applicable records, without my prior consent, not to be unreasonably withheld.

☛ In this and other royalty provision calculations based upon the "otherwise applicable royalty rate," all the other "applicable" reductions (e.g., foreign, record club, etc.) and deductions (freebies, container charges, etc.) come along for the ride.

EXAMPLE 5: Budget and Mid-Line Royalty Three-Fourths

(ii) The royalty rate in respect of the sale of mid-priced records shall be three-fourths (¾) of the otherwise applicable royalty rate as calculated in accordance with the foregoing provisions and the royalty rate in respect of the sale of budget or low-priced records shall be one-half (½) of the otherwise applicable royalty rate as calculated in accordance with the foregoing provisions.

EXAMPLE 6: Mid-Line Royalty Five-Eighths

(h) With respect to so-called "budget line" long playing records, the royalty rate shall be one-half (½) of the otherwise applicable royalty rate. With respect to so-called "mid-price" long playing records, the royalty rate shall be five-eighths (⅝) of the otherwise applicable royalty rate.

EXAMPLE 7: Mid-Line Royalty Two-Thirds

(iv) With respect to records sold on a "price line" or "list category" which is lower than Company's "top priced" line or highest "list category," royalties shall be at the following rates:

(A) with respect to such records sold on a "price line" or "list category" which is sixty (60%) percent to eighty (80%) percent of Company's "top priced" line or highest "list category," royalties shall be at two-thirds (⅔) the rate otherwise applicable; and. . . .

EXAMPLE 8: Definition of Mid-Price Record

(b) "Mid-price Record"—a Record, whether or not previously released, bearing a Suggested Retail List Price in the country concerned in excess of sixty-seven percent (67%) and less than eighty-five percent (85%) of the Suggested Retail List Price applicable to the Top-line Record in the same configuration.

CONTAINER CHARGES

DICK:

The first thing we do, let's kill all the lawyers.

—WILLIAM SHAKESPEARE
Henry VI, Part 2, Act VI, Scene 2

One of the great fictions of royalty computation is the *container charge* (also known as the "packaging charge" or "jacket charge") which has already popped up in examples and discussions. This fiction is based upon the concept that the buyer of a record is really buying two separate things—the recording with the performance and the packaging with the artwork and text—and, accordingly, the overall price should be apportioned between them. Under this theory, I should be able to go into a record store, pick up a $17.99 CD, go to the cashier, remove the disc, pay about $4.00, and leave with the jewel box and booklet. Or, alternatively, I could take just the disc for around $14.00. Yeah, sure.

Although based upon fiction, it is a fact that the container charge is deducted from the royalty computation price, even from recordings which, presumably, have no packaging at all, such as records delivered through electronic transmission (see Example 1 under "Electronic Transmission," page 91). Other than computations where the base royalty itself is reduced (e.g., record club, foreign, etc.), the container charge is the largest single deduction in the royalty computation. Oh, and by the way, it is still deducted from record club sales, foreign sales, and the other categories where the base royalty is reduced.

The historical basis for the container charge is rooted in the days when there was considerable breakage of 78-rpm records, and stores often kept the jackets separately and just reordered the actual disc or discs without jackets. As a consequence, some older agreements specified that royalties would be computed upon the "replacement cost" of records—the cost of the disc only, not including the cost of the jacket. And, in the days of the 45-rpm single, conventional wisdom was that under no circumstance (other, perhaps, than the classic "take it or leave it") should an artist accept a provision which allowed the record company to deduct a container charge for a regular sleeve for a single record, since in most cases 45s were all released with the same standard paper sleeve that was used for all artists on the label. Of course, conventional wisdom didn't always work, and some record companies did manage to write in a deduction for those plain wrappers.

"Container" became the generic term for the physical enclosure which contains the recording—whether it is an album jacket, CD jewel box and booklet, or whatever may be used in any new configuration—as well as the accompanying artwork, covers (front and back), liner notes, etc. And don't forget the curious inclusion of container charges for electronic transmission sales, where there is no actual container.

In the past, an argument against a container charge for a 45-rpm single was usually accepted and there would be no deduction for the packaging. In today's market, however, with CD singles, the container charge for singles has reestablished itself.

The points to look out for in container deduction provisions are the size of the deduction and any special circumstances which might increase the amount of the deduction. For example, it became common with some companies to deduct a higher percentage for a double-fold, or gatefold, album jacket for vinyl records—that is, one that opens up, much like a book. Gatefold albums containing only one disc did cost more to manufacture than single-sleeve jackets, but they were sold for the same price, so there was some justification for taking a higher container deduction. On the other hand, double-pocket jackets, which contained two discs, were sold at a higher price, so there was no justification for the record companies to raise the percentage of the container deduction.

Record companies could try to apply the same reasoning when calculating the packaging deduction for CDs containing more than one disc, the so-called box sets, but so far seem to have relied upon the higher price of the box set without the need for increasing the container charge. The gatefold vinyl album containing only one disc existed because of the need (usually triggered by someone's ego) to include more pictures, artwork, text, or whatever could fit in standard album packaging. With the booklet in today's CD packaging, the space is readily available for such expansion, which, presumably, has made this particular issue moot.

The range of the container charge has fluctuated with the passage of time and, in addition, varies according to the particular configuration of the recording. When the only configurations available were on vinyl, virtually all container deductions were 10%. Then the concept of "special packaging" (see below) arrived, and the deduction for vinyl albums went up to 15%. When cassettes appeared, the deduction for tape packaging generally was 5%, sometimes 10%, above the company's rate for vinyl; for CDs, the deduction was usually 5% to 10% above the rate the company deducted for cassettes. With the passage of time, most companies bumped up their rate at each level by 5%. Do note that the actual percentages deducted for container costs may vary from company to company. Today, the average deduction for most companies is 25% for CDs.

Any provisions providing for higher deductions for special packaging (see Example 4 below) should be examined with care. Sometimes, for example, a company will try to take a higher deduction for special stickers added to the packaging. Since, however, it is common practice for record companies to add ". . . contains the hit . . ." stickers to CD packages, there should be no additional container deduction for this type of sticker.

Often companies will decide that some albums should have special artwork or packaging (e.g., holograms), which is more expensive than regular packaging, and will include contract provisions specifying that the container deduction for such packaging will be higher. In such cases, the artist should try to change the language so that the artist's consent must be obtained before the company orders the "special" artwork which will increase the container charge.

SAMPLE CONTRACT PROVISIONS

EXAMPLE 1: Vinyl 15%, Tape 25%

(g) With respect to all records sold hereunder, royalties on records included in albums, jackets, cartridges, boxes or any other type of package or container (herein collectively referred to as "containers") shall be based solely on the applicable "royalty price" [as defined in subparagraph 5(h) below] of such records and containers less all taxes and also less a container charge equal to fifteen (15%) percent of the applicable royalty price; provided, however, that the container charges in respect of records not in disc form shall be twenty-five (25%) percent of the applicable royalty price.

☛ This provision predates CDs; it is a historic relic. Vinyl records have a 15% deduction for container charges. Records "not in disc" form (tapes) are at 25%.

EXAMPLE 2: Analog 20%, Other 25%

(g) With respect to all analog disc records and analog cassette records sold hereunder, royalties on records included in albums, jackets, cartridges, boxes or any other type of package or container (herein collectively referred to as "containers") shall be based solely on the applicable "royalty price" [as defined in subparagraph (m) below] of such records and containers less all taxes included in the price and also less a container charge equal to twenty (20%) percent of the applicable royalty price; provided, however, that the container charges in respect of all other records shall be twenty-five (25%) percent of the applicable royalty price. In addition, if Company uses a so-called "PPD" basis for the calculation for foreign royalties in any foreign territory, then the foreign container deduction shall be used for such territory rather than the deductions set forth herein.

> ☞ This reflects the Dawn of the Age of CDs. We don't even have a name for a CD except that it is "other" than analog. Also, note the language for foreign container charges in territories specifying a PPD basis and the use of the foreign licensees' container deduction rates, which may be greater than the limits set forth in the agreement.

EXAMPLE 3: Vinyl 15%, Tape 20%, CD 25%

(7) With respect to all records sold hereunder, royalties on records included in albums, jackets, cartridges, boxes or any other type of package or container (herein collectively referred to as "containers") shall be based solely on the applicable "royalty price" [as defined in Subparagraph (9) below] of such records and containers less all taxes and also less a container charge equal to fifteen (15%) percent of the applicable royalty price; provided, however, that the container charges in respect of the records not in disc form shall be twenty (20%) percent of the applicable royalty price and compact discs shall be twenty-five (25%) percent of the applicable royalty price. In addition, if Company uses a so-called "PPD" basis for calculation for foreign royalties in any foreign territory, then the foreign container deduction shall be used for such territory rather than the deductions set forth herein.

EXAMPLE 4: Special Packaging

14.25. *Special Packaging Costs*—Costs incurred by Company in creating and producing Album covers, sleeves and other packaging elements, in excess of the following amounts: (a) five thousand dollars ($5,000) per Album for design of artwork (including the expenses for reproduction rights); (b) four thousand dollars ($4,000) per Album for engraving; and (c) packaging manufacturing costs of twenty-five cents (25¢) per long-playing disc Album unit, twenty-two cents (22¢) per tape cassette Album unit (including the cost of the "C-O" cassette housings), and sixty-six cents (66¢) per compact disc Album unit, for Albums manufactured for distribution in the United States or Canada.

> ☞ In another provision in the agreement from which Example 4 is taken, it is specified that 5% higher container charges are deducted for recordings having special packaging costs. This language cited here is unusual as it actually sets forth a dollar cost scale to determine whether or not a project is "special." Using specified dollar amounts rather than percentages in any of these artist royalty computation determinations can be dangerous. For example, inflation or deflation, manufacturing shortages, substantial cuts in costs, etc., can all have a material and unplanned effect on the royalty. For the record company, any factor that it cannot control becomes an unknown, and unknowns are dangerous.

CROSS-COLLATERALIZATION

We now come to the (from the artist's viewpoint) villain of the piece—cross-collateralization. Of course, one man's villain is another man's (insert "record company's" here) white knight. *Cross-collateralization* provisions, whether they are between a publishing company and a writer or an artist and a record company, give the company the right to recoup monies lost on one agreement from monies made on another, entirely separate agreement. In other words, if an artist owes a record company money under one contract (say, for example, for unrecouped recording costs which are treated as advances) and the artist is due royalties under a different contract (such as a prior recording contract with the company or, say, a songwriter's agreement with a publisher affiliated with the record company), the record company, if it has the right to cross-collateralize, takes the money from the second contract and uses it to offset the debts of the first contract.

Now, isn't that a Jolly Clause.

Almost all agreements drawn up by record companies will have cross-collateralization provisions in them. However, as you will see from the examples at the end of this section, most clauses giving a company cross-collateralization rights do not actually use the term. Heaven forbid that the record company should red-flag the language! What is used instead (and these are the tip-off words) are phrases such as "under this or any other" (see Example 1 below) or, less frequently, "one accounting unit" (see Example 2). Any time those phrases crop up, unless there is some modification to the language, you've got cross-collateralization. In addition, either expressly or implied, the cross-collateralization applies to agreements "heretofore or hereafter" entered into (that's past, present, and future) between the artist and the record company *and any affiliated company.*

Because of cross-collateralization, many seemingly successful artists (if you judge by the number of their recordings which are reported as having been sold) may never actually receive royalty payments from their recording agreements. When there is cross-collateralization in an agreement, the likelihood of money actually reaching the artist's pockets is substantially reduced (if not eliminated). In some cases, artists might just as well view such agreements as vehicles to pull their careers along (the choo-choo train theory of career development) so that income can be generated from other sources, such as personal appearances, merchandising, etc.

The best-case scenario, for the artist, would be to get the cross-collateralization clauses, all of them, removed from the contract. (Yeah. *Good luck!*) This, of course, is virtually impossible. So, what *can* be done?

From the artist's point of view, it is always desirable (but not always possible) to limit the scope of cross-collateralization in the agreement as much as possible. For example, cross-collateralization may be limited only to records recorded under one contract; only to record contracts between the artist and the same company (see Example 4); or only to a portion of another contract, say only the writer's share of royalties under a copublishing/songwriter's agreement that is attached to the recording agreement (leaving a share of the publishing income for the artist). What happens if it is not restricted? If, for example, an artist is under contract to the record company's publishing wing, and cross-collateralization is allowed, the artist may find his or her songwriter's royalties going to pay for his or her unrecouped recording costs under the recording agreement. Clearly, cross-collateralization can be a very costly arrangement for the artist.

Recently, I was advising an artist who was contemplating signing a recording agreement with an independent producer and, at the same time, signing with that producer to be the artist's personal manager. The producer wanted to cross-collateralize all contracts. We made an attempt to limit the cross-collateralization so that the producer/manager did not use income from concerts, merchandising, songwriting, publishing, etc., as a way to recoup recording costs under the recording agreement. The producer/manager did not see the justice in having to give up this lucrative insurance policy (did I mention that he owned the studio and intended to record "hundreds" of cuts looking for the right product and intended to charge the going rate for studio time?). A heart-to-heart talk with the artist convinced him that it was wiser to move on than to sign on to perpetual financial purgatory.

Artists with a proven track record may be able to virtually eliminate cross-collateralization, even, in exceptional cases, between albums, within one agreement. For example, I worked with one successful artist who was signing a new agreement after the expiration of a preexisting agreement with the same company and we were able to negotiate terms wherein each album was a "separate accounting unit" from any other album, as well as from prior recording agreements. This meant that the record company could not cross-collateralize the losses of an unsuccessful album against the profits from a successful album. Short of not having to pay back recording costs at all, you can't do much better than that.

Obviously, the economic consequences of cross-collateralization versus no cross-collateralization can be quite dramatic. The following examples illustrate these consequences.

Example: Albums Are Separate Accounting Units

Artist records two albums. Album #1 costs $200,000 and grosses only $25,000 in royalties, for a net of –$175,000. Album #2 costs $175,000 and grosses $350,000, for a net of $175,000. The result: Artist receives $175,000, the net royalty on Album #2, although Artist is still $175,000 in the red on Album #1.

Example: Albums Are Cross-Collateralized

Same numbers as in the first example. This time, however, the record company keeps the $175,000 from Album #2 to offset the "unrecouped recording costs" of $175,000 on Album #1. Artist receives $0.

A more common example of the sort of devastation which can be inflicted upon an artist through cross-collateralization is as follows:

Example: Artist Is a Singer/Songwriter

Under his recording agreement, which has a provision for cross-collateralization, Artist has signed a songwriter's agreement with a publisher affiliated with the record company. Artist records an album of original songs at a cost of $250,000. The album sells only enough copies to recoup $25,000 of the recording costs, leaving a balance of $225,000 unrecouped. One song on the album does, however, become a big hit and is recorded by several artists. The royalties due Artist pursuant to his songwriter's agreement equal $225,000. The record company, using cross-collateralization, applies the $225,000 songwriting royalty as a "credit" against the unrecouped $225,000 in recording costs under the recording agreement. No "payment" is made. Artist receives $0.

Cross-collateralization can also come creeping up on you out of the dark or out of left field (you can pick your own metaphor). Suppose you have run out one agreement with a record company and have happily moved on to a second company, leaving a large indebtedness behind. With one or both companies (it doesn't matter which), you have a cross-collateralization provision in your agreement. OK, Sunshine, guess what happens when one of these record companies acquires the other one? You got it! Ol' Mr. Cross-Collateralization has come waltzing back into your life, bringing along the prior indebtedness. As you might imagine, that kind of scenario is not all that rare in this era of acquisitions and takeovers. (See Example 3 for references to company "and affiliates.")

Sometimes, references to the right of cross-collateralization in one agreement may be so numerous and scattered—or, perhaps, so well hidden—that trying to deal with each and every one is impractical. A solution to this problem is to add the good old standby "Notwithstanding anything to the contrary contained herein . . ." somewhere in the agreement in connection with a statement specifying the agreed-upon limitation to cross-collateralization (see Example 4).

SAMPLE CONTRACT PROVISIONS

EXAMPLE 1: ". . . This and/or Any Other Agreement"

a. We will compute royalties payable to you hereunder, within sixty days after June 30th and December 31st of each year during which records made hereunder are sold, for the preceding six-month period, and we will render accountings for and pay such royalties, less any unrecouped advances under this and/or any other agreement between you and us, within such sixty days.

EXAMPLE 2: All Agreements as One Accounting Unit

(f) The words "royalty" or "royalties" include royalties payable under this and any other agreement between Company and me. All royalty agreements between Company and me heretofore or hereafter entered into shall be deemed to be one accounting unit.

EXAMPLE 3: ". . . and/or affiliates"

(a) We will compute the total composite royalties earned by you pursuant to this Agreement or any other agreement between the parties hereto . . . and will submit to you the royalty statement for each such period together with the net amount of such royalties, if any, which shall be payable after deducting any and all unrecouped advances and chargeable costs under this Agreement or any other agreement between you and us and/or affiliates. . . .

EXAMPLE 4: Limit on Cross-Collateralization

8. Notwithstanding anything to the contrary contained herein, it is expressly agreed between Artist and Company hereunder that there shall be no cross-collateralization between Artist's royalties hereunder, including the recoupment of Recording Costs, as provided for above in Subparagraph 7(h), and any royalties due Artist as a composer, as provided for below in Paragraph 16.

☛ This prohibits cross-collateralization between the artist's recording agreement and songwriter's agreement.

THE RECOUPMENT OF ADVANCES

Advances are prepayments of prospective royalties. Advances are usually nonreturnable, but recoupable. That is, without an express agreement to the contrary between the parties (and barring fraud of some sort), an artist cannot be made to pay back an advance that has been made as a prepayment of royalties; the company can only recover (recoup) the advance monies from future earnings, in this case royalties. The examples below show typical general contract provisions pertaining to several different types of advances.

Example

Artist enters into a recording agreement with Record Company. Artist receives an advance of $50,000 for signing. (For simplicity, we are ignoring for the time being the question of recording costs, which are covered later in this section.) Artist's only record earns Artist $25,000 in artist royalties from sales. Record Company retains the $25,000 in artist royalties, thereby *recouping* (recovering) $25,000 of the $50,000 advance paid to Artist. Artist is still in a debit position of $25,000. Another $25,000 must be earned by Artist and retained by Record Company to recoup the full advance. Record Company cannot look to Artist for the other $25,000 from any other source but future royalty earnings. Artist will not receive any royalty *payment* until the entire $50,000 has been recouped.

When the subject of advances is brought up, "signing advances" are the kind that usually come to mind. These are paid to induce (translated: "bribe") an artist to sign with the record company. Obviously, advances may also be payable in connection with the exercise of options, at the commencement of option periods, or at any other time upon which the parties may agree. Frequently, advances are payable in connection with some event, such as sales of a single or an album reaching a certain level, or, perhaps, some degree of success in the national charts.

Stories about signing advances of legendary proportions are legion in the industry. I remember quite well the publicity that accompanied the signing of Johnny Winter to Columbia Records in the spring of 1969. It was reported in the press that Columbia had signed Winter for an advance of $300,000, an unheard-of sum in those days for an untried artist. The exact sum comes easily to mind because I specifically remember thinking, "I pity the poor bastard who has to negotiate for Columbia after this." A week or so after that, I received a telephone call from CBS and found out who that poor bastard was going to be—me.

There is another story connected with the Johnny Winter signing which will give you a good idea of the kind of competition which can go on between record companies to sign an artist. It was told to me by a friend (who must remain anonymous) who swears it is true. I cannot personally vouch for the details, but the story certainly illustrates the kind of madness that brings us into this business in the first place.

My friend, who was in the A&R Department of one of the major labels, wanted to sign Winter, but he kept running up against the rumors that Columbia was offering Winter a gigantic sum to sign with them. Nevertheless, he wanted Winter and knew he had to better the Columbia offer to get him. What to do? He didn't want to rely upon the rumors—it wouldn't be the first time that false numbers were thrown out in order to sweeten the pot and increase the fever pitch of the competitors. He needed to know what Columbia was *really* offering. So he flew to New York. After acquiring a few props, he conned someone from the mail room at his label's New York office to join him on a little escapade. Clad in identical jumpsuits and pushing a dolly, they marched over to the CBS building—Black Rock as it was affectionately known—and took an elevator up to the CBS Records Legal Department. With businesslike efficiency, they loaded the "W" file cabinet onto the dolly and disappeared.

Back at their office they quickly rifled through the papers until they found Winter's file, and made a photocopy. Still suited up, they quickly, and nervously, restored the file cabinet to CBS, then rushed back so my friend could review the file.

Aha! A quick glance confirmed his suspicions. Columbia was only offering Winter $30,000, not the reported hundreds of thousands of dollars. My friend triumphantly called Winter's manager and offered $40,000. Winter's manager listened politely, laughed, and hung up, leaving a very puzzled A&R man on the other end of the line. His puzzlement was only increased when Columbia actually did sign Winter for $300,000. Something seemed wrong here. How could there be such a large discrepancy between the file and the actual offer? Rechecking the photocopy of the purloined file, he found the very simple answer. He had grabbed the comedian Jonathan Winters's file, not the Johnny Winter file. So much for industrial espionage.

In addition to signing advances, what other monies are considered recoupable from royalties by the record companies? First and foremost, there are all the costs of the recording sessions, including payments to the engineers, arrangers, musicians, etc.; union costs (some, but not necessarily all); tape; perhaps outboard equipment; and any number of other chargeable costs (see below, "Recording Costs"). Other costs which probably will be treated as advances and are, accordingly, recoupable are "tour support" (not commonly offered by record companies these days), the costs of videos/DVDs (which, generally, have replaced tour support), promotional costs, the purchase price of masters, and, potentially, damn near anything the record company says is money spent on behalf of the artist, unless guidelines are in the agreement. And what about a "loan" to the artist to pay his or her rent for a month? Is this an advance? "Advances" may take many forms, some open, some devious, some previously unthought of.

I cannot stress enough that whenever money passes from the record company to the artist, there should be absolutely no confusion or disagreement between company and artist as to whether or not the transfer is an advance. For many years, monies that were routinely spent on sales efforts, including promotion, were not considered advances. Now, most labels charge some or all promotion costs back to the artist as an advance.

Example

Artist is requested to make a promotional appearance in New York on behalf of Record Company. Artist lives in Los Angeles. Record Company flies Artist to New York and puts him up in palatial splendor at the Plaza. Bill for the trip: $5,000. Is the $5,000 an advance? The answer: Could be.

My position is that money given to the artist is *not* an advance unless there is a piece of paper somewhere specifying that the artist has agreed that these monies were to be an advance. Naturally, not every record company sees the justice and wisdom of my position. Suspect costs, excuse me, advances may show up on statements without explanation or with misleading descriptions. Always try to get it in writing.

Sometime before the demise of ABC Records, I was negotiating a release for an artist from his recording agreement with ABC. Certain guaranteed advances were due the artist from ABC and the total amount still due was in dispute. ABC wanted to offset the amount by certain payments they had made on behalf of the artist, claiming these had been advances. "Prove it," I challenged. They produced canceled checks. No question, the money had been spent. "I never doubted that," I said, "but how do I know those were advances?"

"What else would they be?"

"Perhaps a voluntary contribution," I suggested earnestly, "or a bonus," I added helpfully. "Certainly not an advance. The contract doesn't say anything about this type of payment being an advance. Doesn't mention it at all. I suppose you don't have a separate agreement from my client agreeing that these are advances, do you?"

Silence.

"No. I didn't think so."

Ultimately, the company had to agree that most of the disputed payments could not be considered advances because the company had not documented them as such. Shortly thereafter, ABC changed its form contract, effectively contractually reversing my argument. Under the new language, *any* monies spent "on behalf" of the artist become an advance unless the company states in writing that they *aren't* an advance! (See Examples 1 and 2).

Contracts must be reviewed carefully for both obvious and hidden advances. If they cannot be eliminated or restricted, they should at least be specific enough that the artist will be aware of the ground rules.

Note that when a record company has an agreement with a production entity that is supplying both the artist and the production function, there may be problems connected with the division of advances and the recoupment of such advances between the production company and the artist. (See Example 9.) Indeed, there may not be any sharing at all of the advance or the recoupment of the advance between the production company and the artist. In the artist's worst-case scenario, the production company may keep all of the advances and recoup all of the advances and costs from the artist. (Such a scenario is probably unlikely in this enlightened age—but as a philosopher once said, "All things is possible.")

Recording Costs

The costs incurred by a company in recording masters are one form of recoupable advance. The fact that recording costs are recovered from the artist's royalties means that the artist, not the record company, is actually paying the recording costs. In most instances, recording costs are the largest recoupable cost charged to the recording artist. (Note that despite the fact that the artist pays the recording costs, the record company retains ownership of the masters.) In fact, the company's control over the recording costs, from approval of budget to actual payment, is a major factor in the record company's maintaining control over the recording activities of the artist.

The meaning of the term *recording costs* is fairly standard throughout the music industry: It means the "cost of *recording,*" including studio costs, musician and vocalist costs, engineering costs, tape costs, mixing costs, related costs, and mastering. A common contractual definition— variations on which can be found in Examples 6, 7, and 8 below—is as follows:

> The words "recording costs" mean all costs incurred by Company for and with respect to the production of masters, as distinguished from manufacturing and distribution costs, including, without limitation, the cost to Company of all instrumental musicians, vocalists, conductors, arrangers, orchestrators, copyists, etc.; all studio, tape, editing, mastering and other similar costs in connection with the production of the final master, and all other costs and expenses incurred by Company in producing masters hereunder, from time to time, and which are customarily recognized as recording costs in the phonograph record industry.

As straightforward as this may sound, consider the subcategories in the various areas. For example, the cost of musicians and vocalists includes more than just the union scale being paid to them for their performance. There may be cartage (the cost of bringing in bulky equipment); there are taxes to be paid; there are union P&W payments (contributions to the union pension and welfare funds); there are fees due to copyists, arrangers, and contractors (double scale to the leader); there's the cost of flying that fantastic kazoo player in from England; etc.

As stated above, recording costs include most but not necessarily all union payments required by the unions (AFM and AFTRA). One type of union payment which should *not* be a recoverable cost from artist royalties is "MPTF and like payments." (MPTF stands for Music Performance Trust Funds; "like payments" generally refers to what is known as the Special Payments Funds.) Fortunately, most standard recording agreements expressly exclude these payments, which are made to the American Federation of Musicians, from the definition of recording costs. (See "MTPF and Special Payments Funds," pages 116–119, for more information; also see Example 7 at the end of this section.)

A particularly tricky question, especially for the artist, is whether or not the fees paid to the producer are to be part of the recording costs chargeable to the artist—even if they are deemed to be advances to the producer. This raises the nasty specter of the record company double dipping: recovering the same costs from both the artist and the producer. There are agreements (usually, but not necessarily, production agreements) that are called *all-in* agreements. Under an all-in agreement, the record company agrees to one overall royalty and from that royalty *all* royalties are paid.

Example

Production Company has Artist under contract with a 7% royalty. Production Company signs a recording agreement with Record Company for an all-in royalty of 12%. Production Company hires Independent Producer to produce Artist for a 3% royalty. From the 12% paid to Production Company, Artist receives 7%, Independent Producer receives 3%, and Production Company retains the remaining 2%.

Returning to the question of whether or not the producer fees should be included in the recoupable recording costs to be charged to the artist, when it is *not* an all-in agreement it has been my position (when representing the artist) that fees and advances paid to the producer should not be charged to the artist. I might add that many record companies have chosen not to agree with me on this issue. (Of course, I don't necessarily agree with me either when I represent record companies.)

For those record companies still maintaining their own recording studios, it is important that the artist impose some sort of control over the price of the studio when determining recording costs. Also, be warned that although the studio may be owned by the record company, its use is seldom free and in fact the cost is probably not competitive with the other studios around town.

Artists who are in an "earned" position (that is, the company owes actual royalty payments, not credits, to the artist) should be aware that companies will sometimes try to avoid making the payments due by requiring that more masters be recorded by the artist and thus spending the money owed the artist on the cost of recording the masters. As previously discussed, the method used to guard against this contingency is to restrict the number of masters a record company can demand without the artist's consent.

It is sometimes possible to negotiate an agreement so that part or all of the recording costs are not an advance against royalties. These nonadvance payments are frequently referred to as "flat," or "bonus," payments. There are two ways of doing this: The contract will simply stipulate that the company will bear some or all of the recording costs, or the agreement will provide that all or part of the recording costs will be borne by the record company only if certain levels of sales are reached.

Example

Artist's agreement provides that for each album recorded which sells 100,000 units "through normal distribution channels," Record Company will assume responsibility for one-half of the recording costs and such costs will not be a chargeable cost to Artist. If the album sells 250,000 units through normal distribution channels, the remaining one-half of recording costs will be borne by Record Company and will not be a cost charged to Artist.

Master Purchases

In all but rare instances, the money paid by a record company to acquire ownership of a previously recorded master or masters from an artist, producer, or production company is counted as an advance against earnings. These purchases, the process, and the underlying agreements are all referred to as *master purchases.*

The record company recoups the cost of the master purchase from the royalty due for the sale of the recordings made from the masters; if cross-collateralization is in effect, the record company can also recoup this advance from sales of previous and subsequent recordings for the record company or affiliated companies. It is possible to argue that a "purchase price" is not the same thing as a "recording cost," but they both serve the same purpose—creating or acquiring a product to be released—and they are both usually treated as the same kind of entity when it comes to recoupment.

The Recording Fund

The majority of those agreements today which are either production agreements or agreements in which the artist is either also the producer, or provides the producer, stipulate the use of what is known as a *recording fund.* (Examples 9 through 11 contain recording fund provisions.) Under this type of arrangement, the record company agrees to a specified budget for recording. The difference, if any, between the actual cost and the specified sum goes to the production company and/or artist as a cash advance. The entire amount of the recording fund becomes an advance against royalties. The recording fund is treated as if it were the recording costs, even if a portion is retained by the production company and/or artist.

Example

Artist and Company have agreed upon a budget of $100,000 for an album as a recording fund. The album costs $60,000 to record. Upon completion of the album, Artist is paid (or retains) a cash advance of $40,000 ($100,000 less $60,000 actual cost = $40,000 cash advance to Artist). The entire $100,000 is an advance against Artist's royalty account, $60,000 as recording costs and $40,000 as a cash advance.

It has been argued that this method of paying the artist (and/or production company) the cash difference between the recording fund and the actual monies spent on the recording has led to better "citizenship" in the studio. There is some justification for this: More recordings are brought in on or below budget under recording fund situations than under situations where the record company pays the cost and either pays an advance to the artist or production company separately or pays no advance at all. Nothing makes an artist's behavior more cost-effective than the realization that monies being spent on production might otherwise go into the artist's own pockets.

In addition, under the recording fund arrangement, the artist (or production company) is, at least contractually, responsible for all costs in excess of the recording fund. In this context, the "responsibility" is to actually pay the excess, not just be responsible for recoupment; that is, the offending party must dip into the party's own pockets to pay for the excess amount. Accordingly, if the recording fund is $100,000 and the artist spends $125,000 on an album, the excess $25,000 is the responsibility of the artist. Or at least so it says on paper—certainly this is more honored in the breach than in practice. Recording fund arrangements have reduced the number of cases in which actual costs exceed the approved budget, presumably because the artist, who is dealing with his or her own money, spends more wisely. (As set forth in Chapter 4, "Independent Producer Agreements," pages 206–220, it is best under these circumstances to build in a contingency for going over budget, e.g., only being responsible for costs in excess of 110% of the approved budget.)

Another reason that recording fund projects are more likely to come in "within budget" is that the practice of bundling together recording costs and a cash advance into a recording fund probably results in a higher projected figure than would have been approved for the recording alone. For example, suppose that a reasonable budget for recording a particular album would have been $100,000, but the recording fund is $125,000. Now if it turns out that the album costs the entire $125,000, which is 25% over what would have been the reasonable recording cost, the project is still "within the budget."

Recording fund provisions frequently, though not invariably, have language referring to a "minimum-maximum" (or "no less–no more") range for the size of recording funds. (See Examples 9, 10, and 11.) These *mini/max* provisions provide a floor (the minimum dollar amount for the recording fund) and a ceiling (the maximum dollar amount for the recording fund). If, after applying a specified formula: (1) the resulting dollar amount is less than the minimum, the specified minimum would apply; (2) the resulting dollar amount is greater than the maximum, the specified maximum would apply; or (3) the resulting dollar amount falls somewhere between the minimum and the maximum amount, that figure would be used as the recording fund amount.

Generally, the size of a recording fund will increase after the initial period, usually according to some formula based on sales of a previous album or albums or just the passage of time. In many ways, the rationale is the same as was noted before for justifying royalty accelerations (see the section "Royalty Acceleration," pages 68–71). Typical language is seen in Example 10 below, one provision of which calls for a recording fund advance of "twenty five percent (25%) of the aggregate royalties, less actual returns and credits (after provision for reasonable reserves for returns and credits) earned by Producer from sales of the prior two (2) albums delivered to Company and released through normal retail channels hereunder," but also specifies minimum and maximum fund amounts for the initial period ($100,000 and $150,000, respectively) and the first option period ($125,000 and $200,000), the second option period ($150,000 and $225,000), and the third option period ($175,000 and $250,000). Thus, if in the first option period the aggregate royalties from two albums were $1,000,000, the recording fund for the first option period would still be only $200,000, because 25% of $1,000,000 is $250,000, or $50,000 over the maximum. Note that the formula for determining the recording fund may require an exception for the first and, possibly, the second album inasmuch as there may not be existing numbers to which the formula can be applied.

Another issue involving recording fund agreements is what sum of money should be payable to the production company or artist-producer in the event that the record company chooses not to allow a project to go forward even though there is a contractual guarantee that the project would be recorded and the appropriate recording fund paid. Obviously, the company would prefer not to make any payment. The production company or artist, on the other hand, is entitled to say, "Whoa there, bunky, part of the recording fund is an advance which was going directly into my pocket. What are you gonna do about that?" A good question. The time-honored method is to determine the amount actually "pocketed" by the production company or artist-producer (the amount kept, if any, after deducting recording costs from the recording fund) on the last project, or, perhaps, the average of the last two albums, and pay that amount to the production company. That's another good reason to keep costs in check. There is likely to be a maximum sum specified which the record company will pay.

SAMPLE CONTRACT PROVISIONS

EXAMPLE 1: All Monies (Except Royalties) Advances

12.(f) All monies payable to you or on your behalf or to or on behalf of any person, firm or corporation representing you, other than royalties payable pursuant to this paragraph, shall constitute advances recoupable from any sums payable under this Agreement or under any other agreement between you and us and or our affiliates, subsidiaries, successors or assigns, unless we otherwise consent in writing.

> ☞ Everything "payable" (other than royalties) is an advance. Does that mean it is recouped even if it is "payable" but not actually "paid?" A curious thought. Can future advances be recouped before they are paid? One presumes (and hopes!) not. Also, note the appearance of Mr. Cross-Collateralization ("or any other agreement").

EXAMPLE 2: Advances—General

6.01 All monies paid by Company to you during the term of this agreement, except royalties paid pursuant to Articles 9, 10 and 12, will constitute Advances. Each payment (except such royalties) made by Company during the term to anyone else on your behalf will also constitute an Advance if it is made with your consent, if it is required by law, or if it is made by Company to satisfy an obligation incurred by you in connection with the subject matter of this agreement (of which Company will inform you and allow you to contest if feasible).

> ☞ I am troubled by the inclusion of payments "required by law" being recoupable. Off hand, other than payroll taxes from recording sessions, I cannot think of a payment "required by law" (such as an income tax levy) that does not first have to have been either earned (e.g., a royalty) or somehow vested (e.g., a guaranteed advance). In the first instance, the artist could be charged twice, once by the I.R.S. and once by the record company when it recoups the sum paid to the I.R.S. on behalf of the artist. In the second instance, since all monies other than royalties are already advances, why do these payments have to be restated as recoupable? "Required by law" might also include past transgressions not related to the recording agreement.

EXAMPLE 3: Advance Reduced by Unrecouped Balance

(b) Promptly after the release of an Album hereunder, Company will pay you an Advance in the sum of Seventy-Five Thousand Dollars ($75,000). (No other Advance will be payable in connection with those Recordings.) Each such Advance will be reduced as provided for in [subparagraph number]. If your royalty account is in an unrecouped position (i.e., if the aggregate of the Advances and other recoupable items charged to that account at the time of payment of that Advance exceeds the aggregate of the royalties credited to that account at the end of the last semiannual royalty period), the Advance payable under the first sentence of this subparagraph will be reduced by the amount of the unrecouped balance; provided, however, in any event, Company shall pay Recording Costs in connection with each such new Master Recording in an amount not in excess of a recording budget approved in accordance with the provisions of section [number].

☛ This language is unclear as to whether the record company can reduce the advance by the amount then unrecouped, leaving the balance due the same, or credit the unpaid portion of the advance toward the unrecouped balance, thereby reducing the balance due.

EXAMPLE 4: Recording Fund Payment Schedule

6. (e) Advances

(i) With respect to each newly recorded CD (except the First CD) hereunder, Company shall pay to you an advance in the amount set forth in the following schedule corresponding to the respective CD. Each such advance shall be payable one-fourth (¼) not later than three (3) weeks prior to the commencement of recording of such respective CD (provided, however, that you shall have furnished Company with a letter warranting and representing that such recording shall, in fact, commence at the expiration of said three (3) week period, and further provided that Producer shall have been mutually approved pursuant to subparagraph 2(a) above), one-fourth (¼) not later than five (5) business days following commencement of recording of the master recordings comprising the respective CD, and the balance not later than ten (10) business days following delivery by you to Company of the master recordings of such CD. Notwithstanding anything to the contrary contained in this subparagraph 6(e)(i), if such recording has not commenced at the expiration of said three (3) week period, then, in addition to any other rights of Company hereunder, you shall promptly repay to Company the amount previously paid to you by Company prior to such commencement of recording.

If the CD Is the:	The Advance Shall Be:
Second CD	$400,000
Third CD, if any	$250,000
Fourth CD, if any	$300,000
Fifth CD, if any	$350,000
Sixth CD, if any	$350,000
Seventh CD, if any	$400,000

(ii) The advances specified in subparagraph 6(e)(i) shall be charged against and recoupable at any time from any and all royalties accruing to your credit hereunder. No advances shall be payable hereunder with respect to Artist's recording "singles" sides, except to the extent that such sides are later included in any CD for which an advance may be due pursuant to subparagraph 6(e)(i) above.

(iii) If for any reason (other than Company's hindrance without cause) any of the master recordings to be recorded hereunder are not delivered within thirty (30) days following the expiration of the applicable period specified in subparagraphs 4(a) and 4(b) hereof, you agree to repay to Company, upon Company's written demand therefor, the respective sum previously paid by Company for such respective master recordings pursuant to this subparagraph 6(e).

☛ The recording funds increase with the recording of each subsequent CD (singles don't count) and the increase is not based upon a sales formula.

EXAMPLE 5: Advances for Injunction

(d) Company shall have the right to pay you at any time any additional amounts which may be required to be paid as a condition to Company's petitioning for any injunction pursuant to Section 526 of the California Code of Civil Procedure and Section 3423 (5th) of the California Civil Code ("Additional Payments"). You hereby agree to accept any and all such Additional Payments. All compensation (other than Mechanical Royalties) paid to you hereunder which is not applied to the Annual Payments theretofore due you will be credited toward satisfying the obligation to make Additional Payments as a prerequisite to seeking injunctive relief hereunder. If Company actually makes any Additional Payments and thereafter elects not to seek such injunction, such Additional Payments shall constitute Advances hereunder.

EXAMPLE 6: Definition of Recording Costs

6. Recording Costs; Budget. Company shall engage and pay for the services of vocalists, musicians, arrangers, sketchers, conductors, orchestrators, producers, contractors and copyists in connection with the performance to be rendered by Artist at all rehearsal and recording sessions hereunder. All such payments, together with payroll taxes thereon, payments based on payroll to any labor organization or designee thereof, the cost of cartage and rental of instruments for such recording sessions, studio costs, transportation costs, hotel and living expenses incurred in connection with the preparation and attendance of Artist, the individual producer, musicians and other essential personnel at recording sessions, tape, editing and similar costs in connection with the production of the final tape master, and all other costs generally and customarily recognized as recording costs in the phonograph record industry, shall be deemed additional non-returnable advances to Artist and shall be deducted from royalties payable to Artist by Company under this Agreement. In the event that Artist should delay the commencement or completion of, or be unavailable for, any recording session hereunder, Company shall have the right to charge Artist for all expenses actually incurred by Company by reason thereof, and, unless Artist was unavailable for reason beyond his control Artist shall reimburse Company on demand for all such costs actually incurred and paid for by Company.

☛ Included in recording costs are "transportation costs, hotel and living costs." Also, cross-collateralization seems to be reined in here since the advances are only deductible "under this Agreement" and not under any other agreement.

EXAMPLE 7: MPTF Payments Not Recording Costs

12. Recording costs shall mean and include all minimum union scale payments made to you, all payments made to any other individuals rendering services in connection with the recordings of Masters, all other payments which are made pursuant to any applicable law or regulation or the provisions of any collective bargaining agreement between us or Distributor and any union or guild (including, without limitation, payroll taxes and payments to union pension and welfare funds), all amounts paid or incurred for studio or hall rentals, tape, engineering, editing, instrument rentals and cartage, mastering, transportation and accommodations, immigration clearances, any so-called "per diems" for any individuals (including you) rendering services in connection with recording of the masters, together with all other amounts paid or incurred in connection with the recording of the Masters. Notwithstanding anything to the contrary contained herein, royalties payable by us or the Distributor to the AF of M Music Trust Fund or Special Payments Funds, shall not be deemed Recording Costs. The Recording Costs shall be recouped from all monies payable to you hereunder or under any other agreement between you and us or our affiliates.

EXAMPLE 8: Recording Costs Shared by Artist and Production Company

(b) If Company enters into an agreement with a third party record company pursuant to a so-called "production agreement," Fifty (50%) Percent of recording costs incurred in connection with the recording of masters hereunder shall be deemed to be non-returnable advances to me and shall be charged against my royalties under this Agreement; provided, however, nothing contained herein shall result in a "double recoupment" of my share of recording costs as a result of the prior recoupment of such recording costs by the third party record company. If I should delay the commencement or completion of, or be unavailable for any recording sessions designated by Company hereunder for any reason whatsoever, I agree to pay all expenses and charges actually incurred or paid by Company. Company agrees to pay that portion of recording costs, as defined in Subparagraph 13(f) below, for my travel, housing, meal expenses, etc. in connection with rehearsals and recording sessions scheduled pursuant to the terms of this Agreement.

☛ This is a provision in an agreement between an artist and a production company. They have agreed that when an agreement is reached with a record company, the allocation of recording costs for recoupment shall be shared equally by the artist and the production company. Note the prohibition against "double recoupment," that is, both the record company and the production company independently recouping artist's share of the recording costs.

EXAMPLE 9: Production Company and Artist Share Advances

(i) If Company enters into a production agreement with a third party record company as provided for herein, I shall receive my proportionate share (fifty (50%) percent) of advances made to Company by such third party record company, such share to be computed after the deduction of recording costs actually incurred, it being the intention of the parties hereto that recording costs be recouped "off the top" prior to any distribution of advances from such third party record company, as also provided for in Subparagraph 4.(g) below.

(j) If Company shall serve as its own distributor, as set forth in Subparagraph 4(d) below, conditioned upon my full performance of all the material terms and conditions hereof, Company shall pay me the following advances in the applicable option periods upon delivery of the recording in satisfaction of the minimum recording commitment in respect of the then current period:

(A) The advance shall be an amount equal to fifty (50%) percent of the aggregate royalties, less actual returns and credits earned by me from sales during the immediately proceeding period of this Agreement through normal retail channels hereunder, including reasonably estimated "pipeline" monies. Notwithstanding the foregoing, each such advance, if any, payable pursuant to this Subparagraph 2. (j) shall not be less than nor more than the following applicable amounts:

Contract Period of Recording	Minimum	Maximum
First Option Period	$10,000	$40,000
Second Option Period	$30,000	$75,000

(B) All amounts paid to me pursuant to this Subparagraph 2(j), shall constitute advances hereunder and shall be recoupable from any royalties payable to me hereunder.

☛ This provision illustrates a number of problems which must be considered and dealt with when a production company and an artist enter into an agreement. Subparagraph (i) deals with the sharing of advances between the production company and the artist when the production company enters into an agreement with a record company. Subparagraph (j), with its subparagraphs (A) and (B), deals with an alternative scenario. Presumably unable to make an agreement with a record company, the production company chooses to distribute its own records (becoming the "record company") and sets up its own mini/max formula to determine the advances due the artist. Note the reference to "pipeline" monies in connection with the formula. These are payments which have not yet been actually received by the production company, but are in the pipeline waiting to be distributed in the appropriate accounting period.

EXAMPLE 10: Minimum/Maximum Based on Royalty

7. Advances

7.1 Conditioned upon Producer's and Artist's full performance of all the material terms and conditions hereof, Company shall pay to Producer the following aggregate recording fund advances (inclusive of all recording costs) for each album delivered to Company in satisfaction of the Minimum Recording Commitment, or any required Additional Product, subsequent to the album to be delivered hereunder in satisfaction of the Minimum Recording Commitment in respect of the initial period:

(a) The recording fund advance shall be an amount equal to twenty-five (25%) percent of the aggregate royalties, less actual returns and credits (after provision for reasonable reserves for returns and credits) earned by Producer from sales of the prior two (2) albums delivered to Company and released through normal retail channels hereunder ... (except as to the second album delivered to Company hereunder, fifty (50%) percent of the aggregate royalties less actual returns and credits). ... Notwithstanding the foregoing, each such advance, if any, payable pursuant to this paragraph 7.1 (a) shall not be less than nor more than the following applicable amounts:

Contract Period of Recording	Minimum Fund	Maximum Fund
Initial Period	$100,000	$150,000
First Option Period	$125,000	$200,000
Second Option Period	$150,000	$225,000
Third Option Period	$175,000	$250,000

• • •

7.2 All amounts paid to Producer pursuant to paragraph 7.1 hereof, as well as monies paid by Company to Producer, or on Producer's behalf, at Producer's request, during the term of this Agreement (other than royalties paid pursuant to paragraph 6 hereof), shall constitute advances hereunder and shall be recoupable from any royalties payable to Producer hereunder.

☛ The formula to determine the recording fund for any album, subject to the minimum and the maximum, is that the recording fund equals 25% of the aggregate net royalty earned from the two prior albums (except for the first album, which is at the base rate of $100,000, and the second, which is based on 50% of the first album's net royalty).

EXAMPLE 11: Minimum/Maximum after Second Album

5. During the term of this Agreement:

(a) Unless otherwise expressly agreed to in writing, Company shall pay to Productions the applicable sum listed below (the "Recording Fund") for the applicable Album delivered to Company in satisfaction of the Artist Recording Commitment:

(i) With respect to the First Album: One Hundred and Fifty Thousand ($150,000) Dollars.

(ii) With respect to the Second Album: One Hundred and Seventy Five Thousand ($175,000) Dollars.

(iii) With respect to the Third Album and Fourth Album, the Recording Fund shall be the Formula Amount, but no less than Two Hundred Thousand ($200,000) Dollars and no more than Four Hundred Thousand ($400,000) Dollars.

(iv) With respect to the Fifth Album and Sixth Album, the Recording Fund shall be the Formula Amount, but no less than Two Hundred and Fifty Thousand ($250,000) Dollars and no more than Five Hundred Thousand ($500,000) Dollars.

(b) The "Formula Amount" for a particular Album delivered hereunder in fulfillment of the Artist Recording Commitment shall mean an amount equal to sixty-six and two-thirds ($66\frac{2}{3}$%) percent of the royalties credited to Productions' account from Net Sales Through Normal Retail Channels in the United States of America and Canada (at Company's top-line, full-price category, net of applicable reserves which, for purposes of the Formula Amount only, shall not exceed twenty (20%) percent) of the immediately preceding Artist Commitment Album computed on the last full month preceding the date Productions shall have commenced recording the Album for which the Formula Amount is being calculated.

(c) The Recording Fund for each Artist Commitment Album shall be paid as follows:

(i) One-half ($\frac{1}{2}$) following Productions' notice to Company that recording of the

Commitment Album will commence within thirty (30) days, the date of commencement of recording, the studio where recording will commence, and that recording is scheduled to proceed, without interruption, to completion. Such notice shall also identify the in-studio producer engaged by Productions; and

(ii) The balance following Productions' Delivery to Company and Company's acceptance in accordance with all of the terms and conditions of this Agreement of the Masters comprising the applicable Commitment Album.

(d) Notwithstanding anything to the contrary contained herein, Productions may request an additional disbursement of the Recording Fund after one-half (½) is paid pursuant to Subparagraph 5(c)(i) above, but prior to Production's Delivery and Company's acceptance of Masters; however, the decision to make any additional disbursements of the Recording Fund, other than as provided in Subparagraph 5.(c)(i) and (ii), will be solely in Company's discretion, not to be unreasonably withheld.

(e) Company shall have the right to withhold a reasonable portion of payments to be made on Delivery to provide for anticipated costs which have not yet been paid by Company or billed to Company, which costs are otherwise deductible from payments to be made to Productions.

☛ Subparagraph (c) sets forth when the recording fund is paid.

MPTF AND SPECIAL PAYMENTS FUNDS

One of the provisions of the AFM Basic Agreement, to which all major record companies are signatories, stipulates that the companies must make payments, based on sales, to the Music Performance Trust Fund (MPTF) and Special Payments Funds. The companies are, in effect, paying a royalty to the American Federation of Musicians.

Music Performance Trust Fund and Special Payments Funds monies are collected directly from the record companies by the trustees of those funds. The proceeds from the MPTF are used by the union for free concerts and to promote live music. The proceeds from the Special Payments Fund are distributed to AFM members based upon their recording session activities in the applicable year. Contract provisions sometimes refer to both funds by name, and sometimes to "MPTF and the like."

Any recording of pure spoken word, without music, is, technically, exempt from MPTF contributions. Recordings made outside of the jurisdiction of the AFM are also exempt; for example, an album recorded in London by the London Symphony would not be subject to MPTF payments.

Be wary of contract definitions of recording costs which make general references to "union payments" or contain similarly broad statements. Modify such language by adding terms such as "other than MPTF and like payments," or limit union costs charged to recording to "payments based on payroll." The payroll limitation automatically excludes MPTF from being a recording cost since MPTF payments are based upon sales, unlike pension and welfare (P&W) contributions, which are based upon payroll (that is, the wages of the musicians), and are traditionally included as a recording cost.

There are times when an artist's royalties are not calculated on either a retail or a wholesale price but on a division of the "net royalty" received by the record company from a third party. This is frequently referred to as a "split" royalty. These are usually licenses to use, rather than sell, the recording, such as licensing a recording for use on a soundtrack to a film or, perhaps, the licensing of a recording in connection with an advertising campaign.

In most recording agreements which have a provision for a "split," or division, of net royalties (such as licensing a record for a flat fee to a third party), the record company will deduct MPTF payments in order to reach the net figure. Mechanical licenses, if paid by the company, will also be deducted to reach the net royalty. Artists should carefully examine language dealing with "splitting" proceeds, or payment based upon a "net royalty," to find out just what gets deducted in order to reach net (see the comment following Example 1). Chances are the record company will not change the royalty provisions, but it never hurts to ask.

SAMPLE CONTRACT PROVISIONS

EXAMPLE 1: Not Charged to Artist

(ii) Company shall be solely responsible for and shall make full payment of any and all sums which may become due and payable, on account of the manufacture and sale of records by Company hereunder, to the copyright proprietors, the Music Performance Trust Fund, the Special Payments Fund and any other union or union trust fund having rights in the premises. Such sums paid by Company shall not be chargeable to your credit hereunder.

> ☛ Music Performance Trust Fund, Special Payments Funds, and mechanical license (paid to "copyright proprietors") payments *on account of the manufacture and sale of records by Company*" are not "chargeable" to the artist [emphasis added]. Note that the license of a recording for use on a soundtrack is not a "manufacture and sale," nor, arguably, is a license to a third party (e.g., a foreign licensee or a record club) who might manufacture and sell records, a sale "by Company."

EXAMPLE 2: Union Costs Limited to Those Based on Payroll

6. Recording Costs; Budget. Company shall engage and pay for the services of vocalists, musicians, arrangers, sketchers, conductors, orchestrators, producers, contractors and copyists in connection with the performance to be rendered by Artist at all rehearsal and recording sessions hereunder. All such payments, together with payroll taxes thereon, payments based on payroll to any labor organization or designee thereof. . . .

EXAMPLE 3: Not Recoupable

8. Payments to the AFM Special Payments Fund and the Music Performance Trust Fund based upon record sales (so-called "pre-record royalties"), will not be recoupable from your royalties or reimbursable by you.

PROMOTION COSTS

Historically, promotion costs were considered to be the company's "cost of doing business" and there was no more thought of charging those costs back to the artist than there was of charging manufacturing costs back. As we have seen, times have changed. Now, it is increasingly common for some (usually half) or all promotional costs to be charged against, and recouped from, the artist's royalties. (See Examples 1 and 2.) One can only speculate about what other "cost of doing business" categories will be tomorrow's recoupable costs.

The fact of the matter is that promotion has become a very expensive operation for record companies. Even though the major record companies have extensive (and expensive) in-house promotion teams, there are always "supplemental" (and *very* expensive) independent promotion efforts. It is not uncommon for the costs of promotion for even a moderately successful album not only to exceed the recording costs, but to exceed those costs by a multiple of five, six, or even more. We are talking about a goodly chunk of money here. It is indeed the rare (and I suspect probably nonexistent) album or single that has a successful sales record without the support of an expensive promotion campaign.

Some note should be made of the record industry's time-honored tradition—payola. *Payola* is generally thought to be the practice of paying a radio station, a radio music programer, a disc jockey, or anyone else to play a record on the radio. From a legal standpoint, this definition is actually incorrect. The payment of money to get a record broadcast is not illegal—what is illegal is the payment of money to get a record broadcast *and not disclosing that the payment was made.* In other words, there's nothing illegal about paying a radio station to play your record, there just better be some disclosure made with the broadcast. Without the disclosure, it's break the piggy bank (up to a $10,000 fine), go to the pokey time (up to one year), or both.

With increasing frequency, record companies are using this method—buying airtime and disclosing the fact—to promote recordings. Since there are no meaningful guidelines for what constitutes appropriate disclosure, the disclosures tend to drift into what can only be described as nebulous. Using offhand phrases such as "XYZ Records presents . . . ," the casual listener probably hasn't a clue that they just listened to a paid commercial.

The beauty of all this is that the record companies are really using payola legally, at a far cheaper cost and with more efficiency than in the grand old days of independent promoters.

A brief pause for a true story. Some years ago at the annual convention of one of the biggest of the major record companies, there was a private party for everyone on the company's promotion team. They had come in from all over the country. They were grizzled veterans, they were new guys, they were a mixture of suits and guys with ponytails and earrings. They were the company's frontline troops on the battlefield of promotion. The vice president of Promotion for the company, the commander-in-chief, was touring the room. He went up to one young man and clapped him on the shoulder.

"How's it going, son?"

"Fine, sir."

"Great. You know, I'm aware of your background, we've been keeping an eye on your work. You've been doing a great job for us." A reassuring squeeze to the young man's shoulder. "Keep it up. I think you've got a real future here with us."

"Thank you," said the young man. He then bent over and picked up the tray of dishes he had come for and disappeared back into the kitchen.

As the old saying goes, if a promotion man's lips are moving, he's lying.

SAMPLE CONTRACT PROVISIONS

EXAMPLE 1: 50% of Promotion Costs Charged to Artist

5. With regard to promotion hereunder:

(a) Company will produce for a Video for each album comprising recordings made entirely from masters hereunder which is released in the United States.

(b) Company, in its sole discretion, shall have the right to expend monies in connection with the independent marketing and promotion of any record(s) embodying the masters. Notwithstanding anything to the contrary contained herein, only Fifty (50%) Percent of all such expenditures shall be advances against and recoupable by Company out of any and all royalties becoming payable to Artist under this or any other agreement. Artist shall have the right to consult with Company with regard to the independent marketing and promotion campaigns.

☞ There are a couple of side issues here: it (a) obligates Company to produce a video for each album and (b) limits recoupment to 50% but includes cross-collateralization.

EXAMPLE 2: Minimum Dollar Amount Specified

(c) In addition to the minimum Video budget provided for above, Company agrees to spend a minimum of Two Hundred and Seventy Five Thousand ($275,000) Dollars to promote the release of the album comprising recordings made entirely from the Masters. Company, in its sole discretion shall have the right to expend such monies in connection with the independent marketing and promotion of any record(s) embodying the Masters. Notwithstanding anything to the contrary contained herein, only Fifty (50%) Percent of all such expenditures (excluding mechanical royalties) shall be advances against and recoupable by Company out of any and all royalties (excluding mechanical royalties) becoming payable to Licensor under this or any other agreement. Licensor shall have the right to consult with Company with regard to the independent marketing and promotion campaigns.

☞ I view specified minimum dollar amounts for promotion with some suspicion. Who can tell two, three, four, five, or more albums in advance what will be an appropriate minimum sum to be spent on any given promotion?

ARTIST/PRODUCTION COMPANY ROYALTIES

Music is your own experience, your thoughts, your wisdom.
If you don't live it, it won't come out of your horn.
—CHARLIE "BIRD" PARKER

Before moving on from the royalty provisions, it is appropriate to pause and touch on the royalty relationship between the artist and the production company. The particular focus here is how to reconcile the potential differences between the royalty received by the production company from the record company and the royalty which the production company, in turn, pays to the artist. (For a detailed review of production agreements see Chapter 6, "Production Agreements.")

More and more production agreements are being used to supply artists to record companies. Under these all-in agreements, the production company supplies the artist and the producer to the record company in exchange for an all-in royalty. In other words, the production company receives the total royalty and then disburses royalties to the artist and the producer. In most cases, the production company will sign the artist to a recording agreement before knowing the terms of the agreement it will enter into with the record company (or, indeed, if there will even be an agreement with a record company). The question for both artist and production company becomes "what is a livable royalty," both in rate and calculation, for both parties.

Example

Artist's agreement with Production Company calls for Artist to receive a 50% reduction of royalties for foreign sales. Production Company's agreement with Record Company provides for a 25% reduction in royalties for foreign sales. Result: Artist gets 50 cents on the dollar on what Artist would have received for a domestic sale while Production Company gets 75 cents on the dollar.

Example

Artist's agreement with Production Company provides for a limit on free records of 2 for 10. Production Company's agreement with Record Company provides for a limit on free records of 3 for 10. Result: Production Company gets paid for 10 record sales for every 13 shipped, while Artist is paid for 10 record sales for every 12 shipped. In effect, Production Company must pay Artist for one extra record sale for each 10 shipped.

As you can see, the discrepancies between what an artist has been able to negotiate for royalties and what the production company may or may not receive from the record company create a potential minefield for both parties.

There are three basic ways to approach this problem:

1. Both production entity and artist try to drive as hard a bargain as possible.

2. Production company and artist reach an agreement whereby the artist receives a specified royalty, either a set percentage or, more commonly, according to what is known as a pro-rata agreement, in which the artist's royalties are a proportion of what the production company receives pursuant to its agreement with the record company. This may be an equal split, with 50% of the monies received by the production company from the record company going to the artist and 50% retained by the production company (see Example 4), or in some other proportion.

3. The agreement between production company and artist contains what is known as a flow-through provision, which states that, no matter what the agreement between the artist and the production company provides, the artist will get the benefit of any more favorable royalty computation in the production company's agreement with the record company. (See Examples 1, 2, and 3.)

By using either the second or third method, the parties forestall protracted negotiations over issues which may or may not be important, as well as the possibility of having to renegotiate, or even kill, a deal because the production company cannot afford the deal offered by the record company.

SAMPLE CONTRACT PROVISIONS

EXAMPLE 1: Flow-Through

n. Except as expressly set forth hereinabove, in all other respects your royalty shall be computed in the same manner (i.e., subject to the same exchange rate provisions and the same reserve and liquidation provisions) as our royalty is computed and reduced pursuant to any license agreements entered into by us concerning the distribution of masters.

EXAMPLE 2: Flow-Through

(n) Notwithstanding anything to the contrary contained herein, if any royalty computation provision contained in any agreement Company has with a third party record company for the distribution of the recordings is more favorable than the computation provisions set forth herein, I shall be given the benefit of any such computation. In other words, for example, if the third party distributor grants Company a more favorable container deduction than granted to me hereunder, I shall receive the more favorable rate.

EXAMPLE 3: Flow-Through

(c) Except as expressly set forth hereinabove, and in Subparagraph 3(d), below, in all other respects my royalty shall be computed in the same manner (e.g., subject to the same royalty computation, deductions, reductions, reserves, etc.) as Company's royalty is computed and reduced pursuant to any agreements entered into by Company concerning the distribution and sale of records manufactured from the masters.

EXAMPLE 4: Royalties and Advances Shared Pro-Rata

5. In connection with the sales or other exploitations of the Masters, we shall pay you an amount equal to fifty percent (50%) of the Net Record Royalties (hereinafter defined) actually received by us under any Distributor Agreement. As used herein, the term "Net Record Royalties" in respect of any particular Master shall mean the gross royalty earned and payable to us under the Distribution Agreement in respect of such Master less any and all royalties payable to any third party royalty participant other than the individual producer. Without limiting the foregoing, we shall have the right to retain for our own account fifty percent (50%) of the Net Record Royalties and we shall pay all royalties payable to any individual producer from such royalties retained by us. Your producer royalty, if any, shall be included in your 50% share, i.e., an "all-in" royalty.

6. We shall also pay you an amount equal to fifty percent (50%) of the amount by which all advances or so-called "recording funds" actually paid to us under the Distribution Agreement exceeds (A) any and all advances required to be paid by us (or otherwise deducted from such advances or "recording funds" and paid) to any individual producer of any of the Masters; (B) any and all recording costs in connection with the recording of the Masters paid by us (or otherwise deducted from such advances or "recording funds" and paid); and (C) any other costs deducted by the Distributor from such advances or "recording funds."

> ☛ In this agreement, royalties and advances are shared between the production company and the artist on a 50/50 basis. The division between the parties is negotiated and can be any proportion: 50/50; 60/40; etc. In any division other than 50/50, the artist's share is usually the larger of the two. Notice that the producer royalty (unless the producer is also the artist) comes from the production company's share.

ACCOUNTING

It is all well and good to know how royalties are computed. But when bills are due, a more pressing issue is *when* royalties will be paid. Most record companies account to their artists twice a year—biannually—usually, but not always, within a specified number of days after June 30 and December 31 (see Examples 1 and 3). The number of days may vary from 30 to 45 to 60 to 90, or more, or less. For whatever reason, some record companies have biannual accounting periods which start and end on months other than the obvious months (June and December). Go figure. Some companies account quarterly, every 3 months, which is better for the artist (see Example 2). Some companies account once a year, which is worse for the artist.

Whatever the company's accounting practice, do not expect them to change it just for you. In fact, about the only flexibility you will find in the realm of accounting periods is that sometimes the company will give itself the right to change the accounting period from one 6-month period to another. This one-sided flexibility takes a form such as altering "the 6-month period ending June 30" to "the 6-month period ending August 31," or the like.

The language used in the accounting provisions of the agreements usually specifies that royalties are not due and payable until the record company has actually received payment (see Examples 1 and 3). Accordingly, if records are shipped in accounting period 1, but payment is not received until accounting period 3, the records are reported to the artist as selling in accounting period 3 and paid in accounting period 4. While this is fair, since a record is not actually "sold" until the company receives payment, it does sometimes mean that the artist must wait a long time for royalty payments. With foreign sales, particularly, "actual payment received" clauses can drag out the waiting time considerably—first for the company and consequently for the artist. Payments of royalties for foreign sales are famous for turning up (if at all) years after albums have been shipped.

Example

The foreign licensee sells Record on January 15 and accounts to record company August 29 (60 days after June 30 for sales in the first 6 months). The record company now accounts for this sale as if it took place on August 29 (the date payment is received), which means it accounts to the artist as if the record sold in the second half of the year. The record company pays artist March 1 (60 days after December 31 for sales in the second 6 months). Result: A 14-month delay between "sale" of record and payment of royalty.

Actually, the above example is almost a best-case scenario when it comes to foreign sales. The time required for these payments to come sliding through the pipeline is usually much longer.

The accounting provisions in recording agreements almost always have a clause stating that the artist waives any right to contest the royalty figures unless an objection is made within a specified time period, which may vary from 90 days or less (clearly too short, see Example 1) to 3 years or more (unlikely). Few companies will agree to a period longer than 2 years. The argument for a longer period than 90 days (or whatever) is that the artist needs more than one accounting in order to determine if there is reason to object. After all, with reserves, returns, freebies, etc., it is logical to suppose that it would take several accountings before a pattern could be detected indicating that the record company was not meeting the high moral standard in its accounting procedures which they, at least, would have us believe is the norm. These provisions are always a two-step procedure. The first step is to make a timely objection; the second, if the record company denies the artist's claim, is to file a lawsuit within a specified time period after the record company's denial. In most instances, that period is equal to the period within which the objection was to be filed (e.g., 2 years to file an objection, then 2 years to bring a lawsuit). (See Examples 1 and 3.) As a practical matter, about the most favorable period an artist can receive from a record company is a 2-year period within which to file an objection and a 2-year period within which to file suit after the record company has rejected the artist's claim.

Audits

The question now is, What do you, the artist, do when the suspicion sets in that the record company may have ripped off your royalties? The answer is an audit. Audits allow you to go in and hunt around in the bowels of the company's royalty department and try to trace what happened to your money. The audit may turn up any number of fascinating things—not necessarily all in the artist's favor. (Theoretically, an audit could turn up the horrifying information that there has been an overpayment. Experience has shown, however, that this is very unlikely.)

There is one major problem with audits—they are expensive. Sometimes, if the audit is really just a fishing expedition, the cost may exceed by many times any discrepancy in the artist's favor. Many companies try to discourage fishing expeditions by stipulating in the contract with the artist that no audit may be done on a "contingency" basis; that is, the artist must actually pay the auditor, not bring an auditor in on the promise of a percentage of the presumably enormous proceeds from the presumably successful audit. One friend of mine always insisted he did not care what was in the agreement, all he cared about was what the royalty department thought was in the agreement. Unfortunately, there is often a discrepancy between what is actually in the agreement and what the accounting department *thinks* is in the agreement. He always hoped it would be unnecessary to use an expensive audit to prove to the accounting department they were doing it wrong. A very pragmatic observation on the cost of audits and, I might add, human nature.

Audit provisions frequently provide that the audit must be conducted only by a certified public accountant (see Examples 4 and 5). The company argues that this means that the audit will take place with maximum efficiency and minimum disruption. It also means that an audit will cost the artist more and, accordingly, be less likely to happen. If possible, the artist should liberalize the terms specifying who may conduct the audit, although it is highly unlikely that the company will allow anyone other than a CPA to conduct the audit.

Many agreements also have restrictions on the number of times an audit can take place within a given period, such as a limit of one audit per year. Some agreements expressly exclude manufacturing records from any audit (see Example 5). To be fair to the record companies, manufacturing records are notoriously inaccurate (for example, 10,000 units may be ordered and anywhere from 9,000 to 12,000, more or less, may actually be manufactured; or thousands of copies may be misplaced in warehouses, or pilfered out the back door, or be mislabeled, etc.). This, of course, reveals a problem: Without knowing how many records were manufactured in the first place, it is impossible to do a proper audit of royalty calculations. Suppose, for example, the company claims that only a specified number of CDs has been manufactured—say Z—but then it turns out that X (the number of copies sold) plus Y (the number of copies returned) equals more than Z. Despite this possibility (and perhaps *because* of it), many record companies adamantly refuse to make this information available. The following true story shows the importance of manufacturing data.

A producer who had an album released by a major record company was told that 100,000 albums had been manufactured, no more, no less. He was paid for some 47,000 albums which the royalty statements indicated had been sold. The royalty statements also indicated, however, that some 150,000 albums had been returned. (Kinda brings to mind seven-league boots, purses of gold which are never empty, and the Emperor's new clothes.)

Also remember that the mere fact that you have audited a company and come up with a figure does not mean the record company is going to roll over, play dead, and accept your conclusions. The actual settlement figure is usually a compromise between the two parties.

Finally, some, but not many, companies will agree to pay the cost of an audit if there turns out to be an underpayment of royalties by a substantial amount, usually a minimum 10% variance.

EXAMPLE 1: Biannual Royalty Accounting Periods; 90-Day Time Limit on Objection

(i) Company will compute royalties payable hereunder within sixty (60) days after June 30 and after December 31 of each year for the preceding six (6) month period and will render accountings for and pay such royalties less any unrecouped advances against royalties due me, within said sixty (60) days. Royalties for records sold hereunder will not be due and payable until payment therefor is received by Company.

• • •

15. With regard to the payment of royalties:

• • •

(b) I shall be deemed to have consented to all royalty statements and all other accounts rendered by Company to me and the same shall be binding upon me and not subject to any objection by me for any reasons whatsoever unless specific objection in writing stating the basis thereof is given to Company within ninety (90) days after the date rendered; and if Company gives me notice in writing that it denies the validity of the objection unless suit is instituted within ninety (90) days after Company gave me such notice.

☞ In the case of an objection by the artist and presuming a quick denial by the company of the artist's objection, it is possible that the deadline might come and go before the artist even receives the next accounting. Ninety days to object (if the artist waits to the last possible moment) plus 90 days to bring a lawsuit is still a few days short of 6 months. The only safeguard under these circumstances is for the artist to object and file a lawsuit for each accounting. This is not a satisfactory solution.

EXAMPLE 2: Quarterly Accounting Periods

7. (a) Statements as to royalties payable hereunder shall be sent by us to you on or about the forty-fifth (45th) day after March 31, June 30, September 30, and December 31, of each year during which records made from the Masters are sold, for the preceding three (3) month period, together with payment of accrued royalties, if any, earned by you hereunder during said preceding three (3) month period, less all advances and charges hereunder or under any other agreement between you and us or our affiliates. We shall have the right to retain, as a reserve against subsequent charges, credits, or returns, such portion of payable royalties as shall be reasonable in our best business judgment.

(b) No royalties shall be payable to you in respect to sales of records by any of our licensees until payment thereof has been received by us. All such sales by any such licensee shall be deemed to have occurred in the same accounting period during which our licensees shall have rendered to us accounting statements therefor.

☞ Notice how in the midst of dealing with what appear to be mundane accounting procedures, our old friends cross-collateralization and a "reasonable" reserve make an appearance.

EXAMPLE 3: 2 Years Plus 2 Years

12. Company will compute royalties payable to me hereunder within Forty-Five (45) days after June 30 and after December 31 of each year for the preceding six (6) month period and will render

accountings for and pay such royalties less any unrecouped advances against royalties due me, within said Forty-Five (45) days. Royalties for records sold hereunder will not be due and payable until payment therefor is received by Company. I shall be deemed to have consented to all royalty statements and all other accounts rendered by Company to me and the same shall be binding upon me and not subject to any objection by me for any reasons whatsoever unless specific objection in writing stating the basis thereof is given to Company within Two (2) years after the date rendered; and if Company gives me notice in writing that Company denies the validity of the objection unless suit is instituted within Two (2) years after Company gave me such notice.

> ☞ Under most circumstances, 2 years to object plus 2 years to bring a lawsuit is about as good as most artists may hope for.

EXAMPLE 4: Audit

19. At any time within two (2) years after any royalty statement is due hereunder, Artist shall have the right to audit Company's books and records with respect to the statements relating to the royalties payable hereunder. Such audit

(a) shall only be conducted after at least thirty (30) days written notice to Company,

(b) shall be commenced at a mutually convenient time, and

(c) shall be conducted at Artist's sole cost and expense by an independent certified public accountant designated by Artist.

Such examination shall be made during Company's usual business hours at the place (located within the continental United States) where Company maintains the books and records that relate to the royalties payable hereunder and that are necessary to verify the accuracy of the royalty statements specified in Artist's notice to Company, and Artist's examination shall be limited to the foregoing. Artist's sole right to inspect Company's books and records shall be as set forth in this paragraph 19. Company shall have no obligation to make available any such books and records more than once with respect to each royalty statement hereunder, or more than once during any calendar year.

EXAMPLE 5: Manufacturing Records Excluded

(e) We shall maintain books of account concerning the sale of phonograph records hereunder. You or a certified public account in your behalf may, at your sole expense, examine our said books relating to the sale of records hereunder (but excluding any of our books or records relating to the manufacture of records hereunder) solely for the purpose of verifying the accuracy thereof, only during our normal business hours and upon reasonable written notice. Our such books relating to any particular royalty statement may be examined as aforesaid only within six (6) months after the date due and we shall have no obligation to permit you to so examine our such books relating to any particular royalty statement more than once. The rights herein above granted to you shall constitute your sole and exclusive rights to examine our books and records.

COUPLING

Record companies usually acquire the right to *couple* an artist's recordings with recordings by other artists. More and more, the term *compilation* is being used to describe such releases. (I must say that "coupling" has always sounded friendlier to me than "compiling.") A greatest-hits album which contains hit singles by 10 different artists is a coupled album, or a compilation. Although many provisions dealing with coupling also deal with joint recordings, do not confuse the two terms (see Example 1). *Joint recordings*, which are discussed in the next section, are when two or more artists record a master or masters together.

When a master is coupled with other masters and released as a part of a package, the artist usually continues to receive a royalty, but the royalty is based upon the artist's proportionate contribution to the album.

Example

A's hit single is coupled with nine other hit singles, all by different artists, on a greatest-hits album. A's royalty is 10% of wholesale. On the greatest-hits album he receives a full 10% royalty on one-tenth of the album, or he receives one-tenth of his royalty (1%) on the full album (it's the same thing).

In the above example, A's share is based upon the number of cuts—1 of 10 cuts equals a one-tenth royalty. Determining an artist's proportionate share on the basis of number of cuts is the most common approach, but it is also possible to calculate the artist's royalty on the basis of playing time. For example, suppose there are 10 cuts, but 1 cut by A is half of the playing time of the album; now suppose A has a provision that computes A's share of royalties on the basis of playing time, not the number of cuts. In that case, A's pro-rata royalty reduction would be reduced by only half (50%). If the other nine artists are paid on the number of cuts, regardless of playing time, each of their shares would be one-tenth ($\frac{1}{10}$ or 10%) of their regular royalty. Presuming all 10 artists have the same royalty rate, say 10%, A gets a 5% royalty rate on the whole album (10% x 0.5 = 5%) and each of the other artists receives a 1% royalty rate on the whole album (10% x 0.1 = 1%). You will note this adds up to a 14% royalty paid on the whole album by the record company.

Another modification an artist may wish to use is to provide that the royalty on coupled records is shared proportionately only between artists who receive a royalty (see Example 4). Yes, children, there are royalty-free artists. Not only is there a possibility of a flat buy-out, but what about a fictitious "artist" created by the record company and made up of studio musicians and/or vocalists who receive no royalty? It was once very common for labels to have "groups" which covered current hits with instrumental versions. These fictitious groups usually had names consisting of a number attached to the word "strings," such as, for example, "100 Strings," "1000 Strings," and, probably, continuing upward with some twisted arithmetical formula.

The first thing for an artist to consider when dealing with coupling clauses is whether such a clause should be in the contract at all, and then, if it must remain in the contract, how it should be worded. If the artist is successful in blocking coupling in the agreement, the best that normally can be expected is a restriction modified by language stating that there may be no coupling "without the prior consent" of the artist. It is very unlikely that a record company would ever agree to a flat statement that there shall be no coupling, even if the parties can always agree to the contrary. The consent language remains the camel's nose poking around the tent flaps.

There are valid reasons for not wanting an artist's hit coupled with other recordings. First of all, if an artist has a hit (especially if the artist is a "one-hit wonder"), coupling the hit with others may cut into that artist's full-royalty sales. Why buy an artist's album just to have a copy of a hit on it when you can pay the same price and get an album with hits by other artists also?

It is important that an artist's recordings do not end up being, in effect, a loss leader for other product. The other artists on a compilation may be at a lower royalty, or no royalty at all, and the successful artist's recording may be the sole selling point for the entire album, but the artist only receives a small share of the royalties for the album.

Attempts during contract negotiations to require that the artist's consent be obtained prior to any coupling are usually settled by a compromise. For example, the compromise may allow the record company to couple only on greatest-hits or best-of albums; there may be a provision that there will be no coupling during the term of the agreement; or that no more than two recordings may be coupled in any 1 year; or any other variation which can be agreed upon.

Clauses granting coupling rights are sometimes "hidden" in other provisions, such as royalty computation or grant of rights provisions. See Example 2, which gives the company the right to "otherwise use or dispose of such records, whether . . . in whole *or in part*" [emphasis added]. Or, coupling rights are granted when the artist grants the record company the right "to sell the records in albums, which albums may contain pictures, prose and verse and records embodying performances by other artists." Such language is not uncommon, and these phrases are the tip-off that the company has the right to couple the recordings.

Coupling is not, per se, necessarily a bad thing for an artist, especially a new artist. Being included in a "sampler" album may introduce an artist to an audience which otherwise may not be aware of the artist's existence. Care, however, should be taken in examining provisions dealing with samplers. These recordings are frequently sold at prices which may trigger a no-royalty situation (see Example 1 under "Freebies," pages 75–77). Artists should make sure that all samplers are not automatically dumped into the no-royalty category just because of their description; some sell at full price.

SAMPLE CONTRACT PROVISIONS

EXAMPLE 1: Proportionate Royalty/Prior Consent

(i) In the event the Masters or any of them are coupled on a record with other recordings, the royalty hereunder shall be based upon that portion of the price which the number of Masters which are embodied on such record bears to the aggregate number of all recordings embodied upon on such record; provided that Masters shall not be coupled with other artist's recordings for release in the United States during the term hereof without your prior approval (not to be unreasonably withheld), except for "Best Of" albums, K-Tel packages and sampler packages; and

(ii) the royalty rate payable to you hereunder and the recording costs hereunder with respect to any Master recorded hereunder by you jointly with any other artist or musician to whom we are obligated to pay a royalty in respect of such Master shall be computed by multiplying the otherwise applicable royalty rate and recording costs by a fraction, the numerator of which shall be one (1) and the denominator of which shall be the sum of one (1) and the total number of such other artists or musicians whose performances are embodied thereon.

☛ This is a classic coupling provision: a proportionate royalty based upon the number of cuts and a restriction on coupling which has no teeth.

EXAMPLE 2: Tip-Offs to Coupling Rights

4. I grant to Company:

(a) The results and proceeds of all endeavors under this Agreement, including the exclusive ownership of all masters, positives or negatives thereof and records manufactured therefrom and the exclusive and perpetual right to control and use the same and the performances embodied therein; the exclusive and perpetual right to manufacture, advertise, sell, lease, license or otherwise use or dispose of such records, whether based in whole or in part upon such results and proceeds or to refrain from so doing, in all fields of use throughout the world, upon such terms as Company may approve; the perpetual right to perform publicly such records and the exclusive and perpetual right to permit public performances thereof in any medium and by any means whatsoever.

• • •

(c) The perpetual right to release records recorded hereunder under any trade name or mark, which records may include performances of other artists, and to sell the records in albums, which albums may contain pictures, prose and verse and records embodying performances by other artists.

☛ These grant-of-rights provisions contain three different tip-off phrases which trigger coupling rights without ever using the word. In subparagraph (a) we have "in whole or in part." In subparagraph (c) we have "may include performances of other artists" and "may contain pictures, prose and verse and records embodying performances by other artists."

EXAMPLE 3: Coupling Rights "In Perpetuity, Throughout the Universe"

12. Company's Rights. Artist hereby grants to Company in perpetuity, throughout the universe, the following rights:

• • •

(c) The perpetual right to couple Masters recorded hereunder on records which contain master recordings embodying performances of other artists, and the perpetual right to include records hereunder in packages with records not recorded hereunder.

☛ That's a *long* time and a pretty *big* territory. One can't be too careful.

EXAMPLE 4: Royalty Rate Based on Cuts *and* Time

(b) The royalty rate on a Phonograph Record embodying Master Recordings made hereunder together with other Master Recordings will be computed by multiplying the royalty rate otherwise applicable by a fraction, the numerator of which is the number of Selections embodying Master Recordings made hereunder and contained on the particular record concerned and the denominator of which is the total number of royalty-bearing Selections contained on such record. The royalty rate on an Audiovisual Record containing an Audiovisual Recording made hereunder and other audiovisual works will be determined by apportionment based upon actual playing time on the Record concerned.

☛ This is a good one! It's the only provision I know that combines both the number of cuts and the running time into back-to-back sentences for determining the royalty, albeit for different configurations. Please check out the "multiply the royalty by a fraction" language. This, or similar language, is very commonly used in proportionate royalty provisions.

EXAMPLE 5: Limit on Number of Coupled Albums

8.03. During the term of this agreement in respect of Records, other than Audiovisual Records, manufactured for sale in the United States, Company will not, without your consent couple during any 1 year period more than two (2) Master Recordings made or furnished under this agreement with Recordings not embodying your Performances, except on promotional Records, Records described in the last sentence of paragraph 10.03 [free samplers attached to audio equipment] and Records created by Company's special products operations for sale to educational institutions.

JOINT RECORDING

Joint recordings should not be confused with coupling (compilations), although the principles and royalty computation are virtually identical (see Examples 1 and 2). *Joint recordings* are masters on which two or more artists have performed together, for example, a single-track release of a duet by two solo artists. Except under special circumstances, a joint recording does not apply toward an artist's minimum recording commitment.

The artists performing on a joint recording may not even be under contract to the same record companies. Over the years, more and more record companies have come to accept the view that allowing their artists to record with other artists can be good for business. The arrangements among different record companies when their artists record together can give rise to various combinations when it comes time to release the product. For example, a recording made jointly by two artists under contract to two separate companies may be released by both companies as one cut on an album by "their" artist, or by one of the companies as one cut on an album and by the other company as a single. In some cases, only one of the companies may actually release the recording. Obviously, joint recordings made by artists under contract to separate companies require a great deal of intercompany coordination.

When two or more artists record together there will be an apportioning of royalties among them. Each retains his or her own royalty rate and royalty calculation on an agreed-upon portion of the recording (e.g., 50%–50%; 33.3%–33.3%–33.3%; 60%–40%). Each artist's royalty rate is multiplied by the artist's proportionate share of the recording.

Example

Artist A and Artist B record a duet together. Their record company splits the recording equally (50%–50%) for royalty purposes. Artist A has a base royalty of 10%. Artist B has a base royalty of 8%. Their net royalty computations, by contract, are identical. On this recording, Artist A receives a royalty of 5% and Artist B, a royalty of 4%.

Example

The facts are as in the first example, except that Artist A's royalty is computed upon 100% of sales and Artist B's is computed on 90% of sales. On this recording, Artist A receives a royalty of 5% and Artist B, a royalty of 3.6% (8% x 0.50 = 4% x 0.90 = 3.6%).

Another issue to consider with joint recordings involves the credit to be received by the artists. Who gets top billing? Is the billing "A and B," "B and A," "A with B," or "B with A."

When separate companies are involved, the royalty due each artist will be paid through that artist's record company. After all, the artist is the exclusive "property" of the record company and, technically, is being loaned to the other company. Funneling the royalties through the record company allows the company to use these royalties for recoupment purposes.

The recording costs incurred in joint recordings are also charged back to the artists in proportion to the artist's share of the recording. (See Example 3.)

In each of the following three examples the artist's consent is a legal requirement, in contrast to coupling provisions which, at best, give lip service to the artist's consent. The difference? In coupling the product has already been recorded. Joint recordings require the cooperation of the artist.

SAMPLE CONTRACT PROVISIONS

EXAMPLE 1: Joint Recording Formula

(ii) The royalty payable to you hereunder and the recording costs hereunder with respect to any Master recorded hereunder by you jointly with any other artist or musician to or in respect of whom we shall be obligated to pay a royalty in respect of such Master shall be computed by multiplying the otherwise applicable royalty rate and recording costs by a fraction, the numerator of which shall be one (1) and the denominator of which shall be the sum of one (1) and the total number of such other royalty artists or musicians whose performances are embodied thereon.

> ☞ This is the exact same formula used to royalty-share for couplings, except that rather than being between different artists on different cuts, it's for different artists on the same cut or cuts.

EXAMPLE 2: Joint Recording Definition and Royalty Formula

(a) In respect to Joint Recordings, the royalty rate to be used in determining the royalties payable to you shall be computed by multiplying the royalty rate otherwise applicable by a fraction, the numerator of which shall be one (1) and the denominator of which shall be the total number of royalty artists whose performances are embodied on a Joint Recording. The term "Joint Recording" shall mean any Master Recording embodying your performances and any performances by another artist with respect to which Company is obligated to pay royalties. Company shall not require you to perform for Joint Recordings without your consent, it being understood that your actual performance for a Joint Recording shall be deemed your granting of such consent.

EXAMPLE 3: Joint Recordings and Recording Costs

(i) If, with your consent, any side is recorded hereunder by you jointly with another royalty artist or musician to whom we are obligated to pay a royalty in respect of such side, the royalties payable to you applicable to records produced therefrom shall be reduced proportionately, and only the proportionate share of applicable [recording] costs set forth in paragraph 2, above, shall be charged against your royalties.

UNRECORDED MASTERS

> *Expecting the world to treat you fairly because you are a*
> *good person is like expecting a bull not to attack you*
> *because you are a vegetarian.*
>
>   —DENNIS WHOLEY

When faced with the heartbreak of *unrecorded masters*, what's an artist to do? And just what heartbreak is that, you might ask. The heartbreak of unrecorded masters usually comes in two forms:

1. The artist has not recorded the required number of masters and the company wants the artist to record them.

2. The artist has not recorded the minimum number of masters and the company just doesn't give a damn but the artist wants to either record or receive payment for the unrecorded masters.

The *artist's* failure to meet the minimum recording commitment will usually cause the term of the agreement to be extended, through suspension, automatic extension, or the operation of what we have called open-ended agreements. During the term of the agreement, the company may have the right to reduce the minimum commitment to the number of masters already recorded or, at least, down to one master and pay union scale on that one master, and then either allow the option to expire or exercise the option and move on to the next period (see Example 5). However, sooner or later, at least in California, the agreement will expire—suspension or extension notwithstanding—and if there are unrecorded masters due and the company still wants the unrecorded masters, what then?

Dealing with the question of what is to be done when a contract ends with product still to be delivered has always been a problem area for both artist and record company. If the company wants the recordings, but the artist can't or won't deliver, what can be done? The courts will not make the artist perform (see the section "Equitable Relief," below). Generally, the company must either walk away or sue the artist for damages.

In September of 1987, an amendment to Section 2855 of the California Labor Code (for the language used in Section 2855, see page 28) was enacted which adds some new twists to the law. The amendment deals only with recording agreements. (Our industry has, once more, been singled out for special attention. It makes a guy kinda proud!) Paragraph (1) of subdivision (a) provides that, notwithstanding the provisions of 2855:

> Any employee who is party to a contract to render personal service *in the production of phonorecords in which sounds are first fixed* [emphasis added] . . . may not provoke the provisions of [2855] without first giving written notice to the employer . . . specifying that the employee from and after a future date certain specified in the notice will no longer render service under the contract. . . .

Paragraph (2) further provides that:

> . . . any party to such a contract shall have the right to recover damages for a breach of the contract occurring during its term in an action commenced during or after its term, but within the applicable period prescribed by law.

This hardly breaks new ground, but let us see what happens when we consider paragraphs (1) and (2) together with paragraph (3), which states:

> [If] a party to such a contract is, or could contractually be, required to render personal service in the production of a specified quantity of the phonorecords and fails to render all of the required service prior to the date specified in the notice [provided for in (1)] . . . the party damaged by the failure shall have the right to recover damages for each phonorecord as to which that party has failed to render service in an action which, notwithstanding paragraph (2), shall be commenced within 45 days after the date specified in the notice.

What this all means is that the artist must now give the company notice that he or she intends to evoke the provisions of Section 2855 (limiting the term of the agreement to 7 years), and the company then has 45 days in which to bring an action for the nondelivery of the unrecorded masters. The company now has a shortened period to enforce its rights, but, in exchange, does have a specific and express legal right to pursue damages. By "shortened period to enforce its rights," I mean shortened compared to the normal period allowed a party to bring a lawsuit in a dispute over a written contract. For example, under normal conditions in California, unless expressly waived by the parties or a legal exception, like this amendment, a party has 4 years to bring a lawsuit for an alleged breach of a written contract. This is the trade-off that was worked out to placate both sides on this issue.

Before the 1987 amendment, the 7-year restriction was a chink in the armor of record companies trying to hold onto a recalcitrant artist. Post-1987 attempts by (successful) artists to be released from their contracts crashed against the stone wall of the amendment. The threat of the record companies' counterclaim for damages for undelivered albums invariably resulted in a negotiated settlement—usually a renegotiated agreement accompanied by a handsome advance. Artists such as the Dixie Chicks went up this hill like Jack and Jill and came back down with lucrative new contracts.

In February 2003, the group Incubus filed a lawsuit against Sony Music based upon the 7-year rule, notwithstanding the fact that the group owed Sony four additional albums. Incubus also claimed that "Sony Music has been handsomely rewarded financially . . . while the members of Incubus have received very little compensation . . . " This opened up the specter that record industry accounting methods would be put under the microscope. It had been estimated that Sony had netted more than $35 million from the group's efforts while Incubus had received only $4 million in advances and had yet to receive any royalties.

Predictably, by April of 2003 an accommodation had been reached between the group and Sony. The accommodation reportedly paid Incubus an estimated $8 million advance for the next album, with two additional albums due (plus an option for a fourth album), with each album, including the option album, coming with a $2.5 million advance.

Let's see, if my math is correct, counting the original $4 million advance and adding in all new albums, including the option album, that's $22 million in advances—what do you think the chances are that Incubus will *ever* receive royalties from Sony?

Notwithstanding an artist's belief that being signed to a recording contract will result in recordings being made, most recording contracts either expressly (see Examples 3 and 4) or impliedly (see Examples 1 and 2) provide that the company need not actually record anything. Cases in which the *company* has not allowed the artist to record the minimum, and the artist wants to either record or be compensated, are a different matter. Even though the amendment to Section 2855 gives the artist the right to sue the record company for failing to record the product [for example, the amendment in paragraph (3) refers to "the *party* damaged," which could be the artist], recording agreements usually contain provisions that specify the company's obligations to the artist if the company does not record the minimum number of masters it has committed to record. Generally, these "unrecorded masters" provisions have the legal effect of providing the company with some kind of out, even when the company has agreed in writing to record a specified number of masters. For example, a provision may stipulate that all a record company has to do when it fails to record the contractually specified number of masters is to pay the artist the applicable scale for the unrecorded masters (see Example 1). Now the scale that is applicable to unrecorded masters is usually a very small amount compared to the payments made to an artist for recording an actual album. And when you figure in the potential loss of royalties; loss of earnings as a songwriter for original material recorded; probable higher fees for live performances for having product released; and any number of other loss-of-income possibilities, the "applicable scale" buyout seems hardly adequate.

Some companies take the above concept one step farther, requiring the artist to put the company on written notice within a specified time after the presumed failure, during one of the periods, to record the masters. Under this type of provision, the artist's failure to give the timely notice means that the artist waives the right to record the masters and the right to be paid union scale for the masters which would have been recorded, and, under California law, has no right to sue under the amendment to Section 2855 (having been waived, there are no undelivered masters and, accordingly, no damages to the artist). (See Example 2.)

If the artist or production company has a recording fund, it is wise to attempt to obtain a provision that the agreed-upon fund, or some portion of the fund (see Example 3), should be payable whether or not the album is recorded as long as the failure to record is not the fault of the artist or production company. (For more information on how recording funds are determined, see pages 108–115.) Under these circumstances, most record companies will insist that the payment be a sum equal to the amount or average amount retained from one or more of the preceding recording funds after accounting for recording and producer costs.

SAMPLE CONTRACT PROVISIONS

EXAMPLE 1: Union Scale Payment for Unrecorded Sides

24. Unrecorded Sides: If Company does not record the agreed upon minimum number of sides, Company's liability shall be limited to the agreed union scale payment to Artist for all unrecorded sides, and providing that Company has paid the union scale payment for all unrecorded sides, this Agreement shall remain in force and effect and Artist shall not have the right to terminate same on account of the failure of Company to record the agreed minimum number of sides. Sides recorded hereunder in connection with other Artist(s) under contract to Company shall be counted towards the minimum number of sides to be recorded hereunder, but only if Company so elects.

EXAMPLE 2: Artist to Notify Company

15.(a) If in respect of any period of the term of this agreement we fail, except for causes provided for in paragraph 14 hereof [force majeure], to record master recordings constituting the minimum recording obligation provided for herein, and if, within thirty days after the expiration of such period of the term hereof, you shall notify us by registered mail of your request that we record such of your performances as will fulfill our minimum obligation hereunder, then we shall, at our option within sixty days after our receipt of such request, either record such performances or pay you at the rate of union scale in full settlement of our obligation in connection therewith. In the event that you do not so notify us within such thirty day period, then we shall be under no obligation to you for failure to record master recordings constituting such minimum recording obligation.

EXAMPLE 3: Monetary Payment for Unrecorded Masters

(b) Nothing herein contained shall obligate us to permit you to record the minimum number of

Masters specified herein to be recorded during the initial term or any renewal term hereof, it being understood that our sole obligation to you as to each such unrecorded Master shall be to pay you an amount equal to the minimum union scale payment which we would have been required to pay you had you in fact recorded such unrecorded Master. In the event we shall fail to request you to record the minimum number of LPs required during any renewal term hereof, we shall also pay you the amount of the recording budget approved for such unrecorded LP in paragraph 20(a) hereof minus the amount of the recording costs and producer's advances incurred in connection with the preceding LP actually recorded hereunder.

☛ During the initial period, minimum union scale is paid; thereafter it is a sum equal to the approved album budget less the prior album's recording costs and producer advances.

EXAMPLE 4: One-Half of Recording Fund

9. *Master recordings.*

(a) Company shall have the right during any Period subsequent to the Initial period, by written notice to you, to elect not to record any or all of the master recordings constituting the minimum recording obligation for such Period, and, in the event Company makes such election, Company shall simultaneously with such notice pay you an amount (inclusive of any and all applicable union scale payments) equal to: (i) one-half (½) of the amount of the [recording fund] advance . . . applicable to the LP constituting such minimum recording obligation . . . which such payment shall be deemed to be in full satisfaction of any and all of Company's obligations hereunder in connection with such minimum recording obligation, and the Term shall be deemed to automatically terminate as of the date of such notice and payment.

☛ This provision is unusually generous to the artist, it provides for an automatic payment of one-half of the recording fund and a free ticket to move on. Compare this to Example 3.

EXAMPLE 5: Notice Required; Reduce Number of Masters

(a) If during any period of this Agreement Company fails, except for causes provided for in Subparagraph 6(c) below, to record the minimum number of masters specified, above, and if, within thirty (30) days after the expiration of such period of the term hereof, I shall notify Company by registered mail of my request that Company record such of my performances as will fulfill Company's minimum requirement hereunder, then Company shall, at Company's option within sixty (60) days after Company's receipt of such request, either record such performances or pay me at the rate of union scale in full settlement of Company's obligation in connection therewith. In the event that I do not notify Company within such thirty (30) day period, then Company shall be under no obligation to me for failure to record masters constituting the minimum requirement hereunder.

(b) If, during any period of this Agreement, I fail, except for Company's refusal without cause to allow me to perform, to complete the recording of a sufficient number of satisfactory masters to fulfill my recording obligation, as set forth above, and to deliver to Company any required approval or consent in connection therewith, then, without limiting Company's rights in any such event, Company, by giving me written notice, shall have the option without liability to reduce the minimum number of masters to that number which had been recorded as of the date when such failure began, but in no event less than one (1) master.

RELEASE OF RECORDINGS

If you give me six lines written by the most honest man,
I will find something in them to hang him.

—CARDINAL RICHELIEU

Most record contracts include a clause somewhere which expressly states that the company is not obligated to sell records made from masters recorded under the agreement (see Example 1) or, perhaps, has the right to "refrain" from selling such records (see Example 2). Indeed, many of these provisions also expressly state the company has no obligation to even record the artist (see Example 1).

As we have seen, minimum-commitment provisions regarding the recording of masters are often of little use to the artist trying to get a record company to adhere to these provisions. If this is frustrating for the artist, what about an artist who has a contractual commitment from the record company for the release of the artist's recordings, but the record company will not release the agreed-upon number of records? While not common, it is possible for an artist to negotiate for, and obtain, a release commitment from the record company. My somewhat jaded response to this issue is, So what? As a practical matter, unless the release commitment has teeth, it may be meaningless.

Before discussing the teeth (or lack thereof) in release-commitment provisions, there are some basic questions which need to be addressed. First of all, what is a release? What seems like a rather silly and simple question is, in fact, rather complicated. Is a release shipping records to radio stations, shipping 100 commercial copies into the field, making the record available to anyone who wishes to order it, etc., etc.? It would seem that defining "release" might be helpful, but coming up with a definition acceptable to both parties is practically impossible. Attempts to do so usually run aground for the same reason: There seems to be no way to tie down a definition of "commercially satisfactory." See, for example, Example 4, which defines a "commercial release" as a release by one of the "six" majors or national distribution through either self-distribution or through independent distribution. Nice try, but this still allows the record company to just spread a few records around the country. Arguably, perhaps as few as four individual records, one for each region (most record companies divide up the country into four regions). I wouldn't want to defend this position in court, but the argument can be made. Also, nothing is said about supporting a release with promotion or advertising. Without support, a release is meaningless.

Secondly, there is the question of the number of records, presumably albums, to be released that the artist may be able to get the record company to agree to in the record contract. Record companies are hesitant to make this commitment in the first place; they are even more likely to resist a multiple-release commitment. Even with a cooperative record company, the number of guaranteed releases will be restricted. For a number of reasons, it may not be desirable for an artist to put too great a release burden on the record company. There is such a thing as "too many" releases. For example, it sometimes takes many weeks or months for a record to catch on. If the record company must release a new recording because of a commitment to the artist, previously released product may lose the opportunity to establish itself in the market. Not only might the release of too many records cause a glut in the market, it might also project a picture of desperation. Timing of releases also becomes an issue. There may be special sales programs scheduled, or seasonal considerations (e.g., Christmas sales to stores take place months in advance), or any other number of time-specific issues which could not have been anticipated and which would make a carved-in-stone release schedule a bad idea.

Sometimes contracts have what might be called a "conditional guaranteed release," that is, a commitment to release which becomes effective when a specified event takes place, such as certain sales figures being met, a chart position being reached, a tour being set, etc. (See Example 3.)

Example

The contract between Artist and Record Company provides that if any single sells 250,000 copies, Record Company will release an album. Artist records a single, Record Company releases it, and the single sells 500,000 copies. Record Company is obligated to release an album by Artist. Note that if Record Company had not by that time allowed Artist to record an album, it would now be obligated, contractually, to do so.

Once the terms of the commitment to release have been worked out, what about the penalty if (and when) the record company does not meet those terms? A meaningful penalty is the necessary "teeth" referred to above. Without one, any "commitment" is virtually worthless.

Often, the penalty for nonrelease is that the company may not be able to pick up the next option. If you are asking how effective a club over the company's head *that* is, you are right to wonder. If the company is not interested enough to release, would it be likely to exercise its option anyway? Example 5 below has language allowing the artist to notify the company of his or her intention to terminate the agreement if the company fails to meet the release commitment. There are other possibilities, of course. The agreement may stipulate that a company failing to meet release commitments must make payments to the artist. The problem with monetary penalties is not only that it is very hard to determine what they should be, it is also almost impossible to get a record company to agree to any penalty involving money. It is also probable that if the record company agreed to make a payment, the payment would be used as a credit against unrecouped advances. Sometimes (but this is very rare, so don't count on it) an agreement can be reached which will allow the artist to purchase or reacquire masters which have not been released by the record company.

Note that there is another area where a guaranteed release may be an issue. This is a release commitment not to an artist or a production company, but to a third party. For example, the record company may have entered into an agreement with a film company to release a soundtrack album with a guarantee that the album be released concurrently with the release of the film.

SAMPLE CONTRACT PROVISIONS

EXAMPLE 1: No Obligation to Record or Release

6. Nothing contained in this Agreement shall obligate Company to make or sell records manufactured from masters or to have me in fact record the minimum number of masters specified; provided, however, that in the event more than the minimum number of masters are recorded during any period of this Agreement, Company shall have the right to apply the excess masters against the minimum recording requirement for any subsequent period.

EXAMPLE 2: Right to "Refrain" from Sale

7.02. Without limiting the generality of the foregoing, Company and any Person authorized by Company shall have the unlimited right to manufacture Phonograph Records by any method now or hereafter known, derived from the Master Recordings made hereunder, and to sell, transfer or otherwise deal in the same under any trademarks, trade names and labels, or to refrain from such manufacture, sale and dealing throughout the world.

☛ It somehow feels like bad manners to rub the artist's nose in it that not only does the company have the right not to release recordings, but that the right not to release is "throughout the world."

EXAMPLE 3: Contingent Release

4. . . . Notwithstanding anything to the contrary contained in this Paragraph 4, we agree that (1) during the term of this agreement, the initial release in the United States and not elsewhere of phonograph records made hereunder shall be on the x label, and (2) if any album recorded hereunder reaches the top 100 LP list in BILLBOARD in the United States, such album shall be released in the United Kingdom.

EXAMPLE 4: "Commercial Release" Defined

(h) If at least one album made hereunder is not commercially released during, or scheduled (during the then current period) for commercial release and commercially released within three (3) months after, the Initial Period herein, if Company exercises the option for the 1st Option Period or 2nd Option Period, I may negate such option exercise by giving Company written notice of such negation within thirty (30) days of the commencement of the 1st Option Period or 2nd Option Period. As used herein, "commercial release: or "commercially released" shall mean any release through one of the six "majors" distribution systems or, if distribution is done directly by Company or through so-called "independents," distribution on a national basis.

EXAMPLE 5: Artist's Option to Terminate

(d) Provided Artist is not in breach of this Agreement or in default of its obligations hereunder and if Company is in receipt of completed Masters, satisfactory to Company, sufficient to comprise Artist's applicable Album Commitment, together with all Delivery materials therefor, Company agrees to commercially release each Album (or at least an EP version thereof for the First Album only) required to be Delivered hereunder in the United States within one hundred and twenty (120) days following Artist's Delivery to and Company's acceptance of the applicable Album. If Company shall have failed to commercially release an Album in the United States, Artist shall have the right, within sixty (60) days following the expiration of said one hundred and twenty (120) day period to notify Company in writing of Company's such failure and Artist's desire that the Term of this Agreement be terminated if Company does not within thirty (30) days after Company's receipt of such notice from Artist, commercially release the Album in the United States. If Company shall fail to fulfill any such release commitment, Company shall have no liability whatsoever to Artist, and Artist's only remedy shall be to terminate the Term of this Agreement.

☛ Big deal. The company is not interested in releasing the product so the artist gets to walk away. Wouldn't it be more fun to stick around and annoy them?

EQUITABLE RELIEF

You got to be careful if you don't know where you're going, because you might not get there.
—YOGI BERRA

Like the previously discussed 7-year issue (see "Term of the Agreement," pages 28–34), there is another area of law which is unique to California, but which also can affect the entire music industry for the same reason—an artist can always move to California and have California law apply. It deals with equitable relief, or, at least, the record company's desire to obtain equitable relief against an artist who is attempting to jump ship and record for another company. The term *equitable relief* means different things in different contexts, but for our purposes, it involves having a court make someone either do something or stop doing something when damages in the form of money would not be adequate compensation for the injured party.

Without going into the history of the law of equity (which invariably boils down to stories about men in baggy clothes passing acorns back and forth to transfer farms), equity is that part of the law which strives to do what is just, fair, and right when slapping a price tag on damages suffered just will not suffice to "right the wrong." The history of equity disputes in the entertainment world is actually quite interesting. As a result of a legal precedent set around 150 years ago [*Lumley v. Wagner*, 42 Eng. Rep. 687 (1854)], equity will not force a party to perform under a personal service contract, such as a recording agreement. Mr. Lumley, operator of Her Majesty's Theatre in London, had hired Johanna Wagner to perform twice a week for 3 months. She was to be paid 100 pounds per week for her services (at this time in London a union bricklayer received less than 2 pounds a week—we are talking good money for our diva). Madame Wagner was not only a very famous opera singer and the niece of Richard Wagner, but she was also "cantatrice of the Court of His Majesty the King of Prussia" (whatever the hell that is).

Madame Wagner decided she would not perform for Mr. Lumley, and Lumley fled to the courts asking that she be compelled to perform under the contract. The court ruled that while she could not be forced to sing for Mr. Lumley, she could be enjoined [stopped] from singing for anyone else, the presumption being that she would, having no alternative venues, sing for Mr. Lumley. (Please note that Madame Wagner actually never did sing for Lumley, giving rise to the possibility that since the fat woman never sang, this case may not yet be over.)

As was held in the Lumley case, it is now a generally accepted principal of law that a party cannot be forced by a court of law to perform a personal service contract. *Stopping* someone, however, from performing those services for another is an entirely different matter. Under the proper circumstances, a court will enjoin, or stop, a party from performing some act.

Back in 1919, however, the State of California placed two restrictions on the right to enjoin someone in connection with a breach of a personal service contract. It had to be shown that, first, "the promised service is of a special, unique, unusual, extraordinary or intellectual character, which gives it peculiar value the loss of which can not be reasonably or adequately compensated in damages" (see Examples 2, 3, and 4, below) and that, second, "the minimum compensation for such service is at a rate of not less than six thousand dollars per annum." (See California Civil Code, Section 3423, and California Code of Civil Procedure, Section 526. The language in both sections is virtually identical. Strangely enough, these provisions were originally written into the law to protect rich men from having their jockeys hired away from their racing stables.)

These restrictions have probably created more confusion among non-California lawyers (and, perhaps, California lawyers) than any other entertainment-related law, and there have been a number of court cases which have attempted to explain just how these laws work. At least in California, under these laws a record company could not obtain an injunction against an artist trying to jump ship unless there was a minimum of $6,000 paid to the artist each year (that dollar figure is now higher, but more on that below).

The first really important case dealing with the $6,000 "guarantee" was *Foxx v. Williams*, 244 Cal.App.2d. 223 (1966). Foxx is, as you might have guessed, the late Redd Foxx. Williams was the president and sole stockholder of a record company entitled Dootone Record Manufacturing, Inc. Difficulties had broken out over a number of issues involving a series of record contracts between Dootone and Foxx. A complaint was filed by Foxx against Williams, and Dootone filed a cross-complaint against Foxx. The issues (all of which should sound familiar by now) were computation of the royalty rate; overpayments of royalties; studio costs; extension of the contract; the 7-year statute; rerecording restrictions; the royalty accounting; and, what is important in this discussion, an attempt to enjoin Foxx from performing elsewhere. At the trial level the court enjoined Foxx. However, this judgment was overturned at the appellate level. The appellate decision offers further insight and interpretation of these laws.

After quoting Section 3423 of the Civil Code, the court stated, at page 236:

> At the trial the parties stipulated to the amounts which Foxx had received as royalties each year from 1956 through 1962, but these figures were not broken down to show what portion was paid for recordings made under the 1958 contract. The royalty statement for the six months ending June 30, 1963, which was the accounting period immediately preceding the trial, showed total royalties for the period as $2,682.27, less advances and charges of $156.
>
> We do not place our decision upon the absence of proof of the amount of royalties earned under the 1958 contract. In our opinion this royalty contract does not meet the requirements of the injunctive statute even though it should ultimately appear that the royalties earned, over any given period, should exceed the rate of $6,000 per year.

An injunction forbidding an artist to accept new employment may be a harsh and powerful remedy. The monetary limitation in the statute is intended to serve as a counterweight in balancing the equities. The Legislature has concluded that an artist who is not entitled to receive a minimum of $6,000 per year by performing his contract should not be subjected to this kind of economic coercion. Under the statutory scheme, an artist who is enjoined from accepting new employment at least has the alternative of earning $6,000 or more per year by performing his old contract.

The trial court's solution to the problem was to grant the injunction for only so long as the royalties for each half-year equaled $3,000. This means that the artist is enjoined for 7½ months at a time (6 months plus the 45 days thereafter which the contract allows for the preparation of the royalty statement) without any assurance of earning anything. This is not what the statute calls for.

The portion of the judgment which enjoins Foxx must be deleted.

Now, inasmuch as I have a mortal fear of people trying to do their own agreements without adequate training, I would like to quote, as a coda to the case, some of Williams's testimony:

Q: Now, with respect to Contract 3, who made that one?
A: I did, after research and inquiry in the industry.
Q: Did you consult an attorney?
A: No.

Q: Used somebody else's form again?

A: No, I consulted a number of contracts that were in use at the time and consolidated the items I thought . . .

Q: Took what you thought would be the best from each one?

A: Yes, that is right.

No further comment other than this: Williams lost.

The Foxx opinion held that the $6,000 had to be *guaranteed* in the record contract. Actual royalty earnings in excess of $6,000 did not count because they were not guaranteed, and the injunction was not granted. Accordingly, in California, if the record company wishes to retain the right to enjoin an artist, the record contract must contain language guaranteeing the minimum rate provided for in the two laws. (See Examples 1 and 2.)

The next case of interest with regard to the "$6,000 provision" is *MCA Records v. Newton-John*, 90 Cal.App.3d 18 (1979), where a guaranteed *advance* in the amount of $6,000 or more was sufficient to meet the $6,000 minimum guarantee. Olivia Newton-John, unhappy with her contractual relationship as a recording artist with MCA, tried to sever that relationship. MCA did not take kindly to this attempt and tried to enjoin her from recording for another record company. Since the contract between MCA and Newton-John did not expressly guarantee her $6,000 minimum compensation and probably relying upon the ruling in *Foxx*, she thought, or, more likely, was told, that she could not be so enjoined. Her contract did, however, provide for a recording fund considerably in excess of $6,000, from which she could take the difference between the actual recording cost and the fund amount as an advance. (The difference had, in the past, always been in excess of $6,000.) Ms. Newton-John maintained that the recording costs ate up the entire fund, and hence the required guarantee of $6,000 did not exist. The court said, however, that the fund was within her control, and she could be as profligate or as tight-fisted as she wanted to be. Since she controlled the money and was able to spend it or keep it at her discretion, they ruled that she was, in fact, guaranteed a minimum of $6,000 and MCA was entitled to injunctive relief.

For years after the *Foxx* ruling, it was common practice for record companies to approach the guaranteed compensation question by inserting an option in the record contract which gave the record company the *option* to guarantee the $6,000 minimum compensation. In practice, of course, the option was never exercised by the record company for any reason other than invoking the right to enjoin the artist. Arguably, the option could be exercised, but the money withheld until the artist was no longer in breach of the terms of the recording agreement; regardless, the "guarantee" had been made. (One is tempted to editorialize: *Wink. Wink. Nudge. Nudge.*) This practice effectively ended in 1984 when it was tested in court.

In *Motown Record Corp. v. Brockert*, 160 Cal.App.3d 123 (1984), commonly known as the "Teena Marie Case," the court ruled that an option to pay the $6,000 was not sufficient for injunctive relief; the money had to be guaranteed. The importance of this case, however, was not so much the decision, but the court's analysis of the *intent* of California Civil Code Section 3423 in granting injunctive relief in these types of cases.

> [A]t the time section 3423 was amended [1919] there was a discernable trend toward enforcing negative covenants against the "prima donnas" but not the "spear carriers." [page 137]

In 1919 the sum of $6,000 a year was more than five times the average national wage of $1,142. . . . This is the equivalent to setting the minimum compensation figure at $100,000 today [1984]. . . . By selecting such a large sum, the Legislature indicated an intent injunctive relief not be available against a performer, however capable, who has not yet achieved distinction. The fact that the bill was further amended to provide that the services must be special is a further indication that the Legislature intended the statute to apply only to persons who had attained "star quality" no matter how special their services might be. [page 138]

The court was also quite clear that this clause was meant to provide relief from an existing star, not a prospective star. The record company could not get in at bargain prices and *after* the artist became a star, choose to exercise an option which would *then* guarantee the $6,000:

The option clause would defeat the legislative intent to limit injunctive relief to contracts where not only the services are special or unique but the performer herself is a person of distinction in her field *at the time of entering the contract* [emphasis added]. [page 136]

It must be emphasized that the provisions discussed above apply *only* to injunctive relief. Always remember that even without injunctive relief, record companies may still recover damages from the artist and, under the right circumstances, from any other record company for which the artist performs.

In 1994, just when everything regarding the "$6,000 question" seemed to have settled down and people were even getting around to understanding how it worked, the California Legislature amended the laws. Recognizing that $6,000 in the 1990s bore little resemblance to $6,000 in 1919, they not only upped the ante, they created two different methods of determining what the guaranteed compensation should be to qualify for equitable relief.

Both methods have a sliding scale, with the required minimum growing over the passage of time. The major difference between the two methods, other than the dollar amounts, is that the first method requires the monies to be guaranteed from the inception of the contract (see Example 2). The second, and more expensive, method allows the record company to elect to guarantee, and pay higher minimums *retroactively*, at a later date (see Example 4).

The dollar amounts for the first method are as follows:

Year of the Contract	Guaranteed Payment	Contingent Money from Past Year		Cumulative Total
1	$ 9,000 +	0	=	$ 9,000
2	$12,000 +	0	=	$21,000 (includes year 1 guarantee)
3	$15,000 +	0	=	$36,000 (includes monies paid in years 1–2)
4	$15,000 +	$15,000	=	$66,000 (includes monies paid in years 1–3)
5	$15,000 +	$15,000	=	$96,000 (includes monies paid in years 1–4)

Year of the Contract	Guaranteed Payment	Contingent Money from Past Year		Cumulative Total
6	$15,000 +	$30,000	=	$141,000 (includes monies paid in years 1–5)
7	$15,000 +	$30,000	=	$186,000 (includes monies paid in years 1–6)

If you think that is complicated, catch the second method—generally (and one supposes, affectionately) referred to as the "superstar insurance" method. Under the "superstar insurance" method a record company electing not to contractually guarantee minimum payments may still have the right to injunctive relief if it makes actual payments on a cumulative basis at ten times the minimum rate established for method 1. Here are the numbers:

Year of Contract	"10 Times" Minimum	Cumulative Actual Payment Prior Year's (Years')		Total Paid
1	$ 90,000 +	0	=	$ 90,000
2	$120,000 +	$90,000	=	$210,000 (includes year 1 payment)
3	$150,000 +	$210,000	=	$360,000 (includes years 1–2 payments)
4	$300,000 +	$360,000	=	$660,000 (includes years 1–3 payments)
5	$300,000 +	$660,000	=	$960,000 (includes years 1–4 payments)
6	$450,000 +	$960,000	=	$1,410,000 (includes years 1–5 payments)
7	$450,000 +	$1,410,000	=	$1,860,000 (includes years 1–6 payments)

The superstar method is, presumably, a viable option for small independent record companies that cannot afford the minimum guarantees under the first method.

Unfortunately, the possibilities for interpretation of these revised laws are almost endless, as, undoubtedly, is the potential for the mischief which will be created out of the scramble to make use of them. Do note that these provisions apply to each individual of a group, so, for example, if there are five members in a group, multiply those dollars by five—unless the record company chooses to just guarantee, prospectively or retroactively, just one or two "key" members of the group. Guaranteeing just "key" members can be tricky and dangerous—not only does it engender guaranteed envy from the unguaranteed members, the record company might guess wrong.

How many record companies are going to write into their agreement with a beginning artist, or each member of a group, these kind of per annum guarantees for the course of the contract? What happens if the "guarantees" are not paid? Is that a material breach of the agreement, or does it just mean the record company does not have a contractual right to obtain injunctive relief?

Example 5 below just about covers all the bases of the first method: (1) guaranteed annual payments matching that required by the codes, (2) a mechanism for any shortfall, (3) aggregate excess compensation applied to future years, (4) a provision for additional payments if (God forbid!) the California Legislature raises the minimum again, and, just to be careful, (5) a provision that "excess expenditures" will not be deducted from annual or additional payments—all of this care and attention even though there is an advance of $200,000 which is deemed to be a prepayment of *all* annual payments (subparagraph 12(b) of the example). The provision providing that "excess compensation" will be applied to reduce the annual payment in subsequent years is also found in the codes themselves. It is worth pointing out that in this particular instance the company was dealing with an individual artist and not a group and had, in fact, already advanced a sufficient amount to prepay the entire amount.

The second, or superstar, method is, on its face, more expensive (10 times in fact) than is the first method (see Example 4). As a practical matter, however, I submit that the superstar method is probably cheaper in the long run. First of all, the need to obtain an injunction is relatively rare to begin with, and, even under those circumstances, there are usually alternative options which may be just as or more effective (such as suing the other record company for "interfering with a business relationship"). The cost of the first method, to make the guarantees to each artist, becomes prohibitively expensive when used across the board with a record company's complete roster. It is cheaper to wait and pay 10 times as much when you know you need to and when you can make the decision as to whether or not it is worth it. Besides, any artist a record company would want to enjoin from leaving probably would either already have sufficient guarantees to qualify for an injunction or would have renegotiated the agreement for such guarantees upon achieving success.

If big record companies are finding it hard to sort out their obligations under these provisions, what about the independent producer or production company with limited funds trying to make a deal with an artist that will allow the producer or production company to deliver an artist to a record company which insists that these guarantees must be already in place? (See the section "Injunctive Relief," pages 243–245.) I foresee a thriving cottage industry growing up around the interpretation and application of these laws.

Note: As a matter of practice, when entering into an agreement with a record company where there is a provision granting the company "the right to injunctive relief" or similar language, make sure the language is modified to read as "the right to *seek* injunctive relief." After all, if the record company is after your backside, why make it easy for them? (See Examples 3 and 4.)

SAMPLE CONTRACT PROVISIONS

EXAMPLE 1: Minimum Compensation for Entire Group

(b) Company shall guarantee each member of Group during each year of the Agreement hereunder shall receive compensation at the rate of not less than the minimum amounts set forth in the California Code of Civil Procedure, Section 526 and California Civil Code, Section 3423 (Fifth) or such other applicable statute during such period.

EXAMPLE 2: Incorporate Code Provisions

15. Artist acknowledges that Artist's services hereunder are of a special, unique, unusual, extraor-

dinary and intellectual character which gives them a peculiar value, and that, in the event of a breach by Artist of any material term, condition, representation, warranty or covenant contained herein, Company will be caused irreparable injury and damage. Company shall be obligated to pay Artist compensation at the rate of not less than Nine Thousand ($9,000) Dollars in the first year of this Agreement, in subsequent years of this Agreement, in each such year Company will pay the amounts provided for in California Code of Civil Procedure, Section 526, and California Civil Code, Section 3423 (Fifth). Prior to the end of each such year of this Agreement, Company will pay Artist the difference, if any, between any amounts theretofore received by Artist and the applicable amount provided for herein.

☞ The language "special, unique, unusual, extraordinary and intellectual character" and "peculiar value" and the like in this and other examples is legal mumbo-jumbo the purpose of which is to make sure the elements of equitable relief exist.

EXAMPLE 3: Unique and Extraordinary Services

13.06. Your services are unique and extraordinary, and the loss thereof cannot be adequately compensated in damages, and Company shall be entitled to seek injunctive relief to enforce the provisions of this agreement. (The preceding sentence will not be construed to preclude you from opposing any application for such relief based upon contest of the other facts alleged by Company in support of the application.)

EXAMPLE 4: Superstar Method

21. I acknowledge that my services hereunder are of a special, unique, unusual, extraordinary and intellectual character which gives them a peculiar value, and that, in the event of a breach by me of any material term, condition, representation, warranty or covenant contained herein, you will be caused irreparable injury and damage.

(a) I acknowledge that if you desire to seek injunctive relief, you may invoke the provisions of Section 526(b)(5)(B)(ii) of the California Code of Civil Procedure and Section 3423(Fifth)(e)(B) of the California Civil Code, which provides that injunctive is available if aggregate compensation received by me under this Agreement is at least ten (10) times the applicable minimum aggregate amount required in the statutes, shall apply and you may seek injunctive relief.

(b) I acknowledge that you may pay me the difference, if any, between any amounts theretofore received by me and the applicable amount provided for herein.

☞ Subparagraph (b) makes sure that if earnings and advances are insufficient to match the minimum guarantees, the company can make up the difference.

EXAMPLE 5: Annual Minimum Compensation Guaranteed

12. Company guarantees to pay you annual compensation ("Annual Payments") during each of the first seven (7) "Fiscal Years" (as hereinafter defined) of such amounts as are set forth in subparagraph 12(a), sections (1), (2), and (3) below. You hereby agree to accept all such Annual Payments.

(a) As used in this paragraph, "Fiscal Year" shall mean each consecutive twelve (12) month period during which this agreement is in effect, commencing with the date of commencement of the term of this agreement. At least thirty (30) days before the end of each Fiscal Year, you shall notify Company in writing if you have not received compensation equal to the Annual Payment for such Fiscal Year and the amount of the deficiency, and Company will pay you the amount of the deficiency.

(1) Nine Thousand Dollars ($9,000) for the first Fiscal Year of the agreement;

(2) Twelve Thousand Dollars ($12,000) for the second Fiscal Year of the agreement;

(3) Fifteen Thousand Dollars ($15,000) for each of the third through seventh Fiscal Years of the agreement.

(b) If in any Fiscal Year the aggregate amount of the compensation (other than Mechanical Royalties) paid to you under this agreement exceeds the Annual Payment, such excess compensation shall apply to reduce the Annual Payment for any subsequent Fiscal Years. You acknowledge and agree that the [$200,000] Advance payable to you pursuant to paragraph 7(b) shall satisfy Company's obligation to pay you Annual Payments in respect of the first seven (7) Fiscal Years.

(c) Each Annual Payment shall be due on or before the last business day of the Fiscal Year to which it applies; provided that if this agreement expires or terminates prior to the end of a particular Fiscal Year, the applicable Annual Payment shall be reduced proportionately, or shall be such greater amount, if any, as is required pursuant to California Civil Code Section 3423. Any failure by Company to make an Annual Payment will not constitute a material breach of the agreement.

(d) Company shall have the right to pay you at any time any additional amounts which may be required to be paid as a condition to Company's petitioning for any injunction pursuant to Section 526 of the California Code of Civil Procedure and Section 3423 (5th) of the California Civil Code ("Additional Payments"). You hereby agree to accept any and all such Additional Payments. All compensation (other than Mechanical Royalties) paid to you hereunder which is not applied to the Annual Payments theretofore due you will be credited toward satisfying the obligation to make Additional Payments as a prerequisite to seeking injunctive relief hereunder. If Company actually makes any Additional Payments and thereafter elects not to seek such injunction, such Additional Payments shall constitute Advances hereunder.

(e) Each Annual Payment and Additional Payment, if any, will constitute an Advance and will be applied in reduction of any and all monies (other than Mechanical Royalties) due or becoming due you under this agreement. Notwithstanding anything to the contrary contained herein, whenever in this agreement Company has the right to deduct excess expenditures (including, without limitation, excess Recording Costs, Mechanical Royalties and Special Packaging Costs) from any and all monies otherwise due or becoming due you under this agreement, Company's such right shall not extend to deducting such excess expenditures from any Annual Payments or Additional Payments.

SAMPLING

One of the benefits (or one of the plagues, depending on your point of view) of the electronic revolution is *sampling*, the practice of incorporating a selection or selections from previously recorded material into a new recording. Sampling is a benefit for those who use it to "borrow" material for creative and commercial purposes, a plague for those who are the unwilling "lenders." Obviously, the same artist can be a borrower on one occasion and a lender on another. Whatever your personal views on sampling, the courts have determined that sampling without consent is, in fact, a copyright infringement. (See the section "Sampling" in Chapter 20, "Copyright," pages 532–533.)

Record companies, faced with potential liabilities for unauthorized sampling on product which has been commercially released, have set up very detailed procedures to make sure that any and all samples have been properly cleared (see Example 1, below). I had one student who ran the sampling clearance department for a major label who also insisted on receiving the multitrack studio masters so that he could listen to each individual track separately for undisclosed sampling. Because of the wide diversity of possible sources (commercial recordings, soundtracks from film or television, live concerts, commercials, etc. [in fact, as I was writing this, the radio informed me that the recording I had just heard contained sampling from a Laurel and Hardy film—need I say more?]), any one sample may require multiple consents, for example, from the publisher of the musical composition; the copyright owner of the recording (record company, producer, or artist, etc.); an individual; a film or television company or producer; and so on. The permissions for artists being sampled from commercial recordings can usually be supplied by the record company that holds the copyright, but it is wise to ask for representations that the record company *does* have these rights to grant and will give an indemnification from the artist's claims in case they do not. The artist or, as applicable, the production company will be required to indemnify the record company from claims of unauthorized use of samples (see Example 2).

Permissions have to be granted, usually for a fee, from all of the owners of the rights in and to the sampled materials before there can be any commercial exploitation of the recordings using the samples. In addition to having a requirement for a royalty or a fee, the permission granted may contain other conditions or restrictions, such as, for example, a limitation on the period of time during which the sample may be used (e.g., a license limited to 5 years, etc.) or, perhaps, a limitation as to the territory (e.g., permission granted only for the United States, etc.). The permissions or clearances involving royalties themselves can be regarded as mini–recording contracts. This poses a difficult problem for an artist and/or a production company: Where are these royalties coming from? (You get three guesses, and any of them without the words "out of the artist's royalty" is not a winner.) What if an artist is in an unrecouped position, but, nevertheless, a royalty for a permission to use a sample is due? For the obvious answer, see Example 4. Finally, as discussed in the "Delivery" section (pages 50–54), the artist may be considered to have failed to meet the delivery requirements if all sample clearances have not been received with the other elements (see Example 3).

SAMPLE CONTRACT PROVISIONS

EXAMPLE 1: Permission Delivery Requirements

12. Artist hereby acknowledges that Company's policies with respect to all Samples, if any, embodied in any Master or other recording hereunder are as follows, and Artist agrees to adhere to such policies and warrants and represents that all information supplied by or through Artist to Company in that regard shall be complete and correct:

(a) Prior to Company's authorization of pre-mastering (e.g., equalization and the making of reference dubs or the equivalent thereof in the applicable configurations) for a particular set of Masters, Artist shall deliver to Company with respect to each such Master:

(i) One (1) fully mixed (but not mastered) DAT copy of the applicable Masters;

(ii) A detailed list of any and all Samples (including, without limitation, musical and spoken word recordings derived from motion pictures, television programs, political speeches, commercials, newscasts and Masters by musical recording artists) embodied in each Master and other recording in the form of the Declaration of Sampling attached hereto as Exhibit C;

(iii) A written clearance or license for the perpetual, nonrestrictive use of each such Sample interpolated in each Master in any and all media from the copyright holder(s) of the Sample concerned. It is Artist's responsibility to obtain all required clearances for each Sample interpolated in each Master; and

(iv) Any and all necessary information pertaining to credit copy required by copyright holder(s) of each Sample interpolated in each Master. Artist agrees to treat this matter with the utmost urgency, as Record packaging and artwork cannot be completed until Company receives this information.

EXAMPLE 2: Artist Indemnification for Samples

17. I hereby warrant and represent that the Masters delivered pursuant to this Agreement contain only samples as are listed in Schedule 2, attached hereto and incorporated herein by reference, if any, and that all third parties owning or controlling rights in the samples have consented in writings being attached hereto, to Company's unfettered exploitation of records embodying the samples. [Schedule 2 is a form on which must be listed, for each sample used, the sampled master, the sampled artist, the sampled record company, and the sampled publisher.]

(a) My failure to list samples herein shall be deemed an express warranty and representation that no samples are embodied in the Masters.

(b) Without limiting the generality of those portions of this Agreement which pertain to my indemnification of Company, I expressly indemnify and hold Company harmless from any and all claims relating to:

(i) the use of samples in the Masters (whether disclosed herein or otherwise);

(ii) my failure for any reason to fully perform the attached agreements; and

(iii) the validity or adequacy of any agreement conveying rights to the samples.

EXAMPLE 3: Sample Clearance as Delivery Requirement

13. After Artist has delivered the information provided for in Paragraph 12., above, with regard to any Sample used herein, Artist shall provide Company with a DAT copy of the Master(s) and Company shall listen to and analyze the DAT copy of the Master(s) to confirm the accuracy of the information provided.

(a) In the event that Company's review of the DAT copy identifies Samples in addition to the Samples listed, Company will promptly inform Artist of the discrepancy.

(b) Until Company identifies all Samples and receives written clearances for those Samples identified as requiring clearances, Company will not authorize pre-mastering of any particular set of Masters and will not issue funds or purchase orders with respect to pre-mastering.

(c) Nothing contained in this Agreement shall relieve Artist of Artist's obligation to identify and clear any and all Samples embodied in Masters and other recordings made hereunder. Company's failure to so identify any such Samples shall not be construed as a waiver of any of Company's rights and remedies contained herein, all of which are expressly reserved.

(d) No Master will be scheduled for release and no Master shall be deemed to have been Delivered to Company hereunder (and no Delivery payments, if any, will be paid) until such written Sample clearances (including credit copy, if any) have been obtained and approved by Company.

EXAMPLE 4: Royalty Payments for Sampled Material

10. With regard to any sampled performances or materials contained in any Master recorded hereunder:

• • •

(h) If any such Sample Clearance provides for a royalty payment on net sales of the applicable Master and Producer's record royalty account hereunder is in an unrecouped position at the time such royalties are due, then, notwithstanding anything to the contrary contained herein, Producer shall be solely responsible for making, and shall make, such royalty payment to the applicable third party promptly upon receipt from Company of such third party's accounting statement thereof.

☛ Ahh ha! The perils of sampling: having to dig into your own pocket to pay for it, even if you haven't been paid yourself.

GRANT OF RIGHTS

Every recording agreement has paragraphs which together are known as *grant-of-rights provisions* but which might better be called "stealth provisions." Every time I review, or draft, a recording agreement and come to these provisions I remind myself of the pretty red apple the witch offered to Snow White. Frequently, they are grouped as subparagraphs under one paragraph entitled "Grant of Rights" (see Example 2, below); but they are also sometimes scattered here and there throughout the agreement.

Even when the term "grant of rights" is not used, these paragraphs specify the rights which are being *granted* to the record company by the artist. Note the similarity of the three examples following this section. Their very familiarity sometimes causes the unwary to miss things or to see things which do not exist. (A good example of this is a recent "definitive" edition of the collected works of William Shakespeare where a distinguished board of editors and *nine* proofreaders failed to catch the misprinting of what is arguably the most famous line in English literature as "To be or to be that is the question.")

Whether grouped under one heading or scattered throughout the agreement, grant-of-rights paragraphs are much the same from contract to contract, and they are usually straightforward—if you bother to read them carefully *and* you know the code words. See Example 3, for example, where subparagraph 4(c) grants the company the right to couple recordings without ever using the terms "couple" or "compilation."

Grant-of-rights clauses are likely to be *very long*, and hence a good place to "hide" things. Some of these seemingly innocent babies are little time bombs waiting to be triggered, and many a provision granting rights the artist would *not* want to grant has slipped by without being deleted or even modified. If, for example, you were to carefully make a checklist of the different rights granted to the company that are crammed into subparagraph (a) of Example 2, you would find the following.

In subparagraph (a):

1. The producer grants to the record company sole and exclusive perpetual ownership throughout the Territory of: Masters recorded by Artist; other recordings recorded by Artist; videos using Masters or produced under the contract; Artwork.

2. Producer grants Company ownership throughout the Territory of all right title and interest in the copyrights to the above items.

3. Producer grants that everything described by this list is deemed to be a "work for hire."

4. Producer grants that if anything on the list is not a work for hire, it is deemed transferred to Company anyway.

5. Producer warrants and represents that Company is the sole and exclusive perpetual owner throughout the Territory of everything described above.

6. Producer warrants and represents that everything on the list is free of claims from anyone other than Company.

7. Producer warrants and represents that the Company has the right throughout the Territory to use and control everything on the list.

8. Producer warrants and represents that Company (or Company's designee) throughout the Territory has the exclusive right to copyright everything contained on the list.

9. Producer warrants and represents that copyrights may be issued with Company's name as owner.

10. Producer warrants and represents that copyrights may be issued with Company's name as author.

11. Producer grants Company the right to renew and extend the copyrights.

12. Producer agrees to execute and deliver to Company any documents that Company may "request to effectuate the intent" of the contract.

13. Producer agrees that Company may sign these documents in the name of Producer.

14. Producer agrees that Company may sign these documents in the name of Artist.

15. Producer appoints Company as Producer's agent and attorney-in-fact to sign the documents.

All this in just the first four sentences of a section that goes on for many more paragraphs! Any or all of the foregoing may be a crucial negotiating point. Because of the presumed "boilerplate" status of these clauses, they are frequently not given their just due and just attention. The most innocent of words and phrases, such as "edit to conform to commercial requirements," "use in commercials for any products," "any licensee," "grant to others" and "other merchandise," must be scrutinized for their full meaning within the context.

On the other hand, without the rights granted in these paragraphs, the record company has nothing, and so wholesale deletion is not the answer. In fact, it is an impossibility. Any record company would react with horror and disbelief if the artist suggested that grant-of-rights provisions should be entirely cut. The only thing to do is review all grant of rights provisions carefully and, *if possible*, delete or modify the offending parts without undermining the record company's basic rights. The problem is convincing the record company that a proposed deletion or modification is not "basic."

Portions of many of the grant-of-rights contract provisions at the end of this section are also included in the sections pertaining to the specific issues involved. For a more detailed discussion of those issues, and suggested modifications that the artist may be able to make, see the following sections:

• Coupling: pages 125–128

• Foreign Sales: pages 77–81

- Joint Recording: pages 129–130

- Label: pages 165–166

- Merchandising: pages 177–180

- Name: pages 167–172

- Publicity: pages 173–176

As you read the sample contract provisions below, notice the references to "employee for hire" (Example 1) and "work made for hire" (Example 2). Virtually every recording agreement contains an acknowledgment that the masters which are recorded pursuant to the agreement are works for hire and, accordingly, the record company is the "author" and copyright holder, with all the rights those designations entail (see Chapter 17, "Copyright," pages 530–532).

SAMPLE CONTRACT PROVISIONS

EXAMPLE 1: List of Rights Granted

3. Producer agrees that Company owns and shall have the entire right, tide and interest of whatsoever kind or nature throughout the world in and to each of the Masters and all other recordings recorded by Artist during the term hereof, and all copies thereof, including but not limited to:

a. The exclusive and perpetual ownership of the Masters and all duplicates thereof and all sound recording copyrights therein (and for the purpose of obtaining any such sound recording copyrights and for no other purpose Producer, Artist, and any individual producer shall be deemed to be Company's "employee for hire" so that Company shall be the "author" of any such sound recordings) and records manufactured therefrom and the right to use and control the same and performances embodied therein in perpetuity;

b. The exclusive and perpetual right throughout the world to manufacture, advertise, sell, lease, license or otherwise use or dispose of the Masters, and/or records manufactured from or embodying all or any part of the contents of the Masters or to refrain therefrom in any and all fields of use throughout the world upon such terms and conditions as Company may approve. As used in this agreement, the noun "record" means any device by which sound may be recorded for later transmission to listeners, whether now known or unknown and howsoever used, whether embodying sound alone or sound synchronized with or accompanied by visual images of Artist or another subject including without limitation "tape records";

c. The perpetual right to use and publish and to permit others to use and publish the names, including professional names now used or later adopted of Producer, any individual producer, Artist, and any individual artist, and the individual performers of the group performing on the Masters and the likenesses of and biographical material concerning all such performers who recorded the Masters, for advertising and trade purposes in connection with the sale and exploitation of records produced from the Masters or to refrain therefrom. Said right shall be exclusive during the term hereof and nonexclusive thereafter;

d. The right to release records manufactured from the Masters under the "Company" label or trademark, or such other tradename or mark as Company may elect from a label distributed by one of the following record companies: CBS, Warner Bros., Elektra/Asylum, Atlantic, A&M, Capitol,

Arista, ABC, MCA, Phonogram, United Artists, Polydor and Motown;

e. The right to sell and exploit records manufactured from the Masters on which the performances by other artists are coupled and to sell records manufactured from the Masters in albums which albums may contain pictures, prose and verse and records embodying performances of other artists; provided however, Company agrees not to "couple" records manufactured from the Masters in the United States during the term of this agreement (as it may be extended and/or renewed) without Producer's prior written consent, except on "best hits," "sampler," and anthology type albums.

☛ This is from an agreement between a production company furnishing the services of the artist to another company looking to make a deal with, preferably, a "major."

EXAMPLE 2: An Exhaustive (and Exhausting) Listing of a Label's Rights

7. GRANT OF RIGHTS

(a) Producer acknowledges that Company is the sole, exclusive and perpetual owner, from the inception of recording and throughout the Territory, of all Masters (and other recordings) recorded by Artist pursuant to this Agreement, all Videos embodying those Masters or otherwise produced hereunder and all artwork created for use in connection with the Masters ("Artwork"), which ownership entitled Company, among other things, to all right, title and interest in the copyright in and to the Masters (and other recordings), Videos and Artwork. Each Master and other recording (from the inception of recording), Video and Artwork made under this Agreement or during its Term and the Artist Term, will be considered a "work for hire" for Company; if any such Master, Video or Artwork is determined not to be such a "work made for hire," it will be deemed transferred to Company by this Agreement, together with all the rights and title in and to such materials. Producer warrants, represents and agrees that all masters (and other recordings) and Videos made under this Agreement (including duplicates, work tapes, etc.), the performances contained thereon and the Masters derived therefrom and the related Artwork, from the inception of their creation, are the sole property of Company, in perpetuity, free from any claims by producer, Artist or any other person, and Company has the right to use and control the same subject to the terms herein. Company (or Company's designees) has the exclusive right to copyright all such Masters (and other recordings), Videos and Artwork in its name as the author and owner of them and to secure any and all renewals and extensions of such copyright throughout the Territory. Producer will execute and deliver to Company such instruments of transfer and other documents regarding the rights of Company or its designees in the Masters (and other recordings), Videos and Artwork subject to this Agreement as Company may reasonably request to effectuate the intent of this Agreement, and Company may sign such documents in Producer's name or in the name of Artist (and Producer hereby appoints Company Producer's agent and attorney-in-fact for such purposes).

(b) Without limiting the generality of the foregoing, Company and persons authorized by Company shall have the sole, exclusive and perpetual rights, throughout the Territory:

(i) to manufacture Records by any and all methods now or hereafter known embodying any portion or all of the Performances embodied on Masters and other recordings hereunder; to publicly perform such Records and permit the public performance thereof in any media; to enforce, export, sell, transfer, lease, rent, deal in or otherwise dispose of such Masters and other recordings and Records derived therefrom throughout the Territory under the trademarks, trade-names or labels designated by Company; subsequent to Producer's first right, to remix, edit or adapt the Masters and other recordings to conform to technological or commercial requirements in various formats now or hereafter known or developed, or to edit or eliminate material which might subject Company to any legal action; to use and, with Producer's consent during the Term (not to be unreasonably withheld), authorize the use of the Masters and the recordings for background music, synchronization in motion pictures and television soundtracks and other similar purposes, including, without limitation, use on transportation and in commercials for any products in any and all media, without any payment other than as provided herein (or Company and its subsidiaries, affiliates and Licensees may at their election delay or refrain from doing any one or more of the foregoing);

(ii) the right to manufacture, sell and exploit Records embodying Masters made hereunder together with Masters embodying Performances by other artists, which Records may contain pictures, prose and verse ("Multi-Artist Records"); provided, however, during each year of the Term hereof, Company shall not couple more than two (2) Masters embodying Artist's performance hereunder with Masters embodying the performances of other artists on one (1) Record for release in the United States without Producer's consent. The preceding sentence shall not apply to Sampler records, compilations sold to jukebox operators for placement in coin operated jukeboxes and Records that are sequenced and/or selected by the consumer or similar type Records; and

(iii) to release Records manufactured from the Masters under the name of "[Company]" or such other trade name or mark as Company may elect; provided, however, Company agrees that the initial United States release of Records hereunder shall be on Company's so-called top-line label.

(c) Company and any Licensee of Company each has the perpetual right, without liability to any Person, and may grant to others the right, to reproduce, print, publish, or disseminate in any media the name of Producer, the name, portraits, pictures and likenesses of Artist and the individual producer and all other Persons performing services in connection with the Masters made under this Agreement and the Artist Agreement (including, without limitation, all professional, group and other assumed or fictitious names used by them), and biographical material concerning them for purposes of news and information, advertising, promotion and trade in connection with producer or Artist, the marketing and exploitation of Records hereunder and general good will advertising. The uses authorized by the preceding sentence include, without limitation, the use of those names, portraits, pictures and likenesses of Artist in the marketing of Records and any other merchandise provided for herein. During the Term hereof, Company and its Licensees may, in the Territory, bill, advertise and describe Artist as an exclusive artist of Company and Producer or by a similar designation. With respect to Artist, Company's rights as described in this paragraph will be exclusive during the Term of this Agreement and nonexclusive thereafter. Producer will make Artist available from time to time to appear for photography sessions arranged in connection with the creation of poster and cover art and the like, under the reasonable direction of Company or its nominees, and to appear for interviews with representatives of the media and Company publicity personnel. Producer and Artist will not be entitled to any compensation for such services, except as may be required by applicable union agreements. During the Term hereof, neither Producer nor Artist shall authorize any party other than Company to use the name and likeness of Artist in connection with the advertising or sale of Records.

EXAMPLE 3: Artist Grants Rights

4. I grant to Company:

(a) The results and proceeds of all endeavors under this Agreement, including the exclusive ownership of all masters, positives or negatives thereof and records manufactured therefrom and the exclusive and perpetual right to control and use the same and the performances embodied therein; the exclusive and perpetual right to manufacture, advertise, sell, lease, license or otherwise use or dispose of such records, whether based in whole or in part upon such results and proceeds or to refrain from so doing, in all fields of use throughout the world, upon such terms as Company may approve; the perpetual right to perform publicly such records and the exclusive and perpetual right to permit public performances thereof in any medium and by any means whatsoever.

(b) The perpetual right to use and publish and to permit others to use and publish my name (including any professional name heretofore or hereafter adopted by me), signature, likeness, voice and sound effects, and biographical material concerning me for advertising and trade purposes in connection with the recordings made hereunder or to refrain therefrom.

(c) The perpetual right to release records recorded hereunder under any trade name or mark, which records may include performances of other artists, and to sell the records in albums, which albums may contain pictures, prose and verse and records embodying performances by other artists.

(d) The right to copyright such master recordings in Company's name as the owner and author thereof and to secure any and all renewals of such copyright; provided, however, if, on any date, the performances borne on any master recording subject to this Agreement become property of the public domain in any territory of the world so that persons may reproduce and/or exploit in such territory records of such performances without license from and payment to Company, then, notwithstanding anything herein to the contrary, no monies whatsoever shall accrue to Company hereunder in connection with records hereunder sold in such territory on and after said date insofar as such performances are concerned.

WARRANTIES AND REPRESENTATIONS

> BRABANTIO:
>
> . . . a practiser
> **Of arts inhibited, and out of warrant.**
>
> —WILLIAM SHAKESPEARE
> *Othello*, Act I, Scene 2

The record company will require the artist to make certain warranties and representations in connection with the signing of the contract. A *warranty* is a promise that a certain fact or facts are as represented. A *representation* is a statement about a past or existing fact. Neither should be taken lightly. Suits brought against artists by record companies are usually based upon a breach of one or more warranties and representations.

Two of the most basic warranties and representations are that the artist is free to enter into the agreement and that the artist is free to record all musical works, except as expressly indicated. Usually, there is also a representation that the artist will continue to actively pursue a career as a recording artist and entertainer (see Example 1).

Another important warranty and representation to be made by the artist (or the production company furnishing the artist to the record company) is that the artist either is under no restriction regarding songs which can be recorded or, if there is a restriction against the rerecording of songs previously recorded (see "Rerecording Restrictions," pages 158–164), those restrictions will be set forth in the agreement (see Example 2).

If a production company is furnishing an artist to the record company under a production agreement, the production company will warrant to the record company that the artist is under contract to the production company and that the production company has the right to furnish the artist to the record company. The production company may also be required to make certain warranties and representations on behalf of the artist, such as, for example, that the artist belongs to the appropriate union. (See Example 2.)

Of great importance in reviewing and negotiating the terms of warranty and representation clauses is the issue of *indemnifications*. Where there is a provision or provisions requiring the artist and/or production company to furnish warranties and/or representations, you can be sure there will also be an indemnification clause. Indemnification clauses, sometimes referred to as *hold-harmless* clauses, require the party making a promise or a statement of fact to be responsible for the damages caused if the promise is not kept or the statement of fact turns out not to be true, that is, to hold the "innocent" party harmless.

There are certain precautions which should be taken by an artist (or production company) with respect to indemnification clauses. The first is to limit what it takes to activate an indemnification clause. In a perfect world, the easiest way to limit indemnification would simply be not to breach the contract—to keep your promises and not to lie about anything. Unfortunately, this approach, while commendable, is insufficient. Not all breaches are willful or caused by or within the control of the artist—negligence, accidents, acts of third parties, etc., may cause a breach. Or a representation that triggers indemnification made by a party in good faith may, in fact, be untrue.

What worries me is that many indemnifications are based on "claims" made by third parties (see Example 3). "Claims" are easy to make and frequently have no truth or fact to back them up. One question lawyers are always asked by clients is, Can [he, she, it, they] sue me? My answer is always, Yes. *Anybody* can sue you. Whether they can win is another matter. If I am in an expansive mood when asked the question, I will sometimes also tell the following story.

One time, while working for CBS, I was in the New York offices and ran into a staff attorney I knew who was wandering the hall muttering to himself and shaking his head vigorously. Being a caring and sensitive person, I asked, "You OK?"

"We got sued," he growled.

I shrugged. "So? We're CBS. We must get sued about a dozen times a day."

"You don't understand," he replied. "Some guy down in Texas just sued us for six trillion dollars *claiming* [emphasis added] that CBS entered his house at night through his television set when he was asleep. And while he was asleep, we removed all his internal organs and replaced them with transistors."

He paused and looked longingly at a window, as if he were imagining throwing the offender through that very window. He turned back to me. "And the judge is making us file an answer."

That answer undoubtedly cost CBS several thousand dollars.

Now imagine that you are under contract to CBS, and, instead of CBS entering the house through the television, the man claims you entered his house through his CD player. He is now suing both CBS and you for walking off with his internal organs. Now stretch your imagination a little further and imagine your contract provides that you will indemnify CBS against any "claims."

That's why I worry about indemnifications based upon "claims."

If you think this is far-fetched, cast your mind back several years to when a record company and a group were sued in a wrongful death action by the parents of a young fan who committed suicide after listening over and over to one of the group's recordings.

Another problem with indemnifications based upon claims is that a record company may be more inclined to buy off the claimant and charge the cost back to the artist than it is to spend more money to defend the matter and prove the claim invalid and then eat the costs of the defense because there was no breach. Chew on that possibility for awhile.

The solution is to provide that indemnifications apply only to instances where the claim has been reduced to a "final judgment" in a court of law. While most record companies will agree to this modification, they will also modify the modification, adding that the indemnification applies to a settlement. This, unsurprisingly, usually results in another modification from the artist's representative—the artist must first approve the settlement (see Example 3). "Well, OK," says the record company, "but then the artist must not unreasonably withhold consent," and the company will probably require the artist to post a bond for and/or be responsible for all costs to continue to defend the action. It is also possible that the record company, in lieu of a bond, may withhold the artist's royalties (see Example 4).

Another issue of importance in the indemnification clause is just which payments the artist (or production company) should be responsible for if the clause is triggered by a breach. The record company wants the language to be such that it can recover "all costs" under the indemnification—damages, losses, expenses, and attorneys' fees. Many jurisdictions will not award attorneys' fees unless there is an express written provision granting them. You will note that all four examples below expressly call for the payment of attorneys' fees. Do note, however, that only Example 1 calls for the attorneys' fees to be "reasonable."

In instances where the record company has the right to sue in the name of the artist, I frequently demand that the record company indemnify the artist against any cross-complaint which may occur as a result of a lawsuit filed by the company.

SAMPLE CONTRACT PROVISIONS

EXAMPLE 1: Basic Warranties, Representations, and Indemnification

10. I represent and warrant that I am under no disability, restriction, or prohibition respecting musical works I can record for Company except to the extent, if any, set forth in the Schedule of Restricted Musical Works attached hereto. Any such musical work, if any, I will set forth in the attached Schedule. If there is no such restriction, I will initial the Schedule at the place indicated. My failure to either indicate such restriction or lack of such restriction shall act as my warranty that no such restriction exists, and, in such case, I agree to indemnify Company for any loss, including reasonable attorneys' fees, caused by my recording of a restricted work.

11. I represent and warrant that I am not a party to any agreement which prevents my fulfilling all of my obligations hereunder or which impairs any rights granted to Company hereunder. I agree that during the term of this Agreement I will work diligently at and pursue my career as a recording artist and as an entertainer. I agree to and do hereby indemnify, save and hold Company harm-

less from loss or damage, including reasonable attorneys' fees, arising out of or connected with any of the warranties or representations made by me in this Agreement and which has resulted in a judgment against Company or which has been settled with my consent. I will reimburse Company on demand for any payment made by Company at any time after the date hereof in respect of any liability or claim to which the foregoing indemnity applies.

☛ The artist agrees to "work diligently at and pursue my career as a recording artist and as an entertainer" during the term of the agreement. Anybody have a device that measures diligence?

EXAMPLE 2: Production Company

1. COMPANY [production company] does hereby warrant to [Record Company] that it is the owner of an exclusive employment agreement with ARTISTS, which agreement includes ARTISTS' exclusive services as recording artists and which shall remain in effect for at least the term and any extensions hereof. COMPANY further warrants that it will perform each and every condition contained in said exclusive employment agreement on its part to be performed, and will not during the term hereof violate any of the terms contained in said exclusive employment agreement, so that said exclusive employment agreement will remain in effect for at least as long a period as the term and any extensions hereof. COMPANY further warrants that ARTISTS are members of the American Federation of Musicians and will remain so during the term and any extension of this agreement. COMPANY does hereby agree to provide the services of ARTISTS to record solely and exclusively for [Record Company] in accordance with the provisions of this agreement.

• • •

16. COMPANY warrants and agrees that no prior contract or agreement of any kind entered into by itself or the ARTISTS or by any accompanists (instrumental and/or vocal) selected by COMPANY or ARTISTS to record hereunder, or any prior performance by itself or the ARTIST and said accompanists, will interfere in any manner with the complete performance of the within agreement. . . . COMPANY further warrants and represents that ARTIST and said accompanists have not performed or agreed to perform any composition agreed to be recorded hereunder for any person other than [Record Company] for the purpose of making phonograph records within a period of five (5) years prior to the date hereof or five (5) years prior to the date such composition will be recorded hereunder . . . COMPANY agrees and does hereby indemnify, save and hold [Record Company] harmless from loss or damage (including attorneys' fees) arising out of or connected with any claim by a third party which is inconsistent with any of the warranties or representations made by COMPANY in this agreement. COMPANY will reimburse [Record Company] on demand for any payment made by [Record Company] at any time after the date hereof in respect of any liability or claim to which the foregoing indemnity relates. COMPANY shall, however, have the right to participate in the negotiations for a settlement of such claim.

☛ Paragraph 16 of this example has a "reverse rerecording restriction," the production company warranting and representing that the artist won't record anything previously recorded within one of two specified 5-year periods. (The "reverse" aspect refers to "previously recorded" rather than future recordings.) I have two problems with this provision: (1) Since there is no "earlier than" or "later than" connected to these periods, if there is a conflict, which one prevails? (2) As you will see in the next section, it is quite possible that a preexisting rerecording restriction may be for a period greater than either 5-year period.

EXAMPLE 3: Artist Warrants, Represents, and Indemnifies

12. You hereby agree to and do hereby indemnify, save, and hold us harmless from any and all damages, liabilities, costs, losses and expenses (including legal costs and attorneys' fees) arising out of or connected with any claim, action, demand, or action by a third party which is inconsistent with any of the warranties, representations, or covenants made by you in this contract. You agree to reimburse us, on demand, for any payment made by us at any time with respect to any such damage, liability, cost, loss or expense to which the foregoing indemnity applies to the extent such payment was made pursuant to a final judgment in a court of competent jurisdiction or pursuant to a settlement or compromise approved by or consented to by you. We shall notify you of any such claim, demand, or action promptly after we have been formally advised thereof. Pending the determination of any such claim, demand, or action, we shall have the right, at our election, to withhold payment of royalties or other sums payable to you hereunder in an amount reasonably related to such claim, demand, or action and our estimated attorneys' fees and estimated legal costs in connection therewith.

EXAMPLE 4: Detailed Indemnification

11. You hereby hold harmless and indemnify us from any and all damages, liabilities, costs, losses and expenses (including legal costs and attorneys' fees) arising out of or connected with any claim, demand or action (collectively referred to below as a "Claim") by a third party which is (a) inconsistent with any of the warranties, representations or covenants made by you in this contract and (b) reduced to a final judgment or settled with your consent, which consent you shall not unreasonably withhold.

(a) You agree to reimburse us, on demand, for any payment made by us at any time with respect to any such damage, for any payment made by us at any time with respect to any damage, liability, cost, loss or expense to which the foregoing indemnity applies.

(b) In the event you shall fail to do so, we shall have the right to recoup such payment from any monies payable to you hereunder or under any other agreement between you and us and any of our affiliates.

(c) We shall notify you of any such Claim promptly after we have been formally advised thereof. Pending the determination of any such Claim we shall have the right, at our election, to withhold payment of any monies otherwise payable to you hereunder or under any other agreement between you and us or you and any of our affiliates in an amount reasonably related to the amount of our attorneys' fees and costs in connection therewith and, if we shall determine that such Claim has merit and/or is not spurious, the amount of such Claim.

(d) You shall have the right to post a bond in form, amount and duration and with a bonding company satisfactory to us, and in the event you shall so post a bond, we shall no longer withhold any monies hereunder in connection with the Claim in respect of which such bond shall be posted.

RERECORDING RESTRICTIONS

Rerecording restrictions are usually contained in their own separate clause in the recording agreement. Sometimes, however, they can be found in other provisions—most likely in that black hole called the "grant of rights." In rerecording restriction provisions, the artist is required to agree that for a specified period he or she will not rerecord for anyone else any composition recorded pursuant to the agreement. These important provisions grant the record company a guaranteed period of exclusivity to the artist for these specified compositions. Please note that these provisions do not restrict the artist from recording for any third party after the term of the agreement, only that the artist will not rerecord the same material for the specified time. Also, the artist is not restricted from performing the specified compositions in live performances, television shows, or soundtracks for films, as long as the restricted performances are not released commercially as recordings by anyone other than the record company. Rerecording restrictions are, I feel, legitimate. The record company has invested time and, if the artist is lucky, money and effort and is entitled to a fair chance to make a return on those investments.

The following story about rerecording restrictions was *not* invented, but actually happened to a client of mine. (Frankly, I don't think my inventiveness is developed enough to come up with something like this.)

My client (referred to hereafter as Artist) is a singer, a songwriter, and a producer. Artist had produced quite a few masters of himself which he either released on his own small local label or put aside for future use. Major Label #1 decided they wanted to sign Artist to a recording contract. This was fine with Artist and a deal was entered into between Artist and Label #1. The contract contained a rerecording provision which stated that, for a specified period, Artist would not rerecord anything recorded during the term of the contract. In signing the contract, Artist also listed, as an exhibit, a large number of preexisting masters, including Master #1, a recording of Song. Label #1 asked Artist to submit some of the existing masters for consideration. Artist did, submitting Master #1, along with some nine or ten other masters. Label #1 liked Song, but not Master #1, and requested that Artist rerecord Song for Label #1. Artist did, and recorded another version of Song, Master #2. Label #1 decided not to release any of the albums which they had recorded with Artist and gave Artist a release from the contract.

Time passed. (Imagine shots of pages falling off a calendar.)

Artist was signed to Major Label #2. As part of the agreement, Artist sold various masters to Label #2, including Master #1. After a short period of time, Artist became dissatisfied with Label #2 and a mutual release was agreed upon. Pursuant to the release, Artist regained ownership of the masters. Another page or two falls from the calendar.

Artist was signed to Major Label #3. Master #1 was sold to Label #3 as part of the agreement. This time, Master #1 was finally released commercially. It became a monster hit.

The scene now shifts to the dais of a major charity event, where the presidents of Label #1 and Label #3 (forget about Label #2, it was included only for historical accuracy) happened to be sitting next to each other. Naturally, the president of Label #3 couldn't resist teasing the president of Label #1. Of course, the next morning I received a call from Label #1's attorney. "Artist recorded Song for us. We had a rerecording clause in our contract with him. He's in breach of the contract, and we are entitled to damages," he informed me.

"Actually, yes, he did record Song for you. Yes, he did have a rerecording restriction. And no, he's not in breach of the contract and, no, you aren't entitled to damages," I replied. I then proceeded to explain that Label #3's recording was from Master #1, which predated Label #1's contract and, since it was a preexisting recording and was not, in fact, rerecorded after Label #1's contract, there was no violation of the rerecording restriction. I directed his attention to the exhibit in the original contract which listed Master #1 as preexisting. He graciously accepted my point, and that was the end of it.

There's a moral in there somewhere, I just don't know what it is, other than that music industry fact is stranger than fiction. And I like the story. Back to the business at hand.

There are four problem areas that come up with regard to rerecording provisions:

1. How long is the restriction in effect? 3 years? 5 years?

2. At what point in time does the restriction period begin: (a) from the date of recording; (b) from the date of release; (c) from the expiration or other termination of the agreement, or (d) a combination of these?

3. If a combination, does the period run from the "earlier" or the "later" of the choices?

4. What is the penalty for violating the restriction?

In general, contracts will stipulate that the restriction period begins at a time that is "the later of" some stated combination of 2(a), 2(b), and 2(c) above.

The first thing to review in these provisions is the length of the period (or, in the case of a combination of periods, the periods) of restriction. A review of all the examples at the end of this section will show varying lengths set forth: 2 years, 3 years, 5 years, 6 years. Rarely will any of these individual periods be expressed in writing to exceed 6 years.

The next thing to review is the starting dates for these periods of restriction. The three variations, (a), (b), and (c), set forth above are the most common. Generally, I have no problem with any of them in combination (using two of them in combination is the norm), except when it comes to deciding whether the appropriate period is the "earlier" or the "later" of the two. I especially have a problem if it is the "later" of any combination which includes "the date of release" as a possible starting date. (Example 1 has this provision, but it is at least modified by a 6-year cap.) When does a rerecording restriction run out if it is, for example, the later of 5 years from the date of recording or 3 years from the date of release (without a cap), when the recording is never released? I'll save you the trouble of counting—the answer is: It doesn't.

Obviously, the record company prefers a period running from the "later of" while the artist prefers the"earlier of." Before agreeing to any combination, it is important to review the variations and understand just how the numbers play out. Each of the examples at the end of this section indicates "the later" of the combinations. I suggest you go through them and substitute the "earlier" for the "later" and take note of the big difference between the total length of the periods. If you must accept a "later of" provision, try to put an absolute cap on the length. (See Example 1, where it is 6 years.)

The final element to be dealt with is the penalty imposed if there is a violation of a rerecording restriction. Considering that most of these violations are inadvertent, some of the proposed penalties can be very harsh. Some record companies will insist that there be a forfeiture of all royalties if there is even a single transgression. This is clearly overkill and should be resisted by the artist.

One possible modification, which is more favorable to the artist, is that royalties are forfeited on any recording containing the offending song or songs. The only problem with this solution is that it takes little imagination to picture the offending cut suddenly appearing on every album ever recorded for the record company by the artist. Short of waiving any penalty, the best solution for the artist would appear to use a pro-rata royalty reduction for the song, much like a coupled recording. In other words, if the rerecorded song appears as one of 10 cuts on an album, the artist's royalty will be calculated only on 9 of the 10 cuts.

As discussed in the section "Warranties and Representations," violations of rerecording restrictions are a sufficient breach of the warranties and representations made by the artist to trigger the indemnification clauses. This raises the possibility that, in addition to penalties in the form of reduced or withheld royalties, the artist may also be responsible for legal costs, damages in the form of lost earnings, etc. These costs may be considerable, and they are "hard money" costs in that the artist would be required to pay them out of his or her own money, not just take a reduction in monies owed.

SAMPLE CONTRACT PROVISIONS

EXAMPLE 1: Cap of 6 Years

5. During the term of this Agreement, including all renewals, extensions and days of suspension and all periods added by amendments or by other agreements, I will not perform for the purpose of or myself engage in making records (other than permitted recordings) for anyone other than Company and I will not authorize the use of my name, likeness or other identification for the purpose of distributing, selling, advertising or exploiting records for anyone other than Company; nor will I perform any selection recorded hereunder for the purpose of making records (other than permitted recordings) for anyone other than Company (i) for five (5) consecutive years after the date of expiration or other termination of this Agreement, or (ii) for five (5) consecutive years after the release of the recordings, whichever is the later, but in no event more than six (6) years after the date of expiration or other termination of this Agreement.

EXAMPLE 2: Flawed Formula

9. (a) During the term of this contract, you will not enter into any agreement or make any commitment which would interfere with your performance of any of the terms and provisions hereof nor will you perform or render any services for the purpose of making phonograph records or master recordings for any person, firm, or corporation other than us. For a period of three (3) years after your recording of any selection hereunder or three (3) years after the expiration or termination of the term of this contract, whichever shall be later, you will not perform said selection for any person, firm or corporation other than us for the purpose of making phonograph records or master recordings.

☛ The combination of the later of 3 years after recording or 3 years after the expiration or termination of the contract is kind of silly here. Unless a recording is made *after* the expiration or termination of the contract, there is no way the rerecording restriction can extend beyond three years after the expiration of the contract. Instead of an "either/or" situation, this is a "just is" situation. If the formula were based on "the earlier of" instead of "the later of," it would be meaningful.

EXAMPLE 3: 5-Year/2-Year Formula

3. . . . After the expiration of the term of this agreement, for any reason whatsoever, you will not perform any musical composition which shall have been recorded hereunder for any person other than us for the purpose of making phonograph records or master recordings prior to whichever of the following dates shall be later: (i) the date 5 years subsequent to the date such composition is recorded hereunder, or (ii) the date two years subsequent to the expiration date of the term of this agreement.

EXAMPLE 4: Possible Further Extension

8. Artist shall not perform any selection or portion thereof recorded hereunder for the purpose of making records for any person other than Company at any time prior to the expiration of the later of the following dates (such later date, with respect to any such selection, is hereinafter sometimes referred to as the "Restriction Date"): (a) five (5) consecutive years after the date of delivery to Company of the Master embodying such selection, or (b) three (3) years after the expiration or termination of this Agreement or any subsequent agreement between the parties relating to Artist's recording services.

> ☛ The restriction may run from the expiration or termination of "any subsequent agreement" between the parties. What if there is, say, a 10-year gap between agreements (not unheard of) and artist legitimately rerecorded songs after the first contract expired. Is the artist retroactively in breach?

EXAMPLE 5: Special Provision for Unreleased Masters

(a) Nor will I perform any selection recorded hereunder for the purpose of making records (other than permitted recordings) for anyone other than Company, if Company is the direct distributor, (i) for two (2) consecutive years after the date of expiration or other termination of this Agreement, or (ii) for five (5) consecutive years after the recording of the recordings, whichever is the later. In the event of masters unreleased during the term of this Agreement re-recording restrictions shall exist only for recordings released in the first year after expiration or other termination of this Agreement and shall continue for a period of three (3) consecutive years after the release of the recordings.

KEY MAN CLAUSE

Sometimes an artist is willing to sign with a record company only because of the presence of a particular individual at the record company. That individual may be an executive; a producer; in promotion or marketing; or, perhaps, just a good friend. Whatever the position or the reasoning, the artist insists that the agreement contain what is known as a *key man clause.*

Pursuant to this clause or provision, if the key man or, yes, key woman is no longer at the company, the agreement either automatically terminates or, more frequently, the artist has the option of terminating the agreement. Because of the possibility of losing an artist this way, companies are rather loath to include key man clauses in agreements.

Sometimes being the object of a key man clause can be a mixed blessing for a mid-level executive at a record company. There is a tendency for eyebrows to raise and suspicions to be aired that "somebody" is getting too big for their britches. On the other hand, if the artist is important enough, the key man clause can serve as a form of insurance for an executive against what might be called "premature retirement."

Two stories I particularly like—one true, one probably apocryphal but nonetheless amusing—are apropos.

Key Man Story 1

An artist was signed to a record contract by the company president, who, by some coincidence, also signed the same artist to a personal manager agreement with the president as the artist's personal manager. Somebody in this equation insisted that there be a key man clause in the agreement allowing the artist to terminate the agreement if the president became an ex-president. After achieving stardom, the artist (naturally) sued the record company to terminate the recording agreement on the basis that there was a conflict of interest—what with Mr. President also being Mr. Personal Manager—and the artist wanted nothing to do with *that* man. In mid-litigation, the president was fired from his post. Almost immediately, the artist's lawyer added a new cause of action to the complaint, based upon the key man clause, because . . . well, because, how could anyone expect the artist to remain at this record company without that dear, talented, sweet man at the helm?

Key Man Story 2

A famous reggae artist was negotiating one on one with the president of his record company over a new recording agreement. The artist stated he wanted a key man clause in his agreement stipulating that if anything happened to the president the agreement would end.

"Why?" asked the president, certainly feeling somewhat flattered.

"Because," stated the artist, "if something happened to you, mon, I doan wanna be on the label. If you died, who'm I gonna talk to, huh?"

"Well," replied the president, "I guess if I died, that makes some sense. I suppose we could put a key man clause in."

"Good!" responded the artist."Then I can get out anytime I want to."

Obviously, the president, putting life and limb and the well-being of the company first, decided against the inclusion of the key man clause.

SAMPLE CONTRACT PROVISIONS

EXAMPLE 1: Dual Key Man

23. If either _____ or _____ cease to be actively involved in the operation of Company, for reasons other than illness or death, by giving Company thirty (30) days prior written notice, I may, at my election, terminate this Agreement.

> ☛ This is a unique key man clause. Not only are there two key men, the absence of either of which is sufficient to allow the artist to terminate, but also either of them may leave voluntarily and give the artist the right to terminate. Normally, a voluntary resignation is excluded as a precondition of the artist's right to terminate.

EXAMPLE 2: Delayed Termination

15. Notwithstanding anything to the contrary contained herein, if _____ should cease to serve as President of Company, I may, upon Fifteen (15) Days prior written notice terminate this

Agreement; provided, however, if I am then in production of any Album to be recorded hereunder, such termination shall become effective Three (3) Months from the delivery of the Album, as provided for herein in Subparagraph 6(c), above.

THE MORALS CLAUSE

Some contracts contain what is known as a *morals clause*. This provision gives the record company an opportunity to bail out if the artist happens to be unlucky enough to be caught with his pants down, figuratively and literally. This provision was born in the motion picture industry in the 1920s as a reaction to the shock waves which were generated in the Fatty Arbuckle case.

Fatty Arbuckle was a silent screen superstar of gargantuan proportions (he was, in fact, fat) and, reputedly, appetites. In September 1921, Fatty and a number of friends worked and partied their way up the coast of California. On reaching San Francisco, this merry band of men retired to the Hotel St. Francis for a marathon party. At the party Fatty met a young model named Virginia Rappe. Without going into sordid details, Fatty (in a moment of misplaced passion and, one might add, without benefit of clergy) and Ms. Rappe excused themselves. The temporary union of Fatty and Ms. Rappe (pronunciation can be tricky) resulted in Rappe's demise.

Arbuckle was eventually accused of the rape and murder of Ms. Rappe. After three trials, and an avalanche of bad publicity, Arbuckle was ultimately acquitted of any crime, but it was too late. He had been found guilty in the public's mind, if not of killing Ms. Rappe, at least of being immoral. The scandal ruined Arbuckle's career. His studio was left with massive financial contractual obligations ($3 million per year when a million dollars was really a million dollars), an unusable star, and no practical relief. And so was born the morals clause.

The morals clause allows the record company to terminate a recording agreement for "immoral" acts on the part of the artist. The rationale is that "immorality" reflects not only upon the artist but also upon the record company. The outraged public, goes the argument, will not purchase records made by "immoral" artists and, furthermore, may "punish" the record company for being associated with them.

The problem with morals clauses is that they invariably use vague language such as "tending to offend public morals" or (my favorite; see Example 1), "[If the Artist] becomes involved in any situation, or occurrence, tending to degrade Artist in society, or to bring Artist into public disrepute, contempt, scandal or ridicule, or tending to shock, insult or offend the community, or tending to reflect unfavorably upon Artist or Company." And, quite apart from the fact that it is impossible to tell what any of that language actually means in this day and age, the decision by a record company to evoke the morals clause is quite arbitrary, and hardly ever has anything to do with morality. Basically, the morals clause is just another bail-out provision for the record company, giving the company more leverage in dealing with the artist.

Suppose, for example, one applies the "tending to reflect unfavorably upon Artist or Company" standard to the Milli Vanilli lip-sync matter (being busted for lip-syncing others' voices); if there had been such a clause in the Milli Vanilli record company contract, it is certainly arguable that the company could have terminated the agreement on the grounds that lip-syncing on a record without informing the public "reflects unfavorably upon Artist." And what if the record company knew all along? Would they still have the right to terminate the artist's agreement on the basis of "immoral behavior" when the scandal became public?

And what about the allegations against Michael Jackson (pick your favorite allegation and insert here)? Do they, proven or unproven, by any standard, fall within the parameters of "tending to offend the community," etc.? You betcha they do!

I was once negotiating two contracts with Playboy Records (yes, there used to be a Playboy Records). The form contracts contained a morals clause. I objected, and requested its deletion. Word came back from "Chicago Corporate Legal" that the one clause in the entire agreement which must remain untouched was the morals clause. More bemused than annoyed, I made the ultimate threat—I would go to the press. What would they think of Playboy demanding a morals clause? There was a long silence; then a call was placed to Chicago. After some whispered conversation, it was decided that perhaps a morals clause was not all that important and, yes, it could be removed from both agreements. (I told this story to the lady who was the vice president of Public Relations for Playboy and she told me she would have called my bluff. She might have, but they didn't.)

In negotiating recording agreements, I generally demand the removal of all morals clause–type language. I consider such provisions absolutely inappropriate, which is perhaps more of a comment on the times and the music industry than on anything else. It appears that in the eyes of most record executives the only immoral act is a failure to sell records. If Attila the Hun was selling records, it is doubtful that his label would drop him. Indeed, in certain arenas of the recording industry today, the incarceration of an artist for violent crimes becomes a promotional opportunity, not a cause for termination.

If you are stuck with a morals clause, try to limit the possible use of the clause as much as possible. This may be accomplished by using a phrase such as "convicted of any felony" (or like language) instead of "tending to . . ." or "commits any . . . ." At least this takes the decision as to whether the morals clause can be invoked out of the hands of the record company. The artist's record company may be his sugar daddy, bank, friend, scapegoat, or whatever, but it should not be his priest, and never his conscience.

SAMPLE CONTRACT PROVISIONS

EXAMPLE 1: Morals Clause—"Tending to . . ."

16. If at any time the conduct of Artist, either while rendering services hereunder or in Artist's private life, is without due regard to the best interests of Company or any associated entity, or to social conventions or public morals or decency, or if Artist commits any act, or becomes involved in any situation, or occurrence, tending to degrade Artist in society, or to bring Artist into public disrepute, contempt, scandal or ridicule, or tending to shock, insult or offend the community, or tending to reflect unfavorably upon Artist or Company or any affiliate, or if publicity is given to any such conduct, commission or involvement on the part of the Artist, which occurred previously, Company shall have the right to terminate this agreement.

EXAMPLE 2: Morals Clause—"Substantially Brings . . ."

11. ARTIST'S CONDUCT: Artist will act at all times with due regard to public morals and conventions. If Artist shall have committed or does commit any act, or if Artist shall have done or does anything which shall be an offense involving moral turpitude under federal, state or local law, or becomes publicly involved in any situation violative of public morals or which substantially brings Artist into public disrepute, contempt, scandal or ridicule, or which offends the community or which

reflects unfavorably upon Company, or any production with which Company is associated, then, and in any of such events, Company shall have the right, at its election, to terminate this Agreement within thirty (30) days after such act or thing occurs or becomes known to Company.

☛ This provision is marginally less broad than the first example: "substantially" vs. "tending." It is still pretty vague, although legal "moral turpitude" rears its head. Interestingly, this is the only example which imposes a time limit on the record company's right to terminate.

EXAMPLE 3: Morals Clause—Violation of the Law

5. If your performance should cease to be of the high artistic quality which induced Company to engage you or if you should cease to work seriously at and pursue your career as a performer in the entertainment field or if you should violate or be charged with the violation of any law which subjects you or Company to any hatred, ridicule, contempt or scandal or if you should fail, refuse or neglect to comply with any of your other obligations hereunder, Company, in addition to any other rights or remedies which it may have, may elect to terminate your engagement hereunder by notice in writing and thereby be relieved of any liability in connection with unrecorded masters or otherwise.

☛ Although this is much narrower than the previous examples, it is still flawed..The last time I checked, being "charged" with a violation of a law does not mean you are "guilty" of violating that law. I also note with some bemusement that ceasing to have "high artistic quality" is lumped into the same sentence as being charged with violation of a law.

EXAMPLE 4: Morals Clause—Felony

13. If at any time you are convicted of any felony which would bring you into public disrepute, contempt, scandal or ridicule, Company shall have the right to terminate this agreement.

☛ I once narrowed this even further for a gospel star by insisting the felony had to be for a morals offense. I guess in a case of rape and pillage, pillage alone would not allow the record company to terminate.

LABEL

> *In this lovely land of corrugated cartons and plastic bags, we want our entertainment packaged neatly . . . an attractive label on the outside, a complete and accurate detailing of contents . . . no loose ends, no odd parts, nothing left out.*
>
> —JUDITH CRIST

I'm sure all artists, prior to signing with a record company, wonder on what label they will appear when they are finally able to obtain a recording agreement. Very few ever stop to wonder, and worry, on what label they will appear *after* they have signed with a record company. The obvious answer, "the one with which they signed," is not necessarily true. (That the "obvious" is not always "true" in these agreements should be painfully clear by this point.) Recording agreements usually contain provisions allowing the company to release the artist's recordings made from the masters recorded pursuant to the agreement on any label it chooses (see Example 1). The language usually also makes use of the term "trade name" in addition to the term "label."

All major, and many minor, record companies have more than one label for released product. Sometimes each label is associated with a different type of product (e.g., Sony Music's Columbia Records for popular music and Sony Music's Columbia Masterworks for classical music), and sometimes two or more labels have the same general type of music (e.g., Sony Music's Columbia Records and Epic Records). An artist may sign with a company with the expectation of being released on Label #1 and find his record released on Label #2. In the absence of some restriction in the agreement, the company has every right to do this. For example, all three labels mentioned above are labels of the parent company, Sony Music. Thus an artist signing with any of them is in reality signing with Sony Music, which has the legal right to release the artist on whatever label it chooses (again, absent any restriction to the contrary).

One good reason for getting label restrictions written into an agreement is to keep the record company from releasing the recordings on budget albums, as budget recordings are usually released on different labels. A label restriction may also block the sale or assignment of the artist's agreement to another company. I know of one instance where the sale of a well-known label to one of the majors was almost derailed when it was found that one of the major artists on the label (and one of the main reasons the label was being acquired) had a provision in his contract that his records could only appear on the label being sold. Since the old label name was not going to survive the sale and the artist was adamant that his records would not appear with the purchasing company's label on them, it looked as if the parties had reached an impasse. A solution was finally worked out. The purchasing company formed a new label with a different name and distributed the artist's recordings on the new label.

A restriction such as the one referred to above may very well survive the expiration or termination of an artist's contract with a record company. In fact, there is no end to the mischief which may be caused by one of these provisions. Accordingly, record companies will rarely grant this sort of control (and that's what it is: control) to an artist without, at least, building in exceptions, including rights on sales of the company or catalogue.

And while we are on the subject of labels, tracking label name changes over the years reveals some interesting twists. For example, did you know that Capitol Records started out as Liberty Records, but had to change the name when it was discovered that another company already owned the rights to that name? Funny enough, Capitol Records eventually bought Liberty Records. It is amazing how many labels have moved around from owner to owner and ultimately ended up where there was some sort of "name-connection" magnet in action. In addition to the Capitol/Liberty confluence, how about Sony/Columbia Records/Columbia Pictures? Historically, Columbia Records had nothing to do with Columbia Pictures, but both were acquired by Sony and are now under the same corporate umbrella.

SAMPLE CONTRACT PROVISIONS

EXAMPLE 1: Any Label

7. All recordings made hereunder and all reproductions made therefrom, the performances embodied therein . . . shall be entirely our property . . . we and/or our designees shall have the worldwide right in perpetuity . . . to release records under any trademarks, trade names or labels. . . .

EXAMPLE 2: Any Label Plus Coupling

4. I grant to Company:

• • •

(c) The perpetual right to release records recorded hereunder under any trade name or mark, which records may include performances of other artists, and to sell the records in albums, which albums may contain pictures, prose and verse and records embodying performances by other artists.

☛ This example is part of a grant-of-rights provision and combines the company's right to use any label and the company's right to couple in the same sentence.

EXAMPLE 3: List of Acceptable Labels

d. The right to release records manufactured from the Masters under the "Company" label or trademark, or such other tradename or mark as Company may elect from a label distributed by one of the following record companies: CBS, Warner Bros., Elektra/Asylum, Atlantic, A&M, Capitol, Arista, ABC, MCA, Phonogram, United Artists, Polydor and Motown; . . .

☛ This example is a bit long in the tooth these days, but it illustrates the transitory nature of the record industry; not only are the distribution outlets now consolidated into less than half the number represented here, but several of these labels either don't even exist anymore or their relative importance has been so diminished that they probably would not be included in such a list today.

EXAMPLE 4: Same Label as Major Artists

4. Artist grants to Company:

• • •

(e) During the term of this Agreement, records recorded hereunder shall be released, in the United States, on the label upon which the majority of Company's major artists' recording are released, thereafter, Company shall have the right to release records recorded hereunder under any trade name, trade mark or label.

☛ *After the term* of the agreement, the company may release the recordings on any label, which, of course, could include budget records.

EXAMPLE 5: Same as Best-Selling Artists

8.03. During the term of this agreement in respect of Records, other than Audiovisual Records, manufactured for sale in the United States, Company will not, without your consent. . . .

(a) Initially release any Commitment Album under any Record label other than the label then used by Company for Recordings of Performances by Company's best selling artists in your genre then under exclusive term contract to Company.

NAME

Would a group by any other name sell as sweet? Names are important to both the artist and the record company. The name of an artist (or group) is a valuable commodity and steps should be taken by both the artist and the record company to protect it. This section covers ownership of artist and group names; the next two sections discuss issues pertaining to the use of names for purposes of publicity ("Publicity") and for commercial exploitation beyond the advertising and sale of records ("Merchandising").

Provisions regarding the artist's name and both the artist's and the record company's right to use the name will be found in any properly drafted recording agreement (see all four examples below). There are three aspects addressed in these provisions. The first is the record company's right to use the name in connection with the marketing and sale of the records. There is a recognized "right of publicity" which requires the record company to obtain an express grant from the artist to use the artist's name for commercial purposes (see the next section, "Publicity"). The mere fact that an artist has been signed to an exclusive contract does not, in itself, give the record company the right to use the artist's name on the cover or label or in advertising (see Examples 1 and 3).

The second aspect of using the artist's name covered in the agreements is the company's right to use *any* name—past, present, or future, real or fictional—used by the artist (see Example 3 below and Examples 1 and 3 in the section "Grant of Rights," pages 148–152).

The artist's ownership of the name is usually also set forth in the recording agreement. These provisions exist whether it is the artist's "real" name or a professional name, and whether the artist is an individual or a group.

In recording agreements where the artist is a group, there will usually be an express provision, in addition to the general language dealing with an artist's right to use the name, referring to representations by the group that the professional name used by the group is owned by them. Some companies, apparently sensitive to conflicts over different artists claiming rights to the same name, insist on tangible proof that the artist owns the name. One particularly extreme attempt is found in Example 4 below.

Sometimes, a record company will attempt to claim ownership of an artist's name. This should be unequivocally rejected by the artist as it is a ticket for the artist to ultimately be ripped off by the label. Do not confuse this "name grab" with the customary rights, referred to above, of the record company to use the name for the exploitation of the records made from the masters to be recorded.

How do you determine who owns a name? The question usually comes up in one of three different ways:

1. Does the artist own the name, or does a third party, such as another record company, a production company, producer, manager, etc., own the name?

2. If more than one artist or group claims the same name, how is it determined who actually has ownership?

3. If it is the name of a group, does "ownership" belong severally to the individual members of the group, or only to one of them?

Claims that an artist or group does *not* have a right to the artist's or group's own name are almost always based upon the artist or the group having signed some contract with a third party at some time. Presuming the artist or the group had established the right to the name in the first place (see below), it then becomes a question, depending upon which side you are on, of either attacking or defending the previous contract. There are two usual grounds used by artists in challenging the contract. One is "failure of consideration" (the thing or things of value given to the artist in exchange for the name were not delivered or turned out to be worthless). The other is fraud, generally "fraud in the inducement." "Fraud in the inducement" is a legal term meaning that *#^&% (when I was very young and saw this in comic strips, I thought this was a very elegant curse word, but couldn't figure out how to pronounce it) lied to the artist about the contract; the artist believed what *#^&% told him; and, relying on what *#^&% told him, the artist entered into the contract. If the challenge is successful, the artist gets the name back. If not, it remains owned by the third party.

With respect to the claim by two or more groups or individuals over ownership of the same name, there are two issues: *first use* and *secondary meaning*. Most state laws provide that whoever first uses a commercial name in that state owns the name. However, the real magic words are "secondary meaning."

Names of individuals or groups, or trade names, logos, designs, etc., are protected as trademarks only when they have taken on a special meaning to the public such that, when the name is mentioned, the general public (or customer) associates that name with only *one* source. For example, mention the Beatles and there is no doubt about what group this name refers to.

In addition, for federal trademark protection for a name to apply, it must first be established that interstate commerce is involved in use of the name. This gives the federal government the right to establish that the name has secondary meaning at the federal level and to issue a federal trademark—unless a third party is able to prove, in a timely manner, that they have previously established secondary meaning for that name. (For more information on trademarks, see the section "Trademarks" in Chapter 13, pages 364–366.)

In determining which of two groups will have the right to use a particular name, it is sometimes necessary to consider both first use and secondary meaning. It is also possible for there to be a geographic division of the ownership of a single name.

Example

Two groups are using the name The Woodchucks. Group A has been using the name for 5 years, but have used the name only in the Dallas–Ft. Worth area of Texas. Group B has used the name for 3 years, but has toured nationally and has released a recording. If some other arrangement is not worked out, it is possible that both groups may continue to use the name, but Group A will be restricted to Dallas–Ft. Worth and Group B will be able to use the name in the rest of the country.

The same name may be used by two or more separate parties if there is no chance of confusion in the mind of the public. For example, The Woodchucks rock group and the Woodchucks hardware store can easily coexist. I seriously doubt that any member of the public is going to go into the hardware store and settle down in the midst of the nails, hammers, saws, and garden hoses and expect their favorite recording group to come out and perform.

When it comes to recording by an unknown group, I generally maintain that if the group finds out that there is a rival claim to the name it is using, it is better for the unknown group to record under a new name than it is to take a chance and have to start all over with a different name after the first recording is out, promoted, and, with luck, a hit. My reasoning in giving this advice is that until the "secondary meaning" has been established, there is no real value in the name. I frankly have never heard a group name that by itself guaranteed the success of a group. The name "Beatles" would have no intrinsic value without *those* guys attached to it. Rather than waste time and money, it is easier to change the name and develop the value in the new name. The only client I had who didn't follow this advice ended up paying an enormous amount of money, wasted several years, lost the lawsuit, lost a record contract, and killed the career of the group in question. Seems like a terrible waste over a name I can't even remember today. Of course sometimes a group will find out about a rival claim after the fact, when it is too late to do anything about it. Two examples from my own experience illustrate what can happen when two groups are using the same name and there has already been a release of product from one or both groups.

In the first case, after an album was released by a group on a label I worked for, we received a letter from a group in North Dakota claiming they had a prior right to the name of the artist. It was not practical to pull the album back, scrap it, and produce new covers with a new name. After some quick calculation, it was decided it was cheaper and more efficient not to ship albums to North Dakota. Both groups settled back into obscurity and nothing was heard of either group ever again.

The second case involves a group I had signed to Columbia Records that released an album which sold exceedingly poorly. The group broke up and did not record again. Unfortunately, their disappearance did not stop a group in Washington having the same name from bringing a suit against Columbia Records, claiming Columbia Records had "stolen" the name from them and was trading upon their (self-proclaimed) "success." The group from Washington was looking for a quick settlement by way of a buyout, but Columbia Records didn't see it that way. In fact, the likelihood that the Columbia Records group (a 10-piece black "horn group" with an albino "chick" [that was the official terminology in those days] singer) was trying to trade on the fame and success of the Washington group (a heavy metal band made up of three white guys) by passing themselves off as the other group was considerably less than slim to none. Short of the fact that both groups were breathing and had claims to the name, there was no way to confuse them.

The case dragged on for years, with the Washington group holding out for a substantial sum of money and Columbia Records adamantly insisting it was not going to pay "one red cent." The legal tariff ultimately became too high for the group in Washington, and they settled for a buyout of, as I recall, substantially under $1,000. Again, both groups disappeared into the sunset never to be heard of again.

Both stories illustrate the importance of secondary meaning. In either case, if one or the other group had developed that secondary meaning, there would probably have been a simple solution.

The question that most frequently comes up is, Which member of a recording group owns the name? If there is a formal partnership agreement between the members of a group, the ownership of the name probably will be specified in the agreement. If the group is a corporation, the corporation owns the name and individual rights to the name will be determined by ownership of shares in the corporation. Unfortunately, most groups never bother to formalize their relationship early on, or at all. So what happens when one or more members leave the group, or the group breaks up? Who owns the name? In the absence of an agreement, each member of the group may have a claim to the name. (See the section "Who Owns the Group Name" in Chapter 1, page 7.)

If one or more members of a group leave and the group continues without them, the answer as to who owns the name may depend upon the manner in which the leaving member(s) left the group. With an agreement between the members of the group, the agreement would prevail. Without an agreement, the number of members who leave may make a difference. For example, if three members leave and two remain, does the name go with the majority? A single member leaving under a cloud for transgressions, might not have any rights—or, on the other hand, might. What about the "leader" who fires the other five members of the group? Does he or do the other five members have the exclusive rights to the name? Or do they all? There is no carved-in-stone answer to these questions. The moral is: Have an agreement between the members up front, when everyone is still talking to each other, and get it in writing. Depending on the circumstances, there are a number of possibilities. Stories are legion of different traveling versions of the same group traversing the land, each version being able to trace their lineage back to one or more original members of the group. These different groups, sharing the same name, sometimes divide up the country into exclusive territories, creating the possibility that the "same" group may be performing live in five or six locations spread around the country all in the same night.

I knew one very famous group whose members left, one by one (on friendly terms I might add), until there was only one original member left. The original member, who had retained the rights to the name, put together a new edition of the group, keeping the original name. The surviving member then decided (quite prematurely, it turned out) to retire from the hectic world of rock and roll and left the name to the new members. When the former lead singer–lead guitar decided he wanted to revive the group with the member who had transferred the name to the new group, they were forced to buy back the name. But that, as you might by now have predicted, wasn't the end of it. Recently (nearly 25 years later), I was contacted by the original member who, with the former lead singer, had bought back the name. It seems his partner, the lead singer, had died and there was now a "difference of opinion" with the lead singer's estate as to who owned the name.

SAMPLE CONTRACT PROVISIONS

EXAMPLE 1: Group Name

19. As used in this Agreement the words "I," "me" and every other grammatical variation shall mean each of the signatories hereto, individually, collectively and as a member of the Group; and that the rights of Company and the warranties, obligations, prohibitions and restrictions imposed upon all of the signatories to this Agreement shall be deemed to be applicable to the signatories hereto individually, collectively, as a member of the Group, and/or leaving member. As used in this Paragraph 19 the word "Group" shall be deemed to mean the collective name (herein called "The Name") which appears next to the names of the signatories to this Agreement and is used to designate and identify the signatories from other recording and performing artists.

(a) I warrant and represent that I own all rights in and to The Name and that I have the sole and exclusive right to use and to allow others to use The Name in connection with the manufacture, advertising and sale of records. I hereby grant to Company, and further warrant and represent that Company shall have, the right to use and to allow others to use The Name for advertising and purposes of trade, and otherwise without restriction, in connection with the records made pursuant to this Agreement.

(b) I understand and agree that during the term of this Agreement, I will not authorize or knowingly permit any performances by any person or persons who shall in any way be identified with

The Name (or any name substantially similar thereto), for the purpose of making records for any person rather than Company. Nor will I authorize or knowingly permit, after the expiration of this Agreement, the performance by any person or persons who shall in any way be identified with The Name (or any name substantially similar thereto) of any selection recorded hereunder for any person other than Company for the purpose of making records (i) for five (5) consecutive years after the date of expiration or other termination of this Agreement or (ii) for five (5) consecutive years after the release of the recording, whichever is later, but in no event more than six (6) years after the date of the expiration or other termination of this Agreement. I acknowledge that the use of The Name (or any name substantially similar thereto) contrary to the provisions hereof, would cause Company irreparable injury, and I agree to use my best efforts in assisting Company to prevent any such use.

☛ All the members of this group are individually making warranties and representations and agreeing to be bound by the terms and conditions of the agreement.

EXAMPLE 2: Company Must Approve Name Change

II. Group Name

(a) As used herein, (i) the term "the Original Name" shall mean the name . . . by which the Artist as a group is professionally known as of the inception of this agreement; (ii) the term the "Name" shall mean the Original Name and every other name (if any) by which the Artist as a group may hereafter be professionally known; and (iii) the term "the Re-Record Period" shall mean the period specified in subparagraph 8(b) of this agreement.

(b) You warrant and represent that Artist is, jointly and not severally, the sole and exclusive owner of all rights in and to the Name, including, without limitation, the right to use (and to allow others to use) the Name in connection with the manufacture, sale, advertising and exploitation of records.

(c) You agree that: (i) During the Term, the name shall not be changed nor shall the Artist become associated with any other name other than the Name without the prior written approval of Company; (ii) Company shall have the same rights with respect to the Name as are granted Company with respect to the Artist's name (including any professional name or sobriquet) in Paragraph 7 and 21 hereof; (iii) the same restrictions shall apply to the Name and any name substantially similar to the Name as apply with respect to the Artist's name (including any professional name or sobriquet) under subparagraph 8(a)(ii) hereof; and (iv) neither you, the Artist nor any person deriving any rights from you or the Artist shall use, or authorize or permit any person other than Company to use the Name during the Re-Record Period in connection with any material recorded hereunder for the purpose of making and/or exploiting master recordings or records.

(d) Without limiting the generality of the foregoing or of subparagraph 14(d)(i) hereof, you acknowledge that any use of the Name (or any name substantially similar thereto) contrary to the provisions hereof would cause Company irreparable injury, and you agree that if Company initiates any action (including, without limitation, litigation) aimed at the prevention of such use, you will cooperate therewith and use your best efforts in support therewith.

☛ Regarding ownership of the name, note that subparagraph (b) provides that the name is owned "jointly," not "severally," by the members of the group. Absent any other agreement, this would give each member of the group an ownership interest in the name.

EXAMPLE 3: Company's Right to Use Name

5. We shall acquire the worldwide right in perpetuity to use and to permit others to use your name (both legal and professional and whether presently or hereafter used by you), likeness, other identification, and biographical material concerning you for purposes of trade, and otherwise without restriction, in connection with the master recordings recorded by you during the term hereof, phonograph records derived therefrom, and our record business and products. We shall have the further right to refer to you during the term hereof by your legal or professional name as our exclusive artist and you shall in your activities in the entertainment field use all reasonable efforts to be billed and advertised during the term hereof as our exclusive artist. The rights granted to us pursuant to this paragraph shall be exclusive during the term hereof and non-exclusive thereafter and, accordingly, you shall not during the term hereof authorize or permit any person, firm, or corporation other than us to use your legal or professional name or your likeness in connection with the advertising or sale of phonograph records.

EXAMPLE 4: Federal Trademark Registration

12.(f) Artist shall apply for and obtain in Artist's name, and at Artist's expense, federal registration of a trademark and/or service mark for Artist's professional name and/or logo in connection with the use thereof in all areas of the entertainment industry, including, without limitation, in connection with the recording and sale of phonograph records, the establishment of fan clubs, the rendition of concert and other live performances, and the sale of clothing and other merchandise; provided, however, that if Artist fails to apply for and obtain federal registration of any such trademark or service mark, Company shall thereafter have the right (but not the obligation) to apply for and obtain federal registration of any such trademark and/or service mark, at Artist's expense, and Artist hereby irrevocably appoints Company as Artist's attorney-in-fact, coupled with an interest, for the purpose of applying for and obtaining any such registration. Artist shall execute a separate trademark license agreement in Company's standard form whereby Artist licenses to Company the right to use Artist's trademark, trade name, service mark and logo for the purposes herein set forth.

PUBLICITY

> *All publicity is good, except an obituary notice.*
> —BRENDAN BEHAN

The fact that an artist agrees to be an exclusive recording artist for a record company does not, in itself, give the company the right to use the artist's name and likeness in connection with the business of the record company or in connection with the records manufactured pursuant to the agreement. There are now laws in many states granting individuals the *right of publicity*, which requires that the individual must expressly grant permission for their name and likeness to be used commercially. For example, California Civil Code Section 3344 provides that any person who uses a "name, voice, signature, photograph, or likeness, in any manner, on or in products, merchandise, or goods, or for purposes of advertising or selling, or soliciting purchases of, products, merchandise, goods or services, without such person's prior consent" is liable for damages (see Examples 1 and 2, below). What seems obvious to us now was not always accepted or written into the law.

Long before there was a record industry, a young lady in New York attended a costume ball dressed as a milkmaid. She must have presented a pretty and charming picture because her picture appeared on the society page in one of the local papers. Shortly thereafter, that picture of her dressed as a milkmaid appeared on the label of a local dairy's milk bottles.

The young lady was not amused. Being that she was a prominent society lady, the prospect of appearing on something so commercially common and crass as a milk bottle sent her to court for a legal solution. Try as it might, the court was unable to find any law or legal precedent that said the dairy could not continue to commercially exploit her without her permission. Well, one of the benefits of being socially prominent is that other prominent people take notice of your discomfort. In 1892, an article entitled *The Right to Privacy*, written by Judges Louis Brandeis and Samuel Warren, appeared. Shortly thereafter the New York legislature passed a law banning any such commercial exploitation of an individual without the individual's consent.

Now many states have statutes which provide that a person's name and likeness may not be used for commercial purposes without the person's express consent. Accordingly, record contracts will contain provisions where the artist, individually or, if the artist is a group, collectively, will expressly grant the record company the right to use the artist's name (including any professional name previously used or that might be used in the future), signature, likeness, voice, sound effects (my personal favorite), and biographical material for advertising and trade purposes (see Example 1).

Care should be taken when reviewing these provisions as sometimes companies try to sneak merchandising rights into the agreement under the guise of publicity rights, and artists should be on the lookout for such attempts. See, for example, Example 6 where the artist additionally grants the company the right to license the artist's name and likeness "in connection with the manufacture, distribution and/or sale of *any and all products or services* [emphasis added]."

One way to protect against having the grant of publicity rights being interpreted too widely and ending up granting merchandising rights is to add language to the publicity clauses restricting the rights granted to only the sale and exploitation of the records manufactured from masters recorded pursuant to the contract (see Examples 2 and 3). Some provisions use vague terminology open to interpretation regarding the possible scope of the company's right to use the name and likeness of an artist for things such as "for purposes of trade" (see Examples 4 and 5). When representing an artist, the paranoid streak in me wants to include written limits on the scope of any such "trade."

SAMPLE CONTRACT PROVISIONS

EXAMPLE 1: Basic Right of Publicity—Artist
4. I grant to Company:

• • •

(b) The perpetual right to use and publish and to permit others to use and publish my name (including any professional name heretofore or hereafter adopted by me), signature, likeness, voice and sound effects, and biographical material concerning me for advertising and trade purposes in connection with the recordings made hereunder or to refrain therefrom.

EXAMPLE 2: Basic Right of Publicity—Group
c. [Group grants to Company] [t]he perpetual right to use and publish and to permit others to use and publish the names, including professional names now used or later adopted of Producer, any individual producer, Artist, and any individual artist, and the individual performers of the

group performing on the Masters and the likenesses of and biographical material concerning all such performers who recorded the Masters, for advertising and trade purposes in connection with the sale and exploitation of records produced from the Masters or to refrain therefrom. Said right shall be exclusive during the term hereof and nonexclusive thereafter . . . .

EXAMPLE 3: Artist to Appear for Publicity Purposes

9. Artist shall, from time to time at Company's request, whenever the same will not unreasonably interfere with other professional engagements of Artist, appear for photography, art work and similar reasons under the direction of Company or its duly authorized agent, as well as appear for interviews which Company may arrange, and confer and consult with Company regarding Artist's performances hereunder and other matters which may concern the parties hereto. Artist shall, if requested by Company and subject to Company's reasonable availability, make personal appearances on radio and television and elsewhere and record taped interviews, spot announcements, trailers and electrical transcriptions, all for the purpose of advertising, promoting, publicizing and exploiting phonograph records recorded by Artist hereunder and for other general public relations or promotional purposes related to the record and music business of Company and its licensees. . . .

☛ In addition to granting Company the right to use Artist's name, likeness, etc., elsewhere in the agreement, this provision requires Artist to actually appear for and cooperate with Company's publicity efforts.

EXAMPLE 4: For Purpose of Trade

5. We shall have the worldwide right in perpetuity to use and to permit others to use your name (both legal and professional and whether presently or hereafter used by you), likeness, other identification, and biographical material concerning you for purposes of trade, and otherwise without restriction, in connection with the master recordings recorded by you during the term hereof, phonograph records derived therefrom, and our record business and products. We shall have the further right to refer to you during the term hereof by your legal and professional name as our exclusive artist and you shall in your activities in the entertainment field use all reasonable efforts to be billed and advertised during the term hereof as our exclusive artist. The rights granted to us pursuant to this paragraph shall be exclusive during the term hereof and non-exclusive thereafter and, accordingly, you shall not during the term hereof authorize or permit any person, firm, or other corporation other than us to use your legal or professional name or your likeness in connection with the advertising or sale of phonograph records.

EXAMPLE 5: Promotional Merchandise

8.01. (a) Company and its Licensees shall have the perpetual and exclusive rights during the term of the agreement (and the non-exclusive rights thereafter) throughout the world and may grant others the rights:

(1) to use the names, portraits, pictures and likenesses of you and Producer(s) and all other Persons performing services in connection with Master Recordings and Covered Videos made or furnished under this agreement (including, without limitation, all past, present and future legal, professional, group, and other assumed or fictitious names used by you or them), and biographical material concerning you or them, as news or information, for the purposes of trade, or for advertising purposes, in any manner and in any medium in connection with the marketing and exploita-

tion of Phonograph Records and Covered Videos hereunder, and Company's institutional advertising (i.e., advertising designed to create goodwill and prestige and not for the purpose of selling any specific product or service) your career; and

(2) to reproduce your names, portraits, pictures and likenesses (including, without limitation, all past, present or future legal, professional, group, and other assumed or fictitious names used by you, collectively "Artist's Name and Likeness") on promotional merchandise (i.e., merchandise not intended for resale to consumers) of any kind, without payment of additional compensation to you or any other Person, in connection with the marketing and exploitation of Phonograph Records and Covered Videos hereunder, Company's institutional advertising and your career.

• • •

8.02. (a) You will cooperate with Company, as it reasonably requests, in making photographs and preparing other materials for use in promoting and publicizing you, the Recordings and Covered Videos made under this agreement, at Company's expense and subject to your prior professional commitments.

☛ The proverbial merchandise camel's nose is sniffing around the tent in subparagraph 8.01(a)(2). Artist grants permission for "promotional merchandise" without any payment to artist.

EXAMPLE 6: Any and All Products or Services

5. We shall acquire the worldwide right in perpetuity to use and permit others to use your name (both legal and professional and whether presently or hereafter used by you), likeness, other identification, and biographical material concerning you for purposes of trade, and otherwise without restriction, in connection with the master recordings recorded by you during the term hereof, phonograph records derived therefrom, and our record business and products. In addition, you hereby grant to us the right to utilize and to license others (including companies affiliated with us) the right to utilize your name (both legal and professional), likeness, picture and/or portrait in any manner whatsoever in connection with the manufacture, distribution and/or sale of any and all products or services. In addition to any other services provided for in this contract, we shall credit your royalty account hereunder with one-half of the net sum received by us in connection with our exercise of our rights granted pursuant to the preceding sentence. We shall have the further right to refer to you during the term hereof by your legal and professional name as our exclusive artist and you shall in your activities in the entertainment field use all reasonable efforts to be billed and advertised during the term hereof as our exclusive artist. The rights granted to us pursuant to this paragraph shall be exclusive during the term hereof and non-exclusive thereafter and, accordingly, you shall not during the term hereof authorize or permit any person, firm, or other corporation other than us to use your legal or professional name or your likeness in connection with the advertising or sale of phonograph records.

☛ If the merchandising camel was sniffing around the tent in Example 5, he has moved in, rearranged the furniture, and already sent out for pizza in this example. Artist has given the company the right to license out the artist's name and likeness to *anyone* to attach to *any* product or service. The artist has no right of review.

MERCHANDISING

Merchandising rights refer to the company's right to "market" the artist in areas other than in connection with the sales of the recordings made pursuant to the recording agreement. Obvious examples are posters, T-shirts, and the like. Also included in merchandising are so-called "commercial tie-ins," where the artist is somehow linked to a product, for example, a brand of beer, automobile, shoe, etc.

The granting of merchandising rights is not to be taken lightly. With a successful artist, the license of merchandising rights can be a major profit center. It is not uncommon for artists to make more from the sale of merchandise at a concert than they receive for performing the concert. There is no end to the number of items which may be manufactured, marketed, and sold with an artist's name, likeness, and/or trademark emblazoned thereon.

Some companies argue that merchandising rights are a necessary part of the grant-of-rights section of the recording agreement. The "necessary," of course, refers to the necessity that the company be able to increase bottom-line profits in whatever ways it sees fit. Years ago, companies would readily waive merchandising rights, and might not even ask for them. Now, it is typical for record companies to be adamant that they will not give up merchandising rights, nor will they agree that such rights properly belong to the artist.

When the company is able to pry these rights away from the artist, the artist usually receives in return 50% of the company's net revenue from the merchandising efforts. Having obtained these rights from the artist, the company will in turn license the merchandising rights to a third party, receiving a royalty from the third party. The royalty received by the record company for the licensing of these rights will vary from deal to deal depending upon the type of merchandise, the territory, the length of time the license is in effect, the relative bargaining power of the parties, and any number of other related and unrelated issues. Under normal circumstances, the royalty for a merchandising license will run about 7% of the suggested retail list price of the item. Of course, with an important artist or project, the royalty figure moves upwards into double digits getting as high as the mid-20s and even higher in extraordinary circumstances. When the record company has the merchandising rights and licenses them to a third party, the end result is that the artist receives a royalty equal to one-half of the net royalties received by the record company from the licensee (see Examples 1 and 2). The definition of "net" may get a little dicey since it is obviously something less than "gross," and the question becomes, "less what?" Note in Example 1, below, where the term "Net Income" is used in subparagraph (a) and "net sums" in subparagraph (b). "Net Income" has a definition. "Net sums" is not defined. If you cross-check the subject matter and possible parties covered in the two subparagraphs, the language may not be identical, but it sure looks like the same stuff to me. "Curiouser and curiouser," said Alice while in Wonderland.

There is no logical or legal reason why an artist should not be able to deal directly with any merchandising company, thus eliminating the record company's "middleman" cut. Record companies, however, faced with such a possibility, can always use the classic "take it or leave it" line of argument, which often has persuasive powers that go far beyond logic.

A relatively new merchandising wrinkle in the record industry is the creation by some of the major record companies of separate merchandising companies which not only aggressively woo the companies' own artists, but also go after major artists recording for other labels. This development will obviously foster an industry climate in which more and more companies will negotiate on a "take it or leave it" basis, especially with new artists.

The "right of publicity" is an individual's right (or in the case of a dead individual, the estate's right) to grant or not grant the use of the individual's name and/or likeness for commercial purposes. The right of publicity is an outgrowth and extension of the right of privacy. The difference between the two rights is that the right of privacy deals with a person's right to, literally, privacy, and the right of publicity deals with commercial exploitation. By becoming a "public figure," by choice or by accident, an individual may lose the right of privacy—just stand in the checkout line at any supermarket and you will see ample proof of this. The right of publicity is another matter. For example, the Supreme Court recognized the right of publicity in a 1977 case involving a "human cannonball"(!) when it upheld the cannonball's claim of damages against a television station. The television station telecast the cannonball's entire act and, as a result, he successfully argued, he was damaged from a loss of ticket sales.[2] (This gives new meaning to the term "arc of a story.")

Being a public figure, however, does not give a third party the right to commercially exploit an individual. This is a whole different kettle of fish. Over the years there has been a steady growth of court cases dealing with this issue. One of the earliest indicating the direction of the law in this area was the Nancy Sinatra "These Boots Are Made for Walking" litigation, where a celebrity "soundalike" impersonator was used to sell automobile tires.[3] More recent cases involved Tom Waits[4] and Bette Midler.[5]

California, for example, has a law, California Civil Code Section 990, which protects a celebrity from the unauthorized use of his or her likeness or image for commercial gain. In terms of merchandising, Section 990 clearly limits commercial appropriation of a celebrity's name and likeness for commercial endeavors. There is a clear distinction under California Civil Code Section 990 between a commercial appropriation—such as using a celebrity's likeness on coffee mugs, posters, sweatshirts, etc.—and the use of a celebrity in a dramatic fictionalization. When it comes to using a celebrity as a character in, for example, a television movie of the week, it gets a little fuzzy as to what is and what is not allowed.

Other states also have laws similar to California Civil Code Section 990. Probably the most comprehensive of the laws is Tennessee's Personal Rights Protection Act of 1984. The law could probably and more correctly be called "The Elvis Presley Protection Act of 1984" as it seems to have been passed by the Tennessee Legislature to protect that particular local industry. Section 47-25-1103 of the act expressly grants property rights in the use of the name, photograph, and/or likeness of any individual:

(a) Every individual has a property right in the use of his name, photograph, or likeness in any medium in any manner.
(b) The individual rights provided for in subsection (a) shall constitute property rights and shall be freely assignable and licensable, and shall not expire on the death of the individual so protected, whether or not such rights were commercially exploited by the individual during the individual's lifetime, but shall be descendable to the executors, assigns, heirs, or devisees of the individual so protected by this part.

---

[2] *Zacchini v. Scripps-Howard Broadcasting Co.*, 433 U.S. 562 (1977).
[3] *Sinatra v. Goodyear Tire and Rubber Co.*, 435 F.2d 711, 717–718 (9th Cir. 1970), cert. denied, 402 U.S. 906 (1971).
[4] *Waits v. Frito-Lay, Inc.*, 978 F.2d 1093 (9th Cir. 1992), cert. denied, 506 U.S. 1080 (1993).
[5] *Midler v. Ford Motor Co.*, 849 F.2d 460 (9th Cir. 1988).

To fill in more details on this picture, let's move on to the next section of "The Elvis Presley Protection Act of . . ." Oops, sorry, the Personal Rights Protection Act of 1984, Section 47-25-1104, which under the heading "Exclusivity and Duration of Right" states:

(a) The rights provided for in this part shall be deemed exclusive to the individual, subject to the assignment or licensing of such rights as provided in §47-25-1103, during such individual's lifetime and to the executors, heirs, assigns, or devisees for a period of ten (10) years after the death of the individual.

(b) (1) Commercial exploitation of the property right by any executor, assignee, heir, or devisee if the individual is deceased shall maintain the right as his exclusive property until the right is terminated in this subsection.

(2) The exclusive right to commercial exploitation of the property rights is terminated by proof of the non-use of the name, likeness, or image of any individual for commercial purposes by an executor, assignee, heir, or devisee to such use for a period of two (2) years subsequent to the initial ten (10) year period following the individual's death.

In other words, the Tennessee law allows the right of publicity (and the income flow therefrom) to continue as long as there is no "non-use" for a period of 2 years—potentially, thus, in perpetuity. That's longer than copyright protection.

The commercial use of a celebrity's identity, even implied, may be protected. On June 1, 1993, the United States Supreme Court, without dissent, refused to hear an appeal from the sponsor of a television commercial, Samsung Electronics, which appealed a California federal court decision that said:[6]

[T]he law protects the celebrity's sole right to exploit the value [of] a celebrity identity . . . whether the celebrity has achieved this fame out of rare ability, dumb luck or a combination thereof.

The "rare ability, dumb luck or a combination thereof" in question was that of Vanna White. The ad showed "scenes from the 21st century," including the "Longest Running Game Show, 2012 A.D." in which a robot in a wig, gown, and jewelry, presumably resembling Ms. White, hosted a television game show. The dissenting judge in the 9th Circuit Court wrote: "Under the majority's view of the law, Gene Autry could have brought an action against all other singing cowboys. Sylvester Stallone could sue actors who play blue-collar boxers." (Indeed, perhaps Gene Autry could have sued Sylvester Stallone for slander for his performance in the justly forgotten movie *Rhinestone Cowboy*.)

SAMPLE CONTRACT PROVISIONS

EXAMPLE 1: Merchandising Rights Granted

12. *Company's Rights*. Artist hereby grants to Company in perpetuity, throughout the universe, the following rights: . . .

(a) The exclusive right to use and/or sublicense others to use Artist's name, logo, likeness and/or performance for merchandising and other commercial purposes (but excluding any use constitut-

---

[6]*White v. Samsung Electronics America, Inc.*, 971 F. 2d 1395 (9th Cir. 1992), cert. denied, 508 U.S. 951 (1993).

ing an endorsement of any product), whether related or not related to the manufacture or sale of phonograph records, including, without limitation, in connection with the sale (whether through "flyers," "bouncebacks" and similar album inserts, or otherwise) of t-shirts and other clothing, posters, stickers and novelties. Upon Company's request, Artist shall execute a license agreement to effectuate the foregoing license, which license agreement shall contain standard terms and provisions customarily used in the licensing of name and likeness rights. Company agrees to pay to Artist fifty percent (50%) of the Net Income derived by Company from the merchandising and exploitation of Artist's name and likeness. For purposes of this paragraph 12(e), "Net Income" shall mean the gross income actually received by Company which is derived directly from the advertising or sale of phonograph records.

(b) You hereby grant to us the exclusive worldwide right during the term hereof and non-exclusive right thereafter to utilize and to license others (including companies affiliated with us) to utilize your name (both legal and professional), likeness, picture and/or portrait in any manner whatsoever in connection with the manufacture, distribution and/or sale of any and all products or services during the term of this Agreement, it being understood that a license or contract entered into within the term of this Agreement shall continue in force for the period of such license. In addition to any other compensation provided for in this Agreement, we shall credit your royalty account hereunder with fifty percent (50%) of the net sums earned and received by us in connection without exercise of the rights granted pursuant to the preceding sentence.

> ☛ Note that the only restriction on the company's right to use or license merchandising rights seems to be the exclusion in (a) of the "endorsement of any product." However, look at (b) where the same rights are granted to company and the company may use or license the rights "in any manner whatsoever." This, along with the other inconsistency referred to in the text, makes one wonder whether this is bad drafting or what my first boss referred to as "using the fine Italian hand"—a reference to our old friend Niccolò Machiavelli.

EXAMPLE 2: Types of Products
9. MERCHANDISING

(a) In addition to the rights set forth in Paragraph 4, Artist hereby grants to Company the worldwide right, exclusively during the term of this Agreement and non-exclusively thereafter to use and allow others to use Artist's name (legal and professional), voices, sound effects, signature, likeness, caricature and biographical material throughout the world in connection with merchandising of products of any kind, including without limitation, posters, paperback books and comic books, cartoon and newspaper publications, apparel, hats, novelties, toys, food, drink and other goods and services whether of a similar or dissimilar nature, together with commercial tie-in rights of any kind whatsoever.

(b) In connection with the exploitation by Company of the rights granted in this Paragraph 9, and in addition to any other amounts payable to Artist hereunder, Company will pay Artist an amount, if and when received by Company, equal to Fifty Percent (50%) of the net monies received by Company from persons licensed by Company to exercise any of the merchandising rights. If Company engages directly in the merchandising of such products, other than through a licensee, Company shall pay Artist Fifty Percent (50%) of all monies received by or credited to Company from such exploitation, after deducting Company's actual out-of-pocket costs incurred directly in relation thereto.

ARTWORK AND PHOTOGRAPHS

What is art? Nature concentrated.

HONORÉ DE BALZAC

Some artists want rights of approval over the artwork used on album jackets, photographs used in publicity, biographies, etc., and some want to supply this material. Although my own experience has been that most record company art departments are good at what they do, and are delighted to work with artists, it never hurts to have the right to approve what goes out with your face on it. However, as the following true story illustrates, artist participation may not always expedite the design process (to put it politely).

A major artist came into my office (I was then working for a well-known label) with a flimsy piece of typing paper.

"This is it!!" he exclaimed, waving the paper excitedly.

"This is what?" I replied warily. I had been to the well several times with this artist already—usually to find either a dry well or one filled with snakes.

"My new cover!"

I looked at the paper dubiously. On it were a bass, a guitar, and a snare drum and sticks, arranged somewhat haphazardly and looking very like a not-very-talented second-grader's work.

I immediately started bobbing and weaving. I've spent enough time in the Music War trenches to sense trouble brewing.

"You mean . . . that's the *design* you want?" [Damage control in action.]

"No," he explained patiently, "this *is* the artwork." [A direct hit.]

I squinted at the artwork. Maybe it would go away. Maybe this was a bad dream. "Ah," I replied—words had not failed me, it was just that I could not say what I was thinking.

Taking my exclamation as praise, he pressed on and, with a flourish, presented me with the back cover. "Ahhh," I said recoiling. Time to try a new tack: "There's, ah, stuff missing. It can't go out this way."

"Stuff?"

"Oh, sure. Lots of . . . stuff."

"Like what?"

"Well, the company's address is missing. There's a state law in New York . . . you've got to have an address for people to write to with complaints." ["If I saw this cover," I thought to myself, "I'd want to write and complain."]

"What's the address?" he asked. I told him. "Lemme borrow your pen."

I watched in horror as he scribbled in the address on the back cover. I finally convinced him that he should discuss this with the Art Department. The Art Department, God bless 'em, prevailed. We didn't use the artist's cover.

Some companies are willing to grant artists the right of approval, some aren't. In any case, the real issue is not really approval versus no approval, it is the possibility that any approval process involving the artist will result in lost time (see Example 1). Even when the artist's approval is not required, the one thing most likely to hold up the release of an album is the artwork for the jackets—there are always last-minute corrections which must be made.

Another story from the wonderful world of artists and artwork approval: A friend of mine told me that he was once invited to a meeting where Stevie Wonder was coming in to approve the artwork on his new album. Wonder was led to the desk with the proofs of the cover, ran his hand over the artwork, and declared, "This isn't the shade of brown I OK'd." And so they had to change the shade of brown.

Another possibility is that the artist's requests—or the material actually submitted by the artist—will drive the total cost of the artwork beyond the record company's projected budget. In agreements granting the artist some level of control over artwork for covers and booklets, there will sometimes be a provision dealing with overbudget costs (see Example 3).

If there are approval rights, the company will insist that there be specified periods, usually the shorter the better, during which the artist must register any complaints. If the artist does not communicate disapproval, usually in writing, within a specified period, approval is usually deemed given by default (see Example 5). However, the artist may be able to turn this around, specifying that failure to communicate is deemed to be disapproval.

Sometimes the right of approval granted to the artist by the record company may only extend as far as the approval of photographs containing the artist's likeness. Contracts in the film industry, where this is a more sensitive matter, frequently provide for what is known as a "floor," whereby the artist agrees to approve for use a minimum percentage, usually 50%, of the photographs submitted to him or her for approval.

When I was a baby lawyer at Capitol Records, one of my many jobs (and probably the one that was the most fun) was to clear all album covers, backs, inserts, etc., for legal problems, such as copyright notices, trademarks, libel, clearances, credits, publishing information, and any other thing that caught my eye as being not quite right. I was the "Court of Last Resort"—and the number of problems I found was staggering. To this day, the first thing I do when I pick up a new album—anybody's—after seeing who the artist is, is to look for the copyright notice. I am proud to say that during my entire stay at Capitol Records only one cover was called back, and that was the only cover that wasn't run by me for approval. Of course, to be honest, I would have cleared the cover had they run it past me. Who was I to question the Beatles if they wanted to put dead babies (or, at least, baby dolls) on their cover? (*Historical notes*: Copies of the Beatles cover which was pulled back are now worth a great deal of money. I had the original proofs in my desk—and someone stole them. Another historical note, one I am proud of: I also cleared the *Sgt. Pepper's Lonely Hearts Club Band* cover, stating to the head of the Legal Department, "Oh, no, Skip. Those aren't marijuana plants.")

SAMPLE CONTRACT PROVISIONS

EXAMPLE 1: Artist's Approval in 5 Business Days

12. Prior to the initial release in the United States of each LP released hereunder, Company shall submit to you for your approval the camera-ready artwork which Company has prepared for use on the outside packaging of the applicable LP. You agree to give your approval or disapproval of such camera-ready artwork within five (5) business days after Company's request therefor. Any disapproval of such artwork shall set forth the specific basis for same. If you fail to approve or disapprove of such artwork within said five (5) day period, then your approval shall be deemed granted. You approval under this Paragraph 12 shall not be unreasonably withheld.

☛ "Business days," as a unit of measure of time, excludes weekends and holidays.

EXAMPLE 2: Artist May Submit Photographs for Covers

15. (b) During the Term, you shall have the right to submit to Company pre-approved photographs of, and biographical material concerning Artist to be used by Company for the purposes set forth herein, including, without limitation, the album cover artwork (if applicable) for the initial United States release during the Term of each LP comprising part of the minimum recording obligation hereunder, provided that any such pre-approved photographs and biographical material respecting any particular LP shall be submitted four (4) weeks prior to the delivery of the . . . [masters for the LP].

EXAMPLE 3: Overbudget Costs Charged to Artist

7A.   (b) All costs up to the amount of Five Thousand ($5,000) Dollars which are incurred by Company in connection with the preparation of such artwork hereunder for any particular LP shall be borne by Company and shall not be charged against or recoupable from any royalties accruing to your credit hereunder. If, due to any changes requested by you and incorporated by Company into such artwork, the total cost shall exceed such Five Thousand ($5,000) Dollar amount, then you shall be responsible for such excess.

☛ The average cover budgets for most major label releases is well above this amount
   these days.

EXAMPLE 4: Only Photographs and Biographies Submitted by Artist

12. We shall only use such photographs or biographies of you hereunder in the United States during the term hereof as shall have been submitted by you. However, in the event that you should fail to submit sufficient photographs and biographies within seven (7) business days after our written request therefor, we shall have the right to utilize such photographs and biographies as we shall select.

EXAMPLE 5: Artist's Right of Consultation

8.07. (a) In preparation for the initial release in the United States during the term hereof of each Commitment Album and any Recompilation Album, Company will consult with you regarding the "Album Artwork" (as herein defined). As used herein, the term "Album Artwork" means all artwork, photography or other graphics and related materials for the packaging of the applicable Album. You shall have the right, exercisable, if at all, within five (5) business days after such Album Artwork has been made available to you at Company's offices for review and comment, to disapprove such Album Artwork. Unless otherwise provided in this paragraph 8.07, Company will make such changes in the Album Artwork as you reasonably request.

(b) Company will not be required to make any changes which would delay the release of the applicable Album beyond the scheduled date or which would require Company to incur any Special Packaging Costs. Any premium charges incurred to meet the release schedule because of delays in approvals by you will constitute Advances and may be recouped by Company from any and all monies becoming due to you hereunder. Upon completion of the Album Artwork, Company will determine and advise you if the costs for the manufacturing of the packaging would require Company to incur Special Packaging Costs. If, within five (5) business days thereafter, you notify Company of your objection to such Special Packaging Costs in connection with such Album Artwork, and Company nevertheless uses such Album Artwork, Company shall not recoup Special Packaging Costs hereunder. No failure to so advise you will be deemed a breach hereof, provided that if Company fails to so advise you, Company will not recoup any such Special Packaging Costs.

(c) Company will not be required to make any change which in Company's reasonable, good faith opinion is patently offensive, constitutes an obscenity, violates any law, infringes or violates the rights of any Person, or which might subject Company to liability or unfavorable regulatory action. All matters relating to Company's trademarks, legal obligations, notices or disclosures deemed advisable by Company's attorneys or other requirements will be determined in Company's sole discretion.

NOTICE PROVISIONS

Although generally thought of as boilerplate, the notice provisions of an agreement can be very important. *Notice provisions* provide the official (contractual) method of communicating between parties. Whether a notice was or was not sent or "served" properly may make all the difference in the world in the case of any dispute or conflict between the parties. An option may be deemed not to have been exercised in a timely manner if the conditions of the notice provision were not met. A suspension or demand may be deemed to be improperly made and, therefore, of no force and effect, if the notice conditions were not properly followed by the party giving the notice. Approvals or disapprovals must be communicated pursuant to the notice provisions.

In cases involving automatic exercise of option, timely notice may be relatively unimportant even if the company does not want the agreement to continue since, unless there are firm guarantees in the agreement, the record company can virtually ignore the continuance of the agreement. After all, without guarantees, if the record company neglects to "un-exercise" the option by informing the artist that the artist's services are no longer required, what exposure does the record company have?

How a message is delivered is important. I have a problem if notices provided for in the agreement may be served on the artist in person. Not that I would imply any hanky-panky from a record company—but it certainly might be tempting to claim notice was given orally when perhaps it was not. When I am representing the artist, I always ask for language specifying that notices must not only be in writing, but that they must be mailed "certified or registered, return receipt requested" so as to avoid any future disagreement as to whether a specific notice was given or not. Rarely does the record company object. One exception will be made to the requirement that notices be sent by certified or registered mail; that exception is royalty statements and payments. These may be sent by regular mail (see Example 4).

As with delivery of product, another area to consider is *when* the notice is considered served. Does the notice take place when it is received? (See Example 3.) When it is mailed? (See Example 4.) Within a specified number of days after mailing? Within a specified number of days after receipt? When notices must be given within a specified time period, there should be an agreed-upon starting point at which the day count begins—the notice equivalent of what constitutes delivery (see Examples 1 and 2). Most recording agreements will specify when the count starts. When the agreement does not specify when the count starts, the applicable law must determine. Under California law, for example, unless there is an express provision in the agreement to the contrary, the notice is deemed to have been given upon the date it was deposited with the postal authorities.

Additionally, I recommend, as a safety net, that the notice provision provide that copies of notices to the artist also be sent to the artist's representative. When there are time-sensitive issues—approvals of artwork, for example, which must be made within a short time span—it is important to have a backup. An artist may be on tour or may not bother to open and read mail. There are any number of other reasons why an artist might not take timely action. Record companies will normally agree to this, but they do, however, usually insist that the copy to the representative be a "courtesy copy" (see Examples 3 and 4). If the copy is not sent as a "courtesy" but as a condition, the failure to send the copy might be a failure of a condition and the notice given not effective.

SAMPLE CONTRACT PROVISIONS

EXAMPLE 1: Classic Notice Provision

15. Any notice, demands or the like which are required to be given under this agreement, or which either party may desire to give the other shall be given in writing and may be served upon Artist and Company by depositing the same, postage prepaid, certified or registered, return receipt requested, in any mailbox, chute or other receptacle authorized by the United States Post Office Department, or by telegram addressed to the party at the address shown in the heading of this agreement or such other address as either party may, from time to time, designate by notice given in conformity hereto. The date of deposit of any such notice in the Post Office or telegram office, postage or charges prepaid, certified or registered, return receipt requested, shall be deemed to be the date of service thereof. Statements need not be sent certified or registered, return receipt requested, as provided for above.

> ☞ Note that the notice provision ground rules cut both ways: The artist must also abide by the rules when giving notice to the company.

EXAMPLE 2: Personal Service Permitted

16. All payments or notices which Company may be required or permitted to make to me may be made personally or by depositing same, postage prepaid, in any mail box, chute or other receptacle authorized by the applicable Postal Service for mail addressed to me at the address set forth below my signature or at such other single address as I may designate by written notice mailed to Company at the address set forth above. The date of service of any payment or notice so deposited shall be the date of deposit.

EXAMPLE 3: Courtesy Copy

8. Where ever in this agreement your approval or consent is required we may require you to formally give or withhold such approval or consent by giving you written notice requesting the same and furnishing you with information or material in respect of which such approval or consent is sought. You or [Attorney] shall give us written notice of approval or disapproval within seven (7) business days after such notice is received by you. A courtesy copy of all such notices shall be sent to [Attorney] at the address first set forth herein. In the event of disapproval or no consent, the reasons therefor shall be stated. Failure to give such notice to us as aforesaid shall be deemed to be consent or approval.

EXAMPLE 4: Change of Address

(c) All notices required to be given to a party hereto must be sent to the address of the party first mentioned herein, or to such new address, if changed as described below, in order to be effective. All payments and royalty statements will be sent to Artist's address first mentioned herein. Each party may change its respective address hereunder by notice in writing to the other. All notices, except statements and payments, sent under this Agreement must be in writing, and, except for royalty statements, may be sent only by personal delivery, registered or certified mail (return receipt requested), or by overnight air express (or courier shipment if outside the United States) if such service actually provides proof of mailing. The date of mailing of any such notice will be deemed to be the date of receipt by the receiving party. Facsimile transmissions will not constitute valid notices hereunder, whether or not actually received. All notices to Company must be sent to the attention of the Vice President, Business and Legal Affairs. A copy of all notices to Company must be sent to [Company's outside counsel with address]. A copy of all notices to Artist must be sent to [Artist's counsel with address].

SIDEMAN

Most recording agreements call for the absolute exclusivity of the artist's services for making recordings. Normally, this language is so absolute that a technical and literal reading of the exclusivity language would indicate that the artist could perform no services in the recording industry for anyone else other than the record company to which the artist is signed (see Example 1). (Indeed, some recording agreements use such strong language when it comes to the record company's exclusive rights to the artist's work, likeness, etc., that perhaps thought and consideration should be given to modifying the contract language so that it specifically allows the artist the opportunity to produce another artist.) Many artists, however, must rely on the ability to do what is known as "session work"—appear as a musician and/or vocalist in recording sessions for other artists—in order to survive. This is known as acting as a *sideman*.

In these "more enlightened times," most record companies understand the need to allow the artist to perform *some* recording services in order to eat, to have roofs over their heads, and to engage in other such self-indulgent practices, and are willing, given certain restrictions, to allow the artist to do so as long as the recordings are not going to cut into the record company's own sales of recordings by the artist. In fact, record companies have increasingly realized that it may be very beneficial for one of their artists to appear as a sideman with successful artists.

Generally, artists who wish to perform as sidemen must request special permission from the record company in order to do so. Lacking a special provision (see below), an appeal is made to the record company which then determines whether or not permission will be granted.

Factors that may be taken into consideration by the record company in determining whether or not permission will be granted may be the following: How recognizable is the artist's performance likely to be? Will it be good, or will it be bad, that the artist's work is recognizable? How likely is it that the new recording will be an important release? It may be good, or it may be bad, that the new recording is perceived to be important. Etc., etc.

When the record company does agree to have provisions that allow artists to appear as sidemen written into their contracts, at the very least, these preapproval provisions will stipulate these three conditions:

- The artist's name and likeness will not appear on the cover of the recording.

- The artist's name and likeness will not appear in bigger type or size than any other sideman on the back liner notes.

- The record company will receive a courtesy credit on the cover or liner notes.

Sometimes, the conditions will be more detailed, and other preconditions will be set forth, but these three conditions will almost always be at the core of the preapproval (see Example 3).

Some contracts also contain a provision stipulating that the artist can do a solo or "step-out" performance if the company has given prior consent [see paragraph (vi) of Example 3].

SAMPLE CONTRACT PROVISIONS

EXAMPLE 1: Artist Exclusivity

5. During the term of this Agreement, including all renewals, extensions and days of suspension and all periods added by amendments or by other agreements, I will not perform for the purpose of or myself engage in making records (other than permitted recordings) for anyone other than Company and I will not authorize the use of my name, likeness or other identification for the purpose of distributing, selling, advertising or exploiting records for anyone other than Company . . .

EXAMPLE 2: Three Conditions

8. During the term of this Agreement Artist will not perform for the purpose of nor will Artist engage in making records for anyone other than Company; provided, however, that nothing contained in this Agreement shall prohibit Artist from either producing recordings for third parties or appearing as a so-called "sideman." In connection with any such recording for anyone other than Company, the following conditions shall apply: (i) Artist's name and likeness shall not appear on the front cover of any such recording; (ii) on any liner or insert Artist's name shall not appear in larger size type than any other sideman; and (iii) Company shall receive a courtesy credit which states that Artist appears through the courtesy of Company.

EXAMPLE 3: Group Members as Sidemen

38. Each of the Artists shall be entitled to undertake work with other recording artists as "Session Musicians" PROVIDED ALWAYS THAT:

(i) Artist shall receive a credit on the sleeve of records derived from the recordings of such performances in the form "appears courtesy of (name of Company)." The credit shall not be prominently displayed and the Artists' name shall not be used in any other way in connection with such recordings.

(ii) No more than one member of Artists will appear on each such recording.

(iii) The Artist(s) activities as a session musician will not materially prejudice him/them in the prompt performance of his/their obligations hereunder.

(iv) All performances on such recordings will be background musical (or background vocal) performances.

(v) The likenesses, picture or portrait of the Artist(s) will not be used in any manner in connection with the recording or packaging of any album or single derived therefrom or in any manner in connection with the exploitation or advertising thereof without the prior consent in writing of

Company.

(vi) Artist(s) will not render solo or "step out" performance without the prior consent in writing of Company.

(vii) The Compositions so recorded shall not have been recorded by Artist for Company, and the Artist shall not be restricted from recording the same Compositions for Company thereafter.

> ☞ Of all of these examples, this one is the most restrictive while still granting permission: e.g., in (ii) only one member of the group may appear on a recording; (iii) the recording will not interfere with obligations under agreement; (iv) only background performances; (v) no picture without Company's consent; (vi) no solo or step out performances; and (vii) a limitation on the composition recorded.

GROUP PROVISIONS

Most recording agreements, especially those using pronouns, are written as if the artist is an individual, not a group. Even contracts with groups are frequently written, at least grammatically, in the singular rather than the plural. Most record contracts for groups continue to use the same forms used for an individual and then tack on language such as:

> As used in this agreement, the masculine, feminine, or neuter gender, and the singular or plural numbers shall be deemed to include the others whenever the context so indicates.

Once past the grammatical boilerplate, there are serious issues which must be addressed in group provisions. One of the issues is the name of the group. Most groups have a collective name. The record company will include language in the group provision addressing ownership of the name. Subparagraph (a) in Example 1 is unusual in that it is the record company that ends up owning the name (see the section "Name," pages 167–172).

There will also be language included in the group provision where each individual member of the group, by signing the agreement, acknowledges individual responsibility for all obligations, warranties, prohibitions, and restrictions contained in the agreement (see the opening paragraph of Example 1).

An important issue addressed in group provisions is what happens when old members leave the group and/or new members join the group. With respect to a "leaving member," the contracts will almost always have a provision granting the record company an option to keep the leaving member as an individual artist. There will be a specified period of time after the company is put on notice that the member is leaving, or has left, during which the company may exercise the option to keep the leaving member. [See subparagraph (d) in Example 1.] I have seen periods as short as 5 days and as long as 90 days. What the time period will be may have to be negotiated. The artist naturally wants as short a period as possible, and the record company wants as long a period as possible.

When negotiating leaving member provisions, it is important to include specific language covering the situation in which the record company *does* decide to keep the leaving member under contract. Sometimes the leaving member provision will include an indication of the terms of the agreement to which the leaving member will be deemed signed. Subparagraph (d) of Example 1, for example, provides that the leaving member's "new agreement shall be substantially identical with the provisions of this Agreement."

Sometimes, without such language, or in spite of such language, a new negotiation is necessary to set the terms of the new agreement. Without a renegotiation, the length of the new agreement may extend past the period of the old agreement.

I have always suspected that one day one of these provisions will actually cause a group to break up—after all, if you are a part of a five-piece group, splitting the royalty equally, and you can continue to record as a solo act for 100% of the royalty, why stick around for one-fifth, or 20%, of the royalty?

The situation in which a new member joins the group is less complicated. Normally, the group informs the record company that the new member has joined and, by so joining, the new member agrees to be bound by the terms and conditions of the agreement [see subparagraph (c) of Example 1]. Surprisingly, some contracts do not require the new member to sign off on or otherwise document the relationship. Some contracts give the record company the right to approve or disapprove of the new member.

The comings and goings of new and old members of the group can create an internal problem for the members of the group when it comes to dividing up royalty income and responsibility for the repayment of recording costs and other advances between continuing, former, and new members of the group. Whatever solution they reach may require cooperation from the record company.

Example

A four-member group that splits royalties equally records Album #1 for $200,000. The royalty is $1 per album sold; 100,000 units of Album #1 are sold, reducing the balance owed for Album #1 to $100,000. Member #1 leaves the group, and Member #5 joins as a new member with the same equal royalty split with Members #2, #3, and #4. They record Album #2, also at a cost of $200,000, which sells 400,000 units for a royalty of $400,000. Who gets what?

There are numerous possibilities. It all depends on what the parties, perhaps including the record company, agree to among themselves. As with the question of ownership of the name between the group members, wouldn't it be just peachy if everyone had agreed in writing up front? You betcha it would. (See Chapter 1, "Who Owns the Group Name," page 7.)

(See Chapter 1, "Who Owns the Group Name," page 7.)

```
SAMPLE CONTRACT PROVISIONS
```

EXAMPLE 1: Group Contract Provisions

19. As used in this Agreement the words, "I," "me" and every other grammatical variation shall mean each of the signatories hereto, individually, collectively and as a member of the Group; and that the rights of Company and the warranties, obligations, prohibitions and restrictions imposed upon all of the signatories to this agreement shall be deemed to be applicable to the signatories hereto individually, collectively, as a member of the Group, and/or leaving member. As used in this Paragraph 19 the word "Group" shall be deemed to mean the collective name (herein called "The Name") which appears next to the names of the signatories to this agreement and is used to designate and identify the signatories from other recording and performing artists.

(a) I agree and acknowledge that Company owns all rights in and to The Name and that Company has the sole and exclusive right to use and to allow others to use The Name in connection with the manufacture, advertising and sale of records. I hereby grant to Company, and further warrant and represent that Company shall have, the right to use and to allow others to use my name and The Name for advertising and purposes of trade, and otherwise without restriction, in connection with the records made pursuant to this agreement.

(b) I understand and agree that during the term of this agreement, I will not authorize or knowingly permit any performances by any person or persons who shall in any way be identified with The Name (or any name substantially similar thereto), for the purpose of making records for any person rather than Company. Nor will I authorize or knowingly permit, after the expiration of this agreement, the performance by any person or persons who shall in any way be identified with The Name (or any name substantially similar thereto) of any selection recorded hereunder for any person other than Company for the purpose of making records (i) for five (5) consecutive years after the date of expiration or other termination of this agreement or (ii) for five (5) consecutive years after the release of the recording, whichever is later, but in no event more than six (6) years after the date of expiration or other termination of this agreement. I agree that after the date of expiration or termination of this agreement, I shall have no further claim to, or right to use, The Name, and that The Name shall remain the sole property of Company. I acknowledge that the use of The Name (or any name substantially similar thereto) contrary to the provisions hereof, would cause Company irreparable injury, and I agree to use my best efforts in assisting Company to prevent any such use.

(c) In the event that during the term of this agreement any member of the Group shall leave the Group, and/or cease to perform as a member of the Group, I shall promptly give Company notice in writing to such effect and such leaving member shall be replaced, if the remaining members and Company shall mutually deem it advisable, by a new member who shall be mutually acceptable to such remaining members and Company; and the name of such new member shall thereafter be deemed substituted in this agreement in the place of such leaving member, and such new member, by performing hereunder, shall automatically be bound by all the terms and conditions of this agreement. Upon the request of Company, the remaining members of the Group will duly cause any such new member to execute and deliver to Company such documentation as Company, in Company's judgment, may deem necessary or expedient to carry out or effectuate the purpose or intent of the foregoing sentence. Such leaving member shall thereafter be relieved from further performances hereunder with the Group, but shall continue to be bound individually by the applicable provisions of this Agreement, including, without limitation, the provisions set forth in subparagraph 19(d), below.

(d) I warrant and represent that, in the event that any one or more of the signatories hereto, shall leave the Group as provided in subparagraph 19(c), above, Company shall have, and each member of the Group does hereby grant Company, an irrevocable option on such leaving member's individual and exclusive services for the purpose of making phonograph records. Such option, with respect to any such leaving member, may be exercised by Company by giving such leaving member notice in writing within ninety (90) days after Company's receipt of the notice provided for in subparagraph 19(c), above; and, in the event of Company's exercise of such option, such leaving member shall execute a new term agreement with Company consisting of not less than the remaining balance of the term of this Agreement as it may have been or be extended by the exercise of the options granted to Company herein. Unless specified below, said new agreement shall be substantially identical with the provisions of this Agreement. In the event that during the term of this

Agreement the Group shall completely disband, I shall promptly give Company notice in writing to such effect and, in such event, the provisions of this subparagraph 19(d) shall be applicable with respect to each member of the Group.

☛ In many ways, these Group provisions are similar to grant-of-rights provisions and mini-restatements of other provisions in the agreement, such as re-recording restrictions, etc.

OWNERSHIP OF MUSICAL COMPOSITIONS

The two types of provisions concerning musical compositions most likely to be included in recording agreements are (1) those stipulating that the record company, or, more likely, an affiliated company, has the right to acquire an ownership interest in the artist's musical compositions and (2) those specifying that the company will pay a reduced mechanical license fee for the compositions by the artist (or, in some cases, compositions by other artists) that will be recorded (see "Rate," page 196).

Some record companies are more aggressive than others in pursuing an ownership interest in the copyrights to the musical compositions written by an artist. Note that the record company may not restrict itself to acquiring an interest in only those compositions recorded under the agreement; it may require the transfer of all the artist's copyrights, whether recorded under the contract or not (see Example 3).

And, if the artist successfully fights off the record company's attempt to run off with his or her publishing properties as if they were pirate plunder, the next battle may be over the company's insistence upon a "right of first refusal." That is, if at any time during the term of the recording agreement, and perhaps beyond, the artist tries to sell his music publishing, he must first offer the record company the opportunity to acquire it before it can be sold to any third party.

When the record company, or the publisher designated by the company, is to acquire an interest in the copyrights for compositions, the following four basic questions must be asked:

1. How much of the copyright must be given?

2. Which compositions will be acquired?

3. How much will the artist receive as compensation (if anything)?

4. What will the terms of the songwriter's agreement signed pursuant to the recording agreement be?

The first three of these are discussed below. The fourth question, involving the terms of the songwriter's agreement, is discussed at length in Chapter 9, "Songwriter's Agreements."

There is also a fifth question which, at least for form's sake, should be considered, although in all probability it will not make any difference at all as to whether or not a deal will be made. (After all, at this point, the artist may figuratively—although I have heard of a few instances where one could say "literally"—have a gun at his or her head.) That question is, Is the record company's affiliated publishing company a competent publisher? This too will be discussed later, but the reason I bring it up here is to emphasize that when the record company says "hand over your publishing or no deal," your opinion of the affiliated publisher is not going to affect the outcome. Unless you have some kind of leverage with the record company—for example, you know that you can get a better deal elsewhere—it is unlikely that you will be able to keep your publishing rights away from a company that wants them.

Let's take the first question: *How much of the copyright must be given?* The usual answer from the artist's standpoint is "as little as possible." The record company, understandably, would respond, "all, or as much as can be taken." A copyright is not a monolith, but can be divided up into as many pieces as is necessary to serve the purposes of the parties. As a practical matter, what we are discussing is a division of income and delegation of control.

Since we are discussing the division of income, it is probably a good thing to explain a few basics about just what income we are talking about dividing up here. (The different sources of income are discussed later in Chapter 9, "Songwriters' Agreements," pages 287–297.) As a general rule of thumb, income from those sources for the commercial exploitation of musical compositions is divided between what are known as the *songwriter's share* and *the publisher's share.* Terminology gets a little tricky here, and sometimes you must read or listen to the references in context in order to figure out which "income" is being discussed. Like the old story about Eskimos having nearly a hundred different words to describe "ice," music publishers have many different words to describe income.

The confusion can grow when faced with the common practice of referring to two separate "one hundred percents" when discussing income from the exploitation of musical compositions. One of the "one hundred percents" is the songwriter's share of income (usually one-half of the total income), and the other "one hundred percent" is the publisher's share of income (the other one-half)—adding up to two "one hundred percents." When there is more than one songwriter or publisher for a song, the shares of the respective songwriters and publishers are described as being a percentage share of the appropriate "one hundred percent." For example, equal copublishers would be described as each having a 50% share of the publisher's share.

Perhaps the following example will help sort out the definitions:

Example

Presume a musical composition ("Song") written by Songwriter #1 and Songwriter #2, each with an equal share of songwriters' royalties. The copyright in Song is owned equally by two publishers, Co-publisher #1 and Co-publisher #2.

1. $1,000 is earned by Song (the *gross income*).
2. Copublisher #1 is the administrator and takes an administration fee of 10%, or $100 (*administration income*).
3. The remaining sum is 90% of gross income, or $900 (the net income).
4. The net income, $900, is divided into two equal shares:
    (a) $450 to the songwriters (the *songwriter's share*) of income which is divided:
        (i) 50% of songwriter's share or $225 to Songwriter #1; and
        (ii) 50% of songwriter's share or $225 to Songwriter #2.
    (b) $450 to the copublishers (the *publisher's share*) of income which is divided:
        (i) 50% of publisher's share or $225 to Copublisher #1; and
        (ii) 50% of publisher's share or $225 to Copublisher #2.

Now back to the matter at hand: what share of the copyright ownership (the publishing) the record company is going to claim.

The percentage of ownership transferred to the record company can become a major negotiating point in entering into a record contract. The starting point for most record companies is to ask for full ownership of the copyrights, which is 100% of the publishing. Probably the most commonly negotiated compromise (if there is one) between the artist and the record company regarding ownership of the copyrights is an arrangement whereby the copyrights (and the publishing) are owned 50% by the record company and 50% by the artist. This is what is known as a *copublishing agreement*. (Chapter 10 discusses copublishing agreements in detail.) Do note that the relative percentages are subject to negotiation and agreement and may be any combination, for example, 60%–40%, 75%–25%, etc. The acquisition of the copyrights, or a portion of the copyrights, is usually accomplished with a provision in the recording agreement (see Example 4), but may be done with a separate copublishing agreement, if the copyright ownership is split, or by either a separate or attached songwriter's agreement (see Examples 1, 2, and 3).

The second question to be dealt with when the record company has pried your publishing away from you is, *Which compositions will be acquired?* There are four possibilities:

1. The company acquires an interest in all compositions written prior to the recording agreement and during the term of the recording agreement.

2. The company acquires an interest in all compositions written during the term of the recording agreement.

3. The company acquires an interest only in those compositions recorded by the artist pursuant to the recording agreement.

4. The artist signs a separate exclusive songwriter's contract which may continue after the recording contract has expired or otherwise terminated.

Normally, it is in the artist's best interests that, if all or a share of the copyrights must be given up, the agreement should be restricted to the third possibility: compositions recorded during the term of the recording agreement. If, on behalf of the artist, I am able to obtain that restriction, I usually also try to further restrict the company's rights to compositions which are "initially" recorded pursuant to the terms of the recording agreement. The example below illustrates what can happen if that modification is not made part of the restriction.

Example

Artist is signed to Record Company. Artist's contract provides that any composition Artist records for Record Company shall become the property of Record Company. Artist now writes a song ("Song") which is recorded by another artist on another label. The recording of Song becomes a smash hit. The record goes to #1 and stays there for 36 weeks. There are 347 cover records of Song.

As the legal owner of Song, Artist is happy indeed. Record Company suggests to Artist that, gee, wouldn't it be great to have a recording by the Writer/Artist of the Song. Artist complies and records Song for Record Company. Record Company thereby acquires the copyright to Song, an obviously valuable commodity, for the price of a recording session—which ultimately will be recouped from Artist's royalties.

Having survived, one hopes, the first two questions, the third question—*How much will the artist receive as compensation (if anything)?*—now comes into play. The addition of "(if anything)" to that question is not foolish. The "compensation" in question here is in the form of an advance and/or purchase price for the copyrights. Most record companies take the position that no such compensation is due the artist other than royalties due as a songwriter pursuant to the songwriter's agreement. Unless restrictions are placed on cross-collateralization (see "Cross-Collateralization," pages 101–102), the royalties themselves may never be paid directly to the artist, but may only be used to recoup recording costs and other advances.

Representing the artist, I always argue that recording and publishing are two separate areas and should be independent of each other. Following this logic, if the record company is not interested enough to sign the artist without the publishing, how interested can it be in the artist as a recording artist? Can the artist expect to receive adequate support from such a company?

Also, as a separate matter, the question of payment for the publishing should, logically, be discussed separately from payment for the recording contract. Unfortunately, logic is not always an operating factor in these negotiations. I do, however, feel very strongly that publishing should not be "given away" and that the artist/songwriter should receive some consideration for the publishing above and beyond the songwriter's agreement.

SAMPLE CONTRACT PROVISIONS

EXAMPLE 1: Separate Songwriter's Agreement/All Compositions

8. I grant to Company the right to acquire each and every composition, together with the copyright therein and all renewals and extensions, and I shall, in respect to each composition, execute a separate Songwriter's Agreement, in the form of the agreement attached hereto as Exhibit "A," with a publisher designated by Company. In addition, I shall make reasonable efforts to acquire publication rights to original musical works submitted by me to Company which are not written by me. If I am able to acquire such publication rights, Company shall enter into a Songwriter's Agreement, in the form of the agreement attached hereto as Exhibit "A," with the writer or writers of such original musical work.

• • •

14. The following definitions shall apply to this Agreement:

• • •

(d) The word "composition" means every original musical work (music and/or lyrics) which I have heretofore written or collaborated in writing, not heretofore published by a publisher other than one controlled by me or affiliated with me, or which I write or collaborate in writing during the term hereof and every arrangement of a work in the public domain in the United States of America.

☛ In each of these examples, whatever publishing the record company acquires is acquired by a "publisher designated by" or "affiliated with" the record company, not by the record company itself.

EXAMPLE 2: Only Compositions Written During Term

15. You grant to Company:

• • •

e. The right to acquire each and every Composition and you agree that at Company's request you will execute an assignment of each Composition to a Publisher designated by Company under all of the terms and conditions applicable to the Standard Songwriter's Contract form attached hereto as Exhibit "A." Whether you sign and deliver said form, you and the publisher designated by Company shall be deemed to have executed an assignment of each Composition on that form. You will not collaborate in the writing or arranging of any Composition with any person unless such person is free, jointly with you, to assign his rights in such Composition under the terms of Exhibit "A" hereto and who agrees to do so if and as required under this provision. As used herein, the word "Composition" means every (i) original musical work (music and/or lyrics) you write or collaborate in writing during the term hereof or (ii) arrangement you write or collaborate in writing during the term hereof of a work in the public domain in the U.S.A. Any composition mentioned herein may be licensed for mechanical reproduction to Company at a rate equal to three-quarters (¾) of the minimum statutory rate per record sold, computed and paid in the same manner that other royalties are computed and paid hereunder and any other Composition written or published in whole or in part by you, or a publisher owned or controlled directly or indirectly, by you and recorded hereunder shall be licensed for mechanical reproduction to Company at a rate equal to three-quarters (¾) of the minimum statutory rate per record sold, computed and sold in the manner that other royalties are computed and paid hereunder.

EXAMPLE 3: Owned or Controlled by Production Company or Artist

10. With respect to any musical composition written in whole or in part by Grantor [a production company] and/or Artist, or owned or controlled by Grantor or Artist in whole or part, and or any affiliated subsidiary or parent of Grantor, corporate or otherwise, which is also recorded hereunder, it is agreed that such composition shall be owned and administered by Company's designated publishing company. The designated publishing company shall have the right to copyright or cause to be copyrighted any arrangement, orchestration or interpretation created or furnished by Grantor or Artist hereunder (whether or not reduced to writing or whether or not involving previously copyrighted or Public Domain material), which is in Company's opinion, entitled to copyright, and the right to renew and secure renewals of any such copyright obtained by Company or Company's designated publisher. Grantor and Artist further agree that with respect to any composition covered pursuant to the terms of this paragraph that Grantor shall execute a form single song agreement similar to the one attached to this agreement as Exhibit A.

☛ The net is thrown wide here—it includes any musical composition written by artist and also anybody connected to the production company supplying artist's services.

EXAMPLE 4: Copublishing

30. Each composition written or composed by you during the term of this Agreement and any renewals or extensions hereof, shall be co-published by our affiliated music publishing company and a music publishing company to be designated by you in accordance with the provisions of the Participation Agreement annexed hereto as Exhibit "A." Said Participation Agreement shall be concurrent and coterminous with this Agreement.

RATE

When it is a question of money, everybody is of the same religion.

—VOLTAIRE

Whether or not the record company acquires all or a part of the artist's music copyrights, the record company will undoubtedly also include in the recording agreement a provision granting the company a *rate*. Granting a rate is the music industry shorthand term for obtaining a discount on the *mechanical license fees*, or (more shorthand) the *mechanicals* the record company must pay music publishers for the right to record, manufacture, and distribute recordings of the publishers' copyrighted musical compositions. The rate to be paid is a bottom-line economic issue for record companies. The music business is a business of pennies. The difference in cost of one cent, or even a fraction of a cent, per unit may make the difference whether an artist is signed or not signed to a recording agreement.

By law, other than for public domain songs—that is, songs which no longer have a copyright—mechanical license fees are due for each individual song on a recording. There is what is known as the *statutory rate*, also known as the *compulsory rate*, which is provided for in Section 115 of Title 17 U.S. Code (the Copyright Act of 1976) (see Chapter 20, "Copyright," pages 512–519). When the record company demands or asks for a "rate" it is trying to obtain a rate which is a percentage of the otherwise minimum applicable statutory rate—usually 75% (see Example 1, which uses ¾). The statutory rate changes every two years. For the period 2004–2005, the statutory rate is 8.5 cents per composition or 1.65 cents per minute, whichever is greater. If 8.5 cents is the minimum statutory rate, the agreed-upon rate at 75% would be 6.375 cents per musical composition. The minimum statutory rate for 2006–2007 is 9.10 cents or 1.75 cents per minute, whichever is greater.

Clearly, the total amount owed in mechanical license fees can amount to a considerable sum, especially on CDs with a large number of songs and/or several very long songs. Thus the record company, if it does not itself hold the copyrights, wants contractual assurances that some sort of reduced mechanical rate will be granted to it. And please note that most companies want language assuring such a reduction whether or not the artist has written or cowritten the compositions, or controls or partially controls the rights to them (*controlled compositions*). Recognizing human nature and the desire of artists to retain ownership of the copyrights in songs they have written ("Oh, *this song*? My infant daughter wrote this—not *me!*"), the definition of what constitutes a controlled composition is quite broad. See, for example, subparagraph 20(a) in Example 3. In the record company's never-ending search for bargain basement rates and cost savings, some or all of the following provisions will appear in record contracts:

1. The rate for controlled compositions will not be greater than 75% of the *minimum* statutory rate.

2. Mechanical license fees will be calculated without regard to running time (the minimum rate).

3. The combined mechanical license rates paid for all selections on an album (controlled and/or noncontrolled compositions) will not exceed the percent of the agreed-upon reduction (usually 75% of the "minimum rate") multiplied by some number of cuts (usually 10, but sometimes more or less).

4. If the total amount paid by the company *does* exceed the specified maximums set forth in the two prior paragraphs, the difference will be deducted from the artist's royalties.

The possibilities that the artist will run afoul of these provisions are endless and, potentially, very expensive for the artist. It is especially dangerous when the artist has little or no control over the choice of songs to be recorded.

Faced with provisions that stipulate that "excess" payments shall be charged back to the artist, it is extremely important to fight for some control of the material which goes on the artist's recordings. One approach is to argue that if the artist has no say over the compositions or the number of compositions, the artist should not be charged for the excess sum of money.

In Example 5, subparagraph (b)(ii), the production company furnishing the artist agrees that mechanical license fees on musical compositions in excess of 75% will be the responsibility of the production company. In that example, there seems to be a distinction between "Controlled Compositions" referred to earlier in the paragraph and the "musical compositions" which are the responsibility of the production company. It would appear the production company is responsible for "excess" mechanicals, whether or not they are controlled compositions or musical compositions outside of the production company's control. Once more, we must wonder is this poor drafting, or was this done on purpose?

The record company is going to reduce the payment for use of compositions in any way it can. Generally, these provisions contain language specifying that there will be no mechanical license fees due for material which is in the public domain, sometimes just called "PD" (see Example 1). Sometimes, a mechanical license fee will be paid for public domain works, but at a reduced rate, usually based upon a determination of some percentage of originality as set by the applicable performance society. (For example, ASCAP says that if the song is 75% public domain material and 25% original, the mechanical license fee shall be 25% of the otherwise applicable rate; see Example 2.) There also may be provisions guaranteeing a reduced rate for records sold through record clubs (see Examples 2 and 4). In Example 4, subparagraph 12(b)(i) provides that the rate is to equal 75% of the statutory rate on the *earlier* of (1) the date recording commences or (2) the date the recording is required to be delivered. What, you may ask, is all *that* about? What it is about is the presumption that on the earlier date the statutory rate may be less than it will be at the later date. (As mentioned above, the statutory rate changes every two years and, invariably, gets more expensive with each change; also see Example 5.)

Another contractual issue involves the rate (if any) that will be paid on freebies, budget issues, etc. Example 2 below stipulates that on records sold on "lower-than-top-priced" labels, the rate will not be greater than 50% of the statutory rate per controlled selection or five times the statutory rate per album. And, of course, record companies will try to avoid payment altogether on freebies. Publishers understandably take a quite different view of this issue, insisting that mechanical license fees be paid on all records distributed, whether paid for or not. Who wins the tug of war between these two positions ultimately depends upon the relative bargaining positions of the parties and/or the need to record and release the particular composition.

As you read through the examples, consider the nightmare combination of an artist who has signed over all publishing rights to the record company, has no say over what is to be recorded, has agreed to be responsible for any costs of mechanicals over 75% times 10 cuts, and *then* finds out that the record company's "affiliated publisher" is charging the full statutory rate on all of the 15 original songs written and recorded by the artist. At a statutory rate of 8.5 cents, that's a total mechanical license fee of $1.275 per album ($0.085 × 15 = $1.275); the artist has agreed to be responsible for anything over \$0.6375 cents (\$0.085 × 10 × 0.75 = \$0.6375), which results in \$0.6375 cents (\$1.275 – \$0.6375 = \$0.6375) per album being charged back to the artist's royalties—the same amount the record company pays. How scary is *that!* Let's not even consider recoupment, cross-collateralization, etc.

For more information on mechanical license fees see Chapter 9, "Songwriters' Agreements," pages 269–306; Chapter 14, "Soundtracks," pages 401–405; and Chapter 20, "Copyright," pages 519–521.

SAMPLE CONTRACT PROVISIONS

EXAMPLE 1: Three-Quarters Rate

8. If I record any composition pursuant to this agreement, I will grant or cause to be granted by the publisher of the composition a mechanical license fee for the use of the composition at a rate equal to three-quarters (¾) of the minimum statutory compulsory license fee for each recording manufactured, sold and not returned, provided that, if such composition is an arrangement of a work in the public domain in the United States, I will grant or cause to be granted a "no fees due" mechanical license for the use of the arrangement. I agree that as a part of any assignment I may make of a composition, I will obtain from the assignee an agreement to issue mechanical licenses, as directed by Company, in such a manner as to fulfill my obligations hereunder.

EXAMPLE 2: Variable Rates

11. Mechanical Licenses. Company shall be responsible for payment of mechanical copyright royalties directly to the copyright proprietors . . . licenses shall be in the general form utilized by The Harry Fox Agency, Inc., [7] or otherwise acceptable to Company, and shall provide that (a) mechanical royalties shall only be payable on records sold and for which a royalty is payable to Artist pursuant to paragraph 5 hereof. . . .

(b) no mechanical royalty shall be payable for material which consists of an arrangement of material in the public domain; provided, however, in the event any such material has a new title and substantially different lyrics or a substantial addition of melodic material, then the mechanical royalty rate for such material in the United States and Canada shall be determined by multiplying the otherwise applicable side rate by that percentage which is used by the applicable performing rights society (ASCAP, BMI, etc.) in determining the credits to be given to the publisher of such material for public performance thereof. . . .

(c) the mechanical royalty rate for selections which are written, owned and/or controlled, directly or indirectly, by Artist ("Controlled Selection") shall not exceed the lesser of (i) the Compulsory Rate per Controlled Selection, or (ii) ten (10) times the Compulsory Rate per album, except that (A) with respect to records sold in the United States or Canada to or through a club operation, the rate shall not exceed the lesser of (1) three quarters (¾) of the Compulsory Rate per Controlled Selection, or (2) seven and one-half (7½) times the Compulsory Rate per album, and (B) with respect to records sold in the United States or Canada on any other lower-than-top-priced label, records sold in the United States or Canada to or for resale to any government or its subdivisions, departments or agencies, or military exchanges, or educational institutions or libraries, and premium records sold in the United States or Canada, the rate shall not exceed the lesser of (1) one-half (½) the Compulsory Rate per Controlled Selection or (2) five (5) times the Compulsory Rate per album. . . .

---

[7]The Harry Fox Agency in New York City collects mechanical royalties for compositions owned by its client publishers, deducts its own fee, then pays the rest to the music publisher (see Chapter 10, "Copublishing," page 319).

☛ This paragraph has several different formulas for determining the mechanical license fees to be paid depending upon how and where the records are sold. In addition, mechanicals are due only on records for which artist is due a royalty. In other words, mechanicals are not paid on freebies, promotional copies, etc., and, probably, only on a percentage of sales (e.g., 90%).

EXAMPLE 3: Controlled Compositions/Excess Charged to Artist

20. Mechanical Royalties.

(a) "Controlled Compositions" means a musical work which is written in whole or in part by Artist or which is owned or controlled by you and/or Artist or in which you and/or Artist have a direct or indirect interest in the income to be derived therefrom or from the copyright thereof.

(b) "Statutory Rate" means, with respect to each musical work recorded and embodied on a master recording hereunder, then-current fixed (without regard to playing time) compulsory mechanical royalty rate in effect pursuant to the United States Copyright Act or the Canadian Copyright Act (as the context so requires) at the time of recording of such master recording.

(c) (i) With respect to each Controlled Composition embodied on records hereunder which are sold in the United States and Canada through normal trade channels and pursuant to subparagraph 6(b)(viii), above, the mechanical royalty payable by Company shall not exceed three-fourths (¾) of the Statutory Rate.

(ii) If, with respect to any album containing one (1) LP ("single LP") sold in the United States and Canada through normal trade channels and pursuant to subparagraph 6(b)(viii), above, the sum of:

(A) the aggregate mechanical royalty payable for all Controlled Compositions on such single LP in accordance with subparagraph 20(c)(i), above, plus

(B) the aggregate mechanical royalty payable for all musical works other than Controlled Compositions ("Non-Controlled Compositions") shall exceed ten (10) times the Statutory Rate, the provisions of subparagraph 20(g), below shall apply. Such sum, calculated as set forth in these subparagraphs 20(c)(ii)(A) and (B), is hereinafter referred to as the "LP Formula."

(iii) If, with respect to any album containing more than one (1) LP ("multiple LP") sold in the United States and Canada through normal trade channels and pursuant to subparagraph 6(b)(viii), above, the maximum aggregate mechanical royalty payable for such multiple LP (which maximum shall be determined by aggregating the "LP Formula" applicable to each single LP comprising part of such multiple LP) exceeds that which bears the same ratio to ten (10) times the Statutory Rate that the retail list price of such multiple LP bears to the retail list price of a single LP, the provisions of subparagraph 20(g), below, shall apply.

(iv) If, with respect to any singles record sold in the United States and Canada through normal trade channels and pursuant to subparagraph 6(b)(viii), above, the sum of:

(A) the aggregate mechanical royalty payable for all Controlled Compositions on such singles records in accordance with subparagraph 20(c)(i), above, plus

(B) the aggregate mechanical royalty payable for all Non-Controlled Compositions shall exceed two (2) times the Statutory Rate with respect to seven (7") inch singles records and three (3) times the Statutory Rate with respect to twelve (12") inch singles records, the provisions of subparagraph 20(g), below, shall apply.

(v) If, with respect to any album sold in the United States and Canada to or through a club operation, the mechanical royalty payable for any Controlled Composition exceeds three-fourths of the Statutory Rate, the provisions of subparagraph 20(g), below, shall apply.

(vi) If, with respect to any album sold in the United States and Canada as a premium record or on a "price line" or "list category" which is lower than Company's "top priced" line or highest "list category" record, the mechanical royalty payable for any Controlled Composition exceeds one-half (½) of the Statutory Rate, the provisions of subparagraph 20(g) shall apply.

(d) No mechanical royalty whatsoever shall be payable (i) for controlled Material on records cut out of the Company catalog and sold as discontinued merchandise; (ii) for Controlled Material which is non-musical; (iii) with respect to records distributed by Company which are not "records sold" as defined in subparagraph 28(f), below; or (iv) for Controlled Material which consists of an arrangement(s) of a work in the public domain, except that if any such Controlled Material referred to in this subparagraph 20(d)(iv) has a new title, substantially different lyrics or a substantial addition of melodic material, then the mechanical royalty rate for such Controlled Material in the United States shall be determined by multiplying the applicable mechanical royalty with respect to such Controlled Material by that percentage which is used by the applicable performing rights society (ASCAP or BMI) in determining the credits to be given the publisher of such Controlled Material for public performances thereof and further provided that you shall furnish Company with a copy of a letter or other satisfactory evidence from the appropriate performing rights society setting forth the said percentage. In the event you shall fail to provide Company with such letter or satisfactory evidence of the percentage as aforesaid, then Company shall not be obligated to pay any mechanical royalty whatsoever with respect to such arranged material.

(e) Notwithstanding the foregoing, if, on any date any work becomes property of the public domain in any territory (other than by Company's negligence), no mechanical royalties whatsoever shall become payable in connection with records hereunder manufactured, sold and/or otherwise distributed in such territory on and after said date insofar as such material is concerned.

(f) You and/or Artist warrant, represent and agree that Company shall receive, with respect to all applicable works embodied on all master recordings produced hereunder, "first use" mechanical licenses as such term is understood in the recording industry and mechanical licenses with respect to Controlled Material on terms not less favorable to Company than those set forth in this Paragraph 20.

(g) Without limiting Company's rights, if for any reason Company is required to pay any mechanical royalty(ies) in excess of the limits specified in this Paragraph 20, Company shall have the right to deduct such excess from any and all payments payable to you hereunder. In the event that any such deduction is effected against an advance otherwise payable hereunder, such deduction shall not impair Company's right to charge and recoup, in the manner herein provided, the entirety of the advance which would otherwise have been payable hereunder.

(h) Any assignment or other disposition of the rights in any Controlled Material shall be specifically made subject to Company's rights hereunder.

EXAMPLE 4: Earlier Date to Determine Rate

12. In connection with Mechanical Royalties:

(a) You grant to Company an irrevocable license, under copyright, to reproduce each Controlled Composition on Phonograph Records other than audiovisual Records, and to distribute them in the United States and Canada.

(b) For that license, Company will pay Mechanical Royalties, on the basis of Net Sales, at the following rates:

(i) On Records sold for distribution in the United States: the rate equal to seventy-five percent (75%) of the minimum compulsory license rate applicable to the use of the musical compositions on phonorecords under the United States copyright law on whatever of the following dates is the earlier:

(A) The date of commencement of recording of the Album project (or other recording project) concerned; or

(B) The date of expiration of the time within which the Recording concerned is required to be Delivered to Company.

(ii) On Records sold for distribution in Canada: The rate prescribed in subsection (i) above or the rate equal to seventy-five percent (75%) of the lowest Mechanical Royalty Rate prevailing in Canada on a general basis with respect to the use of musical Compositions on standard Records, whichever is lower.

(iii) The Mechanical Royalty on any Record sold through a record club operation shall be three-fourths (¾) of the amount fixed above. If the Composition is an arranged version of a public domain work, the Mechanical Royalty on it will be half of the amount fixed in subparagraphs (i) and (ii) above. No Mechanical Royalties will be payable for any Records described in subparagraph 8(g) [freebies, surplus, scrap, etc.].

(c) The total Mechanical Royalty for all Compositions on any Album, including Controlled Compositions, will be limited to ten (10) times the amount which would be payable on it under subparagraph 12(b) if it contained only one Controlled Composition. The total Mechanical Royalty on any Single will be limited to twice that amount. The total Mechanical Royalty on any Records which is not an Album or a Single will be limited to three (3) times that amount.

EXAMPLE 5: Production Company and Rate

(b) Production Company shall cause all of the same terms and conditions contained in this Paragraph 13 to be included with the Artist Agreement so that Artist shall be subject to the same limitations and restrictions contained herein. Production Company hereby grants to Company an irrevocable license under copyright to reproduce each Controlled Composition on Records and distribute such Records in the United States and Canada. For that license, Company will pay Production Company or Artist (or the applicable designee) Mechanical Royalties, on the basis of Net Sales (which for purposes of this subparagraph 13(b) only shall include fifty percent [50%] of Free Goods), at the following rates (the "Controlled Rate"):

(i) On audio Records manufactured for distribution in the United States: the rate equal to seventy-five percent (75%) of the minimum compulsory license rate applicable to the use of musical compositions on audio Records under United States copyright law on the earlier of (A) the last date for timely Delivery of the Master concerned and (B) the date of commencement of recording the Master concerned. . . .

(ii) Production Company agrees to indemnify and hold Company harmless from the payment of Mechanical Royalties in excess of the applicable amounts set forth in the provisions of this paragraph ("Excess Mechanical Royalties"). If Company pays any such Excess Mechanical Royalties, Company may recover such payments from any and all monies payable by Company under this Agreement.

INDUCEMENT

When a recording artist is not signed directly to a record company but to an intermediary entity such as a production company, an independent producer, or a loan-out company specializing in "furnishing the services of" artists (an FSO company), the record company requires an acknowledgment from the artist of the artist's relationship to the lending entity, an acknowledgment that the artist has accepted the agreement between the lending entity and the record company, and some legally binding assurance that the artist will abide by the terms of the agreement between the intermediate entity and the record company. (See Chapter 6, "Production Agreements," page 234.) Without such assurance, the record company will not proceed. Frequently, therefore, the agreement between the intermediary and the recording artist will contain a provision wherein the artist expressly agrees to sign the appropriate document, known as an *inducement letter*, when an agreement is reached with a record company or distributor (see Example 1). This or some other provision will also, many times, provide the production company or independent producer with a power of attorney granting the production company or the independent producer the right to sign the document on behalf of the artist or artists if the artist does not sign the document (again, see Example 1).

The inducement letter will be attached, usually as an exhibit, to the record contract being submitted to the lending entity, be it production company, independent producer, or loan-out company. The lending entity will obtain the artist's signature on the inducement letter (or sign for the artist) and return the signed inducement letter to the record company along with the lender's signature to the agreement. The inducement letter frequently states that the artist is "familiar with each term and condition of the Agreement" (see Example 3), despite the fact that the artist may never be given an opportunity to even see the contract, let alone become familiar with each term and condition in it.

In the inducement letter, whether or not the artist has actually reviewed the contract, the artist agrees to all the terms and conditions, warranties and representations, and anything else which happens to be in the contract between the lending entity and the record company. For example, with a nod to the "right of publicity," the artist will verify and expressly grant to the record company the record company's right to use the artist's name and likeness. (See item 3 in Example 2 and the sections "Publicity," pages 173–176, and "Merchandising," pages 1777–180.) Almost always, the inducement letter will expressly state the artist's agreement that the artist will "look solely" to the lending entity for all compensation, not to the record company (see Examples 2 and 3), which means, in the case of a dispute over payment, that the artist may look only to the lender for payment, not to the record company.

Generally, inducement letters are fairly short, usually not more than two pages. In addition to the artist's (or, in the case of a group, the artists') acknowledgment of the existence of the agreement and willingness to be bound by the terms contained therein, there are, more often than not, provisions allowing the record company, under certain circumstances, to exercise any option directly with the artist(s) and/or have the artist(s) signed directly to the record company.

If the artist is allowed to see the agreement as part of signing the inducement letter, the artist may be able to find out what the terms are of the middleman entity's agreement with the record company. By that time, unfortunately, it is too late to object and/or all the juicy parts are likely to be blanked out.

EXAMPLE 1: Artist–Independent Entity: Inducement Clause

(c) You agree to execute any and all documents which we may deem necessary or desirable to effectuate the intention of this agreement, including, without limitation, customary so-called "inducement letters," whereby you agree to provide your services to the Distributor in accordance with the Distributor Agreement, provided that such documents are consistent with the terms hereof, and you hereby irrevocably appoint us your attorney-in-fact for the purpose of executing such documents in your name if you fail so to execute any such documents within fifteen (15) days after our request therefor.

(d) You warrant, represent, and agree to fully and to the best of your abilities perform and discharge all of the obligations, warranties and undertakings contained in any Distribution Agreement insofar as the same are required of you and to the extent we have undertaken to cause the performance and discharge by you of those obligations, warranties and undertakings.

EXAMPLE 2: Sample Inducement Letter

Date:

RECORD COMPANY
Re: PRODUCTION COMPANY

Gentlemen:

Pursuant to an exclusive agreement between the undersigned and PRODUCTION COMPANY (hereinafter referred to as "Production Company"), Production Company is entitled to my exclusive services for the recording of phonograph recordings and for the composing of musical compositions.

I have been advised that Production Company is entering into a written agreement with you (hereinafter referred to as the "Agreement"), pursuant to which Production Company has agreed to furnish my services as a recording artist and composer, all upon terms and conditions which have been fully explained to me by Production Company.

In consideration of your executing the Agreement, and, as a further inducement for you to do so (it being to my benefit as a recording artist and a composer that you execute same), I hereby agree as follows:

1. I confirm, warrant, guarantee, covenant and agree that:

(a) Production Company has the right, insofar as I am concerned, to enter into the Agreement and to assume all of the obligations, warranties and undertakings to you on the part of Production Company therein contained, and Production Company will continue to have such right during the term of the Agreement and thereafter until all said obligations, warranties and undertakings have been fully performed and discharged.

(b) All of the warranties, representations, covenants and agreements on the part of Production Company contained in the Agreement, which concern me, are true and correct.

(c) I will duly and to the best of my ability perform and discharge all of the obligations and undertakings contained in the Agreement insofar as the same are required of me and to the extent which Production Company has undertaken to procure my performance thereof.

2. If, during the term of the Production Company or any extensions or renewals thereof, Production Company shall cease to be entitled to my recording services in accordance with the terms of the Agreement, or, if Production Company shall fail or refuse to convey any of my recordings to you, I shall, at your request, do all acts and things as shall give to you the same rights, privileges and benefits as you have had under the Agreement if Production Company had continued to be entitled to my recording services and if Production Company had continued to deliver to you my recordings, and such rights, privileges and benefits shall be enforceable on your behalf against me.

3. You shall have the exclusive right to use and publish and to permit others to use and publish my name (both legal and professional) and likeness for your advertising and purposes of trade and otherwise, without restriction, in connection with the recordings made under the Agreement, and you have the right to refer to me as your exclusive artist.

4. I shall not, during the term of the Agreement or any extensions or renewals thereof, perform for anyone other than you or Producer for the purpose of making phonograph records, and I shall not, during the period of the re-recording restriction set forth in the Agreement, perform for anyone other than you, for the purpose of making phonograph records, any selection embodied in any recording which shall have been conveyed to you or to which you shall have been entitled under the Agreement.

5. No termination of the Agreement shall operate to diminish my liability or obligation hereunder without your written consent.

6. You may in your own name institute any action or proceeding against me to enforce your rights under the Agreement and under this guarantee, or pursuant to my recording rights contract with Production Company.

7. I shall look solely to Production Company for any and all royalties, recording fees and other monies which shall be payable to me with respect to the making of all recordings under my recording agreement with Production Company and in connection with the manufacture and sale of records embodying said recordings throughout the world.

Very truly yours,

_____

[ARTIST]

EXAMPLE 3: Artist's Inducement and Acknowledgment

In order to induce COMPANY (hereinafter referred to as "Company") to enter into the agreement dated as of _____ (hereinafter referred to as the "Agreement") with LOAN OUT CORPORATION (hereinafter referred to as "Lender"), and in consideration of Company's execution and delivery thereof:

1. The undersigned:

    (a) warrants and represents that the undersigned is familiar with each term and condition of the Agreement;

    (b) consents and agrees to the execution and delivery of the Agreement by Lender;

    (c) agrees to render all of the services therein provided to be rendered by the undersigned;

    (d) to be bound by and duly perform and observe each and all of the terms and conditions of the Agreement requiring performance or compliance on the part of the undersigned;

(e) hereby joins in all warranties, representations, agreements and indemnifications made by Lender;

(f) agrees that if Lender should be dissolved or should otherwise cease to exist or for any reason whatsoever should fail, be unable, neglect or refuse duly to perform and observe each and all of the terms and conditions of the Agreement requiring performance or compliance on the part of the Lender, the undersigned shall, at the election of the Company, be deemed substituted as a direct party to the Agreement in place and in stead of the Company; and

(g) agrees that in the event of a breach or threatened breach of the Agreement by Lender or by the undersigned, Company shall be entitled to legal and equitable relief by way of injunction or otherwise against Lender, or against the undersigned, or against both of us, in Company's discretion, in any event, without the necessity of first resorting to or exhausting any rights or remedies which Company may have against Lender.

2. The undersigned waives any claim against Company for wages, salary or other compensation of any kind for the Agreement, and the undersigned agrees that the undersigned will look solely to Lender for any and all compensation that the undersigned may become entitled to receive for services in connection with the Agreement.

3. The undersigned agrees, confirms and joins in the acknowledgment and agreement setting forth Company's rights in the Agreement, including, without limitation, the "work for hire" provisions, the related assignment provisions (if applicable) and all grants to Company of all rights under the Agreement, including, but not limited to, the right to use the undersign's name and likeness as set forth therein, whether or not the undersign's employment by Lender should expire or be terminated.

4. That all notices served on Lender under the Agreement will be deemed to be notices to me of the contents thereof.

5. The undersigned acknowledges that the rights, privileges, benefits and remedies granted to Lender in my employment agreement with Lender and to producer in the Agreement may be enforced against me directly, jointly and generally, by Company or Company's assignees in the name of Lender or in Company's or Company's assignees' own names and in their behalf in any court of competent jurisdiction, whether or not Lender is a party to the litigation.

6. The undersigned agrees to indemnify, save and hold harmless Company and Company's officers, affiliates, licensees, assignees, agents, employees, attorneys, successors and representatives, as applicable, from and against any and all claims, demands, actions, liabilities, costs, damages and judgments (including, without limitation, attorneys', paralegals' and accountants' fees and costs, whether or not litigation is commenced) arising out of or in connection with any breach or alleged breach of any grants, representations, warranties or agreements herein and the exercise thereof.

7. All of the foregoing shall be to the same extent and have the same force and effect as if the undersigned had agreed to render services to Company as an employee. The undersigned agrees, acknowledges and accepts the foregoing and indicates such agreement, acknowledgment and acceptance by signing in the space provided for below.

DATED: _____

CHAPTER 4

INDEPENDENT PRODUCER AGREEMENTS

Produce! Produce! Were it but the pitifullest infinitesimal fraction of a product, produce it in God's name! 'Tis the utmost thou has in thee: out with it then.

—THOMAS CARLYLE

The agreement between an independent producer and either the artist or the record company is usually quite similar to the artist's own agreement with the record company. The independent producer agreement differs from the production agreement in that the producer and the artist are not considered to be "one package," and separate contracts will be signed with each. More likely than not, the independent producer's agreement will be either directly with the record company or with a production company and not with the artist.

Generally, many provisions of the producer's agreement—royalty computation, accounting, etc.—will be virtually identical to the provisions covering the same subject in the artist recording agreement. Accordingly, for provisions not specifically considered below, the discussions in Chapter 3 with respect to the artist recording agreement will apply, and they will not be repeated here.

However, there are certain provisions that are unique to an independent producer agreement. These provisions will not be found in, or will be different from, those contained in an artist recording agreement. It is those provisions which will be examined here.

DUTIES OF THE PRODUCER

One of the most obvious provisions not included in the artist recording agreement that is included in an independent producer agreement is the one dealing with the actual production of the recording by the producer and the services to be performed by the producer. This provision lays down the rules and regulations to be followed by the producer, such as the controls placed upon the producer by the record company, union requirements, budget requirements, etc.

The following examples provide a virtual checklist of the duties of a record producer. In reviewing the examples, note the record company's oversight and control at every step of the process. Much of what is required of the producer is mundane administrative work, such as, for example, preparing budgets [see (c) in Example 1], preparing and filing session reports for the unions [see (f) in Example 1], preparing and furnishing label copy [see (b) in Example 2)] and even acting as border guard in making sure immigration Form I-9 is signed and turned in to the company for each person [see 4(c)(i) in Example 3].

[see 4(c)(i) in Example 3]

SAMPLE CONTRACT PROVISIONS

EXAMPLE 1: Checklist of Duties

2. In connection with each master produced by me hereunder, I agree that I shall:

(a) produce and record such master recordings in recording studios approved by Company;

(b) work within the framework of a recording budget approved by Company;

(c) submit to Company a fully detailed recording authorization, including, but not necessarily limited to, specification of the proposed budget setting forth, without limitation, all costs or fees paid to individuals, including but not limited to recording artists, sidemen, arranging and copying fees, etc., all studio charges, all union contributions and payments to be made, and the applicable copyright royalty rates due for any compositions recorded; such recording authorization must be submitted to Company at least fourteen (14) days prior to the applicable recording session, and must be approved by Company in writing;

(d) abide by all appropriate union regulations;

(e) maintain and submit all applicable job sheets and obtain appropriate title clearances for any compositions used;

(f) make timely delivery to Company of properly completed session reports, and of all other documents, information and other materials, if any, required by Company, in order to make payment, when due, of union-scale compensation, or in order to effect timely compliance with any other obligations under any applicable agreement with any union or labor organization with reference to such master recordings. I will pay or reimburse Company, upon demand, for any penalties, fines, lateness charges or other costs incurred by reason of my failure to do so. Any such amount paid by Company and not properly reimbursed by me may, at Company's election, and without limiting Company's rights, be applied by Company in reduction of any sums due or becoming due me under this and/or any other agreement between Company and me;

(g) upon Company's request, I shall perform as liaison between Artist and Company in all necessary or appropriate matters;

(h) mix down and edit the recordings and obtain Company's reasonable approval of the same; and

(i) deliver to Company fully edited stereophonic master recordings.

☞ This is a bare-bones checklist. Compare this with the details contained in the following two examples.

EXAMPLE 2: Producer's Creative Duties

12. *Producer's Functions.* Producer shall edit, mix and master a stereo tape, furnish Company with masters and master tapes, and generally perform all other services customarily rendered by producers in connection with producing recording sessions and making satisfactorily finished master recordings. Without limitation of the foregoing, Producer shall do all of the following with respect to the master recordings hereunder:

(a) Developing and furnishing Company with an album concept, an album title, and selection titles for each album.

(b) Furnish Company, in writing, with the label copy (including song titles and any subtitles), names of composers, any show or movie credits, complete publisher line, including the address and telephone number of each publisher, affiliate (BMI, ASCAP, etc.), serial number, timings, any arranger credits, any accompaniment credits, names of engineers, list of musicians with instruments played, exact recording date(s) and studio location(s), indication whether recording is track, sweetening or vocal overdub, producer and/or production company credits.

(c) Furnish Company, in writing, the liner credits for each album.

(d) Edit the master recordings for all types and configurations of records and furnish Company with master recordings in the form of two (2) equalized tape masters, and two (2) masters which are representative of said tape masters, which tapes and masters shall be satisfactory for the manufacture and sale of records. All work parts of whatsoever nature (including, without limitation, any outtakes or tracks recorded during the same sessions as the recording of tracks contained in master recordings delivered hereunder) shall be delivered to Company concurrently with delivery of the foregoing items under this subparagraph 12(d).

(e) Furnish Company, in writing, with the sequence and final timings in connection with the master tapes furnished in accordance with subparagraph 12(d) above. Company shall have the right to prepare the tape sequence for all configurations of tapes.

(f) Make arrangements for the preparation of liner notes for albums and for any photography, including Artist's photograph, in connection with album artwork.

(g) Obtain and furnish Company, in writing, with all consents or clearances required by Company in relation to the use or proposed uses by Company of any of the elements which are within the scope of Producer's functions hereunder. All of the services which Producer is to render hereunder will be rendered in coordination and cooperation with, and shall be subject to Company's approval and the supervision of Company's Artist and Repertoire Department. In the event of any disagreement between Producer and Company relative to Producer's services (as described herein) or the making of master recordings hereunder, Company's decision shall be final.

> ☞ This example has some unusual provisions. In (a) and (f) the record company is giving the producer a higher degree of creative input and independence than is normal. While it is not unusual for a producer to participate in song selection, rarely does a producer have a contractual duty to furnish the "concept" and "title" of an album, and even more rarely does a contract specify that the producer will arrange for an album's liner notes and artwork.

EXAMPLE 3: Producer's Responsibility for Form I-9s

4. You will follow the procedure set forth below in connection with Master Recordings made hereunder:

(a) Except as expressly noted otherwise in this agreement, prior to the commencement of recording in each instance, you shall obtain the approval of Company on each of the following, in order, before proceeding further:

(i) Selection of material, including the number of Compositions to be recorded. Company shall not be deemed to be unreasonable in rejecting any request to record an Album consisting of more than the equivalent of one CD Record. You shall advise Company of the content of each medley before it is recorded.

(ii) Selection of dates of recording and studios where recording is to take place, including the cost of recording there. The scheduling and booking of all studio time will be done by Company.

Company's facilities and the services of its engineers will be used to the extent required by Company's union agreements.

(iii) A proposed budget (which you will submit to Company sufficiently in advance of the planned commencement of recording to give Company a reasonable time to review and approve or disapprove it at least fourteen (14) days before the planned commencement of recording).

(b) You shall notify the appropriate Local of the American Federation of Musicians in advance of each recording session.

(c) Before each recording session:

(i) You will require each background instrumentalist, background vocalist, and other person to be employed in connection with the session to complete and sign the Employee Information and Verification ("Employee") section of a U.S. Immigration and Naturalization Service Employment Eligibility Certificate (Form I-9), unless you have already obtained such a Certificate from the person concerned within the past three years:

(ii) You will complete and sign the Employer Review and Verification ("Employer") section of each such Certificate; and

(iii) You will attach copies of the documents establishing identity and employment eligibility which you examine in accordance with the instructions in the employer section. If any such person is engaged during a session, you will comply with subsections (i) through (iii) above, with respect to that person, before he renders any services.

(d) You will not permit any such person who fails to complete the employee section, or to furnish you with the required documentation, to render any services in connection with Recordings to be made under this agreement.

(e) You will deliver those Certificates and documents to Company promptly, and in no event later than the Delivery of the Recordings concerned.

(f) You will comply with any revised or additional verification and documentation requirements of which Company advises you in the future.

(g) As and when required by Company, you shall allow Company's representatives to attend any and all recording sessions hereunder.

(h) You shall in a timely manner supply Company with all of the information it needs in order: (1) to make payments due in connection with such Records; (2) to comply with any other obligations Company may have in connection with the making of such Master Recordings; and (3) to prepare to release Records derived from such Master Recordings. Without limiting the generality of (2) of the preceding sentence:

(i) You shall furnish Company with all information it requires to comply with its obligations under its union agreements, including without limitation, the following:

(1) If a session is held to record new tracks intended to be mixed with existing tracks (and if such information is requested by the American Federation of Musicians), the dates and places of the prior sessions at which such existing tracks were made and the AFM Phonograph Recording Contract (Form "B") number(s) covering such sessions;

(2) Each change of title of any composition listed in an AFM Phonograph Recording Contract (Form "B"); and

(3) A listing of all the musical selections contained in Recordings Delivered to Company hereunder; and

(ii) You will furnish Company with all of the immigration control documentation required by Subparagraph 4(c), above, at the same time as the AFM and AFTRA session reports, tax withholding forms and other documentation required by Company in order to make the payments to the session musicians and other employees concerned, if any.

(iii) You shall Deliver to Company's A&R Administration Department fully mixed, edited, and unequalized and equalized Master Recordings (including, but not limited to, final two-track equalized tape copy), commercially satisfactory to Company for its manufacture and sale of Records, and all original and duplicate Master Recordings of the material recorded, together with all necessary licenses and permissions, and all materials required to be furnished by you to Company for use in the packaging and marketing of the Records. Each Master Recording will be clearly marked to identify the Artist as the recording artist, and to show the title(s) of the composition(s) and recording date(s).

> ☛ In this detailed list of requirements, the producer is made responsible for obtaining everybody's signatures on immigration Form I-9. And note the requirement, buried in subparagraph 4(h)(iii), that the producer deliver masters which are "commercially satisfactory to Company." In the midst of all these bureaucratic duties suddenly the *very* subjective obligation to be "commercially satisfactory" rears its head.

TERM OF THE AGREEMENT

Lead me not into temptation, I can find the way myself.
—MAE WEST

The length of the term of the independent producer's agreement may be the same as the artist's, the term may be for one recording only, or it may be for any intermediate period. Frequently, a producer's continued tenure as the producer will depend upon the success of the earlier recordings. If, for example, a certain level of success is obtained, the producer may be given the contractual right to produce subsequent recordings (see Example 3, below). If not, the producer's ongoing professional relationship with the artist may be cut short.

Example

A, an independent producer, signs an agreement with Record Company to produce B. The agreement provides that if the first album produced pursuant to the agreement sells 100,000 copies within 6 months of initial release, A will be granted the right to produce a second album with B. If the second album sells 250,000 copies within the first 6 months, then A has the right to produce a third album.

The agreement may or may not provide that the producer will be the exclusive producer for the artist (see Example 1). Most record companies are reluctant to lock themselves into one producer for the life of an artist's contract. The one exception here is the production agreement. By implication, exclusivity is given in production agreements where the producer is the production company. There is, however, usually some "safety valve" (see Example 2) allowing the company to substitute a new producer even in supposedly exclusive agreements. Today an independent producer agreement will almost always be on a project basis and not a term basis. A project may not even be for an album's worth of material. A producer may be brought in for just one song.

Of course, the producer wants the opportunity to continue working with a successful artist. Most independent producers who have contributed to the success of an artist, especially a beginning artist, want the right to record subsequent product with the artist. More than artistic integrity is involved here; there are production fees, royalties, and the opportunity for additional business and notoriety.

SAMPLE CONTRACT PROVISIONS

EXAMPLE 1: Nonexclusive Producer

1. Company engages my personal endeavors in connection with the production of records as an independent producer. My endeavors hereunder are non-exclusive, and Company may, at Company's election, utilize the services of other producers in connection with recordings made by the Artist. I accept such engagement and agree to render services to the best of my ability and of the same high artistic quality as induced Company to engage me, at recording sessions conducted by Company at times and places designated by Company.

☛ Under this provision, the producer literally serves at the will of the record company and can be dismissed at any time.

EXAMPLE 2: Company May Replace Producer

13. If the person(s) mutually approved hereunder to act as Producer shall, for any reason other than Company's refusal without cause to allow such person(s) to perform, fail to perform the services of Producer, or if Artist indicates an unwillingness to perform with such person . . . Company shall have the right, at its election, to designate a person(s), including a member(s) of Company's Artist and Repertoire staff, to be or to replace (as the case may be) Producer.

EXAMPLE 3: Conditional Option to Continue

1. Company engages X's endeavors in connection with the production of records featuring Company's recording artist, A (hereinafter referred to as the "Artist") as a recording artist for the production of one (1) album. . . .

(a) If, within the first six (6) months of commercial release, the first album produced by X hereunder shall sell a minimum of 200,000 units through Normal Retail Channels in the United States ("USNRC Sales"), X shall have the right to produce A's next album recorded pursuant to A's agreement with Company.

(b) If, within the first six (6) months of commercial release, the second album, if any, produced by X hereunder shall sell a minimum of 350,000 USNRC Sales, X shall have the right to produce A's next album recorded pursuant to A's agreement with Company.

PRODUCTION FEE

Producers usually receive some sort of *production fee* for their services. The production fee may be an advance against the producer's royalty (see Examples 1 and 2) or it may not be an advance against royalties (Example 3). If the production fee is an advance, it will be recoupable from the producer's royalties, which, while they may accrue from the first record sold, may not be payable until recording costs have been recouped from the artist. Additionally, the production fee may be variable, based upon the number of selections produced (e.g., $5,000 per selection), or it may be a flat rate for a project (e.g., $50,000 for an album). The producer's agreement will have a provision providing a schedule for when and in what portions the producer will receive the production fee. Most of the agreements will provide for a portion (usually, but not necessarily, one-half) of the fee to be paid on or before commencement. The remaining portion or portions will be paid according to a negotiated schedule, with the final payment due when the masters are delivered and accepted (see Example 4).

Of interest to the artist in all of this is whether or not the production fee, whatever it is, is going to be charged back to the artist as a recording cost. If the producer's production fee is an advance against the producer's royalty, arguably it should not be charged back to the artist as a recording cost. Some recording agreements, however, include the production fee as a recording cost. If the production fee is treated as an advance against the producer's royalties *and* as a recoupable recording cost under the artist's contract, the record company may be able to do what is known as *double dipping*, that is, recoup the cost twice.

Since the artist may never know the production fee terms of the producer's agreement and since the producer's agreement is likely to be entered into *after* the artist–record company agreement, what can the artist do to guard against double dipping? The answer, of course, is to remove any reference to the producer or to production fees from the recording cost provisions of the artist's agreement. Alternatively, the artist can ask for language to be added specifying that if the production fee is an advance against the producer's royalties, it shall not be deemed a recording cost.

SAMPLE CONTRACT PROVISIONS

EXAMPLE 1: Production Fee as an Advance

(b) Recordings made pursuant to any agreement between Company and/or Artist and record companies shall provide a production fee, to be mutually agreed upon, payable to Producer in connection with each master recorded thereunder. Such production fee will be an advance against Producer's royalties.

EXAMPLE 2: Fee Amount Per Selection

2. For the services to be rendered by Producer hereunder, Company agrees to pay Producer the sum of _____ ($_____) Dollars for each selection featuring Artist which is recorded hereunder and accepted by Company as a Master hereunder. All such payments made hereunder shall be deemed to be an advance against the royalties due Producer pursuant to Paragraph 3, below.

EXAMPLE 3: Fee Not an Advance

(ii) Notwithstanding anything to the contrary contained herein, the production fee payable to Producer pursuant to Subparagraph 4(a), above, shall not be deemed to be an advance against producer's royalties under this or any other agreement between Company and Producer.

> ☞ Although the fee is not an advance against the producer's royalty, it most certainly is an advance against the artist in the form of a recording cost. Also, the producer has been able to remove cross-collateralization—an important issue for an independent producer.

EXAMPLE 4: Payment Schedule

6. The Budget that Producer shall prepare will include an advance (the "Advance") of _____ Thousand Dollars ($_____) payable to Producer, which shall be the only amount recoupable from any royalties (other than mechanical royalties) payable to Producer hereunder. Conditioned upon Producer's full and faithful performance of all of the material terms and conditions hereof, Artist shall cause [Record Company] to pay Producer the foregoing amounts as follows:

(a) Fifty percent (50%) upon commencement of Producer's services hereunder; and

(b) Fifty percent (50%) upon delivery and acceptance of commercially and technically satisfactory Masters.

RECORDING COSTS

The independent producer's royalty almost always is treated differently from that of the artist in that recording costs are not recouped from the producer's royalties, but they are recouped from the artist's royalty. (See Examples 1 and 2, below.)

Producers' agreements do, however, frequently contain a provision requiring the producer to be responsible for recording costs in excess of the approved budget. (See Examples 2 and 4.) Although this provision is more honored in the breach than the observance (record companies rarely actually charge this back to the producer—they just go on charging it to the artist), it pays for the producer to object to the inclusion of this paragraph. The usual compromise between the producer and the record company is that the producer will be responsible only for recording costs in excess of 110% of the approved budget.

Another aspect to consider is the record company's control over the purse strings. The producer always runs the risk that if it appears that the production is going to run over budget, the record company will pull the plug on the sessions (see Example 3) or replace the producer with another producer or do both.

I was told a story by a record executive (a friend of mine) about a group whose sales were lagging. What was needed was a hit single. At the request of the group's manager, a well-known producer was brought in to produce one master to be the A side for the single.

The budget for the A side was generous, very generous.

The executive promised the manager of the group that a close watch would be kept on the sessions. Unfortunately, a slight distraction caused my friend to take his eye off the ball. When the session bills came in, the bills exceeded the approved budget by 100%. In other words, the session cost twice the very generous sum which had been allocated. Inasmuch as the recording costs were being recouped from the artist, it was with some discomfort and trepidation that my friend called the manager to break the bad news.

The information was met with a long moment of silence and then he was informed that the manager would be in his office the next morning in person. Now, my friend was in Los Angeles and the manager was on the East Coast, so this was not a simple drive across town.

The meeting took place as scheduled. After hearing my friend's explanation and apology, the manager calmly told him that he was going to kill him. My friend laughed nervously. "You can't do that," he volunteered.

"Why not?"

"They'll know you did it."

"Who's gonna tell? You won't. You'll be dead."

A compromise was suggested by the manager; he would just kill the producer. My friend pleaded for the producer's life and negotiated the deal down to two broken legs for the producer. On behalf of the producer, the record company agreed to eat the amount over the approved budget, thus saving both life and limb.

SAMPLE CONTRACT PROVISIONS

EXAMPLE 1: Recording Costs Charged to Artist

(a) Recording costs of masters recorded hereunder, and pursuant to any agreement with a record company, shall be recoverable from Artist's share of royalties, and Producer's share of royalties shall be payable, retroactively if necessary, from the first record sold.

> ☞ For an explanation of retroactive payment to producer from the first record sold, see the first paragraph of the section "Record One," page 217.

EXAMPLE 2: Excess Recording Costs Producer's Responsibility

6. Company shall pay the aggregate amount of all recording costs, and such recording costs shall constitute advances and shall be charged against the royalties payable to the Artist, if and when earned. It is specifically understood that any amount of recording costs in excess of the amount approved by Company shall be Producer's responsibility, and Producer hereby warrants, represents, covenants and agrees that Producer will pay all such amounts, if any, promptly. If Company shall elect to pay any such excess, and Company is not promptly reimbursed by Producer, then, without limiting Company's rights, Company shall have the right to apply such excess amount in reduction of any sum due or becoming due to Producer under this and/or any other agreement between Company and Producer.

> ☞ Somewhere there may be a case where a producer actually reimbursed the company, I've just never heard of it. Note that if the company reduces the producer's fee by the amount of the excess and also charges the excess to the artist as a part of recording costs, it is double dipping.

EXAMPLE 3: Session Discontinued for Exceeding Budget

(f) We may, at our election, discontinue any recording sessions for the Masters if in our judgment the Recording Costs incurred or to be incurred will exceed the approved Recording Budget or if the Masters being produced will not be satisfactory.

EXAMPLE 4: 110%

9. All recording costs will constitute advances. Any recording costs in excess of 110% the Recording Fund set forth in Paragraph 8, above, or other amount approved in writing by Company will be your sole responsibility and will be paid by you promptly or reimbursed by you if paid by Company.

> ☞ The built-in 10% cushion protects the producer from being responsible for minor overruns.

PRODUCER'S ROYALTY

The royalty for independent producers, including the formulas for the calculation of the royalty, is set forth in the producer's agreement and may or may not be tied into the artist's or production company's royalty. In other words, it may be set forth in full without any reference to the artist's or production company's royalty provisions, or it may either incorporate or make reference to the underlying agreement with the artist or production company (see Example 2, below). Many of the same possibilities which exist for an artist negotiating an agreement will also exist for a producer, such as, for example, a royalty escalation (see Example 1 and the section "Royalty Acceleration" in Chapter 3, pages 68–70).

The traditional (but not universal) range for record producers' royalties is 3% to 4% of the retail price. Three percent of the retail price, with the same formulas for royalty calculation as an artist receives, seems to be the most common producer's royalty rate. Successful producers can receive a royalty equal to or even higher than that of the artist. Because of the likelihood that whatever the producer is producing will, sooner or later, be released with product *not produced* by the producer, a *coupling clause* is usually included in provisions concerning the producer's royalties (see Example 2). When a producer produces more than one artist, the issue of cross-collateralization should also be addressed.

Producers usually do receive, and should request, direct payment of their royalties from the record company (see Example 3).

SAMPLE CONTRACT PROVISIONS

EXAMPLE 1: 3% Royalty with Escalation

7. (a) (i) On full-price Net Sales of Phonograph Records embodying the Master(s) through normal retail distribution channels in the United States ("USNRC Net Sales"), we shall pay or cause Distributor to pay you a royalty of three percent (3%) of the suggested retail list price ("SRLP") of records computed, adjusted and paid in the same manner and on the same basis as our royalties are computed, adjusted and paid pursuant to the Recording Agreement. Notwithstanding the foregoing, solely with respect to (a) full-price USNRC Net Sales of the Album in excess of one million (1,000,000) units, your royalty shall be three and one-half percent (3½%) rather than three percent (3%).

(ii) With respect to other than full-price USNRC Net Sales of Phonograph Records, the royalty rate will be reduced in the same proportion and will be subject to the same terms and conditions (excluding royalty escalations) as apply to our royalty rate pursuant to the Recording Agreement; and

(iii) The royalty otherwise payable to you will not become payable unless and until Distributor has recouped all Recording Costs (as defined in the Recording Agreement), including the Engineering Fee, for the Master(s). Such recoupment will be computed at the "net artist" rate (i.e., the full royalty payable to us less the royalty payable to all producers including you) prorated on the basis of the number of Master(s) embodied on the Album compared to the total number of master recordings on the Album. After such recoupment, your royalty shall be computed retroactively and paid on all records from the first record sold, subject to recoupment of the Producer Advance.

EXAMPLE 2: 3% Royalty; Royalty Paid as Production Company Is Paid

3. (a) (i) With respect to net sales of the Album through normal retail distribution channels in the United States ("USNRC Net Sales"), we shall irrevocably direct Company to pay directly to you a royalty of three percent (3%) of the suggested retail price of the Album (or, if Company computes royalties on a "wholesale" basis, six percent (royalty base price)). With respect to exploitations of the Masters in respect of which we are paid a portion of Company's "net receipts," you shall be entitled to a fraction of the net receipts paid to or credited to our account, the numerator of which is your basic royalty rate hereunder and the denominator of which is the basic royalty rate payable to us under the Company Agreement. The royalty payable to you for foreign sales, singles, budget records, mid-priced records, club sales, compact discs and any contained on the Album for which we are paid a reduced royalty shall be computed by reducing your basic royalty rate in the same proportion that the basic royalty rate payable by Company to us for USNRC Net Sales of the Album is reduced. All royalties payable to you shall be computed, calculated and paid in the exact same manner and at the same time (e.g., container charges, free goods, reserves, etc.) as royalties payable to us by Company are computed, determined, calculated and paid pursuant to our recording agreement with Company. With respect to sales of records embodying Masters produced by you coupled with other master recordings, your royalty shall be multiplied by a fraction, the numerator of which is the number of Masters produced by you on the record in question and the denominator of which is the total number of master recordings embodied on that record. Your royalties as aforesaid shall be payable retroactively to the first record sold after recoupment by Company at the net artist rate of solely the acquisition costs of the Album (it being understood that you shall not be required to "stand behind" or otherwise bear any portion of any "general" artist advances or any other costs [except for the acquisition costs specified earlier in this sentence] that Company may charge against your account). Following such recoupment, your royalty shall be payable both retroactively to the first record sold and prospectively on all records sold thereafter.

(ii) Notwithstanding anything to the contrary contained herein, it is agreed that royalties payable to you hereunder shall not be cross-collateralized against royalties payable to you under any other project which you may produce for us in the future.

(b) Attached hereto as Exhibit "A" are appropriately redacted copies of the royalty clauses and accounting clauses of the recording agreement between us and Company.

☛ This agreement, which is between the producer and a production company, specifies that the producer will be paid as the production company is paid and includes, as Exhibit A, a copy of the production company's royalty provisions. The provision pertaining to record one specifies that the producer be paid from "the first record sold" after recoupment from the artist's royalties of the "acquisition cost" (the cost of purchasing the finished album, which is treated as a recording cost). Provision 3(a)(ii) specifies that the producer's royalty may not be cross-collateralized. Catch 3(b), which mentions "redacted" copies of the royalty clauses. In other words, an "edited" version of the clauses—another example of the juicy parts being removed.

EXAMPLE 3: Direct Payment/Same Calculation as Artist

5. (a) Artist shall provide Company with the "Letter of Direction" substantially in the form attached hereto as Exhibit B authorizing direct payment by Company to Producer. Producer's roy-

alties shall be calculated in the same manner as Artist's royalties with respect to the Master; shall be subject to the same reductions, deductions, exclusions and category variations as is Artist's royalty (including, without limitation, tape, compact disc, new media, foreign sales, record clubs, mid-price, budget, singles, coupling, free goods, discounts, packaging deductions, royalty base, reserve policy, definition of net sales, percentage of net sales accounted on) under Artist's Agreement with Company; and shall be paid at the same time as Artist is paid by Company. Each statement or accounting rendered hereunder shall be binding upon Producer, and not subject to any objection whatsoever, unless Producer serves Artist notice of specific objection, stating the basis thereof, within two (2) years following the date rendered.

RECORD ONE

Most independent producer agreements have a provision granting the producer a royalty which will be credited from the first record sold or, as it is referred to, from *record one*. However, payment is only made retroactively, that is, after the recording costs for the recordings in question have been recouped from the artist's royalties. Once the recording costs have been recouped, the producer is owed royalty payments back to record one. However, if the recording costs are not recouped (hardly an uncommon occurrence), the producer does not receive any royalties.

Example

Producer receives a royalty paid retroactively to the first record sold (from record one) after recoupment of recording costs from Artist. Producer's net royalty is $0.50 per album sold and Artist's net royalty is $1.00 per album. All recording costs are charged back to Artist. They record Album for $100,000 in recording costs.

1. Album's net sales are 99,999 copies: Record Company recoups $99,999 from Artist (99,999 × $1.00 = $99,999). Artist is still $1.00 in the red with unrecouped recording costs. Producer has a "future" interest of $49,999.50 (99,999 × $0.50 = $49,999.50), but until the recording costs are recouped, receives nothing. Payment to Artist: $0.00. Payment to Producer: $0.00.

2. Album's net sales are 100,001 copies: Record Company recoups $100,001 from Artist (100,001 × $1.00 = $100,001). Artist is now $1.00 in the black, having recouped the recording costs of $100,000. Producer now qualifies to receive royalties on all 100,001 sales (100,001 × $0.50 = $50,000.50) since the recording costs are recouped from Artist's royalty. Payment to Artist: $1.00. Payment to Producer: $50,000.50.

Sometimes the record company will not pay the producer a retroactive royalty, insisting instead that the producer royalty does not accrue until all recording costs have been recovered from the artist at the artist's royalty rate. If this were the case in the scenario above, Producer would have no "future" interest in calculation (1), and in calculation (2) Producer would only receive $0.50. Under these circumstances, the retroactive payment makes a considerable difference: $50,000.50 versus $0.50.

Does this require any comment? At first blush maybe not. However, look at the following twist, which may be used to improve a less-than-desirable provision in a producer's contract.

If the producer's royalties do not start to accrue until the recording costs are recouped, the producer should then insist that his or her royalties should also be used to recover recording costs.

This way, with the producer's "contribution" at least the payoff will come sooner. Using the same scenario as above, now recording costs are recouped at the rate of $1.50 per album ($1.00 from Artist and $0.50 from Producer). Consequently, only 66,667 net albums must be sold to recoup the recording costs, and thereafter Artist receives $1.00 per album and Producer receives $0.50 per album. At 100,001 albums sold, Artist now receives $33,334 and Producer receives $16,667.

Compare these examples of cost recoupment with the recoupment previously described (page 217), where the production company may receive royalty payments before both the artist and the producer receive their royalties.

SAMPLE CONTRACT PROVISIONS

EXAMPLE 1: Credited from Record One

6. It is agreed and understood that no royalties shall be payable to you hereunder until such time as recording costs have been recouped from royalties due the Artist for the recording of the Masters hereunder. Upon such recoupment, Company shall credit to your account your share of royalties from sales of such recordings from so-called record one, the first recording sold. Nothing contained in this provision is to imply that any share of recording costs, other than as provided for in paragraph 5(b)(i), above [over budget], shall be recoupable from your royalties hereunder.

> ☞ Being "credited" is not the same as being "paid." The credited monies may be used by the company to recoup advances paid to the producer as production fees; to recoup excess costs over the approved budget; or, heaven forfend, if the company has the right to cross-collateralize against the producer's other contracts, to recoup losses from an entirely different project.

EXAMPLE 2: Recoupment of Production Fee

(b) Notwithstanding anything to the contrary contained herein, no royalty shall be payable to Producer hereunder unless and until Company recoups at the "net artist rate" (i.e., the "all-in" royalty rate payable to Artist less the royalty rate payable to Producer) all recording costs attributable to the album. Following such recoupment, Producer's royalties shall be paid retroactively to the first record sold, subject to the recoupment of the Advance set forth in paragraph 6 herein. For purposes of this agreement, the term "recording costs" and all other terms used herein shall have the same meaning as those terms are used in the Agreement between Artist and Company.

> ☞ Under this provision, unlike the provision in Example 1, the *only* thing which may be recouped from the producer is the producer's advance—the production fee paid to the producer.

EXAMPLE 3: Retroactive to First Record Sold

(c) With respect to sales of records hereunder embodying Masters produced by Producer, royalties shall be payable to Producer retroactively to the first record sold after recoupment by Company at the net artist rate of recording costs of the Album. Following such recoupment, Producer's royalty shall be payable both retroactively to the first record sold and prospectively on all records sold thereafter.

PUBLICITY AND ADVERTISING

The record company will require the producer to agree to provisions granting the record company virtually the same rights it has acquired from the artist for publicity and advertising (see Example 2). The same laws apply to the producer as apply to the artist: Without the express permission of the producer, the record company may not make any commercial use of the producer's name, likeness, biography, sound effects, etc., in connection with the sale of the recordings or in any other manner at all. Accordingly, language similar—if not identical—to that which appears in the artist's recording agreement will appear in the producer's agreement. Note that all the sample provisions below (1 through 4) make use of the word *shall* in connection with the credits to be given producer. "Shall," of course means that the producer *must* receive credit. If the word "may" had been used, it would mean that the record company had permission to give the producer credit but was not required to do so. Big difference.

So what is so different about the producer's agreement that the language about advertising and publicity requires a section of its own? In the artist's agreement, these provisions deal with the company's *right* to use the artist's name, etc. In the producer's agreement, the *right* to use the producer's name, etc., should also be coupled with the company's *obligation* to actually *use* the producer's name in connection with the advertising and sale of the recordings.

There is more than ego involved here. The inclusion of the producer's name in connection with the advertising and sale of the recording is a form of promotion for the producer and can lead to additional work, earnings, fame, success, and who knows what else. The record company may be willing to contractually agree to the inclusion of the producer's name in advertising, but, more likely than not, it will probably insist that the producer's name and credit need not appear in print advertising of less than one-half (or, if pushed vigorously, one-fourth) of a page. Given the possibility that if recording costs are not recouped, the producer will not receive royalties, publicity may be the only real value—apart from the producer's fee, of course—which the producer gets in return for the efforts expended.

In addition, the inclusion of the producer's name becomes very important in many major territories outside of the United States, and may very well generate additional royalties for the producer from neighboring rights. (See Chapter 15, the section on "Neighboring Rights," pages 416–419.)

SAMPLE CONTRACT PROVISIONS

EXAMPLE 1: Producer Shall Be Given Credit

5. Producer shall be given credit in substantially the form specified by Producer on the discs, back cover, and booklet, if any, of all records manufactured from master recordings made pursuant to this Agreement, and any agreement between Company and/or Artist and a record company and in all major advertisements placed directly by Company, or any third party, which relate solely to such records.

EXAMPLE 2: Producer Shall Be Given Credit in All Paid Advertising

(b) The perpetual right to use and publish and to permit others to use and publish Producer's name (including any professional name heretofore or hereafter adopted by Producer), signature, likeness, voice and sound effects, and biographical material concerning Producer for advertising and trade purposes in connection with the recordings made hereunder or to refrain therefrom; provided, however, that Producer shall receive credit on all labels and packaging as producer of the masters recorded hereunder and, likewise, shall receive credit as producer in all paid advertising for records made from master recorded hereunder.

> ☛ Memory fails me, but I suspect that the language of this provision (the obligation to give credit applies to *all* paid advertising) is an oversight on the part of the company rather than a negotiated point. Compare this language with the language in Example 3, below, where the conditions governing the credit to producer limit the credit requirements for print advertising to ads of a certain size ("national half-page or larger") in "trade and consumer press advertising."

EXAMPLE 3: Credit on Half-Page or Larger Ads

7. Conditioned upon Producer's full and faithful performance of all of producer's material services and obligations hereunder, Production Company shall direct Record Company to accord credit with respect to the Masters in the form "Produced by _____" on the labels, liners and/or packaging of records in all configurations embodying the Masters produced hereunder in all national half-page or larger trade and consumer press advertising by Record Company relating to records comprising the Masters. Production Company shall also request that the liner notes on the Album contain a "studio" credit for Producer's studio. No casual or inadvertent failure by Production Company and no failure by a third party to comply with the foregoing credit requirements shall be deemed a breach of this agreement and in no event shall Producer seek or be entitled to injunctive or other equitable relief for failure to comply with any of the credit provisions hereof. Upon Production Company's receipt of Producer's notice of such failure, Production Company shall use reasonable efforts to cause Record Company to prospectively cure any such failure on future manufacturing runs.

> ☛ I do remember this one! I negotiated for the credit for the producer's studio.

EXAMPLE 4: Detailed Credit Obligations

5. (a) Distributor shall have the worldwide right in perpetuity to use and to permit others to use Producer's professional name, likeness and other identification, and biographical material concerning Producer for purposes of trade in connection with the Masters and the phonograph records derived therefrom. We shall instruct Distributor to give Producer production credit on phonorecord labels and liner notes (in all configurations) in substantially the following form: "Produced by _____."

(b) Per your request and subject to the applicable provisions of the Recording Agreement, we shall instruct Distributor to make available to you for your inspection and approval at Distributor's offices photographs and biographies of producer which Distributor desires to use in connection with its exploitation during the Term of phonographs records hereunder in the United States. You shall have the right to approve the same, it being understood that you shall not unreasonably withhold such approval. You shall be deemed to have approved any such photographs or biographies if you shall fail to submit to Distributor in writing your specific objections thereto within five (5) days after we or Distributor have notified you of their availability.

(c) We shall also instruct Distributor to give Producer credit as the producer of the Master(s) completed by Producer in all one-half (½) page or larger advertisements placed by Distributor or under its control in the United States in so-called "nation-wide" trade and consumer publications which such advertisements pertain to records solely embodying the Master(s). We shall also instruct Distributor to use reasonable efforts to accord Producer paid advertising credit as set forth in the preceding sentence in all one-quarter (¼) page advertisements. All production credits given to Producer pursuant to this paragraph shall be in substantially the form set forth in paragraph 5(a) hereinabove. No inadvertent failure on Distributor's part or on the part of Distributor's licensees to provide such credit shall be deemed a breach of this Agreement, with the understanding that we will use reasonable efforts to cause Distributor to correct any such inadvertent failure on future runs after we have been notified by you in writing of any such failure.

> ☛ This is the most detailed credit provision I have in my files for a record producer. It not only contains the normal credit obligations, it even specifies that the producer has the right to approve photographs of producer. In addition, it also says that the record company will "use reasonable efforts" to include producer credits in print advertising as small as one-quarter page.

CHAPTER 5

MASTER PURCHASE

COSTARD:

> . . . a good master of mine,
>> —WILLIAM SHAKESPEARE
>> *Love's Labour's Lost*, Act IV, Scene 1

LEWIS:

> Is purchase of a heavy curse . . .
>> —WILLIAM SHAKESPEARE
>> *King John*, Act III, Scene 1

MASTER PURCHASE AGREEMENTS

Record companies frequently purchase recorded masters from artists, producers, or production companies. Agreements for the purchase of masters deal with the sales of completed (or nearly completed) master recordings to a record company by the owner (be it production company, producer, artist, or financial backer) of the masters. These agreements are usually referred to as *master purchase agreements.*

The independent recording of masters for submission to a record company is a time-honored, expensive, and risky method of trying to obtain a recording agreement for an artist. Unfortunately, a great deal of money is often spent on recording masters without securing a contract. From the record company's point of view, however, the practice is a welcome one. None of the risk of recording an unknown quantity is borne by the record company, but by the artist, production company, sugar daddy, or whoever puts up the money. The record company doesn't have to imagine or guess what an artist's product will sound like. If the company doesn't like what it hears, it passes on the artist and the product, leaving the investor to absorb the financial loss. If the company does like the recording, it can negotiate a master purchase agreement.

In most cases when a record company enters into a master purchase agreement, the record company will want the agreement to be tied in to the company's right to follow through on successful product with future recordings featuring the artist. Rarely, a master purchase agreement will deal only with the specific recording being purchased and not be linked with either an agreement or an option for an agreement with the artist and/or producer. This might happen with a novelty recording, spoken-word recording, concept recording, or any other type of recording that might be viewed as a one-shot opportunity.

When you are selling a master or masters to a record company, the major issues are the purchase price, the royalty, and what happens next. The record company, of course, has its own priorities in addition to the above issues, such as documentation of the transfer of ownership and representations and warranties that all obligations have been taken care of so that the record company will not have unforeseen liabilities. Many of the same issues that apply to the artist recording agreement also apply to the master purchase agreement. For example, the same issues regarding royalty computations, reserves, the granting of mechanical license fees at reduced rates, accounting, etc., are all part of negotiating and entering into this type of agreement Here we will be dealing with those issues and provisions that are unique to the master purchase agreement.

PURCHASE PRICE

The cost of a thing is the amount of what I call life which is required to be exchanged for it, immediately or in the long run.
—HENRY DAVID THOREAU

The purchase price paid for masters is, naturally, of interest to the seller. The negotiated price for masters will fall into one of three categories:

1. Purchase price less than the cost of the masters.

2. Purchase price at the cost of the masters.

3. Purchase price greater than the cost of the masters. (These choices may seem less than inspired, but the list is accurate.)

It is not unusual for the seller to transfer ownership of the masters to the record company for a purchase price less than the actual cost of recording masters. In fact, it is more common than one would think for the masters to be transferred to the record company without any payment at all. Why, you might ask, would anyone do this? The answer is that in this record industry buyer's market it can be incredibly difficult for an artist to sign with any record company, and giving masters away may be perceived as the only way to get a contract. And there is always the chance that royalties generated from commercial sales will be enough to recover the cost of recording. In any event, there are some steps the seller can take to try to minimize the economic burden. The first step is to insist that the seller be paid on sales from record one, as there are no recording costs for the record company to recoup. The second step is to negotiate a higher royalty rate because the seller is bearing the economic risk of the production of the masters. Sometimes, a higher-than-usual royalty will apply to the masters until such time as the recording costs are recouped by the seller, and then the royalty reverts to the regular rate (see Example 3).

Today, the most commonly negotiated purchase price is the actual cost of recording (see Example 1). The agreements usually require the seller to provide proof of the actual costs, including those already paid, those accrued but not yet paid, and those yet to come. I include "accrued" in the equation because sometimes masters are sold, and then remaining bills are paid, sometimes directly, by the record company. The language "yet to come" covers the fact that masters are sometimes sold prior to their completion—a mix is needed, new drums, sweetening, etc.

If the masters are special enough, there is the possibility of negotiating a premium purchase price, over and above the recording costs. This most often comes about as a result of a bidding situation between two or more record companies, probably as a result of some success with independent promotion and/or sales. Except in extremely rare instances, the purchase price will be treated as an advance or as a recording cost and is, accordingly, recoupable from the sale of the recordings. Unless expressly excluded in some manner, the monies paid by the record company will be cross-collateralized against other earnings due the production company or artist (see Example 2).

SAMPLE CONTRACT PROVISIONS

EXAMPLE 1: Cost of Recording

(f) I have recorded a pre-existing album featuring me which is being delivered to Company concurrently herewith. Notwithstanding the fact that the album shall not apply against any minimum recording obligation hereunder, the album shall be subject to all the terms and conditions of this Agreement as if said album had been recorded hereunder. Company agrees to reimburse me, or my designees, the recording costs, not to exceed _____ Thousand ($_____) Dollars, as evidenced by canceled checks, for such album, which shall be deemed to be recording costs hereunder.

> ☛ This purchase price provision is inserted within an agreement signing the artist to a recording agreement. This album is treated as if it were recorded pursuant to the agreement except that the album does not count against the minimum recording obligation. The purchase price is treated as a recording cost.

EXAMPLE 2: Purchase Price Cross-Collateralized

3. Concurrently with the execution of this Agreement, Producer shall deliver the Masters to Company, as provided for in Paragraph 12, below. Upon delivery of the Masters to, and acceptance by, Company, Company shall pay to Producer the sum of _____ Thousand _____ Hundred Dollars ($_____) as the purchase price (hereinafter "Purchase Price") for the Masters hereunder. The Purchase Price shall be deemed to be an advance hereunder and shall be recoupable from this and/or any other agreement between Producer and Company.

EXAMPLE 3: Royalty Adjusted After Recoupment

(a) For records manufactured from the masters transferred hereunder, the royalty shall be the Base Royalty plus Three (3%) Percent (hereinafter referred to as the "Adjusted Royalty") until such time as Artist's royalty account shall be credited with a sum of money equal to the dollar amount [the purchase price] set forth in Paragraph 6, above. Thereafter, the royalty for sales of the recordings shall be reduced to the Base Royalty.

(b) Artist shall be credited, at the rate of the Adjusted Royalty, for all sales of records manufactured from the masters transferred herein from the first such record sold. . . .

> ☛ The artist gets a "bump" in royalties of an extra 3% from record one until the purchase price is recouped, then the royalty is adjusted back down to the base royalty (adjusted royalty minus 3% on sales after recoupment).

INCORPORATION BY REFERENCE

PORTIA:
... that great vow
Which did incorporate and make us one.
—WILLIAM SHAKESPEARE
Julius Caesar, Act II, Scene 1

As stated above, today it is rare for a purchase of masters not to be tied into a recording agreement or at least an option for a recording agreement. This, of course, gives the record company the opportunity to follow up on the success, if there is success, of the project. Record companies are not generally known to be terribly interested in creating success for someone else. Accordingly, most negotiations for a master purchase are for both purchasing the masters and signing the artist to a recording agreement. The two goals may be combined in one agreement, covered in one agreement with an attachment or exhibit, or set forth in two separate agreements. The language of the agreement or agreements will *incorporate by reference* all or some of the terms and conditions of the recording agreement to apply to the masters being purchased.

Incorporation by reference in any agreement saves both ink and space. Why fill multiple pages with formulas for calculating royalties, free goods, returns, etc., when all this can be simply done by stating that these provisions will be the same as set forth in another agreement between the parties? (See Examples 1 and 2.)

SAMPLE CONTRACT PROVISIONS

EXAMPLE 1: "Deemed to Have Been Made"
20.03 The Masters will be deemed to have been made under this agreement for the purposes of Articles 7, 8, 9, 10, 11, 12 and 13. The Masters will be treated under Article 9 as Recordings made during the initial Contract Period of the term of this agreement, and will be deemed "Materials" under paragraph 13.01(d). The five (5) year period referred to in clause (i) of subparagraph 13.02(b) will commence, with respect to each of the Masters, on whichever of the following dates shall be the earlier: (a) the date of Company's initial release of the Phonograph Records derived from the Master concerned, or (b) the date one year after the date of this agreement.

☛ The masters in this provision were purchased under a separate agreement. Elsewhere in this agreement, "Masters" are defined as the recordings acquired through the separate agreement. However, they are now "deemed to have been made" under the current agreement, and so all the provisions of the current agreement apply to the masters.

EXAMPLE 2: Exhibit Incorporated by Reference
15. Producer sells, transfers and assigns to Company all right, tide and interest in and to the Masters set forth in Exhibit "A" and incorporated herein by reference, which embody Artist's performances. The Masters shall be subject to all of the terms and conditions hereof which are applicable to Masters recorded hereunder.

☛ This agreement is a combination recording agreement and master purchase agreement. The titles of the masters being purchased are set forth in Exhibit A and incorporated by reference into the main body of the agreement. These purchased masters are treated in the same manner as are new masters recorded pursuant to the agreement.

TRANSFER OF OWNERSHIP

The purchase of masters includes not only the physical transfer of the master tapes, but also the purchase of the rights inherent in the exploitation of the recordings. This two-part transfer of ownership—ownership of the tapes themselves and ownership of the rights to manufacture and sell the recordings of the tapes—is essential for the record company.

Example

Artist is under an exclusive recording agreement with Company. Independently, while under contract, Artist records an album without any participation on Company's part. Who owns the album? The answer is, *both* of them. Artist owns the masters because Artist paid for them. Company owns the exclusive right to manufacture and sell records made from the masters; Artist is under an exclusive agreement with Company. Accordingly, it is a standoff. Neither can do anything commercially with the masters without the cooperation and agreement of the other.

In master purchase agreements, the transfer sometimes takes the form of an outright sale or transfer as specified in the language used in the agreement (see Example 1). The transfer may also be accomplished by providing that the masters are deemed to have been recorded pursuant to the terms and conditions of a recording agreement being entered into at the same time. (See below, pages 229–230, for a discussion of transfer of copyright in a sound recording.)

SAMPLE CONTRACT PROVISIONS

EXAMPLE 1: Transfer of "All Right, Title, and Interest"

20.01 You hereby sell, transfer and assign to Company irrevocably all right, title and interest in and to the Master Recordings featuring the Artist's performances enumerated in Schedule "A" attached, from the inception of Recording (the "Masters"), including, without limitation, the copyrights in the Masters and the right to secure such copyrights and all renewals and extensions of such copyright, perpetually and throughout the world.

EXAMPLE 2: Transfer of "All Right, Title, and Interest"

(d)(i) You hereby sell, transfer and assign to Company all right, title and interest in and to the master recordings (the "Purchased Masters") of the sides entitled . . . [titles] . . . embodying Artist's performances which will be subject to all of the terms and conditions hereof applicable to master recordings of sides recorded during the Initial Period, except as specifically set forth herein to the contrary.

DELIVERY

Agreements for the purchase of masters will have "delivery" language specifying the details of the physical delivery of the masters and other elements, such as label copy, consents, credit information, clearances, etc., required for the record company to exploit the masters. This is probably the most basic, nuts-and-bolts provision in any agreement for the purchase of master recordings in that the seller is given a checklist of items of items which must be physically delivered to the record company to effectuate the sale (see Example 2).

EXAMPLE 1: When and Where to Deliver

20.02 You will Deliver the Masters to Company at its offices in Los Angeles, California, not later than January 31, _____ . If the Masters have not been so Delivered Company shall have the right to terminate the term of this agreement, at its election and without limiting its rights.

EXAMPLE 2: Delivery Checklist

(vii) Contemporaneously with the delivery of the master recordings of the Masters, you shall furnish Company, in writing, with the following:

(A) the label copy (including song titles and any subtitles), names of composers, any show or movie credits, complete publisher line, including the address and telephone number of each publisher, affiliate (BMI, ASCAP, etc.), serial number, timings, any arranger credits, any accompaniment credits, names of engineers, list of musicians with instruments played, exact recording date(s) and studio location(s), indication whether recording is track, sweetening or vocal overdub, producer and/or production company credits;

(B) the liner credits;

(C) two (2) equalized tape masters, and two (2) reference lacquers which are representative of said tape masters which lacquers and tapes shall be satisfactory for the manufacture and sale of records. All work parts of whatsoever nature (including without limitation, any outtakes or tracks recorded during the same sessions as the recording of tracks contained in master recordings delivered hereunder) shall be subject to subparagraph 9(d) and shall be delivered to Company concurrently with delivery of the foregoing items under this subparagraph 5(d)(vii)(C);

(D) the sequence and final timings in connection with the reference lacquers and master tapes furnished in accordance with subparagraph 5(d)(vii)(C) above. . . .

(E) all consents or clearances required by Company in relation to the use or proposed uses of Company of any of the elements which are within the scope of Producer's function hereunder.

WARRANTIES AND REPRESENTATIONS

Not surprisingly, perhaps, the provisions covering representations and warranties in master purchase agreements are usually longer and more detailed than are the equivalent provisions in an artist's recording agreement. (See the section "Warranties and Representations," Chapter 3, pages 153–157.) This is because the seller is furnishing finished, or at least partially finished, product. Accordingly, many aspects of the creation and production of the masters which might otherwise have been under the control of the record company—from paying recording costs through making and selling records made from the masters—have already taken place.

The record company takes special care to determine that no third parties have any claims to the masters, that the seller has the right to sell the masters and transfer all the rights and interests in the masters, that union payments have been or will be paid, that no copies have been sold, and that permissions have been obtained from all performers. Once the record company has purchased the masters, third parties will look to the record company to make good on unpaid bills and will sue the company in case of alleged transgressions. Of course the seller will also be sued by said third parties, but, correctly or not, the record company is going to be seen as the "deep pocket" and hence the prime target. (If the allegations have merit, the record company will also sue the seller for breaching the warranties and representations.)

Note that in both examples below, virtually all the warranties and representations are in the past tense—things that have or have not been done. They deal with matters that would have been taken care of by the company, one way or another, if the masters had originally been recorded under the company's control. The exception is paragraph (g) in Example 1, which refers to a future obligation.

SAMPLE CONTRACT PROVISIONS

EXAMPLE 1: Warranties and Representations

23. You represent and warrant:

(a) that you are the sole and worldwide owner of the Purchased Masters as well as the sole and worldwide owner and holder of all right, tide and interest, intangible and intangible therein;

(b) that there are no liens or other encumbrances against the Purchased Masters or any part thereof;

(c) that you have the right, on your behalf and on behalf of Artist, Producer and all other persons who participated in or in connection with the making of the Purchased Masters to sell same to Company and to grant Company the rights to use same for records and other purposes described in this agreement;

(d) that Artist and all other persons whose performances are embodied in the Purchased Masters have been paid in full by you and in amounts not less than applicable union scale for services rendered by them in connection with the Purchased Masters;

(e) that all costs incurred in the creation and production of the Purchased Masters have been paid by you;

(f) that no records derived from the Purchased Masters have been heretofore made, distributed or sold;

(g) that you shall promptly enter into the current American Federation of Musicians ("AFM") Phonograph Record Labor Agreement and applicable American Federation of Television and Radio Artists ("AFTRA") Agreements and shall comply therewith and with any renewals, extensions or modifications thereof;

(h) that, without limiting the generality of subparagraph 5(d)(iv)(g) above, the scale wages were paid for all music contained on the Purchased Masters and the contribution to the Pension and Welfare Fund described in Exhibit B of the Phonograph Record Labor Agreement with the AFM has been paid. This representation and warranty is included for the benefit of the AFM (among others) and may be enforced by the AFM or by such person or persons as it may designate;

(i) that, without limiting the generality of subparagraph 5(d)(iv)(g) above, for the direct benefit of the AFTRA and all artists whose performances are contained in the Purchased Masters, that all artists whose performances embodied therein were recorded in the United States of America, its territories and possessions (if any) have been paid the minimum rates specified in the AFTRA Code of Fair Practice for Phonograph Recordings or the applicable code then in effect at the time the recording was made and that all payments due to the AFTRA Pension and Welfare Funds have been made;

(j) that you and/or Artist and/or Producer are not currently a party to any agreement pursuant to which you and/or Artist and/or Producer have granted to any third party any right in and to any of the Purchased Masters for record purposes; and

(k) that, except as expressly specified herein, Company shall have no obligation whatsoever to Artist, Producer or any third party for or in connection with the creation of the Purchased Masters and Company's exercise of any rights therein.

EXAMPLE 2: Warranties and Representations

20.04. You warrant and represent:

(a) You are the sole and exclusive owner of the Masters and all rights in them.

(b) No Phonograph Records have been manufactured from the Masters by you or any other Person, and none of the musical compositions performed in the Masters has been performed by the Artist for the making of any other Master Recordings.

(c) You have not, nor has any other Person, sold or assigned to any other Party or otherwise disposed of any right, title or interest in or to the Masters.

(d) With regard to the Masters:

(1) Each Person who rendered any service in connection with, or who otherwise contributed in any way to the making of the Masters, or who granted to you your rights referred to in this agreement, had the full right, power and authority to do so, and was not bound by any agreement which would restrict such person from rendering such services or granting such rights.

(2) All recording costs and expenses with respect to the making of the Masters have been paid as of the date when the Masters are physically delivered to Company.

(3) All necessary licenses for the recording of the Compositions performed in the Masters have been obtained from the copyright owners, and all monies payable under such licenses or otherwise by reason of such recording have been paid. (The preceding sentence does not apply to any monies payable to those copyright owners in connection with the manufacture or sale of Phonograph Records derived from the Masters.)

(4) All the Masters were made in accordance with the rules and regulations of the American Federation of Musicians ("AFM"), the American Federation of Television and Radio Artists ("AFTRA"), and all other unions having jurisdiction. Without limiting the generality of the preceding sentence: (1) the requirements of paragraph 17 of the Phonograph Record Labor Agreement between the AFM and Company (or the corresponding provisions of any successor agreement) have been satisfied (which warranty and representation is included for the benefit of AFM, among others, and may be enforced by the AFM or by such person or persons as it may designate); and (2) the requirements of paragraphs 31 and 32 of the AFTRA Code Fair Practice for Phonograph Recordings between AFTRA and Company (or the corresponding provisions of any successor agreement) have been satisfied (which warranty and representation shall inure to the benefit of AFTRA and the artists performing on the Masters).

TRANSFER OF COPYRIGHT

Before 1972, musical compositions, artwork, photographs, and liner notes were all protected by U.S. copyright law, but recordings were not. On February 15, 1972, the United States joined most other countries in the world and granted copyrights and copyright protection to recordings, or, to use the terminology from the Copyright Act of 1976, "sound recordings" and "phonorecords." Note that this is a separate copyright from the copyright given to musical compositions, artwork, etc. The copyright symbol for recordings is ℗; for everything else it is ©. Look at the copyright notice on any album released after 1972 and you *should* see both symbols.

Since phonorecords can have a separate copyright, there is usually a provision in the master purchase agreement that provides either for the registration of the copyright in the name of the record company or for the assignment of any such registration to the record company (see Examples 1 and 2).

A detailed discussion of the rights of the copyright holder of phonorecords is given in Chapter 20, "Copyright," pages 510–511. Also relevant is the section "Transfer of Copyright" in Chapter 20, pages 533–534.

SAMPLE CONTRACT PROVISIONS

EXAMPLE 1: Sell, Transfer, and Assign Copyright

20.01 You hereby sell, transfer and assign to Company irrevocably all right, title and interest in and to the Master Recordings featuring the Artist's performances enumerated in Schedule "A" attached, from the inception of Recording (the "Masters"), including, without limitation, the copyrights in the Masters and the right to secure such copyrights and all renewals and extensions of such copyright, perpetually and throughout the world.

EXAMPLE 2: Instruments of Transfer

(vi)   (A) Promptly upon Company's request, you will execute and deliver to Company any Instruments of Transfer and other documents necessary for Company to secure copyright protection in the Masters and you hereby appoint Company as your agent and attorney-in-fact to sign any such Instruments or other documents in your name and to make appropriate disposition of them provided they are consistent with this agreement.

LEASE OF MASTERS

There is one type of transfer of masters that is neither a master purchase nor the artist recording for the company pursuant to a recording agreement. (Note that when an artist records for the record company, such recordings are always done as works for hire and, accordingly, there is no real transfer involved. For a discussion of works for hire, see pages 530–532.) This different type of transfer is a *lease* agreement, whereby the masters are literally leased to the record company for some specified period of time.

Under these circumstances, there usually is not a purchase price, or equivalent, paid for the masters nor are there recording costs to be recouped. There probably will be a payment in the form of a license fee, which will, more likely than not, be recoupable. The ownership of the masters does not transfer to the record company, but remains with the owner. What is transferred for that period is the right to exploit the masters. At the end of the specified period, the rights to the masters revert to the owner.

The lease of masters was once much more common than it is today. In the late 1970s there was a federal investment tax credit available to the "owners" of certain properties, including recorded masters. Thus the owners of recorded masters would lease the masters, retaining, for tax purposes, the ownership of the masters. An entire cottage industry grew up around the leasing of masters for investment tax credit. Partnerships were set up in which the investing partners took investment tax credits on the basis of inflated appraisals from so-called "experts" ("There's an enormous market for accordion music, so this album of accordion music should sell half a million copies, probably more—it's worth at least $1 million!") and the general partners took the cash for the (also inflated) recording costs. These arrangements all came crashing down when the government decided that these tax credits should be disallowed and acted accordingly. A lot of people lost a lot more than their shirts.

Today, masters are generally leased by established artists who at the expiration of the lease period negotiate to relicense the masters, either to the original lessee on a renewal basis or to a new lessee.

One possible reason to lease masters is the presumption that by retaining ownership the artist will have more control over the commercial exploitation of the records. This is not usually correct. In fact, lease agreements generally provide that the rights granted are exclusive during the term of the agreement and that the records manufactured from the masters will remain the property of the record company, along with all the necessary rights to manufacture, sell, and advertise the recordings. (See Examples 1 and 2.) The lease may provide that the record company's right to sell recordings made from the masters will terminate with the termination of the lease, usually with a specified sell-off period (see paragraph 3 in Example 1).

SAMPLE CONTRACT PROVISIONS

EXAMPLE 1: 10-Year Lease

2. The recorded masters of the musical compositions set forth in Exhibit "A," attached hereto and incorporated herein by reference, (hereinafter referred to as the "Masters"), are, effective this date, leased to Company for a period of ten (10) years from the initial commercial release of records manufactured from the Masters. . . . Such commercial release shall take place no later than Ninety (90) days from the date of this Agreement.

(a) During the term of the lease provided for herein, Company shall have all rights in and to the exploitation of the records manufactured from the Masters and sold hereunder. . . .

(b) During the term of the lease provided for herein, the rights granted to Company herein shall be exclusive to Company. . . .

3. Upon the expiration of the lease period set forth in Paragraph 2, above, all of Company's rights in and to the Masters shall revert to Owner subject to Company's right to sell off existing recordings for a period of six (6) months after the expiration of the lease period.

☛ A 10-year lease of a recording would not run afoul of California's 7-year rule. The 7-year rule applies *only* to personal service agreements.

EXAMPLE 2: Rights Granted to Record Company

5. Lessee agrees and acknowledges that Lessee owns and shall have the entire right, title and interest of whatsoever kind or nature throughout the world in and to each of the Masters subject to the rights granted to Lessor hereunder.

• • •

13. During the term hereof, with regard to the records manufactured from the Masters and all copies thereof, Lessor grants to Lessee the following rights:

(a) The exclusive ownership of the records manufactured from the Masters and the right to use and control the same and performances embodied therein during the Term.

(b) During the Term, the exclusive and perpetual right throughout the world to manufacture, advertise, sell, lease, license or otherwise use or dispose of the records manufactured from or embodying all or any part of the contents of the Masters or to refrain therefrom in any and all fields of use throughout the world upon such terms and conditions as Lessee may approve. As used in this agreement, the noun "record" means any device by which sound may be recorded for later transmission to listeners, whether now known or unknown and howsoever used, whether embodying sound alone or sound synchronized with or accompanied by visual images of Artist or another subject including without limitation "tape records."

(c) During the Term, the perpetual right to use and publish and to permit others to use and publish the names, including professional names now used or later adopted of any individual producer, Artist, and any individual artist, and the individual performers of the group performing on the Masters and the likenesses of and biographical material concerning all such performers who recorded the Masters, for advertising and trade purposes in connection with the sale and exploitation of records produced from the Masters or to refrain therefrom.

(d) During the Term, the right to release records manufactured from the Masters under Lessee's label or trademark, or such other tradename or mark as Lessee may elect.

(e) During the Term, the right to sell and exploit records manufactured from the Masters on which the performances by other artists are coupled and to sell records manufactured from the Masters in albums which albums may contain pictures, prose and verse and records embodying performances of other artists; provided however, Lessee agrees not to "couple" records manufactured from the Masters in the United States during the term of this agreement (as it may be extended and/or renewed) without Lessor's prior written consent, except on a "best hits," "sampler," and anthology type albums.

> ☞ This example belies the presumption that leasing leads to greater control by the lessor/artist over the leased masters. The lessor/artist has granted the "perpetual right throughout the world" to the record company to do just about anything with the records manufactured, including license for soundtrack usage [13(b)], release under any trademark [13(d)], and couple with performances by other artists [13(e)].

CHAPTER 6

PRODUCTION AGREEMENTS

> *Has rock music become the rock Cornish hen of the arts, a severely limited life form, genetically trivialized, bearing the same relationship to actual music as body building does to the intricacies of track and field?*
>
> —JIM HARRISON
> *Esquire magazine*

Production agreements are really a hybrid between an artist's recording agreement and an independent producer's agreement that combines most, if not all, of the elements of both. Production agreements are sometimes referred to as *all-in* agreements.

Just what are production agreements? These are agreements whereby a production entity, which can be the artist, the producer, a company, or whatever, supplies all the production elements for a specific project to the record company. In other words, it is an all-inclusive agreement. The production entity supplies to the record company all necessary "elements"—namely, the artist, the producer, and the actual production process, including, possibly, the acquiring of mechanical licenses, liner information, label copy, and so forth—and delivers a finished product (see Example 3).

In this chapter, we are talking about the agreement between a production company and the record company, not the agreements between the production company and the artist or the producer. The production agreement between the record company and the production company will contain royalty provisions, grants of rights, recording commitments, and all the other delightful provisions we have come to love.

First, the production company enters into a recording agreement with the artist, and then the production company, in turn, "supplies" the artist to the record company. In order to provide the production of the masters, the production company, if it is not the producer, by choice or by reason of the requirement from the distributing record company, enters into an independent producer agreement with the producer and also "furnishes" the services of the producer for the recordings. These agreements between the production company and the artist and the production company and the independent producer contain all the standard provisions. With the artist and producer now tied to it, the production company enters into a recording agreement with the record company. The production company receives royalties from the record company, and is responsible for paying the royalties due the artist and the producer out of those royalties (see Example 2).

Sometimes a record company may unwittingly find itself being transformed from a label into a production company. It is not uncommon for an independent record label to enter into an agreement for the distribution of its product and later discover that it is the less-than-proud owner of what is known as a *conversion clause* (see the section "Conversion of Artists" in Chapter 16, pages 440–443). With a conversion clause, the distributor may, under specified conditions, "convert" (acquire) an artist from the original label for the distributor's label. Although the independent label still has the artist under contract, it must now supply the artist to the distributor's label (see Example 1).

Production agreements between the record company and the production entity should always contain an inducement letter or provision. This is either a side letter, exhibit, or acknowledgment signed by the artist, wherein the artist affirms the agreement and agrees to be bound by all of its provisions. These inducement provisions usually contain some language giving the record company the right to sign the artist directly under certain specified circumstances such as default or bankruptcy on the part of the production entity. There may even be circumstances where the record company can take over the production company's agreement with the artist. (For more information on inducement provisions, see the section "Inducement," in Chapter 3, pages 202–205, which provides two sample inducement letters.) The inducement language may also provide for the automatic execution of the option to continue the artist's recording agreement in the event of the exercise of the option to continue the production agreement. This will solve the problem of coordinating the exercise of options between the two agreements.

If the agreement between the artist and the production company provides for a royalty computation that is different from that contained in the agreement between the production company and the record company (for example, one may calculate royalty on the basis of wholesale price and the other on the basis of retail price), the inducement letter may alter the royalty computation to that contained in the agreement between the production company and the record company. However, if the artist and the production company have either a pro-rata or a flow-through provision, the terms and provisions of the two agreements will automatically be synchronized to one another. (Pro-rata and flow-through arrangements are discussed in detail below, under "Royalties.")

Production agreements more and more are becoming the common method of signing, or in this case, providing, artists to record companies. The benefits to both parties—to the record company the probability of using recording funds to keep recording costs in line and to the production company the ability to control the recording process—make them the agreement of choice.

SAMPLE CONTRACT PROVISIONS

EXAMPLE 1: Conversion of Artist

1. Engagement. Reference is made to the Distribution Agreement between the parties hereto of even date. If Company shall exercise the option, known as the Conversion Option, as provided for in paragraph 29 of the Distribution Agreement, with respect to a particular Artist (as defined below) then the parties hereto acknowledge that the terms of this Agreement shall be applicable with respect to that particular Artist. Company hereby engages Producer to furnish to Company, in accordance with the requirements of the Agreement, the following: (a) Producer's services as in-studio producers and executive producers of musical project(s) hereunder and (b) the exclusive recording services of various musical artists as set forth herein.

EXAMPLE 2: Responsible for Royalties to Artist and Producer

8. Conditioned upon Producer's full and faithful performance of all material terms and conditions hereof, Company shall pay Producer an all-inclusive royalty in respect of Net Sales of Records

manufactured from the Masters Delivered hereunder at the applicable rates specified hereinbelow based on the applicable Royalty Base Price of the Record concerned ("Record Royalties"). Producer agrees to be solely responsible for and pay any and all royalties and/or other sums due to Artist and all other artists, musicians, performers and producer(s) which are or may become due by reason of Company's exploitation of the Masters Delivered hereunder.

EXAMPLE 3: Production Company Furnishes the Artist

5. Subject to subparagraph 6(c), below, during each applicable Artist Contract Period, you will cause Artist to perform for the recording of masters and you will cause the production and delivery to Company of the number of masters necessary to comprise one (1) album. . . .
6. (c) You will engage (pursuant to a binding agreement that grants to Company all rights in and to the recording) all artists, producers, musicians, and other personnel for the recording sessions hereunder. Company, at its sole cost and expense, has the right to have a representative attend all recording sessions conducted pursuant to this Agreement.

ROYALTIES

The production company is responsible for the payment of the artist's and the producer's royalties (see Example 1). The production company serves as a middleman between the record company and the artist and producer. The record company will usually pay the entire royalty to the production company, which will, in turn, pay royalties to the artist and to the producer from the monies received from the record company (see Example 1).

Sometimes the production company and the record company will agree to have the record company pay the artist's share of the royalties earned and/or advances directly to the artist.

Generally, the artist receives much the same royalty rate when signing with the production company as when signing directly with the record company. The agreement may call for a specified royalty, such as, say, 10%, or may provide for a pro-rata sharing of the total royalty being paid by the record company (see Example 3). For example, in a *pro-rata* arrangement the artist and the production company may agree to split the royalty equally—50% going to the artist and 50% going to the production company—or in some other proportion, perhaps 60% going to the artist and the remaining 40% to the production company. Another approach sometimes used in the agreement between the production company and the artist is a *flow-through* clause which provides for the artist's royalty computation to be changed to match the method used to calculate the production company's royalty from the record company (see Example 5).

It is not unusual for production agreements to have a higher royalty than the combined royalties of the artist and the producer would have been if the record company had signed separate agreements. This in itself may be adequate justification for an artist or producer to choose to use this form of agreement with a record company.

The production agreement carries an additional benefit to a producer who is also the production entity: Recording costs are almost always recouped from the total production royalty, which includes both the artist and the producer's royalty, plus, maybe, an additional royalty for the production company. Another plus, beyond faster recoupment at a higher royalty, is the fact that, as with a traditional recording agreement between the artist and the record company, recording costs are likely to be chargeable to the artist. This creates an interesting and very tempting opportunity for the production company: By having the recording costs recouped by the record company from the all-in production company royalty, the production company will not only receive royalties before an independent producer would, but the production company also can turn around and recoup the entire recording cost from the artist and end up not being responsible for any part of the cost of recording; that is, the production company has the opportunity to pocket an amount equal to the recording costs before having to make any royalty payment to the artist.

Example

Artist A is signed to B, a production company, who is both producer and production company. A's artist royalty is 10%, and the agreement provides that the recording costs will be recouped from A. B signs with Record Company for 20%, which equals $1.00 per album sold. An album featuring A is produced for Record Company by B at a cost of $100,000. After the album sells 100,000 copies, Record Company begins paying B at the rate of $1.00 per album. B keeps the royalty on the next 100,000 albums sold ($100,000) and does not have to pay artist anything until 200,001 copies of the album are sold, at which point artist begins to receive $0.50 per album.

Arguably, the artist is no worse off under this arrangement than the artist would be if the artist were signed directly to the record company. Presuming that the artist receives the same royalty rate from the production company as it would have from the record company with a direct signing, and using the scenario above, recording costs would be recouped from the artist at the rate of $0.50 per album and the artist would not begin receiving royalty payments until 200,001 copies of the album had been sold.

In fact, in many instances the artist is better off being signed through the production company because, either voluntarily or because of a contractual provision, the production company begins paying the artist upon recoupment of the recording costs based upon the combined royalty of the production company and the artist.

Example

Assume the same facts and numbers as in the example above, except that the artist will be paid when the recording cost ($100,000) is recouped from the combined royalty. Record Company credits the combined royalty of $1.00 per album against the $100,000 recording costs. After 100,000 units are sold, Record Company has recouped the recording costs. Thereafter, Record Company pays the production company $1.00 per album. The album sells an additional 100,000 units for a combined royalty of $100,000. The production company and artist each receive $50,000.

In both examples total sales are 200,000 units. But in scenario 1, the artist receives nothing; in scenario 2, the artist receives $50,000 (see Example 3).

SAMPLE CONTRACT PROVISIONS

EXAMPLE 1: All-Inclusive Royalty

8. Conditioned upon Producer's full and faithful performance of all material terms and conditions hereof, Company shall pay Producer an all-inclusive royalty in respect of Net Sales of Records manufactured from the Masters Delivered hereunder at the applicable rates specified hereinbelow based on the applicable Royalty Base Price of the Record concerned ("Record Royalties"). Producer

agrees to be solely responsible for and pay any and all royalties and/or other sums due to Artist and all other artists, musicians, performers and producer(s) which are or may become due by reason of Company's exploitation of the Masters Delivered hereunder.

☛ The record company pays the total royalty to the production company. In turn, the production company is responsible for paying royalties to the artist and producer. Although not stated in this clause, the all-in royalty paid to the production company does not include mechanical license fees and payments to unions, such as MPTF, based on sales. These remain the obligation of the record company.

EXAMPLE 2: Production Company Responsible for Direct Payment of Royalties to Artist

17. As used herein, the term "Artist Payments" means all sums (other than mechanical royalties) paid by Production Company to Artist (or, at Artist's request, to a third party) during: (i) the period in question, or (ii) during any preceding period to the extent such monies paid during such period exceeds an Annual Payment [for injunctive relief] prescribed in the applicable period and the actual recording costs relating to the Album to be recorded.

EXAMPLE 3: Pro-Rata Royalty for Artist

2. Conditioned upon my full and faithful performance of each and all of the terms hereof, Company agrees, except as otherwise provided, to pay me the applicable amount specified in the Payment & Master Schedule below. Subject to Subparagraph 2.(c)., below, I grant Company Two (2) options, each to renew this Agreement for the period set forth below, said options to run consecutively beginning at the expiration of the initial period, except as otherwise specified in the Payment & Master Schedule below. Each option shall be deemed automatically exercised unless Company notifies me, in writing, to the contrary at least ten (10) days prior to the expiration of the then current period.

PAYMENT & MASTER SCHEDULE

Periods of This Agreement	Duration	Masters	Amount per Master	Royalty
Initial Period	18 Months; or 8 Months following delivery of the minimum recording obligation (whichever is later)	1 album	Scale	50%
1st Option Period	18 Months; or 8 Months following delivery of the minimum recording obligation (whichever is later)	1 album	Scale	50%
2nd Option Period	18 Months; or 8 Months following delivery of the minimum recording obligation (whichever is later)	1 album	Scale	50%

• • •

(b) If Company enters into an agreement with a third party record company pursuant to a so-called "production agreement," Fifty (50%) Percent of recording costs incurred in connection with the recording of masters hereunder shall be deemed to be non-returnable advances to me and shall be charged against my royalties under this Agreement; provided, however, nothing contained herein shall result in a "double recoupment" of my share of recording costs as a result of the prior recoupment of such recording costs by the third party record company. If I should delay the commencement or completion of, or be unavailable for any recording sessions designated by Company hereunder for any reason whatsoever, I agree to pay all expenses and charges actually incurred or paid by Company.

• • •

(i) If Company enters into a production agreement with a third party record company as provided for herein, I shall receive my proportionate share [fifty (50%) percent] of advances made to Company by such third party record company, such share to be computed after the deduction of recording costs actually incurred, it being the intention of the parties hereto that recording costs be recouped "off the top" prior to any distribution of advances from such third party record company, as also provided for in Subparagraph 4(g), below.

• • •

3. The royalties set forth in the Payment & Master Schedule shall be the rate specified for the period in which the applicable master was recorded and shall be the percentage indicated of the monies received by Company from any third party distributor or record company for sales of records manufactured and sold by Company (or by any subsidiary, affiliate or licensee), which contain only records manufactured from masters recorded hereunder, except as otherwise expressly set forth herein where, for example, my recordings are coupled with other recordings (subject to the restrictions provided for herein). Net sales of any record shall be determined cumulatively on the aggregate number of such records sold, for which Company has been paid, after deducting all returns, rebates, credits, cancellations, and exchanges. In computing the number of records manufactured and sold hereunder, Company shall have the right to deduct returns and credits of any nature, including, without limitation, those on account of a one hundred (100%) percent return privilege, defective merchandise, exchange privilege, promotional credits, records not paid for, errors in billing, usable overstock and errors in shipment. Company shall have the right to maintain reasonable reserves against returns hereunder only if Company is the direct distributor of records hereunder.

• • •

(c) Except as expressly set forth hereinabove, and in Subparagraph 3(d), below, in all other respects my royalty shall be computed in the same manner (e.g., subject to the same royalty computation, deductions, reductions, reserves, etc.) as Company's royalty is computed and reduced pursuant to any agreements entered into by Company concerning the distribution and sale of records manufactured from the masters.

• • •

(f) Company will compute royalties payable hereunder within sixty (60) days after June 30 and after December 31 of each year for the preceding six (6) month period and will render accountings for and pay such royalties less any unrecouped advances against royalties due me, within said sixty (60) days. Royalties for records sold hereunder will not be due and payable until payment therefor is received by Company. Notwithstanding anything to the contrary provided for above, if Company has entered into an agreement with a third party record company for the manufacture and distribution of records manufactured from masters recorded hereunder, Company shall account to me hereunder within sixty (60) days of Company's receipt of royalties from such third party record company. Copies of applicable royalty statements from the third party record company shall accompany such accounting to me.

(g) Notwithstanding anything to the contrary contained herein, it is agreed and understood that Company and I shall share equally in advances, net of recording costs, received by Company from any third party record company in connection with any agreement between Company and such third party record company for the manufacture and release of recordings made from masters recorded hereunder on such third party record company's own label in the same proportion as is set forth in the Payment & Master Schedule. Company shall pay me my share of advances hereunder within thirty (30) days of Company's receipt of payment from such third party record company.

☛ This provision represents an across-the-board, pro-rata sharing of the royalty between the production company and the artist. The artist's royalty rate is 50% of the royalties received by the production company from the record company (paragraph 2). In addition, all costs and advances are shared in the proportion between the production company and the artist. Also note that subparagraph 2(b) contains an express restriction against double recoupment.

EXAMPLE 4: Pro-Rata with Double Dipping

6. Conditioned upon your full and faithful performance of all the material terms and provisions hereof, you shall be paid in respect of the sale by us or our Distributor of phonograph records embodying the Masters recorded hereunder and in respect of any other exploitation by us, or Distributor, our Licensees or our Distributor's licensees of such Masters, the following sums upon the terms hereinafter set forth:

(a) (i) In connection with the sales or other exploitations of the Masters, we shall pay you an amount equal to fifty percent (50%) of the Net Record Royalties (hereafter defined) actually received by us under any Distributor Agreement. As used herein, the term "Net Record Royalties" in respect of any particular Master shall mean the gross royalty earned and payable to us under the Distribution Agreement in respect of such Master less any and all royalties payable to any third party royalty participant other than the individual producer. Without limiting the foregoing, we shall have the right to retain for our own account fifty percent (50%) of the Net Record Royalties and we shall pay all royalties payable to any individual producer from such royalties retained by us. Your producer royalty, if any, shall be included in your 50% share, i.e., an "all in" royalty.

(ii) Without limiting the generality of the foregoing, no royalties shall be payable by us to you hereunder unless and until all Recoupable Costs (hereinafter defined) shall have been recouped from royalties payable to you hereunder. Royalties shall be payable to you hereunder respectively after the recoupment of such Recoupable Costs. As used herein, the term "Recoupable Costs" shall mean any and all recording costs, advances, video production costs, or other costs or charges of any nature which are recoupable by the Distributor under the Distributor Agreement and/or by us pursuant to subparagraph 7(d) below.

(iii) Without limiting the generality of anything contained in this contract, you shall not be paid any royalties in respect of any exploitation of the masters for which we do not earn a royalty under the Distribution Agreement.

(b) (i) We shall also pay you an amount equal to fifty percent (50%) of: the amount by which all advances or so-called "recording funds" actually paid to us under the Distribution Agreement exceed (A) any and all advances required to be paid by us (or otherwise deducted from such advances or "recording funds" and paid) to any individual producer of any of the Masters; (B) any and all recording costs in connection with the recording of the Masters paid by us (or otherwise deducted from such advances or "recording funds" and paid); and (C) any other costs deducted by the Distributor from such advances or "recording funds."

(ii) Notwithstanding the foregoing, we shall have the right to retain, for our own account, from the first (or any subsequent) advances or other sums paid by the Distributor to us (i.e., prior to calculating your share thereof pursuant to the provisions of this paragraph 6) any and all direct, out of pocket costs incurred by us in connection with the Demos or other recordings embodying your performances or in connection with obtaining to the Distributor Agreement (including, without limitation, attorney's fees with respect to the negotiating thereof).

☛ The above provision is also a pro-rata arrangement. Note that subparagraph 6(a)(i) has language stating that the production company has the responsibility to pay the producer's royalty, unless the artist is the producer. The effect of subparagraph 6(a)(ii) is that the production company recoups recording costs from the artist's royalty, which means that the production company can lay off *all* recoupable costs on the artist, including, in addition to recording costs, promotion costs, producer's fees, etc. Once the record company recoups the costs from the combined production company/artist royalties, the production company continues to recoup from the artist until a matching amount is reached. In effect, the production company gets to pocket the extra amount before the artist sees a penny. The artist has been double-dipped!

EXAMPLE 5: Production Company's Right to Change Artist's Royalty Computation

7b (iii) At our election, we shall have the right to automatically amend the terms and provisions hereof to comply with the terms and provisions of the Distribution Agreement, including without limitation, those terms and provisions relating to the manner and basis for computing, paying and reducing the royalty payable to you hereunder.

PRODUCTION COMPANY–PRODUCER

The production company supplies the producer to the record company in much the same way as the artist is supplied: The producer signs to the production company, which, in turn, supplies the producer's services as part of the elements being delivered by the production company. (Remember that, among other possibilities, the artist may be acting as the production company, and in that capacity may be supplying an independent producer for the recordings, or an independent producer may be acting as the production company.)

As is true with the royalty due to the artist, the royalty due to the producer is the obligation of the production company and comes out of the overall royalty to the production company. If the independent producer is not part of the production company, the independent producer may insist that producer royalties be paid directly by the record company. This is not something the production company can agree to without first obtaining clearance from the record company, because this separate payment may call for the producer to be paid at a time that the production company is still in a debit position with the record company. If the record company agrees to such an arrangement, the producer's royalty will have to be broken out separately from the royalty paid to the production company. Note that even in a situation in which the production company and/or the artist are still in an unrecouped position, it is possible for a royalty to be due the independent producer. For example, the recording costs on an album produced by an independent producer may have been recouped, but the production company's account may still be in the red because of unrecouped costs from projects unconnected to the independent producer. It is not uncommon for arrangements to be made for the independent producer to be paid notwithstanding the overall unrecouped position of the production company (see Example 2).

One major battlefield in the production agreement may be the issue of the record company's right to replace the production company's producer (the production company and producer usually being one and the same person) with a producer of the record company's choice. While the experience and prior success of the producer may be sufficient to stave off an initial attack by the record company, it is just as likely that the record company will still insist upon the right to substitute a producer at some later date. If the production company and/or the designated producer are without notable experience and success, it is almost a certainty that the record company (especially if it is one of the major labels) will insist on the right to substitute a different producer, either at will or upon certain events happening or not happening.

The solution to the impasse between the production company and the record company is to work out some sort of performance criteria. For example, if the prior album sells x units within x period, the producer has the right to continue, if the sales do not meet x within the period, then the record company has the right to substitute. (Example 3 illustrates this sort of provision.)

What happens if the record company substitutes another producer of its own choosing to record masters pursuant to the production agreement? Certainly there are emotional and practical issues beyond the scope of this book if the production company (which is frequently the same as the artist) does not want the designated producer. However, with regard to the subject of royalties, there are some predictable ramifications. Since the royalty paid to the production company is presumed to include a royalty payment to the producer, there will usually be a reduction in the total royalty paid to the production company to compensate for the royalty which will now, presumably, be paid by the record company directly to the new producer.

Although it might produce an emotionally charged situation, the production company should insist on having some say in negotiating the terms that are included in the "designated" producer's agreement. Since these payments are coming out of the production company's royalties and recording budget, they are of more than passing interest to the production company. In general, the production company (especially if it is also the artist) will have some contractual right of approval of or consent to the choice of producer (see Examples 1, 3, and 5). Using whatever leverage it has, the production company may be able to insert language in the agreement stating that the record company will assume all or a portion of the responsibility for payment of the producer's royalty (see Example 4).

A deal structured as a production agreement—even taking into account the possibility of being bumped as the producer—affords an individual producer a much greater level of protection than does a situation where the independent producer brings an artist to the record company and then signs on as the producer separately. With a production agreement, the production company holds the artist's contract, and it would be extremely hard for the record company to separate the producer from the royalty stream.

SAMPLE CONTRACT PROVISIONS

EXAMPLE 1: Mutual Approval of Producer

26. Each individual producer of masters recorded hereunder shall be subject to the mutual approval of Company and me ("Producer"). I shall be solely responsible for the payment of fees and royalties to any Producer for his services hereunder and I agree to indemnify and hold Company harmless from any claims and expenses (including reasonable attorneys' fees) to the contrary.

EXAMPLE 2: Producer Paid Directly

12. . . . In the event that Company is required to pay royalties to a Producer at a time when Production Company's royalty account is still in a debit position, then Company shall treat such payment of royalties to a Producer as an additional advance to Production Company which shall be recoupable from any royalties otherwise payable to me under this or any other agreement between Company and Production Company.

EXAMPLE 3: Producer's Future Right Subject to Meeting Shipping Criteria

2. *Artist and Producer.*

(a) You will, in accordance with the terms and conditions hereof, furnish to Company the services of (i) (hereinafter referred to as "Artist") and (ii) such person(s) to be mutually approved by you and Company from time to time (hereinafter referred to as "Producer") to produce master recordings embodying Artist's performances. For the purposes hereof, you hereby warrant and represent that (hereinafter referred to as "Name") was Producer of the First LP (as hereinafter defined). Name is hereby deemed mutually approved as Producer of all subsequent LPs subject to subparagraph 2(b), below. . . .

(b) Notwithstanding anything to the contrary contained in subparagraph 2(a), above, if any particular LP (the "Name-Produced LP") produced by Name has not gross shipped (as such term is commonly understood in the recording industry) at least three hundred thousand (300,000) units in the United States within three (3) months after the release through "normal trade channels" (as hereinafter defined) in the United States of such Name-Produced LP, then such person to be mutually approved as producer of the master recordings of any LP(s) to be recorded and delivered in accordance with the terms hereof after the Name-Produced LP shall be, if Company so elects, in its sole and exclusive discretion, a person other than Name.

EXAMPLE 4: Cap on Royalty Paid to New Producer

13. . . . With respect to sales of records embodying performances rendered at recording sessions produced by a person(s) so designated by Company to act as Producer, the Basic Rate accruable under subparagraph 4(a), above, shall be the applicable rate specified therein reduced by the corresponding Basic rate accruable to the credit of such designee(s), but in no event shall such reduction be more than Four (4%) Percent. The advance payable to you pursuant to subparagraph 4(d)(i),

above, with respect to any LP produced by a person(s) so designated by Company to act as Producer shall be reduced by the amount of the fee, if any, payable to such designee.

☛ Here a maximum of 4% of the producer's royalty is chargeable to the production company. Anything over 4% is the responsibility of the record company.

EXAMPLE 5: Production Company's Choice of Producer

(c) You will engage (pursuant to a binding agreement that grants to Company all rights in and to the recording) all artists, producers, musicians, and other personnel for the recording sessions hereunder. Company, at its sole cost and expense, has the right to have a representative attend all recording sessions conducted pursuant to this Agreement.

☛ Although the production company here has the right to choose the producer, Big Brother is still lurking about, as the record company has the right to send a "representative" to any session. Implicit with the representative's presence is the knowledge that one telephone call can stop the project and, perhaps, remove the producer.

INJUNCTIVE RELIEF

The compound relationships of the production company signing the artist directly and then entering into an agreement with a record company for the distribution of the recordings add a new ingredient to the stew when considering the issues of equitable relief and injunctions.

As discussed in Chapter 3, in 1994, the California Legislature revised Section 3423 of the California Civil Code and Section 526 of the California Code of Civil Procedure and created two different methods of determining what the guaranteed compensation should be to qualify for equitable relief ("Equitable Relief," pages 137–144). What had been the plain old "$6,000 question" (see pages 139–143) for anyone wishing to attempt to obtain injunctive relief against an artist or a group had become a whole series of questions. In addition to the questions raised in the earlier discussion, what new issues crop up for a production company, its artists, and the record company?

Is an independent production company going to take on the financial responsibility of guaranteeing an artist, or a whole group, the minimum sums provided for in the laws? This financial responsibility is not insubstantial. It is the rare production company, indeed, that can afford and/or is willing to provide these financial guarantees to one artist, let alone an entire group. Do the math. Without success, this can be a very expensive proposition for an individual or company that is not well-heeled.

Today most production companies choose (usually by default) the "superstar insurance" method instead of making a minimum guarantee. (For an explanation of superstar insurance, see "Injunctive Relief," Chapter 3, pages 142–143.) This is even more expensive (10 times the minimum amount), at least on the back end; but at least it does not include front-end expenses where the risk factor is the highest.

When California's injunctive relief statutes were amended, a section referring to contracts "in writing for the rendition *or furnishing* [emphasis added] of personal services" was changed so that the words "or furnishing" no longer appear. Unless the law is altered, modified, or explained, does the deletion of "or furnishing" from the laws mean that the record company cannot directly obtain injunctive relief against an artist signed through a production company? For whatever it is worth, when the law was first passed in 1994, I called the individual who drafted the amended version and asked why "or furnishing" had been deleted. He was shocked. Apparently, other than me, no one had noticed. The omission was a typo—an error. (For those who love typo error stories: One of the first printed bibles was known as the "Sinner's Bible" because one of the Ten Commandments read: "Thou shall commit adultery.")

If the issue of injunctive relief is not taken care of in the production agreement to the satisfaction of the record company, it is probable that the record company will either handle this through the inducement letter or by requiring the production company to amend its agreement with the artist accordingly. This raises the legal question, Can this be done retroactively and, if not, must a new contract be entered into by the parties? And, if a new contract is required, does this not raise the horrible specter of a renegotiation with an artist who knows going in that he or she now has economic value?

The production company is faced with a "damned if you do, damned if you don't" situation: exposing itself to the potential financial risk of guaranteeing the artist the minimum amounts provided for in the statutes or hoping to be able to renegotiate with the artist when the artist knows there is a deal pending and he/she/they are a wanted and valuable commodity.

The problem becomes even more acute when a production company/record label is signing artists directly, but must be able to furnish the artist(s) to the distributor/record label under a "conversion" provision in the distribution agreement. Must the production company/record label guarantee every artist (including each member of groups) the minimum payments required when perhaps one in one hundred or one in two hundred, at best, may be a candidate for conversion?

SAMPLE CONTRACT PROVISIONS

EXAMPLE 1: Superstar Insurance

(d) Company shall have the right to pay you at any time any additional amounts which may be required to be paid as a condition to Company's seeking any injunction pursuant to Section 526 of the California Code of Civil Procedure and Section 3423 (5th) of the California Civil Code ("Additional Payments"). You agree to accept all such additional payments. All compensation (other than Mechanical Royalties) paid to you hereunder which is not applied to the Annual Payments therefore due you will be credited toward satisfying the obligation to make Additional Payments as a prerequisite to seeking injunctive relief hereunder.

☞ Here the production company relies on the superstar method, potentially more expensive if used, but undoubtedly cheaper in the long run. This is what I recommend to my independent production company clients.

EXAMPLE 2: Production Company Guarantees Payment

(f) For the benefit of Company, Production Company shall guarantee that each member of Group during each year of the Agreement hereunder shall receive compensation at the rate of not less than the minimum amounts set forth in the California Code of Civil Procedure, Section 526 and California Civil Code, Section 3423 (Fifth) or such other applicable statute during such period.

☞ Here the record company locks the production company into having to pay each member of the group the minimum guaranteed amount each year. God help the production company if the agreement doesn't provide some sort of subsidy from the record company.

EXAMPLE 3: Production Company Guarantees Injunction Provision

21. You warrant and represent that you have provisions in your agreement with Artist preserving Company's and your right to seek injunctive relief to prevent the breach of this Agreement by Artist, and accordingly, it is your and Company's mutual intention that this Agreement be interpreted and construed in such a manner as to comply with the provisions of Section 3423 (Fifth) of the California Civil Code concerning the availability of injunctive relief to prevent the breach of a contract in writing for the rendition of personal services.

☛ Here, at least, the record company allows the production company to rely on the superstar method.

CHAPTER 7

OPTION AGREEMENTS

Who controls the past controls the future.
Who controls the present controls the past.
—GEORGE ORWELL

It is not uncommon for a production company or producer to enter into an *option agreement* with an artist prior to taking the plunge of signing the artist to a long-term contract and incurring obligations. It is possible, but less common, for a record company to use an option agreement as an interim step before signing the artist to a term agreement. There is no particular justification for this approach other than that the record company cannot make a decision at that particular time and wants to hold onto the artist without expending money on production, promotion, advertising, etc.

An option agreement may also be referred to as a *development agreement*, where the record company takes the opportunity to "bring along" an artist to the point where it makes sense to sign the artist to a term agreement, which entails significant commitment and expense on the part of the record company. The concept of the option agreement is to tie up the artist for a specified period of time while a decision is made as to whether or not the artist should be signed to a regular recording agreement. We, of course, know who holds all of the cards in making the decision whether or not the option will be exercised. During the option period, the artist is signed to an exclusive, albeit temporary, agreement, which prevents the artist from entering into agreements with anyone else.

Usually, but not necessarily, some recording is done during the option period, whether it be demos (recordings made to demonstrate an artist's talents) or masters. Upon the completion of the recordings, the recordings are shopped, or released, as the case may be, and a determination is made as to whether or not to exercise the option to sign the artist to the term agreement.

Some option agreements may be very short in duration, in which case they will usually incorporate either the terms of or the actual proposed agreement as an exhibit which is deemed to go into effect upon the exercise of the option. In others, all the terms of the final recording agreement are contained in the option agreement. Option agreements involve a double negotiation in that the terms and conditions of the option agreement *and* the terms of the recording agreement must be negotiated, since the recording agreement will go into effect if the option is exercised.

The following sections are a review of those provisions in the option agreements which are either somewhat different from the equivalent provisions in the recording agreement or unique to the option agreement.

TERM OF THE OPTION

The *term of the option* is the period during which the option to exercise the agreement to sign the artist to a longer-term agreement can be exercised by the producer, production company, record company, or whatever. The essence of the option agreement is that the party taking the option has a period of time during which they may or may not choose to proceed into an agreement having a longer term and a greater commitment. The period of time for an option agreement usually, but not always, commences upon the signing of the option agreement and then runs a specified period—such as a period of 90 days, 6 months, 1 year, etc.—usually from either the recording of or the completion of masters, probably being recorded as part of a recording commitment contained in the option agreement (see "The Recording Commitment," page 249, and Example 1 below). Sometimes, no recordings are made during the option period, perhaps because the artist has already recorded masters and somebody wants to "shop" them on behalf of the artist. Under such circumstances the period is most likely to run from the signing of the agreement. Of course, how to determine when the clock actually starts running is limited only by the imaginations of the parties. (A case in point is Example 2, which has a period which commences on signing, but the clock does not start running until the earlier of 10 months from signing or 6 months from the completion of the masters being recorded.) The length of the period is subject to negotiation. The artist, presumably, wants a shorter period; the production entity wants a longer period during which to determine whether or not the option is to be exercised.

The bottom-line question when deciding how long the option is going to run is, Just how long will it take to make this sucker fly? Anything under 6 months is probably too short and anything over 1 year is, I believe, too long. Generally, anything that has been shopped for six months and does not have either an agreement or a pending agreement is probably not going to sell, at least not with the party doing the shopping. The fault may lie with the product or it may lie with the person doing the shopping. Or the timing may just be off. Regardless, there should be some outside date by which something either happens or it is time for all the parties to gather up their marbles and find a new game to play in.

> ### SAMPLE CONTRACT PROVISIONS

EXAMPLE 1: 6 Months from Delivery of Demos

2. Term.

   (a) The term of this Contract ("Term") shall begin on the date hereof and shall expire upon the date six (6) months after the date upon which you deliver to us the Demos.

• • •

   (c) Notwithstanding anything to the contrary contained in the foregoing provisions of this paragraph 2, if we shall not have entered into good faith negotiations with a Distributor with respect to the material terms and conditions of a Distribution Agreement within six (6) months after your delivery to us of the Demos, then you and we each shall have the election, upon written notice to the other, to terminate the Term effective as of the date of that notice and upon such termination neither you nor we shall have any continuing obligations or rights hereunder.

> ☞ After 6 months, unless there is a "good faith negotiation" in progress, either party can terminate with written notice.

EXAMPLE 2: 10 Months from Signing or 6 Months from Recording

5. The option provided for herein shall commence as of the date hereof and shall continue for a period which shall expire the earlier of ten (10) months from the date hereof or six (6) months from the completion of the Masters . . .

EXAMPLE 3: 1 Year; Start Recording within 60 Days

1. This Option Agreement shall commence as of the date hereof, and shall continue in force for one (1) year. . . . Producer agrees that the recording of four (4) master recordings (hereinafter referred to as the "Masters") featuring your performances shall commence no later than sixty (60) days from the date hereof.

EXERCISE OF THE OPTION

The option agreement will have some provision dealing with the procedure for exercising the option. In most cases, unlike recording agreements, the right to exercise will extend up to and include the last day of the term. Indeed, in some cases it even may continue beyond the option period if there is a good-faith negotiation for an agreement in process (see Example 4).

The exercise of the option can be subject to some precondition, such as the sale of the masters produced, a recording agreement, a payment of money, or whatever can be negotiated. The condition may even require that there be an agreement with, for example, a major label or a company having a nationwide distribution system (see Example 2).

SAMPLE CONTRACT PROVISIONS

EXAMPLE 1: 7 Months Within Which to Give Notice

4. (b) Within seven (7) months following completion of the master recordings provided for above, Company shall have the right to give you written notice of its intention to exercise the option provided for herein and concurrently with such exercise the Recording Agreement attached hereto as Exhibit A shall be deemed to become effective. If Company fails to exercise its right by the giving of such written notice as set forth in this subparagraph, the option provided for herein shall automatically expire.

EXAMPLE 2: Distributor Agreement with Major Label Prerequisite for Exercise

2. (b) You hereby acknowledge that we intend to enter into one (1) or more record production and distribution agreements with one (1) or more major record companies or label(s) distributed by a major record company (hereinafter individually and collectively referred to as "Distributor") in one (1) or more territories of the world for the production, manufacture, and sale of recordings embodying your performances. . . . We agree that the Option provided for herein may not be exercised by us unless we have met the pre-requisite for entering into a Distributor Agreement with a record company which meets the definition of being a Distributor. The Term of this Agreement, unless we otherwise give you notice to the contrary in writing, shall be automatically extended to be coterminous and coincide with the term of the Distribution Agreement, including all extensions, suspensions and renewals thereof.

EXAMPLE 3: Option May Be Exercised up to Last Moment

4. The option hereunder may be exercised by us giving you notice in writing at any time prior to

the expiration of such option term. Such notice to you may be given by delivery to you by certified or registered mail to you at your address last known to us. Such notice by mail shall be deemed to have been given on the date on which it is mailed.

☛ Even in option agreements like this, where the option may be exercised at any time up to actual expiration of the option term, procedures on how the exercise-of-option notice is to be delivered are specified.

EXAMPLE 4: Good-Faith Negotiations May Extend Period

5. Notwithstanding anything to the contrary contained in this Agreement, if Company has entered into good faith negotiations with a recognized record company prior to the expiration of this Option Term, the Option Term shall be extended up to thirty (30) days.

☛ Depending on whom you are dealing with, you may want to set some parameters around what constitutes "good faith."

THE RECORDING COMMITMENT

> PROTEUS:
> **I do as truly suffer**
> **As e'er I did commit.**
> —WILLIAM SHAKESPEARE
> *Two Gentlemen of Verona*, Act V, Scene 4

Unlike the equivalent provisions in the recording agreement, the recording commitment in an option agreement usually is not stated in terms of a minimum commitment of number of masters to be recorded (or, perhaps, number of demos, since the commitment sometimes refers to recordings to be shopped for a record deal, which are not necessarily finished masters—see Example 1). Indeed, there may not even be a recording commitment of any sort in an option agreement, since the option agreement is really a license to shop the artist for a specified period of time. It is not uncommon for the material being shopped to be recordings supplied by the artist and not produced or otherwise created by the holder of the option. Under these circumstances, some thought must be given to the option holder's rights after the expiration of the option period. (See below, "Rights on Nonexercise," pages 251–255.)

Arguably, if the agreement is called a *development* agreement, there should be some recording commitment, for is it not the essence of a development deal that there will be development in the form of product being recorded during that period? Of course, essence and reality are not always in agreement. Additionally, it is possible, but not likely, that an option agreement might contain a commitment for additional material, for example, a provision specifying that a minimum of so many masters are to be recorded. From the artist's standpoint, the use of "minimum of" language should be avoided as it gives the other party the opportunity to record additional product without making a long-term commitment to the artist.

Most option agreements do have a requirement for the artist to record a specified number of masters during the option period. Presumably, these masters are then used to shop the artist for a recording agreement. The recording commitment in these agreements usually is in the range of two to four masters to be recorded under the supervision of the producer, production company, or record company. Because of the combination of the speculative nature of the agreements and the costs of recording, it is unusual for the commitment to exceed four masters.

SAMPLE CONTRACT PROVISIONS

EXAMPLE 1: Record Minimum of Four Demos

(a) You shall record for and deliver to us not less than four (4) Demos within thirty (30) days after the date hereof. Upon our request you shall deliver to us that additional number of Demos as we shall reasonably require; and you shall record for and deliver to us that number of master recordings ("Masters") required to be delivered by us to the Distributor pursuant to the Distribution Agreement as and when such recordings are required to be so delivered.

> ☛ Exactly what your mother should have warned you not to do—agree to deliver additional demos in excess of the minimum specified. Compare this with the next two examples.

EXAMPLE 2: Four Masters (No More, No Less)

2. Producer agrees that the recording of four (4) master recordings (hereinafter referred to as the "Masters") featuring your performances shall commence no later than sixty (60) days from the date hereof.

EXAMPLE 3: Two Masters (No More, No Less)

3. You agree to record two (2) masters of selections chosen by Company. . . . Such recording to take place at a studio chosen by Company within sixty (60) days after the date of this Agreement.

EXAMPLE 4: Four Demos, One Album, And . . .

2. (a) During the term hereof you shall record for us (i) four (4) demonstration recordings embodying your performances ("Demos" herein), and (ii) upon our request sufficient Masters to constitute one (1) album of no less than thirty-eight (38) minutes in duration (hereinafter sometimes referred to as the "First Album") and such additional Masters as we may further request.

> ☛ If Example 1 is bad, this is worse. It does not even have the dubious protection of the addition of "reasonably" to the right to require additional recordings.

INCORPORATION BY REFERENCE

Some option agreements are self-contained in the sense that they have all the provisions of a recording agreement contained within the agreement. Other option agreements deal only with the terms of the option agreement and then attach a full-fledged recording agreement as an exhibit to the option agreement and incorporate by reference the terms of the recording agreement if the option is exercised. (See Examples 1 and 2 below and the section "Incorporation by Reference," Chapter 5, pages 225–226.) Again, under either arrangement, there are two parts to the negotiation process: the option itself and the long-term recording agreement that may come out of it.

SAMPLE CONTRACT PROVISIONS

EXAMPLE 1: Exhibit A Incorporated As the Agreement

8. If the Option is exercised, the agreement attached hereto as Exhibit A and incorporated herein by reference (hereinafter referred to as the "Recording Agreement") shall be deemed signed and

effective as of the date of the notice of exercise. The Masters recorded hereunder shall be deemed to have been recorded during the initial period of the Recording Agreement and shall apply to the recording commitment contained in the Recording Agreement.

EXAMPLE 2: Recording Agreement Attached As Exhibit

12.(a) Upon the exercise by Company of the option provided for herein, Artist agrees to be bound by the terms and conditions of the agreement attached hereto as Exhibit A.

RIGHTS ON NONEXERCISE

What happens when the option period expires and there has been no exercise of the option? Generally, the parties each go their separate ways—probably sadder and hopefully wiser. But what of the little bundles of joy which this union has left behind—the masters or demos recorded during the option period? As a practical matter, probably nothing will happen to them. If no deal was made during the option period, it is quite likely that nothing can be done with the masters and they will be allowed to languish on a shelf or in a vault. There is a market, albeit not a thriving market, in these "orphaned" recordings for use on soundtracks of theatrical films, television films and programs, videos, and the like, as, for example, generic rock 'n' roll recordings to be blasting out of a jukebox or playing on a car radio.

The producing entity may wish to have the opportunity to get its recording costs back—or, perhaps, the right to have a commercial release of the recordings in the future (see Example 1). The option agreement usually has provisions which provide that, even if the option is not exercised, the recordings are treated as if it had been. Accordingly, the masters may be used to release commercial recordings, and the provisions of the recording agreement apply to the recordings as if the option had been exercised.

It may be possible for the artist to retain possession of the masters, either for release or as demos for the purpose of obtaining a recording agreement. This may require some form of payback and/or override to the producer (see Example 2). The payback may be a set price. It may be the actual recording costs, usually paid off the top. It may even be some percentage of the advance, if any, received by this artist. The override is usually a percentage royalty paid as if it were a producer's royalty, and sometimes it actually is a producer's royalty (see Example 3). As part of the written contract between the parties, these provisions are enforceable, at least against the artist. If the artist is unable to have the new record company take responsibility for the payback and/or the override, the money will come out of the artist's share.

Sometimes, the option agreement will provide that even if the masters or demos are just "used" by the artist or a third party to obtain a record contract with a different company, after the expiration of the option agreement there must be, if not a payback, at least an override. This "usage" may not even involve commercial release or purchase of the recordings; submission itself may be enough to create the obligation for an override. Indeed, the new company may have hated the submitted recordings and signed the artist *in spite* of them. If this sounds far-fetched, check out Example 4 below, where the override obligation even extends to publishing agreements. Granted, a direct relationship between masters or demos and subsequent signing may be hard to prove or disprove, but the vaguer the language, the more likely it is that disputes will arise. For example, see subparagraph (f)(ii) of Example 4 below, where it would have been desirable to specify some criteria for determining whether or not a future contract has been "based upon" the demos.

EXAMPLE 1: Producer's Right to Use Masters If Option Not Exercised

10. If the option provided for herein is not exercised, notwithstanding anything to the contrary contained herein, Producer shall continue to have the right to manufacture and distribute recordings made from the Masters hereunder. . . . The terms and conditions of the Record Contract shall apply to the recordings so manufactured and distributed as if they had been recorded pursuant to the Record Contract.

☞ The producer may release the recordings whether or not the option is exercised. If the option is not exercised, the terms and conditions of the "Record Contract," which would have applied if the option had been exercised, are incorporated by reference back into the now-expired option agreement and become binding upon the artist.

EXAMPLE 2: Payback and Override

(d) Notwithstanding anything to the contrary contained herein, if we shall not enter into the Distribution Agreement . . . then we shall grant to you all of our right, title and interest in and to any and all Demos and Masters theretofore recorded hereunder and, upon our request, you shall pay to us one-half (½) of the aggregate Recording Costs incurred by us in connection with those Demos and Masters. If, at any time after the expiration of this Contract . . . you enter into a recording agreement or licensing agreement with any third party pursuant to which the Demos or Masters are exploited in the form of Phonograph Records or otherwise, you shall pay or cause to be paid to us an amount equal to one-half (½) of the aggregate Recording Costs of the Demos and Masters (the "Buy-Out Amount") and you shall cause that third party to pay to us a royalty in respect of all phonograph records embodying those Demos and Masters which shall be the equivalent of two percent (2%) of the suggested retail list price of one hundred percent (100%) of net sales of top-line, full-priced Phonograph Records sold through normal retail distribution channels in the United States and which royalties shall be otherwise reduced, calculated and adjusted as your royalty is reduced, calculated and adjusted; provided that such royalty shall be (i) . . . [pro-rata reduction of royalties for release with other recordings] and (ii) payable to us retroactively to the first record sold after the recoupment of the Buy-Out Amount at the aggregate royalty payable to you under your agreement with that third party.

EXAMPLE 3: Override (Long Form)

22. In the event that within one (1) year after the expiration or termination of the term hereof, you shall enter into an agreement (said agreement hereinafter referred to as the "Artist Distribution Agreement") with a third party record distributor (the "Artist Distributor") for the sale, manufacture and distribution after the expiration or termination of the term hereof of records embodying your performances recorded hereunder, you shall cause the Artist Distributor to pay us the following royalties in respect of each master recording recorded hereunder subject to such Artist Distribution Agreement (herein such master recordings are referred to individually as a "Distribution Master" and collectively as "Distribution Masters"):

(a) A royalty at the rate of two percent (2%) of the suggested retail list price (the royalty rate set forth herein is referred to as our "Base Rate") with respect to the exploitation through normal retail channels in the United States of one hundred percent (100%) of net sales of CDs embodying the Distribution Masters (herein referred to as "US CD Retail Sales") based upon the proportionate share of such Distribution Masters to the total number of masters included on any such recording.

(b) Notwithstanding any of the foregoing, in the event the Artist Distributor shall calculate your royalties under the Artist Distribution Agreement based upon the so-called "wholesale price," "sub-distributor price" or any other wholesale-based (rather than retail-based) price of records embodying the Distribution Masters, then Our Base Rate under paragraph 22(a) shall be four percent (4%) in lieu of two percent (2%).

(c) In all other aspects Our Base Rate shall be computed and reduced in the same manner and pursuant to the same policies (i.e., including without limitation, for singles sales, EP sales, club sales, budget sales, discounted records, PX sales, other non-retail sales and foreign sales; packaging deductions and tax deductions; "free goods" records [to distributors, through record clubs or otherwise], cut-outs, overstocks, promotional records, scrap records; reserve and liquidation provisions; exchange rate provisions; etc.) as your basic royalty for U.S. CD Retail Sales for such Distribution Masters ("Your Basic Rate") is computed and reduced by the Artist Distributor under the Artist Distribution Agreement. Notwithstanding the foregoing, in the event that Your Basic Rate shall be paid on the basis of less than one hundred percent (100%) of net sales, Our Base Rate shall be proportionately increased to compensate for such lesser basis upon which Your Basic Rate may be paid.

(d) In connection with any exploitation of a Distribution Master or a video or DVD containing a Distribution Master for which you receive a percentage of the Artist Distributor's "net receipts," in lieu of the royalty provided for above, we shall then receive a fraction of the aggregate amount payable to you under the Artist Distribution Agreement as a result of such exploitation, the numerator of which is Our Base Rate, and the denominator of which is Your Basic Rate.

(e) Without limiting the generality of the foregoing, we shall not be entitled to receive a royalty in respect of any exploitation of a Distribution Master which you, pursuant to the Artist Distribution Agreement, are not entitled to receive payment or credit therefor.

(f) Notwithstanding anything to the contrary contained herein, whenever any of the Distribution Masters are coupled on records with other master recordings, the royalty otherwise payable to us shall be multiplied by a fraction, the numerator of which is that number of Distribution Masters embodied on such record and the denominator of which is the total number of master recordings (including the Distribution Masters) embodied on such record.

(g) In addition to the foregoing, you shall cause the Artist Distributor to pay to us (or if the Artist Distributor shall fail, you shall pay to us) "Our Percentage" (hereinafter defined) of any and all advances payable to you or on your behalf by the Artist Distributor in connection with the Distribution Masters (excluding advances in the form of the recording costs described in paragraph (h), below). As used herein, the term "Our Percentage" shall mean an amount equal to a fraction, the numerator of which is Our Base Rate, and the denominator of which is Your Basic Rate.

(h) The royalty payable to us in respect of a particular Distributed Master under this paragraph 22, shall be payable after the recoupment by the Artist Distributor from the aggregate royalty payable to you under the Artist Distribution Agreement of solely the actual (audio only) recording costs incurred in connection with the recording of the other masters (excluding, specifically, any advances payable to you). Upon such recoupment as aforesaid, our account shall be credited for payment at the next regular accounting date under the Artist Distribution Agreement, of all royalties earned commencing with the next record sold after such recoupment.

☛ Note that the verbiage in this example could have been cut down considerably by the judicious use of incorporation by reference. Of interest also is the provision specifying that the override does not apply if more than 1 year goes by between the expiration of the option agreement and the signing of an artist–third party contract using masters recorded under the option agreement. Also, although the producer (or whatever we call the person or company receiving the override—that's one reason I hate using pronouns in contracts) is obviously entitled to a form of independent producer's royalty as the override, subparagraph (h) does not provide for the royalty to be paid from record one.

EXAMPLE 4: Payback and Override for Contract Based upon Demos

(f) (i) We shall have the right to exploit the Demos in any manner we see fit and to use your name and likeness in connection with the exploitation of the Demos to the same extent as provided elsewhere herein with respect to the Masters. In the event we shall exploit the Demos, we shall pay you royalties in the same manner as provided elsewhere herein with respect to the Masters. All costs incurred by us in connection with the recording, production and/or exploitation of the Demos shall be a direct debt from you to us and to the extent not reimbursed by you, we shall be able to recoup said amount from any monies payable by us to you hereunder or pursuant to any other agreement between you and us or our affiliates.

(ii) Notwithstanding the foregoing, in the event that the term of this agreement expires or is terminated in accordance with the provisions contained herein or by mutual agreement; and in the event thereafter at any time you enter into any recording agreement with any third-party record company, or if you enter into any publishing agreement with any third-party publisher based upon any Demos recorded hereunder, then you shall cause said record company and/or publisher, as applicable, to pay us from the first monies that become payable to you under the applicable recording agreement and/or publishing agreement, the aggregate amount of expenses incurred by us in connection with the production and promotion of the Demos.

CHAPTER 8

VIDEO and DVD

All truth passes through three stages. First, it is ridiculed.
Second, it is violently opposed. Third, it is accepted as
being self-evident.

—ARTHUR SCHOPENHAUER

Very much like Frankenstein's monster, when video first burst onto the scene, it was met with consternation, high hopes, fear, misunderstanding, and all the other emotions that make a good story. Unlike Frankenstein's monster, however, video didn't end up being pursued by a mob of panicked villagers wielding pitchforks and torches. Like Frankenstein's monster, there was some initial question as to its proper classification: Was it (video—not Frankenstein's monster) something to be sold, or was it something to sell with? In fact, it turned out to be both. This inability to put video into a single category is reflected in the contract provisions that deal with the recovery of costs in connection with the filming of videos and DVDs. At the birth of videos, the provisions regarding the granting of rights and exploitation of them grew quite rapidly (a review of some early agreements might even justify the use of the words "out of control"). A look at some of those provisions is in order, even though more recent agreements rarely go into such detail. Video/DVD provisions are now contained routinely within artist recording agreements and, accordingly, must be read and reviewed in that context. Unless noted differently, the provisions of recording agreements also apply to these rights granted by the artist in the recording agreement.

WHAT IS VIDEO?

Video rights first appeared as a gleam in the eyes of record executives years ago. There were some early false starts, such as Scopitone, "video jukeboxes" that were all the rage in the mid-1960s, but had disappeared completely by the end of the decade. Whatever it was going to be, record companies knew it was coming and damned if they were going to be left behind. By the mid- to late sixties, record companies began including "sight and sound" and/or "audiovisual" devices within the definition of "records" and "recordings" (see Example 1).

Rather than provide a blow-by-blow narrative of the history of the videotape in the music industry, I will provide a graphic illustration of the growth and contraction of contractual audiovisual rights (and obligations). The following three examples are in chronological order of their appearance in recording contracts.

In Example 1 the definition of "recording" includes reproductions having "sound synchronized with visual images." By the middle 1960s this definition was already commonplace in recording agreements. Through the '70s and '80s, as technology and commercial possibilities for "video" (which begins to take on a generic capacity beyond just tape configuration) expanded, so did the definitions of video, or "audiovisual," rights in recording agreements (see Example 2). Eventually, most definitions contracted back to rather simple language (see Example 3). Interestingly, the definition used in Example 1 is still very popular and commonly used in record contracts. *Et banum quo antiquius, ea melius* ("And the older a good thing is, the better it gets").

A definition of video currently used in the home video industry that includes DVDs as a "video device" is as follows:

> *Video device* shall mean individual, linear, physical copies of the pictures manufactured on a videocassette, laser disc, DVD, or any other format now known or hereafter devised to be used in conjunction with an in-home, nonbroadcast, reproduction apparatus.

You can see here and in the newer examples that the term "video" has, in many instances, become the generic term for any and all sight and sound devices, be they DVDs or any post-DVD configuration.

SAMPLE CONTRACT PROVISIONS

EXAMPLE 1: "Sound Synchronized with Visual Images"

(b) The nouns "records," "phonograph records," and "recordings" mean and include all forms of recording and reproductions, now known or which may hereafter become known, manufactured or sold primarily for home use and/or school use and/or jukebox use and/or use on or in means of transportation whether embodying sound alone or sound synchronized with visual images.

EXAMPLE 2: "Audiovisual Work"

21. Audiovisual Works.

(a) As used herein:

(i) "Audiovisual work" means a work consisting of a series of related images which are intrinsically intended to be shown by the use of a machine and/or device (including without limitation projectors, viewers and electronic equipment) together with accompanying sounds, if any, regardless of the nature of the material object, such as film, disc or tape, in which the work is embodied.

(A) "Video Clip" means an audiovisual work produced during the Term embodying a master recording of one (1) musical work produced hereunder in synchronization with a visual rendition of Artist's performances, and/or other performances and/or images.

(B) "Program" means an audiovisual work produced during the Term embodying Artist's audio performances in synchronization with a visual rendition of Artist's performances, and/or other performances and/or images, including, without limitation, a compilation, collective work or derivative work which embodies a Video Clip together with other Video Clip(s) and/or other audiovisual works.

(C) Video Clip(s) and Program(s) shall hereinafter sometimes be referred to collectively as "Video(s)."

(ii) Also as used herein:

(A) "Videogram" means a material object, including without limitation, tape, disc or film, embodying a Video or a compilation, collective work or derivative work which embodies a Video together with other Video(s) and/or other audiovisual work(s) intended for non-home use, including, without limitation, videocassettes and videodiscs.

(B) "Exhibition Copy" means a copy of a Video in any material form, including without limitation, tape, disc or film intended for non-home use, including, without limitation, all video jukebox, television and theatrical distribution.

☛ One wonders, What on earth were they thinking? It's sort of like reading predictions of the future from the 1939 World's Fair in New York City—one of which was that by 1960 we'd all be commuting to work in our personal individual helicopters? Happily, most people today stick with something much closer to Example 1.

EXAMPLE 3: "Sight and Sound Device"

(i) "AV Device" shall mean any so-called "audio-visual" or "sight and sound" device intended primarily for home use (e.g. videocassettes, videodiscs).

VIDEO RIGHTS

How does the record company obtain the rights to the videos featuring its artists? Since virtually all agreements, if they do not cover the issue elsewhere, now include videos in the definition of "record," the granting of the rights by the artist to the company in the recording agreement is also a grant of the video rights, throwing them in with everything else. (Note that Example 1 below creates a separate grant of rights just for videos.) By definition then, in many agreements, a video becomes a "record" and is treated as such. Do be aware, however, that under copyright law in the United States, videos and DVDs are not and cannot be "records" (or to be more precise, "phonorecords") as they are "copies" and phonorecords and copies are two different things indeed. (For a more detailed discussion of the distinctions between phonorecords and copies, and the importance of the distinctions, see Chapter 20, "Copyrights," page 497.) Today, it is virtually impossible to make a recording deal, especially with the major companies, without having to include the video rights.

Before there really was a home video market, the inclusion of video in the definition of "records" had already begun. At that time, the standard practice on behalf of the artist was to try to hold open the video rights or at least hold back some position vis-à-vis the royalty until the dust settled on "sight and sound" devices. The usual way for artists to do this was either to tie up the video rights in some manner which would require negotiation or to leave open the amount of the royalty to be paid in connection with video. Video rights were tied up by the artist by simply not granting them, giving the company a right of first refusal to the rights, or requiring the artist's consent before the rights could be exploited. If attempting to tie up the rights didn't work, the next step was to protect the artist through the back door using the royalty. Language providing that the royalty for videos would be negotiated (always, of course, "in good faith") at some future date or that it be consistent with industry standards as they developed offered some moderate control over future usage. As video has grown as an area of exploitation, especially in advertising and promotion, neither of these methods works anymore.

In the early days, there was one slight problem that would inevitably pop up: What if a recording artist appears in a motion picture and then the motion picture is released for home video? Under all the definitions, this became a "recording," even if the performance was strictly dramatic and was not a musical performance. Indeed, in those days of yore, an occasional demand was delivered to film companies from record companies claiming a royalty for the use of recording artists as actors. It does not take much imagination to figure out what probably happened the first time there was even a hint of this to a major recording artist who also happened to be an actor or actress. In most instances, this is not an issue anymore, but video language should always be checked with this possibility in mind (see Examples 3 and 5).

SAMPLE CONTRACT PROVISIONS

EXAMPLE 1: Video Grant of Rights

(e) You agree that (as between you and Company) Company is the sole, exclusive and perpetual owner of each Video including, but not limited to, the sole, exclusive and perpetual owner of all the copyrights of any nature whatsoever in and to each Video and each element or component part thereof, excepting only the copyrights in the underlying musical works. Company, its affiliates, subsidiaries and licensees shall have the sole exclusive and perpetual right to: (i) exhibit, duplicate, manufacture, distribute and exploit by sale, lease, license, rental or other manner each Video (or any portion(s) thereof) and copies thereof for such purposes, at such times and places, and in any and all media, including, but not limited to, "free," "pay," "public," "cable" and "subscription" television, theatrical and non-theatrical distribution, as shall be determined by Company, (ii) manufacture and distribute Videograms and Exhibition Copies, and (iii) allow others to exercise any or all of the aforesaid rights. Company shall have the right to cut and edit each Video (if necessary) for the exploitation of such Video in different media.

> ☞ This provision is from the same contract as Example 2 in the previous section. Apparently, because of the newness of video when the contract was drawn up, the company felt that it was necessary to include a separate grant-of-rights provision for video paralleling the grant-of-rights provision for records.

EXAMPLE 2: Artist's Consent to Video

28. From time to time during the term hereof, Company may request me to perform at sessions for the purposes of embodying my performances on videotape and/or films ("Tapes"):

a. I consent to Company's production of the Tapes as set forth herein.

b. I agree that Company is the sole, exclusive and perpetual owner of the Tapes from inception including, but not limited to, the sole, exclusive and perpetual ownership of all copyrights of any nature whatsoever in and to the Tapes.

c. I consent to the exhibition and exploitation of the Tapes by Company and its licensees for such purposes, at such times and places and in such media as determined by Company and its licensees.

EXAMPLE 3: Company's Exclusive Rights to Artist for Videos

21.(g)(i) You and Artist agree that, during the Term and, with respect to material recorded hereunder during the Restricted period, Artist shall not render and shall not have the right to render any performances (excluding solely non-musical dramatic performances (the "Dramatic Performances")) for any person other than Company (the "Third Party Company") in connection with the creation and/or exploitation of Videos. The foregoing restriction shall not apply to Artist's performances in television and/or motion pictures. Neither you nor Artist shall have the right to authorize, permit or grant to any Third Party Company the right to manufacture and/or distribute Videograms embodying performances other than the Dramatic performances, except that with respect to Artist's performances other than the Dramatic Performances in television and/or motion pictures as described in the next preceding sentence, Company agrees to negotiate in good faith with the applicable television or movie production company(ies) (as the case may be) with respect to the right to manufacture and/or distribute Videograms of the entire television film and/or motion picture film embodying performances other than the Dramatic Performances.

EXAMPLE 4: Artist Agrees to Issue Synchronization Licenses

24. We shall be the sole owner of all worldwide rights in and to Video (including the worldwide copyrights therein and thereto) to the same extent that we own Masters hereunder. You shall issue (or shall cause the music publishing companies having the right to do so to issue) to us at no cost (i) worldwide, perpetual synchronization licenses and (ii) perpetual licenses for public performance in the United States (to the extent that ASCAP and BMI are unable to issue same), for the use of all Controlled Compositions in Videos, which licenses shall be effective as of the commencement of production of the applicable Video. Your execution of this agreement shall constitute the issuance of such licenses by any music publishing company which is owned or controlled by you and/or by any Person owned or controlled by you.

> ☞ Synchronization licenses are discussed below in the sections "Production Costs," page 261, and "Music Rights," page 265, and in Chapter 9, "Songwriters' Agreements," the section "Synchronization Licenses," pages 294–295.) Briefly, under a synchronization license, the publisher of a musical composition gives the producer of a film, television program, video, etc., the right to use the composition in connection with a visual image, that is, to allow the music to be synchronized with the visual image. If the artist has not granted the synchronization rights ahead of time, the artist can use the granting of the license as leverage in a new negotiation.

EXAMPLE 5: Artist May Appear in Films

4. All master recordings recorded by you during the term hereof, from the inception of the recording thereof, and all phonograph records and other reproductions made therefrom, together with the performances embodied therein and all copyrights therein and thereto, and all renewals and extensions thereof. . . . Without limitation of any of the foregoing, we and/or our designees shall have the exclusive worldwide right in perpetuity to dispose of and exploit or license others to exploit or dispose of phonograph records or other reproductions (visual and non-visual) embodying such master recordings, by any method or manner now or hereafter known, in any field of use. Nothing contained in this contract shall be construed to limit your rights to grant to others the right to embody in Videos your dramatic performances in motion pictures, theatrical plays or television shows which are primarily dramatic in nature.

GUARANTEED VIDEO

Video has become increasingly important as a sales and promotional tool. We have entered an era where an artist's career can be made on the basis of a video performance alone, rather than through radio airplay and/or live performances. Video has, in fact, supplanted live touring as the major promotional device subsidized by record companies. Before the emergence of video as a marketing force, "tour support," the financial subsidizing by the record company of touring costs, was frequently asked for by artists' representatives and, not uncommonly, granted by the record company. Today, it is very rare for an artist to receive, at least as a contractual guarantee, tour support from the record company. The monies which may have gone to tour support in the past now go to producing videos. Television has become a major vehicle for promoting an artist and selling records. As a result, artists increasingly demand that they be guaranteed the release of videos for their product. The record companies recognize the value of the videos, but they also recognize the cost and the problems of recoupment (see below, "Video Royalties," pages 263–265).

Like every other provision of a recording contract involving significant expenses, the final shape and form of video provisions have a lot to do with the relative bargaining positions of the company and artist. The artist is probably going to want to make as many videos as possible; the record company is going to resist overcommitment to this very expensive activity—the cost to make a video of one cut from an album can easily be as high as, or higher than, the cost of recording an entire album.

From the artist's point of view, negotiating for guaranteed videos could invoke the ancient curse, "May you get what you wish for." A video may help to generate success (some will insist that without a video success is impossible), but the cost of producing the video will dig the artist's financial deficit hole even deeper. If the artist is pretty sure that a recording agreement will be the launching pad for a successful career, then it makes sense to insist on having a guaranteed video provision in the agreement. For the artist who is less ambitious (or less adventurous), it may be wise to pass on having guaranteed videos and try to minimize recoupable costs.

SAMPLE CONTRACT PROVISIONS

EXAMPLE 1: Good-Faith Negotiation Regarding Video Production

37. Notwithstanding anything to the contrary contained herein, with respect to each newly delivered Album Company agrees to give due and deliberate consideration in good faith to the production by Company of one (1) Video Clip embodying your performances of material contained in such newly delivered Album. If, after such good faith due consideration, Company shall decide in good faith not to produce said Video Clip with respect to such newly delivered Album, then you shall have the right to request in writing that you produce one (1) Video Clip embodying your performances ("Your Video"). If you and Company shall agree, after good faith negotiations, that you shall have the right to produce Your Video, then you shall not have the right to authorize, permit or grant to any third party the right to manufacture and/or distribute Videograms embodying Your Video (or any portion thereof). If Company shall give you the right to produce Your Video, then you shall have the right to grant to a third party the right to exploit Your Video through theatrical exhibition and/or television broadcast or transmission but the right to so exploit Your Video shall be specifically subject to Company's right of first refusal as set forth in Paragraph 39., below.

> ☞ A truly wishy-washy fence straddler. "Company" doesn't really have to do anything, but, by golly, it will consider anything in "good faith." A famous comedian I represented used to refer to this sort of language as *kinderspiel*—"children's talk."

EXAMPLE 2: Company to Produce One Video Per Album

8.08. Company will produce or cause to be produced at least one (1) Covered Video for each of the Commitment Albums released hereunder, provided that you have fully complied with your material obligations to Company hereunder.

EXAMPLE 3: Minimum Budget Guaranteed

(a) Company will produce for a minimum budget of Seventy Five Thousand Dollars ($75,000) a Video for each album comprising recordings made entirely from masters hereunder which are released in the United States.

PRODUCTION COSTS

As stated above, the costs of producing a music video can be both extensive and expensive. Logically, it might seem that with respect to recoupment these production costs should be treated in the same manner as are recording costs. However, further reflection on the dual nature of videos—half product for sale and half sales tool—leads to the conclusion that the two cannot be handled in exactly the same way.

There are two major differences between these production costs and recording costs. The first is that a wider range of costs goes into the making of a music video. The second is how the costs are recouped.

Making a video is like making a short film. It incurs any number of costs which have no comparable equivalent in making a record, such as crews—camera, technical, lighting, production, construction; costumes; makeup artists and hairdressers; drivers; permits; insurance; building materials; etc. (see Example 1). There are a lot of people who must get paid, equipment that must be bought, locations that must be managed, etc. In addition, before a musical composition can be used on a video, the owner of the copyright of the composition must grant a synchronization license. (See comment following Example 4 in "Video Rights," page 259.) Since synchronization licenses apply only to sight and sound usages, they are never a part of the recording costs of a phonorecord.

The recoupment of video production costs reflects the dual nature of music videos as sales tools and as product sold. Frequently, the recoupment procedure is treated differently from that of the recoupment of recording costs, for those costs are recouped from virtually any source, especially if cross-collateralization is present. It is not unusual to have a portion of the music video production costs, either expressly or by implication, borne by the record company. Example 2 provides that only up to 50% of production costs may be recouped from record royalties. The balance must be recouped only from royalties from the sales of videos or DVDs, an unlikely event. As a result, under most circumstances, almost certainly the record company is going to bear that portion of the production cost. Subparagraph (b) of Example 3 gives lip service to the fiction that the production costs will be recouped only from video royalties, but then reality steps in with subparagraph (c), which states that "to the extent production costs are not recouped from Video Royalties" they are recouped from record royalties.

```
SAMPLE CONTRACT PROVISIONS
```

EXAMPLE 1: Definition of Production Costs

(iii) "Production Costs" means all costs incurred or expended in connection with the preparation, pre-production, production, post-production, completion and delivery of the final master tape or film (including a negative, print or other applicable material) of videos, including without limitation, all payments to or for: production companies (including without limitation, video producers, directors, writers and associate producers); technical, lighting and production crews; each and every individual (including Artist) who appears in or who rendered services or performances in or in connection with a Video arising out of the creation thereof; any union, guild, labor organization or trustees thereof pursuant to the terms of any collective bargaining agreement and otherwise; studios, halls and facilities; set construction crews and materials; location and police permits and fees; transportation, living expenses and per diems incurred in connection with location scouting and the attendance of artists and all production personnel at pre-production, production and post-production sessions and the preparation therefor; equipment rental and cartage; insurance premiums paid in connection with the production of Videos; taxes and contingencies (including fees or mark-ups payable to any production company or any other person in connection with Videos); tape, film or other stock; on-line and off-line editing, mixing, special effects, color correction, audio track transfer or dubbing, title cards and similar functions; the creation of videocassette viewing copies from the final master tape or film; payments in connection with the production and utilization of the musical works embodied on Videos including, without limitation, flat fee payments to the publishers of such musical works (or their agents for collection) but excluding any payments in the nature of a royalty or "per unit" fee arising out of or in connection with the distribution and sale of Videos; unreimbursed costs and expenses incurred in the duplication and delivery of copies of Videos (including, without limitation, Exhibition Copies) for licensees (unless such costs and expenses are deducted pursuant to subparagraph 22(a)(v)(B)(3) below); and all other costs and expenses (excluding Company's overhead costs and services of Company's employees) incurred with respect to Videos which are now or which become generally recognized as production costs of audiovisual works.

☛ Note how much more extensive this definition is than the definitions of recording costs given in Chapter 3, page 106 and pages 110–116.

EXAMPLE 2: Up to 50% Recouped from Record Royalties

(c) In addition, to the extent Production Costs are not recouped from Video Royalties, notwithstanding anything to the contrary, up to Fifty (50%) Percent only of the Production Costs in connection with any such Video shall also be recoupable from record royalties payable to Licensor. Notwithstanding the foregoing, in connection with the making or use of the Video, any scale payments made to Artist and health, pension, and welfare payments in connection therewith made to the applicable union(s), shall be recoupable from either recording royalties under this Agreement or any video royalties payable under this Agreement. Nothing contained in this Agreement shall be deemed to grant the right or allow Company to deduct Production Costs pursuant to any recoupment provision contained herein more than one time.

EXAMPLE 3: Production Cost Recoupment

(b) In the event Company shall pay any production costs in excess of the Production Budget (which Company has no obligation to do so), then Company shall have the right to deduct an amount equal to such excess costs from any monies payable by Company to Artist hereunder. All production costs in connection with each Video shall be recoupable from Video Royalties in respect to each Video.

(c) In addition, to the extent production costs are not recouped from Video Royalties, One Hundred (100%) Percent of the production costs in connection with any such Video shall also be recoupable from record royalties payable to Artist hereunder with respect to Artist's recording services.

VIDEO ROYALTIES

Get your facts first and then you can distort them as much as you wish.
—MARK TWAIN

Provisions in earlier record contracts which dealt with the royalties due from the various areas of exploitation of video suffered from overambitious expectations for the commercial future of music videos. These early provisions were very long and very convoluted, with such arcane headings as "Videogram Transactions" and "Exhibition Transactions," and might run well over six single-spaced pages. This approach led to the necessity of using phrases like "The Videogram Share of Videogram Net Receipts and License Net Receipts and Exhibition Net Receipts and Your Share of Exhibition Net Receipts . . ." where each defined term then spun off pages of paragraphs and sub-paragraphs of other definitions and issues.

Happily, today the size and complexity of video royalty provisions have been reduced considerably. Most provisions now provide for a division of income from licenses to third parties. When the videos are sold to the public at retail, there is a royalty, which is structured much liked the royalties used for the sales of records.

SAMPLE CONTRACT PROVISIONS

EXAMPLE 1: Definition of Video Royalties

27. As used herein, your "Video Royalties" shall be defined and determined as follows:

(a) In respect of Videos licensed by us, your Video Royalties shall be one-half (½) of our Net Video Receipts.

(b) In the event that we shall distribute Videos ourselves, rather than licensing the distribution to third parties, your Video Royalties shall be computed as if the Videos were records under Paragraph 5, above, with the following adjustments to the provisions thereof:

(i) The rate of your Video Royalties for Videos with a suggested retail list price less than or equal to Twenty ($20) Dollars, shall be Fifteen (15%) Percent.

(ii) The rate of your Video Royalties for Videos with a suggested retail list price greater than Twenty ($20) Dollars, shall be Twenty (20%) Percent.

(iii) In computing your Video Royalties, the suggested retail list price shall be deemed to be Ninety (90%) Percent of the posted price (as of the commencement of the applicable accounting period hereunder) at which our distributing company's branch distributors shall offer the applicable Video to their customary subdistributors.

(iv) You shall be solely responsible for any Participant Payments and we shall have the right to deduct from your Video Royalties pursuant to this subparagraph 27.(b) any such payments made by us.

(c) In the event we couple a particular Video or Videos in a compilation of videos which are not Videos hereunder ("Other Videos"), and the monies paid to us in respect thereof are not specifically allocated as among the Videos and Other Videos, your Video Royalties shall be the otherwise applicable Video Royalties (i.e., as if such compilation consisted solely of Videos hereunder) multiplied by a fraction, the numerator of which is the number of Videos included in such compilation and denominator of which is the aggregate number of royalty-bearing videos (including Videos) included in such compilation.

EXAMPLE 2: Video Royalties

9.06. Company will pay you royalties as follows in connection with the following uses of Audiovisual Records (including for sales of Audiovisual Records which contain Covered Videos):

(a) (1) Company will pay you a royalty (the "Net Receipts Royalty") in the amount equal to fifty percent (50%) of Company's "Net Video Receipts" (defined below) derived from all uses of Audiovisual Records which produce revenues directly for Company other than as described in sub-paragraph 9.06(b) below.

(2) "Gross Receipts," in this subparagraph 9.06(a), means all monies actually received by Company (or credited to Company's account against advances previously received) in the United States which are specifically allocated to the exploitation of Audiovisual Records. "Net Video Receipts" means Gross Receipts, less all direct out-of-pocket expenses, taxes, adjustments, and collection costs incurred by Company in connection with the exploitation of such Audiovisual Records, all payments required to be made to Persons other than you or any other "Royalty Participant" (as hereafter defined), including, without limitation, to unions or guilds or to publishers of non-Controlled Compositions and "Independent Interests" (as hereinafter defined) in Controlled Compositions in connection with the production and/or exploitation of such Audiovisual Records and any Covered Videos embodied therein, and a distribution fee equal to twenty percent (20%) of those Gross Receipts. Any item of expenses which is actually recouped from Gross Receipts under this section will not be chargeable against royalties under paragraph 5.02. If any item of revenue or expenses is attributable to an Audiovisual Record or a Covered Video and to other audiovisual works, the amount of that item includible in Gross Receipts or deductible in computing Net Video Receipts will be determined by apportionment based upon actual playing time of the Record concerned.

(3) You shall be solely responsible for and shall pay any and all monies payable to the Producers, to the producers and directors of the visual portion of the Audiovisual Records or Covered Videos, to the publishers of Controlled Compositions and to any other Person (except publishers of non-Controlled Compositions or of Independent Interests in Controlled Compositions which are embodied in the Audio Visual Records or Covered Videos and any unions or guilds or their funds) who are entitled to a royalty or any other payment in respect to the exploitation of the Audiovisual Records (each such person being herein referred to as a "Royalty Participant"). Notwithstanding the foregoing, if Company shall pay or be required to pay any such monies directly to any Royalty Participant, then Company shall have the right to deduct same from any and all royalties payable to you hereunder.

(b) If Company or Company's Distributor manufactures and distributes Audiovisual Records embodying one or more Covered Videos, then Company will pay you royalties at the rates and in the manner set forth in subparagraph 9.06(b), rather than the Net Receipts Royalty payable to you pursuant to subparagraph 9.06(a).

(1) On Net Sales of Audiovisual Records distributed in the United States: twenty percent (20%) of the applicable Royalty Base Price for such Audiovisual Records, and on Net Sales of Audiovisual Records distributed outside of the United States: fifteen percent (15%) of the applicable Royalty Base Price for such Audiovisual Records.

• • •

(4) The royalties payable in accordance with this subparagraph 9.06(b) shall be inclusive

of all royalties that may be payable to all Persons (other than unions or guilds and their funds), including without limitation, Royalty Participants and the publishers of both Controlled Compositions and non-Controlled Compositions or Independent Interests. If Company makes any payments to any Person with respect to any such Audiovisual Record, then Company shall have the right to deduct such payments from royalties otherwise payable to you with respect to Audiovisual Records.

☛ Notice in subparagraph 9.06(b)(1) how royalties for the sale of videos are treated using the same basic principles as are royalties for records. Here, "Royalty Base Price" is the equivalent of "applicable wholesale price."

MUSIC RIGHTS

Try as I like to find the way,
> **I can never get back by day,**
> **Nor can remember plain and clear**
> **The curious music that I hear.**
>> —ROBERT LOUIS STEVENSON
>> *A Child's Garden of Verse*

In connection with the use of videos there are two types of music licenses which must be taken into consideration. One, the synchronization license, has already been touched on with regard to video usage and will be discussed again below. The other type of license, the mechanical license, is the license which allows the record company the right to sell copies of the video. This has been discussed before, but in a different context. Both of these licenses are issued by the publisher or publishers, that is, the copyright owners, of the musical compositions being used.

We have already dealt with the fact that mechanical licenses are required for the distribution and sale of recordings. There is, however, a very important difference between the issuance of a mechanical license for a video and issuance of a mechanical license for a record. This is going to get technical here, so be patient for a moment or two.

Under Section 115 of the Copyright Act of 1976 a compulsory license is available in connection with the release of "phonorecords." The introductory clause of Section 115 specifically states that "the exclusive rights . . . to make and distribute *phonorecords* . . . are subject to *compulsory licensing* . . ." [emphasis added]. (See Chapter 17, the section "Section 115—The Compulsory License," pages 512–516.) Section 115 also provides for a statutory rate for mechanical licenses for music included on a phonorecord. Section 115 does *not*, however, provide for a compulsory license or a statutory rate for "copies." Because videos are "copies" and not "phonorecords," there is no compulsory license or statutory rate which applies to the licensing of music rights in a video. What does this mean? It means that a mechanical license is still required to market and sell videos. The record company cannot rely upon Section 115 for a compulsory license and a statutory rate; the company must negotiate with the music publisher for such a license. Since the publisher is not required by law to grant such a license, nor is there an established rate as there is with a phonorecord, the publisher can hold out for top dollar. The mechanical license fee, if granted, is at a negotiated rate. It may, like a mechanical for a record, be based upon a per unit price; it may, unlike a mechanical for a record, be based upon a royalty (see Example 2); or it may be just about anything the copyright owner can extract from a desperate record company.

Mechanical license fees are, however, frequently waived for videos, especially on videos other than pure music videos, such as, for example, a soundtrack of a film released as a home video or DVD. Even with a waiver of mechanical license fees, in some foreign territories a mechanical license fee will be collected by law.

As with the mechanical license for videos, there is neither a compulsory license nor a statutory rate in connection with synchronization licenses, so the record company is also at the mercy of the copyright proprietor when it comes to the synchronization license. As noted earlier, the synchronization license fee is charged against the artist's royalty as a production cost (see Example 3).

SAMPLE CONTRACT PROVISIONS

EXAMPLE 1: Synchronization License Fees Waived for Owned Compositions

c. I consent to the exhibition and exploitation of the Tapes by Company and its licensees for such purposes, at such times and places and in such media as determined by Company and its licensees and I agree that Company and its licensees shall have the right to use all musical compositions that were written by me in whole or part, or are owned or controlled directly or indirectly by me in whole or in part or by a publishing company owned or controlled directly or indirectly by me in whole or part ("Owned Compositions"), and that appear on the Tapes with no further payment for the use of such Owned Compositions, except pursuant to Paragraph 28.e.(i) hereof and except for any public performance fees payable to the applicable performing rights societies.

• • •

e. (i) I hereby acknowledge that Company and/or Company's licensees shall have the right to sell and/or rent primarily for home use any form of reproduction of the Tapes reproduced or manufactured hereunder. Company and I shall negotiate in good faith concerning a royalty with respect to such sale and/or rental.

☞ Although the artist/writer/publisher has waived all synchronization fees for the use of the composition, the mechanical license fees are to be negotiated for the sale of copies.

EXAMPLE 2: $100 Synchronization Fee

(d) (i) For each Controlled Composition embodied on Videos, you warrant, represent and agree on behalf of any music publishing company which is the publisher of such Controlled Composition owned or controlled by you that Company shall receive upon request (and effective as of the commencement of production of such Video) a non-exclusive, worldwide and perpetual synchronization and other necessary use license(s):

(A) for promotional purposes free of charge or royalty, for the purpose of reproducing such Controlled Composition in Videos and exhibiting, duplicating, manufacturing and distributing copies of such Videos;

(B) For a one-time fee of One Hundred ($100.00) Dollars for each such Controlled Composition (which fee shall be a Production Cost) for the purpose of reproducing such Controlled Composition in Videos and exhibiting, duplicating, manufacturing, distributing and otherwise exploiting Videograms and Exhibition Copies embodying such Videos by sale, lease, license, rental or other manner (except, with regard to the sale and rental of such Videograms, the provisions of subparagraph 2 l(d)(i)(C) below shall instead apply), which such fee shall become due and payable within ten (10) business days following the first such commercial exploitation; and

(C) for a royalty in an aggregate amount equal to that proportion of (1) four (4%) percent of Videogram Net Receipts (as hereinafter defined) attributable to the sale or rental of each such Videogram by Company or by an Affiliated Entity, or (2) twenty (20%) percent of License Net Receipts (as hereinafter defined) attributable to each sale or rental of each Videogram by a Third Party (as hereinafter defined) as reported to Company in the United States by such Third Party, which the number of Controlled Compositions embodied in any such Videogram bears to the total number of musical works embodied thereon; provided, however, that the amount payable by Company with respect to each Controlled Composition in each such Videogram sold shall not be less than three-fourths (¾) of the then-current Statutory Rate nor more than one and one-half (1½) times the then-current Statutory Rate.

(ii) Promptly upon request you shall execute and deliver to Company the licenses referred to in subparagraph 21(d)(i) above. If, for any reason, Company does not promptly receive any such license, then same shall be deemed to have been granted *ab initio* (on such terms and conditions as aforesaid).

(iii) Without limiting Company's rights, if, for any reason, Company pays to the publishers of Controlled Compositions any sums in excess of the limits set forth in subparagraph 21 (d)(i) above, then Company shall have the right to deduct such excess from any and all monies accruing to your credit hereunder. In the event that any such deduction is effected against an advance otherwise payable hereunder, such deduction shall not impair Company's right to charge and recoup in the manner herein provided, the entirety of the advance which would otherwise have been payable hereunder.

☛ There's a lot going on in here, and much of the language is somewhat fuzzy around the edges—that is, poorly drafted. For controlled compositions there is an agreed-upon $100 fee—cheap in the world of synchronization licenses (albeit without bothering to call it a synchronization license—which is charged back to the artist anyway, as, indeed, are any "excess" publishing payments. (Ain't life grand!) Subparagraph (C) provides for a mechanical based upon a percentage—provided that the royalty will not be "less than three-fourths (¾) of the then-current Statutory Rate nor more than one and one-half (1½) times the then-current Statutory Rate." We've got a minimum floor and maximum ceiling (no less than but no more than) for the mechanical license fee. This is hunky-dory—except for one *slight* technical problem: There is no statutory rate for videos. Oh well, I'm sure the intentions were good, even if the legal drafting wasn't.

EXAMPLE 3: Free Licenses or Fees Deducted from Artist's Royalties

(d) As set forth in paragraph 12.02 below, you shall issue (or cause the music publishing company[ies] having the right to do so to issue) (1) worldwide, perpetual synchronization licenses, and (2) perpetual licenses for public performance in the United States (to the extent that ASCAP and BMI are unable to issue same), to Company at no cost for the use of all Controlled Compositions in any such Covered Videos effective as of the commencement of production of the applicable Covered Video (and your execution of this agreement shall constitute the issuance of such licenses by any music publishing company[ies] which is owned or controlled by you or by any Person owned or controlled by you). In the event that you shall fail to cause any such music publishing company[ies] to issue any such license to Company, or if Company shall be required to pay any fee to such music publishing company[ies] in order to obtain such license, then Company shall have the right to deduct the amount of such license fee from all monies becoming due to you under this agreement. Notwithstanding the foregoing, although the synchronization license is perpetual and remains in effect, if the costs incurred with respect to any such Covered Video is entirely recouped, then after such recoupment, and only with respect to prospective commercial uses of such Covered Video, at your written request prior to such prospective commercial uses of such Covered Video, Company and you shall negotiate in good faith with respect to compensation consistent with the then-current Company standards, to be paid by Company for such a synchronization license for the Controlled Compositions used in such Covered Video.

☛ The last sentence in this example (besides being hard to follow) is one I've never seen in any other agreement. It gives the artist the right, after full recoupment, to come back and negotiate a retroactive synchronization fee "consistent with the then-current Company standards." A rather meaningless—and meatless—bone thrown to the artist.

CHAPTER 9

SONGWRITERS' AGREEMENTS

I cannot write in verse, for I am no poet. I cannot arrange the parts of speech with such art as to produce effects of light and shade, for I am no painter. Even by signs and gestures I cannot express my thoughts and feelings, for I am no dancer. But I can do so by means of sounds, for I am a musician.

—WOLFGANG AMADEUS MOZART

Songwriters' agreements are the agreements between a songwriter or songwriters (or writer, or composer, or lyricist) and a music publisher or publishers. In most cases, the publisher will be the owner or co-owner of the copyright of the musical compositions in question. (One exception is a participation agreement; see the first paragraph of Chapter 10, "Copublishing Agreements," page 310.)

A music publisher may be an independent company or it may be owned by a record company, a film company, or an individual (yes, including an artist, producer, and/or songwriter). Just about any individual, company, or organization that wishes to be a music publisher can be. (To dramatize this in my classes, I routinely offered to make anyone a publisher by placing my open hand on his or her forehead and saying the magic words: "My child, you are a publisher.")

Recall that the rules of the performing rights societies in the United States (ASCAP, BMI, and SESAC) require that no publisher may simultaneously belong to more than one performance rights society. Because record companies do not want to be limited to signing writers belonging to only one of these societies, they generally "own" two or more publishing companies, to have at least one publisher affiliated with ASCAP or BMI. (See the example in the section "Publishing," Chapter 2, page 26.) When a record company acquires publishing rights from an artist or production company in a recording agreement, the record company's publisher will invariably be labeled as being "affiliated with" or "designated by" the record company.

Songwriters' agreements are generally one of two types:

1. The first, for lack of a better term, may be called *nonexclusive*. Under these agreements, the songwriter has written, assigned, and/or sold the copyright of a specified composition or compositions to the publisher.

2. Under *exclusive* agreements, the songwriter's services as a songwriter are exclusive to the publisher for a specified period of time and any compositions written within that period are the property of the publisher.

Many of the provisions of songwriters' agreements are identical to or similar to the corresponding paragraphs in artist recording agreements. Here we discuss the various provisions of songwriters' agreements that are unique to songwriters' agreements, somewhat different from recording agreements, or of particular interest. Also, unless expressly pointed out to the contrary, the provisions discussed below apply to both exclusive and nonexclusive agreements.

TERM OF THE AGREEMENT

In the strict sense of the word, only exclusive songwriters' agreements would have a "term." The songwriter is signed for a specified term, such as, for example: 1 year; 1 year plus four 1-year options; coterminous with the songwriter's contract as a recording artist; etc.

By definition, there is no term for nonexclusive songwriters' agreements, which are, in effect, acquisitions of one or more specified copyrights. A nonexclusive agreement is a one-time transaction, with the composition or compositions in question being transferred to the publisher. The songwriter is not under an exclusive obligation to the publisher and is free to write for, or sell to, another publisher. All that happens with this type of contract is that the copyright is transferred, in one form or another, from the writer to the publisher. Unless specified otherwise (and ignoring the possibilities of reversions), the term of the transfer of rights in the copyright, under both types of agreement, is usually for "the life of the copyright." (See the section "Term of Copyright," Chapter 20, pages 526–527). Some of these agreements may be *inferred* to have a "term" or "period" because there may be a provision in the agreement for a reversion of the rights back to the songwriter if, within a specified period of time, the composition is not, for example, recorded and released commercially.

The previous discussions of term of the agreement (see pages 28–34) and exercise of options (see pages 35–41) with regard to artist recording agreements are applicable to exclusive songwriters' agreements, as are the discussions on advances (pages 103–105). Usually, under those exclusive songwriters' agreements that are tied into an artist's recording agreement, the periods of the two agreements will be connected so that if the recording agreement's option is exercised, the option for the songwriter's agreement is also deemed exercised. This is called a *coterminous* arrangement; both agreements will terminate at the same time, so that if one agreement is terminated before the natural expiration of the agreement, it causes the other agreement to terminate as well.

There are other songwriters' agreements which may be categorized as "exclusive" which are not tied into recording agreement, but nevertheless tie the songwriter exclusively to the publisher for the term of the agreement. For example, a songwriters' agreement attached to and/or incorporated by reference into a recording agreement may be in the form of a "single-song" agreement; no length of time is given, but instead the agreement specifies the creation or transfer of one or more songs which have yet to be written, each pursuant to a single-song agreement. Note that the names of the songs are usually not specified, but are indicated as "to be designated." Agreements of this type fall into the exclusive category because they are used to document songs written during the term of the exclusivity.

All the provisions in "Sample Contract Provisions: Agreement Tied to Record Contract" (beginning on page 271) illustrate exclusive songwriters' agreements tied directly to recording contracts. They are from recording contracts, not from songwriters' agreements. In each instance, the exhibit incorporated into the recording is a single-song agreement which applies to each composition acquired.

The provisions in "Sample Contract Provisions: Agreement Independent of Record Contract," beginning on page 272, are exclusive songwriters' agreements having their own independent term; that is, they are not tied into any recording agreement. Note the similarity to the language used in recording agreements. In fact, the mere substitution of "artist" for "writer" and "record company" for "publisher" would allow either agreement, at least for the equivalent provisions, to pass for the other. This exemplifies a certain thriftiness in the music industry. Why create entirely new language when a simple name change will do the job?

There is a third group, sort of a hybrid type, in which an exclusive songwriter's agreement is tied into a record contract with a record company that is not affiliated with the music publisher. These are dealt with in a section of their own.

SAMPLE CONTRACT PROVISIONS: AGREEMENT TIED TO RECORD CONTRACT

EXAMPLE 1: Part of Record Contract Grant of Rights

15. You grant to Company:

• • •

e. The right to acquire each and every Composition and you agree that at Company's request you will execute an assignment of each Composition to a publisher designated by Company under all of the terms and conditions applicable to the Standard Songwriter's Contract form attached hereto as Exhibit "A." Whether you sign and deliver said form, you and the publisher designated by Company shall be deemed to have executed an assignment of each Composition on that form. You will not collaborate in the writing or arranging of any Composition with any person unless such person is free, jointly with you, to assign his rights in such Composition under the terms of Exhibit "A" hereto and who agrees to do so if and as required under this provision. As used herein, the word "Composition" means every (i) original musical work (music and/or lyrics) you write or collaborate in writing during the term hereof or (ii) arrangement you write or collaborate in writing during the term hereof of a work in the public domain in the U.S.A.

☛ Anything written or cowritten by the artist during the term of the recording agreement is assigned to the record company. By signing the recording agreement, the artist is "deemed to have executed" a songwriter's agreement attached as an exhibit for each composition, whether or not the artist actually signs a copy of the form agreement. Also note the use of the terminology "a publisher designated by Company," language that is always used in recording agreements. This allows the record company to place the copyright with the appropriate (vis-à-vis ASCAP or BMI) publishing company.

EXAMPLE 2: Form Single-Song Agreement Attached

10. With respect to any musical composition written in whole or in part by Grantor [a production company] and/or Artist, or owned or controlled by Grantor or Artist in whole or in part, and/or any affiliated subsidiary or parent of Grantor, corporate or otherwise, which is also recorded hereunder, it is agreed that such composition shall be owned and administered by Company's designated publishing company. The designated publishing company shall have the right to copyright

or cause to be copyrighted any arrangement, orchestration or interpretation created or furnished by Grantor or Artist hereunder (whether or not reduced to writing or whether or not involving previously copyrighted or Public Domain material), which is in Company's opinion, entitled to copyright, and the right to renew and secure renewals of any such copyright obtained by Company or Company's designated publisher. Grantor and Artist further agree that with respect to any composition covered pursuant to the terms of this paragraph that Grantor shall execute a form single song agreement similar to the one attached to this agreement as Exhibit A.

EXAMPLE 3: Artist to Make "Reasonable" Effort to Acquire Compositions Not Written by Artist

8. I grant to Company the right to acquire each and every composition, together with the copyright therein and all renewals and extensions, and I shall, in respect to each composition, execute a separate Songwriter's Agreement, in the form of the agreement attached hereto as Exhibit "A," with a publisher designated by Company. In addition, I shall make reasonable efforts to acquire publication rights to original musical works submitted by me to Company which are not written by me. If am able to so acquire such publication rights, Company shall enter into a Songwriter's Agreement, in the form of the agreement attached hereto as Exhibit "A," with the writer or writers of such original musical work.

EXAMPLE 4: Copublishing (Company Affiliate and Company Designated by Artist)

30. Each composition written or composed by you during the term of this Agreement and any renewals or extensions hereof, shall be co-published by our affiliated music publishing company and a music publishing company to be designated by you in accordance with the provisions of the Participation Agreement annexed hereto as Exhibit "A." Said Participation Agreement shall be concurrent and coterminous with this Agreement.

☞ A publishing equivalent of "you show me yours and I'll show you mine."

EXAMPLE 5: Coterminous Period

14. The initial term of this agreement shall commence upon the date hereof and continue for the initial term of the [Recording] Agreement. It is the intention of the parties hereto that the term hereof be coterminous with the term of the Agreement, as same may be renewed or extended from time to time. Accordingly, each extension or renewal of the term of the Agreement shall automatically extend the term hereof for the same period. The phrase "the term hereof" or "the term of this agreement" as used in this agreement, shall refer to the initial and any extensions or renewal terms hereof in accordance with the foregoing.

SAMPLE CONTRACT PROVISIONS: AGREEMENT INDEPENDENT OF RECORD CONTRACT

EXAMPLE 1: 1 Year Plus Four 1-Year Options

1. Publisher hereby employs Writer and Writer undertakes and agrees to render his exclusive services to Publisher in the writing and composing of original musical compositions, numbers and works (the "Compositions") for a period of one (1) year from the date hereof (the "Term") both alone and in collaboration with others, as designated, directed, selected and required by Publisher, as an employee for hire.

• • •

3. During the Term and each exercised option year as hereinafter provided, Writer shall not write or compose, or furnish or dispose of, any musical compositions, numbers, works, or material, or any rights or interests therein whatsoever, other than for and to Publisher, except as specifically set forth herein.

• • •

22.(a) Writer hereby grants to Publisher four (4) separate options, each of which shall, upon the exercise thereof by notice in writing by Publisher to Writer at least thirty (30) days prior to the expiration of the Term or exercised option year, as the case may be, extend the Term for one (1) year.

☛ This is the traditional, classic language used for directly signing a songwriter to an exclusive agreement with a publisher.

EXAMPLE 2: 3 Years Plus Two 1-Year Options

1. *Employment.* Publisher hereby employs Writer to render his services as a songwriter and composer and otherwise as may be hereinafter set forth. Writer hereby accepts such employment and agrees to tender such services exclusively for Publisher during the term hereof, upon the terms and conditions set forth herein.

2. *Term.* The initial term of this agreement shall commence upon the date hereof and shall continue for three (3) years. Writer hereby grants to Publisher two (2) separate and irrevocable options, each to renew this agreement for a one (1) year term, such renewal term to run consecutively beginning at the expiration of the initial term hereof, all upon the same terms and conditions as are applicable to the initial term except as otherwise provided herein. Each option shall be exercised by Publisher by written notice to Writer at least ten (10) days prior to the expiration of the then current term.

EXAMPLE 3: 2 Plus 2 Plus 2 Years

1. This agreement shall commence as of the date hereof and shall continue in force for a term which shall consist of an initial period of two (2) years from such date, and the additional period or periods, if any, by which such term may be extended through our exercise of one or more of the options granted to us herein. Each year of the term hereof is sometimes hereinafter referred to as a "contract year."

• • •

25. You hereby grant us the option to extend the term of this agreement for a first additional period of two years upon all of the terms and conditions herein contained, except that the advances referred to in subparagraph 10(e) shall each be $_____ rather than $_____ and the weekly advance referred to in subparagraph 10(f) shall be $_____ per week rather than $_____.

26. If we have exercised the option granted to us in paragraph 25 hereof, you hereby grant us the option to extend the term of this agreement for a second additional period of two years upon all of the terms and conditions herein contained, except that the advances referred to in subparagraph 10(e) shall each be $_____ rather than $_____ and the weekly advance

referred to in subparagraph 10(f) shall be $_____ per week rather than $_____ .

☛ With the exercise of options the advances, guaranteed yearly and weekly, increase.

EXAMPLE 4: Later of 1 Year from Commencement or Delivery
1. TERM

1.01. (a) The term of this agreement (the "Term") will begin on the date hereof and continue, unless extended or sooner terminated as provided herein, for one (1) Contract Period, as such term is defined in paragraph 1.01(c) below (such Contract Period is sometimes referred to as the "Initial Period").

(b) Writer hereby grants Publisher three (3) separate options to extend the Term for additional Contract Periods (sometimes referred to as "Option Periods") on the same terms and conditions applicable to the Initial Period except as otherwise provided herein. Publisher may exercise such of its options hereunder by sending Writer a written notice at any time prior to the expiration of the then-current Contract Period.

(c) Each "Contract Period" hereunder shall commence upon the expiration of the previous Contract Period (provided that the Initial Period shall commence on the date hereof) and shall continue until the later of (i) one (1) year from the date of commencement thereof, or (ii) thirty (30) days after the date on which Writer satisfies the Minimum Delivery Obligation (as defined in paragraph 3 below) for such Contract Period.

☛ The provisions in this agreement regarding the "term" (periods running the later of the commencement date of each period or the delivery of the minimum delivery obligation) make this songwriter's agreement the equivalent of the open-ended recording agreement.

WRITER AS RECORDING ARTIST

It is a reflection on the state of the music industry that many agreements that I have referred to as being exclusive but not tied into recording agreements are still, one way or another, conditional upon the writer becoming a recording artist (see Example 1). In ancient times (pre-Beatles), artists were not expected to write their own songs. There were exceptions, of course, most notably with instrumental artists, but not even giants like Duke Ellington and Count Basie wrote all their own songs. (Everyone thinks Duke Ellington wrote "Take the 'A' Train," his theme song, but it was Billy Strayhorn who wrote it. By the way, Lawrence Welk inevitably referred to that song as "Take A Train.")

Before the era when it became fashionable, if not essential, for the artist to also write the material being performed, the Brill Building in New York was famous for the songwriters and song pluggers who worked there supplying songs to artists. In those days, music publishers hired composers by the score on an exclusive basis. Songs were cranked out on the basis of "such and such artist is looking for a ballad for his new album," etc. After the Beatles arrived on the scene, it became more and more expected that artists should write and record their own compositions, rather than use independent songwriters' work. Now many, if not most, exclusive songwriter agreements are based on the presumption that the songwriter will become a recording artist. The (presumably) guaranteed outlet for songs which comes with a recording agreement sets in motion some internal accelerations of advances and other ripples through the agreement.

EXAMPLE 1: Periods Tied into Delivery under Separate Record Contract

4. (a) If Writer enters into an exclusive recording agreement ("Recording Agreement") with a Major Record Company, as such term is defined in paragraph 4.(c) below, during the Term, then Writer shall cause such Major Record Company to give Publisher written notice (the "Acceptance Notice") promptly following the date when the Major Record Company accepts as delivered, pursuant to the Recording Agreement, each Album required to be delivered thereunder. Writer shall deliver to Publisher, simultaneously with the delivery to the Major Record Company of each Album, a Recording of such Album and complete information regarding the songwriters and publishers, including the applicable writing and ownership shares, of the musical compositions embodied on such Album. Unless sooner terminated or extended as provided for herein, the Contract Period during which such Recording Agreement is executed, and each successive Contract Period hereunder, shall end on the date which is thirty (30) days following the later of (i) the date on which Publisher receives the Acceptance Notice with respect to the Album which, if Publisher were to exercise its option for the immediately succeeding Contract Period, would constitute the Minimum Delivery Obligation for such Period, or (ii) the date on which Publisher receives written notice from the Major Record Company that it has placed such Album on its schedule for new releases.

(b) In the event Writer enters into a Recording Agreement during the Term and such Recording Agreement terminates prior to the expiration or termination of this agreement, then the terms of subparagraph 3.(c) above shall apply with respect to the expiration of the Contract Period in effect at the time of such termination and with respect to the duration of any subsequent Contract Periods. Notwithstanding the foregoing, in no event shall the Contract Period in effect at the time of such termination end sooner than the date which is thirty (30) days following the termination of the Recording Agreement.

(c) As used herein, "Major Record Company" shall mean a company which distributes Records primarily through only one (1) of the six (6) major record distribution systems (i.e., PGD, Sony, BMG, WEA, CEMA, or MCA/Uni); provided, however, that "Major Record Company" shall not mean a record company which distributes Records embodying the Album constituting the applicable Minimum Delivery Obligation hereunder primarily through an alternative distribution system (e.g., ADA and RED), notwithstanding that such record company may also distribute other Records through a major record company distribution system, or that such alternative distribution system may itself be affiliated with a major record company distribution system.

☛ This agreement is in the form of an option agreement which is conditional upon the writer entering into a recording agreement with a third party. Another "historical" document: six—count 'em, six—majors.

EXAMPLE 2: Songwriting Commitment and Advances Tied to Record Contract
3. MINIMUM DELIVERY OBLIGATION

3.01. (a) During each Contract Period, Writer will Deliver to Publisher the applicable "Minimum Delivery Obligation" as follows:

(i) With respect to paragraph 1.01 above [no recording agreement], the Minimum Delivery Obligation shall be four (4) New Compositions that have been recorded and commercially released through normal retail channels in the United States.

(ii) With respect to paragraph 1.02 above [recording agreement], the Minimum Delivery Obligation shall be New Compositions constituting one hundred percent (100%) of one (1) Album, which Album has been accepted by a Major Record Company pursuant to the terms of the Recording Agreement and commercially released through normal retail channels in the United States. Notwithstanding anything to the contrary expressed or implied in the preceding sentence, to the extent any Album, or portion thereof, consists of "live" or "greatest hits" Recordings of Compositions which have been previously released on Master Recordings embodying Writer's performances, such Compositions shall not count toward fulfillment on Writer's Minimum Delivery Obligation.

(b) Notwithstanding anything to the contrary expressed or implied in paragraph 3.01(a)(ii) above, it is understood and agreed that if the number of New Compositions embodied on any Album required to be Delivered hereunder constitutes less than fifty percent (50%) of the total number of Compositions embodied on such Album, neither such Album nor such New Compositions shall apply in reduction of Writer's Minimum Delivery Obligation hereunder, it being understood and agreed that Publisher shall nonetheless have all rights hereunder with respect to such New Composition and shall pay Writer the applicable Advance subject to the terms of paragraph 6.03 below.

• • •

6.03. The Advance provided for in paragraph 6.02 for each Contract Period applies only if Writer satisfies the Minimum Delivery Obligation in such Contract Period. If Writer fails to satisfy such Minimum Delivery Obligation by the end of the applicable Contract Period, then Publisher, in addition to the other remedies hereunder, may pay, in lieu of the applicable Advance provided in paragraph 6.02, an Advance equal to the product of (a) the otherwise applicable Advance, and (b) a fraction, the numerator of which is the number of New Compositions embodied on the applicable Album which are subject to exclusive exploitation hereunder and the denominator of which is equal to the Minimum Delivery Obligation. In no event shall such fraction exceed one (1). If Publisher has, prior to the end of the applicable Contract, paid Writer an Advance in excess of the reduced Advance provided by the operation of this paragraph 6.03, Publisher may require Writer to repay the amount of such excess in accordance with the provisions of paragraph 10.05(a)(iii) below.

☛ This is a tough one for the writer. The minimum delivery obligation is out of the writer's control. Even if the writer isn't under contract as a recording artist (to a "Major Record Company," no less), there must be four new compositions commercially released [3.01(a)(i)]. It gets even more complicated if the writer *is* under contract to a Major Record Company [3.01(a)(ii) and 301(b)].

EXAMPLE 3: No Separate Recording Agreement, No Advances

6.02. Subject to paragraph 6.03, below, and subject to Writer's full and faithful performance of its obligations hereunder Publisher shall pay Writer the following sums at the following times, all of which sums shall constitute Advances hereunder:

• • •

(c) If Artist enters into a Recording Agreement during the Term:

(i) (A) Publisher shall pay Writer an Advance of Five Thousand Dollars ($5,000) promptly following Publisher's receipt from the applicable Major Record Company of written confirmation that it has entered into a Recording Agreement with Writer which Recording Agreement contains a commitment for at least one (1) Album.

(B) If New Compositions constitute at least eighty percent (80%) of the first Album delivered by Writer and accepted by the Major Record Company pursuant to the Recording Agreement, Publisher shall pay Writer an Advance of Five Thousand Dollars ($5,000) promptly following Publisher's receipt of the Acceptance Notice, together with the other materials required to be delivered to Publisher pursuant to the terms of paragraph 1.02(a) above, with respect to such first Album.

(C) Notwithstanding the provisions of paragraph 6.02(c)(i)(B) above, if New Compositions constitute less than eighty percent (80%) (the "Advance Obligation") of the first Album delivered by Writer and accepted by the Major Record Company pursuant to the Recording Agreement, the Advance provided in paragraph 6.02(c)(i)(B) shall be reduced proportionately by multiplying such Advance by a fraction, the numerator of which is the number of New Compositions embodied on the applicable Album which are subject to exclusive exploitation hereunder expressed as a percentage of the total number of Compositions on such Albums, and the denominator of which is eighty percent (80%).

(ii) The Advance, if any, provided in paragraph 6.02(b) shall be payable promptly following Delivery to, and acceptance by, Publisher of the Minimum Delivery obligation for the applicable Contract Period.

☛ Although not as complicated as Example 2, this agreement poses the same problems for the writer.

THE SONGWRITING COMMITMENT

> **I crave our composition may be written,**
> **And seal'd between us.**
>   —WILLIAM SHAKESPEARE
>   *Antony And Cleopatra*, Act II, Scene 6

As in recording agreements, the commitment to deliver a specified unit or units is important. In recording agreements, the commitment is to deliver masters, sides, albums, or some other entity, often with some specification as to length (e.g., "sufficient to constitute one (1) album of no less than 35 and of no more than 74 minutes in duration"). In songwriters' agreements, "songs" or "musical compositions" are the unit to be delivered.

In nonexclusive songwriters' agreements, the commitment is to deliver specific compositions. Usually the specific composition being purchased or assigned is a result of negotiation on a song-by-song basis. In those exclusive songwriters' agreements that are tied into a recording agreement, the commitment will generally be the compositions recorded or written, as the case may be, during the term of the recording agreement. It is possible that some songwriters' agreements tied into recording agreements will also, by definition, include all compositions written prior to the agreement (see Example 3).

In songwriters' agreements that are exclusive and independent of a recording agreement, the commitment is handled in much the same manner as is the record commitment in recording agreements (see Example 1). In these instances the commitment is the obligation of the writer to write and deliver a specified minimum number of musical compositions to the publisher (see Example 1). The size of the commitment will vary from publisher to publisher and from writer to writer. The commitments always seem to be in terms of "a minimum of" so many compositions. Interestingly enough, publishers don't seem to push their luck by adding "or more as requested by Company" or similar language, as record companies do in recording agreements.

For some reason, writers are treated as either being more subject to self-imposed creative restrictions than are recording artists or less likely to be able to deliver additional product. I suppose the justification behind this line of thought is the knowledge that an artist can always record someone else's song. The number of compositions to be delivered is subject to negotiation. If forced to come up with an "average" number, I would say it is about one song every 3 weeks for a total of 16 to 18 compositions per year.

A factor to be considered in negotiating the commitment for compositions is the songwriter in question. Can he or she deliver enough compositions? Failure to do so will probably draw the same threats of suspension or termination as with recording agreements, except with songwriters' agreements, there is the added threat that the periodic advance (a feature that many songwriters' agreements have) will be cut off. Some writers have to be threatened, cajoled, tricked, begged, forced, and bribed to fulfill their commitment. Other writers crank out songs at such an alarming rate that the publisher is deluged with a flood of material, much of it second-rate. From the publisher's point of view, it is important to develop a feel for a writer's capacity and desire to write prior to negotiating the commitment.

Usually, the publisher will have some provision dealing with the acceptability of the compositions. Because of the subjective nature of what is "acceptable" or, heaven forbid, "commercial," the concept of acceptability to the publisher is a tricky area to deal with. At some point, both parties must rely upon the professionalism and good faith of the other. One way of approaching this problem is set forth in Example 2, where any compositions in excess of five which are rejected by the publisher as being unacceptable become the sole property of the writer and the writer is free to do with them anything the writer wishes to do. This sort of approach offers some protection against the publisher rejecting submissions, while still retaining ownership, in order to use a back-door method of increasing the minimum commitment.

SAMPLE CONTRACT PROVISIONS

EXAMPLE 1: Minimum Commitment of 15 Compositions per Year

(c) During each year of the initial term hereof and during each renewal term hereof Writer shall deliver to Publisher not less than fifteen new and original musical compositions composed solely by Writer (hereinafter such obligation for each such year and each renewal term hereof, if any, on the part of Writer is referred to as the "Minimum Commitment"). If Writer shall not comply with the foregoing Minimum Commitment for any year of the initial term or any renewal term hereof prior to thirty days before the expiration of such year or renewal term hereof then such year or renewal term shall be automatically suspended until thirty days after Writer shall comply with such applicable Minimum Commitment. The foregoing is without prejudice to such other rights and remedies Publisher may have in respect of Writer's failure to comply with such applicable Minimum Commitment.

EXAMPLE 2: Submissions Must Be "Satisfactory"

13.(a) In respect of each Contract Year of the term hereof and not less than thirty (30) days prior to the end of such Contract Year, you shall complete and deliver to us a minimum of twenty (20) musical compositions written and composed entirely by you which are satisfactory to us and are accepted by us (according to our normal and usual standards) as Compositions hereunder ("Minimum Delivery Commitment"). Notwithstanding the foregoing, all musical compositions rejected by us as unsatisfactory in excess of five (5) during any Contract Year hereof shall revert to you and shall thereafter be your sole and exclusive property. Compositions written by you prior to the term of this agreement shall not count in reduction of your Minimum Delivery Commitment. You shall complete and deliver to us a minimum of ten (10) such musical compositions which are satisfactory to us and are acceptable by us (according to our normal and usual standards) as Compositions hereunder during the first six (6) months of each Contract Year of the term hereof. In the event that with respect to any yearly period of the term hereof, you have failed to deliver to us the minimum commitment for such Contract Year and/or have failed to deliver any portion of the minimum commitment with respect to the prior Contract Year, then, notwithstanding anything to contrary contained herein and without limiting our rights in any such event, we shall have the option without liability, by giving you written notice thereof, to extend the expiration date of the current Contract Year and/or suspend the operation of paragraph 10(e) and (f) [advance payable upon the commencement of each year and an additional weekly advance] hereof until sixty days following the date of the completion of delivery to us by you of the aforesaid minimum commitment(s) by Certified or Registered Mail, return receipt requested. Notwithstanding the foregoing, the Minimum Delivery Commitment for the initial Contract Year of the term hereof shall be fifteen (15) rather than twenty (20) of such compositions.

(b) Notwithstanding anything to the contrary set forth in subparagraph 13(a) above, in the event that you collaborate as a writer of musical compositions with other writers . . . , each such collaborated musical composition shall count as two-thirds (⅔) of a Composition for the purposes of your Minimum Delivery Commitment.

☛ There are two iffy provisions here. The first is that old bugaboo "standards," where the acceptability of compositions is subject to the publisher's "normal and usual" standards. The other is the sentence that begins with "You shall complete and deliver to us. . . ." Although the record company undoubtedly meant the 10-composition minimum to exclude prior compositions, the syntax is unclear.

EXAMPLE 3: Commitment Equals Controlled Compositions

2. The "Compositions" hereunder shall be deemed to be each and every Controlled Composition as defined in paragraph 8 of that certain recording agreement of even date between Record Company and Artist, an individual doing business as Production Company (hereinafter referred to as the "Recording Agreement"). Notwithstanding the foregoing, in no event shall this agreement be applicable to (i) any Controlled Composition in which Publisher has heretofore acquired any interest including without limitation all Controlled Compositions recorded under that certain Agreement dated as of between Record Company and Artist nor to (ii) any Controlled Composition in which Publisher shall hereafter acquire any interest from any person, firm or corporation other than Artist.

EXAMPLE 4: Periods Extended for Nondelivery

(f) Writer guarantees to deliver to Publisher in each year constituting the Term and each exercised option year a minimum of eighteen (18) new and original Compositions (excluding existing Works and arrangements of public domain material). If Writer fails to meet such guarantee during the Term or any exercised option year, as applicable, this agreement shall be extended automatically without payment of further advances until such guarantee shall be met and the time for the exercise of all subsequent options shall be extended for an amount of time equal to such automatic suspension.

SONGWRITER COMPENSATION

No man but a blockhead ever wrote, except for money.

—SAMUEL JOHNSON

Just "how," "what," and "what for" is a songwriter compensated by a publisher? Like the recording artist, the songwriter is paid royalties that are divided into various categories and are paid at varying rates. Songwriters' royalties are the money due to a songwriter for the use of a portion of the copyright for a song written by the songwriter. (For a more detailed discussion of this somewhat confusing statement regarding "a portion of the copyright," see the section "Exclusive Rights in the Copyright," Chapter 20, pages 502–504.)

Basically, copyrights are made up of multiple rights, all of which can be licensed collectively, individually, or in various combinations—you can chop those suckers up into as many little pieces as you want. With each use of a right, the songwriter should receive a payment. In the discussions on recording agreements the "royalty rate" usually meant the percentage figure to be paid to the artist. Unlike recording agreements, in songwriters' agreements, the royalties are usually described in both percentage numbers and in specified dollar figures, or, more correctly, cent figures. (Most of the royalty categories are based on a percentage; one category, the exception, sheet music, is based on a specified cent rate per copy sold.)

The following discussions are a breakdown of the areas of compensation.

PURCHASE PRICE

Never give a sucker an even break or smarten up a chump.

—W. C. FIELDS

In nonexclusive songwriters' agreements, where the songwriter has written, assigned, and/or sold the copyright of a specified composition or compositions to the publisher, there is frequently a "purchase price," although for a number of reasons the purchase price is not generally referred to as such. One reason for avoiding the terminology may be a fear of creating a sales tax problem. Another reason may be the concept of the "employee for hire," which is difficult to reconcile with a "purchase price." Another, quite basic, reason is that these sums are usually an advance, and therefore such a term would, arguably, be inaccurate (see all three examples below).

Please note that although the purchase price concept is more likely to appear in nonexclusive songwriters' agreements, it may, and frequently does, appear in what I have referred to above as exclusive songwriters' agreements (see Example 2). The most obvious case in which there is a purchase price is when a preexisting composition is being acquired (see Example 3). The publisher acquires the composition by paying the songwriter an agreed-upon sum of money; this payment is usually, though not necessarily, treated as an advance against the royalties to be paid to the songwriter pursuant to a songwriters' agreement.

Example

Songwriter sells "Song" to Publisher for a payment of $500. As a part of the sale, Songwriter enters into a songwriters' agreement with Publisher which provides that the $500 payment is an advance against royalties to be earned pursuant to the agreement.

As an aside, I'd like to express the hope that the days when a songwriter might sell all rights of any nature, including the songwriter's share of royalties, for a flat sum are in the past. I recall hearing somewhere that W. C. Handy sold all rights to "Memphis Blues" for $25. The story may be apocryphal, but it does make a point.

Sometimes, in entering into an exclusive songwriters' agreement, the publisher acquires the rights to all preexisting compositions that have not already been assigned. Sometimes the songwriter is paid for these preexisting compositions, sometimes they get thrown into the pot for free. When representing the songwriter, I try to get some additional payment for such compositions.

SAMPLE CONTRACT PROVISIONS

EXAMPLE 1: $500 Advance/"Purchase Price"

4. In consideration of this contract, the Publisher agrees to pay the Writer as follows:

(a) $500.00 as an advance against royalties, receipt of which is hereby acknowledged, which sum shall remain the property of the Writer and shall be deductible only from payments hereafter becoming due the Writer under this contract.

☛ This agreement was for the purchase of one song.

EXAMPLE 2: $1 Advance

8. [Paragraph from recording agreement] I grant to Company the right to acquire each and every composition, together with the copyright therein and all renewals and extensions, and I, as appropriate, shall, in respect to each composition, execute a separate Songwriter's Agreement, in the form of the agreement attached hereto as Exhibit "A," with a publisher designated by Company. In addition, I shall make reasonable efforts to acquire publication rights to original musical works submitted by me to Company which are not written by me. If I am able to acquire such publication rights, Company shall enter into a Songwriter's Agreement, in the form of the agreement attached hereto as Exhibit "A," with the writer or writers of such original musical work.

• • •

1. [Paragraphs from Exhibit "A"] Subject to the terms of this agreement, Writer hereby irrevocably, exclusively and absolutely sells, assigns, transfers and delivers to Publisher, its successors and assigns, the original musical composition written and composed by Writer, now entitled "Song" (herein called "Composition"), which title may be changed by Publisher; including the title, words and music thereof, and all rights therein; all copyrights including all rights included in Section 106 of the United States Copyright Act of 1976 and the rights to secure copyrights and extensions and

renewals of copyrights (to the extent they exist) in the Composition and in arrangements and adaptations thereof, throughout the world; any and all other rights that Writer now has or to which Writer may be entitled or that Writer could or might secure hereafter if this agreement had not been entered into, throughout the world; and for Publisher, its successors and assigns to have and to hold said copyright and all rights of whatsoever nature thereunder existing.

• • •

3. In consideration of this agreement, Publisher agrees to pay Writer as follows:

(a) An advance of One Dollar ($1.00) in hand paid, receipt of which is hereby acknowledged, which sum shall be deductible from any payments hereafter becoming due Writer under this or any other agreement between Publisher and Writer.

☛ This is a "purchase" through a recording agreement. Each of the artist's compositions is automatically "acquired" pursuant to the songwriter's agreement attached as Exhibit "A." In subparagraph 3(a), the artist/songwriter is "in hand paid" the grand sum of $1.00, which in turn is an advance which is cross-collateralized. In fact, the artist probably will never see the $1.00, except, perhaps, on an accounting statement. The old "$1.00 in hand paid, receipt of which is hereby acknowledged" is the time-honored legal fiction that *something* of value changed hands to legitimize the transfer of property or rights.

EXAMPLE 3: Purchase of Preexisting Works

22.(e) Upon the execution and delivery of this agreement Writer shall assign, transfer, set over and deliver in the form provided in subparagraph 15(b) hereof all music, lyrics, titles and compositions created by Writer prior to the date hereof and owned or controlled by Writer or Participant on the date hereof (referred to as "existing works") a schedule of which is annexed hereto and made a part hereof and shall execute an assignment of the copyrights (if any) of all existing works to Publisher subject to the terms and conditions of this agreement and the following special provisions:

(i) Publisher shall pay Writer the sum of Twelve Thousand ($12,000.00) Dollars which shall be an additional advance against and deductible from any and all royalties and other sums payable to Writer (other than the payments provided for in subparagraph 22(b) above) and/or Participant hereunder realized from the exploitation of any of the Compositions or existing works.

EXCLUSIVE AGREEMENTS AND SONGWRITER'S GUARANTEED ADVANCE

> *And one must remember that in those cheap times four hundred dollars was a salary of almost inconceivable splendor.*
>
> —MARK TWAIN
> *Life on the Mississippi*

In exclusive songwriters' agreements, other than those that are tied into a recording agreement, there is usually a system of guaranteed compensation payable to the songwriter as consideration for the songwriter granting the publisher the exclusive right to the compositions. These payments are almost never referred to as a salary. They are advances and are treated as such because (1) they are, and (2) treating the songwriter as a salaried "employee" (as distinct from an "employee for hire") may create problems for the publisher with respect to withholding taxes, employee benefits, etc. (For a discussion of work-for-hire arrangements, see "Work for Hire," pages 530–532.)

Advances may be paid weekly, biweekly, in one yearly payment, or some combination of these (see Example 1). In most cases, advance payments due the songwriter will increase with the passage of time. Advances may also be tied into "something" happening, most likely the release of recorded product containing compositions written pursuant to the songwriter's agreement with the publisher (see, for example, Example 5). These advances and the songwriter's participation in ownership of the copyrights are usually the most hotly contested matters in the negotiations over these exclusive songwriters' agreements.

Under this sort of arrangement, the writer will, in almost all instances, be a writer for hire, which makes the compositions composed works for hire, and accordingly, the publisher becomes the author for purposes of copyright.

SAMPLE CONTRACT PROVISIONS

EXAMPLE 1: Yearly and Weekly Advances

10. For your services rendered hereunder, and for the rights granted herein to us, with respect to the compositions, we shall pay or cause to be paid to you the following aggregate amounts:

• • •

(e) Promptly after the execution of this agreement, we will pay you the sum of $2,200.00, and, on the commencement of the second Contract Year, we shall pay you an additional sum of $2,200.00 and such sums shall constitute advances and shall be charged against your royalties under this agreement between you and us.

(f) We will pay you the additional sum of $150.00 per week during the initial term of this agreement and such sums shall constitute advances and shall be charged against your royalties under this agreement between you and us.

• • •

25. You hereby grant us the option to extend the term of this agreement for a first additional period of two years upon all the same terms and conditions herein contained, except that the advance referred to in subparagraph 10(e) shall be $3,600.00 rather than $2,200.00 and the weekly advance referred to in subparagraph 10(f) shall be $200.00 per week rather than $150.00.

26. If you have exercised the option granted to us in paragraph 25 hereof, you hereby grant us the option to extend the term of this agreement for a second additional period of two years upon all the same terms and conditions herein contained, except that the advance referred to in subparagraph 10(e) shall be $5,000.00 rather than $2,200.00 and the weekly advance referred to in subparagraph 10(f) shall be $250.00 per week rather than $150.00.

27. All sums paid to you pursuant to paragraphs 25 and 26 hereunder shall constitute advances and shall be charged against your royalties under this agreement between you and us.

☛ Note that the amount of the advances increases with the exercise of options for additional years.

EXAMPLE 2: Advances Paid in Three Installments

19. Conditioned upon Writer's full and faithful performance of all the terms and provisions hereof, Publisher shall pay to Writer the following sums at the following times, each of which sums shall

constitute an advance recoupable from any and all royalties otherwise payable to Writer hereunder under any other agreement between Writer and his publishing designee and Publisher relating to the Compositions hereunder, or under the Participation Agreement.

(a) The sum of Five Thousand Dollars ($5,000) for the first one year period of the initial term hereof, payable as follows: The sum of Two Thousand Dollars ($2,000) promptly after execution hereof; the sum of One Thousand Five Hundred Dollars ($1,500) promptly after the date six months after execution hereof, and the sum of One Thousand Five Hundred Dollars ($1,500) promptly after the date nine months after execution hereof;

(b) The sum of Five Thousand Dollars ($5,000) for the second one year period of the initial term hereof, payable as follows: The sum of Two Thousand Dollars ($2,000) promptly after commencement of the second year one year period of the initial term hereof; the sum of One Thousand Five Hundred Dollars ($1,500) promptly after the date six months after commencement of said one year period, and the sum of One Thousand Five Hundred Dollars ($1,500) promptly after the date nine months after the commencement of said one year period;

(c) The sum of Five Thousand Dollars ($5,000) for the third one year period of the initial term hereof, payable as follows: The sum of Two Thousand Dollars ($2,000) promptly after commencement of the third year one year period of the initial term hereof; the sum of One Thousand Five Hundred Dollars ($1,500) promptly after the date six months after commencement of said one year period, and the sum of One Thousand Five Hundred Dollars ($1,500) promptly after the date nine months after the commencement of said one year period;

(d) The sum of Six Thousand Dollars ($6,000) for the first renewal term hereof, if any, payable one-third (⅓) promptly after the commencement of said renewal term, one-third (⅓) promptly after the date six months after commencement of said renewal term, and one-third (⅓) nine months promptly after the commencement of said renewal term;

(e) The sum of Six Thousand Dollars ($6,000) for the second renewal term hereof, if any, payable one-third (⅓) promptly after the commencement of said renewal term, one-third (⅓) promptly after the date six months after commencement of said renewal term, and one-third (⅓) nine months promptly after the commencement of said renewal term;

EXAMPLE 3: Weekly Advances
22.(b) During the Initial Period and each exercised option year Publisher shall pay Writer the following weekly sums which shall be advances against and deductible from royalties and other sums payable to Writer or Writer's publishing company:

(i) During the Initial Period	$300.00
(ii) During the first exercised option year	$325.00
(ii) During the second exercised option year	$375.00
(iv) During the third exercised option year	$425.00
(v) During the fourth exercised option year	$500.00

EXAMPLE 4: Writer Designates Payment Schedule
ADVANCES:

(a) For the initial term of the Agreement, the sum of Thirteen Thousand ($13,000) Dollars, Three Thousand ($3,000) Dollars of which has been paid, receipt of which is hereby acknowledged, and the remaining Ten Thousand ($10,000) Dollars to be paid upon execution hereof.

(b) For the first option period, the sum of Thirteen Thousand ($13,000) Dollars payable during such period in such manner as Writer shall in writing designate.

(c) For the second option period, the sum of Thirteen Thousand ($13,000) Dollars payable during such period in such manner as Writer shall in writing designate.

☛ This example is unusual in that the songwriter gets to specify, in the option period, when and in what installments the yearly advance will be paid. Normally, the only practical reason for any choice other than full payment on commencement, apart from some self-imposed "allowance," would be a delay for tax purposes. Note also that this is the only example that does not have an increasing advance with the passage of time.

EXAMPLE 5: Advances Tied to Record Contract

6. *Advances.* Subject to any rights and remedies which may be available to Publisher in the event of a material breach of this Contract on the part of Writer and/or Participant, Publisher shall make advances to Writer as set forth below, each of which shall constitute an advance recoupable from all writer royalties and Participant's share of the publisher's share of net income.

(a) With respect to the first Qualifying Album, Publisher will advance to Writer the sum of Ten Thousand Dollars ($10,000), payable as follows:

(i) Five Thousand Dollars ($5,000) within five (5) business days after the execution of this Contract;

(ii) In addition to the foregoing advances, Publisher shall also make available to Writer during the first eighteen (18) months of the term hereof a marketing and promotion fund in an amount not to exceed Five Thousand Dollars ($5,000), which shall be disbursed with the mutual consent of Writer and Publisher. Any portion of this fund remaining as of the expiration of the above-mentioned eighteen (18) month period shall be paid to Writer.

(iii) In the event that the first Qualifying Album is released nationally in the United States by a Major United States Record Company, then Publisher shall pay to Writer as an additional advance the sum of Fifteen Thousand Dollars ($15,000) within ten (10) business days after the later of:

(A)   United States Release of the first Qualifying Album by such Major United States Record Company and

(B)   the full execution of the Long Form Agreement.

(b) As to any subsequent Qualifying Albums:

(i) The advance payable for the second Qualifying Album, if any, shall be Thirty Five Thousand Dollars ($35,000) less the aggregate amount of the unrecouped balance of advance payments previously paid to Writer hereunder, calculated as of the end of the accounting period immediately preceding the accounting period in which such payment is due, but not less than Seventeen Thousand Five Hundred Dollars ($17,500). However, if an amount equal to two-thirds (⅔) of the royalties earned by Writer and Participant hereunder calculated as of the end of the accounting period immediately preceding the accounting period in which such payment is due exceeds Thirty Five Thousand Dollars ($35,000), and provided that Writer is then in a recouped position, then Publisher shall pay Writer the excess amount up to a maximum of Seventy Thousand Dollars ($70,000) as an advance payment.

(ii) The advance payment for the third Qualifying Album, if any, shall be Forty Five Thousand Dollars ($45,000) less the aggregate amount of the unrecouped balance of advance payments previously paid to Writer hereunder, calculated as of the end of the accounting period immediately preceding the accounting period in which such payment is due, but not less than Twenty Two Thousand Five Hundred Dollars ($22,500). However, if an amount equal to two-thirds (⅔) of the royalties earned by Writer and Participant hereunder calculated as of the end of the accounting period immediately preceding the accounting period in which such payment is due exceeds Forty Five Thousand Dollars ($45,000), and provided that Writer is then in a recouped position, then Publisher shall pay Writer the excess amount up to a maximum of Ninety Thousand Dollars ($90,000) as an advance payment.

(iii) The advance payment for the fourth Qualifying Album, if any, shall be Sixty Thousand Dollars ($.60,000) less the aggregate amount of the unrecouped balance of advance payments previously paid to Writer hereunder, calculated as of the end of the accounting period immediately preceding the accounting period in which such payment is due, but not less than Thirty Thousand Dollars ($30,000). However, if an amount equal to two-thirds (⅔) of the royalties earned by Writer and Participant hereunder calculated as of the end of the accounting period immediately preceding the accounting period in which such payment is due exceeds Sixty Thousand Dollars ($60,000), and provided that Writer is then in a recouped position, then Publisher shall pay Writer the excess amount up to a maximum of One Hundred and Twenty Thousand Dollars ($120,000) as an advance payment.

(iv) The advance payment for the fifth Qualifying Album, if any, shall be Seventy Five Thousand Dollars ($75,000) less the aggregate amount of the unrecouped balance of advance payments previously paid to Writer hereunder, calculated as of the end of the accounting period immediately preceding the accounting period in which such payment is due, but not less than Thirty Seven Thousand Five Hundred Dollars ($37,500). However, if an amount equal to two-thirds (⅔) of the royalties earned by Writer and Participant hereunder calculated as of the end of the accounting period immediately preceding the accounting period in which such payment is due exceeds Seventy Five Thousand Dollars ($75,000), and provided that Writer is then in a recouped position, then Publisher shall pay Writer the excess amount up to a maximum of One Hundred and Fifty Thousand Dollars ($150,000) as an advance payment.

The Advance payments due for each Qualifying Album (in addition to the first Qualifying Album), if any, shall be payable within thirty (30) days after the later to occur of: (a) United States Release of the applicable Qualifying Album, (b) the date in which Publisher must exercise its option to reject a Qualifying Album as provided above or (c) full execution of the Long Form Agreement.

(c) The advance for the particular Qualifying Album is predicated on that Album containing at least eight (8) newly written and previously unrecorded Compositions entirely subject hereto that have been licensed to the record distributor at not less than three-quarters (¾) of the then current statutory rate in effect on the date of the initial United States commercial release of such Album or the equivalent. If any Album shall contain less than the above, the advance relating to that particular Album shall be reduced in the proportion that the mechanical royalty payable upon the Writer's portion of musical compositions subject hereto, bears to eight (8) times three quarters (¾) of the statutory rate in effect on the date of the initial United States release of such Album. In making this determination, musical compositions only partially subject hereto are to be counted against the minimum required number of Compositions per Album as fractional Compositions. For example, using the mechanical copyright royalty rate currently in effect, if an Album contains only five (5) Compositions that are one hundred percent (100%) subject hereto a mechanical royalty rate of $0.2475 would be payable for those Compositions ($0.0660 × 0.75 × 5) and the advance for that Album would be reduced in the proportion that $0.2475 bears to $0.396 ($0.0660 × 0.72 × 8). Notwithstanding anything to the contrary, no advance shall be due Writer if an Album shall contain less than five (5) Compositions one hundred percent (100%) subject hereto.

(d) Further, notwithstanding the foregoing, if a Qualifying Album is released by a Major Independent Record Company, then the advances payable pursuant to subparagraph 6(b) above shall be reduced by one half (½). No advance shall be due with respect to any Album released by a person or entity which is not a Major United States Record Company or Major Independent Record Company.

☞ This songwriters' agreement is obviously driven by the songwriter's position as a recording artist. With the release of the artist's future albums, the advances as a songwriter become substantially larger. Of particular interest is subparagraph 6(a)(ii), which provides for a marketing and promotion fund for the first Qualifying Album. The publisher is kicking in money to help promote the recording, subject to the mutual consent of the songwriter and publisher.

SONGWRITER'S SHARE OF MECHANICAL LICENSE FEES

A major source of income from the use of musical copyrights is the mechanical license fee, the fee paid by the record company to the publisher for the use of the copyrighted composition on a recording that will be sold to the public.

As a practical matter, there is a ceiling placed upon the rate that must be paid to the publisher by the record company when a musical composition is used without obtaining prior approval. This, however, does not alter the opportunity to negotiate a lower rate with the publisher (or, frequently, the publisher's representative, such as an administering publisher or a private collection agency like The Harry Fox Agency, Inc.) in advance of using the product. This ceiling is the compulsory license fee, commonly called either the "compulsory" or the "statutory" rate, and is set by the Copyright Act of 1976, whereby any party can "mechanically" reproduce a musical composition without first obtaining the consent of the publisher. There are, of course, other restrictions and conditions that apply to the compulsory license. For more details on the compulsory license, see pages 512–521, which discuss the provisions of Section 115 of the Copyright Act of 1976.

As discussed earlier, before January 1, 1978, the statutory rate was 2 cents per record manufactured. Under the new Copyright Act of 1976, which became effective January 1, 1978, the statutory rate for each composition was initially 2¾ cents, or ½ cent per minute of playing time or fraction thereof, whichever was greater, for each record manufactured and sold. The new act also established a formula for progressively increased payments for compositions in excess of 5 minutes.

The statutory rate increases every 2 years, in the even-numbered year. For the period 2004–2005, the statutory rate is 8.5 cents per unit or 1.65 cents per minute of playing time, whichever is greater, which represents a 425% increase over the 1909–1978 rate. After a 70-year period in which the statutory rate had stayed at 2 cents, the record companies were in for a considerable economic shock at the new, ever-increasing sticker price. Well, my little dumplings, the record companies weren't going to stand for it. Not, of course, that they were going to change or break the law. No siree! What they would do, with increasing vigor, was not only to insist on lower mechanical license fee rates at every opportunity but also to stipulate that the recording artist be responsible for "excess fees" charged.

Accordingly, record companies frequently attempt to license the use of musical compositions at less than the statutory rate. In some instances, such as budget records and record clubs, the record company *must* obtain a special rate; otherwise it cannot economically afford to put out the package. Note that if a recording artist happens to control the copyrights, this might be a method of controlling the ability of the record company to re-release recordings on budget offerings.

In virtually every instance, the compensation due the songwriter from the publisher for mechanical license fees received by the publisher is one-half (50%) of the amount collected. Most of the mechanicals collected are from the sale of records, but there may also be mechanical license fees received from the use of the musical compositions on videos, especially from the release on home video of films containing the compositions on the soundtrack.

SAMPLE CONTRACT PROVISIONS

EXAMPLE 1: 50% of All Net Sums
3. In consideration of this agreement, Publisher agrees to pay Writer as follows:

• • •

(g) A royalty of fifty (50%) percent of all net sums actually received by Publisher from any license issued authorizing the manufacture of the parts of instruments serving to mechanically reproduce the Composition in the United States of America.

☛ You can't get more basic than this.

EXAMPLE 2: Mechanicals Combined with Other Categories
7. **Compensation.** Provided that Writer shall faithfully and completely perform the terms, covenants and conditions of this agreement, Publisher hereby agrees to pay Writer for the services to be rendered by Writer under this agreement and for the rights acquired and to be acquired hereunder, the following compensation based on the musical compositions which are the subject hereof:

• • •

(c) Fifty percent (50%) of any and all net sums actually received (less any costs for collection) by Publisher in the United States from the exploitation in the United States and Canada by licensees of Publisher of mechanical rights, electrical transcription and reproduction rights, motion picture and television synchronization rights and all other rights (excepting printing rights and public performing rights) therein, whether or not such licensees are affiliated with, owned in whole or in part by, or controlled by Publisher.

PUBLIC PERFORMANCE FEES

Vegetables of all kinds now began to fill the air, and Freddie,
abandoning his Art as a wash-out, sought refuge behind the piano. But
this move, though shrewd, bought him only a temporary respite. No
doubt this audience had had to deal before with singers who hid behind

pianos. It took them perhaps a minute to find the range, and then some kind of a dried fish came dropping from the gallery and caught him in the eye. Very much the same thing, if you remember, happened to King Harold at the battle of Hastings.

—P. G. WODEHOUSE
The Masked Troubadour

Generally speaking (there are always exceptions), the two areas that generate the most earnings for a songwriter are mechanical license fees and public performance fees. Public performance fees are those fees paid to both the songwriter and the publisher by the applicable performance society (e.g., ASCAP) for "public performance for a profit." Section 101 of the Copyright Act of 1976 defines what it means to "perform or display a work 'publicly' (see page 497), but for the purposes of this discussion, assume that the term *public performance* refers to radio play and television play; music played for a live audience, including in clubs and concert halls and during breaks in sporting events; and, in most cases, music played in stores. In other words, we are talking about just any public performance of music. Copyright law grants the copyright owner the right to control the use of the copyrighted material. With a few minor exceptions (not important for this discussion), the only area where the copyright owner of musical compositions does not have complete control over the use of the copyrighted material is the area of the compulsory license.

Accordingly, the copyright owner—the publisher—of a musical composition has the absolute right to grant or not grant what are known as *small performance rights*, the right to publicly perform the copyrighted work for a profit. These rights are "small" only in comparison to the "grand" rights, which are the rights to perform the work as part of a dramatic production, such as an opera or a musical comedy. For example, a grant of the grand rights is required to produce a musical on Broadway; a grant of the small rights is sufficient to be able to play a song from that musical on the radio. Because it would be extremely difficult for individual publishers to separately license these rights to radio stations, networks, concert halls, hotels, etc., separate licensing agencies, or performance societies as they are sometimes called, have developed.

Performing rights societies were briefly discussed in Chapter 2 (pages 8–9), and will be visited in much more detail in Chapter 15, "Performance, Performing, and Neighboring Rights." Chapter 15 deals with both "performing" and "performance" rights societies; the distinction between the two is technical. To add to the confusion, some foreign societies are both. In the United States, there is currently no performance rights society; U.S. performing rights societies are ASCAP, BMI, and SESAC. They license the right to perform songwriters' compositions. The fees referred to in this chapter are those collected by ASCAP, BMI, and SESAC and paid out to songwriters.

It is interesting to note that many performing and/or performance rights societies in other countries are governmental or quasi-governmental agencies. In addition, in some countries, the collection of a public performance fee by one of these societies may be triggered by events that would not trigger a collection in the United States. For example, in France, it is possible to collect from five—yes, five—different societies for the same use of the same piece of music. It is possible for Americans to be eligible for these payments.

As stated earlier no single corporation may be affiliated with both ASCAP and BMI. However, one corporation may own two subsidiary corporations, one affiliated with ASCAP and the other with BMI. Many publishers do not have a SESAC affiliate. It is much smaller than its two rivals. A songwriter can be affiliated with only one performing rights society at a time. There are songwriters who drift back and forth between the three societies, now signed to one, now signed to another. The songwriter enters into written agreements with whichever society he or she chooses to affiliate with for the collection of his or her share of performance fees.

In the past, it was common practice for a performing rights society to offer a "signing advance" to songwriters. These advances were negotiated, and were paid by the particular society against that songwriter's income from performance fees. Some time ago, ASCAP and BMI ceased giving signing advances. Despite recurrent rumors that the societies plan to reinstitute this practice, to date they have not.

Commonly, after deducting a portion for administration fees, the gross performance fees for each composition are divided equally between the publisher(s) and the songwriter(s). The performing rights society will pay the publisher's share of performance fees directly to the publisher and the songwriter's share directly to the songwriter. This is important to the songwriter as it means that the performance fees cannot be used by the publisher, and perhaps an affiliated record company, to recover advances either directly or through cross-collateralization.

In some instances, participants are not treated equally, although arguably they are, since each *has the potential* to reach some favored position. For example, BMI will give bonuses to publishers and composers whose cumulative performances reach certain levels. In other words, if a song is performed enough times, the publisher and writer receive additional compensation.

Where do the performance fees come from? The performing rights societies license the rights to public performance for profit of copyrighted musical compositions. The most obvious source of such income are the radio stations. Radio stations pay a license fee to the performing rights societies for the right to broadcast the compositions. Television networks also obtain licenses. Concert halls, or at least the promoters of concerts in halls, are required to obtain licenses. Nightclubs that play music are required to obtain a license. There have even been successful lawsuits requiring clothing stores to obtain a license for playing a radio for its customers. Hotels that have piped music into rooms have also been required to obtain a license.

In the past, a store with two or fewer speakers for piping music throughout the store was not required to obtain a license. If, however, there were more than two speakers, a license was required. This all changed when the Fairness in Music Licensing Act of 1998 (see pages 522–526 for more information on this act) was passed, which provided for many more exceptions than had previously been the case.

As a point of paranoia, there were, and still are, private "music police" who go undercover to bust violators who have not paid the fees required under the law. After polite and increasingly threatening calls from ASCAP and BMI, if the offender does not give in and obtain a license, the enforcement of performing rights violations by the performing rights societies ultimately leads to litigation. At fairly regular intervals ASCAP and BMI will file lawsuits against stores, bars, and other establishments using copyrighted music without proper licensing. These lawsuits are given maximum public exposure as a warning to other offenders. This happens on a much smaller scale than the carpet-bombing techniques used by the RIAA to nail miscreant downloaders, but the goal is the same: Scare the general population of potential offenders by making an example of some average Joe or Josephine.

Enforcement of performing rights in countries outside of the United States can be even stricter.

For example, in England, pub performers must file a report as to what compositions are to be performed before performing them. After the performance, the report is to be checked and any additional songs or differences in the program are to be noted. Failure to report properly can lead to jail sentences for the performers.

Once the payments have been acquired by the performing rights societies, how are they divided up? ASCAP and BMI have different formulas for calculating how the monies collected will be allocated for payment to the songwriter(s) and publisher(s) of each particular composition after deducting operational and administrative costs. (ASCAP claims that 80% of its collections are paid to its members; BMI claims 85%.) ASCAP's formula is based upon recorded air checks, using tape recordings of actual radio broadcasts from across the country. BMI uses a system that requires each station to log in all compositions broadcast and send the log into BMI. Each society naturally has irrefutable proof that its system and formula is superior. (For a more detailed examination of both the ASCAP and BMI systems of logging and accounting for performances, see Chapter 15, the sections "ASCAP," pages 409–410, and "BMI," page 411.)

Performing rights societies are almost a nonissue in songwriters' agreements, and there are generally only two provisions in these agreements that may make reference to them. The first is a reference, more often than not implied, to the particular society with which the songwriter or the publisher is affiliated. By "implied," I mean that the performance society may not be named at all, but reference may be made simply to a particular publisher who is affiliated with, for example, BMI. In most songwriters' agreements tied into recording agreements, there will not even be a specific reference to a publisher by name, let alone one of the societies, but rather to "a publisher designated by the Company," or the like. Note that the affiliation of the songwriter is usually the factor that determines the affiliation of the publisher, which is why most publishing organizations have more than one publishing company. The second provision deals with the division of performing rights society payments, or rather the nondivision, since the publisher and the songwriter are each paid separately and directly. You will note that Examples 2 and 3 following this section both boil down to "Don't look to us to pay you for public performance fees." In addition, Examples 1 and 3 explicitly state that the songwriter agrees that "Writer" has no claim to the publisher's share of public performance fees.

SAMPLE CONTRACT PROVISIONS

EXAMPLE 1. Writer Has No Claim to Publisher's Share

4. Writer agrees that Writer shall not be entitled to receive any part of monies received by Publisher from any performance rights society for the use of the composition throughout the world.

EXAMPLE 2: Songwriter Paid Directly

6. As full consideration for the services to be rendered by Writer hereunder, and for the rights granted herein, Publisher shall pay to Writer:

• • •

(f) Publisher shall not be required to pay royalties to Writer for public performance of the Compositions. Writer shall receive royalties for public performances from the performing rights society with which Writer is or may, in the future, become affiliated.

EXAMPLE 3: Song Writer Paid Directly; Writer Has No Claim to Publisher's Share

7. Compensation. Provided that Writer shall faithfully and completely perform the terms, covenants and conditions of this agreement, Publisher hereby agrees to pay Writer for the services to be rendered by Writer under this agreement and for the rights acquired and to be acquired hereunder, the following compensation based on the musical compositions which are the subject hereof:

• • •

(d) Writer shall receive his public performance royalties throughout the world directly from the performing rights society with which he is affiliated, and shall have no claim whatsoever against Publisher for any royalties received by Publisher from any performing rights society which makes payment directly (or indirectly other than through Publisher) to writers, authors and composers.

PRINT RIGHTS

> **Think, when we talk of horses, that you see them**
> **Printing their proud hoofs i'th' receiving earth.**
>
> —WILLIAM SHAKESPEARE
> *Henry V*, Prologue

Print rights, the rights exercised when a composition is reproduced in printed form, are probably the third most important source of earnings after, and pick your own order, mechanical fees and performance money. The reproduction can be in the form of sheet music, folios, songbooks, lyrics only, lyrics printed on liner notes to an album, etc. The right to reproduce the composition in this form is reserved to the copyright proprietor of the composition and may be licensed by that copyright proprietor to third parties, retained, or not used at all. Unlike the case of a compulsory license for recorded versions of a composition, a copyright proprietor cannot be forced to allow the reproduction of the composition in printed form. (See the discussion on pages 502–504 regarding Section 106 of the Copyright Act of 1976.)

With respect to songwriters' agreements, compensation to the songwriter for print rights is usually specified as a cent amount (sheet music) or is based upon a percentage (for every other type of print right).

Historically, when sheet music sold for 10 cents, the sheer music rate of compensation to the songwriter was usually set at 5 cents, reflecting an equal split between the songwriter and the publisher. For many years, as the price for sheet music rose, the songwriter's share stayed mired in the in the nickel range. Ultimately, the royalty began to creep upward.

Current agreements may specify from 4 cents (very low these days) to 15 cents for each piece of sheet music sold, with the most common rate being between 8 cents and 12 cents. (I did have one songwriter's agreement years ago with a major company that specified a royalty of 18½ cents for each piece of sheet music sold—and this at a time when the normal royalty was 5 cents. I never found out why we were getting such a high rate because I was afraid to ask.)

Traditionally, the method of sale of printed copies, be they sheet music, folios, compilations, or whatever, had no affect on the royalty rate. This is still the case today. Cent-amount royalty calculations apply whether the sale involves a copy printed by the sales outlet or is an Internet download.

A note on terminology. In the following sample provisions, "Piano copy," "pianoforte copy," and "sheet music" are all the same thing: sheet music of a single musical composition. "Folios," "song books," "compilations," "octavos," and like editions are collections of compositions. The collection may be of songs all by one songwriter, who would then receive the full royalty, or a collection of compositions by different songwriters, in which case the songwriter would receive a pro-rata share of the royalty.

SAMPLE CONTRACT PROVISIONS

EXAMPLE 1: Classic Print Royalty

3. In consideration of this agreement, Publisher agrees to pay Writer as follows:

• • •

(b) A royalty of five ($.05) cents per copy on all regular piano copies sold and paid for in the United States of America.

(c) A royalty of five ($.05) cents per copy on any form of orchestration thereof sold and paid for in the United States of America.

(d) A royalty of ten (10%) percent of the wholesale selling price for each of any song book, song sheet, folio, or similar publication containing the Composition for which the Publisher is paid in the United States of America, except that in the event that the Composition is used, in whole or in part, in conjunction with one or more musical compositions in a folio or Album, Writer shall be entitled to receive that portion of ten (10%) percent which the Composition shall bear to the total number of musical compositions contained in such folio or Album.

• • •

(h) For "professional material" not sold or for resale, there shall be no royalty.

(i) In the event that new music or lyrics are added to the Composition, the royalties set forth above shall be divided between Writer and the new writer or composer, if any, in equal shares.

☞ This is it, kids! You understand this breakdown of categories and you know everything you need to know about this type of provision. The numbers may vary a little (not much) and so may the language, but this is pretty much what there is out there on royalties on print rights.

EXAMPLE 2: More of the Same . . .

10. For your services rendered hereunder, and for the rights granted herein to us, with respect to the Compositions, we shall pay or cause to be paid to you the following aggregate amounts:

(a) In respect of the Compositions written and composed solely by you, if published by us or with our consent or at our direction and during the life of the copyright therein:

(i) $.06 per copy for each regular piano and vocal copy of any of the Compositions alone, sold, and not returned, in the United States of America and/or the Dominion of Canada and for which we are paid.

(ii) Except with respect to sales of folios or composite works containing any of the Compositions, 10% of the wholesale selling price (after trade discounts, if any) for each band part and/or orchestration of any of the Compositions sold, and not returned, in the United States of America and/or the Dominion of Canada and for which we are paid.

(iii) Such percentage of 10% of the wholesale selling price (after trade discounts, if any) of any folio or composite work containing any of the Compositions and published by us and sold, and paid for and not returned, in the United States of America and/or the Dominion of Canada as the number of Compositions therein bears to the total number of musical compositions included in said folio or composite work; if any of the Compositions are included in a folio or composite work which is not published by us, that portion of 50% of the net monies received by us from the sale of such folios and composite works in the United States of America and/or the Dominion of Canada as the numeral one (1) bears to the total number of compositions included in said folio or composite work which are copyrighted by us.

EXAMPLE 3: And Still More of the Same . . .

6. As full consideration for the services to be rendered by Writer hereunder, and for the rights granted herein, Publisher shall pay to Writer:

(a) Seven ($.07) cents per copy, for each and every pianoforte copy of the Compositions sold by Publisher in the United States and Canada, paid for and not returned.

(b) Ten (10%) percent of the wholesale selling price (after trade discounts, if any) for each and every printed copy of each and every other arrangement and edition of the Compositions published and sold in the United States and Canada by Publisher, paid for and not returned, except that in the event that the Composition shall be used or caused to be used in whole or in part in conjunction with one or more other musical compositions in a folio or Album, Writer shall be entitled to receive that portion of said ten (10%) percent which the Compositions shall bear to the total number of musical compositions contained in such folio or Album.

• • •

(d) Publisher shall not be required to pay any royalties for professional or complimentary copies or any copies which are distributed gratuitously to performing artists or orchestra leaders or for advertising or exploitation purposes or copies disposed of below cost.

SYNCHRONIZATION LICENSES

Another area of earning for the songwriter is the songwriter's share of *synchronization license fees*, or *sync fees*, which are the license fees charged by the copyright proprietor to a third party who wishes "to synchronize visual images with the musical composition." Use of the term "synchronize" does not mean that the music has to be synchronized to the visual in the same way that one might lip-sync to a song, only that it is to accompany the visual image. Accordingly, musical compositions used as instrumental background scores for film and television require a synchronization license. The same is true for songs featured on soundtracks and music videos. The fee received for the sync license is generally divided equally between the publisher(s) and the songwriter(s).

Sync licenses are required for the use of the copyrights of musical compositions for film soundtracks whether the music used is recorded originally for the film or taken from preexisting recordings. Sync rights are also required for television and videos, both for broadcast and for sale for home use.

The decision as to whether a synchronization license will be granted or not remains in the control of the copyright proprietor, the publisher, or, in the case of copublishers, the administrating publisher. As discussed in Chapter 7, there is no statutory rate here, as with compulsory mechanical license fees, and the copyright proprietor has the right to refuse to license the use. As a result, the price of the fee can be any price the licensee is willing to pay. I have seen sync fees for individual songs run from no fee at all, a "freebie," to many thousands of dollars. In fact, I have one report of an instance where the sync fee was $250,000—per note! (Before your eyebrows rise up any higher in astonishment, I must admit that it was only a four-note composition—still a lot of money by any standard.)

The publisher's absolute control over whether or not a sync license will be granted leads to many anguished moments for film producers who have not taken the necessary steps to clear the rights before using the music. We have all seen films where the extras are dancing to "something," but probably not the music we are hearing. (For some reason, it is usually a downstairs disco with the good guy pursuing the bad guy—it must have something to do with stairs and strobe lights.) What probably happened was that a specific piece of music was used and then, to the horror of the producer, it was discovered that the piece was either not available or available only for some horrendous sum of money. In such cases, another piece of music has to be substituted on the soundtrack, leaving moviegoers with an uneasy feeling that something is wrong.

Although this discussion is primarily concerned with the songwriter's share of the earnings from synchronization licenses, it is appropriate to mention some important information regarding the granting of these licenses. Film producers frequently insist upon a "flat" buyout when obtaining sync licenses for areas such as, for example, mechanical licenses in connection with video release. If you have any bargaining power and are granting a synchronization license, *don't* do it— don't give away these areas of potential income by waiving mechanical license fees. There is money to be made out there from all the various uses of the music, many of which have no impact, pro or con, on the film producer. There is no reason why the publisher should not retain these rights and just waive them when appropriate.

SAMPLE CONTRACT PROVISIONS

EXAMPLE 1: Classic Synchronization Royalty

3. In consideration of this agreement, Publisher agrees to pay Writer as follows:

• • •

(f) A royalty of fifty (50%) percent of any and all sums actually received by Publisher from motion picture and television synchronization rights in the United States of America.

EXAMPLE 2: Synchronization Royalty

8. Provided that Writer shall duly perform the terms, covenants and conditions of this Contract, Publisher shall pay Writer, for the services to be rendered by Writer hereunder and for the rights acquired by Publisher hereunder, the following compensation based upon the exploitation of the Compositions:

• • •

(c) (i) Fifty percent (50%) of any and all Receipts actually received by Publisher in the United States from the exploitation in the United States by licensees of mechanical rights, grand rights, electrical transcription and reproduction rights, digital broadcast or transmission rights, motion picture and synchronization rights, dramatization rights and other rights therein [except print rights, which are covered in subparagraphs (A) and (b) above, and public performance rights, which are covered in subparagraph (d) below].

MISCELLANEOUS INCOME

Most songwriters' agreements have a catchall provision that provides that any other income, of any nature, that is received by the publisher and not otherwise provided for or described in the songwriter's agreement is to be divided equally between the publisher and the songwriter.

The types of income that can be called "miscellaneous" are varied and may range far afield from what one normally might think of as music publishing. Examples range from the obvious, such as the licensing of a musical composition for an advertising campaign, to the more subtle, such as merchandising rights. For example, a perfume might be named after a song. A song title might be used for the title of a motion picture (e.g., *Stand by Me*). A character from a song might be spun off into animation, toys, and any number of commercial uses (e.g., *Rudolph The Red-Nosed Reindeer*). The income from the various uses of a composition covered under these miscellaneous provisions is split 50–50 between the writer(s) and the publisher(s) (see Examples 1 and 2).

With new technology, the lines between income categories have become blurred. Take the licensing fees in the United Kingdom for "ringtones": the tones callers hear when they call someone else's cell phone. A performance rights group formed by the alliance of the Performing Rights Society and the Mechanical Copyright Protection Society (see Chapter 15, "Performance, Performing, and Neighborning Rights," pages 414–415) issues blanket licenses to wireless phone companies for the public performance fees (an annual minimum fee of £850 against the greater of 5% of gross revenues or 5p per file supplied) and mechanical licenses (an advance of £500 against the greater of 10% of gross revenues or 10p per file supplied). On the face of it, this use could possibly fall into at least four different royalty categories: (1) mechanical licenses, (2) public performance, (3) foreign, and/or (4) miscellaneous. Ultimately, it probably doesn't really matter which categories apply as the end result remains the same: The writer gets 50% of the income.

SAMPLE CONTRACT PROVISIONS

EXAMPLE 1: Miscellaneous Income

10. For your services rendered hereunder, and for the rights granted herein to us, with respect to the Compositions, we shall pay or cause to be paid to you the following aggregate amounts:

• • •

(d) 50% of all net sums received by us solely with respect to the Compositions written and composed solely by you from any use of such Compositions not dealt with elsewhere in this agreement, provided you are not paid, or to be paid, for such use directly or indirectly by a third party.

EXAMPLE 2: "Catchall" Provision

7. Provided that you have faithfully and completely performed the terms and conditions of this Agreement, for any net income received by Publisher which is not provided for in Paragraph 6, above, and for which you do not receive direct payment of the so-called writer's share, Publisher shall pay you Fifty (50%) Percent of such net income.

SONGWRITER'S SHARE OF FOREIGN RECEIPTS

I only know two tunes—one is "Yankee Doodle" and the other isn't.

—ULYSSES S. GRANT

As with recording agreements, it would be unusual for a songwriter's agreement to specify "full" payment for foreign sales, licensees, etc., because of the licensor/licensee situation that exists between the publisher and the foreign licensees. Remember that foreign licensees may be independent companies, affiliated companies, or owned subsidiaries (see Example 1).

There is, however, one area where the songwriter will receive a "full" songwriter's royalty for foreign activities. That area is the collection, by foreign performing rights societies, of public performance royalties that are then accounted directly to the songwriter through the songwriter's affiliated domestic performing rights society (see Example 1). Note that the word "full" is in quotes. It is perhaps the wrong word to use in this situation. First of all, the societies collect handling fees before remitting earnings. It also takes forever (or longer) for the monies to arrive. Even more important is the fact that very few, if any, American writers ever receive their "full" royalty from foreign sources. This is not necessarily the fault of the publisher, unless, of course, ignorance is considered a "fault." At least in most cases the ignorance is not malicious.

The copyright laws in most foreign countries, especially in Europe, are set up to provide an advantage to the native publisher and writer. This is the intellectual property equivalent of countries setting up trade barriers to give an advantage to native manufacturers or farmers. Most American publishers are, unknown to them, taken advantage of in ways unimagined in our simple, straightforward, and trusting industry. (I hope the tongue-in-cheek irony was not too subtle in the preceding sentence.) As a result of the publishers losing out, the writers also suffer. (For a more detailed, and really scary, discussion of such matters, see the discussion on the infamous "Black Box," pages 355–357.)

Additionally, there are sources of performance royalties that are available from some of the foreign societies that are not available in this country. There is, for example, the licensing of public performance rights to soundtracks of motion pictures. In this country when you go down to your local movie theater to see a film, the theater does not pay a public performance fee for the use of the music. In many countries outside of the United States, however, every time a film plays at the local theater a performance fee is due and payable to the local performance society and, in turn, is to be paid to the publisher and the writer. Another example is in the area of mechanical licenses for video rights. Although mechanical license rights are sometimes acquired on a flat buy-out rate, some countries make it a legal requirement that the mechanical license fees be paid despite the fact that they had been contractually waived.

The potential income from songwriters' royalties from foreign sources is enormous. Songwriters who had, at best, received a few hundred or so dollars in foreign royalties have, after being properly plugged into the system, found themselves the surprised recipients of thousands or even millions of dollars. That is not a typo—from hundreds of dollars to millions of dollars. It can be better than winning a lottery.

Usually, the royalty payable to the songwriter by the publisher is either 50% of the otherwise applicable royalty and/or 50% of the publisher's net receipts from the foreign sources. With respect to these provisions covering the reduction of royalties from foreign sources, some are expressly set forth in the songwriter's agreement and some are included either by implication or reference. (Other foreign sources of income from the exploitation of music are discussed in Chapter 15, "Performance, Performing, and Neighboring Rights," the section "Neighboring Rights," pages 416–419.)

SAMPLE CONTRACT PROVISIONS

EXAMPLE 1: 50% of Any and All Net Sums

(e) Fifty percent (50%) of any and all net sums, after deduction of foreign taxes, actually received (less any costs of collection) by Publisher in the United States from sales, licenses and other uses of the subject musical compositions in countries outside of the United States and Canada (other than public performance societies as hereinabove mentioned in (d) above) from collection agents, licensees, subpublishers or others, whether or not same are affiliated with, owned in whole or in part by, or controlled by Publisher.

☛ This example covers all the bases. It provides (1) a royalty, 50%, based on: (2) "any and all net sums," with "net sums" being defined as (a) monies actually received in the United States after deductions of foreign taxes and costs of collection; (b) from all sources outside the United States and Canada; (c) except public performance fees, which are paid directly to the songwriter.

EXAMPLE 2: Foreign Print Royalty 50% of Net Sums

10. For your services rendered hereunder, and for the rights granted herein to us, with respect to the Compositions, we shall pay or cause to be paid to you the following aggregate amounts:

• • •

(c) 50% of all net sums received by us solely with respect to the Compositions written and composed solely by you due to the sale outside of the United States of America and/or Canada of sheet music, folios, band parts and/or orchestrations of such Compositions.

☛ This provision deals only with print rights. The songwriter receives 50% of all net sums received by the publisher for foreign sales of printed copies of the compositions. Note that Canada is included with the United States as a domestic territory.

NONSHARED ADVANCES

Traditionally, by implication, and sometimes by express contract provision, advances received by the publisher are not shared with the songwriter until they are actually earned. Since the songwriter's royalties are for actual sales, an advance to the publisher from a third party, such as a foreign subpublisher, is not a sale. An advance against print sales, for example, is not an actual sale, it is a recoupable payment against anticipated sales. Once recoupment of the advance begins, the songwriter's portion becomes due.

In most instances, advances to a publisher are for an entire catalogue, not just one writer's work. Accordingly, until there are actual sales or other collections, it is impossible to apportion monies among the various writers on any basis that makes sense. And, of course, if the advance is not recouped, the publisher may keep the unrecouped portion as it is not technically due the writers.

SAMPLE CONTRACT PROVISIONS

EXAMPLE 1: Advances Not Shared

7. Compensation. Provided that Writer shall faithfully and completely perform the terms, covenants and conditions of this agreement, Publisher hereby agrees to pay Writer for the services to be ren-

dered by Writer under this agreement and for the rights acquired and to be acquired hereunder, the following compensation based on the musical compositions which are the subject hereof:

• • •

(j) In no event shall Writer be entitled to share in any advance payments, guarantee payments or minimum royalty payments which Publisher shall receive in connection with any subpublishing agreement, collection agreement, licensing agreement or other agreement covering the subject musical compositions or any of them.

DEMONSTRATION COSTS

Songwriters' agreements frequently contain a provision which, although related to the recording costs provisions in recording agreements, is unique to songwriters' agreements. It deals with the costs of the recording of demos (demonstration records) of musical compositions. Demos are made for the purpose of selling something. A recording artist makes demos in order to get a record agreement. A songwriter, or more usually a publisher, makes demos in order to sell songs. In the past, making a demo recording was generally a basic, bare-bones production. Today, with the advent of computers and state-of-the-art home studios, most demos are more elaborate.

The costs of making demos are sometimes charged to the songwriter and sometimes paid entirely by the publisher, but most often they are equally divided between the songwriter and the publisher (see Example 1). When it comes to selling the song, the songwriter is treated almost as a partner of the publisher. To extend the analogy, consider demos as sales tools for marketing a product (the song) to potential buyers (recording artists and their producers); this marketing cost is split between the "partners." Obviously, having a decent home studio may allow artists to side-step this whole issue.

In many cases it is wise to place one particular restriction upon the publisher with respect to demos, which are frequently recorded by the songwriters themselves. This restriction forbids the publisher to make any commercial use of the demos without the prior consent of the songwriter. There have been artists who were embarrassed by the commercial release of old publisher's demos featuring performances best forgotten. Publishers are usually willing to include a provision restricting the commercial use of the demos (see Example 3).

SAMPLE CONTRACT PROVISIONS

EXAMPLE 1: Half of Demo Costs As Advance; Cross-Collateralization
8. Publisher shall specify, and pay the costs of, the talent, studio and all other items expended in the production of demonstration records embodying performances of the Composition. One-half (½) of all such costs so paid by Publisher shall constitute an advance and shall be charged against the royalties payable to Writer under this or any other agreement between Writer and Publisher.

☞ Just a little reminder: Cross-collateralization can show up anywhere.

EXAMPLE 2: Half of Demo Costs Recoupable
12. Writer hereby agrees that Publisher may charge against and recoup from royalties otherwise payable to Writer hereunder one-half (½) of the costs advanced by Publisher for the preparation and recording of demonstration records embodying one or more of the Compositions.

EXAMPLE 3: No Commercial Use of Demos

(d) Publisher at its sole discretion shall reasonably make studio facilities available for Writer so that Writer, subject to the supervision and control of Publisher, may make demonstration records of the musical compositions hereunder and also for Writer to perform at such recording sessions. Writer shall not incur any liability for which Publisher may be responsible in connection with any demonstration record session without having first obtained Publisher's written approval as to the nature, extent and limit of such liability. In no event shall Writer incur any expense whatsoever in behalf of Publisher without first having received written authorization from Publisher. Writer shall not be entitled to any compensation (in addition to such compensation as may be otherwise provided for herein) with respect to services rendered in connection with such demonstration record recording sessions. Publisher shall advance the costs for the production of demonstration records, one-half (½) of such costs shall be deemed additional nonreturnable advances to Writer and shall be deducted from royalties payable to Writer by Publisher under this or any other agreement between Writer and Publisher relating to any of the Compositions hereunder, or under the Participation Agreement between Writer and Publisher. All recordings and reproductions made at demonstration recording sessions hereunder shall become the sole and exclusive property of Publisher, free of any claims whatsoever by Writer or any other person deriving any rights from Writer. Notwithstanding the foregoing, Publisher shall not commercially exploit any such demonstration records embodying the performances of Writer without Writer's written consent, which consent shall not be unreasonably withheld.

COWRITERS

Included in most songwriters' agreements, usually in the grant-of-rights section, are provisions dealing with cowriters. These provisions deal not only with the situations where two or more writers originally wrote a song, but also with the publisher's right to add cowriters. It is sometimes possible to add language specifying that the original songwriter will have the first right to alter lyrics or add lyrics for the composition. If the songwriter does get such a provision, it usually applies only to English-language versions. If, of course, the songwriter is bilingual or multilingual, it may be possible to write the provision such that the songwriter will have the first right to add lyrics in the other language.

Usually, provisions dealing with the division of royalties between cowriters provide that the royalties, and the costs, be divided equally between them. This, of course, does not mean that the royalties have to be divided equally if the parties agree otherwise (see Example 1).

SAMPLE CONTRACT PROVISIONS

EXAMPLE 1: Division of Royalties to Cowriters

10. The term "Writer" shall be understood to include all the authors and composers of the Composition. If there are more than one, the covenants herein contained shall be deemed to be both joint and several on the part of the writers and the composers and the royalties hereinabove to be paid to Writer shall, unless a different division of royalty be specified, be due to all the writers and composers collectively, to be paid by Publisher in equal shares to each. This agreement may be executed by writers and composers in several counterparts.

EXAMPLE 2: Company's Right to Change Music and Words

4. (c) You hereby consent to such changes, adaptations, dramatizations, transpositions, editing and arrangement of the Compositions and the setting of words to the music and of music to the words and the change of title thereof as we deem desirable (hereinafter collectively called "change(s)"); we will notify you of any change other than a dramatization, and we shall not use or effect any such change if you object thereto, provided that in no event shall you unreasonably object to any such changes in the Compositions in order to make them suitable and proper for use outside of the United States of America, and to authorize others to make such changes, without your approval. If words are set to the music which alone is transferred to us pursuant to the provisions hereof, and/or if music is written for the words alone which are transferred to us pursuant to the provisions hereof, we shall have the right to deduct, from the monies payable to you hereunder, the costs of such new words and music, as the case may be, not to exceed one-half of the amounts payable to you hereunder and the amounts payable to you hereunder shall be reduced accordingly.

☛ Note that the writer's right to object to changes is limited. The writer may not "unreasonably object" to changes done to make the composition suitable for use outside of the United States. And if the writer supplies music and lyrics separately, the publisher has the right to have lyrics written for the music, or music written for the lyrics, with the costs, including up to one-half of the royalty, deducted from the original writer's royalties.

EXAMPLE 3: Publisher's Right to Add New Music or Lyrics

18. Writer acknowledges that Publisher has the right to substitute a new title or titles for the Composition and to make any arrangement, adaptation, translation, dramatization or transposition of the Composition in whole or in part, and in connection with any other musical, literary or dramatic material, and to add new lyrics to the music of the Composition or new music to the lyrics of the Composition. Writer's royalties hereunder for any such Composition shall be reduced in such a manner as to reflect the contribution of any new contributor to the Composition, but in no instance may Writer's royalties be reduced by more than one-half (½).

SONGWRITER WARRANTIES AND REPRESENTATIONS

The publisher in both exclusive and nonexclusive agreements will require the songwriter to make certain warranties and representations in connection with the compositions being transferred and/or written pursuant to the agreement. As stated before, a *warranty* is a promise that a certain fact or facts are as represented. A *representation* is a statement about a past or existing fact. The most obvious representation and warranty that the publisher will require of the songwriter is that the copyright(s) for the composition(s) being assigned or written pursuant to the agreement be free and clear from any claims disputing ownership or from any claim of copyright infringement (see Example 1). If it is an exclusive agreement, there is almost always a representation that the songwriter is free to enter into the agreement and to deliver the musical composition required by the agreement.

These clauses frequently include indemnification provisions, whereby the songwriter agrees to be responsible for any loss caused by a breach or misrepresentation of any representation or warranty (see Example 2). As with recording agreements, care should be taken in determining what fact or occurrence triggers the indemnification. (For example, does a claim of copyright infringement trigger indemnification, or does an actual judgment against the songwriter trigger indemnification?) Indemnification clauses usually include provisions granting the publisher the right to withhold royalties due the songwriter in their entirety until a settlement or judgment has been reached. These types of clauses should be reviewed carefully, and the definition of what triggers the obligation should be limited as much as possible.

SAMPLE CONTRACT PROVISIONS

EXAMPLE 1: Warranties, Representations, and Indemnification

2. Writer warrants and represents that Writer is the sole author and composer of the title, music and/or lyrics constituting the Composition; that said title, music and lyrics are Writer's own original work and creation, and that neither said music, title or lyrics nor any part thereof are a copy of any other copyrighted work or infringe or violate any rights of any third party; and that no adverse claim exists thereon. Writer further warrants and represents that Writer has not sold, assigned, leased, licensed or in any way disposed of or encumbered any of the rights herein granted to Publisher and that Writer has the right to make this agreement.

• • •

7. Writer hereby authorizes Publisher at its absolute discretion and at Writer's sole expense to employ attorneys and to institute or defend any action or proceedings and to take any other proper steps to protect the right, title and interest of Publisher in and to the Composition. Publisher may settle, compromise or in any other manner dispose of any matter, claim, action, or proceeding and may satisfy any judgment that may be rendered. All or any expenses so incurred and other sums paid by Publisher shall be paid to Publisher on demand by Writer.

(a) Writer agrees to and does hereby indemnify, save and hold Publisher harmless from loss or damage, including attorney's fees, arising out of or connected with any claim by a third party which is inconsistent with any of the warranties, representations, covenants or agreements made by Writer in this agreement.

(b) The decision as to whether any claim should be made or any legal action should be brought against any alleged infringer of the copyright in the Composition shall be made solely by Publisher; the extent of the prosecution of any such claim or action and/or the terms of any settlement or compromise of any such claim or action, and the decision whether to prosecute or abandon such claim or action, shall be decided solely by Publisher.

(c) Whenever in Publisher's opinion its right, title or interest to the Composition is questioned or there is any breach of any of the covenants, warranties or representations contained in this agreement, Publisher may withhold any and all royalties which may be or become due to Writer hereunder until such question is settled or such breach repaired, and to apply such royalties to the repayment of all sums due Publisher hereunder.

> ☛ The first paragraph in this example, which deals with the warranties and representations, is pretty standard and requires no modification for the songwriter. Paragraph 7, the indemnification, is another story. The songwriter would be wise to negotiate for changes to this provision. Publisher has "absolute discretion" to deal with any claims and "all or any expenses" are to be paid by the writer. It is certainly cheaper and easier for the publisher to pay with the songwriter's money than it is to successfully defend against any claim, no matter how wacko.

EXAMPLE 2: Writer Is Not to "Unreasonably" Withhold Consent to Settlement

10. Writer warrants and represents and undertakes and agrees that the Compositions (and all existing works as hereinafter defined) and each and every part thereof, will be original and will not infringe upon any other musical or lyric material and that Writer will hold Publisher harmless by reason of any and all claims in respect thereof and any and all obligations incurred by Publisher in settling, paying and defending any and all claims and any and all litigation arising therefrom including reasonable attorneys' fees. Publisher shall have the right to defend any and all actions and proceedings instituted upon the same, and, with the prior consent of Writer, which consent will not be unreasonably withheld, to settle the same before or after suit, for such amount and upon such terms as Publisher shall in its sole discretion deem advisable.

EXAMPLE 3: Writer Represents That He Has Not Elsewhere Agreed to a Controlled Composition Clause

10. *Warranties; Indemnification.*

(a) Writer and Participant [co-publisher] hereby warrant, represent, covenant and agree as follows: (i) Writer and Participant have the full right, power and authority to enter into and perform this Contract and to grant to and vest in Publisher all rights herein set forth, free and clear of any and all claims, rights and obligations whatsoever; (ii) all of the Compositions and all other results and proceeds of the services of Writer hereunder, including all of the titles, lyrics and music of the Compositions and each and every part of thereof, delivered and to be delivered by Writer hereunder are and shall be new and original and capable of copyright protection throughout the entire universe; (iii) no Composition shall, either in whole or in part, be an imitation or copy of, or infringe upon, any other material, or violate or infringe upon any common law or statutory rights of any party including, without limitation, contractual rights, copyrights and rights of privacy; (iv) Writer has not sold, assigned, leased, licensed or in any other way disposed of or encumbered any Composition, in whole or in part, or any rights herein granted to Publisher, nor shall Writer sell, assign, lease, license or in any other way dispose of or encumber any of the Compositions, in whole or in part, or any of said rights, except under the terms and conditions hereof, (v) Writer nor anyone acting on Writer's behalf or deriving rights from or through Writer has received or will receive an advance, loan or other payment from a performing rights society, record company or other third party which is or may be recoupable from (or otherwise subject to offset against) monies which would otherwise be collectible by Publisher hereunder (in the event of a breach of this subparagraph 10(a)(v), Publisher shall be entitled to reimburse itself from monies otherwise becoming due to Writer hereunder to the extent that monies are not collectible by Publisher by reason thereof), (vi) neither Writer nor anyone acting on Writer's behalf or deriving rights from or through Writer is or will be subject to a "controlled compositions" clause under which (aa) Compositions are or may be subject to being licensed to a record company in the United States and/or Canada at less than seventy five percent (75%) of the full statutory mechanical license rate in effect on the date of manufacture and sale of each specific record embodying a Composition (however the record company may impose a maximum of ten (10) times such rate with respect to Album-length records and two (2) times such rate with respect to singles); (bb) mechanical royalties may be payable on less than fifty percent (50%) of Album-length "free goods" distributed for resale; (cc) Compositions are subject to inclusion in home video devices except in consideration of a royalty of six cents ($.06) per Composition per copy on sales and a pro rata share of four percent (4%) of wholesale on rentals thereof (based upon comparative running time) or (dd) a combination of two or more of the foregoing.

(b) Writer and Participant shall indemnify Publisher against any loss or damage Publisher may suffer, including reasonable attorney's fees and costs of suit, occasioned by or arising out of any claim, demand or action which is inconsistent with any agreement, representation, grant or warranty made or assumed by Writer and/or Participant hereunder which is reduced to final judgment or settled with Writer/Participant's written consent, which consent shall not be unreasonably withheld or delayed.

☛ This contract provision is a good example of how an artist/songwriter and a publisher may find themselves at cross-purposes with respect to other entities with which the songwriter may be dealing. It includes a warranty and representation that the writer, who is also the copublisher, has not agreed and will not agree to a "controlled composition" clause (a clause in a recording agreement that provides for a reduced mechanical rate for any composition written or controlled by the artist) on less favorable terms than the then-current industry norm. In effect, the songwriter has to warrant that there are and will be no outstanding cross-collateralization provisions with other parties that are less than specified rates. If the limits set forth in the example were more stringent, it could put a serious crimp in the songwriter's chances to get a deal with a record label. One aspect of this agreement that is favorable for the songwriter is that the writer is responsible for costs arising out of indemnification only when the claim has either been reduced to a final judgment or settled with the writer's consent. This is significantly better than Example 1, where the publisher has the discretion to deal with claims and all expenses are to be paid by the writer.

GRANT OF RIGHTS BY THE SONGWRITER

BONA:
Your grant, or your denial, shall be mine:
—WILLIAM SHAKESPEARE
Henry VI, Part 3, Act III, Scene 3

Each of the various songwriters' agreements, the exclusive and the nonexclusive, will have grant-of-rights provisions, which are sometimes quite similar to the equivalent provisions in artist recording agreements. The grant of rights is usually contained in several paragraphs which set out the various rights that are being granted to the publisher by the songwriter. As in artist record agreements, these paragraphs are usually fairly similar from contract to contract. The rights granted in these paragraphs are what the publisher has negotiated and agreed to pay for.

Like the grant-of-rights provisions in a recording agreement, most of which deal with the exploitation of the recordings, these grants deal primarily with the exploitation of the rights in the musical compositions, such as, for example, the right to change titles and lyrics, the right to license others to record, etc. (see Example 2). Along with the obvious grants of rights, such as ownership of the copyright, the writer also grants the publisher the right to use his or her name, likeness, biography, and the like in connection with the exploitation of the musical compositions (see Example 1). This provision also gives the publisher the right to use the songwriter's likeness on the cover of sheet music or, perhaps, in a "personality" songbook. (A personality songbook is sort of a hybrid between a songbook and a celebrity scrapbook, combining printed music with photographs of and personal information about the songwriter.)

As you read the following grant-of-rights provisions, remember my earlier admonition that these provisions are a jolly good place to hide all sorts of nasty things.

SAMPLE CONTRACT PROVISIONS

EXAMPLE 1: Grant of Rights: Single-Song Agreement

1. Subject to the terms of this agreement, Writer hereby irrevocably, exclusively and absolutely sells, assigns, transfers and delivers to Publisher, its successors and assigns, the original musical composition written and composed by Writer, now entitled "Song" (herein called "Composition"), which title may be changed by Publisher; including the title, words and music thereof, and all rights therein; all copyrights including all rights included in Section 106 of the United States Copyright Act of 1976 and the rights to secure copyrights and extensions and renewals of copyrights (to the extent they exist) in the Composition and in arrangements and adaptations thereof, throughout the world; any and all other rights that Writer now has or to which Writer may be entitled or that Writer could or might secure hereafter if this agreement had not been entered into, throughout the world; and for Publisher, its successors and assigns to have and to hold said copyright and all rights of whatsoever nature thereunder existing.

• • •

6. Writer hereby expressly grants and conveys to Publisher the copyright of the Composition, with renewals, and with the right to copyright and renew the Composition, and the right to secure all copyrights and renewals of copyrights and any and all rights the Writer may at any time be entitled to, and agrees to sign any and all other papers which may be required to effectuate this agreement. Writer hereby irrevocably authorizes and appoints Publisher, its successors or assigns, as Writer's true and lawful attorney, with full power of substitution and delegation, in Writer's name and in Writer's place and stead, or in Publisher's name, to take and do such action, and to make, sign, execute, acknowledge and deliver any and all instruments or documents which Publisher, from time to time, may deem desirable or necessary to vest in Publisher, its successors, assigns and licensees, any of the rights or interests granted by Writer hereunder.

7. Writer hereby authorizes Publisher at its absolute discretion and at Writer's sole expense to employ attorneys and to institute or defend any action or proceedings and to take any other proper steps to protect the right, title and interest of Publisher in and to the Composition. Publisher may settle, compromise or in any other manner dispose of any matter, claim, action, or proceeding and may satisfy any judgment that may be rendered. All or any expenses so incurred and other sums paid by Publisher shall be paid to Publisher on demand by Writer.

• • •

9. Writer grants to Publisher the perpetual right to use and publish Writer's name (including any professional name heretofore or hereafter adopted by Writer), likeness, voice and sound effects and biographical material, or any reproduction or simulation thereof in connection with the printing, sale, advertising, distribution and exploitation of music, folios, recordings, performances, and otherwise with respect to the Composition, and for any other purpose related to the business of Publisher, its affiliated and related companies, or to refrain therefrom.

☛ Note the unrestricted indemnification in Paragraph 7. And what about Paragraph 9, which practically gives the publisher carte blanche to use the writer's name and likeness for anything it pleases, including, perhaps, advertising and merchandising?

EXAMPLE 2: Grant-of-Rights Shopping List

3. *Grant of Rights.* Writer hereby irrevocably and absolutely assigns, transfers, sets over and grants to Publisher, its successors and assigns each and every and all rights and interests of every kind, nature and description in and to the results and proceeds of Writer's services hereunder, including but not limited to the titles, words and music of any and all original musical compositions in any and all forms and original arrangements of musical compositions in the public domain in any and all forms, and/or all rights and interests existing under all agreements and licenses relating thereto, together with all worldwide copyrights and renewals and extensions thereof, which musical works have been written, composed, created or conceived, in whole or in part, by Writer alone or in collaboration with another or others and which may hereafter, during the term hereof, be written, composed, created or conceived by Writer, in whole or in part, alone or in collaboration with another or others, and which are now owned or controlled and which may, during the term hereof, be owned or controlled, directly or indirectly, by Writer, alone or with others, or as the employer or transferee, directly or indirectly, of the writers or composers thereof, including the title, words and music of each such composition, and all worldwide copyrights and renewals and extensions thereof, all of which Writer does hereby represent are and shall at all times be Publisher's sole and exclusive property as the sole owner thereof free from any adverse claims or rights therein by any other person, firm or corporation.

Writer acknowledges that, included within the rights and interests hereinabove referred to, but without limiting the generality of the foregoing, is Writer's irrevocable grant to Publisher, its successors, licensees, sublicensees and assigns, of the sole and exclusive right, license, privilege and authority throughout the entire world with respect to the said original musical compositions and original arrangements of compositions in the public domain, whether now in existence or hereafter created during the term hereof, as follows:

(a) To perform said musical compositions publicly, whether for profit or otherwise, by means of public or private performance, radio broadcasting, television, or any and all other means, whether now known or which may hereafter come into existence.

(b) To substitute a new title or titles for said compositions or any of them and to make any arrangement, adaptation, translation, dramatization or transposition of said compositions or any of them, in whole or in part, and in connection with any other musical, literary or dramatic material, and to add new lyrics to the music of any of said compositions or new music to the lyrics of any of said compositions, all as Publisher may deem expedient or desirable.

(c) To secure copyright registration and protection of said compositions in Publisher's name or otherwise as Publisher may desire at Publisher's own cost and expense and at Publisher's election, including any and all renewals and extensions of copyrights, and to have and to hold said copyrights, renewals, extensions and all rights of whatsoever nature thereunder existing, for and during the full term of all said copyrights and all renewals and extensions thereof.

(d) To make or cause to be made, and to license others to make, master records, transcriptions, sound tracks, pressings, and other mechanical, electrical or other reproductions of said compositions, in whole or in part, in such form or manner and as frequently as Publisher's sole and uncontrolled discretion shall determine, including the right to synchronize the same with sound motion pictures, and the right to manufacture, advertise, license or sell such reproductions for any and all purposes, including, without limitation, private performances and public performances, radio broadcast, television, sound motion pictures, wired radio, phonograph records and any and all other means or devices whether now known or which may hereafter come into existence.

(e) To print, publish and sell, and to license others to print, publish and sell, sheet music, orchestrations, arrangements and other editions of the said compositions in all forms, including, without limitation, the inclusion of any or all of said compositions in song folios, song books, mixed folios or lyric magazines with or without music.

(f) Any and all other rights of every and any nature now or hereafter existing under and by virtue of any common law rights and any copyrights and renewals and extensions thereof in any and all such compositions.

(g) Writer grants to Publisher, without any compensation other than as specified herein, the perpetual right to use and publish and to permit others to use and publish Writer's name (including any professional name heretofore or hereafter adopted by Writer), Writer's photograph or other likeness, or any reproduction or simulation thereof, and biographical material concerning Writer, and the titles of any and all of the compositions hereunder, and for any other purpose related to the music business of Publisher, its affiliated and related companies, or to refrain therefrom. The right shall be exclusive during the term hereof and nonexclusive thereafter. Writer shall not authorize or permit the use of a name or likeness or biographical material concerning him, or other identification, or any reproduction or simulation thereof, for or in connection with any musical composition covered by this agreement, other than for Publisher. Writer grants Publisher the right to refer to Writer as Publisher's "Exclusive Songwriter and Composer" or other similar appropriate appellation, during the terms hereof.

EQUITABLE RELIEF

With exclusive songwriters' agreements, which are by nature ongoing, the question of equitable relief also becomes an issue. Equitable relief is not an issue in nonexclusive agreements in that there is no need or reason to restrain the composer from working elsewhere. As discussed before, *equitable relief* means the right to go to court to obtain a ruling that is "just, fair, and right, in consideration of the facts and circumstances of the individual case." Since songwriters' agreements are personal service contracts, the courts will not make a recalcitrant songwriter write songs, but under the proper circumstances will grant an injunction and *stop* the songwriter from writing for anyone other than the publisher. (For a complete discussion of equitable relief, and especially as it applies to California law, see the section "Equitable Relief," Chapter 3, pages 137–144.)

As in artist recording agreements in California, the (formerly $6,000, but now) $9,000-plus provision also applies to exclusive songwriters' agreements (see page 141 and Example 1, below). By law, if there is no guarantee in an exclusive songwriter's agreement that the songwriter is to receive a minimum of $9,000 the first year and the appropriate amounts in subsequent years, the agreement cannot be enforced by an injunction, other than by use of the "superstar insurance" clause. Even if royalties payable under the songwriter's agreement exceed the required minimum, if the minimum is not guaranteed in the agreement an injunction cannot be obtained and the contract cannot be enforced unless the sums, and/or additional payments, at least match the minimum under the superstar insurance clause—10 times the minimum provided for in the $9,000 plus provision.

Now, suppose the songwriter is an exclusive writer because his or her recording agreement says so. What happens if, under California law, the publisher wants to get an injunction to stop the songwriter from going to another publisher? Can the earnings from the recording agreement and the songwriter's agreement be combined in order to meet the minimum dollar requirements for the California law to allow an injunction, or must they be considered separately? In fact, two opposing arguments can be made, depending on whose side you are on, the writer's or the publisher's. Since I don't know which side I may be on, I will keep my thoughts to myself.

SAMPLE CONTRACT PROVISIONS

EXAMPLE 1: Minimum under California Law Guaranteed

9. Writer acknowledges that Writer's work hereunder is of a special, unique, extraordinary and intellectual character which gives it peculiar value, the loss of which cannot be reasonably or adequately compensated in damages in an action at law, and that a breach by Writer of any of the provisions of this Agreement will cause Publisher irreparable injury.

(a) Writer expressly agrees that Publisher is entitled to injunctive and other equitable relief to prevent a breach of this Agreement or any portion thereof, which relief shall be in addition to any other rights or remedies, for damages or otherwise, which Publisher may have.

(b) Publisher shall be obligated to pay Writer at the rate of no less than Nine Thousand ($9,000) Dollars in the first year of this Agreement, in subsequent years of this Agreement, in each such year Publisher shall pay Writer the amounts provided for in California Code of Civil Procedure, Section 526, and California Civil Code, Section 3423 (Fifth). Prior to the end of each such year of this Agreement, Publisher shall pay Writer the difference, if any, between any amounts theretofore received by Writer and the applicable amount provided for herein.

EXAMPLE 2: Company Has Right to Make Up Minimum for Equitable Relief under California Law

15. In the event that you shall not receive the applicable sum provided for in California Code of Civil Procedure, Section 526, and California Civil Code, Section 3423 (Fifth) during any applicable year hereunder, you shall so notify us on a date not later than thirty (30) days prior to the end of that one (1) year period and we shall pay you, as a non-returnable advance recoupable from any and all monies payable to you hereunder, prior to the expiration of such one (1) year period, the amount by which the applicable sum exceeds the aggregate amount of all monies theretofore paid to you hereunder during that one (1) year period.

> ☛ And what happens if the artist does, or even doesn't, give the company notice and the difference isn't paid? And then the company wants to exercise its rights for injunctive relief? Presumably, under the precedent established in the "Teena Marie Case" (see page 140), the company has blown it and will not be able to make up the minimum amount.

EXAMPLE 3: Loan-Out Company to Make Minimum Payment

(k) Participant [Writer's publishing company loaning the services of Writer] warrants, represents, and agrees that Writer shall receive from Participant during each consecutive twelve (12) month period of the Term ("Term Calendar Year") compensation of no less than the sums provided for in California Code of Civil Procedure, Section 526, and California Civil Code, Section 3423 (Fifth) in respect solely of that [individual] member of Writer's services under this Agreement. If, for any reason, Participant shall fail to pay to Writer at least such applicable sum during any Term Calendar Year, Publisher shall have the option to pay to Writer an amount which, when added to the amounts, if any, so paid by Participant to Writer during that Term Calendar Year, shall equal the required sum. Publisher may, without limiting its other rights and remedies, deduct that amount from any monies payable by Publisher hereunder or under any other agreement between Participant and/or Writer and Publisher or Publisher's affiliates. No longer than thirty (30) days prior to the end of any Term calendar Year, Participant shall advise Publisher in writing if Participant has not complied with Participant's obligations pursuant to this paragraph.

☛ This is a loan-out agreement, in which Participant is furnishing the services of Writer to Publisher. Accordingly, it is Participant's obligation to make the minimum payments to Writer, not Publisher's. Publisher is, however, prepared to step in with a checkbook to pick up the slack if Participant falls short in any year. Note that Publisher has the right to deduct the payments using cross-collateralization from this or other agreements, including those with "Publisher's affiliates."

CHAPTER 10

COPUBLISHING AGREEMENTS

That love is merchandised whose rich esteeming
The owner's tongue doth publish every where.
—WILLIAM SHAKESPEARE
Sonnet 102

When the copyright for a musical composition is owned by more than one entity, the co-owners need an agreement indicating the shares of the copyright owned by each entity, the compensation to be paid to each, how costs are shared, who administers the copyright, and any number of other areas that require clarification. These agreements are called *copublishing agreements*.

It is usually presumed that copublishing agreements mean two parties, each owning an equal share in the subject copyrights. In fact, while this configuration is probably the most common, the number of co-owners can, theoretically, be infinite and the division of the ownership between the parties can be in any conceivable (or sometimes inconceivable) proportion.

One type of copublishing agreement is the *participation agreement*. Generally speaking, in terms of sharing income, there is no real difference between a copublishing agreement and a participation agreement, other than the possible psychological implication of "togetherness" suggested by the term "participation." However, there is a significant difference in the ownership of the copyrights. The participation agreement usually implies participation without any share of copyright ownership. In effect, a participation agreement may be like an administration agreement in that neither the participant nor the administrator necessarily owns any piece of the copyright, but they do, however, receive some share of the income from the exploitation of the copyright. (See the section "Administration" below, pages 316–318.)

Copublishing agreements may be for a limited, specified period of time or for the life of the copyright. The agreements may be for a specified territory or for the entire world (or, indeed, the entire universe). The parties to the agreement may be individual artists or corporate giants. Most of the boilerplate provisions in copublishing agreements are quite similar to the equivalent provisions in artist recording agreements. For example, the notice provisions and provisions dealing with accountings can be treated in the same manner as discussed earlier with regard to artist recording agreements. Additionally some provisions equivalent to those found in songwriters' agreements (also previously discussed) would be treated similarly. However, areas which are of prime importance when entering into one of these agreements and those which are unique to copublishing agreements do require some consideration.

WHICH COMPOSITIONS?

Copublishing agreements may be for a single composition or for an entire catalogue. They may be for past, present, and/or future compositions. The essence of the copublishing agreement is that compositions are jointly owned by the parties.

As with songwriters' agreements, it is possible to divide copublishing agreements into two groups: exclusive and nonexclusive. Nonexclusive copublishing agreements are for one or more specified songs. The songs are usually either identified in the body of the nonexclusive agreement or, especially if a number of songs are being transferred, in an exhibit or schedule attached to the agreement. In nonexclusive copublishing agreements, the parties are free to enter into other copublishing agreements with other parties or to keep all the publishing themselves on compositions not included in the agreement. Exclusive copublishing agreements provide that all publishing rights acquired during the period of the agreement by, usually, one of the copublishers will be jointly owned and copublished by the publishers. Exclusive copublishing agreements should always have a provision for adding new titles (see Example 1). Not surprisingly, copublishing agreements are commonly entered into pursuant to a recording agreement whereby the publishing company affiliated with the record company acquires, and copublishes, copyrights with the publishing company affiliated with the artist, producer, and/or production company.

SAMPLE CONTRACT PROVISIONS

EXAMPLE 1: Schedule of Compositions "Added to From Time to Time"

This Co-Publishing Agreement is made and entered into as of the 1st day of September, _____, by and between [Company #1] (hereinafter referred to as the "Administrator"), and [Company #2] (hereinafter collectively referred to as "Co-Publisher") and in consideration of the terms and conditions contained herein, Administrator and Co-Publisher agree to jointly own the copyrights and all rights in and to the musical compositions set forth in Schedule "A," as such Schedule shall be added to from time to time (hereinafter individually and collectively referred to as the "Compositions").

EXAMPLE 2: Copublishing Agreement Tied to Recording Agreement

30. Each composition written or composed by you during the term of this [recording] Agreement and any renewals or extensions hereof, shall be copublished by our affiliated music publishing company and a music publishing company to be designated by you in accordance with the provisions of the Participation Agreement annexed hereto as Exhibit "A." Said Participation Agreement shall be concurrent and co-terminous with this Agreement.

☛ Here the record company has acquired the copyrights to all compositions written during the term of the recording agreement. The artist has a "participation" in the publishing income, but no copyright ownership. The Participation Agreement is attached and incorporated by reference into the recording agreement.

EXAMPLE 3: Copyrights Owned Jointly

8. I grant to a publisher designated by Company and to a publisher designated by me the right to acquire each and every composition, together with the copyright therein and all renewals and extensions, and I, as appropriate, shall, in respect to each composition, execute a separate

Songwriter's Agreement, in the form of the agreement attached hereto as Exhibit "A," with a publisher designated by Company and with a publisher designated by me. In addition, I shall make reasonable efforts to acquire publication rights to original musical works submitted by me to Company which are not written by me. If I am able to acquire such publication rights, the publishers designated by Company and me shall enter into a Songwriter's Agreement, in the form of the agreement attached hereto as Exhibit "A," with the writer or writers of such original musical work. The copyrights in any composition or original musical work, as provided for herein, shall be owned jointly by the publishers designated by Company and me, with the publisher designated by Company having all administrative rights in such works.

EXAMPLE 4: Ownership and Income Split Differently

6. The music publishers formed by the Label shall be administered by Publisher on the following terms:

(a) Copyrights in the musical compositions recorded pursuant to the Recording Agreement shall be owned in equal shares by Publisher and Copublisher.

(b) Notwithstanding the ownership set forth in Subparagraph 6.(a), above, the net publishers' share of income from the exploitation of the copyrights shall be divided between Label, Copublisher and Publisher in equal shares.

> ☛ Note that notwithstanding the 50–50 ownership of the copyrights by the publisher and copublisher, the income is divided into equal thirds. The record company (which happens to own the publisher) gets one-third of the net publishers' share of income, so the record company/publisher gets two-thirds of the publishing income and the artist gets one-third even though the artist owns 50% of the copyrights.

TERM OF THE AGREEMENT

The term of a copublishing agreement may be precisely specified, partly specified, or implied. Because copublishing agreements deal with co-ownership, and co-ownership is usually (but not always) for the life of the copyright, the most common term for a copublishing agreement is for "the life of the copyright" of the compositions. Note that this creates a situation in which it is possible for the length of the agreement to be determined song by song. If there is no expiration that cuts across the board and affects the entire agreement, parts of the agreement can expire while other parts remain in effect.

Many copublishing agreements, usually those which deal with specified predetermined compositions, will not even mention a term for the agreement, but will provide for co-ownership of the copyrights in the compositions. In the absence of any other language, the co-ownership of the copyright makes the term of the copublishing agreement the life of the copyrights. On the other hand, it is certainly not uncommon for a copublishing agreement to be for a specified period of time not related to the life of the copyright, for example, 5 years. Presumably, under these agreements, at the expiration of the term some transfer or assignment or even reassignment of rights, if not the whole copyright, takes place. If the parties continue to own their shares, a de facto copublishing agreement continues, even though the signed agreement expires. In such cases, the expiration usually means that the parties can no longer add compositions to the agreement.

EXAMPLE 1: Life of the Copyrights As Implied Term

1. Company and Participant shall jointly own the following undivided interests in the Compositions, including all of the worldwide right, title and interest, including the copyrights, the right to copyright and the renewal rights, therein and thereto.

☛ Since there is no specific language relating to the length of the term of the agreement, and the copyrights are jointly owned, the (implied) term is the life of the copyrights.

EXAMPLE 2: Life of the Copyrights As Implied Term

WHEREAS, it is the intention of Publisher and Co-Publisher that they shall jointly own, in the shares hereinafter described, the musical composition or the musical compositions (hereinafter referred to individually and collectively as the "Compositions") listed or described below, so that the entire worldwide right, title and interest, including the copyrights, the right to copyright and the renewal rights in and to the Compositions shall be owned by Publisher and by Co-Publisher. . . .

EXAMPLE 3: Life of the Copyrights As Specified Term

1. Publisher and Co-Publisher shall jointly own the Compositions, so that fifty (50%) percent of the entire worldwide right, title, and interest, including the copyright, the right to copyright, and the renewal right, if any, therein and thereto, shall be owned by Publisher, and fifty (50%) percent shall be owned by Co-Publisher.

(a) The term of this Agreement, except as expressly set forth below, shall be for the life of the copyrights in the Compositions.

(b) The rights of the parties hereto in and to each of the Compositions shall extend for the term of the copyright of the Composition in question and of any derivative copyright obtained there-from in the United States of America and throughout the world and for the terms of any renewals or extensions thereof, if any, in the United States of America and throughout the world.

☛ Since the term is for the life of the copyrights and, presumably, not all the "lives" of the copyrights are identical, this agreement will, from time to time, "die" in pieces.

TERRITORY

A man's feet should be planted in his country, but his eyes should survey the world.
—George Santayana

Sometimes, copublishing agreements apply only to certain territories. For example, the publishers may co-own the copyright(s) in one or more territories, but in other territories, the copyright(s) may be owned by one or the other publisher (see Example 1), or perhaps even neither of them. This is much more likely to happen in agreements for the administration of the copyrights rather than in a copublishing agreement (the distinction being *ownership* versus *participation*). Copyright ownership can be divided in innumerable ways, not the least of which is on a territory-by-territory basis. As a practical matter, this territorial division, if it exists, is normally based upon country boundaries, but it could, in theory, be divided into much smaller territories. A copyright owner could, in a fit of madness, assign co-ownership to 50 different individuals, each to co-own and copublish in a different state within the United States.

SAMPLE CONTRACT PROVISIONS

EXAMPLE 1: Territory Is the United States and Canada

2. TERRITORY: Co-Publisher's rights hereto in and to each of the Compositions shall extend for the term of this Agreement for the United States of America and Canada (hereinafter referred to as the "Territory"). All rights in and to the Compositions outside of the Territory shall remain the sole property of Publisher.

EXAMPLE 2: Territory Is the World

3. The rights in and to the Compositions granted to Co-Publisher hereunder by Publisher shall be for the life of the copyright in each such Composition and for the entire world.

EXAMPLE 3: Territory Is the Universe

11.16. "Territory": The universe.

☛ "The universe"? Rumor has it that this is the new name for Starbuck's smallest cup size for coffee. It's a big place.

OWNERSHIP

Since co-ownership is the essence of copublishing, ownership division is given prominent attention in the copublishing agreement. The ownership division usually has a direct effect on how the money from the exploitation of the compositions is shared, and affects each party's share of the costs expended. Nothing is more basic than how the money is divided. Thus the ownership, or the "split," of the copyright or copyrights between the copublishers becomes a prime battleground in the negotiation of the agreement. Contractually, although the profits and costs can be divided between the parties in any ratio and without any relation to the ownership of the copyrights, normally there is a correlation between the ownership and the division of money. Although arrangements like those in either of the examples below are possible, a relationship between copyright ownership and share of income like that described in Example A is far more common.

Example A

A and B each own 50% of the copyright in "Song." The publishers' share of income (gross income less the songwriter's share) is divided equally between A and B; 50% goes to each.

Example B

The same facts as above, except by agreement, A receives 75% of the publishers' share and B receives 25% of the publishers' share of income.

Note that co-ownership does not necessarily mean equal ownership. Although most often copyright ownership will be split evenly among copublishers, it is certainly not uncommon for the percentage split between the parties to be unequal, for example 75%–25%, 66⅔%–33½%, etc. (See Example 1, below.) With more than two copublishers, even more variation is possible, for example, 50%–25%–25%, 50%–30%–20%, etc.

EXAMPLE 1: Copublisher's Share Increases with Each Option Period

1. Company and Co-Publisher shall jointly own the following undivided interests in the Compositions, including all of the worldwide right, title and interest, including the copyrights, the right to copyright and the renewal rights, therein and thereto, subject to the provisions of subparagraph 22(c) of the Writer's Agreement:

(a) Compositions delivered during the first year of the Writer's Agreement: Company 75% and Co-Publisher 25%

(b) Compositions delivered during the first option year of the Writer's Agreement: Company 70% and Co-Publisher 30%

(c) Compositions delivered during the second option year of the Writer's Agreement: Company 65% and Co-Publisher 35%

(d) Compositions delivered during the third option year of the Writer's Agreement: Company 60% and Co-Publisher 40%

(e) Compositions delivered during the fourth option year of the Writer's Agreement: Company 50% and Co-Publisher 50%.

☛ This copublishing agreement is linked to an exclusive songwriter's agreement, and the copublisher's increasing percentage is the publishing equivalent of a recording artist's accelerated royalty.

EXAMPLE 2: Conditional Copublishing Agreement

WHEREAS, it is the intention of Publisher and Co-Publisher that they shall jointly own, in the shares hereinafter described, the musical compositions (hereinafter individually referred to as "Composition" and collectively referred to as "Compositions") listed or described below, so that the entire worldwide right, title and interest, including the copyright, the right to copyright and any and all renewal rights, in and to the Compositions shall be owned by Publisher and by Co-Publisher in the percentages set forth below:

All musical compositions to be acquired by Publisher pursuant to its exclusive songwriter's agreement of even date herewith (hereinafter referred to as the "Agreement") with Writer (hereinafter referred to as "Composer"), which musical compositions pursuant to paragraph 20 of the Agreement shall be delivered to Publisher after the rendition of a semi-annual accounting statement rendered during the term of the Agreement for a semi-annual accounting period ending December 31st, which statement shall reflect that Composer has earned, in the aggregate, compensation in excess of One Hundred Thousand ($100,000.00) Dollars pursuant to Paragraph 7 of the Agreement.

Percentages	
Publisher	75%
Co-Publisher	25%

• • •

8. . . . The copyright in each such composition acquired hereunder shall be owned seventy-five (75%) percent by the publisher designated by Company and twenty-five (25%) percent by the pub-

lisher designated by me. The publisher designated by Company shall retain all administrative rights in and to the copyrights.

☛ Under this provision, the copublishing relation begins only after the writer has proved the writer's "worth" by earning an aggregate minimum of $100,000 from royalties as a songwriter. After meeting this earnings benchmark, the writer becomes the copublisher and acquires a 25% ownership of the copyrights.

EXAMPLE 3: 50%–50% Split

The "Compositions" hereunder shall be deemed to be each and every Controlled Composition as defined in paragraph 8 of that certain recording agreement of even date between Record Company and Artist, an individual doing business as [Production Company] (hereinafter referred to as the "Recording Agreement"). Notwithstanding the foregoing, in no event shall this agreement be applicable to (i) any Controlled Composition in which Publisher has heretofore acquired any interest including without limitation all Controlled Compositions recorded under that certain Agreement dated as of between Record Company and Artist nor to (ii) any Controlled Composition in which Publisher shall hereafter acquire any interest from any person, firm or corporation other than Artist.

Percentages	
Publisher	50%
Co-Publisher	50%

ADMINISTRATION

Usually the right to *administer* the copyrights in a copublishing agreement is exclusive to one party, referred to as the "administrator" or the "administering publisher," although there is no rule or law that says that there must be only one. Administration will be discussed at much greater length in Chapter 11, "Administration Agreements." For this discussion, it is sufficient to say that what we are examining is the right to manage the exploitation of the compositions, such as the granting of mechanical licenses, synchronization licenses, print rights, etc. (see Example 1). The administrating publisher collects the money from the rights that are granted to third parties, and generally also collects the publishers' share from ASCAP or BMI on behalf of the copublishers. In addition, the party doing the administration is very likely to be rewarded with an administration fee (see Example 2). (The administration fee is discussed below, under "Costs.") It is possible to have performance monies from ASCAP or BMI paid directly to each party, but the administration fee is generally still paid to the administering publisher. Note that the nonadministering publisher does not have the right to grant third parties the right to use the compositions, even if the nonadministering publisher or publishers own the majority of the copyrights in question.

SAMPLE CONTRACT PROVISIONS

EXAMPLE 1: Exclusive Administrator

3. Company has the sole, exclusive and worldwide right to administer and exploit the Compositions, to print, to publish, sell, dramatize, use and license any and all uses of the

Compositions, to execute in its own name any and all licenses and agreements whatsoever affecting or respecting the Compositions, including but not limited to licenses for mechanical reproduction, public performance, dramatic uses, synchronization uses and sub-publication, and to assign or license such rights to others. This statement of exclusive rights is only in clarification and amplification of the rights of Company and not in limitation thereof.

EXAMPLE 2: Administrator's Duties and Rights

3. Copublisher hereby acknowledges and agrees that Company, its successors, assigns, licensees and sub-publishers, shall have the exclusive right throughout the world to administer and exploit all rights of every kind, nature and description in and to the Compositions, together with the exclusive right to manage and administer all copyrights and renewals and extensions thereof, including but not limited to the right to:

(a) issue licenses with respect to mechanical and electrical reproduction of the Compositions throughout the world on phonograph records, pre-recorded tapes, piano rolls and transcriptions, or by any other method now known or hereafter devised for sound reproduction.

(b) publicly perform the Compositions and license such right in all media including radio and television broadcasting.

(c) grant licenses for the recording of Compositions in and with motion pictures and television productions produced throughout the world, of making copies of its recordings thereof, and importing such copies into all countries of the world.

(d) print, publish and sell printed music throughout the world in the form of sheet music, arrangements, song books, albums, folios or educational works.

(e) translate the lyrics or create new lyric versions of the Compositions into all languages other than English, and make or have made, band, choral, orchestral, or other arrangements of the Compositions.

(f) enjoy and license all additional rights granted by the United States Copyright Act of 1976 not specifically set forth herein.

(g) Company will prepare and file all copyright forms, Notice of Use forms and other documents required to be filed with the Copyright Office in the United States and foreign countries, and will file with the appropriate performing rights societies all documents required to be filed with said societies.

• • •

5. Company shall pay to Participant the applicable percentages indicated in Paragraph 1 hereof of the Net Income actually received and derived by Company from the exploitation of the Compositions. "Net Income" is defined as the gross receipts derived by Company from the exploitation of the Compositions including the publisher's share of public performance fees paid by the applicable performing rights society, less the following:

(a) An administration fee of ten (10%) percent of the Gross receipts after the deduction of any collection fees.

☛ Paragraphs 3(a) to 3(g) are a representative checklist of what an administrator does.

EXAMPLE 3: Copublisher As Administrator

2. Participant agrees that Co-Publisher shall be the joint owner of an undivided fifty (50%) percent

interest in and to the copyrights in the Compositions and Co-Publisher shall administer and control the same on behalf of the parties hereto.

3. Co-Publisher shall have the sole and exclusive right to administer and protect the Compositions on behalf of both parties, and shall have the sole right to designate on behalf of both parties hereto all persons, firms or corporations to administer the Compositions throughout the world, including within the United States and Canada and, on behalf of or in the names of both parties, to enter into agreements with said persons, firms or corporations which may be affiliated with Owner to sub-publish or otherwise deal with the Compositions.

COSTS

A hamburger by any other name is more expensive.

—ANONYMOUS

The costs involved in the administration and exploitation of the compositions are usually borne by the parties in direct proportion to their ownership of the copyright. Accordingly, if two publishers own a copyright in equal shares, each will be responsible for one-half of the publishers' share of costs. I say "publishers' share of costs" because there may be some costs charged to the songwriter, such as one-half of the demo costs; perhaps a share of third-party administration; copyright registration fees; collection costs; attorneys' fees; etc. Usually, the administrating publisher pays the costs and then recoups the nonadministrating publisher's share from earnings collected.

One cost is the fee given to the party who administers the copyright, called the *administration fee*. This fee usually ranges from 10% to 25%, although it can certainly be higher, lower, or even nothing at all (see Example 3). The administration fee is usually deducted off the top using either the gross sums received for the composition or the adjusted gross publishers' share of income. *Gross sums* are the total payments received for the exploitation of the compositions. Subject to the deduction of costs, which may or may not come off the top (depending upon the language in the contract), the gross sums are divided, generally equally, between the publisher(s) and the writer(s). The share retained by the publisher(s) is the *gross publishers' share*.

Example

A owns 50% of the copyright in "Song." B owns 50% of the copyright in "Song." They are to share the net publishers' share of income equally, 50% to each. The copublishing agreement between A and B provides that A shall administer the copyright. For the administration of the copyright, A is to receive an administration fee of 10% of the publishers' share of income. After the administration fee is deducted, the income is shared equally. As a result, for each $1 that is received as publishers' income, A gets 10 cents off the top, and the remaining 90 cents is divided equally, 45 cents to each publisher. However, because of the payment of the administration fee, A actually receives 55% of the total, or 55 cents, and B receives 45%, or 45 cents.

Note that under normal circumstances, other costs, such as those described below, would be deducted from the 90 cents before dividing the spoils. If, for example, 20 cents out of every dollar goes for costs, that 20 cents is first deducted from the 90 cents, leaving 70 cents to be divided between A and B, so A gets 45 cents (10 cents + 35 cents) and B gets 35 cents.

Other costs which may be deducted are the songwriter's share of royalties; copyright registration fees; advertising; attorneys' fees; printing costs, engraving costs, and other costs involved with the print rights; the cost of preparing lead sheets (written transcriptions of the notes and chords of musical compositions with or without lyrics); demonstration costs, to the extent that they are not recouped from the songwriter; and any other costs which the administering publisher may include unless restrictions of some sort are included in the copublishing agreement (see Example 1). There may also be costs deducted that are paid to *collection agents* (see Example 2), usually The Harry Fox Agency, Inc. The Fox Office, as it is referred to, issues mechanical licenses to record companies giving them the right to record and release compositions to the public and then collects mechanical license fees from the record companies on behalf of the various publishers it represents. This is done for a fee, usually based upon a percentage of the monies collected. The Fox Office also conducts periodic audits on behalf of its clients.

It is important to determine the order in which costs are deducted. Some of these deducted costs are based upon percentages that may, in turn, already be based upon an adjusted figure. For example, if a 10% administration fee is "taken off the top" rather than after the deduction of all other costs, then the administrator taking the administration fee pushes a higher pro-rata burden on the other publisher and, conversely, bears a lesser share of the costs.

Example

A and B have a copublishing agreement, again sharing the net publisher's share equally. Pursuant to the copublishing agreement, A receives a 10% administration fee, but the language of the agreement provides that all other costs are deducted first. Presume that for each $1 of publishers' share, 20 cents in costs are deducted, leaving 80 cents. A's 10% administration fee (8 cents) is deducted, leaving 72 cents to be divided. A receives 44 cents (8 cents + 36 cents) while B receives 36 cents.

With this arrangement, B gets 1 cent more per every dollar than in the example above. This may not seem like much, but remember: The music business is a business of pennies, and whether they come from heaven or from copyrights, they do add up.

SAMPLE CONTRACT PROVISIONS

EXAMPLE 1: 15% Administration Fee Off the Top

4. Co-Publisher shall pay Publisher fifty (50%) percent of the net publisher's share actually received by Co-Publisher in the United States and earned after the date hereof on account of the Compositions (and remaining after deduction of an administration fee to Co-Publisher of 15% of the gross publisher's share, royalties payable to writers, unrecouped advances, if any, and other chargeable amounts hereunder, and the costs of printing, engraving, copyrights, trade advertising and other direct costs and expenses paid or incurred by Co-Publisher with respect to the Compositions hereunder).

☛ This is a "stealth off the top" administration fee. While the contract is expressly silent regarding the order of deductions, do note that the 15% administration fee is first in line in the recitation of deductible costs. The fee in Example 2, while lower, is also right there at the top of the list of costs.

EXAMPLE 2: 10% Administration Fee Off the Top

5. Company shall pay to Publisher the applicable percentages indicated in Paragraph 1 hereof of the Net Income actually received and derived by Company from the exploitation of the Compositions. "Net Income" is defined as the gross receipts derived by Company from the exploitation of the Compositions including the publisher's share of public performance fees paid by the applicable performing rights society, less the following:

(a) An administration fee of ten (10%) percent of the Gross receipts after the deduction of any collection fees;

(b) Royalties and other sums which shall be paid by Company to the writer(s) of the Compositions in accordance with the provisions of the Writer's Agreement;

(c) Collection and other fees customarily and actually charged by The Harry Fox Agency, Inc. or other collection agent which may be used by Company, to the extent that fifty (50%) percent thereof has not been recouped from royalties payable to the writer(s) of the Compositions;

(d) Exploitation expenses of Company with respect to the Compositions, including, without limitation, registration fees, advertising and promotion expenses directly related to the Compositions, the cost of making lead sheets, and the cost of producing demonstration recordings;

(e) Attorneys' fees, if any, actually paid by Company for any agreement (other than the within agreement) affecting the Composition; and

(f) The costs of printing, engraving, arranging and editing printed editions of the Compositions, provided that Company actually incurs such costs.

EXAMPLE 3: No Administration Fee

5. Company shall pay to Participant such percentage of the net income derived by Company from the Compositions as shall conform to Participant's share of each Composition, and shall retain the remaining net income for its own account. "Net Income" is defined as the gross receipts less the following:

(a) Royalties which shall be paid by Company to Composer pursuant to the Agreement and royalties which shall be paid by Company to any other writers of the Compositions pursuant to any other songwriter's agreements between Participant and any such other writers (true copies of which latter agreements shall be submitted by Participant to Company promptly upon execution thereof), it being understood that in no event shall any royalties exceed the royalties provided for in paragraph 7 of the Agreement;

(b) Administrative and exploitation expenses of Company with respect to the Compositions including, without limitation, registration fees, advertising and promotion expenses directly related to the Compositions, the costs of producing demonstration records to the extent such costs are not recoupable from Composer's or other writer's royalties; and

(c) Attorneys' fees, if any, actually paid by Company for any agreements (other than the within agreement) affecting solely the Compositions or any of them.

☛ Although there is no administration fee as such, administrative expenses [listed in paragraph (b)] are taken. Note that in agreements which specify an administration fee, these expenses are taken *in addition to* the fee.

EXAMPLE 4: Administration Fee Higher for Cover Records

5. Administrator shall pay to Publisher #1, Publisher #2 and Publisher #3 the following percentages of the net income derived by Administrator from the Composition:

Owner	Percentage of net income payable
Publisher #1	16⅔%
Publisher #2	66⅔%
Publisher #3	16⅔%

Monies payable hereunder to Publisher #2 shall include, and Publisher #2 warrants, represents and agrees that it shall pay, any and all royalties which shall be payable to the Composers. "Net Income" is defined as the gross receipts less the following:

(a) An administration fee of fifteen percent (15%) of the gross receipts, which fee shall be retained by Administrator for its own account, provided, however, that said fee shall be increased to twenty-five percent (25%) with respect to all income (including, without limitation, mechanical royalties and public performance fees) earned from the exploitation of a cover record of the Composition (the term "cover record" being defined as any recording of a Composition other than a recording by the Composers thereof or a recording in existence prior to the term hereof);

(b) Administration and exploitative expenses of Administrator with respect to the Composition including, without limitation, registration fees, advertising and promotion expenses directly related to the Composition, the costs of transcribing for lead sheets, and the costs of producing demonstration records; and

(c) Attorneys' fees, if any, actually paid by Administrator for any agreements (other than the within Agreement) affecting solely the Composition. For the purposes of subparagraph (a) above, public performance fees for any accounting period attributable to a cover record of the Composition shall be computed (if not separately reported to Administrator) as that proportion of the total public performance fees received by Administrator for said accounting period with respect to said cover record bears to the total mechanical royalties received by Administrator for said accounting period with respect to the Composition.

☛ This is an interesting provision on several levels. First, the "split" of net income between the three publishers: It appears that Publisher #2 is receiving four times the share of each of the other publishers, but when the composers' share (50%) is deducted from Publisher #2's share, each of the publishers receives the same amount—an equal one-third of the net publishers' share. Second, note that the administration fee is based upon "gross receipts," not "net income," and is the first sum taken off the top before any other costs are deducted; accordingly, unless Publisher #2 is making up the difference (unlikely), the composers are bearing half the costs along with the three publishers. Third, there is a higher administration fee if there is a cover record—a new recording by someone other than the Composers—a "reward" based, presumably, on the "extra" work done by the administrator to obtain the new recording. Finally, the provision handles the tricky problem of proportioning the two different administration fees between non–cover record and cover record performances of the same composition against public performance fees from ASCAP or BMI, since neither ASCAP nor BMI report which version received the credit for public performance. The answer is to credit in the same proportion as mechanical license fees are received for the different versions during the same period. In other words, if the original version accounted for 90% of mechanical license fees during that period and the cover record accounted for the other 10%, 90% of the performance fees would bear an administration fee of 15% and the remaining 10% would be at 25%.

PERFORMING RIGHTS

> *I must tell you I take terrible risks. Because my playing is very clear, when I make a mistake you hear it. Never be afraid to dare.*
>
> —VLADIMIR HOROWITZ

As in songwriters' agreements, copublishing agreements have a statement regarding small performance rights, in this case the division of the publishers' share of public performance fees, usually collected by ASCAP, BMI, or SESAC.

Unlike the division of public performance fees between publisher and songwriter, the division between copublishers is subject to their own agreement. For example, the performing rights societies will pay over the complete publishers' share to one publisher; divide them between publishers in the same ratio as their respective copyright shares; or pay the shares in some entirely different manner, as directed by the copublishers.

Example

Publisher A and Publisher B each own an equal share of the copyright in "Song." A is the administering publisher. Pursuant to instructions from both publishers, ASCAP pays A the entire publishers' share of public performance fees. A then accounts to B for B's share.

Example

Publisher A and Publisher B each own an equal share of the copyright in "Song." A is the administering publisher. Pursuant to instructions from both publishers, ASCAP pays one-half of the publishers' share of public performance fees directly to each publisher.

Example

Publisher A and Publisher B each own an equal share of the copyright in "Song." A is the administering publisher and receives an administration fee of 10%. Pursuant to instructions from both publishers, ASCAP is to pay each publisher directly in the following manner: A receives 55% of the entire publishers' share of public performance fees and B is paid the remaining 45%.

In the last example, even though A and B each own an equal share of the copyright, A receives 55% and B receives 45%. This is not entirely arbitrary, as you will note that A has retained the 10% administration fee by receiving 10% off the top and splitting the remaining 90% equally with B (see Example 1). A and B could just as easily have instructed ASCAP to pay A 87% and to pay B 13%. Generally, nonadministering publishers prefer to be paid directly by the performing rights society for the same reason songwriters appreciate being paid directly for their writer's share—the monies not only get paid more quickly, but they also are not available for offset, recoupment, or cross-collateralization (see Example 3).

EXAMPLE 1: Direct Payment, Including Administration Fee

6. Small performing rights in the Compositions, to the extent permitted by law, shall be assigned to and licensed by the public performance [sic] society to which the parties belong. Said society shall be and is hereby authorized to collect and receive all monies earned from the public performance of the Compositions and shall be and hereby is directed (subject to its rules and regulations) to pay directly to Company and to Participant, in the shares set forth below, the entire amount allocated by said society as the publisher's share of the public performance fees for the Composition:

Company: Fifty-five percent (55%)

Participant: Forty-five percent (45%)

☞ A 10% administration fee is factored in here: 10% off the top to Company and the remaining 90% shared equally by Company and Participant. Note that in this and the following two examples the common mistake is made of referring to "performance" societies, when ASCAP, BMI, and SESAC are in fact performing rights societies. Not to worry. Generally, only picky books like this make the distinction.

EXAMPLE 2: Administrator Receives Full Payment

6. Small performing rights in the Composition, to the extent permitted by law, shall be assigned to and licensed by the public performance [sic] society to which Administrator belongs. Said society shall be and is hereby authorized to collect and receive all monies earned from the public performance of the Composition in the United States and Canada, and shall be and hereby is directed (subject to its rules and regulations) to pay the Administrator the entire amount allocated by said society as the publisher's public performance fees for the United States and Canada.

☞ Here the administrator collects directly and divvies up the money, keeping its share and paying the balance to the publisher.

EXAMPLE 3: Direct Payment After Recoupment of Advances

6. Small performing rights in the Compositions, to the extent permitted by law, shall be assigned to and licensed by the applicable public performance [sic] society. Said society shall be and is hereby authorized to collect and receive all monies earned from the public performance of the Compositions and to pay directly to Company one hundred (100%) percent of the same sums as are allocated by said society as the publisher's share of public performance fees. At such time as the Term hereof has expired and all advances paid to Participant or to Writer, pursuant to the Writer's Agreement, have been fully recouped, Company and Participant shall execute such letters of direction to the applicable performing rights society authorizing and directing such society to pay directly to Participant and to Company their respective portions of the publisher's share of public performance fees, which portions shall be computed in accordance with the provisions of Paragraph 5 above.

☞ Until Company has recouped advances paid to Participant [the copublisher] and to Writer, Company receives 100% of public performance royalties. After recoupment, each receives direct payment of their publisher's share of the public performance royalties.

ARM'S LENGTH

Some copublishing agreements contain a provision stating that if the administering publisher is affiliated with a record company, there will be what is known as an *arm's-length* relationship when it comes to mechanical licenses and other licenses. Arm's-length provisions refer to the obligation of the administering publisher to deal with itself and affiliated companies as if they were not affiliated. This requires the administering publisher to charge, for example, a full statutory mechanical license fee if, under the same circumstances, a full rate would be charged to an unrelated company (see Example 2). Some companies refuse to agree to an arm's-length restriction and will, in fact, license to themselves at less than the going rate.

SAMPLE CONTRACT PROVISIONS

EXAMPLE 1: Attempt to Specify Arm's-Length Rates

4. Administrator shall be entitled to receive and collect and shall receive and collect all gross receipts from the Composition. . . . In the event Administrator or its subsidiaries or affiliates in the United States or Canada shall print and sell any printed editions of the Composition, gross receipts with respect thereto, for the purposes of this agreement shall be deemed to be as follows: Thirty-five cents ($0.35) for each copy of sheet music in a standard piano/vocal notation sold, paid for and not returned, twelve and one-half percent (12½%) of the suggested retail list price of each instrumental, orchestral, choral, band or other arrangement of the Composition in a standard piano/vocal notation sold, paid for and not returned, and ten percent (10%) of the suggested retail list price of each instrumental, orchestral, choral, band or other arrangement of the Composition in other than a standard piano/vocal notation sold, paid for and not returned, and in the case of any folio or songbook containing the Composition and other musical compositions, after deduction of an administration fee to Co-Publisher of 15% of the gross publisher's share, royalties payable to writers, unrecouped advances if any and other chargeable amounts hereunder, and the costs of printing, engraving, copyrights, trade advertising and other direct costs and expenses paid or incurred by Co-Publisher with respect to the Compositions hereunder. . . .

☞ I hate the theory behind this provision. The presumption is that by contractually setting a specific rate, be it a dollar or cent figure or a set percentage, you are automatically getting an arm's-length rate. This is the equivalent of agreeing to a set dollar amount for your salary over the next 25 years without factoring in inflation or a cost-of-living index. Percentages, at least, may be worth more as underlying wholesale or retail prices increase—but a set dollar or cent figure? C'mon! What if, for example, an artist making records during the vinyl age, who didn't believe in a percentage royalty (many didn't—it takes some thought), decided that, based on the fact that an LP album had a retail price of $4.98 (they once did), the once and future royalty should be $0.50 per album? Today, when CDs retail for, say, $17.98, the artist would still be receiving a $0.50 royalty.

EXAMPLE 2: Copublisher Must Consent to Rate

23. Notwithstanding anything to the contrary contained herein, Company agrees not to issue mechanical licenses for Compositions hereunder to any record company which is affiliated with or a subsidiary of Company hereunder at less than then current statutory rate without first obtaining the prior written consent of Co-Publisher.

EXAMPLE 3: Arm's-Length Agreement

10.(h) In arriving at the "net sums received by us" as used herein, without limitation, in the event we or any subsidiary of ours directly licenses the Compositions to third parties and/or collects all mechanicals due therefrom, we may deduct from gross monies received pursuant to each such license commissions in the amount equal to that which would be charged by The Harry Fox Agency, if The Harry Fox Agency rather than we or our subsidiary were the licensing agent. Notwithstanding the foregoing, we shall not deduct such commissions with respect to licenses from us directly to Record Company. We shall endeavor to deal on our normal "arm's-length" basis with respect to licenses from us to Record Company.

RIGHT OF FIRST REFUSAL

The meek shall inherit the earth but not its mineral rights.
—J. PAUL GETTY

A provision that is rarely, if ever, found in recording agreements but occurs quite frequently in co-publishing agreements is one known as a *right-of-first-refusal* provision. These provisions restrict one publisher, usually the nonadministering copublisher, from disposing of its share in the copyright for the composition(s) without first offering the share to the other publisher on the same terms as they have been offered to a third party who may wish to acquire the copyrights. The other publisher, usually the administering publisher, may dispose of its share without making an offer to the copublisher (see Example 1).

When faced with one of these right-of-first-refusal provisions while representing the publisher on the short end of the stick, I usually, though not always with success, try to strike the provision. Another approach is to work out a compromise where it is a mutual obligation and/or does not apply to the sale of an entire catalogue. A demand that the right of first refusal be mutual is invariably met with a combination of horror and mirth. The publisher *without* the right of refusal probably has less than one or two dozen copyrights in its catalogue. The other publisher may literally have hundreds of thousands of copyrights in its catalogue. The idea that the larger publisher, when offered hundreds of millions of dollars for its catalogue, must stop and first offer the catalogue to the little publisher at the same price is ludicrous and unworkable. OK, I reply, What about this? There will be mutual rights of first refusal over individual songs which are copublished by the two publishers, but both are free to make a sale of their entire catalogues without having to first offer the catalogue to the other. Usually, this is accepted as a compromise (see Example 3).

One of the problems with a right of first refusal has to do with the negative effect of a time lag when you are trying to close a deal. Negotiations and deal making have rhythms of their own. To postpone the consummation of a deal while the agreement is submitted to the other publisher (especially when the reviewing publisher may exercise its right to purchase the share) can put a terminal strain on that deal. Many potential buyers are unwilling to negotiate an entire deal and incur costs if there is the possibility of finding at some point that they have done all the work for someone else who has a right of first refusal.

One way to put some limits on the damage a right of first refusal can do to a developing deal is to make as short as possible the time period during which the party having the right of first refusal can exercise the option. Another possibility is to provide that when the party having the right of first refusal rejects the offer, and the agreement between the copublisher and the third party falls through, the copublisher does not, when negotiating future deals, have to go back to the party with the right of first refusal.

Example

Party #1 offers you $100 for your 50% interest in a song. You offer the interest in the song to your copublisher for $100, who says no. Party #1 then, for whatever reason, does not purchase the interest in the song. Thereafter, you do not need go back to the copublisher on future offers.

If the above arrangement is not acceptable (and it often isn't), perhaps you can obtain language stating that you do not have to go back to the copublisher if a subsequent offer for the same property is the same or higher than the one the copublisher has already turned down.

Example

Party #1 offers you $100 for your 50% interest in a song. You offer the interest in the song to your copublisher for $100, who says no. Party #1 then, for whatever reason, does not purchase the interest in the song. A few months later, another party offers you $101 (or $110 or $125—it doesn't matter how much over $100 it is). You can accept the offer without going back to the copublisher.

SAMPLE CONTRACT PROVISIONS

EXAMPLE 1: Time Limit on Right of Refusal

10. Participant shall not sell, transfer, assign or otherwise dispose of or encumber its interest under this agreement or its earnings therefrom without first offering same to Company, in writing, at the same price and upon the same terms as any such contemplated sale, transfer, assignment or encumbrance. Company shall have a period of fourteen (14) business days from the date of receipt of written notice from Participant setting forth the price and of other terms of the contemplated sale, transfer, assignment or encumbrance in which to notify Participant of its willingness to accept or reject such offer. If Company rejects any such offer, Participant may enter in an agreement with such third party on terms not less favorable to Participant than those offered to Company.

EXAMPLE 2: One-Sided No First Refusal If Entire Catalogue Is to Be Sold

11.(a) Participant shall not sell, transfer, assign or otherwise dispose of any interest in the copyright of any Composition without first offering to Company the right to buy or acquire such interest in the copyright of such Composition at the same bona fide price and pursuant to the same bona fide terms as may be offered to Participant by any responsible, prospective and unrelated third party, which terms may, however, only provide for payment of cash in one lump sum or installments. Participant agrees to give Company written notice of any such bona fide and acceptable offer as described above (which notice shall set forth the name of the prospective purchaser, the price, and all other terms of such offer) and Company shall have a period of fifteen (15) business days after receipt of such notice in which to notify Participant whether or not it desires to acquire such interest in the copyright of such Composition at the price and pursuant to the terms set forth in such notice. In the event Company fails to give Participant written notice within said fifteen (15) business day period that it is exercising its option to buy or acquire such interest in the copyright, Participant shall have the right to accept the bona fide offer by the prospective purchaser, but only as set forth in Participant's notice to Company, provided, however, that if Participant does not accept such bona fide offer from the prospective purchaser within thirty (30) business days after expiration of said fifteen (15) business day period, the procedure set forth in this subparagraph shall again be followed by Participant before Participant may dispose of such interest in the copyright of such Composition.

(b) Company may not dispose of any interest in the copyright of any Composition without following the procedure set forth in subparagraph 11(a) above; provided, however that Company may dispose of all its interest in the copyrights of all the Compositions without following such procedure in connection with the disposition of its entire catalog of musical compositions.

☛ The right of first refusal for the sale of any composition applies to both parties, but is expressly excluded if Company, but not Participant, is selling its entire catalogue. Guess who the dominant copublisher is in this relationship.

EXAMPLE 3: Mutual No First Refusal for Entire Catalogue

23. Neither Company nor Participant shall sell, transfer, assign or otherwise dispose of or encumber its interest under this agreement or its earnings therefrom without first offering same to the other party, in writing, at the same price and upon the same terms as any such contemplated sale, transfer, assignment or encumbrance. The party to whom such offer is made shall have a period of five (5) business days from the date of receipt of written notice from the other setting forth the price and of other terms of the contemplated sale, transfer, assignment or encumbrance in which to notify the offering party of its willingness to accept or reject such offer. If the party to whom such offer is made rejects any such offer, the other party may enter in an agreement with such third party on terms not less favorable than those offered; provided, however, that the terms of this paragraph 23 shall apply to any sale of either parties' entire catalogue.

CHAPTER 11

ADMINISTRATION AGREEMENTS

It serves me right for putting all my eggs in one bastard.
—Dorothy Parker

Administration agreements are like copublishing agreements, but they aren't—if you follow my drift.

Administration agreements create an arrangement whereby one publisher manages copyrights for another publisher or copyright owner. Usually, but not necessarily, when an administration agreement is discussed, co-ownership is not an issue. If it were, the resulting agreement would be more properly classified as a copublishing agreement (usually with one party administering the copyrights).

Since we are really dealing in labels here, this chapter, except as specifically noted, focuses on those agreements where the administering publisher is not an owner or co-owner of the copyrights in question but is functioning as the administrator of the rights.

The management of copyrights involves much more than just sitting on top of a pile of copyrights and waiting for money to come in the mail. Since any person owning even one copyright is, in effect, a publisher, it should be obvious why many "publishers" do not have the requisite knowledge, or time, to adequately represent their own interests. For example, copyright holders may have monies due from any combination of the following: mechanical licenses, synchronization, sale, arrangement, adaptation, grand and small performance rights, print, translation, dramatization, retransmission, merchandising, and neighboring rights (see Example 1, paragraph 5, in the section "Duties of the Administrator," page 331).

Location may also be a factor. Even fully-staffed publishing companies have foreign subpublishers who administer their interests outside of the United States.

SAMPLE CONTRACT PROVISIONS

EXAMPLE 1: Administrator Has Exclusive Rights

This Administration Agreement is made and entered into as of the 1st day of September, _____, by and between [Administrator] (hereinafter referred to as the "Administrator"), and owner/publisher [Owner] (hereinafter referred to as "Owner") and in consideration of the terms and conditions contained herein and the sum of One ($1.00) Dollar, the receipt of which is hereby acknowledged, Owner hereby grants to Administrator the exclusive rights to act as administrator of all rights in and to the musical compositions set forth in Schedule "A," as such Schedule shall be added to from time to time (hereinafter individually and collectively referred to as the "Compositions").

EXAMPLE 2: Administrator Has Right to License Subpublishing

3. Administrator shall have the sole and exclusive right to administer and protect the Compositions on behalf of Publisher, and shall have the sole right to designate on behalf of Publisher all persons, firms or corporations to administer the Compositions throughout the world, including within the United States and Canada and, on behalf of or in the name of Publisher, to enter into agreements with said persons, firms or corporations which may be affiliated with Administrator to subpublish or otherwise deal with the Compositions.

☛ The administrator has the right to negotiate and make foreign subpublishing deals for the publisher. Since the administrator undoubtedly has other deals with the foreign subpublisher, there is a potential problem for the publisher in this agreement to be a victim of cross-collateralization for advances made to administrator for other deals.

EXAMPLE 3: Exclusive Grant of Rights

5.02 *Administration*. During the Retention Period, Publisher and its Licensees will, subject to all restrictions contained in this Agreement, have the sole and exclusive right, throughout the Territory, with respect to Your Interest in the Compositions to:

(a) License, and cause others to license, the exploitation of the Compositions, including, without limitation, the right to license: (i) broadcast and other public performances, (ii) the manufacture, distribution and sale of Phonograph Records and video devices embodying the Compositions, (iii) the synchronization of the Compositions in connection with motion pictures, videos, television programs and commercials, provided that Publisher shall not without your prior consent, issue an exclusive synchronization license for such purposes, (iv) the use of the Compositions in any technology or configuration in respect of which musical composition may be licensed, and (v) the use of the Compositions in connection with merchandising activities.

(b) Administer and grant rights in the Compositions.

(c) Collect all monies earned during or prior to the Retention Period with respect to the Compositions (including, without limitation, any amounts collectible by Publisher pursuant to the [preceding] Agreement), no matter when actually paid or payable, and all performance royalties payable to you with respect to the Compositions by the applicable performing rights society (hereinafter collectively the "Societies"), but excluding any songwriter share of public performance income and excluding any income derived from the rights specifically reserved to you hereunder. In addition to the rights that the applicable performing rights society(ies) may have to license public performance uses of the Compositions, Publisher shall have the right to license the public performance uses of the Compositions directly and all income received by Publisher in connection with such license shall be deemed Gross Income and subject to accounting hereunder, provided that if any of the Gross Income derived from such direct license constitutes the "writer's share" of public performance royalties, then such writer's share will be paid directly to you by Publisher (without regard to recoupment) at the time, and in the manner that royalties are payable to you hereunder. In addition, for two years following the expiration of the Retention Period (the "Collection Period"), Publisher shall, notwithstanding anything herein, have the sole and exclusive right to collect all monies earned for uses of the Compositions made during the retention period.

(d) Make arrangements of, or otherwise adapt or change, the Compositions in any manner, provided that Publisher shall not make, or authorize the making of, material changes in the lyrics of the Compositions without your consent. Your consent will not be required, however, for any foreign language changes in the lyrics of the Compositions, gender changes, and other changes that are required for the uses contemplated (e.g., uses in Phonograph Records), provided that royalties or fees paid to local adapters, arrangers and lyricists shall, where possible having regard to the terms of the Writers Agreements, be deducted from the "writer's share" of income. In this regard, Publisher shall provide you with copies of all agreements where such royalty obligations extend beyond the expiration of the Term hereof.

(e) Otherwise administer and exploit the Compositions and act as the music publisher of the Compositions.

DUTIES OF THE ADMINISTRATOR

Just what is it that the administrator actually does in the pursuit of administrative nirvana? The duties of the administrator are many and varied, but all deal with either the protection of the copyright, the exploitation of the copyright, or the collection and disbursement of the proceeds of the exploitation.

Note that almost all administration agreements call for the administering party to be the exclusive administrator. Administration works best where there is one focal point for control of the exploitation and licensing of the copyrights. Although not common, there are copublishing agreements in which there is more than one administrator, and each *coadministrator* has a separate right to carry out the administrative functions.

The following examples offer a good cross section of provisions dealing with what is expected from administrators.

SAMPLE CONTRACT PROVISIONS

EXAMPLE 1: Administrator's Duties

4. COPYRIGHT ADMINISTRATION: Administrator shall have the right to secure, in the name of Owner, and at Owner's expense, the copyright registration, including any renewal registration, with respect to the Compositions under any law now in effect or hereafter enacted throughout the Territory.

(a) Administrator shall administrate the copyrights and interests in the Compositions in all fields of use, on a sole and exclusive basis, throughout the Territory.

(b) The Administrator's rights, powers, privileges and duties with respect to the administration of the Compositions, as hereinafter more particularly stated, shall extend and apply to any and all contracts and licenses heretofore made or issued by or on behalf of or for the benefit of Owner and hereafter made or issued by or on behalf of or for the benefit of Owner, with respect to the Compositions and rights therein and proceeds therefrom in all fields of use throughout the Territory, including without limitation, mechanical, electrical transcription, reproduction, synchronization, audio-visual, performance, dramatization, printed matter and publication and neighboring rights and usages and all other rights and usages relating to the reproduction, adaptation, distribution, performance, display, and preparation of derivative works, as well as all other rights and usages of the Compositions now known or hereafter coming into existence during the term hereof.

(c) In connection therewith, the Administrator shall have the right to adapt, arrange, revise, edit and translate the Compositions, and to provide or cause to be written new and original music therefor or lyrics therefor in any language other than the English language.

5. COLLECTIONS: Administrator shall have the sole and exclusive right throughout the Territory to collect and receive all royalties, revenues, monies, income and all other compensation or advances accrued or paid with respect to the Compositions, and/or appoint others to do so. The rights granted herein include, but are not limited to, the right to collect royalties, payments and settlements from or relating to:

(1) Mechanical licenses;

(2) Synchronization;

(3) Sale;

(4) Arrangement;

(5) Adaptation;

(6) Grand rights;

(7) Performing rights;

(8) Small performing rights;

(9) Performance rights;

(10) Print;

(11) Translation;

(12) Dramatization;

(13) Re-transmission;

(14) Merchandising;

(15) Neighboring rights; and

(16) Any other use and other disposition now or hereafter known accruing heretofore or hereafter, including, but not limited to so-called "pipeline monies."

• • •

9. ATTORNEY IN FACT: Owner hereby constitutes and appoints Administrator its true and lawful agent and attorney in fact, to make, execute and deliver any and all documents, instruments and writings, in its name and to take any other action upon Owner's prior written approval, not to be unreasonably withheld, in its name which in the reasonable judgment and discretion of the Administrator is necessary or desirable to carry out the purposes of this Agreement, including, without limitation, the following:

(a) To prepare, execute, file and register claims of copyright in the Compositions and, to the extent applicable, renewals, extensions and dispositions of termination or reversionary and extension rights of the same, in the name of Owner as copyright proprietor.

(b) To endorse all checks and drafts received by the Administrator with respect to the Compositions for deposit only, and to deposit all such checks, drafts and other receipts in the account of Administrator and Owner relating to this Agreement.

☛ This example could serve as a manual for a beginning administrator.

EXAMPLE 2: Short Form List of Administrator's Duties

3. Company has the sole, exclusive and worldwide right to administer and exploit the Compositions, to print, to publish, sell, dramatize, use and license any and all uses of the

Compositions, to execute in its own name any and all licenses and agreements whatsoever affecting or respecting the Compositions, including but not limited to licenses for mechanical reproduction, public performance, dramatic uses, synchronization uses and subpublication, and to assign or license such rights to others. This statement of exclusive rights is only in clarification and amplification of the rights of Company and not in limitation thereof.

EXAMPLE 3: Worldwide Exclusive Right to Administer

3. Publisher hereby acknowledges and agrees that Administrator, its successors, assigns, licensees and subpublishers, shall have the exclusive right throughout the world to administer and exploit all rights of every kind, nature and description in and to the Compositions, together with the exclusive right to manage and administer all copyrights and renewals and extensions thereof, including but not limited to the right to:

(a) issue licenses with respect to mechanical and electrical reproduction of the Compositions throughout the world on phonograph records, pre-recorded tapes, piano rolls and transcriptions, or by any other method now known or hereafter devised for sound reproduction.

(b) publicly perform the Compositions and license such right in all media including radio and television broadcasting.

(c) grant licenses for the recording of Compositions in and with motion pictures and television productions produced throughout the world, of making copies of its recordings thereof, and importing such copies into all countries of the world.

(d) print, publish and sell printed music throughout the world in the form of sheet music, arrangements, song books, albums, folios or educational works.

(e) translate the lyrics or create new lyric versions of the Compositions into all languages other than English, and make or have made, band, choral, orchestral, or other arrangements of the Compositions.

(f) enjoy and license all additional rights granted by the United States Copyright Act of 1976 not specifically set forth herein.

(g) Administrator will prepare and file all copyright forms, Notice of Use forms and other documents required to be filed with the Copyright Office in the United States and foreign countries, and will file with the appropriate performing rights societies all documents required to be filed with said societies.

EXAMPLE 4: Administrator to Make "Best Efforts to Exploit" Compositions

2. In consideration of the terms and conditions contained herein:

(a) Administrator shall administrate and exploit the copyrights and interests in the Compositions in all fields of use, on a sole and exclusive basis, throughout the universe.

(b) The Administrator's rights, powers, privileges and duties with respect to the administration of the Compositions, as hereinafter more particularly stated, shall extend and apply to any and all contracts and licenses heretofore made or issued by or on behalf of or for the benefit of Owner and hereafter made or issued by or on behalf of or for the benefit of Owner, with respect to the Compositions and rights therein and proceeds therefrom in all fields of use throughout the universe, including without limitation, mechanical, electrical transcription, reproduction, synchronization, audio-visual, performance, dramatization, printed matter and publication rights and usages and all other rights and usages relating to the reproduction, adaptation, distribution, performance, display, and preparation of derivative works, as well as all other rights and usages of the Compositions now known or hereafter coming into existence during the term hereof (hereinafter referred to as "Licensed Usages").

3. The Administrator agrees to use its best efforts to exploit the Compositions hereunder.

(a) The Administrator shall have the sole and exclusive right throughout the universe to grant licenses and/or to collect and receive all royalties, revenues, monies, income and all other compensation or advances accrued or paid with respect to the Licensed Usages; and

(b) In connection therewith, the Administrator shall have the exclusive right to adapt, arrange, revise, edit and translate the Compositions, and to provide or cause to be written new and original music therefor or lyrics therefor in any language.

☛ The "best efforts to exploit" part of this example means that the administrator's tasks extend beyond the usual administrative duties of registration, collection, accounting, and the like [subparagraphs 2(a) and 2(b)] to the "plugging" and placement of the compositions for exploitation.

EXAMPLE 5: Coadministration

1. The parties hereto shall jointly own the musical compositions set forth in the annexed Exhibit "A" (hereinafter referred to as the "Composition"), in the shares set forth in Exhibit "A," including all of the worldwide right, title and interest, the copyright, the right to copyright, and any and all renewal rights therein and thereto, for the full term of copyright and all extension and renewal terms in each and every country of the world.

2. Each party shall have the separate right in the United States and Canada to administer and exploit the Composition, to print, publish, use and license the use of the Composition, and to execute any and all licenses and agreements whatsoever affecting or respecting the Composition, including, but not limited to licenses for mechanical reproduction, print uses, public performances and synchronization uses and subpublication, subject to the following terms and conditions:

(a) All worldwide synchronization rights (including, but not limited to, all licenses for use of the Composition in motion pictures, television programs, radio and television commercials and audio visual devices) are expressly reserved to Publisher. Without limiting the generality of the foregoing, the parties agree that [Film Company] is hereby issued an irrevocable, perpetual and worldwide license, without charge, for the use of the Composition in synchronization with the theatrical motion picture currently entitled "[Film]" and all sequels, remakes and episodic television programs derived therefrom (collectively and individually the "Picture") and for the performance of the Composition in the Picture, for exploitation in any and all media now known or hereafter known or hereafter devised (including, but not limited to audio-visual devices in any configuration), and in trailers, advertisements, featurettes and other promotions of the Picture, without limitation as to the number, time and/or duration of such uses and without any obligation to pay further sums for any such use.

(b) Notwithstanding the foregoing: (i) Publisher agrees to issue or cause to be issued a customary synchronization license at a customary rate in connection with the on-camera performance of the Composition by the recording artist who [Film Company] may decide to record the Composition for possible use in the Picture and/or Soundtrack Albums in a non-dramatic television program (e.g. "Solid Gold"); (ii) from and after the date occurring one (1) year after the release of the Picture,

Co-Publisher shall have the right to grant licenses for the synchronization of the Composition in a television program or other motion picture, provided, the Composition may not be used as the title and/or theme song for any such television program and/or motion picture without Publisher's prior written consent; (iii) Publisher will give due consideration to any synchronization use of the Composition requested by Co-Publisher or Co-Publisher's subpublishers which cannot be granted by Co-Publisher pursuant to this paragraph 3(a), provided that Publisher's decision will be final in all such matters; and (iv) Publisher agrees to negotiate any agreement or license for the synchronization of the Composition other than in connection with the Picture (including without limitation, advertising, promotion and ancillary uses thereof) on an "arm's-length" basis in accordance with customs and practice in the music industry.

(c) All worldwide matching folio print rights with respect to the music in the Picture and with respect to the music on the Soundtrack Album derived from the Picture ("Soundtrack Album"), and worldwide sheet music rights with respect to the Composition, are expressly reserved to Publisher and any related print licenses will be issued on a competitive basis with each party receiving their appropriate share derived therefrom. Publisher and Co-Publisher shall each have the nonexclusive right to license the use of the Composition in mixed folios and mixed songbooks.

(d) Except as provided in paragraph 3(a) and (b) above, no licenses or agreements affecting or respecting the Composition shall be exclusive.

(e) (i) Subject to paragraph 3(d)(ii) below, no mechanical license shall be issued by any party at less than the then current statutory rate (with reduced rates to be permitted, however, in any such licenses, for those types of sales or distributions for which music publishers customarily grant such reduced rates to non-affiliated record companies), Co-Publisher shall not grant a mechanical license for the first right to reproduce the Composition on phonorecords without Publisher's prior written consent.

(ii) Without limiting the generality of the foregoing, Publisher and Co-Publisher hereby agree that the Composition shall be deemed a "Controlled Composition" (as such term is defined under the applicable distribution agreement with respect to the Soundtrack Album) and shall be subject to the "Controlled Composition" provisions contained therein, including, without limitation, the issuance of mechanical licenses at a rate less than the current statutory rate.

(f) A true copy of each license or agreement issued by one party shall be promptly furnished to each other party.

☛ This long and convoluted example shows just how messy coadministration can be.

TERM OF THE AGREEMENT

> FORD:
> ### . . . stand under the adoption of abominable terms,
> —WILLIAM SHAKESPEARE
> *The Merry Wives of Windsor,*
> Act II, Scene 2

Inasmuch as administrators are not copyright owners, administration agreements, unlike copublishing agreements, are rarely for the life of the copyright, but for periods similar to those in artist recording agreements, songwriters' agreements, distribution agreements, etc. As with other types of agreements, the term may be for an initial period plus one or more option periods. The agreement can, of course, be for a specific period of time, such as, for example, one 5-year period (see Example 1). If the administration agreement provides for payment of advances by the administrator to the publisher, there is very likely to be a provision that allows for an extension of the term of the agreement if said advances have not been recouped (see Example 6). (This is, by the way, not unusual. Publishing is, after all, the cash cow of the music business, and it often makes financial sense for a publishing administrator to pay an advance, albeit recoupable off the top, for the right to administer and take a percentage of the publishing income for so doing.)

As with the other types of agreements, when there are option periods, provisions are usually included dealing with the exercise of options. Unlike the other types, however, with administration agreements there is a reasonable possibility of making the exercise of the option a mutual decision between the parties.

SAMPLE CONTRACT PROVISIONS

EXAMPLE 1: Five-Year Term

2. The term of this Agreement shall be five (5) years, commencing upon the date hereof. During this period, Administrator shall serve as the exclusive administrator of the Compositions.

EXAMPLE 2: Decision to Extend Term Must Be Mutual

1. TERM OF AGREEMENT: The term of this Agreement shall be for an initial period of three (3) years from the date hereof. There shall be one (1) additional three (3) year period which shall continue upon the expiration of the initial period unless either party hereto gives the other party written notice of such party's intention to terminate this Agreement, such notice to be given, if it is given, no later than sixty (60) days prior to the expiration of the initial period.

EXAMPLE 3: Administrator's Decision to Extend Term

1. Publisher hereby agrees that Administrator shall be the exclusive administrator of the musical compositions, numbers and works specified in Schedule 1 (the "Compositions") for a period of one (1) year from the date hereof (the "Term").

• • •

3. Publisher hereby grants to Administrator four (4) separate options, each of which shall, upon the exercise thereof by notice in writing by Administrator to Publisher at least thirty (30) days prior to the expiration of the Term or exercised option year, as the case may be, extend the Term for one (1) year.

EXAMPLE 4: $300,000 Minimum in Initial Term Before Administrator Can Exercise First Option

2. Term. The initial term of this agreement shall commence upon the date hereof and shall continue for three (3) years. Publisher hereby grants to Administrator two (2) separate and irrevocable options, each to renew this agreement for a one (1) year term, such renewal term to run consecutively beginning at the expiration of the initial term hereof, all upon the same terms and conditions as are applicable to the initial term except as otherwise provided herein. Each option shall be exercised by Administrator by written notice to Publisher at least thirty (30) days prior to the expiration of then current term; provided, however, that if Publisher has not received a minimum

of $300,000 from the Catalogue during the initial period of this Agreement Administrator may not exercise the first option provided for herein.

EXAMPLE 5: Term Tied to Individual Compositions

1. TERM OF AGREEMENT: The term of this Agreement shall be for an initial period of five (5) years from the date hereof; provided, however, that in the case of individual Compositions for which Publisher's rights expire prior to the expiration of this Agreement, the term for such individual Compositions shall expire coterminously with such expiration.

> ☛ If the copyright on any composition in the catalogue which is being administered expires, the "term" for that particular copyright expires with it, even though the agreement may continue to run.

EXAMPLE 6: Term Tied to Recoupment of Advance

4. TERM/RETENTION PERIOD.

4.01 The "Initial Term" of this Agreement shall mean the period commencing upon the date hereof and continuing for five (5) years thereafter.

4.02 In the event that upon the expiration of the Initial Term, all Advances made hereunder have not been fully recouped, then the Term of this Agreement shall continue for the "Extended Term." The "Extended Term" shall mean the period commencing upon the expiration of the Initial Term and continuing until the earlier of the following two dates, namely:

(a) the date upon which all Advances made hereunder are fully recouped; and

(b) the date two years after the expiration of the Initial Term.

4.03 The "Term" of this Agreement shall mean the Initial Term and, if applicable, the Extended Term.

4.04 The period during which the Publisher shall retain the rights acquired by it pursuant to this Agreement (the "Retention Period") shall be for the Term hereof. Subject to Publisher's rights hereunder during the Collection Period, as hereinafter defined, upon the expiration of the Retention Period with respect to any Composition hereunder, you shall have the sole and exclusive right to collect all monies with respect to such Composition, regardless of when such monies are earned.

· · ·

5.02 . . . Collect all monies earned during or prior to the Retention Period. . . . In addition, for two years following the expiration of the Retention Period (the "Collection Period"), Publisher shall, notwithstanding anything herein, have the sole and exclusive right to collect all monies earned for uses of the Compositions made during the Retention Period.

> ☛ The administrator has given the publisher an advance for the honor (and profit) of administering the publisher's catalogue. Honor, however, only goes so far. The term of the agreement may be extended up to another 2 years if the advance is not recouped in the initial period.

TERRITORY

Administration agreements usually contain provisions dealing with and certainly specifying the territory or territories involved in the grant of the right to administer the copyrights. It is not unusual for administration agreements to be limited to specified territories rather than being granted on a worldwide (or even universewide) basis. Additionally, provisions may be required to describe what limitations, if any, apply to the territory covered by the administration agreement.

Many domestic publishers are not really qualified to act as administrators outside of the United States and, accordingly, the territory may be restricted to the United States, leaving foreign publishing to be either administered by foreign subpublishers or, perhaps, not administered at all. For the U.S. publisher, foreign markets represent fertile fields to be tilled which, alas, are usually left fallow—even when the domestic publisher thinks all is being done that can be done.

SAMPLE CONTRACT PROVISIONS

EXAMPLE 1: Territory Is Entire World
3. The administration rights in the Compositions granted to Administrator hereunder by Publisher shall be for the life of the copyright in each such Composition and for the entire world.

EXAMPLE 2: Territory Is United States and Canada
4. The right of Administrator to administer the Compositions shall be for the United States of America and Canada only (hereinafter referred to as the "Territory"). All administration rights in and to the Compositions outside of the Territory shall remain the sole property of Publisher.

EXAMPLE 3: Foreign Territories Specified
3. Administrator shall, on behalf of Publisher, administer the musical compositions set forth in the annexed Exhibit "A" (hereinafter referred to as the "Compositions"), in the countries which presently constitute the European Union, including those non-EU territories for which GEMA presently collects performance royalties.

> ☛ The territory covered by this agreement includes those nations that are a part of the European Union (Austria, Belgium, Denmark, Finland, France, Germany, Greece, Ireland, Italy, Luxembourg, the Netherlands, Portugal, Spain, Sweden, and the United Kingdom.) Also included are those countries subsequently added to the EU after the agreement was signed and "non-EU territories for which GEMA" collects performance royalties. [For more information on GEMA (Gesellschaft für musikalische Aufführungs und mechanische Vervielfältigungsrechte) see the list of foreign performance and performing rights societies starting on page 413].

COMPENSATION

The trouble with the rat race is that, even if you win, you're still a rat.

—LILY TOMLIN

The administrator receives a percentage of the income for the administration services performed. Much of the information about administration fees in the section on copublishing agreements also applies in this context. The fee is negotiable and generally may be somewhat higher than administration fees in copublishing agreements. It usually ranges between 10% and 25% of the gross receipts from the exploitation of the compositions, but may be higher or lower. As with copublishing agreements, some items may be deducted before calculating the administration fee, for example, collection fees paid to third parties such as the Fox Office. Fees deducted by subadministrators may also be deducted prior to determining the dollar amount of the administration fee. As in co-publishing agreements, the order in which costs are deducted affects the ultimate sum received by the administrator. Additionally, the administration fee may increase or decrease, depending upon circumstances or the sources of the income. (See Example 2, where the administration fee is adjusted from 15% to 25% of income earned from exploitation of a cover record.)

SAMPLE CONTRACT PROVISIONS

EXAMPLE 1: 20% Fee

6. *Compensation*: In compensation for the services performed by Administrator hereunder, Administrator shall retain Twenty (20%) Percent of One Hundred (100%) Percent of all Gross Receipts collected from all sources and shall remit the remaining Eighty (80%) Percent to Owner. Statements setting forth the monies received by Administrator in respect of the Compositions, the deductions therefrom and the monies payable by Administrator to Owner hereunder shall be sent by Administrator to Owner quarterly within fifteen (15) days after the end of each quarterly calendar period. Statements shall be accompanied by payments by Administrator to Owner of all monies actually received by Administrator on behalf of Owner under the terms of this Agreement during the period covered by such statement, deducting therefrom the payments or deductions permitted by this Agreement.

EXAMPLE 2: Higher Fee for Cover Records

(a) An administration fee of fifteen percent (15%) of the gross receipts, which fee shall be retained by Administrator for its own account, provided, however, that said fee shall be increased to twenty-five percent (25%) with respect to all income (including, without limitation, mechanical royalties and public performance fees) earned from the exploitation of a cover record of the Composition (the term "cover record" being defined as any recording of a Composition other than a recording by the Composers thereof or a recording in existence prior to the term hereof).

EXAMPLE 3: Higher Fee Due to Advance

6. ROYALTIES. Provided that you have fully complied with all of your material warranties, representations and obligations provided for in this Agreement, Publisher shall credit your royalty account with the following amounts with respect to its exploitation of Your Interest in the Compositions in the Territory.

6.01 *Public Performance Income*. 60% of Net Income derived from the publisher's share of public performance income collected by Publisher with respect to performances of Your Interest in the Compositions. . . .

6.02 *Mechanical Income*. 60% of Net Income derived from Publisher's exploitation of Interest in the Compositions for use in Phonograph Records, except that Publisher shall pay you 30% of such Net Income derived from Cover Recordings.

6.03 *Synchronization and Commercials Income and Video Uses Secured by Publisher*. 50% of Net Income derived from Publisher's exploitation of Interest in the Compositions in commercials, motion pictures, television programs, videos and other audiovisual works where such use is secured by Publisher.

6.04 *Other Synchronization and Commercial Income and Video Uses*. 60% of Net Income derived from Publisher's exploitation of Interest in the Compositions in commercials, motion pictures, television programs, videos and other audiovisual works not described in subparagraph 6.03.

6.05 *All Other Uses*. 60% of Net Income derived from Publisher's exploitation of Interest in the Compositions for uses not specifically described above.

☛ The administration fees in this agreement (which are the difference between 100% of net income and the percentages of net income paid to the owner of the compositions) are unusually high—ranging from a low of 40% to a high of 70% (for mechanicals on cover records)—because the administrator had advanced a substantial sum to the owner.

COSTS

Administering copyrights creates expenses, and administration agreements need to specify how these costs are treated. Although the administrator may, as a practical matter, at least have to front the money for the administration costs (see Example 1), the ultimate cost of administering the copyrights is always charged back to the copyright owners and recovered from the income generated from the exploitation of the copyrights (see Example 2).

The administrator collects the income from the exploitation of the compositions and, before distributing to the copyright owner, deducts expenses and the administration fee. The items that constitute costs can be quite varied, including, for example, registration fees, advertising and promotion expenses, demo recording costs, the costs of lead sheets, dubbing costs, the costs of adaptations, arrangements, revisions, translations, editing, writing new lyrics or music, etc. There are costs involved in the protection of the copyrights, such as legal fees and litigation costs. There are also costs involved in the preparation of print copies of the copyrights if, in fact, the publisher is responsible for these costs (engraving, printing, etc.) rather than making these costs the responsibility of the assignee of the print rights. Those items which are generally accepted as overhead, such as rent, telephone, utilities, etc., are usually borne by the administrator as its cost of doing business, and attempts to charge these costs to the copyright owner should be rejected.

SAMPLE CONTRACT PROVISIONS

EXAMPLE 1: Lists of Expenses to Be Charged Back to Owner

7. EXPENSES: Owner shall be responsible, upon Owner's prior written approval, not to be unreasonably withheld, for the following expenses; provided, however, that any such expenses paid by Administrator shall be reimbursed by Owner but solely from monies received as a direct result of Administrator's collection efforts, including, but not limited to:

(a) Upon Owner's prior written approval, not to be unreasonably withheld, administrative and exploitation expenses, if any, actually paid by Administrator with respect to any of the Compositions including, without limitation, registration fees, advertising and promotion expenses directly related to any of the Compositions, the costs of transcribing for lead sheets, the costs of any adaptations, arrangements, revisions, translations, editing or new lyrics or music, and the costs of producing demonstration records, it being understood that no such expenses shall be incurred without the prior written approval of such expense therefor by Owner;

(b) Upon Owner's prior written approval, not to be unreasonably withheld, attorneys' fees, if any, actually paid by Administrator for any agreements affecting any of the Compositions; and

(c) Upon Owner's prior written approval, not to be unreasonably withheld, the costs actually incurred by Administrator of printing, engraving, arranging, editing and distributing printed editions of any of the Compositions.

☛ At least the owner's prior written consent is required—for what that's worth, since consent is "not to be unreasonably withheld."

EXAMPLE 2: Net Receipts Paid to Publisher

5. Administrator shall pay to Publisher the net receipts from the exploitation of the Compositions. "Net receipts" is defined as the gross receipts derived by Administrator from the exploitation of the Compositions, including the publisher's share of public performance fees paid by the applicable performing rights society, less the following:

(a) An administration fee of Seventeen and One-Half (17.5%) Percent of the gross receipts after the deduction of any collection fees;

(b) Royalties and other sums which shall be paid by Administrator to the writer(s) of the Compositions in accordance with the provisions of the Writer's Agreement;

(c) Collection and other fees customarily and actually charged by The Harry Fox Agency, Inc. or other collection agent which may be used by Administrator, to the extent that fifty (50%) percent thereof has not been recouped from royalties payable to the writer(s) of the Compositions;

(d) Exploitation expenses of Administrator with respect to the Compositions, including, without limitation, registration fees, advertising and promotion expenses directly related to the Compositions, the cost of making lead sheets, and the cost of producing demonstration recordings;

(e) Attorneys' fees, if any, actually paid by Administrator for any agreement (other than the within agreement) affecting the Composition; and

(f) The costs of printing, engraving, arranging, and editing printed editions of the Compositions, provided that Administrator actually incurs such costs.

☛ The administration fee has been tossed into the list of expenses, but since the fee language in (a) specifically states that the 17.5% administration fee is based on gross receipts after deduction of collection fees as set forth in (c), it makes no difference in what order the expenses are paid. Also note that this administrator has the responsibility of making payments to the writers.

OBTAINING INFORMATION FROM THE COPYRIGHT OWNER

Frank and explicit; that is the right line to take when you wish to conceal your own mind and to confuse the minds of others.

—Benjamin Disraeli

In order to do the job right, any administrator needs access to information about the individual copyrights. Who is the writer—or is it writers? Is the composition to be placed in ASCAP or BMI—or, in the case of co-writers, possibly both? What is the song's title? Does the administrator have a complete copy (or recording or demo tape) of the song? In the case of coadministrators, it is necessary for information to be shared between the coadministrators. How will this sharing of information be handled? All these questions, and many more, have to be answered in order for the administrator to fulfill all necessary duties and obligations. There is no end to the mischief that can be generated when there is no information or, worse, misinformation. The foundation of all successful publishing enterprises is obtaining and maintaining complete, accurate records.

In a way, the deceptively simple and banal provisions which specify the mechanics of how information and materials will flow from the publisher to the administrator are the lynchpins of the administrative agreement. Without the flow of information from the publisher, there is no way to administer nor is there any practical reason to have entered into the agreement in the first place.

SAMPLE CONTRACT PROVISIONS

EXAMPLE 1: Information to Be Supplied by Copyright Owner

8. Information: In order to perform the services to be performed by the Administrator hereunder, Owner shall:

(a) Provide the Administrator with copies of all the Compositions;

(b) As and when appropriate, furnish the Administrator with a schedule of Compositions setting forth as to each of the Compositions:

(1) the title thereof;

(2) the date of registration of a claim to copyright therein;

(3) the copyright registration number of the same (including, as applicable, for the renewal term of copyright);

(4) the name and address of the writer or writers;

(5) the date of service of any termination notice, if any, and the termination date set forth therein, and copies of all applicable documents relating to the above;

(c) Furnish the Administrator with a legible lead sheet and demonstration tape, or recording, of each of the Compositions together with a written statement of the name and address of the copyright proprietor or proprietors and of the writer or writers and the title thereof (if the same does not appear on such lead sheet) and the approximate date when the first commercial recording was or is to be released embodying the same;

(d) Furnish Administrator with copies of all contracts between Owner and Publisher an any other writers or composers of the Compositions; and

(e) Will also furnish the Administrator with copies of all assignments, contracts or other instruments under which Owner acquired title or any right or interest in the copyright in and to any of the Compositions, including copies of all contracts as well as any other instruments respecting any rights or interests in the Compositions and with any pertinent data relating thereto.

CHAPTER 12

FOREIGN SUBPUBLISHING AGREEMENTS

EMILIA:

And pour our treasures into foreign laps,

—WILLIAM SHAKESPEARE

Othello, Act IV, Scene 3

Foreign subpublishers is the designation used to identify publishers in territories outside of the United States who are administering copyrights for American publishers in the designated foreign territories. *Foreign subpublishing agreements,* agreements with foreign subpublishers, are basically administration agreements. They are not set up as copublishing agreements, but unless care is taken in negotiating an agreement with the foreign subpublisher, the subpublisher may treat the copyrights as if it were a co-owner, or indeed the sole owner, of the copyrights. Because we are dealing in foreign territories, there are several areas of difference between these agreements and the administration agreements and copublishing agreements previously discussed. Probably the most important difference between foreign subpublishing agreements and our homegrown administration agreements is the possibility that some permanent transfer of rights may take place without the knowledge or consent of the copyright owner, and this may occur in spite of language specifying periods less than the life of the copyrights. Another important difference is the fact that foreign subpublishing agreements, unlike domestic administrative agreements, almost always bring an advance of money to the domestic publisher.

Hidden dangers lurk beneath the surface of these agreements and the relationships created by them. For the U.S. publisher licensing administrators' tasks to foreign publishers, the most vicious monster lurking under the bed is the infamous "Black Box," where uncollected publishing monies languish until they are collected—or appropriated. The best defense against this monster and the others creeping around these agreements is, first, knowledge that they exist (many don't) and, second, strategies for taming them. (See "The Black Box and Other Evil Companions," pages 355–357.)

SAMPLE CONTRACT PROVISIONS

EXAMPLE 1: Exclusive Right to Administer in Territory

This Sub-Publishing Agreement is made and entered into as of the 15th day of May, _____, by and between [foreign publisher], (hereinafter referred to as the "Sub-Publisher"), and [domestic publisher] (hereinafter referred to as "Publisher") and in consideration of the terms and conditions contained herein, Publisher hereby grants to Sub-Publisher the exclusive rights to act as administrator in the Territory, as defined below, of all rights in and to the musical compositions set forth in Schedule "1," as such Schedule shall be added to from time to time (hereinafter individually and collectively referred to as the "Compositions").

EXAMPLE 2: Subpublisher As Exclusive Administrator

1. Subject to the terms and conditions set forth herein, Publisher hereby appoints Sub-Publisher, and Sub-Publisher accepts such appointment, as the exclusive administrator of the Compositions in France (hereinafter referred to as the "Territory"). All rights in and to the Compositions outside of the Territory shall remain the sole property of Publisher.

TERM OF THE AGREEMENT

A true friend stabs you in the front.
—OSCAR WILDE

As stated above, it is rare that a domestic publisher enters intentionally into a foreign subpublishing agreement in which the term is the life of the copyright. As a practical matter, if the foreign publisher is allowed to take out the copyright in the local territory in its own name, the foreign publisher may, in fact, have the publishing, or at least a portion of it, for the life of the copyright. Generally, however, these agreements are for a limited period of time, allowing the domestic publisher licensing the copyrights to either renegotiate the agreement or move on to greener pastures (see Example 4). In practice, because it takes some time for a subpublisher to gear up and get the registration and collection moving along and into the pipeline, it is extremely rare to find any of these agreements having a term of less than 3 years. In fact, most foreign performance societies will reject any subpublishing agreements for their territories that are less than 3 years, and some will not allow member publishers to enter into agreements in their territories unless the minimum period is 5 years.

With the proper ammunition, a domestic publisher is usually able to obtain an advance from a foreign subpublisher in return for giving the subpublisher the right to publish the compositions in the applicable territory. Upon the expiration of the term of the agreement, the domestic publisher is in a position to negotiate a new agreement, either with the same subpublisher or a new subpublisher, and with the new agreement, another advance is likely to come galumphing along. Accordingly, the length of the term is important if for no other reason than that each separate agreement is a possible source of cash. Of course, it may also be important to have a limited term so that you can allow the agreement to expire if your present subpublisher just isn't doing the job. Or, perhaps, on a more Machiavellian level, you previously received a substantial advance from your present subpublisher which has yet to be recouped from your share of royalties and now the opportunity arises to move to a different subpublisher for a fresh start and a new pot of advance monies.

SAMPLE CONTRACT PROVISIONS

EXAMPLE 1: Term of 5 Years or Expiration of Rights

1. TERM OF AGREEMENT: The term of this Agreement shall be for an initial period of five (5) years from the date hereof; provided, however, that in the case of individual Compositions for

which Publisher's rights expire prior to the expiration of this Agreement, the term for such individual Compositions shall expire coterminously with such expiration.

☞ For compositions which revert to other publishers during the term, the rights to subpublish revert also.

EXAMPLE 2: 5-Year Term

2. The term of this Agreement shall be five (5) years, commencing upon the date hereof. During this period, Sub-Publisher shall serve as the exclusive publisher of the Compositions in the Territory.

EXAMPLE 3: 3-Year Term; Option for Second 3-Year Term on Payment of Additional Advance

1. *Term of Agreement*: The term of this Agreement shall be for an initial period of three (3) years commencing January 1, _____. Subpublisher shall have an option for one (1) additional three (3) year period which, if exercised as provided for below, shall commence upon the expiration of the initial period; provided, however, that Sub-Publisher may not exercise said option unless, concurrently with such exercise, Sub-Publisher pays to Publisher, as an advance, the greater of either Twenty-Five Thousand Dollars ($25,000) or a sum equal to Fifty (50%) Percent of Publisher's earnings hereunder during the initial period of this Agreement.

☞ Note that the advance necessary to trigger the option period in this agreement might be hefty indeed, as it is the *greater* of $25,000 or a sum equal to 50% of the publisher's earnings during the initial term.

EXAMPLE 4: 6-Month Extension for Recoupment

6. Sub-Publisher shall pay to Publisher an advance in the sum of Fifty Thousand ($50,000) United States Dollars. The advance shall be recoupable from Publisher's earnings hereunder. If the advance provided for hereunder is not recouped upon the expiration or other termination of this Agreement, the Term of this Agreement shall be extended until the earlier of such recoupment or six (6) months.

☞ If the $50,000 advance has not been recouped prior to expiration, the period of this agreement may be extended up to 6 months past the contract expiration date, giving the subpublisher a maximum of an extra 6 months to recoup the advance. Thereafter, the publisher is free to sign a new agreement with the subpublisher or any other potential subpublisher and, perhaps, collect another advance.

TERRITORY

Clearly, the designation of territory is extremely important in foreign subpublishing agreements. It is possible, for example, to sublicense the publishing for the entire world outside of the United States. In my opinion, the smart money position in most cases is to license on a territory-by-territory basis. Usually, the aggregate advances will be greater than the advance which would be obtained if worldwide rights were licensed. Also, of course, cross-collateralization can be avoided when agreements are made with nonaffiliated subpublishers in the various territories: no affiliation, no cross-collateralization.

EXAMPLE 1: Territory: U.K. and PRS Territories

2. TERRITORY: Sub-Administrator's rights hereto in and to each of the Compositions shall extend for the term of this Agreement throughout the area set forth in Exhibit "A," attached hereto and incorporated by reference (hereinafter referred to as the "Territory").

• • •

EXHIBIT "A": TERRITORY

As used herein, Territory shall be deemed to be: United Kingdom of Great Britain; Northern Ireland; Eire; and "PRS" territories.

☛ The Performing Rights Society (PRS) is the United Kingdom's (and a whole lot of what used to be the British Empire's) equivalent to ASCAP and BMI. Founded in 1914, the PRS administers, licenses, collects, and disburses revenue from the public performance of musical works.

EXAMPLE 2: Territory: Italy

4. Subpublisher's rights herein in and to the Compositions shall be for Italy only (hereinafter referred to as the "Territory"). All rights in and to the Compositions outside of the Territory shall remain the sole property of Publisher.

EXAMPLE 3: Territory: France and Belgium

(a) Company shall publish and administrate the copyrights and interests in the Compositions in all fields of use, on a sole and exclusive basis, in France and Belgium only ("Territory").

ADVANCES

As mentioned above, it is very likely that, given a moderate level of commercial importance or a significant number of copyrights, the foreign subpublisher will advance money for the right to represent the copyrights in the applicable territory (see Example 2). The advances are recouped out of the licensor's share of the income from the exploitation of the copyrights and the resulting collection of funds in the territory. The publisher's share, depending upon the agreement, may be based either on gross receipts or on net receipts (see Example 3 and the following section, "Fees"). The net share will be determined by taking the gross receipts and deducting applicable (or allowable) costs and the subpublisher's share of the income.

Advances in foreign subpublishing agreements (if there are to be advances), unlike advances in recording agreements, are most likely to be signing advances; that is, they are tied into the signing of the agreement. Of course, in such cases "finished product" (specified songs or an entire catalogue) is usually being delivered to the subpublisher, and it may be possible to have additional advances payable upon the exercise of options for subsequent periods. If one is fortunate (or sly) enough, there is the possibility of having what might be termed a *rolling advance*. This is an advance that is automatically replaced when it is recouped. (See Example 1 for an illustration of a rolling-advance provision.)

Example

The publisher receives a $25,000 advance from the supublisher under an agreement that calls for a rolling advance. In the first accounting period, $15,000 is recouped. In the second accounting period, the publisher's earnings are an additional $15,000. Having earned back the $25,000 advance, plus an additional $5,000, the publisher is now paid $5,000 as a royalty plus an additional $25,000 to renew the rolling advance.

SAMPLE CONTRACT PROVISIONS

EXAMPLE 1: Rolling Advance

6. *Advance.* Sub-Publisher shall pay to Publisher advances in the sum and manner as set forth in Exhibit B, attached hereto and incorporated by reference. Said advances shall be recoupable, but non-returnable, from Publishers share of Gross Receipts, as provided for above. Upon recoupment of each advance hereunder, a new advance of an equal sum shall accompany the statement indicating such recoupment; provided, however, that no additional advance will be due after the expiration date of this Agreement, subject to the provisions of the next sentence in this Paragraph 6. In the event that any such advance is unrecouped upon expiration or other termination of this Agreement, this Agreement shall be extended until the earlier of such recoupment or six (6) months.

☞ Note that this provision extends the term of the agreement by as much as 6 months if the advance has not been recouped by the end of the initial period. Many rolling-advance provisions include language terminating the automatic advance before the expiration of the agreement, frequently 6 months, sometimes more.

EXAMPLE 2: Signing Advance

2. During the term hereof, Sub-Publisher shall have the sole and exclusive right to administer and protect the Compositions in the Territory on behalf of Publisher. Concurrently with the execution of this Agreement, Sub-Publisher shall pay Publisher the sum of Ten Thousand ($10,000 US) United States Dollars as an advance against Publishers share of income hereunder.

EXAMPLE 3: Waiving New Advance Upon Recoupment Lowers Subpublisher's Fee

6. ADVANCE: Sub-Administrator shall pay to Publisher advances in the sum and manner as set forth in Exhibit "B," attached hereto and incorporated by reference. Said advances shall be recoupable, but non-returnable, from Publisher's share of Gross Receipts, as provided for above.

Upon recoupment of each advance hereunder, Publisher shall have the option to:

(a) Either require a new advance of an equal sum, which shall be paid within thirty (30) days of Publisher's notice to Sub-Administrator of Publisher's election; provided, however, that no additional advance will be due after the expiration date of this Agreement and that, in the event that any such advance is unrecouped upon expiration or other termination of this Agreement, this Agreement shall be extended until the earlier of such recoupment or six (6) months; provided, however, if Publisher requests a new advance at any time during the second or third year of this Agreement, this Agreement shall automatically be extended an additional two years on the same terms and conditions contained herein and the compensation to Sub-Administrator shall remain Twenty (20%) Percent.

(b) Or, Publisher may elect to forgo the new advance and, in which, case, the compensation to Sub-Administrator on distributions thereafter, notwithstanding the provisions of Paragraph 5, above, shall be Fifteen (15%) Percent.

(c) Upon receipt of any statement indicating that the then current advance has been recouped, Publisher shall have thirty (30) days within which to give Sub-Administrator written notice of Publisher's election of either (a) or (b), above.

> ☛ This is an optional rolling advance. The agreement starts with an advance. Upon recoupment of the advance, the publisher has the choice of either taking a new advance or waiving the advance. Taking the advance during the second or third years of the agreement will automatically extend the agreement another 2 years. Accepting additional advances also leaves the subpublisher's fee at 20%, while waiving the advance reduces the fee to 15%.

FEES

How is the money split between the publisher and the subpublisher? In practice, the fees retained by the subpublisher under subpublishing agreements will, in most cases, be about the same as the fees retained by the administrator in administration agreements. Depending, as always, upon the relevant negotiating positions of the parties, the subpublisher's share of the income usually ranges from 15% to 25%, although recently the percentage has been edging toward the higher end of the range and even beyond.

There is one circumstance, however, in which the foreign subpublisher's share of the income is likely to increase well beyond 25%. If there is a cover record done in the territory, especially one done in the language (other than English) spoken in that particular locale, the subpublisher's share of the income—either from the cover recording only or, perhaps, from any recording of the composition—may increase to 50% (see Example 4).

SAMPLE CONTRACT PROVISIONS

EXAMPLE 1: 20% of Gross Receipts

5. COMPENSATION: In compensation for the services performed by Sub-Publisher hereunder, Sub-Publisher shall retain Twenty (20%) Percent of One Hundred (100%) Percent of all Gross Receipts collected from all sources and shall remit the remaining Eighty (80%) Percent to Publisher.

(a) Statements setting forth the monies received by Sub-Publisher in respect of the Compositions, the deductions therefrom and the monies payable by Sub-Publisher to Publisher hereunder shall be sent by Sub-Publisher to Publisher quarterly within fifteen (15) days after the end of each quarterly calendar period. Statements shall be accompanied by payments by Sub-Publisher to Publisher of all monies actually received by Sub-Publisher on behalf of Publisher under the terms of this Agreement during the period covered by such statement, deducting therefrom the payments or deductions permitted by this Agreement. At Publisher's request Sub-Publisher shall provide Publisher with copies of local Society statements and reports as submitted to Sub-Publisher.

(b) Publisher or a designee in its behalf and at its sole cost and expense may, at reasonable intervals, examine the books of Sub-Publisher pertaining to the Compositions during Sub-Publisher's usual business hours and upon receipt of thirty (30) days' advance written notice.

> ☛ It is important to understand the difference between agreements in which the domestic publisher's share is based on gross receipts (Examples 1 and 2) and those in which the

domestic publisher's share is based upon net receipts (Example 3). In agreements based on gross receipts, which are relatively common, the costs are borne by the foreign subpublisher, that is, subtracted from the fee. Agreements that specify that the foreign subpublisher's fee will be a percentage of net receipts must have provisions dealing with how costs and expenses are to be recouped.

EXAMPLE 2: 25% of Gross Receipts

6. Subpublisher shall retain Twenty-Five (25%) Percent of One Hundred (100%) Percent of all Gross Receipts collected from all sources in the Territory and shall remit the remaining Seventy-Five (75%) Percent to Publisher.

EXAMPLE 3: 20% of Net Publisher's Share

5. Company shall retain from the net publisher's share actually received by Company in Italy and Greece during the Term on account of the Compositions a fee of Twenty (20%) Percent. . . .

EXAMPLE 4: Subpublisher's Share 50% for Cover Records

(a) Sub-Publisher's share of gross receipts shall be twenty (20%) percent, which share shall be retained by Sub-Publisher for its own account, provided, however, that said fee shall be increased to fifty (50%) percent with respect to all income (including, without limitation, mechanical royalties and public performance fees) earned from the exploitation of a cover record of the Composition (the term "cover record" being defined as any recording of a Composition in French originally recorded in the Territory and not in existence prior to the term hereof);

> ☛ A cover record is a cover record whether it is in English, French, or Swahili. The increased fee is probably immaterial if limited just to the cover record, as in this example. Where there is potential grief for a domestic publisher is the situation in which the cover record causes the fee to go to the higher level for *all* recordings of the composition—including the original version which was covered.

COSTS

In both copublishing agreements and administration agreements there is always a provision or provisions dealing with the recoupment of costs and expenses connected with the exploitation of the compositions. This is not necessarily so in foreign subpublishing agreements, many of which more closely resemble agreements for the foreign distribution of recordings in that most, if not all, costs are assumed by the foreign company and are not borne by or paid by the domestic company. Some subpublishing agreements do provide for the recoupment of costs from the domestic publisher's share of income or for the costs to be deducted prior to the computation of the relative shares of the parties. Agreements that refer to the publisher's share being based upon gross receipts, gross income, or the like are agreements where the expenses are not being charged back to the domestic publisher. Conversely, those foreign subpublishing agreements that refer to net receipts, net income, and such usually have provisions dealing with the recoupment of costs.

Examples 1 and 2 below illustrate these two methods of paying costs and expenses incurred in the subpublishing, or administration, if you will, of the copyrights in the specified territory. Example 1 is based on gross receipts. The formula is simple. The fee split is 75%–25%. For each 100 French francs that are collected, 25 are retained by the subpublisher and (the dollar equivalent of) 75 French francs are paid to the copyright owner. All costs and expenses come out of the subpublisher's fee. Example 2 is based on net income. The expenses *and* the subpublisher's 20% fee are taken off the top. So, if expenses are 10 francs per 100 francs, 10 francs for expenses plus 20 francs for the subpublisher's fee are taken off the top, leaving 70 francs for the domestic publisher. Obviously, if the percentage taken as a fee is the same, a subpublishing agreement based on gross receipts is better for the copyright owner than one based on net receipts.

SAMPLE CONTRACT PROVISIONS

EXAMPLE 1: Gross Receipts
6. Subpublisher shall retain Twenty-Five (25%) Percent of One Hundred (100%) Percent of all Gross Receipts collected from all sources in the Territory and shall remit the remaining Seventy-Five (75%) Percent to Publisher.

EXAMPLE 2: Net Income
3. Subpublisher shall pay to Owner the Net Income actually received from the exploitation of the Compositions. "Net Income" is defined as the gross receipts from the exploitation of the Compositions in the Territory including the publisher's share of public performance fees paid by the applicable performing rights society, less the costs specified below and Subpublisher's share of Twenty (20%) Percent of the Gross Receipts.

PAYMENT

> *When choosing between two evils*
> *I like to try the one I've never tried before.*
> —MAE WEST

When negotiating subpublishing agreements, careful attention should be paid to language dealing with the mechanics of payment. Many complex issues are involved, such as currency exchange rates, blocked funds, method of payment, etc., and care should be taken to provide for contingencies. As you make your way through the examples, consider the following possibilities.

1. The currency exchange rate in Country A fluctuates wildly during a 1-week period, from 10% higher than the norm to 10% lower. Which day and exchange rate applies for the conversion into dollars?

2. The subpublisher's territory is 15 different countries, 5 of which have blocked funds laws which do not allow money to be transferred out of the country. What happens to the royalties from these countries?

3. If money is not wired into the domestic subpublisher's account, and instead payment is made by mail, what happens when a check that has supposedly been mailed is delayed for weeks?

SAMPLE CONTRACT PROVISIONS

EXAMPLE 1: "Payment" Defined
7. PAYMENT: With regard to Publisher's compensation, as provided for above:

(a) As used herein, the words "payment," "pay," "payable," "paid" or words of similar meaning when applied to obligations of Sub-Publisher to Publisher mean the actual receipt by Publisher by the date payment was to have been made in the amount and currency specified herein or by Publisher of a bank transfer of funds to Publisher's account unencumbered and immediately withdrawable.

(b) Sub-Publisher shall timely obtain all governmental permits necessary to make all payments to Publisher as and when required under this Agreement, including advances.

(c) Unless specified otherwise, the following currency conversion provisions shall apply:

(1) Any amounts payable under this Agreement, regardless of the currency of the Territory, shall be paid in United States dollars, unless Publisher specifies otherwise. Sub-Publisher shall make whatever currency conversion is necessary to make such payments, and all costs of currency conversions including, without limitation, banking charges, permit fees, and transmittal costs, shall be borne solely by Sub-Publisher and shall not reduce any amounts due Publisher in such bank or other depository as may be designated by Publisher, or promptly pay such funds to such persons or entities as Publisher may from time to time designate in writing.

(2) As to amounts payable to Publisher not expressed in a particular currency, Sub-Publisher shall convert such amounts from the currency in which they were originally earned directly into United States dollars, or such other currency as Publisher may specify, at the rate of exchange prevailing at the close of the accounting period for which Sub-Publisher was obligated to account to Publisher for such payments. If Sub-Publisher pays such amounts later than under this Agreement (whether voluntarily or as a result of an audit or otherwise), then the exchange rate used at the time of such later payment may not be less favorable to Publisher than if Sub-Publisher had paid when required.

8. BLOCKED FUNDS. In the event that Sub-Publisher shall be prohibited or restricted from making payment of any monies at the time when same are due and payable to Publisher hereunder by reason of the laws or currency regulations within the Territory, Sub-Publisher shall promptly so advise Publisher in writing. Sub-Publisher shall, upon Publisher's request, deposit any such blocked funds to the credit of Publisher in a bank or banks or other depository in the Territory designated in writing by Publisher, or pay them promptly to such persons or entities as Publisher may designate in writing.

☛ Both Examples 1 and 2 go into great detail over the mechanics of making the payment and then, almost as an afterthought, throw in "Oh, by the way, there's this rather rude possibility that we can't send you the money anyway. Terribly sorry. Blocked funds. Government, you know."

EXAMPLE 2: Payment Procedures

6. KEEPING OF RECORDS. In connection with the keeping of records, Subpublisher agrees to maintain true, accurate and complete books and records, in the currency or currencies of the Territory, of all of the Subpublisher's transactions in connection with the Compositions and the exercise of Rights Licensed herein.

(a) All accountings by Subpublisher shall be on a cash basis.

(b) For all purposes of this Agreement (including, but not limited to, accounting for royalties, Gross Receipts, payment and recoupment of the advance, submitting statements, keeping books and records and making any payments to Publisher hereunder) the Compositions shall be treated as separate and distinct from all other copyrights and songs licensed by Subpublisher.

7. STATEMENTS: AUDIT RIGHTS. With regard to statements hereunder:

(a) Sub-publisher agrees to furnish to Publisher quarterly, a detailed report regarding the earnings attributable to the Compositions in the Territory.

(1) Each report shall be in the English language and shall contain such information, reported in the local currency or currencies of the Territory, as is customary in the industry, including, without limitation, detailed cumulative and current periodic statements of the Gross Receipts, the permitted deductions therefrom, all other expenses (regardless of whether deductible) incurred in connection with the sales or license of the Compositions and any other information requested by Publisher.

(2) Each such report shall be furnished to Publisher within thirty (30) days after the close of the period for which such report is made.

(3) Subject to the provisions of Paragraph 9, below, Subpublisher shall currently with the delivery of each report pay to Publisher any sums to which it is entitled.

(4) All sums paid to Publisher pursuant to this Agreement shall be sent to the address specified above or to such other payee and/or address as Publisher may from time to time designate in writing.

8. PAYMENT, REMITTANCES, AND CURRENCY EXCHANGE

(a) As used herein, the words "payment," "pay," "payable," "paid" or words of similar meaning when applied to obligations of Subpublisher to Publisher mean the actual receipt by Publisher by the date payment was to have been made in the amount and currency specified herein or by Publisher of either:

(1) cash;

(2) a bank transfer of funds to Publisher's account unencumbered and immediately withdrawable;

(3) the unconditional clearance of a check or bank draft drawn on a United States bank; or

(4) the draw down by Publisher of a previously approved and existing Letter of Credit from a United States bank pursuant to the terms thereof.

Payment in any other manner shall not be deemed "paid" to Publisher until the proper amount and currency are actually received and available for expenditure by Publisher, and Subpublisher takes the risk that any transfer of funds (whether due to the method of transfer, failure to obtain necessary permits, or otherwise) will not be so received by Publisher within the time periods herein required for particular payments.

(b) Subpublisher shall timely obtain all governmental permits necessary to make all payments to Publisher as and when required under this Agreement, including the advance. Subpublisher shall also pay without limitation any tax, levy or charge, however denominated, imposed or levied by any jurisdiction in the Territory against Subpublisher, Publisher, or the Compositions (excluding only taxes based on Publisher's net income), including, without limitation, quotas, value added taxes, so-called "remittances" and similar taxes, licenses, contingents, turnover taxes, import permits and duties, and national, state, county, city or other taxes, however denominated, relating to or imposed upon the advance or any part thereof, any other amounts payable to Publisher, or other material, or the right or privilege to use the same in connection with the Compositions. It is the intent hereof that the advance and any other amounts payable to Publisher shall be net amounts, free and clear of any tax, levy or charge of whatsoever kind or nature however denominated, and if Subpublisher claims it is required to deduct any taxes or other sums from any such amounts, Subpublisher shall present the original government receipt showing the amount paid and deducted. Any tax, levy or other charge paid by Subpublisher pursuant to this Paragraph shall be deemed paid on Publisher's behalf and Publisher shall have the right to treat such payments for all purposes as payments made solely by Publisher. Subpublisher may, after presentation to Publisher of the original government receipt indicating that any of the foregoing taxes have been duly paid, recoup the same as an expense from subsequent sums payable to Publisher hereunder.

(c) Unless specified otherwise, the following currency conversion provisions shall apply:

(1) Any amounts payable under this Agreement, regardless of the currency of the Territory, shall be paid in United States dollars, unless Publisher specifies otherwise pursuant to Subparagraph 8(c)(5), below. Subpublisher shall make whatever currency conversion is necessary to make such payments, and all costs of currency conversions including, without limitation, banking charges, permit fees, and transmittal costs, shall be borne solely by the Subpublisher and shall not reduce any amounts due Publisher in such bank or other depository as may be designated by Publisher, or promptly pay such funds to such persons or entities as Publisher may from time to time designate in writing.

(2) With regard to the recoupment of the Advance (or any part or multiple of it), then, for the purpose of determining such recoupment, Subpublisher shall convert each payment made by Subpublisher on account of the Advance into the local currency of the Territory, using the exchange rate in effect at the time of such payment. If Subpublisher pays any part of the Advance later than when required under the Agreement, then the exchange rate used at the time of such later payment may not be less favorable to Publisher than if Subpublisher had paid when required.

(3) As to amounts payable to Publisher not expressed in a particular currency, Subpublisher shall convert such amounts from the currency in which they were originally earned directly into United States dollars, or such other currency as Publisher may specify pursuant to Subparagraph 8(c)(5), below, at the rate of exchange prevailing at the close of the accounting period for which Subpublisher was obligated to account to Publisher for such payments. If Subpublisher pays such amounts later than under this Agreement (whether voluntarily or as a result of an audit or otherwise), then the exchange rate used at the time of such later payment may not be less favorable to Publisher than if Subpublisher had paid when required.

(4) Whenever it is necessary to determine the exchange rate under this Paragraph 8, the applicable exchange rate shall be the exchange rate then prevailing at the Chase Manhattan Bank in New York City. Nothing contained in this Paragraph 8 regarding the exchange rate to be applied to a late payment will authorize such late payment, nor waive any right or remedy which Publisher may have as a result of such late payment.

(5) Publisher may, from time to time, designate any amount payable under this Agreement to be paid in the local currency of the Territory, or any other currency; in either case, all payments shall be made pursuant to this Paragraph 8, in such currency and at such depository as Publisher may have designated.

(d) Any sums payable to Publisher under this Agreement which are not paid when due shall bear interest from the due date until the date of payment at a rate per annum two (2%) percent higher than the prime rate charged from time to time by Chase Manhattan Bank in New York. The foregoing interest payment shall be in addition to any other rights Publisher may have hereunder or at law.

9. BLOCKED FUNDS. In the event that Subpublisher shall be prohibited or restricted from making payment of any monies at the time when same are due and payable to Publisher hereunder by reason of the laws or currency regulations within the Territory, Subpublisher shall promptly so advise Publisher in writing. Subpublisher shall, upon Publisher's request, deposit any such blocked funds to the credit of Publisher in a bank or banks or other depository in the Territory designated in writing by Publisher, or pay them promptly to such persons or entities as Publisher may designate in writing.

☛ That's an awful lot of words to move money from point A to point B.

DUTIES OF THE SUBPUBLISHER

The various duties of the foreign subpublisher are carried out to protect the interests of the copyright owner in the territory covered by the subpublishing agreement. Of course, part of protecting the interests includes collecting the monies earned. The foreign subpublisher, in effect, becomes the publisher's surrogate in the licensed territory. Note the word "surrogate." The subpublisher does not, and should not, own the copyrights. In fact, when entering into subpublishing agreements for foreign territories, it is extremely important *not* to assign the copyrights to the foreign subpublisher. The price to be paid for not following this advice can be steep and painful. (See the comment following Example 2.)

SAMPLE CONTRACT PROVISIONS

EXAMPLE 1: Subpublisher's Right to Administer

3. Sub-Publisher has the sole, and exclusive right in the Territory to administer and exploit the Compositions, to print, to publish, sell, dramatize, use and license any and all uses of the Compositions, to execute in its own name any and all licenses and agreements whatsoever affecting or respecting the Compositions, including but not limited to licenses for mechanical reproduction, public performance, dramatic uses, synchronization uses and to assign or license such rights to others. This statement of exclusive rights is only in clarification and amplification of the rights of Sub-Publisher and not in limitation thereof.

EXAMPLE 2: Subpublisher's Duties

3. The Sub-Publisher agrees to use its best efforts to exploit the Compositions hereunder.

(a) The Sub-Publisher shall have the sole and exclusive right throughout the Territory to grant licenses and/or to collect and receive all royalties, revenues, monies, income and all other compensation or advances accrued or paid with respect to the Licensed Usages; and

(b) In connection therewith, the Administrator shall have the exclusive right to adapt, arrange, revise, edit and translate the Compositions, and to provide or cause to be written new and original music therefor or lyrics therefor in any language, other than English, in current and general use in the Territory.

4. Publisher hereby constitutes and appoints Sub-Publisher its true and lawful agent and attorney in fact, to make, execute and deliver any and all documents, instruments and writings, in its name

and to take any other action in its name which in the reasonable judgment and discretion of the Publisher is necessary or desirable to carry out the purposes of this Agreement, including, without limitation, the following:

(a) To prepare, execute, file and register claims of copyright in the Compositions and, to the extent applicable, renewals, extensions and dispositions of termination or reversionary and extension rights of the same, in the name of Sub-Publisher as copyright proprietor.

(b) To collect royalties, monies and all other compensation or advances for Licensed Usages of each and all of the Compositions throughout the Territory heretofore accrued and unpaid and hereafter accruing during the term hereof, and to receive all accounting and royalty statements in connection with the foregoing; and to execute and deliver receipts for any and all such collections if necessary to do so.

(c) To endorse all checks and drafts received by the Sub-Publisher with respect to the Compositions for deposit only, and to deposit all such checks, drafts and other receipts in the account of Sub-Publisher.

(d) To collect all monies and payments arising from or in connection with settlement agreements of any kind or nature executed by Publisher and/or with respect to the Compositions, and to execute and deliver receipts for the same, and to endorse and deposit checks and drafts and all other receipts in connection with the foregoing in the said account of Sub-Publisher.

(e) Sub-Publisher shall furthermore have the incidental right, power and authority to execute any and all other or additional documents, instruments or other writings that may be necessary to carry out the foregoing acts, in the name of and for the benefit of Publisher.

☛ Subparagraph 4(a) provides that the compositions will be registered with the name of the subpublisher as the copyright owner in the territory, giving a literal meaning to the term "exploit the compositions." A domestic publisher should *never* allow a subpublisher, sublicensee, or administrator to register the copyright in its name. In some countries there are rights which remain with the first person filing the copyright which remain with the subpublisher even after the agreement has expired or been terminated. Compare this example with the next one, which specifies that the subpublisher will secure the copyright registration in the territory *in the name of the original or designated owner* (emphasis added).

EXAMPLE 3: Copyright to Remain in Publisher's Name

3. COPYRIGHT ADMINISTRATION: Sub-Publisher shall have the right to secure, in the name of the original or designated owner, and at Sub-Publisher's expense, the copyright registration, including any renewal registration, with respect to the Compositions under any law now in effect or hereafter enacted throughout the Territory.

(a) Sub-Publisher shall administrate the copyrights and interests in the Compositions in the fields of use itemized in Paragraph 4., below, on a sole and exclusive basis, throughout the Territory.

(b) The Sub-Publisher's rights and duties with respect to the administration of the Compositions, as hereinafter more particularly stated, shall extend and apply to any and all contracts and licenses heretofore made or issued by or on behalf of or for the benefit of Publisher and/or the owner of the Composition and hereafter made or issued by or on behalf of or for the benefit of Publisher or such owner, with respect to the Compositions and rights therein and proceeds therefrom in the fields of use set forth below throughout the Territory.

4. COLLECTIONS: Sub-Publisher shall have the sole and exclusive right throughout the Territory to collect and receive all royalties, revenues, monies, income and all other compensation or advances accrued or paid with respect to the Compositions, and/or appoint others to do so in the areas of use set forth below. The rights granted herein include the right to collect royalties, payments and settlements from or relating to:

(1) Mechanical licenses;

(2) Arrangement;

(3) Adaptation;

(4) Performing rights;

(5) Small performing rights;

(6) Performance rights;

(7) Print;

(8) Re-transmission; and

(9) Neighboring rights;

accruing heretofore or hereafter, including, but not limited to so-called "pipeline monies."

THE BLACK BOX AND OTHER EVIL COMPANIONS

I am not a crook.
—RICHARD MILHOUSE NIXON

We will now take time for a fairy tale of sorts. The value judgments implied, if any, should really be based upon how the particular parts of the story affect you. The bad guys can be good guys if you are able use them for your own purposes. The story begins after the end of World War II. The major music publishers from the various European nations—former friends and foes—met to discuss this brave new world they were about to enter and how to make the most of it. With admirable foresight, they decided that American music would be the next big thing.

"How," the question was posed, "are we to make the most of this?" And make the most of it they did. The rules and regulations dealing with the exploitation of music and, more importantly, the collection of the proceeds from such exploitation and, even more importantly, who got to keep the lion's share were established throughout Europe. And, my sweet innocents, who do you think got the benefit of these rules and regulations? I fervently hope that this far along in the book there is no confusion as to who was able to reap the benefits.

There were a number of different approaches to the task of writing the rules so that the foreign publisher would have the opportunity to, shall we say, legally appropriate monies that would otherwise have gone to the American publishers. The most creative—and dangerous—of these is what is known in most countries as the Black Box, the place where unclaimed publishing monies are placed until they are collected.

"Collected by whom?" you may ask. A very good question. The monies are collected by the owner of the copyright in that territory, as indicated on the local rolls (more on this below). Of course, if a song has not been filed with the local performing rights societies or somehow not put into the "collection machinery" or has been misidentified because no one bothered to cross-reference the English title with the title used in the local language (who knew that "Ciao Giuseppe" was "Hey Joe"?) or has fallen behind a file cabinet or any one of a thousand other mishaps, the monies collected in the territory for the exploitation of that song become what is known as "unallocated funds." And where do unallocated funds go? They are placed into the Black Box and, after a discreet passage of time of a year or two, divided up among—ta daaa!—those writers and publishers who are the members of that country's performance and performing rights societies. It goes without saying that the members of that country's performing rights societies do not include the American publisher and the American who wrote the song. And just how many of these performing and performance rights societies exist outside the United States?

How about well over 1,000. And guess what, Bunky? Some major territories have up to five or six different societies, each collecting—*and paying*—for different rights, so that one performance may trigger payments from each society.

Most American publishers would be amazed to learn this information—that is, if they believe it at all. There is a common misconception in this country that other countries operate the way we do, except that where we have ASCAP, BMI, and SESAC, the foreign countries usually have only one society. It is true that they usually have only one analogous to our performing rights societies, but they also have other societies—performing and performance—for purposes that do not exist in this country.

As always, the distinction between "performing" and "performance" is technical and confusing. The term *performance society* is used here in a generic sense to mean an organization which administers rights granted to its members pursuant to copyright laws and/or international conventions, and, in the process, collects and disburses revenue in connection with the exploitation of these rights. Some of the organizations are private; some are governmental or quasi-governmental. Some of them are national in scope, some are multinational in scope, and some may be said to be both national and multinational, such as, for example, GEMA and SACEM. (The organizations that are both national and multinational usually, at the multinational level, deal with same-language nations and/or former colonial states.) Some specifically perform activities not usually undertaken by performance societies, such as lobbying governments.

Most of these societies are conceptually similar to ASCAP and BMI, but many of them administer and collect for rights which do not exist here in the United States, such as broadcast mechanicals, royalties for theatrical performance of the work, royalties pursuant to the doctrine of neighboring rights (see Chapter 15, page 416), etc. In fact, considerable sums of money may be generated without the release of a recording. It should also be clear that without proper administration, much of the income generated outside of the United States through the collection of these royalties will wind up in the Black Box.

Example

A 30-minute cartoon incorporates an opening theme, a title song, a closing theme, and 15 minutes of background music. Following the cartoon is 2 minutes of advertising accompanied by the same background music. In France, the 15 minutes of background music would generate around $60,000 in royalties per televised episode and the music for the commercial would generate around $600 per airing.

Similar rules apply to other countries.

An important fee not collected in America that is collected in most foreign territories is the one paid for public performance, in movie theaters, of film soundtracks (the fee does not apply to video or television "performance").

Example

Film has a soundtrack controlled by Publisher. *Film* is distributed in Italy and has a theatrical release. In Italy, 10% of the box office gross is paid as a fee for the public performance of the soundtrack. *Film* does the equivalent of $1,000,000 at the box office. Publisher and composer receive $100,000 ($1,000,000 × 0.10 = $100,000).

I would like to emphasize we're talking *gross* here! (That's more than the biggest movie star in the world gets!) The distributor doesn't get paid on gross because the exhibitor takes his share and costs (which include the public performance fee) off the top. The distributor in turn takes his share and costs from this amount and (presumably) remits the adjusted amount to the producer, who, in turn, takes his share and costs from this adjusted amount before sharing with anyone else.

To make it even better, this share of box office gross is collected for the publisher by the government! That's like having the IRS do collection work for you. In Italy, when you go to see a film, your ticket stub isn't a receipt for admission, it's a receipt for your use of the music. I hope you are getting an idea of the amount of money that can be earned by music in the territories outside of the United States.

Now back to the American publishers' problem when it comes to sharing in this largess. First of all, if the foreign subpublisher has managed to get itself named as the copyright owner in the territory (a very, very unsatisfactory arrangement from the domestic publisher's point of view, as discussed above), the subpublisher will be able to collect all the monies for the exploitation of the copyrights. Now, there are some foreign publishers who feel that what the American publishers don't know won't hurt them. Why confuse them?

As for the monies that flow into the Black Box, if the American publisher has had the copyright registered in its name in the territory and makes the claim for them, the money *can* be collected. Indeed, with proper police work and paperwork, in most jurisdictions a publisher and/or writer can recapture black box funds retroactively. How far back you can go varies by society and circumstance. In most instances you can go back 3 to 5 years. Ultimately, the real villains in the piece are the U.S. publishers, songwriters, producers, record companies, film producers, and, dare I say it, entertainment attorneys who are ignorant of the potential in the foreign markets and how the rules and regulations work. For years, and to this day (whatever day this is), many, if not most, Americans dismiss the foreign market as relatively unimportant or too hard to collect from.

It doesn't have to be.

CHAPTER 13

MERCHANDISING

I can make what merchandise I will.
—WILLIAM SHAKESPEARE
The Merchant Of Venice, Act III, Scene 1

As discussed in Chapter 3, *merchandising rights* refer to a company's right to market a person, a group, a thing, a concept, or whatever for commercial gain. Also usually included under merchandising are commercial tie-ins, where the licensed property is somehow linked to a product. For a successful artist, merchandising, along with publishing and live performance, is part of the triumvirate of potential cash cows, producers of *real* money that comes right to the artist, free from the gravitational pull of record companies attempting to recoup it—free, that is, if the recording artist has not signed away merchandising rights to the record company. In light of the potential in merchandising for generating vast sums of money, it is hoped that an artist, in signing with a record company, will take any reference to merchandising, express or otherwise, extremely seriously.

Merchandising can be a very important and *very large* source of income. For example, a successful artist may gross $100,000 in ticket sales for one evening's performance in a stadium setting; with the proper merchandising and marketing, income from the sale of products at the same concert may account for more than twice that amount.

Basically, merchandising deals with the creation and/or licensing of products which are somehow tied into a personality, a name, a logo, a song, a likeness, etc., which allows the products to have value in the marketplace. A licensed name and/or logo can be slapped on virtually anything—ballpoint pens, T-shirts, coffee mugs, posters, you name it.

This chapter deals with the issue of the artists themselves licensing merchandising rights to licensees who provide manufacturing and marketing and pay for the privilege.

TERM OF THE AGREEMENT

FORD:
. . . stand under the adoption of abominable terms,
—WILLIAM SHAKESPEARE
The Merry Wives of Windsor, Act II, Scene 2

Licensing agreements have varying lengths of time. The rights licensed may be for a period as short as one night (for example, the right to sell a particular poster or T-shirt at a single concert) or they may be "in perpetuity" (see Example 1 under "Merchandising" in Chapter 3, page 179). Some merchandising agreements are tied into and coterminous with other agreements, such as an artist's recording agreement, a production company's agreement with an artist and/or with the record company (see Example 1, below), or even a record company's distribution agreement with a distribution company (see Example 2, below.)

A merchandising license may be for a specified period with or without options for additional periods of time (see Example 3, below). Many agreements are for relatively long periods of time because it takes time and money to develop, market, and exploit a product. Frequently, the licensee who is creating a product around the licensed rights owns all rights to that product and just sticks the artist's name on it. Licensing agreements are not personal service contracts, so the California 7-year restriction (see Chapter 3, page 28) does not apply to them.

SAMPLE CONTRACT PROVISIONS

EXAMPLE 1: Term Coterminous with Production Company/Record Company Agreement

4. The period of this Agreement (the "Term") shall commence on the date of the Agreement between Company and Producer during which period Producer shall furnish the right to use Artist's name and likeness, as provided for herein, and shall terminate with the expiration or other termination of the Agreement between Producer and Company dated as of [a date different from the date of this Agreement].

☛ Note that even when a merchandising agreement is entered into after a recording agreement has commenced, it can still be coterminous with the recording agreement.

EXAMPLE 2: Term Coterminous with Distribution Agreement

2. TERM. The term of this Agreement (the "Term") shall commence on the date hereof and continue for a period of time which is coterminous with the Distribution Agreement entered into between [Distributor] and Company on even date herewith, subject to the provisions of paragraph 11 below.

• • •

11. Upon the expiration or other termination of this Agreement, [Distributor's Licensee] and its licensees shall have the non-exclusive right to continue to sell for a period of six (6) months following such expiration or termination, all Merchandise in [Distributor's Licensee's] possession, subject to [Distributor's Licensee's] continuing obligation to pay royalties thereon as set forth herein; provided, however, at the end of such six (6) month period, all Merchandise in [Distributor's Licensee] possession or control shall, at Company's option, either:

(a) Be shipped by [Distributor's Licensee] to Company at Company's expense; or

(b) be destroyed by [Distributor's Licensee] under the supervision of Company, or upon Company's written instructions be destroyed by [Distributor's Licensee] without such supervision, provided [Distributor's Licensee] furnishes owner with an affidavit of such fact signed by a principal officer of [Distributor's Licensee].

☛ This agreement is between the distributed label and a licensee of the distributor. The same form of contract would work equally well, with minor alterations, for an artist licensing directly to a merchandiser.

EXAMPLE 3: Stand-Alone Agreement; Initial Period of 3 Years with Options

1. TERM OF AGREEMENT: The term of this Agreement shall be for an initial period of three (3)

years from the date hereof. The extent of the rights granted hereunder is defined in the GENERAL TERMS AND CONDITIONS, attached hereto as Exhibit "A", and incorporated herein by reference. Representative agrees to use its best efforts consistent with Representative's best business judgment with respect to market conditions in each country within the Territory to exploit the market for the Properties in the Territory so as to insure the widest possible sale of the Properties in the Territory.

☛ This agreement, which involved use of an artist's name on clothing, had ongoing 1-year options after the initial period, exercisable only if either certain sales levels generated specified royalties in the prior period or the company actually made up the difference between actual sales and contractual levels with a cash payment. Such "made up" payments are nonrecoupable.

TERRITORY

> *Hello Kitty is an icon that doesn't stand for anything at all. Hello Kitty never has been, and never will be, anything. She's pure license; you can even get a Hello Kitty car! The branding thing is completely out of control, but it started as nothing and maintains its nothingness. It's not about the ego, and in that way it's very Japanese.*
>
> —Tom Sachs

As in all licensing agreements, the territory to which the rights apply is an issue which must be dealt with in some detail. The rights in merchandising agreements can be licensed on a worldwide (or universewide!) basis (see Examples 1 and 2) or on a territory-to-territory basis (see Example 3). Factors that affect the territory to be licensed are the type of product being licensed and the fame or notoriety of the licensor in the particular territory. In merchandising agreements, the virtues of licensing on a territory-to-territory basis are the same as in other agreements—the probability of a higher aggregate advance, avoiding cross-collateralization, etc.

With merchandising agreements, however, it is often the case that the licensee is the party owning and, indeed, possibly even creating, the product which is being sold while the licensor may be just attaching a name to this product. Under those circumstances, it may be very hard to avoid granting the rights on a worldwide basis. Although hard, it may not be impossible.

There are American stars who will not lend their name to a product in the United States, but who feel no compunction about doing so in another territory. This is quite common with products licensed in Japan.

SAMPLE CONTRACT PROVISIONS

EXAMPLE 1: Entire World

3. The rights granted to Licensee hereunder by Licensor shall be for the entire world (hereinafter referred to as the "Territory")....

EXAMPLE 2: Entire Universe

12. *Company's Rights.* Artist hereby grants to Company in perpetuity, throughout the universe, the following rights: ...

EXAMPLE 3: Limited Territory

2. TERRITORY. The Territory shall mean Germany, Austria and Switzerland as their political boundaries exist on the date of this Agreement, exclusive of non-contiguous colonies, possessions and similar non-contiguous areas, unless otherwise expressly stated in the Agreement. The Territory also does not include any foreign nations' military and other governmental installations geographically located within the Territory, nor foreign-based companies' oil rigs and other marine installations located within the Territory.

☛ Note the exclusions in the last sentence of this example. There are companies that cater exclusively to such "territories," which include, in addition to military post exchanges (PXs) and other government installations and marine installations, in-flight entertainment on airplanes.

EXAMPLE 4: United States and Canada Only

1. *Grant of Rights*. Company hereby grants to Merchandiser for the Term (as hereinafter defined) throughout the United States and Canada (the "Territory"), the exclusive right to manufacture, distribute, advertise and sell, and to authorize (subject to Company's prior written approval) third parties to manufacture, distribute, advertise and sell, through any and all means and methods [the Product]. . . .

RIGHTS LICENSED

The rights licensed may be the use of a name, likeness, sound, or whatever the fertile minds of marketing geniuses come up with. If attaching it to a product makes that product marketable, it can be merchandised.

SAMPLE CONTRACT PROVISIONS

EXAMPLE 1: Clothing

7. RIGHTS LICENSED: Artist hereby grants to Licensee, and Licensee hereby accepts from Artist for the term of this Agreement for the Territory only, the exclusive right to use Artist's name (hereinafter referred to as the "Name") for the purpose of exploitation in connection with clothing articles, during the term of this Agreement (hereinafter referred to as the "Rights Licensed").

• • •

(b) Notwithstanding anything to the contrary contained herein, or in Exhibit "C", the following rights are expressly excluded from the Rights Licensed hereunder:

    (1) Sweaters;

    (2) Scarves; and

    (3) Commercial tie-ins, as that term is generally understood;

☛ *Commercial tie-ins* are generally understood to mean linking the artist's name to a specific commercial brand which would imply an endorsement of that product. If the artist *is* the "product," it is not a commercial tie-in.

EXAMPLE 2: Perfume

1. Licensor grants to Licensee the sole and exclusive right to use Licensor's name, likeness and signature in the Territory (as hereinafter defined) only for the purpose of creating, manufacturing,

marketing, selling and otherwise exploitation in connection with perfumes (hereinafter referred to as the "Product").

EXAMPLE 3: Video Games

2. The rights licensed herein to Company from Artist shall be the right to use Artist's name and likeness (the "Rights") in connection with video games (hereinafter referred to as the "Games") and the creation of an animated character based upon Artist for use only in connection with the Games.

EXAMPLE 4: Just About Everything

5. Company hereby grants to Licensee for the Term throughout the world (the "Territory"), the exclusive right to manufacture, distribute, advertise and sell, and to authorize third parties to manufacture, distribute, advertise and sell, through any and all means and methods, whether now or hereafter known, including, but not limited to, wholesale, retail, mail order, premiums and at live performances, all types of products and merchandise, whether now or hereafter known, including, but not limited to, T-shirts, sweatshirts, hats, buttons, posters and books (collectively "Merchandise"), embodying (a) the name, photographs or likeness of, or biographical material concerning any artist which enters into an exclusive recording agreement with Company during the term of this Agreement ("Artist"), (b) any words or symbols which identify Artist or (c) any trademarks, trade names, service marks or similar properties relating to Artist, including artworks prepared by or for Licensee in connection with the sale of audio recordings containing Artist's performances (collectively the "Property").

> ☛ The language "through any and all means and methods, whether now or hereafter known, including, but not limited to, wholesale, retail, mail order, premiums and at live performances" is about as inclusive as it gets. The inclusion of "live performances" means that the licensee, not the label (the Company) or the artist, controls sale of posters, etc., at concerts. The label (the Company) needs to tie up all these rights exclusively when signing *any* artist in order to not be in breach of the agreement.

ROYALTY

The royalty which will be paid to the licensor for the license of merchandising rights depends upon several factors, including, but not limited to, the following: the value of the rights being licensed (i.e., how important and famous is the artist?); the territory (is it local or worldwide?); the scope of the license (is it for one individual product or a whole family of products?); the length of time for the license to run; the type of product; etc.

In those instances where the artist has granted the merchandising rights to another party (for example, a record company) who will, in effect, act as the middleman, the merchandising royalty coming to the artist will be a share, usually 50%, of the royalty received by the other party from third parties (see Example 1). As stated in Chapter 3, it is certainly to the artist's benefit to deal directly with the licensee rather than through a middleman. The royalty, whether payable directly to the artist or to the middleman to be shared with the artist, will vary depending on the factors listed above. Generally, however, the royalty payable by the licensee will range from 1% to 50%. Sometimes the royalty is not expressed as a percentage but as a specified rate per unit (e.g., $1 per unit sold) or a flat rate (e.g., $10,000 per year). There may also be barter arrangements (e.g., a free automobile).

EXAMPLE 1: 50% of Net Monies

(b) In connection with the exploitation by Company of the rights granted in this Paragraph 9, and in addition to any other amounts payable to Artist hereunder, Company will pay Artist an amount, if and when received by Company, equal to Fifty Percent (50%) of the net monies received by Company from persons licensed by Company to exercise any of the merchandising rights. If Company engages directly in the merchandising of such products, other than through a licensee, Company shall pay Artist Fifty Percent (50%) of all monies received by or credited to Company from such exploitation, after deducting Company's actual out-of-pocket costs incurred directly in relation thereto.

EXAMPLE 2: 50% of Net Receipts

(a) An amount equal to fifty (50%) percent of all Net Receipts hereunder. As used in this Agreement, "Net Receipts" means all gross receipts, royalties, fees and other monies actually received by or credited to Company from sales of Merchandise derived from the Property less (i) all costs incurred in the manufacture, distribution, marketing, sale, licensing and exploitation of such Merchandise, including but not limited to all transportation, shipping, postage, fulfillment and handling charges, (ii) all applicable commissions, taxes and duties, and (iii) all other expenses directly or indirectly related to the exploitation of such Merchandise including a fifteen percent (15%) contribution towards Company's overhead,

☞ Note the 15% "contribution towards Company's overhead." Welcome to the world where you get to contribute to the costs of water, power, telephone, paper, and executive bonuses.

EXAMPLE 3: 35% of Net Income

4. Licensor agrees to pay to Artist thirty-five (35%) percent of the Net Income derived by Company from the merchandising and exploitation of Licensor's name and likeness in connection with the Licensed Product. For purposes of this Agreement, the term "Net Income" shall mean the gross income actually received by Company which is derived directly from such use of Licensor's name and likeness in connection with the Licensed Product less direct expenses actually incurred by Company, including but not limited to:

(1) costs of collection,

(2) commissions and/or royalties payable to any third parties,

(3) manufacturing costs,

(4) costs of packing, shipping, postage, insurance, and

(5) advertising and promotion expenses.

EXAMPLE 4: 20% of Gross Receipts

4. COMPENSATION: In compensation for the Rights granted to Licensee hereunder, Licensee shall pay Licensor a royalty equal to Twenty (20%) Percent of One Hundred (100%) Percent of all Gross Receipts collected from all such sources. "Gross Receipts" shall mean the aggregate of all gross monies of every kind (including, without limitation, all sums invoiced to purchasers and other licensees, any awards, subsidies by governmental agencies or others, and any other allowances) derived or realized by Licensee or by its subsidiaries, licensees or assigns, from the lease, license, rental, dealing in or distribution of the Properties and the exercise of any Rights Licensed to

Licensee under this Agreement, all without any deductions whatsoever; . . .

☞ Even though the percentage figure is lower in this example than in the first three examples (20% versus 50% and 35%), since the percentage is of gross rather than net receipts, the actual dollar amount would probably be higher.

ADVANCES

Advances? Do we have advances? Good lordy, we sure do! That is, if we are licensing directly and at arm's length—when a record company, for instance, takes the merchandising as its just due and licenses to itself, you can bet there will be no advance. As a general rule of thumb, when a potential licensee wants to negotiate a licensing agreement, the licensee is willing to pay an advance for the right. Presumably the merchandising rights under consideration involve a known factor, for example, a successful artist, rather than an unknown factor, for example a first-time artist who has just signed a recording agreement. Since there is a known factor, the element of risk is, presumably, reduced. Reduce the element of risk and what do you get? You betcha! Advances! With the right breaks and factors, advances can be astronomical.

SAMPLE CONTRACT PROVISIONS

EXAMPLE 1: Recoupable Advance
6. ADVANCE: Licensee shall pay to Licensor advances in the sum and manner as set forth in Exhibit "B", attached hereto and incorporated by reference. Said advances shall be recoupable, but non-returnable, from Licensor's share of Gross Receipts, as provided for above.

EXAMPLE 2: Signing Advance and Option Advances
5. In connection with the rights granted to Company herein, Company agrees to pay Licensor an advance of Two Hundred and Fifty Thousand ($250,000) Dollars against the royalty provided for below. If Company chooses to extend the term of this Agreement beyond the initial period provided for in Paragraph 1, above, for each option exercised by Company, Company shall pay to Licensor an additional advance in the sum of Two Hundred and Fifty Thousand ($250,000) Dollars or a sum equal to Fifty Percent (50%) of the royalties earned during the preceding period, whichever is greater.

☞ Each option, if exercised, comes with an advance. Each option advance has a "floor" of $250,000, but will go higher if 50% of the royalties for the prior period exceed $250,000. A later provision provides for a retroactive adjustment if 50% of royalties exceed $250,000 but are not reported prior to the option exercise. The icing on the cake here would be to have the "floor" in subsequent periods increase to match the highest amount paid in the previous period.

TRADEMARKS

YORK:
   . . . that's the golden mark I seek to hit.
                        —WILLIAM SHAKESPEARE
                        Henry 6, Part II, Act I, Scene 1

Inherent in any merchandising is the exploitation of a name and/or an image: a trademark. I might, for example, manufacture the best athletic shoes in the business, but I won't be able to stay in business and prosper unless I can attach some famous athlete's name to them. "Branding" (establishing the recognition value of a name or trademark) creates the intrinsic worth of the name or trademark, which in turn creates opportunities to merchandise products using the name or trademark. A trademark may be a word or words and/or a logo (a graphic design).

Because the potential value of a name or trademark is huge, steps should be taken to protect them. The best protection is to register the trademark or name. When a trademark or name becomes so well known that when the name or trademark is mentioned or seen, the public associates that name or trademark with only *one* entity, the name or mark has developed what is known as secondary meaning (see Chapter 3, page 169). Secondary-meaning status—what is sometimes referred to as a "common-law trademark"—does give the owner some protection. However, registering a trademark with the United States Patent and Trademark Office gives the owner several benefits the common-law owner does not have.

- It provides nationwide notice and evidence of the trademark owner's claim.

- It allows the owner to sue in the federal courts for infringements.

- It can be used as a basis for obtaining registration in foreign countries.

- It can be filed with U.S. Customs Service to block imports of unauthorized goods using the mark.

The notice of registration ® may only be used after the registration has been finalized—a process which can take a considerable amount of time—and any use of ® before that is against the law. It is, however, legal to use either TM (trademark) or SM (service mark) before the registration is final.

Note that in the context of protecting a trademark or name, the "name" here is probably a group name as opposed to an individual performer's name. Group names, when registered, are generally granted a service mark rather than a registered trademark. A trademark identifies the object being sold or exploited (e.g., an automobile, soap, etc.) while a service mark is used for providers of services (e.g., an airline or a band).

In applying for trademark or service mark registration, the applicant must specify the "class" of the goods or services being registered. There are 45 separate classes of good and services. It is possible—and sometimes desirable—to register a mark in more than one class, but a separate registration fee is due for each class being registered. For those in the music industry, the classes of particular interest are:

- Class 9. Apparatus for recording, transmission, or reproduction of sound or images; magnetic data carriers, recording discs

- Class 15. Musical instruments

- Class 25. Clothing, footwear, headgear (let us not forget T-shirts and baseball caps sold at concerts)

- Class 41. Entertainment and cultural activities

Part of the requirement for registering a trademark or service mark is a declaration that the mark is either already "used in commerce" or that the registrant "intends to use the mark in commerce." Since the registration of trademarks and service marks is a federal matter, it is necessary to show that the marks have been, or will be, used in interstate commerce. (In theory, that means it's gotta cross over a state line somewhere, but there are enough exceptions that you don't have to worry about it.)

As noted elsewhere, the value of a trademark comes from what you make of it. The best damn name or logo in the world has very little value if the product it stands for isn't very good.

CHAPTER 14

SOUNDTRACKS

A film is—or should be—more like music than like fiction.
It should be a progression of moods and feelings. The theme,
what's behind the emotion, the meaning, all that comes later.
—STANLEY KUBRICK

Everybody in Hollywood knows their own job plus music.
—ALFRED NEWMAN

The first use of music with motion pictures had nothing to do with the artistic value of the music, the emotional impact on the audience, or enhancing the action on screen. The original function of the music was as "white noise": to cover the loud and annoying sound of the projector. Of course, it did not take long to realize that music accompanying films could have entertainment value of its own. (Arguably, with some soundtracks, we have come full circle.)

Before the advent of talkies, the precursor of soundtracks existed in connection with the exhibition of silent films. While the films may have been silent, the theaters were not. The smallest theaters had a piano playing along with the film. The large, fancy theaters had grand pipe organs and even full orchestras for some films.

In the smaller theaters, the piano player mostly improvised music and/or played existing selections that, in the player's judgment, fit the action on the screen. For the major releases, however, a score would be composed, and sheet music to accompany the film would be made available for the orchestra, string quartet, pipe organ, or lonely piano.

The release of *The Jazz Singer* changed all this. The talkie had arrived, and in that first talkie smash, Al Jolson not only talked, he also sang. More importantly, at least for our purposes, music became part of the film. Although the music and voices in *The Jazz Singer* were on discs, and therefore not technically a "soundtrack," the principle is the same, and music was now an integral part of filmmaking. Composers, serious and otherwise, began to make contributions to soundtracks.

With modern technology, many of today's composers are also the performing artists—and many film soundtracks are being created in home studios. I believe that if Mozart were alive today, he'd be cranking out soundtracks in his back bedroom and making piles of money.

The process of creating and exploiting soundtracks involves just about every aspect of the music industry, probably more so than any other field of endeavor in the music industry. There are composing, recording, publishing, performance, synchronization, mechanical, and print rights; video release; record release; theatrical release; and the list goes on and on—potentially encompassing virtually every area and issue related to the commercial exploitation of music.

Soundtrack music is generally classified into two groups: songs and scores. *Songs* can be title songs, opening credit songs, closing credit songs, songs performed on camera, songs coming out of radios and jukeboxes, etc. *Scores* are the background music, usually instrumental, used to create moods, enhance action, etc.—you know, the "tum-tee-tum-tee-tums" under car chases. Scores for television also include what are known as "bumpers," the music leading into and coming out of commercial breaks. There is also a third group, actually more of a subgroup, called *source music,* which may be either songs or scores (see pages 393–394). Source music is defined by how it is used, not the form of the music, and it is almost always a preexisting work.

Soundtracks are not, of course, limited to motion pictures. This discussion also relates to the creation and exploitation of music for television, video, laser discs, computer games, and CD-ROM interactive programs, not to mention music on chips inserted into toys. In any situation where there is a "visual" use (such as film, video, television, laser disc, etc.), be it for entertainment, for educational use, for commercial use, or whatever, there will probably be music "attached" to that visual in some manner. That usage requires permission and a license from the copyright owner of the music.

Various parties get directly involved in the process of adding "sound" to "sight": producers, directors, music supervisors, composers, performers, publishers, distributors (of films, television programs, videos, records, etc.), and the performing and performance rights societies. In this chapter the word *producer* is used to designate both record producers and film, television, etc., producers. It is one of the unfortunate linguistic challenges of the entertainment industry that the same title is used for two different jobs, and, accordingly, care must be taken to read any reference to "producer" in context. When I am referring only to film or television producers, I will use "film producer."

In most cases, the film producer of a project hires a music supervisor to gather the materials for the soundtrack—be it the creation of new songs and score, the licensing of existing songs and score, or a combination of new and old. The music supervisor discusses the project's needs with the film producer, and probably the director, and then proceeds to attempt to meet those needs. A composer is chosen and hired, and the film is then "spotted"—that is, decisions are made as to where music is to be inserted. It is not unusual for the composer to come into the game very late and to be up against extremely tight deadlines for composing and recording the score. After the spotting decisions have been made, the composer retires to whatever retreat or haven has been carved out and works like crazy with a video of the project (if the composer is lucky). The composer may perform the music electronically, and/or live musicians may perform it, with or without the composer's participation. Next, the music is integrated into the film or project by the music editor. Once the music is in the soundtrack and the project is released commercially, there are various income streams possible for the composer, publisher(s), etc.

The following discussion and examples give an overall look at the various issues, problems, and possibilities connected with the creation and exploitation of soundtracks for both film and television.

DUTIES OF THE MUSIC SUPERVISOR

> *When I was growing up, there were two things that were unpopular*
> *in my house. One was me, and the other was my guitar.*
>
> —BRUCE SPRINGSTEEN

It is the music supervisor's job to oversee the creation of the soundtrack, whether that involves composing and recording new music or licensing and acquiring preexisting music. The job requires a combination of creative and business talents and activities—from the creative decisions of selecting the best composer for the project through and beyond the business aspects of negotiating the deal, from the creative decisions of mood and placement of music to the actual recording of the music. Sometimes the music supervisor must also act as the producer of the recording sessions for the soundtrack and, if there is one, the soundtrack album for commercial release (see Example 2). In addition, the music supervisor is responsible for all administrative duties, such as applying for all necessary licenses, doing session reports, making payments to musicians, etc. In short, a music supervisor *supervises*.

SAMPLE CONTRACT PROVISIONS

EXAMPLE 1: Music Supervisor's Duties

WHEREAS, Supervisor provides music supervision for the creation, licensing and exploitation of music scores (hereinafter individually referred to as the "Score" and collectively as the "Scores") and/or sound recordings (hereinafter individually referred to as the "Recording" and collectively as the "Recordings") for use, individually and collectively, for soundtracks of motion pictures (hereinafter individually referred to as the "Soundtrack" and collectively as the "Soundtracks");

• • •

2. For the Film hereunder, Supervisor shall supervise all aspects of the creation and delivery of the Score and Soundtrack and perform all services customarily performed by music supervisors in the motion picture industry, including without limitation, obtaining all agreements with parties performing services, facilities and materials in connection therewith.

(a) Supervisor shall be responsible for payments to the composer of the Score (hereinafter referred to as the "Composer") and to all other parties entitled to compensation in connection with creation of the Score and Soundtrack from the Budget, as defined below.

(b) Notwithstanding the foregoing, Supervisor shall not be responsible for the compensation payable to the music editor for the Film, compensation and other costs in connection the music editor, music editing, magnetic transfers of items delivered hereunder, and other aspects of post production shall be the responsibility of Company.

(c) Composer shall be signed to a work for hire agreement in the form set forth as Exhibit B-1 or B-2, as appropriate, and incorporated herein by reference (hereinafter referred to as the "Composer's Agreement").

3. Supervisor shall be responsible for supplying the Composers for the creation of the Scores, musicians, engineers, etc., for the creation of the Recordings, and all materials in connection therewith, including, without limitation, cue sheets, etc. All persons, facilities and services contemplated by this Agreement shall be employed or engaged by Supervisor. All personnel shall sign W4 forms and INS forms. Creative personnel such as musicians, performers, etc., shall sign work for hire agreements in the form set forth as Exhibit C, attached hereto and incorporated herein by reference.

• • •

4. For each Film, Supervisor shall deliver the Delivery Elements set forth in Exhibit A on or before the Delivery Date specified in Exhibit A. Except as expressly set forth herein, Company shall own all results and proceeds hereunder and all items delivered hereunder, including, without limitation, all masters of Recordings, as works for hire under United States Copyright Law. Delivery shall be

accomplished at a place designated by Company; if such place is not in Los Angeles, the cost of delivery shall be borne by Company.

5. Company and Supervisor shall determine the budget (hereinafter referred to as the "Budget") for the Soundtrack of the Film, as specified in Exhibit A, and the Budget shall be disbursed to Supervisor pursuant to the Payment Schedule specified in Exhibit A.

☛ This example is a pretty good road map to the duties of the music supervisor in the creation, production, and delivery of the finished soundtrack. Don't be misled by the seemingly offhand reference to cue sheets. These very important documents provide information on the length, title, composers, and publishers of musical selections included on soundtracks of films, television programs, and other audiovisual media. Performing rights societies rely on cue sheets to determine royalties due for the public performances of the soundtracks. Also note subparagraph 2(c), which requires the composer (Exhibit B-1) or the company furnishing the composer's services (Exhibit B-2) to sign a work-for-hire agreement to make sure the compnay owns the copyright for the ensuing work.

EXAMPLE 2: Music Supervisor/Recording Session Producer

1. Engagement: Company engages Supervisor to produce and record master recordings embodying the compositions set forth on Schedule A attached hereto. Supervisor agrees to render such services to the best of Supervisor's ability at recording sessions conducted by Supervisor at times and places mutually designated by Company and Supervisor. Supervisor shall record and re-record each selection until a fully edited and equalized two-track stereophonic tape master, acceptable to Company as technically and commercially satisfactory for the production of Records, is made and delivered to Company. "Records" is defined as "phonorecords" is defined in the U.S. Copyright Act.

EXAMPLE 3: Composer as Music Supervisor

WHEREAS, Composer has the ability to create or acquire musical compositions (hereinafter individually and collectively referred to as the "Compositions") and so-called music videos (hereinafter individually and collectively referred to as the "Videos") for use as the soundtrack of and, in the case of the Videos, in, the Film (hereinafter individually and collectively referred to as the "Sound-track"); NOW, THEREFORE, in consideration of the mutual covenants, representations, warranties, agreements and obligations set forth herein, the parties hereto agree as follows:

1. Producer hereby engages Composer to provide Compositions, Videos and the Soundtrack for the Film. It is agreed that Composer will provide underscore, and a minimum of six (6) songs and Videos for the Film.

☛ In this agreement, the composer is, in effect, also serving as the music supervisor. This is not uncommon, especially for composers who are hired for smaller independent films.

DUTIES OF THE COMPOSER

It is difficult to produce a television documentary that is both incisive and probing when every twelve minutes one is interrupted by twelve dancing rabbits singing about toilet paper.

—Rod Serling

The soundtrack composer is usually an employee for hire, rather than a salaried employee, who is hired to create the score and, sometimes, songs for the soundtrack of a film, television show, etc. (For more information on work for hire, see below under "Employment Status," pages 357–377.) Composers serve under the direction and goodwill of the film producer and/or the director, usually through the offices of the music supervisor. They may also be hired to create soundtracks for any one of a number of different projects, such as interactive games, videos, etc.

The composer is chosen on the basis of artistic ability, style of music, availability, cost (remember after all, this is a business), and the composer's ability to deliver on time. As stated above, the composer is probably the last creative step brought into the production procedure and is frequently not hired until the last possible moment (or later). Those desiring to become successful soundtrack composers must be prepared to work extremely long hours and under extreme time pressures. If you can't take pressure, people yelling at you (with or without justification), and long hours, don't bother to apply for this position.

Frequently the soundtrack composer also is expected to act as, or at least perform the duties of, the music producer (see Examples 1, 2, and 3). Composers are commonly under contract to their own companies, which loan out, lend, or furnish the services of (FSO) the composer to the motion picture or television producer. (For more information on loan-out agreements, see pages 378–380.)

Some successful film and television composers subcontract portions of their work to other composers in order to meet their commitments. I was told a story by two composers who frequently work together as a team about an early experience with a famous composer. The composer had a weekly commitment to a 1-hour television show, and the duo had agreed to ghostwrite the music. Months would go by without ever seeing the composer, while every week one or the other of them would go by a vegetable stand in Palm Springs where the farmer would hand them a scrap of paper, sometimes the back of an envelope, with anywhere from five to ten bars written on it. This was the "theme" for the week. They would crank out the music for the week based on the theme and then wait for the following week's visit to the vegetable stand for the next week's work.

SAMPLE CONTRACT PROVISIONS

EXAMPLE 1: Score and Soundtrack

1. SERVICES: Company hereby engages Composer as a music composer in connection with the feature motion picture presently entitled "_____" (hereinafter referred to as the "Film").

(a) The period of employment shall commence on the date hereof and continue (unless Company elects to abandon the project earlier) until the date that Company and the producer of the Film (hereinafter referred to as the "Producer") approve the final music score for the Film, which shall contain background and incidental music, main and end title music, underscore, orchestrations, and arrangements (all hereinafter collectively referred to as the "Score"), as set forth below, and, as required and requested by Company, the recording of the recordings of the Score for the soundtrack (hereinafter referred to as the "Soundtrack") of the Film and for the possible release of a commercial recording of the Soundtrack (hereinafter referred to as the "Soundtrack Album").

(b) During the period of employment, Composer shall, on an exclusive basis, personally render all services customarily rendered by a music composer in the motion picture industry in connection with the creation of the Score and the Soundtrack, as requested by Company, including, but not limited to writing, composing, orchestrating, arranging, conducting, recording and adapting the Score. Composer shall, as requested, consult with Company, Producer and/or persons designated by Company or Producer, including, without limitation, the director and individual producer of the Film, at times and places reasonably specified regarding the Score and the Soundtrack.

(c) In connection with the Score and the Soundtrack, as requested, Composer shall prepare, or cause to be prepared, and deliver to Company orchestral scores of the Score, lead sheets, and cue sheets.

(d) If Composer shall be required to perform additional services hereunder after the initial scoring sessions as a result of any edits or other changes in the Film which occurred after the initial scoring, Composer shall perform such services pursuant to the terms and conditions of this Agreement. Notwithstanding anything to contrary contained herein, if Composer is required to create additional music and/or recordings for trailers for the Film after the initial scoring sessions, such services shall be pursuant to a separate agreement to be negotiated in good faith between Composer, Company and Producer.

(e) All of Composer's services hereunder, including the delivery of masters of the Soundtrack, except as otherwise expressly provided for herein, shall be completed on or before (hereinafter referred to as the "Delivery Date").

> ☛ In this agreement, the composer is both writing and recording the score. Until the finished score and recordings are delivered, the composer's services are exclusive to the film company. This exclusivity is usually not a problem for a composer, since normally the period is very short (usually too short!) and there is little time to work on another project anyway.

EXAMPLE 2: Length of Score

3. SERVICES: Composer shall provide the following services pursuant to the terms and conditions of this Agreement:

(a) Write, compose, arrange, orchestrate, prepare and submit to Producer, and, if requested by Producer, to collaborate with others in the writing, composition, orchestration, preparation and submission of music suitable for use as the complete background score for the Film.

(b) To record the Score in synchronized and timed relation with the Film.

(c) To provide Producer with cue sheets and other documentation connected with the Score.

• • •

(e) To deliver to Producer the master recording of the Score. As used herein, the term "deliver to Producer," or words of similar connotation, when used in connection with master recordings shall mean delivery to a studio or other facility designated or approved by Producer, of fully mixed, leadered, sequenced and equalized stereophonic master tapes, in configuration acceptable to Producer, synchronized and in timed relation to the Film, satisfactory to Producer, in proper form for the soundtrack of the Film; and delivery of all original session tapes and any derivatives, duplicates or reproductions thereof to Producer or any other location designated by Producer.

(f) The Score supplied to Producer shall be no less than Thirty (30) Minutes in length and no more than Fifty (50) Minutes in length.

> ☛ It is very common for these agreements to specify parameters for the length of the score. From the composer's point of view, it is wise to include as much music as possible on the soundtrack for (in this case) the film, inasmuch as performance royalties are based upon the amount (in minutes and seconds) of music contained in the soundtrack. For example, I have

a cowriter's share of an 8-second title theme for an animated cartoon and recently received a check for $35 for broadcast of the cartoon in Spain. Think about a 60-minute score for a film which is broadcast both domestically and in territories around the world—the potential earnings for the composer are considerable.

EXAMPLE 3: Score and Title Song

1. SERVICES: Composer shall render all services usually and customarily rendered by composers/conductors/orchestrators in the motion picture industry and as required by Producer. Such services shall include, without limiting,

(a) the composing, copying, arranging, conducting, contracting and production of original music for Producer's 23-minute [animated] Picture;

(b) the services of no more than six (6) musicians and a synthesizer player for a title song (which shall include up to three (3) versions for approval by Producer);

(c) an end title or other song which shall have appropriate versions and variations on the main title song for the different animals in the Program;

(d) underscoring for the Program; and

(e) up to three (3) demos of master (comparable) quality for the title song (all collectively "musical material").

☛ Service provisions like those in this example are somewhat unusual (though not unusual enough to raise eyebrows) in that the composer is to deliver both score and songs and, in addition, is to provide up to three demos. Most composers doing work for soundtracks do either scores or songs, but not both.

EXAMPLE 4: Composer and Record Producer

1. Services.

• • •

(b) Composer shall render all other services generally rendered by composers in the television industry, all of which may be rendered alone or in collaboration with others, as directed by Company and in a conscientious, professional and timely manner to the best of Composer's ability in accordance with Company's directions and instructions. Composer will provide the following:

1. Composition
2. Orchestration
3. Conducting
4. Musicians
5. Copying/Supplies
6. Cartage/Rentals
7. Recording Studio
8. Tapes
9. All Appropriate Fringes on Labor Charges.
10. A copy of the AFM Contract verifying that the appropriate fringes have been paid as well as a log reflecting the hours used in recording the synthesizer score.

In the event that Composer requests Company to handle the AFM payroll and fringe payments on his behalf, Company will do so and deduct these amounts from the $_____ fee.

☞ In this agreement, Composer is functioning as both composer and record producer and has been given a budget to cover all costs of creating and recording the score. Session costs of the musicians, including fringe benefits (e.g., payments to union pension and welfare funds) will, at the composer's request, be paid by the film producer, but the sums paid will be deducted from the composer's budget. The composer's fee for all this is the difference between the budget and the actual costs.

DUTIES OF THE FILM PRODUCER

There are provisions which companies sometimes "conveniently" leave out of soundtrack agreements. These provisions deal with what is normally the responsibility of the film producer and their absence should not only be noted but corrected by the composer when entering into the soundtrack agreement. Normally, these "producer responsibility" items are in the area of what might be referred to as postproduction matters—music editing, transfer costs, rescoring, etc.—or in connection with the acquisition of rights to source music—synchronization licenses, master use licenses, etc. Unless the composer has agreed for some reason ("if you don't somebody else will") to perform what are normally the producer's duties and/or have the costs come out of the composer's budget, the film producer's duties should be spelled out in the contract so that the composer will not get stuck with those costs. The composer's concern about costs charged to the composer's budget is a serious concern because in many instances the composer's fee is the difference between the actual cost and the composer's budget, and these additional costs can eat away any profit margin, which may constitute the sole cash fee to the composer.

Composers should be careful not to volunteer for, or be forced into agreeing to, things that will be detrimental to their position. For example, after-the-fact costs, such as a request to include additional music after the original delivery, if borne by the composer, will not only eat into the composer's net income, but may actually put the composer in the red on out-of-pocket costs for the project. I've seen this happen too many times to young composers trying to make a name for themselves working on an underfunded low-budget film.

SAMPLE CONTRACT PROVISIONS

EXAMPLE 1: Changes and Travel Expenses Film Producer's Responsibility

18. In the event of any changes in the Score and/or Recordings at any time after Composer has scored and recorded any Soundtrack hereunder on behalf of Producer, which are requested by Producer, all out-of-pocket costs to third parties other than Composer, except as expressly set forth herein, shall be borne by Producer. There will, however, be no additional charge to Producer for the services of Composer in connection with the Score or to Composer for services performed in connection with such changes.

• • •

(b) In the event the Budget does not include transportation, hotel, local transportation, living expenses, etc., and Producer shall require that Composer or any personnel travel outside of the Los Angeles area, such costs shall be borne by Producer.

☞ Here the producer is responsible for all additional costs of composing and recording that are necessary as a result of changes made in the film *after* the composer has delivered the score (e.g., different edits, new scenes shot).

EXAMPLE 2: Film Producer Responsible for Licenses

(b) Music Production elements hereunder include, but are not limited to, all recording costs incurred in connection with recording the score, recording studio, engineer and tape, musicians, contractors, cartage and rentals, copying and supplies, fringes and payroll taxes and processing fees. Producer and Lending Corporation agree that acoustic musicians shall be used to augment the electronic score, the number of musicians to be mutually agreed upon. Music Production elements do not include costs of Synchronization and Performance Licenses, Master Use Licenses, Music Supervisor, Music Editor, mag and transfer costs or AFM Special Payment Fund or re-use or new use fees. Notwithstanding the above, upon Producer's written approval, Producer will pay costs to third parties for pre-recorded music for playback on the set.

EXAMPLE 3: What Company Will Provide

(b) Company will provide the following:
1. Music Editor
2. Sync and Re-use fees of outside songs
3. Vocalist costs

EXAMPLE 4: What Costs Will Not Be Charged to Composer

(f) Notwithstanding anything to the contrary contained herein, the following costs shall be borne by Producer and shall not be charged to or against Composer hereunder:

(i) Mag stock and transfers, including transfers of any kind required for the Score and the Soundtrack in connection with the Show;

(ii) Licensing of music, if any, not composed by Composer hereunder;

(iii) Reuse, new use, supplemental market fees and other residual type payments generated under the American Federation of Musicians Basic Agreement;

(iv) As provided for in subparagraph 1.(d), above, re-scoring and/or re-recording required for creative reasons outside of the control of Composer after the delivery to and acceptance by Producer of the masters of the Soundtrack;

(v) Lyricist and vocalist related expenses unless furnished by Composer and/or Lender hereunder;

(vi) Sidelining, if any;

(vii) Pre-score, if any; and

(viii) Music editors.

☛ There are many composers out there who regret not having a provision like this in their contract.

EMPLOYMENT STATUS

The music supervisor, composer, recording artists, etc., will probably be employed by the film producer under a work-for-hire arrangement, making them employees for hire and making the film producer the legal "author" of any work created under that arrangement. Absolute ownership of all rights in and to the material created by the employee for hire is vested in the employer. With few exceptions, employees for hire are not eligible for any of the benefits available to people who are hired as permanent employees. All of the examples below are work-for-hire arrangements.

Most film contracts for "creative" parties (in addition to composers, these are screenwriters, directors, actors, designers, animators, etc.) include a waiver of "moral rights" (*droit moral*), a term which refers to the creator's broad right to maintain the integrity of his or her work even when the creator does not hold the copyright. In theory, the waiver of moral rights prevents the composer from legally being able to object to any changes and alterations to his or her score (see Example 4 and the section "Grant of Rights" below, pages 381–385, as well as Example 1 in that section).

SAMPLE CONTRACT PROVISIONS

EXAMPLE 1: Definition of Work for Hire

2. WORK MADE FOR HIRE: Company shall be the sole and exclusive owner of all the results and proceeds of Composer's services hereunder, including acts, poses, plays and appearances of Composer and all literary, dramatic and musical material, as well as inventions, designs and photographs, drawings, plans, specifications and sound recordings containing all or any part of any of the foregoing written, supplied or improvised by Composer, whether or not in writing.

(a) The foregoing shall constitute works prepared by Composer as an employee of Company within the scope of Composer's employment hereunder and, accordingly, the parties agree that each and all of the foregoing are and shall be considered "works for hire" for Company.

(b) Company is and shall be considered the author of said material for all purposes and the owner of all the rights comprised of the copyright in and to said material and any and all patents, trademarks and other rights thereto. Composer hereby grants to Company all rights which Composer may have in and to all such materials as Composer's general employer.

(c) It is the express intent of the parties hereto that the results and proceeds of Composer's services hereunder are created to be a work for hire as provided for in the Copyright Act which specifies:

"A 'work for hire' is—

(2) a work specially ordered or commissioned for use as a contribution to a collective work, as a part of a motion picture or other audiovisual work, as a translation, as a supplementary work, as a compilation, as an instructional text, as a test, as answer material for a test, or as an atlas, if the parties expressly agree in a written instrument signed by them that the work shall be considered a work made for hire." . . .

☛ It is very rare to find one of these contracts that does not provide that the composer is working under a work-for-hire arrangement. See the comment to the next example.

EXAMPLE 2: Copyright in Producer's Name

5. COPYRIGHT OWNERSHIP: Inasmuch as the Score is a work for hire, Producer shall have the right to secure, in the name of Producer, and at Producer's expense, the copyright registration, including any renewal registration, with respect to the Score under any law now in effect or hereafter enacted throughout the world.

☛ The employer here is a film company, the work for hire is the score, and the employee for hire is the composer. There needs to be no assignment of copyright from composer to company because the film company becomes the "author" of the score from the instant it is created. Because the score is a work for hire, the composer has no right of reversion of the copyright.

EXAMPLE 3: Loan-Out Work for Hire

(d) Lender and Composer hereby acknowledge and agree that Producer has specially ordered and commissioned the Materials as "works made for hire" as defined in the U.S. Copyright Act ("Act"), that the Materials are and shall be considered "works made for hire," and that the Materials are and shall be deemed to be the sole and exclusive property of Producer, who is and shall be deemed to be the sole author thereof. To the extent, if any, despite the intentions of the parties hereto, that the Materials are not considered "works made for hire" in accordance with the Act, Lender and Composer hereby irrevocably grant and assign to producer exclusively, perpetually and throughout the universe all ownership in all copyrights (including without limitation, the right to make derivative works) and all rights, title and interest of every kind whatsoever known or hereafter devised (including without limitation, in any and all media known or hereafter devised) in and to the Materials. Without limiting the foregoing, Lender and Composer shall have no right whatsoever in, or to exploit, the Materials.

EXAMPLE 4: Moral Rights—Certificate of Authorship

7. (a) Composer agrees that all musical material written or composed by Composer hereunder is a work made for hire and shall automatically become the property of Producer; and accordingly for this purpose Producer shall be deemed the author thereof. Producer as author shall own the copyright therein forever with the right to make such changes therein and such uses thereof including but limited to derivative works, as Producer may determine as author, and Composer hereby waives the "moral rights" of authors as said term is commonly understood throughout the world. Composer further agrees to execute, acknowledge and deliver to Producer in connection with all such musical material a certificate in substantially the following form:

CERTIFICATE OF AUTHORSHIP

I, the undersigned, hereby certify that I composed or will have composed (or collaborated in the composing of) the original numbers, parts and arrangements as more particularly set forth in Exhibit "A" attached and made a part hereof, as a "work-made-for-hire" (as such term is defined in the U.S. Copyright Act of 1976), for Company pursuant to an agreement between the undersigned and Company dated as of _____.

I hereby certify that the works separately composed by me were not copied or adapted from any other work, except as indicated thereon.

I hereby authorize and direct Company to insert in said Exhibit "A" the titles of said individual works, as such titles are determined by Company.

(Notarial Acknowledgment)

(Exhibit "A" attached)

☛ Certificates of authorship are generally part of film and television soundtrack agreements. Because of very detailed and precise delivery requirements of foreign film and television distributors, film and television companies usually demand more detailed documentation than do record companies.

LOAN-OUT AGREEMENTS

As noted above, many of the composer agreements for soundtracks are so-called *loan-out*, or *lender*, agreements, where the composer is, in fact, employed not by the film producer but by a corporation that furnishes the services of the composer to the film producer (see Examples 1 and 2).

These loan-out agreements are not unique to composers or soundtrack agreements. Indeed, our old friend the production agreement, with a production company signing the recording artist directly and then, in turn, providing the artist to a record company, is, in fact, a loan-out agreement. Loan-out agreements are used by many different professions in addition to that of composer—recording artists, record producers, actors, film and television directors and producers, writers, executives, doctors, and (yes) lawyers. One practical, though not technical, difference between a production agreement and a loan-out agreement is that the loan-out corporation is more likely than not to be owned by the *lendee* whereas the artist being furnished by the production company may or may not be the owner of the production company.

Basically, loan-out agreements exist for two reasons. First, having a loan-out corporation allows for flexibility in tax accounting and estate planning, with the most obvious advantage being that the producer is not required to withhold personal income tax for the loan-out corporation as it would for an individual. Second, loan-out agreements are a way to reduce liability risks. In simple terms, unless a plaintiff obtains a judgment "piercing the corporate veil" (that is, a judgment that holds that the corporation is a corporation in name only), the liability stops at the corporation and does not reach the individual. Conversely, unless *respondeat superior* can be proved, the assets of the corporation are be protected from the acts of the individual. (*Respondeat superior* is the legal principle that an employer is responsible for the illegal acts of his or her employee when those acts were carried out in the scope of the employee's duties for the employer.) Asset protection, presuming the assets are worth protecting, is very important. There are some rather complicated and expensive legal ways of protecting assets using several legal entities, both domestic and foreign. The use of loan-out agreements is a first simple step toward asset protection.

Note that with loan-out agreements, as with production agreements, the composer will have to sign an inducement letter in one form or another. (Example 4 is a lengthy inducement letter. Also see Chapter 3, pages 202–205, for more information on inducement.)

SAMPLE CONTRACT PROVISIONS

EXAMPLE 1: Lending Company Agrees to "Cause Composer to Comply"

5. SERVICES: Company [lending Composer] agrees to cause Composer to comply with all the requirements, directions and requests, and with all the rules and regulations made by Producer in connection with the regular conduct of its business; to render services during Composer's employment hereunder whenever and wherever and as often as Producer may require in a competent, conscientious and professional manner, and as instructed by Producer in all matters, including those involving artistic taste and judgment, but there shall be no obligation on producer to cause or allow Composer to render any services, or to produce, release, distribute, advertise or exploit any motion picture or to continue with any of the above once begun.

➡ Since Composer is the employee of the lending company and since the film company's agreement is with the lending company, the film company, at least in theory, cannot issue instructions to the Composer directly but must go through the lending company, which will then instruct the Composer accordingly. Of course, since almost all of these loan-out companies are owned by the composers, we have the delightful fiction of instructing the composer, as lender, to instruct himself or herself to perform.

EXAMPLE 2: Lending Company Agrees to Exclusivity

(b) During the period of employment, Lender shall furnish to Producer the exclusive services of Composer to personally render all services customarily rendered by a music composer in the motion picture industry in connection with the creation of the Score and the Soundtrack, as requested by Producer, including, but not limited to writing, composing, orchestrating, arranging, conducting, recording and adapting the Score. Composer shall, as requested, consult with Producer and/or persons designated by Producer, including, without limitation, the director and individual producer of the Film, at times and places reasonably specified regarding the Score and the Soundtrack.

EXAMPLE 3: Lender's Warranties and Representations

9. WARRANTIES AND REPRESENTATIONS: Lender represents, warrants and agrees that:

(a) Lender is free to enter into this Agreement and that neither Lender nor Composer is subject to any conflicting obligations or disability which will or might prevent Composer from, or interfere with, the execution and performance of this Agreement, or which will or might conflict with or impair the complete enjoyment of the rights granted to Producer hereunder;

(b) neither Lender nor Composer will employ any person to serve in any capacity, nor contract for the purchase or lease of any article or material, nor make any agreement committing Producer to pay any sum of money for any reason whatsoever in connection with the Film or for services to be rendered by Composer, or otherwise, without first obtaining the prior written approval of Producer;

(c) all material of Lender or Composer referred to herein will be wholly original with Composer or in the public domain throughout the universe, and neither the Film nor any part thereof shall infringe upon or violate any copyright of, or the right of privacy of, any person or constitute a libel or slander of any person, and shall not infringe upon or violate any other right of any person; and

(d) at all times, Lender and Composer shall promptly comply with all of Producer's instructions, directions and requests in all matters.

EXAMPLE 4: Inducement Letter

INDUCEMENT AND ACKNOWLEDGMENT

In order to induce _____ (hereinafter referred to as "Producer") to enter into the agreement dated as of _____, _____ (hereinafter referred to as the "Agreement") with [Loan-out Company] (hereinafter referred to as "Lender"), and in consideration of Lender's execution and delivery thereof:

1. The undersigned:

(a) warrants and represents that the undersigned is familiar with each term and condition of the Agreement;

(b) consents and agrees to the execution and delivery of the Agreement by Lender;

(c) agrees to render all of the services therein provided to be rendered by the undersigned;

(d) agrees to be bound by and duly perform and observe each and all of the terms and conditions of the Agreement requiring performance or compliance on the part of the undersigned;

(e) hereby joins in all warranties, representations, agreements and indemnifications made by Lender;

(f) agrees that if Lender should be dissolved or should otherwise cease to exist or for any reason whatsoever should fail, be unable, neglect or refuse duly to perform and observe each and all of the terms and conditions of the Agreement requiring performance or compliance on the part of the Lender, the undersigned shall, at the election of the Producer, be deemed substituted as a direct party to the Agreement in place and in stead of the Lender; and

(g) agrees that in the event of a breach or threatened breach of the Agreement by Lender or by the undersigned, Producer shall be entitled to legal and equitable relief by way of injunction or otherwise against Lender, or against the undersigned, or against both of us, in Producer's discretion, in any event, without the necessity of first resorting to or exhausting any rights or remedies which Producer may have against Lender.

2. The undersigned waives any claim against Producer for wages, salary or other compensation of any kind for the Agreement, and the undersigned agrees that the undersigned will look solely to Lender for any and all compensation that the undersigned may become entitled to receive for services in connection with the Agreement.

3. The undersigned agrees, confirms and joins in the acknowledgment and agreement setting forth Producer's rights in the Agreement, including, without limitation, the "work for hire" provisions, the related assignment provisions (if applicable) and all grants to Producer of all rights under the Agreement, including, but not limited to, the right to use the undersign's name and likeness as set forth therein, whether or not the undersigned's employment by Lender should expire or be terminated.

4. The undersigned agrees that all notices served on Lender under the Agreement will be deemed to be notices to me of the contents thereof.

5. The undersigned acknowledges that the rights, privileges, benefits and remedies granted to Lender in my employment agreement with Lender and to Producer in the Agreement may be enforced against me directly, jointly and generally, by Producer or Producer's assignees in the name of Lender or in Producer's or Producer's assignees' own names and in their behalf in any court of competent jurisdiction, whether or not Lender is a party to the litigation.

6. The undersigned agrees to indemnify, save and hold harmless Producer and Producer's officers, affiliates, licensees, assignees, agents, employees, attorneys, successors and representatives, as applicable, from and against any and all claims, demands, actions, liabilities, costs, damages and judgments (including, without limitation, attorneys', paralegals' and accountants' fees and costs, whether or not litigation is commenced) arising out of or in connection with any breach or alleged breach of any grants, representations, warranties or agreements herein and the exercise thereof.

7. All of the foregoing shall be to the same extent and have the same force and effect as if the undersigned had agreed to render services to Producer as an employee.

The undersigned agrees, acknowledges and accepts the foregoing and indicates such agreement, acknowledgment and acceptance by signing in the space provided for below.

• • •

DATED: As of
(Composer)

EXCLUSIVITY

You've got to take the bitter with the sour.
—SAMUEL GOLDWYN

Many composer agreements have some form of *exclusivity* provisions in them. These usually provide that the composer's services will be exclusive until the scoring for the project in question is completed or, at the very least, that the producer will have the contractual right to a first call for the composer's services during the period required for the composing and recording of the score. Regardless of the form of exclusivity used, it probably will not be a burden to the composer because, as mentioned before, in most cases, the composer's work will be done at a dead run at the last possible moment. As a practical matter, the composer probably will barely have enough time to perform the services required, let alone take on other projects that might compete for the composer's time.

SAMPLE CONTRACT PROVISIONS

EXAMPLE 1: Exclusive During Employment
(b) During the period of employment, Lender shall furnish to Producer the exclusive services of Composer to personally render all services customarily rendered by a music composer in the motion picture industry in connection with the creation of the Score and the Soundtrack, as requested by Producer, including, but not limited to writing, composing, orchestrating, arranging, conducting, recording and adapting the Score. Composer shall, as requested, consult with Producer and/or persons designated by Producer, including, without limitation, the director and individual producer of the Film, at times and places reasonably specified regarding the Score and the Soundtrack.

➨ In addition to providing exclusive services, the composer must be available for consultations with people who think they know more about composing than does the composer.

EXAMPLE 2: Nonexclusive; First Position Rights
(c) Composer's services hereunder shall be non-exclusive, but Company shall be in so-called "first position" with respect to such services, and Composer shall not render any outside services which would prevent the work to be done hereunder from being completed within Company's schedule.

EXAMPLE 3: Period of Exclusivity Specified
2. START DATE: Composer's services hereunder will commence on or about _____ (the "Start Date"), and shall be completed not later than _____. During said period, Composer's services shall be rendered exclusively to Producer.

GRANT OF RIGHTS
As is true with other agreements previously examined, such as artist recording agreements and songwriters' agreements, the company will insist that the composer, music supervisor, recording producer, etc., expressly agree to a grant of rights not only in and to the created compositions, recordings, performances, services rendered, etc., but also to rights of publicity, such as the right to use name and likeness (and, of course, our old friend, sound effects), and other similar rights in

connection with the exploitation of the soundtrack. These provisions may be combined with or in addition to work-for-hire provisions (see Examples 1 and 3).

As mentioned above, many of these provisions contain a waiver of the artist's "moral rights," that is, the legal right of an artist to protect the integrity of his or her work. This right exists under American copyright law only for the creators of a work of visual art, but it does exist for other types of artists in many of the major foreign territories in one form or another. Since the foreign market is very important in the exploitation of films and television, producers are very careful not to grant composers or other creative talents the right to insist on any unwanted "integrity" of the producer's commercial product. Producers and distributors may be able to shrug off money damages, but the mere hint of the possibility that the exhibition and/or distribution of a film or television show may be enjoined or stopped strikes real fear into their hearts.

SAMPLE CONTRACT PROVISIONS

EXAMPLE 1: Grant of Rights

5. Employee for Hire grants to Company:

(a) The results and proceeds of all endeavors under this Agreement, including the exclusive ownership of all the proceeds of Employee for Hire's services and the exclusive and perpetual right to control and use the same; the exclusive and perpetual right to manufacture, advertise, sell, lease, license or otherwise use or dispose of such proceeds of Employee for Hire's services, whether based in whole or in part upon such results and proceeds or to refrain from so doing, in all fields of use throughout the universe, upon such terms as Company may approve.

(b) The perpetual right to use and publish and to permit others to use and publish Employee for Hire's name (including any professional name heretofore or hereafter adopted by Employee for Hire), signature, likeness, voice and sound effects, and biographical material concerning Employee for Hire for advertising and trade purposes in connection with the proceeds of Employee for Hire's services hereunder or to refrain therefrom.

(c) The perpetual right to release the proceeds of Employee for Hire's services under any trade name or mark, which may include the proceeds of Employee for Hire's services of others, and to sell or otherwise license the proceeds of Employee for Hire's services.

(d) The right to copyright such the proceeds of Employee for Hire's services Company's name or in the name of Company's assignees as the owner thereof and to secure any and all renewals of such copyright.

(e) Employee for Hire hereby waives any so-called "*droit moral*" rights of any nature which Employee for Hire may have, if any, in the proceeds of Employee for Hire's services hereunder.

☛ With the exception of subparagraph (e) waiving "*droit moral rights*" (which I suppose translates as "moral right rights"), these provisions could easily be used in any work-for-hire agreement.

EXAMPLE 2: Producer's Right to Composer's Name and Likeness

16. Composer hereby grants Producer the right to issue and authorize the issuance of publicity concerning Composer and to use Composer's name, voice, likeness and biographical data in connection with the distribution, exhibition, advertising and exploitation of the Film. Without limiting the generality of the foregoing, Producer may use Composer's name, voice and likeness in connection with

publications, by-products, merchandising, commodities and services of every kind, provided reference is made to the Film or the material upon which the Film is based, or any part thereof, or to Composer's employment hereunder, and provided Composer is not represented as using or endorsing any such item.

☞ Note the similarity between this provision and similar provisions in recording agreements regarding the recording company's use of the artist's name and likeness for merchandising purposes.

EXAMPLE 3: Both Lender and Composer Grant Rights

3. *Rights.* (a) Lender [the company providing the Composer's services] and Composer hereby acknowledge and agree that producer or its designees is and will be the author(s), owner(s) and proprietor(s), exclusively, perpetually and throughout the universe, of all rights of every kind and character whatsoever (including, without limitation, all copyrights in all jurisdictions and all renewals and extensions thereof), whether known or hereafter devised, in and to Composer's services and performances hereunder and all results and proceeds thereof, regardless of their state of completion, including, without limitation, the Score, the Songs, all sound recordings and mechanical and proceeds, and any and all music, lyrics, titles, ideas, inventions and other material written, composed, created, submitted, added, improvised, interpolated and invented by Composer in connection with the Mini-Series (Composer's services hereunder, the results and proceeds thereof, and all of the foregoing are collectively referred to as "Materials").

(b) The rights acquired by Producer include, without limitation, the complete, unencumbered, exclusive and perpetual right throughout the universe to exhibit, record, reproduce, broadcast, televise, transmit, publish, copy, print, reprint, vend, sell, lease, distribute, license, perform and use the Materials for any purpose, in any similar or dissimilar manner, and in any media (including, without limitation, videograms) by any means whether known or hereafter devised, and whether separately or in synchronization or timed relation with the Mini-Series or any excerpts thereof, or any motion picture, or any video or music video, or on any Phonorecord, or otherwise all upon such terms and conditions as Producer in its sole discretion may approve, and to permit others to do any or all of the foregoing, or to refrain therefrom, and to advertise, publicize and promote the Mini-Series in any and all media, whether known or hereafter devised.

(c) Without limiting the rights of Producer set forth herein, Producer may add to, subtract from, substitute, arrange, rearrange, revise, translate, adapt and change the fundamental nature of the Materials and the Mini-Series in any manner, may interpolate the Materials with any materials written by others, and may interpolate lyrics and any other material written by others with the Materials, and Composer hereby waives throughout the world the "moral rights" of authors, as such term is commonly understood.

(d) Lender and Composer hereby acknowledge and agree that Producer has specially ordered and commissioned the Materials as "works made for hire" as defined in the U.S. Copyright Act ("Act"), that the Materials are and shall be considered "works made for hire," and that the Materials are and shall be deemed to be the sole and exclusive property of Producer, who is and shall be deemed to be the sole author thereof. To the extent, if any, despite the intentions of the parties hereto, that the Materials are not considered "works made for hire" in accordance with the Act, Lender and Composer hereby irrevocably grant and assign to producer exclusively, perpetually and throughout the universe all ownership in all copyrights (including without limitation, the right to make derivative works) and all rights, title and interest of every kind whatsoever known or hereafter devised (including without limitation, in any and all media known or hereafter devised) in and to the Materials. Without limiting the foregoing, Lender and Composer shall have no right whatsoever in, or to exploit, the Materials.

(e) Lender and Composer hereby grant to Producer the perpetual right to issue and authorize publicity concerning Composer and to use and publish and to permit others to use and publish Composer's names and likenesses and biographical data on a non-exclusive basis in connection with the exploitation of the Mini-Series and/or the musical compositions embodied in the Soundtrack and the advertisement, promotion, marketing and/or publicizing thereof, or to refrain therefrom. Lender and Composer hereby warrant and represent that Lender and/or Composer is not a party to a recording agreement or other agreement that would conflict or in any way interfere with the rights of Producer in this Paragraph 3 or elsewhere in this agreement, or with any other rights of Producer hereunder, or with any exercise of Producer's rights obtained in this agreement.

(f) Without limiting the generality of the foregoing, Producer will have the right to sell, assign, license or otherwise transfer or dispose of the Materials, including, without limitation, the Score and the Songs and all or any part of its rights with respect to the Score and the Songs and all or any part of its rights in and to the other results and proceeds of Composer's services hereunder including, without limitation, the Soundtrack relating to the Mini-Series, the use of the Composer's name and likeness, and all of the Lender's and Composer's representations and warranties hereunder, to any person (person being defined in this agreement to include persons, corporations, companies, firms, associations and any other entities), including, without limitation, the right to assign for publication Producer's and/or its designees' interest in and to the Score and the Songs, and the right to nominate or designate the actual publisher thereof (which may, but need not be, a publisher owned or controlled by Producer) and the administrator of the various rights protected by copyright. Producer may, when selling, assigning, licensing or otherwise transferring or disposing of any and/or all of the foregoing rights to a publisher, recording company, a distributor of the Mini-Series or other third party, reserve to itself and its affiliates, parent and subsidiary companies, and successors, free from payment of any fees, royalties or other consideration whatsoever to Lender or Composer, any or all of the foregoing rights, including, without limitation, any and all of the foregoing rights, including without limitation, any and all such rights useful or necessary for or related to any and all exploitation, distribution, performance, recording, broadcasting, synchronization, reproducing, creating, displaying, publicizing, promoting and/or advertising of motion pictures, videograms and/or television programs (including, without limitation, all television films, episodes of any television series, videotape films, music videos and any films produced electronically or otherwise) by any and all methods and means together with all licenses necessary for performance or exhibition of such motion pictures, videograms and/or television programs subject to the then-existing rights of public performance societies outside of the United States. Should Producer assign, license or otherwise transfer such rights to a distributor of the Mini-Series, such distributor may, when assigning, licensing or otherwise transferring such rights to a publisher, reserve equivalent rights to itself.

(g) Producer will have the right to make Phonorecords (including, without limitation, compilation Phonorecords) and videograms embodying all or any portion of the Score and the Songs (whether or not embodied in the Mini-Series) and the right to designate any record company(ies), and/or distributor(s) for purposes thereof.

(h) Lender and Composer will perform all acts and execute and deliver all documents Producer deems necessary to secure or confirm any right herein granted to producer or acknowledged, including, without limitation, the letters of direction to ASCAP or BMI, as applicable, attached hereto as Exhibit "E."

(i) Neither the expiration nor termination of this agreement shall affect Producer's right, title and interest in and to the Materials, or any other of Producer's rights hereunder.

RETENTION OF RIGHTS

There are situations in which the composer, and sometimes other parties, can retain certain rights in and to a soundtrack. The most common is when a film producer is unable to pay a composer the asking price for creating the soundtrack and, in exchange for a lesser price, lets the composer retain all or part of the copyright in the score, songs, and/or soundtrack recordings (see Examples 2 and 4). Sometimes established composers, on the basis of prior successes, are able to ask for and get the retention of all or part of the publishing rights. Sometimes composers are able to retain rights because the producer doesn't know any better. Film and television producers are notoriously ignorant when it comes to knowing the value of music publishing. To quote our old friend Shakespeare, they, "Like the base Indian, [who] threw a pearl away Richer than all his tribe," give away the publishing.

Obviously, it would always be desirable for the composer, music supervisor, or whoever to retain some or all of the publishing rights if possible, as those rights can be an important source of income. Usually, however, the film producer hangs on to the publishing for dear life even though he or she may not have the faintest idea of what to do with it.

Some years ago, I had a conversation with a film producer/distributor who at that time, after some 20 years in the business, had over 120 films in his library for which he claimed he owned all the publishing to the music. These were films that received a great deal of television play and a surprising level of video sales both domestically and outside of the United States. The potential earnings from performance royalties and mechanical royalties were astronomical.

When I asked what kind of earnings he had collected, I got a funny look from him and he informed me he had never received a penny. Seems he had never filed any paperwork with ASCAP or BMI or any of the foreign societies, nor had he pursued any of the ancillary rights in the music. The suggestion that he might want to do something about this situation fell upon deaf ears. He was afraid someone might steal from him the money he wasn't earning or collecting anyway. Go figure.

SAMPLE CONTRACT PROVISIONS

EXAMPLE 1: Music Supervisor Retains 50% of Copyright

8. For each of the Scores created hereunder by Composers, Music Supervisor grants Producer a synchronization license irrevocably granting Producer an unrestricted right to use the Score in connection with the Film and the exploitation of the Film throughout the universe in perpetuity, in all media. For that portion of the copyright in the Score that Music Supervisor is able to retain, Music Supervisor grants Producer a Fifty (50%) Percent royalty participation in Music Supervisor's net publishing income of any kind or nature with respect to any of the Scores.

(a) Music Supervisor shall administrate and collect the proceeds from all fields of use of the Score. Within thirty (30) days of the end of each calendar quarter for which there are royalties due Producer hereunder, Music Supervisor shall pay over to Producer a sum equal to Fifty (50%) Percent of Music Supervisor's net publishing income with respect to all such receipts during the preceding calendar quarter, together with an accounting statement summarizing such receipt and copies of accounting and royalty statements received in connection therewith.

(b) As used herein, "net publishing income" shall mean that portion of monies received from the exploitation of the copyrights in the Scores, other than as paid for herein by Producer in connection with the creation of the Scores and the synchronization of the Scores with the Films, less third party payments, such as to writers and composers, administrators, performance and performing rights societies, collection agencies, etc.; provided, however, that no such third party administrators, performance or performing rights societies, collection agencies may be affiliated with Music Supervisor, or, if affiliated, such payments shall not be deducted from publishing income to determine the "net publishing income."

☛ In this agreement, the composer worked as an employee for hire and the copyrights created are owned equally between the film producer and the music supervisor. The music supervisor retains administrative rights and collects all income and disburses to the composer the writer's share and one-half of the net publishing income to the film producer.

EXAMPLE 2: Producer Assigns Copyright to Composer

26. Producer assigns to Composer all of Producer's rights (including Producer's ownership and administration of copyrights) in and to the Score with respect to the Picture, except for the following reserved rights to Producer throughout the universe in perpetuity:

(a) the exclusive right to record the Score (in whole or in part) in any manner, medium or form (whether now known or hereafter invented) with respect to the Picture and any and all versions and trailers thereof, and all remakes, and sequels and versions and trailers thereof and all merchandising, publishing and other subsidiary and ancillary exploitation of all the foregoing.

(b) the exclusive right to publicly perform the Score (in whole or in part) as so recorded in all media and by all devices now known or hereafter invented subject to the collection of customary performance fees by customary performing rights societies (or if they shall not be authorized to so act then Composer shall negotiate the relevant fee in good faith and if the Composer cannot agree with the particular licensee then the matter shall be submitted to binding arbitration before the American Arbitration Association in Los Angeles under its rules).

☛ This agreement, which was a work-for-hire agreement, made Producer the original copyright owner, but in this provision Producer assigns the copyright to Composer subject to the reservation of the rights set forth in subparagraphs (a) and (b). The rights "reserved" by Producer are those which are covered by a synchronization license. Composer ends up owning the entire copyright in the score and Producer has an irrevocable synchronization license. Note, however, that Producer has failed to obtain the right to release the music on video without having to pay a mechanical license fee—a common mistake made by filmmakers, as is discussed in more detail below in the section "Mechanical Fees," pages 401–405.

EXAMPLE 3: Supervisor Assigned Copyright

6. As further consideration for the services performed by Supervisor hereunder in connection with the composing and recording of the Soundtrack of the Film, Producer, subject to the rights reserved by Producer in Paragraph 7., below, assigns to Supervisor all of Producer's rights, title and interest in the copyrights in and to the Score.

EXAMPLE 4: Copyright Retained by Composer

2. Composer shall have the right to secure, in the name of Composer, or Composer's designee, at Composer's expense, the copyright registration, including any renewal registration, with respect to the Compositions, the Videos and the Soundtrack under any law now in effect or hereafter enacted throughout the universe.

CREDIT

> CHARLES:
>
> **I wrestle for my credit;**
>
> —WILLIAM SHAKESPEARE
> *As You Like It*, Act I, Scene 1

As in all areas of the business of "show," credits are important. Credits can not only generate future work, but are also capable of generating income. Obviously, the credits on a film or television program aid in identifying performances when the film or television program is broadcast. There is, however, another, less well known, reason for insisting on complete soundtrack credits. Having a credit attached to a film or television program can make certain "performers" eligible for a royalty income stream from countries outside the United States. In some countries, the definition of eligible performers may include the composer—especially a composer/performer who also acts as a conductor or featured musician (see Example 4)—the producer of the recordings, or other individuals or companies. (See Chapter 15, "Neighboring Rights, pages 414–419.) Without dwelling on the details here, suffice it to say that sometimes the credit given to an individual or company is the determining factor in deciding whether or not royalties are being generated or who is to be the recipient of such royalties.

SAMPLE CONTRACT PROVISIONS

EXAMPLE 1: Individual Screen Credit

6. CREDIT: In connection with the use of the Score and recordings in connection with any Film or other exploitation, Composer shall be accorded individual screen and advertising credit:

(a) Composer grants to Producer the perpetual right to use and publish Composer's name (including any professional name heretofore or hereafter adopted by Composer), likeness, voice and sound effects and biographical material, or any reproduction or simulation thereof in connection with the printing, sale, advertising, distribution and exploitation of music, folios, recordings, performances, and otherwise with respect to the Score, and for any other purpose related to the business of Producer, its affiliated and related companies, or to refrain therefrom.

(b) Composer shall be afforded a credit as composer(s) in any Film using any Score to the extent that Producer is able to contractually require the producer of each such Film to provide such a credit. Producer agrees to use its best efforts to provide that Composer shall receive such a credit.

The position, size, prominence, style and form of any such credit shall be determined by such producer in its sole discretion.

(c) No casual or inadvertent failure to comply with any provision hereof relating to credit to be accorded to Composer shall constitute a breach of this Agreement by Producer. The rights and remedies of Composer in the event of any such breach shall be limited to the right to recover damages, if any, in an action at law, and in no event shall Composer be entitled by reason of any such breach to terminate this Agreement or any other agreement with respect to the Scores or the Films or to enjoin or restrain the exhibition of the Film.

(d) The credit provisions hereof are subject to standard motion picture exclusions.

☛ The language "individual screen and advertising credit" means that the composer does not share the credit for the score with any other individual. Note, however, that the credit provision is "subject to *standard* [emphasis added] motion picture exclusions," which can be troublesome. For example, one "standard" may be that the composer's credit need not appear in print advertisements that are a quarter page or smaller.

EXAMPLE 2: Single Card Credit on the Same Card

7. If Supervisor and Composer have fully performed the services to be performed hereunder, Producer shall accord the following credits to Supervisor and Composer on positive prints of each Film (single card credit on the same card) and in all paid advertising issued or controlled by Producer, in a size of type and placement at Producer's discretion, subject to customary and exculpatory provisions:

MUSIC BY (Composer)

MUSIC SUPERVISION BY
(Music Supervisor)
(Company Name)

☛ "Single card credit on the same card" means that when the film's credits appear on screen the composer's and the music supervisor's name will appear on the screen together without having to share the space with any other person.

EXAMPLE 3: Credit Provisions

7. CREDITS: Subject to Composer's full performance of all services and obligations required by Supervisor hereunder, subject to customary and exculpatory provisions:

(a) Composer shall be accorded a "Music by" credit:

(1) On Screen, on a separate card shared with Supervisor, in a size of type no less than the larger of Fifty (50%) Percent of the size of the regular title or the "Directed By" credit accorded the director and in the main titles if the "Directed By" credit is in the main titles, placement at Producer's discretion; and

(2) In paid ads issued or controlled by Producer, in a size of type and placement at Producer's discretion.

(b) No casual or inadvertent failure to comply with credit requirements shall be deemed a breach of this Agreement. The sole remedy of Composer for a breach of any of the provisions of this Agreement shall be an action at law for damages, it being agreed that in no event shall Composer seek or be entitled to injunctive or other equitable relief by reason of any breach or threatened breach of any of the credit requirements, nor shall Composer be entitled to seek to enjoin or restrain the exhibition, distribution, advertising, exploitation or marketing of the Film.

(c) Composer hereby grants Supervisor the right to issue and authorize the issuance of publicity concerning Composer and to use Composer's name, voice, likeness and biographical data in connection with the distribution, exhibition, advertising and exploitation of the Film. Without limiting the generality of the foregoing, Supervisor may use Composer's name, voice and likeness in connection with publications, by-products, merchandising, commodities and services of every kind, provided reference is made to the Film or the material upon which the Film is based, or any part thereof, or to Composer's employment hereunder, and provided Composer is not represented as using or endorsing any such item.

☛ The size and placement of a credit are important. In this provision, the composer's credit shall be no less than 50% of the size of the director's credit. In addition, the credit will appear in the "main titles" with the director's credit. The rules of the Directors' Guild of America provide that if the main credits are at the front end of the film the director's credit will be the last credit to appear before the film starts, and if the credits are at the end of the film, it will be the first credit to appear. In the majority of released films, the main credits are at the front of the film, and what are known as "below the line" credits are at the end of the film. The rule of thumb for credits is that the higher you are in the pecking order, the closer you are to the director's credit. Lawyers, if they receive a credit, usually appear before the line reading "no animals were harmed in the making of this film."

EXAMPLE 4: "Composed and Performed By"

6. Subject to Composer's full performance of all services and obligations required by Producer hereunder:

(a) Composer, as composer and performer of the Compositions, shall be afforded single card credit in the main titles of the Film as follows: "ORIGINAL MUSIC COMPOSED AND PERFORMED BY [Composer]"

(b) Composer shall be accorded a music production credit on screen.

(c) Composer's publisher designee(s) shall be accorded credit on screen.

(d) Featured performers, producers, etc., requiring credit for Videos, etc., will be accorded credit on screen.

EXAMPLE 5: Conditional Credit

4. CREDIT: Subject to Producer's customary provisions and exclusions, Composer shall be accorded credit as follows:

(a) On Screen: If over one-half (½) of the underscore to the Picture as first generally televised consists of music composed solely by Composer, Composer shall receive single card credit and in the same size (i.e., height) as the credit to the individual screenplay writer in substantially the following form: "Music, Lyrics and Score by [composer]."

(b) Paid Ads: If the entire underscore of the Picture as first generally televised consists of music composed solely by Composer, Composer also shall be accorded credit in all paid print advertisements in newspapers, trades and other periodicals, provided that the screenwriter of the Picture receives credit in any such print advertisements (and further provided any such paid print advertisements is/are not "teaser," "award," "nomination" etc. type paid print ads.)

☛ The negotiated credit provisions apply if the composer furnishes over one-half of the score for this television movie. Note that the credit requirement does not apply to "teaser," "award," "nomination," etc., or to paid print ads, for example, an ad stating that the director has been nominated for an Emmy or an ad congratulating the director for winning an Emmy.

SOURCES OF INCOME

Getting down to the bottom line (if that is not redundant), just what are the sources of income for the lucky participants? Depending on what a party has contributed to a soundtrack, the types of potential income are varied and each relates to a different area of interest. We shall tiptoe through the different sources of income and, at the same time, examine the different issues. It is probably easiest to approach this subject in a somewhat chronological manner, starting with the creation of the soundtrack and tracking the income generated by the exploitation of the soundtrack by the different sources.

For the sake of discussion, unless otherwise noted, the following sections presume that a music supervisor and a composer have been hired to create a score for the soundtrack of a theatrical film. For the sake of this hypothetical scenario, and to make as many points as possible, we will also presume that the composer retains not only the writer's share of income generated by the exploitation and use of the music, but also the entire publisher's share of the income for the music.

Creating the Soundtrack

The producer of the film hires both the music supervisor and the composer to create the soundtrack. The supervisor receives a fee for the services rendered, usually a set fee, which is part of the film's budget. Some supervisors, however, provide all services—composer, recording, musicians, etc.—for a flat fee, much like the way in which a recording fund is supplied to a production company. This is especially likely to happen when the budget allocated for music is, to state the issue politely, sparse. The supervisor's personal fee under these circumstances is the spread between the budgeted amount and the actual expense (see Example 2). The supervisor may also receive deferred payments, shares of the publishing, royalties on soundtrack albums, and/or a share of any advances paid for the placement of a soundtrack album with a record company for commercial release.

Usually, the composer is paid a fee for composing the score for a soundtrack, and, if the composer is also performing as an artist (e.g., performer and/or conductor), these services are included in the fee (see Examples 1 and 3). Depending upon the relative bargaining positions of the composer and the producer, the composer may retain all or a part of the publishing of the music created by the composer for inclusion on the soundtrack. The reason for using the phrase "created by the composer" is to exclude publishing rights to so-called source music, which, presumably, is not controlled by any of the parties to begin with. (See the following section for a more detailed discussion of source music.)

SAMPLE CONTRACT PROVISIONS

EXAMPLE 1: Flat Fee—Songwriter's Agreement

2. COMPENSATION: Subject to the provisions of this Agreement and provided that Company and

Composer shall keep and perform all covenants and conditions to be kept and performed by Company and Composer hereunder, Producer agrees as full compensation for services rendered and for all rights granted to Producer hereunder to pay Company as follows:

(a) The sum of _____ Thousand ($_____) Dollars, in installments as follows:

(1) One-Third (1/3rd) thereof upon Producer's request for the commencement of the services to be performed hereunder;

(2) One-Third (1/3rd) thereof upon delivery of the Score and all other delivery elements required to Producer; and

(3) One-Third (1/3rd) thereof upon delivery of the answer print of the completed Film.

(b) It is mutually agreed that the guaranteed compensation specified in this Paragraph 2 is a "flat fee" and, except as expressly provided for herein, Company shall not be entitled to any additional or overage compensation for any of the services rendered.

(c) It is expressly understood that the above compensation includes all applicable pension, health and welfare payments.

(d) In addition, in connection with the Score, Composer shall also receive:

(i) A royalty of six ($.06) cents per copy on all regular piano copies sold and paid for.

(ii) A royalty of six ($.06) cents per copy on any form of orchestration thereof sold and paid for.

(iii) A royalty of ten (10%) percent of the wholesale selling price for each of any song book, song sheet, folio, or similar publication containing the Score or any portion of the Score for which Producer is paid, except that in the event that the Score is used, in whole or in part, in conjunction with one or more musical compositions in a folio or Album, Writer shall be entitled to receive that portion of ten (10%) percent which the Score shall bear to the total number of musical compositions contained in such folio or Album.

(iv) A royalty of fifty (50%) percent of all net sums actually earned by the Score and received by Producer for regular piano copies and/or orchestrations thereof, for the use of the Score in any folio or composite work, or other use in countries outside the United States.

(v) A royalty of fifty (50%) percent of any and all sums actually received by Producer from motion picture and television synchronization rights.

(vi) A royalty of fifty (50%) percent of all net sums actually received by Producer from any license issued authorizing the manufacture of the parts of instruments serving to mechanically reproduce the Composition.

(vii) For "professional material" not sold or for resale, there shall be no royalty.

(viii) In the event that new music or lyrics are added to the Score, the royalties set forth above shall be divided between Composer and the new writer or composer, if any, in shares to be determined, in good faith, by Producer.

(ix) Composer agrees that Composer shall not be entitled to receive any part of monies received by Producer from any performance rights society for the use of the Score throughout the world.

(e) Notwithstanding anything to the contrary contained herein, if Producer requires Composer to supply any Score in excess of the maximum provided for below, other than the provisions of Subparagraph 2.(d), above, the only additional payment required of Producer will be the actual cost of recording such additional Score.

☛ The composer gets a fee, payable in equal thirds: (1) at commencement of the composer's services; (2) upon delivery to the producer of the finished and recorded score; and (3) upon delivery of the finished film. The agreement also incorporates songwriters' agreement language.

EXAMPLE 2: Net of Budget—50% of Net Proceeds from Record Royalties

5. Producer and Supervisor shall determine the budget (hereinafter referred to as the "Budget") for the Soundtrack of each such Film, as specified in Exhibit A, and the Budget shall be dispersed to Supervisor pursuant to the Payment Schedule specified in Exhibit A.

• • •

(c) Producer and Supervisor agree and acknowledge that Supervisor's compensation hereunder, other than as expressly set forth herein, shall be the difference between actual expenditures and the Budget. The Budget shall be paid, in its entirety, to Supervisor for disbursement on the schedule set forth in Exhibit A for each such Film project. Except as expressly set forth herein in this Agreement or with Producer's express agreement, there shall be no additional charge to Producer for the Score, Recording and/or Soundtrack beyond that indicated as the Budget in Exhibit A.

6. Supervisor shall be Producer's exclusive agent for placing any soundtrack Album based upon a Soundtrack created hereunder. Supervisor shall not have the authority to enter into any such soundtrack Album agreement without Producer's prior consent. If Producer accepts the terms and conditions of any such soundtrack Album agreement, from the proceeds therefrom Supervisor shall receive an advance equal to the sum indicated as the Album Advance in Exhibit A from the first monies payable pursuant to such soundtrack Album agreement.

(a) After the Album Advance has been recouped from proceeds from the soundtrack Album agreement, the net proceeds thereafter shall be divided equally between Producer and Supervisor. As used herein, the net proceeds shall be deemed to be the net monies received therefrom after required payments to third parties such as Composer, performers, musicians, etc., if any.

(b) Notwithstanding the foregoing, if the first proceeds from the soundtrack Album agreement are insufficient to pay the Album Advance, it is agreed that the difference between the amount so received and paid to Supervisor and the amount of the Album Advance shall be treated as a deferred payment due Supervisor and Supervisor shall continue to receive the proceeds until the Album Advance has been paid to Supervisor.

☛ The supervisor's fee comes out of the difference between the approved budget and what is actually spent. To augment the fee, the supervisor is given the exclusive right to make a deal for the soundtrack album with record companies and to keep any advance, up to a specified amount. After the advance is recouped, royalties from the album are divided equally between the supervisor and the film producer.

EXAMPLE 3: Flat Fee

3. Subject to the provisions of this Agreement and provided that Composer shall keep and perform all covenants and conditions to be kept and performed by Composer hereunder, Producer agrees as full compensation for services rendered and all rights granted to Producer hereunder to pay Composer _____ Thousand ($_____) Dollars, payable as follows:

(a) _____ Thousand ($_____) Dollars concurrently with the execution of this Agreement; and

(b) _____ Thousand ($_____) Dollars upon delivery of the Compositions, Videos and Soundtrack to Producer by Composer.

(c) The payment provided for herein for the production of the Compositions, Videos and the Soundtrack is a "flat fee" and Composer shall not be entitled to any additional payments, except as expressly provided for herein, for such services.

Source Music

Not all music is originally created just for the soundtrack. There is frequently a need for a preexisting recording as source music. *Source music* is generally used to evoke a time or place as part of the story being shown. For example, "Don't Sit Under the Apple Tree," "The White Cliffs of Dover," "Praise the Lord and Pass the Ammunition," "Der Führer's Face," and so forth might be licensed to establish World War II as the setting of a film. The licensing of source music usually also means the licensing of a particular recording of it. For example, it isn't good sense to obtain a synchronization license of "Der Führer's Face" without also licensing the original recording by Spike Jones.

The recording is licensed from the applicable record company using what is generally called a "master use license" (see below). The license will call for a payment to be made to the record company, which is usually divided with the artist. The license will also usually provide for a royalty if the licensed master is used in a soundtrack album. Another license that must be obtained, one that is separate from the master use license for the recording, is the synchronization license from the music publisher for the use of the song itself.

Sometimes the combined cost of the synchronization license and the master use license is prohibitive. A synchronization license for source music doesn't do a film producer much good without the master use license, but one viable option in such cases is to get a synchronization license from the music publisher and create a new "soundalike" recording for the film.

SAMPLE CONTRACT PROVISIONS

EXAMPLE 1: Source Music as Separate Budget Item

(a) Notwithstanding anything to the contrary contained herein, it is agreed and acknowledged that for any so-called "source music," compositions and/or sound recordings, licensed from third parties for use in the Soundtrack of any Film, Supervisor may not be able to provide work for hire agreements, ownership, participation, or like rights as otherwise provided for herein and that in any such instance such failure is not a breach of the terms of this Agreement. All agreements for use of any so-called "source music" from third parties shall conform to industry standards and shall provide Producer with, as appropriate, master use rights and/or synchronization rights.

(b) If Producer requests the inclusion of "source music" in any Film, source music, unless expressly stated to the contrary, shall be deemed to be in addition to the Budget set forth in Exhibit A for such Film.

☛ The costs of source music are frequently handled under a separate budget from the costs for the score, or are at least a separate budget item. In situations where the supervisor is given a budget and the supervisor's fee is taken from the difference between the budget and costs, usually the costs of source music will be borne by the film producer.

EXAMPLE 2: Source Music Distinguished from Scores and Recordings

11. Supervisor represents, warrants and agrees that the Scores and the Recordings, other than so-called "source music" will be wholly original or in the public domain throughout the world, and neither the Scores nor the Recordings nor any part thereof shall infringe upon or violate any copyright of, or the right of privacy of, any person or constitute a libel or slander of any person, and shall not infringe upon or violate any other right of any person.

> ☞ Because source music consists of preexisting compositions and, usually, preexisting recordings, source music is not part of the supervisor's warranties and representations made to the film producer. Those warranties and representations show up in the separate agreements entered into with the music publisher (for the synchronization license) and the record company (for the master use license).

EXAMPLE 3: Artist's Share

(d) In respect of any Master licensed by Company for use on a soundtrack or on a soundtrack Album, you shall receive Fifty (50%) Percent of Company's "net receipts" received by Company from such usage(s). As used herein, "net receipts" and similar terms mean royalties or flat payments received by Company that are solely attributable to Masters hereunder, less all costs incurred by Company in connection with the exploitation concerned (including, without limitation, manufacturing and duplicating costs, advertising expenses, mechanical royalties and other copyright payments, union or guild payments, etc.).

> ☞ When a master use license is issued to a film producer by a record company for the use of a recording in a soundtrack, the income generated from the license fee is usually divided equally between the record company and the artist, based upon "net receipts received" by the record company. Costs which are deducted to reach "net receipts" are normally third-party costs, for example, a commission given to a third party for brokering or "placing" the recording in the soundtrack.

Soundtrack Albums

Beyond obtaining the music as cheaply as possible for their films, the only other thought most film producers have about the soundtrack is the possibility of getting a soundtrack album released and, if they are really lucky, a hit single with lots of airplay just before and as the film is opening. With the right kind of soundtrack, hope springs eternal for album sales in sufficient quantity to create royalties pouring into the gross income pot for the film (where they can be absorbed and written off so that "net income" need not be shared with third parties). For the supervisor and/or composer, royalty participation from the soundtrack album should be calculated and paid based upon only the sales of the album, not the net profits of the film. If the royalty is allowed to become part of the net profits of the film, the likelihood of any royalties ever being paid is considerably lower than nil. Film studio accounting methods would shame the most rapacious Byzantine tax collector. Interestingly, there have been films, even box office successes, where the net earnings from the soundtrack album have exceeded those from the film itself.

EXAMPLE 1: Supervisor's and Producer's Cut of Album Deal

6. Supervisor shall be Producer's exclusive agent for placing any soundtrack Album based upon a Soundtrack created hereunder. Supervisor shall not have the authority to enter into any such soundtrack Album agreement without Producer's prior consent. If Producer accepts the terms and conditions of any such soundtrack Album agreement, from the proceeds therefrom Supervisor shall receive an advance equal to the sum indicated as the Album Advance in Exhibit A from the first monies payable pursuant to such soundtrack Album agreement.

(a) After the Album Advance has been recouped from proceeds from the soundtrack Album agreement, the net proceeds thereafter shall be divided equally between Producer and Supervisor. As used herein, the net proceeds shall be deemed to be the net monies received therefrom after required payments to third parties such as Composer, performers, musicians, etc., if any.

(b) Notwithstanding the foregoing, if the first proceeds from the soundtrack Album agreement are insufficient to pay the Album Advance, it is agreed that the difference between the amount so received and paid to Supervisor and the amount of the Album Advance shall be treated as a deferred payment due Supervisor and Supervisor shall continue to receive the proceeds until the Album Advance has been paid to Supervisor.

EXAMPLE 2: Composer Royalty from Soundtrack Album

6. SOUNDTRACK ALBUM: If a Soundtrack Album is released commercially, Composer shall receive the royalty provided for below for Composer's performances and services as provided for herein:

(a) Composer shall receive a royalty of Six (6%) Percent, computed, paid and defined in the same manner and in all aspects as provided for in the agreement between Supervisor and/or Producer and the record company distributing the Soundtrack Album.

(b) No record royalties shall be payable hereunder to Composer unless and until Supervisor and/or Producer and the record company have recouped advances pursuant to the agreement for the commercial release of the Soundtrack Album.

☞ This provision for record royalties for the composer sets the composer's royalty rate at 6% and incorporates by reference the royalty provisions of any future agreement with a record company for the commercial release of the soundtrack album.

EXAMPLE 3: "Usual and Standard Recording Costs" Recouped

10. In connection with a soundtrack Album, if any, containing the Score hereunder, Producer shall pay or cause to be paid to Composer a royalty which shall be a percentage of the net retail selling price on ninety percent (90%) of all such records sold, as such price, such number of records and applicable percentage are classified, computed and accounted for in accordance with the usual and standard practices of the record company concerned. Such record company may recoup from such royalties its usual and standard recording costs. . . .

☞ This example, concerning the basis of a composer's royalty for a soundtrack album, is placed here as a test for the reader. If your eyebrows did not rise in indignation at the use of the terms "usual and standard," it is time to go back to the beginning of the book and start all over.

Synchronization Licenses

Synchronization licenses are required in connection with any use of music (other than public domain music) on a soundtrack. This is the license to *synchronize* the music with a visual image. (For a detailed discussion of the topic, see Chapter 9, "Songwriters' Agreements," pages 294–295.) Synchronization licenses for the score are usually addressed in the agreement with a composer to create a score for the soundtrack, and the license fee is included in the compensation provided for in the agreement (see Example 1). Songs and source music not created by the composer will also require synchronization licenses, which must be obtained from the respective music publishers for each individual piece of music.

There are instances where rights to songs or scores are granted for free or for a very modest sum in exchange for being included in the film or program. The trade-off for the free or modest license fee, other than exposure or generosity, is the possibility of income from performance royalties and mechanical license fees.

On the other hand, synchronization fees can be quite lucrative. They are issued by the copyright owner (i.e., the publisher), and, since there is no compulsory provision in the U.S. Copyright Act granting anyone the right to synchronize music, the fee must be negotiated. Because the publisher can simply say no, there is nothing the producer can do other than increase the offer or not use the music. The average going rate for a synchronization license for a song for use in a major studio feature film is around $25,000. I have personally participated in negotiating license fees that ran into six figures (not counting the numbers after the decimal point).

Clearly, it is good business for a film producer to try to obtain a synchronization license ahead of time, rather than after it is too late, so that he or she can negotiate with the copyright owner ("if we can't get it cheap, we'll have to use another song," etc.). Note that, contrary to the belief of many film producers, a synchronization license does not, in and of itself, grant a mechanical license for the inclusion in and sale of the music in audiovisual works, such as videocassettes. (See the discussion of mechanical fees below, pages 401–405.)

SAMPLE CONTRACT PROVISIONS

EXAMPLE 1: Synchronization License Included in Agreement

4. The Compositions, Videos and Soundtrack shall remain the property of Composer, or Composer's designee, and this Agreement shall constitute a synchronization license to use same in the Film throughout the universe in all media in perpetuity.

EXAMPLE 2: Composer's Share of Synchronization License Fees 50%

10. For your services rendered hereunder, and for the rights granted herein to us, with respect to the Compositions, we shall pay or cause to be paid to you the following aggregate amounts:

• • •

(b) In respect of any of the Compositions written and composed solely by you, if usage is licensed by us to any other person, firm or corporation, whether in the United States of America, Dominion of Canada or any other foreign country throughout the world, 50% of all net sums received by us in respect to the Compositions from any such licenses issued by us, or on our behalf, authorizing the use of any and/or all of the Compositions for any of the following:

    (i) Phonograph records
    (ii) Electrical transcriptions

(iii) Sound synchronization of the Compositions in motion pictures

EXAMPLE 3: Grant of Rights

1. GRANTED RIGHTS: For good and valuable consideration, the receipt of which is hereby acknowledged, and subject only to the "Reserved Rights" set forth below, Licensor hereby irrevocably grants to Company and its successors and assigns, in the Territory [the world] and for the Term [in perpetuity], in all media and languages, and by any and all means whether now known or hereafter devised (including but not limited to in connection with theatrical and televised motion pictures, and on all forms of home video devices), the non-exclusive but otherwise unlimited right to record the Composition in synchronization and timed relation with the Picture and to manufacture, reproduce, distribute, exploit, transmit, broadcast, and import copies of the Picture containing the Composition, and, subject to paragraphs 3 and 4, to perform the Picture containing the Composition. The rights hereinabove granted shall specifically include, but not be limited to, such rights as may be required to utilize the Composition in clips and in works which advertise and promote the Picture, and in storage and retrieval devices which embody the Picture substantially as generally released (which for this purpose shall be deemed to include so-called Editor's and/or Director's cuts, versions adapted for the visually or hearing impaired, or other similarly altered versions) provided that viewers are not invited to manipulate the images and/or audio program material of such devices in a non-linear progression. For the purposes hereof, the inclusion of "chapter stops" or other addressable locator codes of any kind on the applicable storage device shall not be deemed to constitute non-linear manipulation.

2. RESERVED RIGHTS: This License does not authorize or permit any use of the compositions not expressly set forth herein and it does not include the right to alter the fundamental character of the music of the Composition; the right to use the title or subtitle of the Composition as the title of the Picture; and the right to use the story of the Composition as the story of the Picture. Further, no sound records produced pursuant to this license are to be manufactured, sold and/or used separately or independently from the Picture without the prior written consent of Licensor.

☞ The grant of rights here is pretty broad. On the other hand, it doesn't contain the following provisions, which producers hate but which are not unusual: limiting the territory (e.g., North America only), limiting the period (e.g., 5 years), and/or limiting the configuration (e.g., theatrical release only), all probably requiring the producer to come back sometime in the future to renegotiate. Pity the poor producer who can't somehow edit the composition out of the film and needs to enlarge the rights granted. For an analogous situation, think of being in the most expensive fish restaurant in town with limited funds, your hot date orders lobster, and the menu reads: "Lobster—Market Price."

EXAMPLE 4: Television

13. As used herein, "television" shall also include means by which the Picture is broadcast or sent by "streaming" via the Internet and similar mediums whether now known or hereafter devised, provided that in connection with such streaming end-users are prohibited from capturing and recording the Picture for multiple viewing, it being agreed that streaming the Picture via the Internet in such a manner as to allow an end-user to capture and record the Picture for multiple viewing shall be deemed equivalent to the manufacture and sale of a home video device, rights for which are herein granted to Producer by Publisher.

(a) Notwithstanding the broad grant of rights set forth in Paragraph 6, above, the right to exhibit the Picture incorporating the Compositions on television in the United States shall be available only after a valid public performance license has been obtained by Producer or its successors or assigns from ASCAP, BMI, from Publisher directly, or from an entity having authorization to issues such licenses on behalf of Publisher. As used herein, "television" shall also include means by which the Picture is broadcast or sent by "streaming" via the Internet and similar mediums whether now known or hereafter devised, provided that in connection with such streaming end-users are prohibited from capturing and recording the Picture for multiple viewing, it being agreed that streaming the Picture via the Internet in such a manner as to allow an end-user to capture and record the Picture for multiple viewing shall be deemed equivalent to the manufacture and sale of a home video device, rights for which are herein granted to Producer by Publisher.

(b) It is understood that clearance by performance rights societies in such portion of the Territory as is outside of the United States will be in accordance with their customary practices and the payment of their customary fees.

> ☛ The license for television broadcast is conditioned upon clearance from performing rights societies in the appropriate territories. Note that video streaming on the Internet is included in the definition of "television."

Master Use License

Any time a preexisting recording is used in a soundtrack, a *master use license* is required in order to complete the documentation of rights acquired by the producer of the film. Generally speaking, any source music, unless it is a soundalike recording, is going to need a master use license. The producer needs this documentation (and more) in order to obtain errors and omission (E&O) insurance for the film.

Errors and omission insurance serves a double purpose. The first is that before an insurance company will issue an E&O insurance policy, the company will go through every element of the film with a fine tooth comb to make sure all necessary rights have been granted (e.g., master use licenses, synchronization licenses, story and script rights, etc.), and that there are no copyright or trademark infringements, no libels or slanders committed, or any other missteps which may lead to litigation. Having, in theory, cleared every aspect from potential liability, the insurance company then issues an insurance policy for any liability which may have slipped past the microscopic examination. Without E&O insurance no one—distributor, licensee, network, television station, etc.—is going to touch the film.

As with synchronization licenses, master use licenses are not compulsory, and fees are negotiable. It is quite common for both the master use fee and the synchronization fee to match each other, even though the licensors are probably different entities. The two different owners may allow one to set the price, with the understanding that price will apply equally to each individual license.

SAMPLE CONTRACT PROVISIONS

EXAMPLE 1: Simple Grant to Use Master Recording

(a) Whereby Owners are the owners of the certain master recordings described below. Owners, hereby grant to Licensee a non-exclusive license to use the master recording(s) embodying the performances of the artists(s) known professionally as _____ ("Artist") comprising the compositions (hereinafter "Compositions") listed on schedule "A" ("Licensed Masters(s)") annexed hereto and made a part of this Agreement, for the purpose of manufacturing, distributing and selling phonograph records, tapes and compact discs ("Records"). Under this Agreement Licensee is granted the limited right to include the Licensed Master(s) in the following manner: Subject to the terms and restrictions set forth herein, inclusion in the theatrical feature film entitled "_____" (hereinafter referred to as the "Film").

☛ Both this example and the next refer to nonexclusive rights. Most master use licenses (and synchronization licenses) are in fact nonexclusive. Sometimes an exclusive license is granted—always for a price of course—but hardly ever for anything other than a limited period.

EXAMPLE 2: Nonexclusive Assignable Rights

2. Grant of Rights: [Record Company] grants to Producer:

(a) the non-exclusive right to synchronize the Recording with the Picture, including the right to publicly perform, distribute, reproduce, manufacture, transmit, broadcast, export and import copies of the Picture containing the Recording in all languages including use in methods, means and devices now known and hereafter known throughout the universe (hereinafter referred to as the "Territory");

(b) the non-exclusive right as may be required to use the Recordings in trailers, in clips and in works which advertise and promote the Picture, including, but not limited to, clips which may be viewed and/or transmitted by means of the Internet; and in storage and retrieval devices which embody the Picture substantially as generally released; and

(c) As used herein, the term "Producer" shall also be deemed to include the successors and assigns of Producer.

EXAMPLE 3: Credits

2. CREDIT: Provided the Master is embodied in the Picture, Producer shall have the right and the obligation to accord Licensors customary screen credit in connection therewith in the main or end titles of the Picture. All characteristics of such credit shall be at Producer's sole discretion. The parties agree that any inadvertent failure to comply with the foregoing credit provision shall not be deemed a breach hereunder.

☛ The significance of credits with regard to possible royalty streams for foreign countries is discussed above, page 387.

Performing Fees

The public performance of soundtracks, with or without the attached visual element, generates performance fees for the composer and publisher and, in some instances, for the producer and performers.

Every time a film or television program is broadcast in the "civilized world" over television, be it network television, local television, cable television, satellite broadcast, or whatever, performance fees, at least in theory, are generated for the publishers and composers of the music. The language covering the generation of these fees is hedged somewhat by the fact that the performances have to be noted and *logged* by the applicable performing rights societies. In this regard, not all societies are created equal, and, unfortunately, American societies are not as efficient as many of their foreign counterparts when it comes to logging in *all* performances. The radio broadcast of soundtrack albums, or singles from such albums, also results—if logged and with the proper filing of cue sheets—in performance money coming to the composers and publishers.

In many countries outside of the United States, when a film is shown at the local theater, a performance fee, usually based upon a percentage of the box office gross, is collected, generating performance royalties for the composers and the publishers. This is not the case in the United States, where there is no public performance fee for the publishers and writers of film music heard during the public exhibition of a film at your quaint neighborhood theater or multiplex.

As mentioned previously, the sums of money generated by these theatrical performances in other countries can be enormous. They are, however, rarely collected for Americans because of our irrational belief that nothing that doesn't exist within our borders could possibly exist outside of our borders.

There are also fees and income generated for "performers" from performances in those mysterious (to Americans) areas called *copyright-related rights* and *neighboring rights,* which presently do not exist in this country but may exist sometime in the future. Under some circumstances, Americans can collect this income.

Another source of income which exists in other countries but not in the United States, one which is a subspecies of mechanical fee, is created by the broadcast of the soundtrack. This fee is known as a *broadcast mechanical.*

For more information on income that may be generated by public performance, see Chapter 9, the section "Public Performance Fees," pages 288–292, and Chapter 15, "Performance, Performing, and Neighboring Rights," pages 406–428.

SAMPLE CONTRACT PROVISIONS

EXAMPLE 1: Performance Fees Not Paid by Publisher

(f) Publisher shall not be required to pay royalties to Writer for public performance of the Compositions. Writer shall receive royalties for public performances from the performing rights society with which Writer is or may, in the future, become affiliated.

EXAMPLE 2: Writer Paid Directly

7. Compensation. . . .

(d) Writer shall receive his public performance royalties throughout the world directly from the performing rights society with which he is affiliated, and shall have no claim whatsoever against Publisher for any royalties received by Publisher from any performing rights society which makes payment directly (or indirectly other than through Publisher) to writers, authors and composers.

EXAMPLE 3: Performance Fee Not Paid by Producer

15. Composer shall look only to Composer's performing rights society for such monies to which Composer may be entitled [for public performances] . . . and Composer shall not under any circumstances look to Producer with respect to accountings or payments relating thereto.

Mechanical Fees

Our old friend the "mechanical" should be no stranger to by now. Obviously the sale of soundtrack albums and singles, if any, culled from a soundtrack album will result in income based upon mechanical license fees. In this respect, there is no difference between a soundtrack recording being released and any ordinary recording. The same rules apply to the sale of soundtrack music as to the sale of "phonorecords."

However, there is another mechanical license that comes into play with regard to soundtracks. A surprising number of film producers and, dare I say, attorneys who should know better, refuse to accept the fact that these mechanical rights exist. I am speaking about the mechanical license fee due for soundtrack music included on films and the like that are released on videocassettes, laser discs, games, and other devices that "mechanically" reproduce the music.

Under the United States Copyright Act, there is a distinction between "phonorecords" and "copies," with audiovisual works being considered as copies and hence excluded from any compulsory license provisions. (For the Copyright Act's definition of those terms, see Chapter 20, "Copyright," pages 495–496.) Since the compulsory license provision of the Copyright Act for use of the music in sales of audiovisual works does not apply to copies and since audiovisual works are copies and not phonorecords, the producer or distributor of DVDs, videos, or other audiovisual works must obtain an express license from the music's copyright owner or agent, either directly or through the film's producer who has obtained the express license with the right to further assign the license or the rights granted for the use of the music. These rules are also generally true outside of the United States.

Absent an express waiver by the copyright owner of payment for videocassette sales, the royalty or fee is a negotiated rate. Similar rules apply in other countries. Without a compulsory license provision available for videos, the negotiated rate does not have a ceiling the way the rate does for the reproduction of phonorecords. Accordingly, the negotiated rate for video rights is generally more varied than it is for recordings.

Since the rate for DVDs and other forms of audiovisual works is open for negotiation, bargaining power plays a significant part in what rate and rights are granted to the producer by the copyright owner of the music. Sometimes an agreement cannot be reached and a piece of music is either not used at all or may appear in the theatrical and television release of a film, but will be missing from the DVD version.

The most common arrangement in setting a license fee is a flat buyout as a part of the synchronization license for the use of the music in the work, but it is important to note that there must be express language in the synchronization license waiving mechanical fees in order to accomplish this. Another approach is to specify a percentage of the retail or wholesale price of the product sold. Sometimes a per-unit royalty rate is expressed in dollars and/or cents. Sometimes there is an advance against a set number of units sold, with additional advances due for sales in excess of the stated number of units. The license may be in perpetuity or for a stated number of years. If a specific time period is given, at the end of that period either there must be a renegotiation or the music must be removed from copies sold after that date. The license may also be granted for worldwide use or on a territory-by-territory basis.

Unfortunately, many film producers do not understand the distinction between a synchronization license granting the right to use the music in a film and the need for a separate license to "mechanically reproduce" the music when DVDs and other audiovisual works are sold. It is not unusual for them to believe they have acquired mechanical rights when in fact they have not. In these cases, the copyright owner of the music (again, absent an express waiver or buyout), has the right to refuse permission for the music to be used as a part of the soundtrack of a film. The question is, what happens when the film producer goes ahead and releases the film on a DVD with a mechanical license.

Probably the most important case in the United States dealing directly with this subject is *Cohen v. Paramount Pictures Corp.*[1] Cohen was the copyright owner of a music composition and granted a synchronization license to the producer of a film who, in turn, assigned all rights in the film, including music licenses which had been obtained from Cohen, to Paramount Pictures Corporation. Paramount subsequently released the film on videocassette. Cohen maintained that the synchronization license did not extend to video, Paramount contended that it did.

In determining what rights had been reserved and what rights had been granted, the court reported, at page 853:

> To resolve this case, we must examine the terms of the license, in order to determine whether the license conveyed the right to use the composition in making and distributing videocassette reproductions of "Medium Cool." The document begins by granting the licensee the "authority . . . to record, in any manner, medium, form or language, the words and music of the musical composition . . ., to make copies of such recordings and to perform said musical composition everywhere *all in accordance* [emphasis added] with the terms, conditions, and limitations hereinafter set forth. . . .
>
> The . . . license herein granted to perform . . . said musical composition is granted for: (a) The exhibition of said motion picture . . . to audiences in motion picture theatres and other places of public entertainment where motion pictures are customarily exhibited. . . . Although the language of the license permits the *recording and copying* of the movie with the musical composition in it, in any medium, or form, nothing in the express language of the license authorizes *distribution* of the copies to the public by sale or rental.
>
> One of the separate rights of copyright, as enumerated in section 106 of the Copyright Act, is the right "to distribute copies or phonorecords of the copyrighted work to the public by sale or other transfer of ownership, or by rental, lease, or lending." 17 U.S.C. [section] 106(3). Thus the right to distribute copies of the videocassette by sale or rental remained with the grantor under the reservation of rights provision in paragraph 6, unless in some way it is encompassed within the right to *perform* the work.

The *Cohen* court makes a distinction between public performance and private performance based on language in Section 101 of the United States Copyright Act:

> To "perform" a work means to recite, render, play, dance, or act it, either directly or by means of any device or process or, in the case of a motion picture or other audiovisual work, to show its images in any sequence or to make the sounds accompanying it audible. . . .
>
> To perform or display a work "publicly" means—
>
> (1) to perform or display it at a place open to the public or at any place where a substantial number of persons outside of a normal circle of a family and its social acquaintances is gathered; or

---

[1] *Cohen v. Paramount Pictures Corp.* 845 F2nd 851 (9th Cir 1988).

(2) to transmit or otherwise communicate a performance or display of the work to a place specified by clause (1) or to the public, by means of any device or process, whether the members of the public capable of receiving the performance or display receive it in the same place or in separate places and at the same time or at different times.

The court also held, again at page 853, that:

The limitation on the right to perform the synchronization with the composition in it is found in paragraph 4 [of the agreement] and that paragraph limits the right to perform, or to authorize others to perform, to: 4(a) exhibition of the motion picture to audiences in motion picture theatres and other places of public entertainment where motion pictures are customarily shown, and 4(b) exhibition of the motion picture by means of television, including pay television, subscription television, and "closed circuit into homes" television.

It is obvious that the distribution of videocassette through sale and rental to the general public for viewing in their homes does not fit within the purpose of category 4(a) above which is restricted to showing in theatres and other similar public places.... The words of that paragraph [4(b), television broadcast] must be tortured to expand the limited right granted by that section to an entirely different means of making that film available to the general public—the distribution of individual videocassette to the general public for private "performances" in their homes. The general tenor of the section contemplates some sort of broadcasting or centralized distribution, not distribution by sale or rental of individual copies to the general public.

The *Cohen* decision thus held that:

• A producer's reservation of the "right to publicly perform" the music—via exhibition of the film to audiences in theaters "and other places of public entertainment" *or* by means of television—is *not*, by itself, a reservation of the "videocassette" or "private performance" rights necessary to justify the right to distribute videocassettes.

• Without an express grant of rights, the reservations which have been retained must be examined to determine if the license includes the right to distribute videocassettes by sale or rental. Unless the license does explicitly grant that right, it remains with the grantor.

There have been some cases wherein the courts granted videocassette rights based upon general language in prior licenses. Those cases all dealt with licenses which were granted prior to the existence of videocassettes as a technology and as a product that could be sold or rented to the public for home use. They were all decided under what is known as a "future technologies" theory: The original grant was broad enough to encompass future technologies then unknown when the grant was made. If the language in the original grant was not broad enough, the right was not granted. As a result, most agreements now use language such as "now known or hereafter known." Paramount, in the *Cohen* case, unsuccessfully argued the "future technologies" theory. The court, at page 854, dismissed Paramount's contention:

Thus, in 1969—long before the market for videocassettes burgeoned—Cohen could not have assumed that the public would have free and virtually unlimited access to the film in which the composition was played; instead, he must have assumed that viewer access to the film "Medium Cool" would be largely controlled by theatres and networks. By the same token, the original licensee could not have bargained for, or paid for, the rights associated with videocassette reproduction. . . . The holder of the license should not now "reap the entire windfall" associated with the new medium.

The courts have set forth a narrow rule of license interpretation, requiring grants or broad future technologies clauses before holding that a licensee has the rights to exploit a work in a particular medium. It is necessary to determine what happens as a result of a film producer's attempt to grant rights beyond the scope of the license it has obtained from the copyright owner. Granting distribution rights to videocassette distributors without the right to do so is, of course, a copyright infringement under United States copyright law. It is basic schoolyard law and logic: *You simply cannot give away what you don't have.*

As noted in the previous section, in many countries there also exists a broadcast mechanical, which is very similar in concept to the other forms of mechanical licenses and fees, except that it is triggered not by sales but by broadcast. The underlying principle is that a copy must be made of any film or program before it is broadcast on television, and a mechanical license fee is due for that copy. The broadcast mechanical is usually due from each station broadcasting the copy, although some countries limit the total number of individual stations that must pay, say, for example, only the first 13 stations.

Since broadcast mechanical license fees are based on running time, the fees can be substantial, especially if you are dealing with the score for a soundtrack. For example, the broadcast mechanical fee in the U.K. is, give or take depending upon the exchange rate, around $350 per 30 seconds, which works out to a cool $84,000 for a 2-hour soundtrack.

SAMPLE CONTRACT PROVISIONS

EXAMPLE 1: Writer Paid 50% of Mechanical License Fees
3. In consideration of this agreement, Publisher agrees to pay Writer as follows:

• • •

(g) A royalty of fifty (50%) percent of all net sums actually received by Publisher from any license issued authorizing the manufacture of the parts of instruments serving to mechanically reproduce the Composition in the United States of America.

EXAMPLE 2: Broadcast Mechanicals
7. Compensation. Provided that Writer shall faithfully and completely perform the terms, covenants and conditions of this agreement, Publisher hereby agrees to pay Writer for the services to be rendered by Writer under this agreement and for the rights acquired and to be acquired hereunder, the following compensation based on the musical compositions which are the subject hereof:

• • •

(e) Fifty percent (50%) of any and all net sums, after deduction of foreign taxes, actually received (less any costs of collection) by Publisher in the United States from sales, licenses and other uses of the subject musical compositions in countries outside of the United States and Canada (other than public performance societies as hereinabove mentioned in (d), above) from collection agents, licensees, subpublishers or others, whether or not same are affiliated with, owned in whole or in part, or controlled by Publisher.

☛ While not expressly mentioned (probably because the publisher is unaware of their existence), this is where "broadcast mechanicals" would pop up in a songwriters' agreement. Since broadcast mechanicals do not exist in the United States, by default the concept is covered in this foreign income subparagraph (see Chapter 9, the section, "Songwriters' Share of Foreign Receipts," pages 296–298). There are two potential problems. (1) Whether or not the publisher knows this right exists, has the publisher taken the right steps to have these royalties collected? (The answer is, Quite likely not.) (2) If these royalties are collected by a public performance society (such as, for example, the MCPS in England), is it not to the benefit of the writer to be affiliated and paid directly, and not rely on the publisher?

Miscellaneous Income

In addition to the other areas of compensation, there are miscellaneous sources of income for the various parties who share in the income stream from the exploitation of the music contained in a soundtrack. There can be print rights involving some or all of the music contained in the soundtrack. There can be sheet music sales of a song or songs from the soundtrack, perhaps even for the entire score. There can also be merchandising spin-offs somehow triggered by the music, such as, perhaps, a music box or figurine, based on a character in a film, that plays or sings a song from the film.

There are even cases in which the composer, in exchange for services rendered, contribution to the project, or whatever, is given a cut of the profits. A discussion including examples of the net profit structure and accounting practices of the film and television industries is beyond the scope of this work, and the space taken up by such an effort would make this book look tiny by comparison. Nevertheless, Example 2 does show a provision wherein the composer receives a share of the producer's share of net profits.

SAMPLE CONTRACT PROVISIONS

EXAMPLE 1: 50% of Miscellaneous Income

10. For your services rendered hereunder, and for the rights granted herein to us, with respect to the Compositions, we shall pay or cause to be paid to you the following aggregate amounts:

• • •

(d) 50% of all net sums received by us solely with respect to the Compositions written and composed solely by you from any use of such Compositions not dealt with elsewhere in this agreement, provided you are not paid, or to be paid, for such use directly or indirectly by a third party.

☛ You can't get more "miscellaneous" than all sums "not dealt with elsewhere."

EXAMPLE 2: Composer Gets Percentage of Net

6. CONTINGENT COMPENSATION: If the Soundtrack of the Film, as released, was composed by Composer, and Composer has performed as indicated above, and if Composer receives credit in accordance with the provisions of Exhibit A and if this Agreement has not been terminated by the default of Composer, then Producer will pay Composer, as contingent compensation, as follows:

(a) An amount equal to One (1%) Percent of Producer's share of net profits from the Film.

CHAPTER 15

PERFORMANCE, PERFORMING, AND NEIGHBORING RIGHTS

KING RICHARD:
... No more shall be the neighbor to my counsels.
—WILLIAM SHAKESPEARE
King Richard III, Act IV, Scene 2

A discussion is necessary here to differentiate between *performing* rights societies and *performance* rights societies. The terms are often used interchangeably—a sin I must confess to committing in weaker moments—but they mean quite different things. Performing rights refer to the rights in the *material being performed*, e.g., musical compositions. Performance rights refer to the rights in the *performance itself on* behalf of the "performer"—a job description much broader than would appear from the title. Some societies function as both performing rights and performance rights societies (e.g., SACEM, in France), which only adds to the confusion.

We earlier touched on the existence of performing rights societies such as ASCAP and BMI here in the United States. There are also foreign societies which function much like ASCAP and BMI, although, indeed, many of them perform many more functions than do ASCAP and BMI, as we shall see. These societies, some of which are multinational, operate on the basis of the copyright laws of the various countries.

There are also rights that exist which are similar or apparently related to rights based upon copyrights, but which are not based upon copyright law, for which royalties are collected by performance rights societies. These rights, known as neighboring rights and also as copyright-related rights, although common in many territories outside of the United States, were not recognized in this country despite many efforts over the years to change the situation. Because the United States does not recognize these rights, millions of dollars are lost every year by performers, producers (including record companies), and others.

The concept of copyright-related rights may seem foreign to American law. These are rights granted, literally, as an afterthought, to intellectual property rights which may have been overlooked in copyright laws or under conventions. It would not be incorrect to state that these rights have "quasi-copyright" protection. Although arguably foreign to American jurisprudence, copyright-related rights have existed in the United States. For example, prior to February 15, 1972, copyright protection did not exist in sound recordings in the United States; however, certain local jurisdictions had copyright-related laws against record piracy.

Most recently, with the passage of the Digital Performance Right in Sound Recording Act of 1995 (see pages 509–510, 511, and 514–515), a performance right arrived on our virgin shores. This performance right provides a royalty to performers and the copyright owners of recordings played on the Internet and over satellite radio. At this writing, the royalty rate that has been established is 7 cents per song played per 100 listeners. The royalties are put into a pool and distributed 50% to the copright owners of the recordings, 45% to the "featured performers," and 5% to "nonfeatured performers" (backup singers and session musicians).

AMERICAN PERFORMING RIGHTS SOCIETIES

The TV business is a cruel and shallow money trench, a long plastic hallway where thieves and pimps run free, and good men die like dogs.
—HUNTER S. THOMPSON

There's also a negative side.
—DUCKMAN

Quotes run together and featured as full-page ads in *Daily Variety* and the *Hollywood Reporter*, February 5, 1996

The publisher of music, as the copyright owner of the music, has, under U.S. copyright law, the right to grant, or to withhold, permission for the public performance for profit of the controlled compositions. (Remember that the composer of a work does not have the right to grant these rights unless the composer is also the publisher/copyright owner.) Because of the sheer volume of potential licensees—from networks to local stations to mom-and-pop clothing stores on the corner—publishers cannot individually license each user, let alone audit all uses to see if there has been an unauthorized (infringing) performance. Accordingly, a system of clearinghouses—the performing rights societies—has evolved to handle the multitude of licenses and to police the use of the musical compositions. As mentioned elsewhere, here in the United States there are three performing rights societies which monitor performances and collect money on behalf of their publisher and composer members for the public performance for profit of music: ASCAP (American Society of Composers, Authors and Publishers), BMI (Broadcast Music, Inc.), and SESAC (Society of European Stage Authors and Composers). Obviously, how and what they find directly affects payments made to their members.

ASCAP operates as a not-for-profit organization. BMI is owned by various entities, but operates as a quasi not-for-profit organization, and SESAC gleefully operates as a private, for-profit company. To quote the cochairman of SESAC: "Because we are a private company, we have the privilege of doing whatever we want."

It hasn't really mattered what SESAC wanted to do, as it is dwarfed by ASCAP and BMI and has been of little or no real importance in the overall scheme of things. In 1992, however, SESAC was acquired by new owners, who committed themselves to making the smaller company competitive with ASCAP and BMI. In 1993 SESAC announced that they had developed a computerized per-play system for logging and licensing music performances that was claimed to be superior to the blanket licensing systems used by ASCAP and BMI. (The three systems are described in more detail below.) Although SESAC has made a concerted move to challenge the monopoly-like positions of its two larger competitors, their efforts, to date, have had little impact.

The blanket licenses offered by ASCAP and BMI both give their licensees unlimited access to their catalogues in exchange for license fees generally based upon the type and size of the user (radio, network television, local television, concert hall, clothing store, etc.). For years the standard fee from ASCAP and BMI for commercial radio stations was based on the stations' gross advertising revenue, usually around 2.5%. BMI still collects fees in this way, but ASCAP has changed its collection method. The change came as something of a shock. ASCAP, which has been under an antitrust decree for nearly half its existence, had been restricted by the government for years from making significant changes in its operation. In October of 2004, a federal district judge approved a new agreement between ASCAP and the Radio Music License Committee, an association of broadcasters representing most of the nearly 12,000 commercial radio stations in the United States. Under the agreement, revenue-based license fees have been replaced by a set payment schedule.

The total amount, over $1.7 billion, is spread over a period of years, retroactively back to 2001 and forward through 2009. Included in the blanket license granted to the radio stations is the right for the stations to stream ASCAP compositions on their Internet Websites. A similar agreement was made between ASCAP and the Television Music License Committee, a not-for-profit organization that represents over 1,200 local stations in their negotiations with ASCAP, BMI, and SESAC. This agreement, however, which covers an 11-year period (retroactively from 1998 and forward to 2009), uses a different concept for determining fees. The rate from April 1998 through November 20, 2004, remained at the rate the stations had been paying—$98.1 million per year. On December 1, 2004, the rate went to $85 million per year. And, starting in 2006, the rate will increase yearly based on the previous year's increase in the Consumer Price Index.

ASCAP

There are two golden rules for an orchestra: start together and finish together. The public doesn't give a damn what goes on in between.

—SIR THOMAS BEECHAM

ASCAP was originally formed in 1914 by composer Victor Herbert and a number of his Broadway composer pals. The story, as told to me—correctly or incorrectly, I've heard different versions—was that Herbert and a friend were having dinner in New York with Italian opera composer Giacomo Puccini (*Madame Butterfly*, *La Bohème*, etc.) at Luchow's, a famous restaurant (alas, now closed) featuring heavy German cuisine, dark wood paneling, dead animal heads protruding from walls, and rotating music groups performing live (oompah bands in lederhosen and string quartets in formal wear). One of the groups (presumably the string quartet, but, who knows, it could have been the oompah band) played one of Victor Herbert's songs. Puccini was shocked to learn that Herbert received no payment for the use of his music by the restaurant. In Europe, he explained, he received money—lot of money—for the public performances of his music.

Needless to say, the next day Herbert put the word out that there should be a meeting. He was joined by 11 other composers, Irving Berlin, John Philip Sousa, and Jerome Kern included, and, voilà, ASCAP was formed. Purportedly, the first public establishment to obtain an ASCAP license for live performances, for an annual fee of $180, was Rector's Restaurant on Broadway in New York City.

Another version has it that Victor Herbert was dining at Shanley's, also in New York City, when he heard one of his songs being played without his permission. He sued the restaurant and then formed ASCAP. Although it is true Herbert sued Shanley's for the unauthorized public performance of his music,[1] the Luchow's story rings truer. While Herbert was born in Ireland, he was raised in Germany and had a lifelong affection for German food and beer.

Whether or not either of these stories is correct, it is true that ASCAP was formed in 1914, and for many years it was the only game in town and had a virtual monopoly on licensing public performance rights for music in the United States.

ASCAP collects for public performances of its members' music by monitoring "public performances for profit." The revenue collected from licensees (radio and television broadcasters, theaters, concert halls, bars, hotels, etc.) is allocated to the works of members based upon the method of performance. For example, television revenues are distributed to members on the basis of television performance, etc. ASCAP uses two logging systems to determine what it calls its "survey": the *sample* and the *census*. The sampling method is by far the more important of the two. ASCAP describes the method as follows:

> [The sample] is *random, stratified*, and *disproportionate*. A *random* sample is scientific by definition. It is determined solely by mathematical probability and leaves no room for personal discretion. The randomness extends to the time periods of the day, and to the days of the year. Under this system, every performance has a chance of coming into the survey.... [The] sample is *stratified* because licensees are classified into groups that have significant common characteristics.... [They] are stratified by media (e.g., local radio, local television); by type of community (e.g., metropolitan, rural); by major geographic regions (e.g., New England, Middle Atlantic, Pacific); and by size of the licensee in terms of annual fees to ASCAP (e.g., $1,000 to $10,000; $10,000 to $20,000 and so on).
>
> Thus, rather than draw a random sample ... [ASCAP] draw[s] a random sample simultaneously from each of 432 "stratified cells." ...
>
> [The] sample is *disproportionate* because the depth of the sample varies with the amount of the fees paid by licensees within each stratified cell. A station which pays ASCAP $20,000 in license fees is sampled twice as much as a station which pays ASCAP only $10,000. The greater the licensing fees, the greater the sampling depth. All radio and television stations that pay $10,000 or more per year are included in the sample each year.[2]

According to ASCAP the sampling method used in its survey is "determined solely by mathematical probability" and is done by recorded air checks of radio and television stations. When a musical composition is identified from the recorded air checks, it is fed into the formula and, theoretically, a representative allocation of collected fees is made based upon the percentage of "plays" credited to the composition. Since sampling is a collection of a small amount of data to extrapolate larger, representative numbers, depending upon the formula used, it may be statistically accurate, but not necessarily quantitatively accurate.

---

[1] The suit went all the way up to the United States Supreme Court, where Herbert won. In the opinion of the court, Justice Oliver Wendell Holmes states: "If music did not pay, it would be given up. Whether it pays or not, the purpose of employing it is profit and that is enough...." Herbert's right to receive payment was protected. It sounds like a nearly hundred-year-old argument against unauthorized free downloading.

[2] *The ASCAP Survey and Your Royalties*, 1992.

For example, I had a client who had received considerably less than $100 over a 3-year period from ASCAP for the soundtrack of a television program that solicited contributions to a charity. The program was shown so many times that anyone who has ever channel-surfed would recognize it instantly. Because of the nature of the show, basically a paid 30-minute commercial, we were able to obtain certified proof of broadcast for each broadcast. Applying the BMI formula (see below) to these broadcasts, the performance royalty for my client (as both publisher and composer) would have been almost $60,000. ASCAP's response: "We didn't pick it up in the sample."

The census method is used mainly for broadcasts aired by the major television networks, ABC, CBS, and NBC (the Fox network, and the other second-tier networks, are not included). Program logs and cue sheets are supposed to be provided to ASCAP by the networks and program producers. ASCAP does make audiotapes and videotapes of the performances in order to verify the information received from the networks and the program producers.

Local television surveying is based upon a two-part system. The first part is based upon a census system for syndicated programming. According to the *The ASCAP Survey and Your Royalties*, the "syndicated programming" covered by the ASCAP census includes both syndicated shows and series as well as films "on those stations which account for the largest fees distributed on the basis of local television performances." The second method involves a combination of cue sheets, tapes, regional issues of *TV Guide*, and information supplied by TV Data, the company which provides programming information for newspapers.

Public broadcasting is surveyed using the sampling method, although, according to ASCAP, fewer hours are sampled because the fees paid by public stations are much lower than those paid by commercial broadcasters.

When it comes to cable television, different methods are used for surveying. First of all, ASCAP distinguishes between programs that are originated by cable operations (for example, HBO, Arts & Entertainment, etc.) and those that are *secondary transmissions*, which are over-the-air broadcasts picked up by cable and retransmitted to cable subscribers. For secondary transmissions, performances are based upon samples of the local television stations being retransmitted by the cable companies.

Cable-originated programming is surveyed in different ways depending upon the source of the program. HBO programming uses a census basis, that is, program logs and cue sheets. Other cable systems, including American Movie Classics, Arts & Entertainment, Black Entertainment Television, Bravo, Comedy Television, Cinemax, CNN, CNN Headline News, Country Music Channel, Lifetime, The Movie Channel, MTV, The Nashville Network, Nickelodeon, Playboy, Prism, Showtime, Turner Network Television, and USA Network, use a sample basis.

The one exception to ASCAP's method of assessment and allocation is for performances of what ASCAP calls "serious" or "standard" (a.k.a. "classical") music. Symphony and concert halls and educational institutions submit programs for "serious music" concerts. For such works, the license fee received is multiplied by 5. However, if the artist is paid less than $1,500 at an educational institution, the normal sample basis is used. Any background music is logged by census.

ASCAP claims that 80% of revenue collected is distributed to its members.

BMI

I've outdone anyone you can name—Mozart, Beethoven, Bach,
Strauss. Irving Berlin, he wrote 1,001 tunes. I wrote 5,500.
—JAMES BROWN

BMI was formed in 1939–1940 as an alternative to ASCAP. At the time, ASCAP operated as a relatively closed society. In order to join ASCAP as a writer, a writer had to have had a minimum of 5 hit songs published. As a result, there were only about 1,100 writers who had ASCAP membership. ASCAP publishers numbered only about 140, and about 15 controlled 90% of the music played on the radio. Between 1931 and 1939, ASCAP's license fees to radio stations increased by 448%. The word was out; another big licensing fee jump was in the works—a 100% increase in 1940. In the fall of 1939, a number of radio station owners got together in Chicago and agreed that if ASCAP could do it, so could they. Thus was BMI—with cheaper license fees and a more open-door policy on membership for writers and publishers—born.

By the end of 1940, 650 stations had signed on with BMI and, after their licenses had run out with ASCAP, only about 200 small stations remained with ASCAP. 1941 was a lean year for the radio audience. BMI was just getting up to speed, ASCAP was effectively locked out of the market, and many stations relied on public domain compositions for radio play—Stephen Foster's (*I Dream of*) *Jeanie with the Light Brown Hair* was one of the most played compositions that year.

BMI is a performance rights society and deals only with the licensing and administration of public performance for profit. It collects license fees from the users of the music and then allocates the revenue to its member publishers and composers. The revenue collected from licensees is allocated to the works of members based upon the logging of performances.

Unlike ASCAP, BMI relies on the logging of performances rather than the sampling of broadcasts. BMI uses some 500,000 hours of broadcast logs for determining members' shares of revenue collected from users. According to *The BMI Story* (BMI, 1987):

> [A] scientifically chosen representative cross section of stations is logged each quarter. The stations which are being logged supply complete information as to all music performed. These lists or logs are put through an elaborate data processing system in which eventually each performance is multiplied by a factor which reflects the ratio of the number of stations logged to the number licensed. If, for example, BMI licenses 500 stations of a certain kind and 10 of them were logged during a given period, every performance of a song listed would be multiplied by 50 and the writer and publisher would receive credit for 50 performances every time the work appeared on a log.

Television theme and cue music is logged with the aid of cue sheets prepared by the producer which list all works performed in the program. The number of performances of music in motion pictures, syndicated film series, and certain other types of TV shows are counted with the aid of cue sheets and computerized data similar to that used by about 110 regional editions of *TV Guide*, which provides information for a virtual census of all syndicated programs and motion pictures shown on local TV. In addition, BMI does a sampling on TV stations which mirrors station-originated local music usage.

BMI claims that 85% of revenue collected is distributed to its members.

SESAC

SESAC and SESAC Latina (a branch of SESAC devoted exclusively to Spanish-language music) use a computerized system for the identification and tracking of musical compositions which, according to SESAC, allows them to monitor 10 times more airplay than ASCAP and BMI combined and to charge broadcasters on an actual per-play basis for the use of SESAC compositions. SESAC maintains that this tracking and payment method allows it to pay its composers and publishers higher royalties than are paid by ASCAP and BMI.

INTERNATIONAL COPYRIGHT OVERVIEW

Copyright protection exists in one form or another almost everywhere in the world—sort of. In fact, the details of copyright protection vary from country to country. There are various international conventions and treaties which attempt to establish some sort of relationship or connection between the different copyright laws of the signatory countries. You are about to learn more than you probably want or need to know about international conventions and treaties on copyright—feel free to move on to the next section if your curiosity is not aroused.

Do be aware that, in spite of these conventions and treaties, there is no one-stop location where a copyright holder can drive up to the copyright equivalent of a drive-through window, sign a registration form, and drive off with a one-size-fits-all copyright registration giving protection around the world. Also, no copyright holder from one country is going to get more protection in any other country than is offered to domestic copyright holders in that country.

The granddaddy of international copyright conventions is the Berne Convention for the Protection of Literary and Artistic Works of September 9, 1886. The Berne Convention was revised numerous times, at different places, over the years: Berlin (1908); back to Berne (1914); on to Rome (1928); then to Brussels (1948); up to Stockholm (1967); and finally to Paris (1971). The last amendments were made in 1979. That's a lot of plastic surgery, but the old gal (since it's the "granddaddy," maybe that should be the old boy) still looks pretty good. Good enough for the United States to sign on in 1989.

At the moment, 151 countries are signatories to the Berne Convention. One of the basic tenets of the Berne Convention is that each signatory country must grant the same copyright treatment to nationals from other member countries as they do to their own nationals. The United States was tardy (what's 103 years among friends?) in becoming a signatory because of its early refusal to accept certain concepts which were part of the package, such as *droit moral* and different requirements requiring notice, registration, and term of copyright.

The United States was not the only country having problems becoming a signatory to the Berne Convention. A number of developing countries were hesitant to join, believing they were better off not having the strict regulations contained in the Berne Convention. Developing countries are invariably resistant to copyright regulations until, of course, they develop their own intellectual properties that need protection from other developing countries (for example, China; see below, page 424). The Soviet Union and many Latin American countries also held out until relatively late in the game.

Through the United Nations Educational, Scientific and Cultural Organizations (UNESCO), an alternate choice to the Berne Convention was developed. This was the Universal Copyright Convention (UCC) of September 1952. The UCC was less stringent than the Berne Convention. The United States signed on to the UCC in 1955, as did a lot of those less developed folks. Most of the Berne Convention members at that time also signed on to the UCC. Why not? This linked them with the United States.

For those countries who are signatories to both the Berne Convention and the UCC and find themselves with a conflict between the two, the terms of the Berne Convention take precedent over those of the UCC. Once the United States and most of the UCC signatories joined the Berne Convention, the UCC became more of a historical footnote than an operating convention.

The Convention for the Protection of Producers of Phonograms Against Unauthorized Duplication of Their Phonograms, which focuses on piracy issues, was adopted in Geneva in 1971.

The next international agreement of importance came into being with the establishment of the World Trade Organization (WTO). The Marrakesh Agreement Establishing the World Trade Organization was signed in Marrakesh, Morocco, on April 15, 1994. An "annex" to that agreement was the Agreement on Trade-Related Aspects of Intellectual Property Rights (TRIPS).

The heritage of TRIPS—as a "descendant" of the WTO, it helps to calm the troubled international trade waters for the purposes of protecting and opening the international marketplace for intellectual properties—is obvious. Among other things, TRIPS reinstated foreign copyrights which, under United States law, had fallen into public domain for not meeting American copyright requirements; installed a form of "most favored nations" for intellectual property rights; and generally helped large corporations protect their intellectual property rights around the world.

Next came the World Intellectual Property Organization (WIPO) Performances and Phonograms Treaty drawn up at Geneva in December 1996. The Preamble of the WIPO treaty reads as follows:

The Contracting Parties,

Desiring to develop and maintain the protection of the rights of authors in their literary and artistic works in a manner as effective and uniform as possible,

Recognizing the need to introduce new international rules and clarify the interpretation of certain existing rules in order to provide adequate solutions to the questions raised by new economic, social, cultural and technological developments,

Recognizing the profound impact of the development and convergence of information and communication technologies on the creation and use of literary and artistic works,

Emphasizing the outstanding significance of copyright protection as an incentive for literary and artistic creation,

Recognizing the need to maintain a balance between the rights of authors and the larger public interest, particularly education, research and access to information, as reflected in the Berne Convention,

Have agreed as follows: . . .

WIPO was meant to beef up international copyright protection in the new digital age and led directly to the U.S. Congress passing the Digital Millennium Copyright Act. (See Chapter 21.)

FOREIGN SOCIETIES

The following alphabetical list of foreign organizations is not all-inclusive, but does cover the major performance societies around the world which are important in the administration and collection of revenue from the exploitation of music copyrights.

APRA (Australasian Performance Rights Association) is a multinational performing rights society based in Australia that also covers New Zealand, New Guinea, Fiji, Papua, Western Samoa, and Ross Dependency. It licenses, administers, and collects and distributes revenues for the public performance of music.

BUMA (formally known as Het Bureau voor Muziek Auteursrecht, now known as Vereniging Bureau voor Muziek Auteursrecht) is a multinational performing rights society which collects in the Netherlands as well as a number of former Dutch colonies.

CMRRA (Canadian Musical Reproductions Rights Agency Limited) (CMRRA) is a mechanical rights society serving Canadian publishers and composers.

GEMA (Gesellschaft für musikalische Aufführungs und mechanische Vervielfältigungsrechte) is (in addition to being a mouthful) both a performing rights and a mechanical rights society. A multinational society, it represents its members throughout the German-speaking world, including some former German colonies, and, more and more, in countries that were former members of the U.S.S.R. GEMA also services countries which do not fit into the above linguistic or geographic categories, such as South Korea, Taiwan, Iran, and Turkey.

IFPI (International Federation of the Phonographic Industry) is a multinational organization for record companies and their video equivalents. Its closest equivalent in the United States is the Recording Industry Association of America (RIAA). RIAA, which is affiliated with IFPI, represents the interests of the American record industry. The IFPI states that "any company, firm or person producing sound recordings or music videos which are made available to the public in reasonable quantities is eligible for membership."

JASRAC (Japanese Society for Rights of Authors, Composers and Publishers) is a multinational performing rights and mechanical rights society. JASRAC is meticulous when it comes to attention to detail and monitoring the multitude of categories and subcategories of public performances (the formulas for live performances differ depending on a number of factors, including type of music, number of seats and/or tables, and the square footage of the location).

MCPS (Mechanical Copyright Protection Society), based in the United Kingdom, does many of the same things the Harry Fox Agency does in the United States. However, the term "mechanical rights" in the United Kingdom encompasses rights which are beyond the mechanical rights provided for in U.S. copyright law. MCPS makes blanket agreements with broadcasters in the broadcasters' capacity as original programmers making use of members' music. The licenses deal with "mechanical reproduction" and not the transmission of the copyrighted works. This is what is known as a "broadcast mechanical." A broadcast mechanical, which does not exist in the United States, is based upon the presumption that a broadcaster will make a copy of the work for broadcast purposes.

PPL (Phonographic Performance Limited) licenses, administers, and collects and distributes revenues for the public use of sound recordings in the United Kingdom. The English Copyright Act of 1956 created a copyright covering the public use of sound recordings. This performing right is separate and distinct from the rights of publishers and composers, which are administered and collected by the PRS (see below). (Presently, there is no equivalent provision in American law providing for a royalty to the producers and performers of sound recordings based upon the public performance of the sound recordings.) PPL controls the licensing of sound recordings in all formats for public performance. PPL licenses all broadcasting—radio and television, BBC and commercial—for the use of sound recordings. PPL also licenses discos, shopping malls, theaters, cinemas, football stadiums, etc., which make use of sound recordings and play ("perform") them for the public. Membership in the PPL is made up of producer/copyright owners and performers of sound recordings. (See also the discussion of VPL, below.)

PRS (Performing Rights Society), a multinational organization, is the equivalent to ASCAP and BMI for the United Kingdom (and a whole lot of what used to be the British Empire). Founded in 1914, the PRS is a performing rights society administering, licensing, collecting, and disbursing revenue from the public performance of musical works. The PRS collects royalties in much the same way that ASCAP and BMI do in the United States—by granting blanket licenses to broadcasters and other users which gives them the right to publicly perform the works controlled by the societies.

SABAM (Société Belge des Auteurs, Compositeurs et Editeurs) is a multinational performing rights and mechanical rights society which administers and collects in Belgium, Burundi, and Rwanda. For many years, Belgium as a territory was considered to be relatively unimportant. In agreements, the territory was invariably lumped together with Holland and/or Luxembourg ("the Benelux") and/or France. In 1985, Brussels enacted a cable retransmission law which provided for a performance royalty to be collected from societies from neighboring countries which had previously received programming from Belgium by reason of proximity rather than by contract. Since the first year's collection for such retransmission of American films and television programs alone amounted to some $80 million, the importance of Belgium as a separate territory is now established. (The only real question I've ever had about SABAM is why it isn't called SBACE.)

SACEM (Société des Auteurs, Compositeurs et Editeurs de Musique) is multinational performing rights society for France and over 30 other territories, most of which, but not all, were formerly part of the French empire. SACEM administers and collects for performing rights, performance rights, broadcast royalties for producers and performers (*droits voisins*), and neighboring rights.

SDRM (Société pour l'Administration du Droit de Reproduction Mechanique) is a multinational mechanical rights society for France, Belgium, Luxembourg, and the former colonies of France. Of particular interest for soundtrack music is the fact that when it comes to home video sales, the producer or distributor, notwithstanding anything attempted in the agreements, cannot waive the mechanical royalties in connection with the sale of the video. SDRM collects a royalty of either 8% of the retail price or 11% of the dealer price, less value-added tax, on each copy sold.

SIAE (Società Italiana degli Autori ed Editori) is a government-controlled performing rights and mechanical rights society which is managed by a board of directors mostly made up of major Italian music publishers (isn't there a saying about not letting the fox manage the henhouse?). SIAE licenses, administers, collects, and distributes revenues for mechanical rights and public performance of music, including performance royalties generated from the theatrical exhibition of motion pictures.

SOCAN (Society of Composers, Authors and Music Publishers of Canada) is now the only performing rights society in Canada. Formed in 1990, it represents a merger of the two prior existing performing rights societies in Canada: Composers, Authors and Publishers Association of Canada (CAPAC) and the Performing Rights Organization of Canada (PROCAN). PROCAN deals only with performing rights—the right to perform the work in public or to broadcast the work—in Canada.

STEMRA (StichtingStemra), based in the Netherlands, is a multinational mechanical rights society affiliated with BUMA. STEMRA is important as a mechanical rights society in that 70% to 80% of all recordings and videos for Germany, Belgium, Denmark, and the United Kingdom are manufactured in Holland.

SUISA (Schweizerische Gesellschafifur die Rechte die Urheber Musikalischer Werke), which operates almost exactly like GEMA, is a performing rights and mechanical rights society.

VPL (Video Performance Limited) licenses, administers, and collects and distributes revenues for the public use of music in the form of sound recordings synchronized with videotape in any form in the United Kingdom. This right exists on behalf of the producer/copyright owner (which may be a record company) and performer of the sound recording used with the video and is separate and distinct from the rights of the publisher and composer of the underlying music. Presently, there is no equivalent provision in U.S. law to provide for a royalty to the producers and performers of sound recordings based upon the public performance of the sound recordings. This is not a synchronization license for the underlying music, nor is it a master license granting the video producer the right to use the sound recordings. These are both licensed, or refused a license, separately. VPL licenses the public performance of these sound recordings synchronized with the video tape after the initial licenses have been obtained to use the music and the recording. VPL licenses all broadcasting, BBC and commercial, for the public use of sound recordings synchronized with videotape. VPL also licenses any establishment, such as discos, clubs, hotels, shopping malls, etc., which may play ("perform") them for the public. Membership in the VPL is made up of producer/copyright owners and performers of sound recordings. (See also the discussion of PPL, above.)

NEIGHBORING RIGHTS

> BOYET:
>
> **Warily**
> **I stole into a neighborhood thicket by,**
>> —WILLIAM SHAKESPEARE
>> *Love's Labor's Lost*, Act V, Scene 2

Certain rights which are not explicitly covered by American copyright law, and consequently are not recognized in the United States either by law or by custom, do exist in other countries, either through international conventions, national laws, or both. These rights, known as *neighboring rights*, are *related to* rights conferred by copyright statutes in that they rely on the preexistence of something eligible for protection by copyright and concern the exploitation or use of the copyrighted material.

Although the type of use of copyrighted materials that falls within the scope of neighboring rights varies from country to country, in general, neighboring rights are the rights retained by performers, phonogram producers, video producers, and broadcast organizations (and others as defined by various territories) in the product of their creative activity. Depending on the country, neighboring rights may also include related rights in photographs, portraits, first-edition books and typographical arrangements; lending and rental rights; tape software and hardware levy rights (fees collected on the sale of digital recorders and blank digital tapes and discs); as well as the rights of individual producers and authors to legal protection of the artistic integrity of their work (*droit moral*).

The legal concept of *droit moral* (moral rights) originated in France; it is expressly provided for in Article 6*bis* of the Berne Convention:

> Independently of the author's economic rights, and even after the transfer of the said rights, the author shall have the right to claim authorship of the work and to object to any distortion, mutilation, or other modification of, or other derogatory action in relation to, the said work, which would be prejudicial to his honor or reputation.

The only jurisdictions which come close to the French-model protection of the moral rights of artists—"artists" in the broadest sense of the word—are those countries that have adopted that model. The essence of the French version of *droit moral* is that notwithstanding "economic" arrangements (sale, lease, gift, etc., of a work) the artist still retains certain specific and important rights in and to that work. Under French law, the artist may not legally waive those rights. There are four key rights in the French laws governing *droit moral*:

1. The right of display or disclosure. Even after sale or transfer, the artist has the legal right to determine whether or not the work can be shown to the public.

2. The right of attribution. The artist has the right to choose whether or not his or her name will be attached to the work.

3. The right of retaining or protecting quality. The artist has the right to protect the work from any modification or distortion which may prove to be professionally embarrassing or harm the artist's reputation.

4. The right to recall the work. The artist has the right, retroactively, to withdraw the work from public display.

I know of no law in the United States that comes close to 1 (right of display) or 4 (right to recall), although there are no doubt contracts entered into by private individuals with consideration and all the other elements which make a contract enforceable that reflect those concepts.

As to the other two rights (attribution and protection of quality), U.S. copyright law does not specifically recognize the moral rights of authors, at least not in the language common to most European copyright statutes. There are, however, two sections of the U.S. Copyright Act that do refer to a work's integrity, one implicitly and one explicitly. Section 115 states that a compulsory license for use of a nondramatic musical work does not give the arranger or performer the right to "change the basic melody or fundamental character of the work." Section 106A, the Visual Artists Rights Act of 1990 (added to the Copyright Act of 1976 in October 1990), recognizes that authors of a work of visual art (painting, drawing, print, or sculpture) have the right to "attribution and integrity," even after transfer of ownership.

"Attribution" under Section 106A means that the visual artist has the right to claim authorship—or, in other words, receive "credit"—for the work of visual art. The section also provides that not only may the visual artist "prevent the use of his or her name as the author of any work of visual art which he or she did not create," but also may prevent the use of his or her name as author of visual art "in the event of a distortion, mutilation, or other modification of the work which would be prejudicial to his or her honor or reputation." "Integrity" refers to the visual artist's right to "prevent any intentional distortion, mutilation, or other modification of that work which would be prejudicial to his or her honor or reputation." These rights of the visual artist are subject to the exceptions for fair use provided for in Section 107 of the 1976 act.

There is a California law, California Civil Code Sections 986 and 987, which, in addition to granting California artists a piece of subsequent sales of their fine art, also grants, albeit not by name, certain *droit moral* protection. Section 987(a) provides:

> (a) The Legislature hereby finds and declares that the physical alteration or destruction of fine art, which is an expression of the artist's personality, is detrimental to the artist's reputation, and artists therefore have an interest in protecting their works of fine art against any alteration or destruction; and that there is also a public interest in preserving the integrity of cultural and artistic creations.

which certainly walks like and quacks like *droit moral*.

Section 987(d) also walks like and quacks like *droit moral*. Section 987(d) provides:

> The artist shall retain at all times the right to claim authorship, or, for a just and valid reason, to disclaim authorship of his or her work of fine art.

Terminology becomes ticklish in any discussion of neighboring rights as to who or what is eligible to receive royalty fees for a particular use. For our purposes, the use of the term "author" is not correct in either the legal or the general sense of the word. (We have already seen that under U.S. copyright law the author of a work for hire is not the person who created the work, but the employer of that person.) Often the person entitled to a neighboring rights fee is a performer. However, there are entities (or individuals) who clearly are not performers but who are afforded protection and remuneration under neighboring rights. For example, in Germany broadcast organizations and photographers are covered by neighboring rights. In addition, who or what is a "performer" may vary from country to country, as will be seen below.

To avoid confusion, it is perhaps best to speak of the *recipient* of the rights, or more precisely the recipient of the royalties generated from the various uses of the rights. This is sort of backwards engineering: You start with the end result and then work backwards to figure out what made it work.

What qualifies as a neighboring right, and who or what qualifies as the "recipient" in a particular country, may vary as you move from country to country.

Neighboring rights differ from copyrights in several ways. As already pointed out, neighboring rights involve an exploitation or use of copyrighted material, but the beneficiary (or, to use our terminology, the recipient) of the fees collected for the use need not be the owner of the underlying copyright. For example, a record producer may be eligible for performance royalties when a recording is broadcast even though the producer may not own any copyright in the musical composition or in the phonorecord.

The derivative works contained in neighboring rights differ from rights in other derivative works which are protected by copyright, such as a translation of literature to another language, an arrangement of a musical work, etc. For example, Section 103 of the Copyright Act of 1976 states:

(a) The subject matter of copyright as specified by section 102 includes compilations and derivative works, but protection for a work employing preexisting material in which copyright subsists does not extend to any part of the work in which such material has been used unlawfully.

(b) The copyright in a compilation or derivative work extends only to the material contributed by the author of such work, as distinguished from the preexisting material employed in the work, and does not imply any exclusive right in the preexisting material. The copyright in such work is independent of, and does not affect or enlarge the scope, duration, ownership, or subsistence of, any copyright protection in the preexisting material.

Under the Copyright Act, the derivative works which are eligible for copyright protection, while derivative, are new-copyright works because of the creative and original change to the preexisting work. However, in the area of neighboring rights, the derivative works are not commonly seen as creations of new works, but as *interpretations* of existing work. Whether a work is seen as a "new work" or an "interpretation" is an important technical and legal distinction. If it is a new work, copyright laws, not neighboring rights laws, apply. By classifying a derivative work as an "interpretation" in jurisdictions recognizing neighboring rights, the recipients are eligible to receive royalties. In general, however, neighboring rights are usually narrower in scope than those granted by copyright law, and are limited to reproduction rights, public performance rights, broadcast rights, and, in some countries, moral rights.

Another difference between neighboring rights and copyright is length of term. In most countries having copyright laws, the term of copyright is now the life of the author plus a specified period of time. In the United States, for example, the period of copyright is the life of the author plus 70 years, or, in the case of a work for hire, 95 years from publication. Neighboring rights, on the other hand, are usually limited to a fixed period, expressed in years, from the fixation of the work or the publication of the work. According to international conventions, the minimum term of protection of neighboring rights is 20 years.

THE ROME CONVENTION OF 1961

The Berne Convention, although recognizing that the rights of performers, phonogram producers, and broadcasters warranted some degree of protection, did not grant copyright protection of such rights. In 1936, Austria granted performers and producers a form of neighboring rights. Italy followed suit in 1941. This problem was finally addressed on a broader scale in The International Convention for the Protection of Performers, Producers of Phonograms and Broadcasting Organizations of 1961, more commonly known as the Rome Convention, which granted protection of neighboring rights.

The Rome Convention provides for the protection of neighboring rights to citizens of the signatory nations and, interestingly, some other nations. Although the quality and degree of protection differ according to national laws, many nations have ratified the Rome Convention or have laws granting similar protection. The protection of the neighboring rights of foreign nationals is generally based upon reciprocal treatment under national laws and membership of international conventions.

Presently there are 76 countries that are signatories to the Rome Convention. The United States is not a party to the Rome Convention and, accordingly, does not grant neighboring rights. Because of this, the protection afforded to U.S. nationals by the laws of foreign nations, based on reciprocity, is quite limited.

In general, the terms of the Rome Convention cover performers' rights, producers' rights, and the rights of broadcasting organizations, subject to some variation from territory to territory. The Rome Convention provides for "national treatment" of the rights granted by the local laws. Article 2 reads as follows:

> 1. For the purposes of this Convention, national treatment shall mean the treatment accorded by the domestic law of the Contracting State in which protection is claimed:
>
> (a) to performers who are its nationals, as regards performances taking place, broadcast, or first fixed, on its territory;
>
> (b) to producers of phonograms who are its nationals, as regards phonograms first fixed or first published on its territory;
>
> (c) to broadcasting organisations which have their headquarters on its territory, as regards broadcasts transmitted from transmitters situated on its territory.

Because of the local nature of the applicable laws, who or what qualifies as a performer, producer, or broadcasting organization may vary from country to country.

Performers' Rights

In the terms of the Rome Convention, a "performer" is an actor, singer, musician, dancer, or other person who acts, sings, delivers, declaims, plays in, or otherwise performs literary or artistic works. The performer must perform in "literary or artistic works," not sports events. In order to qualify as a performer for these purposes the performer may not be a mere extra. According to Article 4 of the Rome Conveention, nonnationals are granted "national treatment" in a Rome Convention territory as "performers":

> ... if any of the following conditions are met:
>
> (a) the performance takes place in another Contracting State;
>
> (b) the performance is incorporated in a phonogram which is protected under Article 5 of this Convention;
>
> (c) the performance, not being fixed on a phonogram, is carried by a broadcast which is protected by Article 6 of this Convention.

This is known as a "point of attachment" in the quaint language favored in international treaties and conventions. It means the act, thing, or circumstance that is a precondition which must be met in order to qualify a performance for inclusion in the terms of the treaty and, as a result, generate the right to receive a royalty.

The rights granted to performers by the Rome Convention as performers' rights are the right to control the:

1. Fixation [incorporation in a "material object," e.g., disc, tape] of a live performance

2. Broadcast of a live performance

3. Subsequent reproduction of the fixation

4. Broadcast of such a fixation

The first two rights, the control of the fixation and broadcast of a live performance, are the rights to either authorize or forbid the use of a live performance. What constitutes a "live performance" may vary from one country to another. A public performance before a live audience, such as a concert, will be deemed to be a live performance in every jurisdiction; but a recording session in a studio may or may not be deemed to be a live performance, depending upon the local regulations.

The third right, the right to control a subsequent reproduction of the fixation of the performance, is permitted only if the reproduction is for a different purpose from that for which the performer originally granted permission. For example, the grant of the right to reproduce a fixation for broadcast purposes is not a grant of the right to reproduce the fixation for home video use. In a way, this right, although not a payment in itself, is somewhat analogous to reuse payments to musicians who perform for the recording of a soundtrack for a film and then receive a reuse payment when the soundtrack is licensed for release as a soundtrack recording.

The fourth right, the right to control broadcast of such a fixation, is more like a compulsory license in that the performer need not authorize each such use, but must be equitably compensated after the use. The collection and distribution of such "equitable compensation" is usually done through collecting societies which monitor such performances and collect and distribute royalties on behalf of performers. Among the signatory countries, the trend today seems to be to grant more extensive rights to performers than are provided for by the Rome Convention, for example, a wider range of rights protecting the reputation and/or integrity of performers and their works.

Producers' Rights

For the purposes of the Rome Convention, a "producer" is the person or entity credited as the producer. Accordingly, credit becomes an issue beyond career and ego issues. The official definition for "producer of phonograms" in Article 3(c) of the Rome Convention is "the person who, or the *legal entity* [emphasis added]which, first fixes the sounds of a performance or other sounds;

Use of the term "legal entity" means that the record company, not just the producer, is eligible to participate as a producer. Frequently the determination as to which, individual or company, gets to participate may come down to which, if either, bothered to file the necessary papers.

The three basic protected rights of producers are the right:

1. To reproduce the work in question

2. To control the public performance of the work in question

3. To control the broadcast of the work in question

The first of the producer's rights, the right to control the reproduction of the work, gives the producer the right to authorize or prohibit reproduction of a fixation of the work. The Rome Convention grants the producer the right to prohibit the reproduction of the fixation whether the fixation is direct, such as broadcast, or indirect, such as the reproduction of a tape as a part of home taping (unless allowed by the private-use exception of the Rome Convention, which is a matter of national law).

The second and third rights, the right to control the public performance of the work in question and the right to control the broadcast of the work in question, depend upon the national laws of the particular jurisdiction. In some jurisdictions, the right may be absolute; in others, it may operate like a compulsory license requiring equitable remuneration to be paid to the producer after the broadcast.

In the case of the producer's eligibility to enforce these rights, the phonogram itself must qualify. On the face of it, since the United States is not a signatory to the Rome Convention, it would seem that recordings first released in the United States would not qualify. There is, however, a way for U.S.-released recordings, and other nonsignatory-based recordings, to qualify. Article 5, 2. of the Rome Convention states:

> 2. If a phonogram was first published in a non-contracting State but if it was also published, within thirty days of its first publication, in a Contracting State (simultaneous publication), it shall be considered as first published in the Contracting State.

In other words, if an American label's recording is released domestically and then, within 30 days, is released in one of the signatory countries, say, the United Kingdom, France, or Burkina Faso, the recording qualifies for protection under the Rome Convention of 1961. However, since exceptions under local laws are allowed, there is a always possibility that the signatory country may have opted out from the simultaneous-publication option contained in Article 5, 2. Under Article 5, 3. any signatory country may decide to negate Article 5, 2. within its own territory. Article 5, 3. reads as follows:

> 3. By means of a notification deposited with the Secretary-General of the United Nations, any Contracting State may declare that it will not apply the criterion of publication or, alternatively, the criterion of fixation. Such notification may be deposited at the time of ratification, acceptance or accession, or at any time thereafter; in the last case, it shall become effective six months after it has been deposited.

This is just one example of why it is impossible to make general statements about how the Rome Convention works. The application of any particular rule may vary from territory to territory on anything from the length of time of protection to actual protection itself.

BROADCASTING ORGANIZATIONS

In all countries, broadcasting has strong connections with the national government through licensing and regulation. Many countries have government-owned broadcasting, such as the British Broadcasting Company in the U.K. and Radio Audizioni Italiane in Italy. Broadcasting is seen as a public service providing news and information as well as entertainment.

To qualify as a "broadcasting organization," the broadcaster must meet the following definition, set forth in Article 6, 1. of the Rome Convention:

> 1. Each Contracting State shall grant national treatment to broadcasting organizations if either of the following conditions is met:
>   (a) the headquarters of the broadcasting organization is situated in another Contracting State;

(b) the broadcast was transmitted from a transmitter situated in another Contracting State.

Of course, there is a provision allowing any signatory country to partially opt out of the provisions of Article 6, 1. Article 6, 2. provides:

2. By means of a notification deposited with the Secretary-General of the United Nations, any Contracting State may declare that it will protect broadcasts only if the headquarters of the broadcasting organization is situated in another Contracting State and the broadcast was transmitted from a transmitter situated in the same Contracting State. Such notification may be deposited at the time of ratification, acceptance or accession, or at any time thereafter; in the last case, it shall become effective six months after it has been deposited.

The rights given to broadcasting organizations by the Rome Convention include the following:

1. The right to authorize or prohibit rebroadcasting

2. The right to authorize or prohibit the fixation of a broadcast

3. The right to authorize or prohibit the communication to the public of a broadcast

The right to authorize or prohibit rebroadcasting is the equivalent of the right to authorize or prohibit the reproduction of a work. In this sense, the reproduction which is authorized or prohibited is the right not only of rebroadcast but also of simultaneous relay of the program. The right to authorize or prohibit the fixation of a broadcast is simply the right to control the copying of the work. Finally, the right to authorize or prohibit the communication to the public of a broadcast is treated in much the same manner as the requirement for a mechanical license for compositions, including, in some territories, a compulsory license with designated fees.

NATIONAL LAWS ON NEIGHBORING RIGHTS

The aspects of neighboring rights that are operative in a given country depend on that country's copyright laws, on relevant laws separate from the body of copyright laws, and on what international conventions and treaties the country is signatory to. The most important international conventions include those discussed above on pages 412–413 as well as the Rome Convention.

Various international organizations have developed over the years to lobby for both copyright protection and protection of neighboring rights for the individuals, companies, organizations, and industries which are affected by the granting or withholding of these rights. Some of the prominent organizations are the International Federation of the Phonographic Industry (IFPI, including IFPI Latin America), the International Federation of Musicians (FIM), the International Federation of Actors (FIA), the Recording Industry Association of America (RIAA), the Association of South-East Asian Nations (ASEAN), and the Music Industry Association. There are also organizations representing the interests of composers (International Confederation of Societies of Authors and Composers [CISAC]); broadcasters (European Broadcasters Union [EBU]); and motion picture producers (Motion Picture Export Association of America [MPEAA]). There are also governmental and quasi-governmental organizations such as the UNESCO, the International Labor Office (ILO), WIPO, and the Council of Europe.

Through, or, perhaps in spite of, the efforts of these groups, many nations around the world have recognized many neighboring rights. For example, the rights of producers of phonograms to remuneration when their recordings are broadcast, transmitted, or otherwise communicated to the public is presently recognized in about 60 different nations (but not the United States), and music videos are now protected as cinematographic or audiovisual works pursuant to the laws of some 120 different countries.

In dealing with neighboring rights, the Rome Convention provides that individual countries who are signatories to the convention may make reservations with regard to certain provisions of the convention. Countries may not, however, make any reservation regarding the protection that must be extended to foreign nationals. With regard to reservations, signatory countries will fall into one of four categories:

1. Countries making no reservations, granting protection if any one of the criteria for protection ("points of attachment") in a particular category is met (e.g., the majority of Latin American countries).

2. Countries which protect foreign nationals and publication excluding fixation (e.g., Germany and the U. K.).

3. Countries which protect foreign nationals and fixation excluding publication (no countries at this time).

4. Countries which protect on fixation only (the Nordic countries and Italy).

In the following sections, some important aspects of various countries' copyright laws and positions on neighboring rights are discussed.

China

The People's Republic of China has come relatively late to the world of copyright protection. Its first copyright act didn't go into effect until June of 1991. The latest version was adopted in October 2001. There's nothing particularly new in China's copyright law, and the law reflects the fact that China has signed just about every international convention and treaty signed by the United States. Although China, like the United States, is not a signatory to the Rome Convention, Chinese copyright laws do reflect an acceptance of many neighboring and copyright-related rights.

The law recognizes copyright protection for foreign nationals in Chapter 1, Article 2:

> Any work of a foreigner or stateless person which is eligible to enjoy copyright under an agreement concluded between the country to which the foreigner belongs or in which he has habitual residence and China, or under an international treaty to which both countries are party, shall be protected in accordance with this Law.

France

France ratified and became a signatory to the Rome Convention on July 4, 1967. The French laws protect performers, producers of phonograms, producers of videograms, and audiovisual communication enterprises. *Audiovisual communication enterprises* include those legal entities which make available to the public sounds, images, documents, data, or messages of any nature via electromagnetic waves or via cable. These enterprises have the right to authorize making these sounds, images, etc., available to the public by sale, rental, or exchange. They also have the right to control the telediffusion and communication of these materials if the public must pay an entrance fee to view and hear them.

A *performer* under the French law is one who acts, sings, delivers, declaims, plays in, or otherwise performs: literary or artistic works, variety acts, circus acts, or puppet acts. Performers who are considered "ancillary" by professional practices are excluded from the protection of neighboring rights. In France, every performer must be employed under a service or employment contract in order to qualify as a "performer" under the Rome Convention.

Under the laws of France, the neighboring rights reserved for performers are:

1. The right to receive payment for the use of the performances. The payment is in the nature of a compulsory license in that the performer need not authorize each such use, but must be equitably compensated after the use.

2. The moral right (*droit moral*) not to have performances altered and to detract from the respect for the name, authorship, and interpretation of the performer. There is no time limit attached to this right. Upon the death of the performer the right is passed on to his or her heirs.

Producers of phonograms are the individuals and/or companies responsible for the initial fixation of sound in a phonogram. The producer has the right to authorize the reproduction of the sound recording.

Neighboring rights, regardless of nationality, were granted in France in the form of remuneration for works fixed for the first time in France if the first use was prior to July 3, 1967. For a first use after that date, France will grant such right and protection to other nationals based upon the reciprocal treatment afforded to French nationals by other countries.

Germany

Germany ratified the Rome Convention on October 21, 1966. German law recognizes the difference between neighboring rights and copyrights. The German law provides for the protection of the copyright-related rights of performers, producers of phonograms and films, and broadcasters. Works protected include photographs, scientific editions of works and texts not protected by copyright, and posthumous editions

Under German law, for purposes of neighboring rights, a "performer" is anyone who recites or performs a work or who participates artistically in the performance of a work. Variety artists and athletes are not included in the definition of performer. The performer has the right to give or withhold consent to the use of the performance and to receive royalties for the use of the performance. Originally, the period of protection granted to the performer was 25 years from fixation of the performance, but it was recently increased to 50 years. "Fixation" is used in the same sense it is used in American copyright law. A work is fixed in a tangible medium when its embodiment is sufficiently permanent or stable to permit it to be perceived, reproduced, or otherwise communicated for a period of more than transitory duration.

In Germany, producers of phonograms have the exclusive right to reproduce and distribute phonograms. The reproductions which are protected are the manufacture of copies and the rerecording of phonograms.

Interestingly, Germany is among the very few countries which afford neighboring-rights protection, in addition to copyright protection, to photographers. Photographs taken as a matter of routine by professional photographers and photographs taken by amateurs are both protected by neighboring rights. The period of protection of economic and moral rights for professional photographers is 75 years following the death of the photographer; for amateur photographers, it is 20 years.

Italy

Italy's copyright law of 1941 recognized the neighboring rights of producers of phonograms, performers, broadcasters, authors of sketches for theatrical scenes, photographs, written correspondence, portraits, and engineering drawings.

In Italy, under the Rome Convention, producers of phonograms have the right to control reproduction, duplication, and distribution as well as the right to receive equitable remuneration. The producer also has the right to oppose any use which would prejudice the producer's commercial interests in the phonograms.

The protection granted to broadcast organizations in Italy under neighboring rights includes the right to approve or prohibit reproduction, duplication, and distribution and the right to receive equitable remuneration for any such uses. The producer's rights permit the producer to oppose any use which would seriously prejudice the producers' commercial interests. To add a little bite to the rights granted to broadcast organizations, in Italy rights of transmission are also protected by criminal law.

Japan

Japan's first copyright law was enacted in 1868 and the most recent copyright law was enacted in 1971. The 1971 law has been amended and updated as Japan has continued to sign on to the various international conventions and treaties, including the Rome Convention of 1961, WIPO, TRIPS, and the usual suspects. As a signatory to the Berne Convention in 1899, Japan has recognized neighboring rights for over 100 years. Japanese copyright law expressly includes neighboring rights for performers, producers, broadcasting organizations, and "wire diffusion organizations."

Latin America

With the exception of Cuba and Belize, all the countries in Latin American are signatories to the Rome Convention and incorporate all or a substantial part of the convention in their national laws.

Russian Federation

Copyright in Russia is based both on legislation enacted by the Supreme Soviet of the U.S.S.R. or, more currently, the Russian Federation and on administrative orders, which might be termed "quasi-legislation" but which have the force of law. The Russian Federation is a signatory to the Rome Convention of 1961 and, accordingly, recognizes neighboring rights.

The Federation's Law on Copyright and Related Rights was first adopted on July 9, 1993; the most recent version was adopted on July 19, 1995. Title III of the law is devoted entirely to neighboring rights and affords protection to performers, producers, broadcasting organizations, and cable-distribution organizations. Performers, for example, are granted the following exclusive rights:

- The right of attribution

- The right to protection of the performance against any distortion that might prejudice the performer's honor or dignity

- The right to exploit the performance in any form, including the right to be paid for every such use

The only exception to the right of exploitation is the Russian Federation's equivalent to U.S. fair-use provisions.

Sweden, Denmark, Norway, Finland, and Iceland

Sweden, Denmark, Norway, Finland, and Iceland are all signatories to the Rome Convention. All five countries have cooperated with regard to the treatment of neighboring rights, and their protections under neighboring rights, with few exceptions, are remarkably similar. In general, these countries provide and recognize neighboring-rights protection for:

1. Performers. Performers have the right to authorize, or to decline to authorize, the recording of their performances, the broadcast of their performances, and/or the duplication of the recordings or broadcasts.

2. Producers of phonograms. The protection afforded to producers of phonograms extends to sound recordings, including the soundtrack of audiovisual recordings. The audio material afforded protection includes all sounds on sound recordings, regardless of their nature: bird songs, traffic sounds, music, etc. The producer of phonograms has the right to authorize, or withhold authorization of, the duplication of the sound recordings by either mechanical or electromagnetic reproductive processes.

3. Broadcast organizations. Broadcast organizations have the right to authorize, or withhold the authorization of, the broadcast of their programs to the public, the rebroadcast of the programs, the recording of the broadcast, and the making of copies of the recording of the broadcast. The protection afforded to the broadcast organization applies to all types of broadcast, regardless of the content of the program.

Spain

Spain became a signatory to the Rome Convention in 1991. The laws of Spain regarding intellectual property are based upon the concept that intellectual property, and the rights related thereto, belong to the author or the creator of the works.

Foreign authors, performers, producers, and broadcasters are protected by virtue of the conventions to which Spain is a party. While coming late to the Rome Convention, Spain was a signatory to the Berne Convention, the Universal Copyright Convention, and the Geneva Convention of 1971 for the Protection of Producers of Phonograms Against Unauthorized Duplication of Their Photographs.

In terms of neighboring rights, Spanish laws also protect performers, phonogram and audiovisual producers, broadcasting organizations, and photographs and certain types of published editions. In Spain, performers are afforded rights in and protected for their artistic and/or literary works. As in some other countries, variety artists and circus performers are excluded from protection. The performer has the right to authorize, or withhold such authorization for, reproduction and/or fixation of the performer's artistic or literary work and for broadcasting or other communication to the public of the performer's artistic or literary work.

United Kingdom

The United Kingdom ratified the Rome Convention on May 18, 1964. In addition, the Copyright Act of 1956 was extensively amended in 1988 to give copyright protection to the equivalent of neighboring rights, as understood in other jurisdictions. The Copyright Act was further modified by The Copyright and Related Rights Regulations 2003. There are also copyright-related rights; for example, protection is granted to foreign nationals, but on the basis of reciprocity rather than on the basis of national treatment. In the United Kingdom, what otherwise would have been neighboring rights in sound recordings, film, broadcasts, and cable programming are now subject to copyright protection.

The 1988 amendment to the Copyright Law of 1956 created provision for the protection of performers in compliance with the Rome Convention. Performances which are protected include the performances of literary works, dramatic works, musical works, and variety acts. Jugglers and acrobats are also protected.

The performer has the right to authorize, or withhold authorization of, the recording, broadcast, or other reproduction of the performance for any purpose other than use in private home use. There are, however, two exceptions: (1) where there is difficulty in establishing the identity of the performer and (2) in some cases where the performer unreasonably withholds consent. Performers' rights in the U.K. to assign rights are more limited than assignment rights generally are under copyright law.

Moral rights (*droit moral*) under the 1988 amendment are not conferred on performers or other "copyrightless" persons except for film directors, who are entitled to the right to be identified and the right to object to the "derogatory" treatment of the created work.

CHAPTER 16

DISTRIBUTION AGREEMENTS

A man who carries a cat by the tail learns something
he can learn in no other way.

—Mark Twain

Distribution agreements are those agreements between two record companies where one company (the distributor) agrees to distribute the recorded product of another company (the distributed label) on the distributed company's own label. These agreements are different from the recording agreements between record companies and artists or production companies in that the distributing company generally does not participate in the production of the recordings. The signing of artists and the production of the recordings are the responsibility of the distributed label.

The distributed label, in theory, up to the actual point of distribution of the product, operates just like a major record company. The essence of distribution agreements is that the distributed label operates as if it were (as indeed it is) an independent label which is distributed through the distribution network controlled by the distributing label. In most instances the choice of product to be distributed is controlled solely by the distributed label. Finished product—not only finished masters and artwork, but usually finished manufactured product also—is delivered to the distributing company.

The distributing company's job is to do the actual selling. However, it is still the distributed label's obligation to promote and advertise its own product. This may or may not be done in coordination with the distributing label. The label being distributed makes its own A&R decisions and is responsible for the production or acquisition of product, the signing of its own artists, the packaging of the finished product, and, in most cases, the actual manufacture of the finished product.

The release of the distributed label's recordings is coordinated with the release schedule of the distributing company. The distributing company may or may not have its own record label or labels. Obviously, if the distributor is part of or affiliated with one of the remaining majors, it will have its own product. Other distributors, most of the indies, either do not have their own record labels or, if they do, the owned labels are really secondary to the distribution wing of the company.

The distributor receives the finished product from the distributed label (in many cases the distributor manufactures on behalf of or coordinates the manufacture of the product on behalf of the distributed label, with, of course, all costs remaining as the responsibility of the distributed label). The distributor then proceeds to sell, or at least to attempt to sell, the product (1) to retail outlets, (2) to other distributors (so-called one-stops, which usually sell to outlets which cannot meet the original distributor's credit requirements), and, sometimes, (3) directly to the public, for example through the Internet. (For a more detailed definition of one-stops, see the section "Inventory," pages 451–453.)

Labels enter into distribution agreements primarily because running a successful distribution operation is extremely complex—and very expensive. It requires an infrastructure, ideally a national network including not only a sales force, but also warehousing facilities, branch offices, office staff, etc. It also, of course, requires "professionals," people who know the market, the buyers, and all the tools of the trade. An independent record label could, of course, distribute its own recordings, but could never hope to do so on the scale of a company dedicated to distribution.

Ultimately, the relationship between a distributor and a label that it is distributing resembles the relationship between a record company and an artist. If the distributed label is successful and powerful, it is treated accordingly by the distributor. If the distributed label is smaller and less successful, it may be treated with the same level of disregard shown by a record label to an artist who has not yet had a hit.

TERM OF THE DISTRIBUTION AGREEMENT

Time is a great teacher, but unfortunately it kills all its pupils.
—HECTOR BERLIOZ

The term of a distribution agreement, like the term of a recording agreement, is usually stated in terms of an initial period and option periods. Often, the initial period is for more than one year (see all three examples below). This is because setting up a functional distribution relationship and getting the kinks out is so complex that it may take an entire year just to make the system run smoothly.

Making the machinery work is a very important step in creating a successful distribution relationship. The distributed label has to set up channels of communication with the distributor so that they can work effectively together. Deadlines for manufacturing, delivery of product, preparation and delivery of artwork, advertising materials, release dates, and a myriad of details have to be worked out. Product has to be put into the pipeline and sales efforts coordinated. Without the machinery, the whole endeavor may be doomed.

After the initial period, the question of options must be considered. Options are usually the sole decision of the distributing company, although it is possible to negotiate for conditional options to exercise based upon performance.

It is a common misconception, by the way, that *anyone* can obtain a distribution agreement. Most distributors have to be selective regarding long-term relationships—there are just so many spaces available on a distributor's roster. Distributors look for a combination of product flow and deep pockets, and it is not unusual for provisions to be included which allow the distributing company to terminate the agreement if there are inadequate sales (see Example 1).

SAMPLE CONTRACT PROVISIONS

EXAMPLE 1: Minimum Sales Requirement

a. The term of this AGREEMENT shall commence on May 1, _____ , and shall continue for an initial period of two (2) years (the "Initial Period"). Company hereby grants to Distributor two (2) options each to extend the term of this Agreement for an additional period of one (1) year, said options to run consecutively beginning at the expiration of the Initial Period. Each option to be exercised not less than thirty (30) days prior to the end of then current period.

b. Notwithstanding the foregoing, Distributor shall have the right to terminate this Agreement unilaterally in the event that the volume of sales of Records distributed pursuant hereto does not exceed the sum of One Million Dollars ($1,000,000.00) during each year of the term.

☛ No 1-year first periods here or in the following examples.

EXAMPLE 2: 3 Years Plus Two 1-Year Options

1. Commencing on the date hereof, this Distribution Agreement shall continue for an initial period of Three (3) Years. Distributor is granted two (2) options to extend the term of this Distribution Agreement, each such option to be for a period of one (1) year running consecutively from the expiration of the proceeding year period.

EXAMPLE 3: 14 Months Plus Three 1-Year Options

3. Term.

(a) The Term of this Agreement shall commence on the date hereof and continue, unless extended as otherwise provided herein, for a first contract period (the "First Contract Year") ending on the date fourteen (14) months from the date hereof.

(b) Company hereby grants to [Distributor] three (3) separate, irrevocable and consecutive options ("Options"), each to renew the Term of this Agreement for additional Contract Periods (referred herein as "Second Contract Period," "Third Contract Period," and "Fourth Contract Period"). The Second, Third and Fourth Contract Periods, if exercised, shall each extend for a period of twelve (12) months after the commencement of such Contract Period. [Distributor] may exercise an Option to renew the Term hereof for an additional Contract Period by giving Company written notice at least thirty (30) days prior to the expiration of the previous Contract Period. [Distributor] shall not be entitled to exercise the Option for the previous Contract Period, as applicable.

☛ The 14-month initial period, while close to the "traditional" 1-year period seen in recording agreements, includes what might be regarded as a start-up period, or lead time, to get product ready for actual release, including such activities as notifying the salespeople in the field, sending advertising material to retail buyers, getting manufacturing parts, sending artwork off for printing of covers, manufacturing the product and combining the recording with the artwork, and carrying through with all of the tasks required to sell the finished product to the public.

TERRITORY

Distribution agreements are for a specified territory. The rights of the distributor will be restricted to the specified territory, whether it is limited (for example, just the United States; see Example 1) or extensive (for example, the entire universe). The distributed label may license worldwide to one company or make agreements on a country-by-country basis. There are advantages and disadvantages to both approaches. Generally, for a "real" label, it is preferable to license distribution rights on a country-by-country basis. (By "real label" I mean a record company with an ongoing flow of product with various artists, as opposed to a company which may, in fact, be operated by the one and only artist on the label with only one or two albums released over a period of time.) Not only does this give the label a more hands-on control of its destiny, it also avoids cross-collateralization. It is generally much easier to obtain a country-by-country arrangement in a distribution agreement than it is an artist's recording agreement or even a production agreement.

SAMPLE CONTRACT PROVISIONS

EXAMPLE 1: Territory Is the United States

3. "Territory" shall mean and refer to the entire United States, and its territories and possessions.

   a. Company hereby appoints Distributor as its exclusive distributor of Records in the Territory, and grants to Distributor the exclusive right to distribute and sell Records in the Territory during the term of this Agreement, including any extensions thereof. During the term of this Agreement, Company shall not itself distribute Records to the Territory, or license or allow any other Person other than Distributor to distribute Records in the Territory.

EXAMPLE 2: Ships, Aircraft, Oil Rigs, and Marine Installations Count

2. As used herein, the term "Territory" shall be deemed to be the countries set forth in Schedule "A." The Territory shall include each such country as its political boundaries exist on the date of this Agreement, inclusive of non-contiguous colonies, possessions and similar non-contiguous areas, unless otherwise expressly excluded. Unless expressly excluded, the Territory also includes any nation's military and other governmental installations geographically located within the Territory, ships and aircraft flying the flags of all countries within the Territory, and oil rigs and other marine installations located within the Territory.

EXAMPLE 3: North America Is Territory

1. (f) (i) "Territory" means and refers to North America.

   (ii) "Manufacturing Territory" means and refers to the United States, its territories and possessions, and shall include military and PX sales.

• • •

2. (a) Subject to the terms and conditions contained herein, Company hereby appoints [Distributor] as its sole and exclusive distributor in the Territory during the Term hereof:

   (i) for all Records manufactured from the Masters in the Manufacturing Territory; and

   (ii) for purposes of causing distribution of Records by licensing throughout the Territory or any part thereof for all purposes including but not limited to master use licenses in any and all media now known or hereafter developed, and grants and licenses to [Distributor] the sole and exclusive right and obligation to distribute and sell all Records whether through Major Label Branch Distribution, Independent Distribution, licensing or otherwise in the Territory during the Term, including any extensions thereof.

   (b) Without limiting the generality of the foregoing, [Distributor] and any person authorized, pursuant to the terms of this Agreement, by [Distributor] shall have the sole and exclusive rights, during the Term throughout the Territory or any part thereof to:

   (i) distribute and sell Records by any and all means through Normal Record Retail Channels in the Manufacturing Territory;

   (ii) license the Masters for distribution of Records or rights in and to the Masters throughout the Territory;

DISTRIBUTOR'S OBLIGATIONS

DICK:

[H]e can make obligations, and write court-hand.

—WILLIAM SHAKESPEARE
Henry VI, Part II, Act IV, Scene 2

The distributor's main obligation is, of course, to distribute. But just what does it mean to "distribute"? The whole distribution process requires many steps and many functions. Example 1 specifies, in broad terms, the various functions which must be performed by the distributor in the course of fulfilling its obligations. Example 2 goes into much more detail.

As stated above, it is extremely important for the distributed label to communicate with the distributing company in order to allow all the following functions and obligations to work for the benefit of the companies. Depending on the size and prosperity of the distributed company, there may be a need for more than one person to work as liaison with the distributor.

As you read the following two examples, which list the multifarious tasks of the distributor, consider the folly and futility of self-distribution unless you have a lot of money and an experienced staff.

SAMPLE CONTRACT PROVISIONS

EXAMPLE 1: Distributor's Contractual Obligations

6. Distributor's Obligations:

a. Subject to the full and faithful performance by Company of all its obligations under and pursuant to this Agreement, Distributor shall furnish, during the term of this Agreement and at Distributor's expense:

(i) Warehousing of Company's inventory of Records at Distributor's distribution centers and, if applicable, storage of components, such as jackets, sleeves, and inserts, subject to the provisions of Paragraph 13. hereof.

(ii) Soliciting sales of Company's Records to Distributor's accounts.

(iii) Order fulfillment, by picking, packing and shipping Records to Distributor's customers from Company's inventory at Distributor's distribution centers.

(iv) Processing of Record returns, subject to the provisions of Paragraph 10. and 15. hereof.

(v) Billing and collection for Records shipped by Distributor to its customers.

(vi) Sales reports pertaining to sales of records hereunder.

b. Distributor shall, at Company's sole expense,

(i) deliver promotional Records furnished by Company and marked as promotional product to Company and to radio stations designated by Company, and

(ii) distribute Company's merchandising materials furnished by Company to Distributor's customers in the manner that Distributor normally distributes such items.

c. Distributor shall distribute to its customers co-op advertising funds furnished by Company as the parties may from time to time agree.

EXAMPLE 2: Distributor's Obligations as Basic Services

6. [Distributor's] *Obligations*.

(a) [Distributor] shall furnish, during the Term and thereafter, as applicable, and at [Distributor's] expense, the following basic services ("Basic Services") throughout the Manufacturing Territory as set forth in subdivisions (i) through (vi) hereinbelow:

(i) Shipment of Records by surface transportation (or any other mode utilized by [Distributor] for the majority of its own records) from the plants where such Records are manufactured (whether they are _____'s plants or those of _____'s subcontractors or otherwise) to Distribution Centers or to any other Major Label Branch Distributor's distribution centers utilized by [Distributor]. Notwithstanding anything to the contrary contained herein, [Distributor] reserves the right in its discretion to change its Major Label Branch Distributor for the Records and/or for its own records, and if [Distributor] makes such change, it shall be deemed to modify all applicable references hereunder to the new Major Label Branch Distributor. Company shall pay for any air transportation of Records requested by Company or for any transportation of Records not manufactured by _____ to Distribution Centers.

(ii) Warehousing of Company's inventory of Records at Distribution Centers or at any other Major Label Branch Distributor's distribution centers utilized by [Distributor] and, if applicable, storage of components, such as jackets, sleeves, and inserts, subject to the provisions of Paragraph 15 hereof.

(iii) Subject to sufficient quantities of Records being on hand, timely and accurate order fulfillment, by causing the picking, packing and shipping Records to [Distributor's] customers from Company's inventory of Records at Distribution Centers or at any other Major Label Branch Distributor's distribution centers utilized by [Distributor]. [Distributor] may consolidate shipments of Company's Records with [Distributor's] own records or those of other Persons that [Distributor] distributes; likewise may consolidate shipments of [Distributor's] records with records of other Persons.

(iv) Processing of Record distributed by [Distributor], subject to the provisions of paragraphs 8, 10, 11 and 17 hereof.

(v) Billing and collection for Records shipped by [Distributor] to its customers, and crediting for Returns. In this connection, [Distributor] will be responsible for any delay in payment, nonpayment (or other so-called bad debts owed by its customers), and [Distributor] shall bear all credit risk for its customers (each to the same extent as is responsible for payment, nonpayment and credit risks on behalf of [Distributor] in the fulfillment agreement [Distributor] and _____). If Company wishes to sell Records to any Person that is not presently a [Distributor] customer, Company so shall advise [Distributor] in writing. [Distributor] shall then promptly either (A) qualify such Person as a [Distributor] customer, and establish an appropriate credit limit in the reasonable business judgment of [Distributor] in which case [Distributor] shall bear all credit risk for such customer; or (B) decline to grant credit to such Person, in the reasonable business judgement of [Distributor] in which case Company shall not sell Records to such Person; provided that Company may assume the respective risk if, and to the extent that, [Distributor] is able to obtain _____'s agreement thereto.

(vi) Sales and inventory reports pertaining to sales, Returns and Inventory of Records hereunder and receipt of Records by Distribution Centers. Upon Company's request, [Distributor] will supply such information to Company via a so-called electronic mailbox, provided that Company shall be solely responsible for and pay all costs connected therewith, including, but not limited to, installation and all data access or transmission charges imposed by third party vendors, e.g., AT&T.

(b) For the Manufacturing Territory, [Distributor] will, on Company's written request, distribute merchandising materials to [Distributor's] customers in the manner that [Distributor] normally distributes such items. Any such merchandising materials shall be furnished by Company at Company's sole cost and expense. Company also shall pay [Distributor's] actual fulfillment costs to pick and pack such materials, and all actual postage, freight or shipping charges attributable to such distribution. All such costs shall be allocated if product originated by more than one (1) label is sent in the same shipment.

(c) [Distributor] will not spend money for customer advertising unless Company previously has allocated funds to [Distributor] for such purpose. [Distributor] will implement and administer customer advertising as requested by Company in writing. Provided that Company is not in material default hereunder, [Distributor] shall advance, at [Distributor's] actual cost, customer advertising funds previously allocated in writing by Company, which shall be deducted from the net proceeds otherwise payable to Company in the month in which [Distributor] credits its customers on account of the advertising. Subject to paragraph 18 hereinbelow and [Distributor's] then current policies, [Distributor] or its subcontractor will examine all advertising claims submitted by its customers; furnish reports thereof to Company; and credit to its customers advertising funds pursuant to Company's previous allocation. Upon Company's written request, [Distributor] will furnish Company with copies of advertising claims submitted by its customers; provided, however, that (i) [Distributor] shall have no obligation to furnish Company with copies of any claim after more than one (1) year from the date upon which such claim is submitted; and (ii) in no event shall [Distributor] be required to furnish Company with copies of backup materials or "tear sheets" accompanying co-op advertising claims for print media, provided that [Distributor] shall make all such backup materials available for review by Company upon request at [Distributor's] offices.

(d) [Distributor] will, on Company's request, prepare artwork in connection with the marketing of the Records, including but not limited to posters, bin dividers and header cards, which shall be subject to the prior approval of Company as well as the terms and conditions contained herein. All actual, out-of-pocket costs, excluding [Distributor's] in-house art staff, shall be at Company's sole cost and expense, including but not limited to separations, film and chromolin costs, and shall be reimbursed by Company to [Distributor] upon Company's receipt of invoices(s) therefor, which sum Company shall promptly pay, or [Distributor] may deduct the amount of any such charge from any sums otherwise payable to Company therefor.

(e) In connection with the exploitation of the Masters and Records derived therefrom pursuant to subparagraph 2(b)(ii) and (iii), [Distributor] shall cause the licensing and dissemination of all elements and material necessary to make reasonable inquiries and solicitations to manufacture Records or otherwise in furtherance thereof, [Distributor] shall be entitled to enter exclusive licensing agreements in order to cause the exploitation referred to herein and [Distributor] shall consult with Company in connection therewith.

COMPANY'S OBLIGATIONS

The company whose product is being distributed also has certain specified obligations under the distribution agreement. There is much more to being on the supply end of a distribution agreement than simply recording masters and turning over records for sale. The distributed company must give not only the manufactured product to the distributor, but also information of pending releases, advertising materials, etc. (see Examples 1 and 2). If the distributed company does not meet all of its obligations, the working relationship between the distributed label and the distributor will not be effective.

This chapter already set forth one common misconception about distributors—that finding a distributor is a simple task (it often isn't). Another misconception is that distributors function as full-service companies, furnishing support in all areas of a record company's operation. In fact, the distributor-distributee relationship is a business relationship between two companies formed for the sole purpose of having the distributor carry out distribution functions. The distributed label is a record company, and the mere fact that another company is distributing its product does not get it off the hook from having all the responsibilities of any record company: paying its artists, paying rent, obtaining licenses, etc., as specified in the two examples below. And, just as artists must pay close attention to the accountings received from record companies, it is important for distributed labels to pay careful attention to the accountings received from distributors.

SAMPLE CONTRACT PROVISIONS

EXAMPLE 1: Distributed Label's Obligations

5. Company's Obligations: Company shall be solely responsible for all activities, and shall pay all costs, expenses and charges incurred in connection with:

a. Obtaining the Masters, including (without limitation) all costs arising out of the creation of or the acquisition of Company's rights in the Masters, and all steps required to utilize the Masters in the manufacture of Records;

b. The manufacture of finished Records from the Masters of a quality satisfactory to Distributor, including (without limitation) the procurement of all raw materials and labor, the assembly of all component parts into finished Records, and the packing of finished Records into Distributor's standard box-lot quantities ready for distribution by Distributor, subject to any Manufacturing Agreement the parties may negotiate;

c. Obtaining a Universal Product Code manufacturing Number from the Uniform Code Council, Inc., and ensuring that appropriate bar code is correctly applied to Company's Records;

d. The timely delivery of Records f.o.b, to Distributor's distribution centers, in satisfactory condition and in quantities sufficient to meet Distributor's product flow requirements;

e. The payment of all freight charges for shipment of the Records by air or surface transportation from the plants where the Records are manufactured to Distributor's distribution centers;

f. The procurement, in writing, of all necessary rights, licenses, consents, authorizations and clearances to record, manufacture, use, sell, advertise, promote and distribute the Records, including (without limitation) (i) mechanical licenses for all copyrighted compositions embodied in any record, (ii) authorizations from each artist and any other Person whose name, likeness, performance or services are embodied in any Record or in any advertising or promotional materials in connection therewith, and (iii) all consents and clearances necessary to use any copyrights, trademarks, trade names, artist names, group names, artwork or any similar intangible property rights of any Person in or on Records and accompanying printed materials;

g. The advertisement, promotion, and merchandising of Records in a professional manner, including (without limitation) the preparation of artwork and design layouts of all types, the furnishing or merchandising posters and displays for distribution by Distributor, the securing of radio and television air play, and the furnishing of all similar materials and services; and

h. The payment of all royalties, fees, costs and other sums payable to any person in connection with the Masters or Distributor's distribution of Records derived therefrom, including (without limitation) all royalty and fees payable to artists, producers, musicians, publishers, writers and other persons; all mechanical license fees; and all synchronization license fees.

EXAMPLE 2: Distributed Label's Obligations

5. Company's Obligations. Company solely shall be responsible for all activities, and shall pay all costs, expenses and charges incurred in connection with:

(a) All creative and artistic aspects of the content of Masters, and obtaining Masters, including, but not limited to, all costs arising out of the creation of or the acquisition of Company's rights in Masters, and all steps required to utilize the Masters in the manufacture of Records.

(b) For the Manufacturing Territory, the manufacture of finished goods in the form of Records from Masters, in such configurations and quantities that Company determines, including, but not limited to, the procurement of all raw materials and labor, the assembly of all component parts into finished goods Records, and the packing of finished goods Records into [Distributor's] standard box-lot quantities ready for distribution by [Distributor]. The parties hereto acknowledge that Company is simultaneously entering into the Manufacturing Agreement with [Distributor] regarding the manufacture of Records.

(c) Obtaining a Universal Product Code Identification Number from the Uniform Code Council, Inc., and ensuring that appropriate bar code appears on all Records.

(d) For the Manufacturing Territory, the delivery of Records f.o.b, to Distribution Centers in satisfactory condition if and only if Company desires that such Records be distributed from a Distribution Center other than the Distribution Center to which [Distributor] would normally deliver such Records.

(e) Scheduling the release of Company's Records, it being understood and agreed that [Distributor] shall solicit sales of Company's Records to [Distributor's] accounts utilizing essentially the same commitment of staff and resources as [Distributor] utilizes for its own records and that Company shall not be required to maintain any sales staff for such purpose. Notwithstanding the foregoing, the release of the Records in Canada shall be subject to subparagraph 4(b)(ii).

(f) The procurement, in writing, of all necessary rights, licenses, consents, authorizations and clearances to record, manufacture, use, sell, advertise, promote and distribute Records, including, but not limited to, (i) mechanical licenses for all copyrighted compositions embodied in any Record, (ii) authorizations from each artist and any other Person whose name, likeness, performance or services are embodied in any Record or in any advertising or promotional materials used in connection therewith, and (iii) all consents and clearances necessary to use any copyrights, trademarks, trade names, artist names, group names, artwork, patents or any similar intangible property rights of any Person in or on Masters, Records and accompanying printed materials.

(g) The advertisement, promotion, and merchandising of Records in Company's discretion, including, but not limited to, the preparation of artwork and design layouts of all types, the furnishing or merchandising of posters and displays for distribution by [Distributor], promotion of radio and television for the purpose of attempting to secure air play, and the furnishing of all similar materials and services.

(h) The payment of all royalties, fees, costs and other sums payable to any Person in connection with the exploitation of the Masters or the sale and distribution of Records derived therefrom, including, but not limited to, all royalties and fees payable to artists, producers, musicians, publishers, writers and other Person(s); all mechanical license fees; all payments which may be required based on the sales of Records pursuant to any applicable union or guild agreement, e.g., AFofM and AFTRA, to a trustee, agent or fund under any successor agreement; Company's pro rata share of dues payable by [Distributor], if any, to the Recording Industry Association of America, Inc. ("RIAA"); provided, however, that [Distributor] shall not collect RIAA dues on Company's behalf if Company establishes and maintains throughout the Term its own RIAA membership; and all synchronization license fees; excluding, however, those costs of sales and distribution incurred by [Distributor] to perform its obligations set forth below.

☛ These two long samples could virtually serve as a how-to manual for the creation and operation of a record label.

EXCLUSIVITY

> HUMPTY DUMPTY:
> **When I use a word . . . it means just what I choose it to mean— neither more nor less.**
>
> —LEWIS CARROLL
> *Through the Looking Glass*

Within the specified territory, the distributor will generally be the exclusive distributor of the licensed product. There are, however, exceptions to exclusivity. For example, the distributed label will frequently exclude record club sales from the distribution agreement (see Example 3). Example 1 illustrates exclusivity language with another type of exception.

SAMPLE CONTRACT PROVISIONS

EXAMPLE 1: Exclusive to Specified Market

a. Company hereby appoints Distributor as its exclusive distributor of Records to the Secular Market in the Territory, and grants to Distributor the exclusive right to distribute and sell Records to the Secular Market in the Territory during the term of this Agreement, including any extensions thereof. During the term of this Agreement, Company shall not itself distribute Records to the Secular Market in the Territory, or license or allow any Person other than Distributor to distribute Records to the Secular Market in the Territory.

• • •

e. "Secular Market" shall mean and refer to all customers regularly serviced by Distributor through its normal distribution channels, exclusive of religious bookstores, clubs and aftermarkets.

☛ This agreement allows the distributed label to use an alternative method of distribution for sales to religious bookstores and religious record clubs.

EXAMPLE 2: Distributor's Right Not to Distribute Rejected Product

12. Distributor is not required to distribute Records manufactured from any Master pursuant to this Agreement. In the event that Distributor (for whatever reason) elects not to distribute any one of Company's Records, it shall thereupon notify Company. Upon its receipt of such notice from Distributor, Company shall have the right to distribute such Records by some alternative manner.

☛ In this agreement, the distributor can "elect not to distribute" any of the company's records, a practice known as "cherry-picking" (see Example 2 in the next section). Any recording which is rejected (frequently, the reasons for rejection in such agreements are questionable language and/or content) can be distributed through alternative distribution systems. Sometimes included in the agreement is a requirement that any rejected product be distributed under a different label name. This is to prevent another distributor's product being returned through the system of the first distributor.

EXAMPLE 3: Record Club Sales Excluded

7. Notwithstanding the otherwise exclusive scope of this Agreement, Company reserves the right to license record clubs to manufacture and distribute Records derived from Masters embodying the performances of artists under contract with Company, provided that: (i) this reservation of rights is limited to albums of sound recordings manufactured for sale and distribution and actually sold and distributed by direct mail or mail order, in accordance with merchandising method known and understood in the mail order business as "subscription" or "club" plan (as distinguished from individual over-the-counter sales by retail store outlets receiving their Records from Record distributors); (ii) no Record manufactured from a Master, Records derived from which are also distributed by Distributor, shall be offered or shipped by any such record club either for sale or as a free or bonus Record until four (4) months after Distributor's release of that Record; (iii) any such record club shall have the right to distribute Compact Discs only of those masters that Distributor has released in Compact Disc form; and (iv) as between Distributor and Company, Company shall be solely and exclusively responsible for all costs and expenses in connection with any agreement between Company and any such record club, including (without limitation) those connected with furnishing Masters and artwork, mechanical and artist royalty payments, A.F.M. payments, taxes, and administrative, overhead and accounting charges.

PRODUCT

When a label enters into a distribution agreement with a distributor it is usually for all the recorded product within the control of the licensing company (see Example 1). Sometimes, however, the distributor is given the right to cherry-pick, that is, to reject some product. Example 2 below gives the distributor the right to pick and choose product based upon content—sort of a distribution morals clause. Some agreements use vaguer language, giving the distributor the right to distribute only the recordings it judges to be "good" product, rejecting recordings it judges to be "poor." Such language, which makes some notion of "quality" the determining factor, should be discouraged for the same reasons that language in recording agreements referring to "commercial acceptability" should be discouraged. Note that when the distributor has the right to reject product, the distributed label should have the right to release the rejected product elsewhere.

When a distributor is making the decision as to whether or not to enter into an agreement with a label, the amount of product likely to be involved is as important as the potential success of the product. For maximum profit, the distribution pipeline needs product flowing through it at all times, and the distributor may be much more interested in distributing the product of a company which will have a steady flow of material than the product of a company which will release only one successful album a year.

SAMPLE CONTRACT PROVISIONS

EXAMPLE 1. Distributor to Accept "Every Master"
1. Company hereby licenses to Distributor, and Distributor hereby accepts from Company for the term of this Agreement for the Territory only each and every master recording owned or controlled by Company (hereinafter referred to as the "Master" or "Masters" as appropriate).

EXAMPLE 2: The Right to Cherry-Pick
1. Notwithstanding anything to the contrary contained herein, Company shall have the right to reject any Record based upon Company's sole determination that language or subject matter contained on such Record may bring Company into public disrepute, contempt, scandal or ridicule. If Company rejects any such Record, you may license the distribution to a third party without being in contravention of the exclusivity provisions of Paragraph 3, above; provided, however, that such release shall be on a different label than the label distributed pursuant to this Agreement.

EXAMPLE 3: Distributor Has Right to Distribute "Each and Every Master"
1. During the term of this Agreement, Company grants to Distributor the right to manufacture and sell in the Territory phonograph records manufactured from each and every master recording which is presently owned by or which shall be owned by Company or otherwise acquired by Company.

EXAMPLE 4: All Recordings Released on Specified Labels
2. Company hereby grants to Distributor for the term specified herein an exclusive license to distribute in the Territory phonograph records produced from tapes or matrices of all recordings released by Company on the "X" label and the "Y" labels.

☛ Many record companies having more than one label release a specific genre on each label, e.g., Label #1 for rock music; Label #2 for rap music; Label #3 for country music; etc.

CONVERSION OF ARTISTS

Power corrupts; but absolute power is really neat.

—JOHN LEHMAN,
Former Secretary of the Navy

Built into many distribution agreements, especially those where the distributor is advancing monies to the distributed label, is a provision known as a *conversion clause*, giving the distributor, under certain specified conditions (usually some level of success); the option to "convert" an artist from the distributed label to the distributor's label. In most cases, the artist will still be under contract to the distributed label, but the distributed label is obligated to assign the artist's services to the distributor. (Be aware, however, that some distribution agreements have a provision which allows the distributor to actually walk away with the artist without any ongoing participation by or royalty to the distributed label. The artist contracts may have been put up as collateral for costs, such as manufacturing costs, advanced by the distributor and the distributor takes the contract for failure to pay the debt. Sometimes a distributor will blatantly steal an artist and take the risk of being sued by the distributed label. If an artist is converted, the distributed label suddenly finds itself, at least with regard to that artist, also converted—into a production company which is supplying the artist to the distributor record company. Both types of conversions, needless to say, are often unwelcome.

When there is a conversion clause, there will almost always be some sort of production agreement waiting in the wings in case the distributor decides to swoop down and snatch up the artist (or more politely, to exercise the conversion option). The terms may be stated in a separate agreement (see Example 1, which is a separate production agreement signed concurrently) but are more likely to be attached to the distribution agreement as an exhibit (see Example 2). The terms and conditions of the production agreement need to be worked out, and often require lengthy negotiation.

During the negotiations over one distribution agreement in which I was representing the label, the distributor insisted that there be a conversion clause, and also wanted my client (a small, undercapitalized record company) to guarantee the minimum payments required in California for equitable relief for each artist, including each individual in groups, just in case any of the artists might be converted at some future date. The cost would have been prohibitive and we successfully fought off the requirement.

If a conversion option related to level of success is included in the distribution agreement, the required level of success, usually described in amount of sales necessary to trigger the option, must be negotiated (see Examples 1 and 2). Numerous other issues must also be addressed. For example: How long does the distributor have to exercise the option? What happens when the distribution agreement ends? What about the distributed label's licensees, such as foreign companies, who think they have the rights to the artist in their territory? What happens to the existing recordings?

SAMPLE CONTRACT PROVISIONS

EXAMPLE 1: Separate Production Agreement in Case of Conversion

29. *Conversion of Artists.* If, at any time during the Term of this Agreement, a Record featuring an Artist obtains sales of one hundred and fifty thousand (150,000) full-priced units sold through Normal Record Retail Channels in the Territory, within any consecutive six (6) week period, Distributor shall have the option (herein the "Conversion Option") to immediately convert and assign the recording services of such Artist to the Production Agreement ("Production Agreement") which is currently being executed by the parties hereto. Distributor shall be entitled to exercise the Conversion Option within thirty (30) days of the satisfaction of the condition contained in the previous sentence by providing notice of its intention to Company. If Distributor exercises its Conversion Option for a particular Artist, Company shall immediately (i) deliver to Distributor the Masters of such Record that is currently being distributed and licensed by Distributor, (ii) execute the attached assignment of the applicable Artist Agreement, and (iii) execute any other documents which distributor deems necessary to carry out the intention of the Conversion Option. If Distributor exercises the Conversion Option, Company shall thereafter cause Artist to record and deliver all future Masters recorded by that Artist subject to and in accordance with the terms and

conditions of the Production Agreement. Notwithstanding anything to the contrary contained herein, if Distributor exercises its Conversion Option pursuant to Paragraph 29, said conversion shall be subject to any licenses which have been previously granted by Company; provided, however, that Company hereby acknowledges that it shall not grant any rights pertaining to any Artist which is subject to this Agreement to any third party for greater than a record by record basis.

☛ Note the second half of the last sentence. Talk about your built-in poison pill! Based on the potential that one or more of Company's artists may be converted in the future, Distributor has made it virtually impossible to enter into meaningful foreign distributions.

EXAMPLE 2: Production Agreement Attached

18. Label agrees that if any recording featuring an Artist hereunder sells a minimum of Two Hundred and Fifty Thousand (250,000) regular full-priced sales in the United States, within a consecutive period of Four (4) Months, Distributor shall have an option (hereinafter referred to as the "Artist Option") to cause Label to assign the Recording Agreement for such Artist to Distributor.

(a) Distributor may exercise the Option at any time within Two (2) Months following any such Four (4) Month period by giving Label written notice of its intention to exercise the Option. Concurrently with the exercise of any such Option, if any, Distributor shall pay Label the sum of Twenty-Five Thousand ($25,000.00) Dollars. The payment provided for herein shall be deemed to be a bonus to Label and shall not be treated as an advance under either this Agreement or the Production Agreement, as defined below.

(b) If Distributor exercises any such Option, the terms and conditions of the Production Agreement attached hereto as Exhibit "C" and incorporated herein by reference (hereinafter referred to as the "Production Agreement") shall become effective as of the date of the Option exercise.

(c) If Distributor exercises any such Option for an Artist, Company shall:

(i) execute the assignment attached hereto as Exhibit "D" and incorporated herein by reference (hereinafter referred to as the "Assignment") assigning Label's recording agreement with the Artist to Distributor; and

(ii) execute any other documents required by Distributor in order to effectuate the assignment of such Artist's services to Distributor.

(d) If Distributor exercises any Option, Company shall thereafter produce Masters featuring Artist pursuant to the terms and conditions of the Production Agreement, it being agreed and understood that Artist shall thereafter be Distributor's exclusive recording artist.

(e) Pursuant to the terms and conditions of the Production Agreement, Label will record and deliver all future Masters recorded by that Artist.

☛ The production agreement is attached to the distribution agreement as an exhibit, as is an assignment transferring the artist's agreement to the distributor. This transfer of the artist's agreement to the distributor places the record company in a weaker position than it would be if a traditional production agreement had been signed in the first place. Under most production agreements the artist is supplied by the production company, meaning the production company retains basic control. Under the arrangement in this distribution agreement the record company is reduced to the position of being an independent producer.

EXAMPLE 3: Incorporation by Reference of Distribution Agreement

1. ENGAGEMENT.

Reference is made to the Distribution Agreement between the parties hereto of even date. If Company shall exercise the option, known as the Conversion Option, as provided for in paragraph 29 of the Distribution Agreement, with respect to a particular Artist (as defined below) then the parties hereto acknowledge that the terms of this Agreement shall be applicable with respect to that particular Artist. Company hereby engages Producer to furnish to Company, in accordance with the requirements of the Agreement, the following: (a) Producer's services as in-studio producers and executive producers of musical project(s) hereunder and (b) the exclusive recording services of various musical artists as set forth herein.

• • •

3. DESIGNATION OF ARTIST.

(a) At such time as Company shall exercise the Conversion Option for a particular artist with the above, such artist will be deemed an "Artist" hereunder, and Producer shall deliver to Company an inducement agreement ("Inducement Letter") in the applicable form annexed hereto as Exhibit "A" which is executed by such Artist. Producer warrants and represents that each such Artist shall have theretofore executed a recording agreement with Producer (individually and collectively the "Artist Agreement") granting Producer the rights and authority to perform its obligations and duties under this Agreement.

(b) *Artist Agreement.* Each Artist Agreement shall provide for the recordation and Delivery of Masters in accordance with Paragraph 4 hereinbelow. Producer shall comply with all the provisions of the Artist Agreement and will cause each Artist to perform each and every term and condition contained in the Artist Agreement to the best of his ability. Producer shall exercise each and every renewal option available to Producer under the Artist Agreement in accordance with Paragraph 4 below, unless Company shall advise Producer to the contrary, in which case it shall be within the discretion of Producer to exercise the renewal option for such Artist for Producer's own behalf (in such instance Company shall have obligation to Producer with respect to future recordings for such Artist and no rights in and to such recordings). Producer shall not waive any of its rights under any Artist Agreement in full force and effect so that Company shall have the benefits of Artist's exclusive recording services. Producer shall immediately notify Company in writing of any notification to Producer by the Artist of any claim or allegation that Producer is in breach of the Artist Agreement with such Artist and the specific details thereof.

☛ In this case, the production agreement, which is separate, automatically goes into effect when the distributor exercises its right to convert the artist.

REPRESENTATIONS AND WARRANTIES

> *Always behave like a duck: keep calm and unruffled on the surface, but paddle like the devil underneath.*
> —Jacob Braude

Distributors demand representations and warranties from the distributed label for the simple reason that they do not wish to be sued. The distributed label is required by the distributor to make a very wide and comprehensive set of representations and warranties (see Example 1).

Because the distributor does not have hands-on control of the creation of recordings, the obtaining of mechanical licenses, the creation of artwork, and all the other processes which go into making the product, it must rely upon the professionalism of the distributed label to avoid lawsuits. Notwithstanding the fact that the distributed label will ultimately be responsible for misdeeds, such as, for example, copyright infringements, the distributor can very easily be swept up in the net of potential defendants in a lawsuit. Indeed, a distributor may very well be included as a target defendant simply because of the perception that the distributor has deeper pockets than does the distributed label. The warranties and representations in distribution agreements are oriented more to "business" and "license or ownership" issues than are the equivalent provisions in artist and production company agreements because a record label has many more opportunities to get into trouble.

SAMPLE CONTRACT PROVISIONS

EXAMPLE 1: Scope of Representations and Warranties

4. Company's Representations and Warranties: Company covenants, represents and warrants to Distributor as follows:

a. Company is a corporation in good standing and is duly qualified to do business in the State of California. Company has the right, power and authority to enter into this Agreement, and to grant to Distributor the exclusive rights set forth herein. Company will comply with all applicable laws and trade regulations, and will not do anything that may curtail or impair any of the rights granted herein.

b. With respect to each Record furnished to Distributor hereunder, Company presently is, and at the time of the manufacture, distribution, and sale of such Record will be the sole owner, assignee or licensee in the Territory of: (i) the Master from which such Record is derived, (ii) all performances embodied in such Record, (iii) the right to manufacture and distribute such Record in the Territory, (iv) all applicable sound recording copyrights in such Record, (v) all applicable copyrights in the graphic materials used in connection with the packaging, merchandising and commercial exploitation of such Record, (vi) all trademarks and trade names used in or on such Record, and (vii) the right to license Distributor to distribute such Record in the Territory. Prior to Distributor's distribution of each Record hereunder, Company shall register such sound recording and other copyrights with the United States Copyright Office, and shall file such trademarks with the United States Patent and Trademark Office.

c. There are presently no liens, encumbrances, claims, demands, disputes, litigation (or any other form of judicial or regulatory proceedings, pending or threatened), limitations of rights, or obligations upon, concerning or in connection with the Masters, Records derived therefrom, or the rights granted to Distributor hereunder, and there shall be none during the term hereof. If, contrary to this representation and warranty, any such pending or threatened claim, demand, dispute or litigation should arise during the term hereof, Company shall immediately notify Distributor thereof in writing. All costs of recording the Masters have been paid in full. All of the performers and other Persons whose services were furnished in connection with recording the Masters (and each selection thereon) were flee to furnish such services, without such conduct constituting a violation of any contract, contractual restriction or duty owed to any Person. There are no outstanding judgments, writs, garnishments or attachments against Company or Company's property. Company shall not suffer or allow any such liens, encumbrances, claims, disputes, limitations of rights, obligations, judgments, writs, garnishments or attachments to arise during the term hereof, other than those granted to Distributor herein.

d. Company presently has, and at the time of the manufacture and distribution of Records hereunder will have, the uncontested right and license to reproduce mechanically all compositions embodied in such Records, including all copyrighted compositions. In the event of any dispute as to the validity of Company's mechanical license, Company authorizes Distributor (though Distributor shall not be required to take such action) to withhold from distribution to Company or bill Company for a sum equal to all mechanical license fees that would otherwise be payable by Company to be held by Distributor until the final resolution of any such dispute. Prior to its release of any Record hereunder, Distributor may (but shall not be required to) request Company to furnish Distributor with actual copies of Company's mechanical licenses for any or all of the compositions embodied on such Record, which Company thereupon promptly shall furnish to Company.

e. The Masters, Records derived therefrom and all other materials and services furnished by Company hereunder, including (without limitation) advertising and promotion activities, album jackets and other packaging, artwork, liner notes, credits, merchandising materials and similar items and services (i) shall comply with all applicable laws and regulations, including those concerning obscenity, and (ii) shall not violate, breach or infringe any contractual right, common law right or statutory right of any living or deceased person whatsoever, including (without limitation) rights with respect to patents, trademarks, trade names, copyrights, defamation, and rights of privacy and publicity.

f. The Masters have been and will be recorded in all respects in accordance with the applicable rules and regulations of the American Federation of Musicians. . . .

g. All AFTRA members whose performances are embodied on Masters have been, and will be, paid not less than the minimum rates specified. . . .

h. The Masters have been, and will be, recorded in accordance with the rules and regulations of all other unions having jurisdiction over the recording thereof.

i. All Records shall be on one of Company's labels bearing such label's logo. Company shall not use any label or trademark owned by Distributor or licensed to Distributor by any other party.

EXAMPLE 2: Distributor Indemnified

21. Company hereby agrees to and does hereby indemnify, save, and hold Distributor harmless from any and all damages, liabilities, costs, losses and expenses (including legal costs and attorneys' fees) arising out of or connected with any claim, action, demand, or action by a third party which is inconsistent with any of the warranties, representations, or covenants made by Company in this contract. Company agrees to reimburse Distributor, on demand, for any payment made by Distributor at any time with respect to any such damage, liability, cost, loss or expense to which the foregoing indemnity applies to the extent such payment was made pursuant to a final judgment in a court of competent jurisdiction or pursuant to a settlement or compromise approved by or consented to by Company. Distributor shall notify Company of any such claim, demand, or action promptly after Distributor has been formally advised thereof. Pending the determination of any such claim, demand, or action, Distributor shall have the right, at Distributor's election, to withhold payment of royalties or other sums payable to Company hereunder in an amount reason-

ably related to such claim, demand, or action and Distributor's estimated attorneys' fees and estimated legal costs in connection therewith.

☛ Where there are representations and warranties, an indemnification is never far behind.

DISTRIBUTION FEES

Don't think there are no crocodiles because the water is calm.
                                                    —MALAYAN PROVERB

The distributor will take a distribution fee off the top of the wholesale price received from the distributor's customers, which may be retail outlets or subdistributors, or may even be reached directly, for example, through the Internet. The distribution fee is generally in the area of 22% to 25%, give or take a percentage point. There are frequently additional percentages taken by the distributor for cash discounts, special sales programs, etc.

The distribution fee is usually based upon net sales (see Examples 1 and 2). In order to determine net sales returns, rebates, credits, and adjustments are deducted from gross sales. From the remaining sum after the deduction of the distribution fee, the distributor will also withhold a reserve before paying the adjusted net amount to the distributed label. The payment to the distributed label will also be subject to recoupment of costs which may have been advanced by the distributor on behalf of the distributed label (such as, for example, manufacturing costs, cooperative advertising costs, etc.). In addition, the distributed label will receive no payment for free goods distributed.

EXAMPLE 1: Company's Share After Deducting Distribution Fee
8. *Company's Percentage of Sales and Returns*:

a. Subject to Paragraph 10. [statements] hereof, with respect to Net sales of Records in the Territory (i.e. Gross Sales of Records less returns, rebates, credits and adjustments) by Distributor, Distributor shall pay the following amounts ("Company's Percentage") to Company: Seventy-Eight Percent (78%) of Distributor's Net Sales computed at Distributor's subdistributor price (or Seventy-Eight Percent (78%) of Distributor's price to independent distributors and military exchanges on sales to those classes of customers) in the Territory for such Records.

b. For this purpose, a "sale" shall occur upon Distributor's shipment of Records to a customer in response to an order. The dollar amount of Sales shall be computed by multiplying the number of units of each Record shipped times Company's percentage of the subdistributor price (or Company's Percentage of Distributor's price to independent distributors and military exchanges on sales to those classes of customers) for such Record applicable at the time of shipment ("Gross Sales"). Net sales shall be determined by deducting from Gross Sales the amounts provided herein for returns, rebates, credits and adjustments, if any. The dollar amount of returns shall be computed by multiplying Company's Percentage of the subdistributor price (applicable at the time of the return) times the number of Records returned except, in the case of Free Goods Returns (as defined in Paragraph 9.d. hereinafter), Distributor shall be entitled to deduct One Hundred Percent (100%) of the applicable subdistributor price times the number of Free Goods Returns.

EXAMPLE 2: Distribution Fee
8. Distribution Fee; Net Sales; Company's Percentage of Net Sales.

(a) In consideration of the Basic Services to be performed by Distributor hereunder, and subject to the terms and conditions contained in this Agreement, Distributor shall be entitled to a distribution fee ("Distribution Fee") equal to twenty-four percent (24%) of "Net Sales" of Records made under this Agreement in the Territory.

FREE GOODS

When freebies are dealt with in distribution agreements, they appear to gain respectability: "freebies" become "free goods." But no matter what they call it, a freebie is a freebie is a freebie. (See the section "Freebies," pages 75–77). Free goods are used to prime the sales pump. For example, the distributor may make the following offer to a retail store: "Buy 100, and we will ship you 130 copies, but we will only charge you for 100." Promotional freebies, records given to radio stations, reviewers, etc., are also considered free goods (see Examples 1 and 2).

Because distribution agreements are, after all, sales agreements, the mechanics of every factor affecting sales are very important. The agreement must take into account the facts that the distributor's job is to sell the product and move as many units as possible but at the same time the product is owned by the distributed label and the distributed label is responsible for orchestrating and financing promotional efforts. The distribution agreement lays down the rules and regulations between the parties with respect to free goods.

SAMPLE CONTRACT PROVISIONS

EXAMPLE 1: Value of Free Goods Shipped Incorporated in Invoice Price

9. Promotion Records, Free Goods and Sales Programs

(a) No payment will be due from Distributor to Company on account of Distributor's or Company's distribution of Promotional Records, it being understood that Distributor will not distribute Promotional Records without Company's prior written consent. As used in this paragraph 9(a), a "Promotional Record" is a noncommercial Record (i.e., specifically identified both on the Disc or Cassette and the accompanying packaging materials as for promotional purposes only and not for resale) which Company gives away or furnishes on a "no-charge" basis for promotional purposes to disc jockeys, newspaper or magazine reviewers, or radio or television stations or networks. Except as provided for herein, Company shall undertake any distribution of Promotional Records entirely at its own cost and expense. Upon Company's written request, Distributor will undertake to mail promotional Records on Company's behalf, Company to furnish labels pre-printed with the names and addresses of all recipients; if Distributor does so, Distributor may charge Company its then-prevailing fee for such service, which sum Company shall promptly pay, or Distributor may deduct the amount of any such charge from any sums otherwise payable to Company hereunder. Commercial Records (i.e., finished goods Records suitable for resale to consumers) shall not be used as Promotional Records unless they are marked in such a manner so as to prevent their return to Distributor; if they are so returned, Distributor may mark such Records as promotional or cutout product prior to their delivery to Company or fulfillment, at its then-prevailing prices for such service and charge Company therefor, which sum Company shall promptly pay, or Distributor may deduct the amount of any such charge from any sums otherwise payable to Company hereunder.

(b) No payment shall be due from Distributor to Company on account of Distributor's distribution of Free Goods. All Free Goods shall be furnished by Company to Distributor at Company's sole cost and expense. As used in this subparagraph 9(b), "Free Goods" also include Promotional Records which are Commercial Records marked by Distributor on Company's behalf. Distributor shall not distribute Free Goods without Company's prior written approval. Company may initiate Free Goods sales programs, subject to Distributor's advice, by advising Distributor in writing of Company's Records to be included in the program, and the amount of Free Goods that Company approves. Company hereby acknowledges and approves application of Distributor's standard Free Goods policy (as it may be amended from time to time) with respect to single Records. The procedure to be used for determining the number and dollar amount of Free Goods Returns shall be determined according to the principles established for Distributor's last in first out accounting system. *Distributor represents and Company acknowledges that Distributor's current Free Goods policy is implemented by incorporating the value of Free Goods shipped into the invoice price for the respective records, i.e., Free Goods are included in the prices charged to customers* [emphasis added]. If such policy changes during the Term, Distributor shall notify Company thereof in writing and, if such policy changes in such a manner so as to have a material negative effect on Net Sales hereunder, Distributor shall use reasonable efforts to prorate Returns between Records sold and Free Goods in the same manner as the shipments are originally invoiced.

☛ The significance of the italicized passage is this: Even though the distributed label is not paid for the free goods (although it has cost the company money to manufacture them), the distributor manages to get paid for them by incorporating their costs into the prices charged to customers, the total of which will be used to calculate the net upon which the distributor's fee is based.

EXAMPLE 2: Free Goods

9. Free Goods and Sales Programs:

a. No payment shall be due from Distributor to Company on Records given away or on Records furnished to Company for promotional purposes or on Records furnished as a sale inducement or otherwise to disc jockeys, radio and television stations or networks, independent distributors, subdistributors and dealers, Distributor may assess Company a reasonable charge to emboss Records as promotional or cut-out product. Albums distributed as sales inducement records to independent distributors, subdistributors and dealers ("Free Goods") shall not be distributed without the prior consent of Company. Company hereby acknowledges and approves application of Distributor's standard Free Goods policy (as it may be amended from time to time) with respect to single Records. Pursuant to such policy, Distributor shall be permitted to bill its customers for and report only a percentage of the units shipped as sold, the remainder being Free Goods.

b. Distributor shall be entitled to charge to Company, and Company shall pay to Distributor, the actual dollar amount of discounts on Records given to Distributor's customers under discount programs requested or approved by Company. Company may participate in sales programs initiated by Distributor applying to some or all of Distributor's own product, by requesting same and advising Distributor in writing of Company's Records to be included in the program, and the size of the discounts Company approves.

c. If Company desires to furnish prizes or "spiffs" to Distributor salesmen and district managers, such programs must be approved in writing by Distributor and paid by Company for distribution by Distributor. In the event Distributor advances funds for any such prizes or "spiffs," it shall be entitled to reimbursement of the amount of such payments from any moneys due to Company from Distributor.

d. Distributor shall be entitled to charge to Company the full subdistributor price on account of returns of Records initially distributed as Free Goods ("Free Goods Returns"). For each monthly accounting period hereunder, the number of Free Goods Returns during such monthly accounting period shall be deemed to be that fraction of all Records returned during such accounting period, the numerator of which is the number of Records distributed as Free Goods during the six (6) month period immediately preceding the applicable accounting period ("Base Period") and the denominator of which is the gross number of Records shipped during such base period. Such fraction, as determined for each monthly accounting period during the term of this Agreement, shall be referred to hereinafter as the "Free Goods Return Rate." Solely with respect to the period from the commencement date of this Agreement through and including six months thereafter (the "Interim Period"), the amount of Free Goods Returns in each monthly accounting period ending on a date during the Interim Period shall be deemed to be twenty percent (20%) of the total number of Records returned during such accounting period ("Interim Free Goods Return Rate").

• • •

[10.] c. Distributor shall be entitled to deduct and retain a two percent (2%) cash discount from any payment mailed on or before the last day of the second full calendar month following the end of the monthly period with respect to which such payment is due, and a One-Half of One Percent (½%) allowance for bad debts.

d. At its option, Distributor also shall be entitled to deduct from any payment owing to Company (or, if such amount is insufficient, to charge and bill Company for) (i) subject to paragraph 9.d. dealing with Free Goods Returns, Company's Percentage of any actual credits, rebates and adjustments for returns received, issued or committed by Distributor to be issued, as of the statement date, but not included in the determination of net sales for the monthly period covered by the statement; (ii) a reserve against future credits, rebates and adjustments for returns of twenty-five (25%) of gross sales per month for albums and fifty percent (50%) of gross sales per month for singles ("Reserve"); (iii) any deficiency necessary to restore Company's cumulative Reserve account to the full amount specified in Paragraph 10.d. (ii) less any amount paid pursuant to Paragraph 10.e.; (iv) the amount of any overpayment by Distributor to Company which is the result of incorrect accounting, clerical error, mistake or inadvertence; and (v) any and all other sums that may be due hereunder from Company to Distributor.

RESERVES

> *There is safety in reserve, but no attraction.*
> *One cannot love a reserved person.*
> —JANE AUSTEN

In the same manner the record company holds back a reserve from the recording artist against returns of recorded product, the distributor holds back a reserve from shipments of the distributed label's product. The reserve, however, is likely to be liquidated more quickly for the distributed label than it would be for a recording artist. Since the distributed label needs the cash flow in order to operate—for everything from recording new product through the promotion and marketing of product—a shorter liquidation period is very important. In most instances, distribution agreements will provide for a liquidation schedule which calls for the distributor to hold the reserve for each month for a period of 6 months and, beginning in the seventh month, liquidate the reserve at the rate of one-sixth per month until liquidated.

SAMPLE CONTRACT PROVISIONS

EXAMPLE 1: Higher Reserve for Singles

d. At its option, Distributor also shall be entitled to deduct from any payment owing to Company (or, if such amount is insufficient, to charge and bill Company for) . . . (ii) a reserve against future credits, rebates and adjustments for returns of twenty-five (25%) of gross sales per month for albums and fifty percent (50%) of gross sales per month for singles ("Reserve");

• • •

e. One-sixth (1/6th) of the Reserve taken in the first (1st) month of this Agreement shall be liquidated and reported on each monthly statement for the seventh (7th) through twelfth (12th) months of this Agreement, and on such basis thereafter. By way of illustration, in the eighth (8th) month of this Agreement, one-sixth (1/6th) of the Reserve taken in the first (1st) month shall be liquidated and reported, together with one-sixth (1/6th) of the Reserve taken in the second (2nd) month; in the ninth (9th) month of this Agreement, one-sixth (1/6th) of the Reserve taken in the first (1st) month shall be liquidated and reported, together with one-sixth (1/6th) of the Reserve taken in the second (2nd) month and one-sixth (1/6th) of the Reserve taken in the third (3rd) month; and so forth. Upon its being liquidated and reported, the amount of the Reserve shall be applied and credited to Company's account, subject to paragraphs 10.f. through 10.h. The Reserve shall be reduced by the amount so applied.

f. Until it is actually paid by Distributor to Company, or otherwise reduced, the Reserve shall be accounted for separately each month but owned by Distributor; and shall be subject to all of Distributor's charges, offsets and recoupment rights, including (without limitation) those set forth in Paragraph 10.g. and 10.h. Company shall not earn the Reserve until it actually is due and paid by Distributor to Company.

g. At its option, Distributor may (but shall not be required to) retain and apply all or part of the Reserve against any sum due from Company to Distributor, including (without limitation) (i) the full amount of any current, cumulative or prospective credits, rebates and adjustments for returns received, issued or committed by Distributor to be issued, as of the statement date, but not included in the determination of net sales for the monthly period covered by the statement, (ii) any deficiency necessary to restore Company's cumulative Reserve account. The Reserve shall be reduced by the amount so applied.

h. No part of the Reserve shall be applied and credited to Company's account for any month in which returns exceed Gross Sales. In that case, the portion of the Reserve scheduled for liquidation may either be retained and applied to Distributor's account . . . or retained and rescheduled for liquidation as if first taken in the month retained. The Reserve shall be reduced by any amount retained and applied to Distributor's account.

☛ While the distributor withholds 25% for albums, for singles the reserve is increased to 50%—one more indication that singles are treated as a tool for selling albums. Presumably, singles will be pumped into the marketplace at a rate which will cause a higher level of returns.

EXAMPLE 2: Liquidation of Reserve at One-Sixth Per Month

12. RESERVES

(a) Distributor shall have the right to withhold a reasonable portion of Company's Percentage of Net Sales as a reserve on account of future credits, rebates, adjustments for Returns or other sums payable by Company to Distributor ("Reserve"). Each Reserve shall be held for six (6) months and shall be liquidated at a rate of one-sixth (1/6) per month over the next six (6) months.

(b) Subject to paragraph 12(a) above, until it is actually paid by Distributor to Company, or otherwise reduced, any Reserve shall be accounted for separately each month but owned by Distributor, and shall be subject to all of Distributor's charges, offsets, deductions and recoupment rights as set forth herein. Company shall not earn any Reserve until it is actually payable by Distributor to Company. No creditor of Company shall have any claim to any portion of any Reserve that has not been earned by Company. Any Reserve is not intended by the parties to constitute a security device, but rather is a means to compute when Company's Percentage is earned.

☛ Note subparagraph 12(b). Ownership of the monies being held in reserve is retained by the distributor. Until it is due and payable, neither the record company nor any third party creditor can make any claim on the money.

EXAMPLE 3: Liquidation Begins in Seventh Month

12. Distributor may withhold a reserve hereunder against future returns of Records or other sum due Distributor by Company hereunder. The reserve shall be withheld on a monthly basis and shall be used to secure Distributor against future returns, rebates, charges, offsets, etc. from the distribution of Records hereunder. The reserve shall not exceed Twenty-Five Percent (25%) and, starting in the Seventh (7th) month after such withholding, shall be liquidated at the rate of One-Sixth (⅙th) per month until liquidated; subject, however, to Distributor's credit for actual returns, rebates, charges, offsets, etc.

INVENTORY

Never invest your money in anything that eats or needs repairing.

—BILLY ROSE

The distributor places the distributed company's product into warehouses and other distribution centers for shipping to customers: subdistributors (distributors who buy product from another distributor under a license and then resell the product), one-stops, or stores. Note that one-stops, while not technically subdistributors, function as if they were. One-stops (named for "one-stop shopping") buy product from other distributors and then sell the product to retail stores and others selling to the public, at a higher price than would have been charged by the original distributors. Traditionally, one-stops have been the source of product for small independent retail stores (a.k.a. mom-and-pop stores), which may buy from the one-stops for any number of reasons, such as not being able to meet the distributor's credit requirements, being too small for the distributor to deal with, or just plain convenience.

Because of the logistics of handling the distributed label's product, distribution agreements provide for the various rights, obligations, and problems which deal with the storage of inventory of the recorded product. Included in the problems of storage are issues such as who must provide the insurance for loss through fire, theft, etc. (sometimes it is the record company, sometimes it is the distributor—see Example 1); what happens if the record company's product is not selling and is cluttering up the warehouse (see Example 2); and any one of the other myriad problems encountered when goods and belongings are stored with a warehousing facility.

SAMPLE CONTRACT PROVISIONS

EXAMPLE 1: Risk of Loss Borne by Company

13. Inventory:

a. The inventory of Records and related components furnished to Distributor by Company (including finished goods, jackets, inserts, and other components) stored in Distributor's warehouses ("Inventory") shall be Company's property. . . . The risk of loss of the Inventory in Distributor's possession due to any casualty, theft or obsolescence shall be borne by Company, and Company shall obtain all-perils insurance coverage for loss or damage to such Inventory. Company shall name Distributor as an additional insured thereunder, and furnish to Distributor a certificate of insurance.

EXAMPLE 2: Distributor Entitled to Scrap Excess Product

a. Distributor shall be entitled to scrap shop-worn Records returned to Distributor, and Distributor shall report such scrapping to Company. "Shop-worn" Records are those Records, in any configuration, which by Distributor's standards are deemed to be so damaged or excessively handled as to be unsalable and not economically salvageable. At its sole cost and expense, Company may take a physical inventory of its Inventory then stored at Distributor's distribution facilities. . . . The book inventory of Company's Records and components, reduced by units so scrapped shall be subject to a shrinkage allowance of four percent (4%) for any unexplained disappearances. For this purpose, overages of any items shall be combined with shortages of any other items to determine net shortages. Distributor shall not be liable for Records scrapped or for unexplained shortages within the net shrinkage allowance. Distributor's sole liability for unexplained shortages in excess of the shrinkage allowance shall be the cost of replacing such excess shortages, or the reasonable market value of the excess missing Inventory, whichever is lower. Distributor may elect to replace excess missing Inventory in satisfaction of such liability and, if requested, Company shall furnish Masters and components, and otherwise cooperate to enable Distributor to do so.

• • •

d. From and after the expiration of one (1) year following the Commencement Date of this Agreement (and as of the end of each monthly period thereafter), Distributor may, by written notice to Company, require Company to remove that portion of the Inventory from Distributor's distribution centers which exceeds fifty percent (50%) of Distributor's net unit sales of the Records in the six (6) month period immediately preceding the date of such written notice. Company shall, within thirty (30) days after such notice, remove such excess Inventory from Distributor's custody, but Company shall not be entitled to dispose of such Inventory except pursuant to the terms and provisions of this Agreement. If Company fails to remove such excess Inventory within such thirty (30) day period, Company hereby authorizes Distributor to sell such excess Inventory as "cut-outs" or to scrap such excess Inventory at Distributor's election.

☞ Distributors recycle returns, reshipping the records back into the field as new orders come in for the product. Sometimes the records never leave sealed boxes, but sometimes they need to have new shrink-wrap applied. If a particularly well-traveled copy goes out and comes back enough times, it will begin to look a little shabby and the distributor reserves the right to scrap the record. (Just for the record, shrink-wrap serves no purpose other than making the product look unused. In fact, the shrink-wrapping on vinyl LPs actually often caused damage by warping the disks.) Paragraph (d) gives the distributor the right to remove excess product which is not selling from the warehouse.

TERMINATION

Now and then there is a person born who is so unlucky that he runs into accidents which started out to happen to somebody else.
—DON MARQUIS

Distribution agreements are not like recording agreements, where the record company owns the recordings in perpetuity even after the artist is no longer under contract to the company. At the expiration of a distribution agreement, the distributed label picks up its marbles and moves on. Accordingly, provisions must be made covering various issues, for example, inventory, reserves, changing bar codes, etc.

One very important termination provision is how to handle returns which, for whatever reason, dribble back to the distributor after the distributed label has moved on. Now, the prospect of being responsible for returns in the normal course of business is one thing for a distributor—they don't like it, but it is part of the business—but to be responsible for returns after the end of the relationship is intolerable. Therefore distributors will take steps to ensure that the responsibility, financial and otherwise, for dealing with post-termination returns rests with the record company (see Examples 1 and 2). One method of providing protection is to require new bar codes to be placed on the existing product, usually by stickering over the old bar codes. The new codes enable the new distributor to determine whether a record is its responsibility or solely the responsibility of the record label.

SAMPLE CONTRACT PROVISIONS

EXAMPLE 1: Company Financially Responsible for Returns

a. . . . at the end of the term of this Agreement Company shall promptly instruct Distributor with respect to the disposition of all Inventory. Company shall remove its Inventory from Distributor's custody within thirty (30) days after Distributor's written demand for such removal. The cost of such removal (including charges from Distributor's loading services, if any) and storage charges from and after the thirty-first (31st) day following such written demand shall be paid by Company.

b. Upon the termination of this Agreement . . . Company shall be solely responsible for all returns of Records. Distributor may continue to accept returns from Distributor's customers, but Distributor shall not be obligated to Company to do so for any records no longer distributed by Distributor hereunder. If Distributor continues to accept returns, Company shall pay to

Distributor, upon Company's receipt of Distributor's invoice therefor, One Hundred Percent (100%) of the amount credited by Distributor in the ordinary course of business to its customers on account of such returns. Notwithstanding anything to the contrary contained in this Agreement, and during the six (6) month period immediately preceding, and the six (6) month period immediately following, any termination of this Agreement, whether by expiration of the term, notice of termination, or otherwise: (i) Distributor shall be entitled to withhold from any funds otherwise payable to Company reasonable reserves against returns . . . and (ii) Distributor shall have no obligation to credit Reserves to Company's account whatsoever until the rendition of the statement for the seventh (7th) monthly accounting period following the termination of this Agreement.

c. From and after the expiration or termination of the term of this Agreement, Company hereby agrees that it shall accept all returns of Records distributed hereunder; and, for the benefit of Distributor and Distributor's customers, Company shall give a credit or refund, whichever is requested by the customer, in the amount that such customer paid to Distributor for such Record. In addition to the foregoing, any successor distributor of Records shall be required by Company to accept all returns tendered to such successor distributor of Records distributed by Distributor; and, for the benefit of Distributor and Distributor's customers, such successor distributor shall give a credit or refund, whichever is requested by the customer, in the amount that such customer paid to Distributor for such Record. . . .

☛ In subparagraph (c) the record company agrees to accept all returns for which the first distributor may have been paid and to repay or credit the customer or have the new distributor repay or credit the customer. If the new distributor pays, it will almost certainly charge this back to the record company. This can become *very* expensive for the record company, which has already absorbed the manufacturing costs and is now required to pay the wholesale price for each unit on product it probably never received payment for in the first place.

EXAMPLE 2: Optional Cutout Notice; Special Reserve

(b) From and after the expiration or termination of this Agreement pursuant to paragraphs 3, 17(a) 20 or otherwise, Label, or Label's successor distributor of records through normal retail channels in the Territory shall be and remain financially responsible for all returns of records distributed hereunder. Distributor may propound a cutout or delete notice to its customers, but shall not do so unless requested by Label in writing. If Distributor accepts any returns, and credits its customer therefor, Distributor may charge and bill Label the actual invoice price for such unit, determined pursuant to Paragraph 8, above, in the same manner that the actual invoice price is determined during the Term, which sum Label shall promptly pay upon receipt of such bill, or Distributor may deduct such amount from the Reserve.

(c) During the six (6) months immediately preceding the expiration or any earlier termination of this Agreement, whether by expiration of the Term, notice of termination or otherwise, Distributor shall be entitled to withhold from any funds otherwise payable hereunder to Label a Reserve against anticipated post-termination Returns equal to Label's "Returns Percentage" over the immediately previous twelve (12) consecutive months times Gross Sales in the month during which such Reserve is taken. For this purpose, Label's "Returns Percentage" shall be a fraction equal to the dollar amount of Returns (as determined in accordance with the provisions of

Paragraph 11) during the immediately previous twelve (12) consecutive months divided by Label's Gross Sales over such period. After the expiration or earlier termination of this Agreement Distributor shall debit any post-termination Returns against such Reserve. Subsequent to a period of six (6) months after the expiration or earlier termination of this Agreement, Distributor shall liquidate and report the balance of the Reserve then on hand no later than twelve (12) months thereafter. Notwithstanding the foregoing, Distributor shall not take or hold a cash Reserve if Label posts a letter of credit with Distributor in the amount of Label's prospective Returns liability, as determined by Distributor in the exercise of its reasonable business judgment. Distributor shall not exercise its rights under this Paragraph 17(c) in Label's contracts with a successor Major Label Branch Distributor of records upon the expiration or termination of this Agreement, and such successor Major Label Branch Distributor agrees in writing to accept this Agreement, and such successor Major Label Branch Distributor agrees in writing to accept all Returns distributed by Distributor in the Territory pursuant to this Agreement which are tendered to such successor Major Label Branch Distributor and, for the benefit of Distributor and Distributor's customers, to give a credit or refund, pursuant to such successor Major Label Branch Distributor's policies, in the full amount that such customer paid to Distributor for such Record.

☛ This agreement represents a rather civilized approach to the return issue. The record company is responsible for the returns, but subparagraph (b) specifies that the record company has the option to have the distributor put out a notice that the product will either be deleted or cut out, thus avoiding being saddled with returns. If the record company wants to keep the product in circulation (which probably means it is selling), it has the opportunity to make appropriate arrangements and the financial exposure may be minimal. Subparagraph (c) gives the distributor the right to establish a special reserve for post-termination returns.

CHAPTER 17

MANUFACTURING AND SECURITY AGREEMENTS

A common mistake that people make when trying to design something completely foolproof is to underestimate the ingenuity of complete fools.

—DOUGLAS ADAMS

The last chapter discussed distribution agreements. Almost all distribution agreements have a manufacturing agreement attached. Where there is a manufacturing agreement, there will be a security agreement.

MANUFACTURING

Distributors that have their own manufacturing plants will probably insist that those plants (and the outside plants they have agreements with) do the manufacturing. In the case of a label being tacked onto another label's distribution agreement, the "sublabel" will have to abide by the distributing label's existing manufacturing agreement. Please note that many distributor/manufacturers have their own plants, but may also use other manufacturers (even other distributor/manufacturers) for overflow manufacturing needs (say, a rush release for 2 million units of one CD on top of normal manufacturing demands) or for different recording configurations.

The following examples are from distribution agreements and from manufacturing agreements entered into separately, but coterminously, with distribution agreements.

SAMPLE CONTRACT PROVISIONS

EXAMPLE 1. Record Label to Use Distributor's Designated Manufacturer

3. Company shall order all of its Disc, Compact Disc, Cassette and Promotional Record manufacturing requirements from Manufacturer for Records to be distributed pursuant to the Distribution Agreement between Company and Distributor in the Territory during the Term. Except as otherwise provided herein, Manufacturer shall furnish the materials and services to manufacturer Records ordered by Company specified in Exhibits A, B, C and D attached hereto and incorporated herein.

EXAMPLE 2: Distributor to Be Manufacturer

7. During the period hereof, Company shall not itself manufacture records in the Territory, or license or allow any party other than Distributor to manufacture records to be distributed through

normal retail channels by means of a system of major branch distribution or independent distribution in the Territory. Company may, however, at its election, order Records from Distributor, under and pursuant to this Agreement, and at the prices set forth herein, for purposes other than Distributor's distribution under and pursuant to the Distribution Agreement (hereinafter sometimes referred to as "Non-Distributor Records"). Distributor shall undertake such manufacturing of Non-Distributor Records subject to availability of components and other production elements. Non-Distributor Records must be numbered or otherwise identified so as to readily distinguish them from records sold by Distributor.

☞ The nondistributor records referred to here may be records for export out of the territory or records of a particular type specified as nonexclusive under the distribution agreement.

EXAMPLE 3: Record Label Responsible for Manufacturing

5. COMPANY'S OBLIGATIONS. Company solely shall be responsible for all activities, and shall pay all costs, expenses and charges incurred in connection with:

(a) Obtaining Masters, including, but not limited to, all costs arising out of the creation of or the acquisition of Company's rights in Masters, and all steps required to utilize Masters in the manufacture of Records.

(b) The delivery of Masters, color separations and label copy to a location in Los Angeles, California, designated by Distributor in the following forms:

(i) With respect to Discs and Cassettes, a high quality, fully edited and equalized two-track Master tape (DAT or analog) from which lacquer Masters and running Masters can be manufactured hereunder. Company may supply its own lacquer Masters of a quality technically satisfactory to Manufacturer (but not running Masters) f.o.b. Manufacturer's manufacturing facility.

(ii) With respect to Compact Discs, actual parts suitable for the manufacture of Compact Discs.

(c) Selecting the carrier and method of transportation to deliver Masters, packaging Masters, arranging for their shipment and delivery to a location designated by Manufacturer, and the payment of all freight charges for the shipment of Masters to Manufacture's facilities in California.

(d) Obtaining Components for all Records; and their delivery in good condition to Manufacturer's manufacturing facility, freight charges prepaid. Company acknowledges that Manufacturer is not required to commence the manufacture of Records unless sufficient Components are on hand.

EXAMPLE 4: Delivery Requirements for Manufacturing

9. MANUFACTURING

9.01. Distributor will have the right, but not the obligation, to manufacture Records distributed hereunder during the term of this Agreement, subject to the terms and conditions set forth in this paragraph.

9.02. The masters ("Masters") from which Distributor will manufacture phonograph records will be delivered to Distributor by you at places designated by Distributor. Each Master will be in the form of a two-track stereo tape, fully edited, mixed, equalized and leadered, in a form suitable for the manufacture of phonograph records and tapes. All configurations of record product to be manufactured hereunder will be fully sequenced by you. Lacquer masters and tape running masters will be made by you and the actual cost thereof will be paid by you. Distributor will have the right to reject any master which is technically deficient, in that it does not meet Distributor's then current prevailing standards for audio and engineering quality, or which Distributor reasonably deems to be offensive to reasonable standards of public morals or which may infringe on the rights of others. If Distributor so rejects any Master, you, at your own cost, will supply to Distributor a substitute Master which does not embody such defect. If, in Distributor's best business judgment, it determines that the initial sequencing of Masters is not technically suitable for the manufacture of any configuration of records, then you will have the first opportunity to perform the resequencing in order to meet Distributor's deadlines. You will also deliver with each Master full and accurate copyright and label information including any and all approvals, consents and necessary sideartist clearances.

9.03. You will supply to Distributor, at your sole cost and expense, film from the camera-ready artwork to be used by Distributor for the inserts for each Record manufactured hereunder.

9.04. Distributor will have the right to use the same label backdrop will be used for all Records manufactured hereunder. Your logo and trademark appearing on the label backdrop will remain your sole property.

> ☛ In the middle of paragraph 9.02 did you notice: "Distributor will have the right to reject any master . . . which Distributor reasonably deems to be offensive to reasonable standards of public morals . . ."? I don't notice here (or elsewhere) any provision allowing the distributed label to release the offending recordings elsewhere. Also, in spite of antiquated language for delivery materials—manufacture of phonograph records and "tapes" and "Lacquer masters and tape running masters"—this is a form currently being used by one of the largest distributors in the world.

EXAMPLE 5: Payment Deferred

6. *Invoice*. If Manufacturer so elects, Manufacturer may invoice Company for CDs manufactured hereunder as such CDs are completed, and Manufacturer will deduct such invoice charges within ninety (90) days from the date of invoice from Company's Net Proceeds earned by Company hereunder. If Company's Net Proceeds are insufficient to pay said manufacturing costs, then Manufacturer will send Company written notice and Company will pay Manufacturer said sum within ten (10) days following Manufacturer's written demand therefor.

7. *Sales Tax*. Company acknowledges that the transactions to be completed hereunder are not sales, or otherwise subject to sales or use taxes. Moreover, if such taxes are determined to be applicable, Company agrees to be responsible for the total amount of any such taxes and will hold Manufacturer harmless therefrom.

> ☛ This method allows the label to defer payment and apply income from sales from this or other product against manufacturing costs. Not so the method in the next example.

EXAMPLE 6: Payment Prior to Manufacture

12. Distributor will charge you per Record manufactured by Distributor in accordance with its then-current rate card charges for similar quantities of records. You will be responsible for and pay all manufacturing costs as described above prior to the manufacture of Records hereunder. If Distributor so elects, Distributor may invoice you for Records manufactured hereunder as such Records are completed, and Distributor will deduct such invoice charges within thirty (30) days from the date of invoice from your Net Proceeds earned by you hereunder. If your Net Proceeds are in-

sufficient to pay said manufacturing costs, then Distributor will send you written notice and you will pay Distributor said sum within ten (10) days following Distributor's written demand therefor.

> ☞ This is scary when you learn that under the distribution agreement it is literally possible for almost a year to pass before payment is received by the label for a CD sold within a month of manufacture. The distribution agreement has quarterly accountings and payments, due 60 days after the close of the calendar quarter. The distributor will accept a 120-day invoice period from its customers. Now try to follow this: You pay for the CD's manufacture on January 1. It is manufactured on January 15. It sells on February 15. The 120-day billing cycle (rounded out to 4 months) results in payment being received by the distributor July 15. The accounting period in which payment is received closes at the end of September. Payment to the label is made 60 days later, mailed at the end of November to be received early in December. Editorial note: *SCARY!!* For even scarier agreements, see the next section.

SECURITY

Security agreements are, to my way of thinking, about as scary as any music industry agreements can get. The distributor/manufacturer demands that manufacturing costs be paid, on time, one way or another. Usually the manufacturing agreement comes with a security agreement, either separate or included in the manufacturing agreement. In addition to the understanding that manufacturing costs come off the top (after, of course, the distribution fee), the security agreement will normally contain at least two of the following:

1. All of the label's assets must be put up as collateral (see Example 2);

2. The label must post a bond (see Example 4); and/or

3. The principal or principals of the label must sign personal guarantees (see Example 4).

Any one of the above is scary. Any combination can be terrifying.

SAMPLE CONTRACT PROVISIONS

EXAMPLE 1: Grant of Security Interest

1. *Grant of Security Interest.*

Debtor has heretofore incurred certain monetary obligations to Secured Party in accordance with certain terms and conditions contained in the Distribution Agreement, attached hereto and incorporated herein by reference. The parties anticipate that from time to time Secured Party will distribute on behalf of Debtor goods described as follows:

(a) Certain phonograph records, pre-recorded tapes, sound and/or videodiscs, on _____ or any parent and/or subsidiary of the same, as more specifically set forth in the Distribution Agreement.

In order to induce Secured Party to manufacture, sell, distribute and commercially exploit such goods, or to finance the manufacture of such goods, Debtor hereby grants to Secured Party a security interest in the collateral described below.

This agreement is a master security agreement and is not a contract to require the sale, consignment, or provision of goods and will not be deemed a promise that any goods will be sold or provided to Debtor.

EXAMPLE 2: Everything You Can Think of Is Collateral

1. Grant of Security Interest.

In order to secure the due and punctual performance by Debtor of its financial obligations under the Manufacturing Agreement and the Fulfillment Agreement, Debtor hereby grants to Distributor a security interest in the Territory in and to all of its rights, title and interest in and to:

(a) All existing and hereafter acquired inventory of Debtor, including, but limited to phonograph records, cassettes and compact discs, and video products, together with the elements with which they are packaged into finished goods, including, but not limited to, all jackets, inserts, boxes and other components, and all proceeds of their sale or other disposition in the Territory, wherever situate, now or hereafter held by Debtor, or by Distributor.

(b) Without limiting the generality of subparagraph 1(a), all record masters and other audio and audio-visual master recordings, whether or not now in existence, owned or controlled, directly or indirectly, by Debtor, or by any other person or entity who or which is, directly or indirectly, affiliated with Debtor by common ownership or control, regardless of the nature of the business, including, but not limited to, those identified on Schedule A [the Masters] which is incorporated herein by this reference; and all production components utilized to manufacture or derive finished goods from such masters, including, but not limited to, lacquers, mothers, stampers, metal parts and running masters.

(c) All existing and hereafter acquired contracts in respect of the Territory for artists, producers, production companies, authors and composers now or hereafter under contract to Debtor or to any other company owned or controlled, directly or indirectly, by Debtor or by any other person or entity who or which is, directly or indirectly, affiliated with Debtor by common ownership or control, including, but not limited to, those artist and publishing contracts identified on Schedule B which is incorporated herein by this reference; and all rights deriving therefrom, including, but not limited to, the right to commercially exploit all masters previously delivered by such artists, or to be delivered in the future; all copyright rights, and the right to compel such artists to deliver masters exclusively to Distributor in the future, in the event of Debtor's default hereunder.

(d) All existing and hereafter acquired compositions owned or controlled by Debtor, including, but not limited to, those identified in Schedule C which is incorporated herein by this reference; and all rights deriving therefrom, including, but not limited to, the right to commercially exploit such compositions in the Territory by any means, all Territory-wide copyrights, and any and all ancillary or related rights. Notwithstanding the foregoing, nothing contained in this Agreement shall prohibit Debtor from entering into an agreement with a third party or parties, for the subpublishing or other music publishing administration in the Territory of compositions owned or controlled by Debtor; provided, however, that Debtor shall be obligated to fully advise each such third party of Distributor's rights and interests hereunder with respect to such compositions and to expressly reference such rights and interests in each such agreement.

(e) All existing and hereafter acquired licenses, rights, copyrights, accounts, proceeds, hereafter acquired property, and other contract rights associated with or necessary for the manufacture and distribution of phonograph records, cassette tapes and compact discs, owned and controlled by Debtor, sufficient to enable Distributor to commercially exploit in the Territory all Collateral (as such term is hereinafter defined) hereunder in the event of Debtor's default.

(f) All accounts receivable due from Distributor under the Distribution Agreement.

(g) All of Debtor's existing and hereafter acquired furniture, fixtures and equipment (including, but not limited to, all recording studios and related equipment), and all replacements, additions, substitutes, accessories and proceeds (including insurance proceeds) related to or derived from any of the foregoing, but specifically excluding any real estate of Debtor.

All items in subparagraph 1(a) through and including 1(g) above are hereinafter collectively referred to as the "Collateral."

> ☞ I promised you scary. About the only thing missing is the family dog and somebody's first-born. While correct in this context, I find it depressing that the designation "Debtor" is already applied to the distributed label. You miss a payment and BAM!, the security agreement kicks in.

EXAMPLE 3: What Does the Collateral Cover?

3. *Obligations Secured.* The Collateral is security for the payment in full of:

(a) The failure to pay for goods consigned by Secured Party to Debtor, upon such payment becoming due or the failure to return such consigned goods on Secured Party's request.

(b) All existing obligations of Debtor to Secured Party arising out of the purchase, by Debtor, or other acquisition by Debtor, of goods or other personality from Secured Party;

(c) All obligations of Debtor to Secured Party arising hereafter on account of consignment, purchases, or other acquisition, of goods or other personal property by Debtor from Secured Party;

(d) All other obligations owed by Debtor to Secured Party, whether now existing or hereafter arising; and costs and expenses, including reasonable attorney's fees, expended by Secured Party to enforce or foreclose the security agreement or in any way incurred by Secured Party with respect to its security interests.

> ☞ Different agreement, but it's still "Debtor." It's like a visit from the Ghost of Christmas Yet to Come.

EXAMPLE 4: Post Bond and Personal Guarantee

3.03. Within five (5) days following execution hereof, [Label] will provide [Distributor] with an irrevocable letter of credit with [Distributor] as the beneficiary in the amount of Five Hundred Thousand Dollars ($500,000) for each period of this Agreement (as extended, if applicable) plus six (6) months. [Distributor] will have the right to use this letter of credit to recover any and all outstanding debts to [Distributor] hereunder, as determined in [Distributor]'s best business judgment and in accordance with the terms hereof. [Label] and MCA agree that notwithstanding the execution of this Agreement, the effectiveness and commencement of the term of this Agreement is expressly conditioned upon [Distributor]'s timely receipt of the aforementioned letter of credit. If such letter of credit is not received by [Distributor] within five (5) days from the date of execution hereof, without limiting its other rights, [Distributor] may elect, at its sole discretion, and at any time, to terminate the term of this agreement.

(a) Notwithstanding the foregoing, [Distributor] will have the right periodically, at [Distributor]'s sole discretion to review the status of [Label]'s account. If [Label]'s account is unrecouped and the unrecouped balance exceeds the sum of the amount secured by the letter of credit, then within ten (10) days following written notice from [Distributor], [Label] will provide [Distributor] with an additional letter of credit in an amount equivalent to [Label]'s anticipated unearned balance for the next six (6) months as estimated by [Distributor] in its sole discretion. If [Label] fails to provide [Distributor] with such additional security within ten (10) days following [Distributor]'s request therefor, [Distributor] will have the right, without limiting its other rights and remedies, to terminate the term of this Agreement by written notice to [Label], and [Label] will immediately pay to [Distributor] any and all of [Label]'s then unsatisfied obligations hereunder.

(b) If [Distributor] utilizes the letter of credit to satisfy any of [Label]'s outstanding debts hereunder in accordance with the terms hereof, [Label] will promptly provide [Distributor] with an additional letter of credit in an amount sufficient to cover the balance then due and owing [Distributor]. If [Label] fails to provide [Distributor] with such additional security within ten (10) days following [Distributor]'s request therefor, [Distributor] will have the right, without limiting its other rights and remedies, to terminate this Agreement by written notice to [Label], and [Label] will immediately pay to [Distributor] any and all of [Label]'s then unsatisfied obligations hereunder.

• • •

PERSONAL GUARANTEES

I have read the foregoing Agreement and agree to be bound by the terms and conditions contained therein. Furthermore, I personally guarantee to [Distributor] any and all of the obligations applicable to [Label]'s Manufacturing Agreement with [Distributor], dated _____. [Distributor] is hereby authorized to seek any and all remedies at law, equity or otherwise, against me personally in connection with the preceding sentence.

☛ A $500,000 bond does not come cheap; plus, of course, the bonding company will want its own collateral—something more valuable than $500,000—in order to issue the bond. Also, there's a hell of a lot of "Distributor's sole discretion" in subparagraph (a).

CHAPTER 18

FOREIGN DISTRIBUTION AGREEMENTS

The world is getting to be such a dangerous place,
a man is lucky to get out of it alive.

—W.C. FIELDS

Foreign distribution agreements (or, as they are sometimes referred to, foreign licensing or foreign sublicensing agreements) are in some ways quite similar to domestic recording agreements and production agreements and are certainly quite similar to distribution agreements; but, like any distant cousins, they do have their distinct differences (or, less charitably, their distinct peculiarities). To the uninitiated—someone familiar with domestic recording agreements, but unfamiliar with foreign distribution—these agreements may seem to have a certain distorted and warped configuration (but only to the "uninitiated" of course).

The relationship between the parties in a foreign distribution agreement is different than that between a record company and an artist or a production company. In these agreements, the record company is not producing for or selling to the foreign distributor, but rather *licensing* the use of masters owned or controlled by the record company. As a licensor, the record company wants to, and, in some instances, must, impose controls over the use of those masters. These imposed controls, generally speaking, would be unthinkable in a recording agreement with an artist or producer. With the foreign distribution agreement, the unthinkable becomes the ordinary.

If the label being licensed is not currently successful or does not have an established roster of artists, it is more than likely that the foreign licensee will require that the contractual relationship begin with an import arrangement whereby the domestic company will export finished product to the foreign company at a set price. When the product sells a specified number of units, or sales reach a certain plateau, the import agreement will automatically become a licensing agreement, where the foreign licensee will manufacture the product under license rather than import finished goods.

For the purposes of this discussion, we will presume that the record company–foreign distributor relationship has progressed beyond the import agreement stage and that the parties are proceeding with a foreign distribution agreement, whereby the foreign distributor is to distribute the record company's product in the territory. The following sections examine, sometimes in detail, sometimes in passing, some of the ways in which foreign distribution agreements differ from domestic agreements. Insights into how these different provisions actually work with regard to the foreign agreement can be discovered by comparing these provisions with the corresponding provisions found in domestic artist recording agreements and domestic distribution agreements.

Keep in mind that all but one of what's left of the major United States domestic record company distributors are owned by foreign entities and that one—Warner Bros.—was, for all practical purposes, bought by a Canadian toward the end of 2003. This may lead to the foreign entity putting pressure on a record company entering into a domestic distribution agreement in the United States to make a worldwide deal rather than dealing on a territory-by-territory basis. Yet there are many good reasons to pick foreign distributors on a territory-by-territory basis, including avoiding cross-collateralization problems, having more hands-on control over the distributor, and the possibility of getting higher advances. In addition, the affiliated distributor in a given territory may be very weak.

TERRITORY

The majority of domestic recording agreements between record companies and artists or production companies provide that the record company obtains the rights granted therein for the entire world. Indeed, some agreements go so far as to talk about the entire universe, including astral bodies now known and unknown. Foreign distribution agreements, on the other hand, are almost always quite explicit in limiting the territory covered by the agreement. (Recall that Example 2 in the section "Territory" in Chapter 16 specified, among other "territories," oil rigs and marine installations.)

Foreign distribution agreements are generally licenses for a specific territory, and, accordingly, the territory must be defined with specific detail. The scope of the definition of the territory is of great importance to both parties. The definition becomes increasingly important in areas where there is a great deal of importing and exporting of product between countries, such as the European Union. With the coming of the European Union, most of western Europe has become part of one giant market, a market that is, in fact, the largest trading market in the world. In addition, most of the countries in western Europe are deregulating their broadcasting industries, allowing for more radio and television stations and the concomitant probability that more and more music will be broadcast. There are opportunities to be explored (and exploited) here.

With these changes comes some risk for Americans, such as the threat of national "content" regulations which may require that specified percentages of a broadcast's content be of local origin. The French government, for example, has been quite vocal in demanding that limitations be placed on the amount of "foreign" (that's us) material broadcast over the airwaves.

SAMPLE CONTRACT PROVISIONS

EXAMPLE 1: Colombia and Venezuela
WHEREAS, Licensee is in a position to provide manufacturing and/or marketing facilities for phonograph records in:

COLOMBIA

VENEZUELA
(hereinafter referred to as the "Territory");

EXAMPLE 2: Germany, France, Italy, and Spain
2. In consideration of the terms and conditions contained herein, Company hereby leases to Lessor and grants to Lessor the exclusive right and license to use the Masters for the purpose of manu-

facturing and selling records therefrom, during the term of this Agreement in: Germany; France; Italy; and Spain only (hereinafter referred to as the "Territory").

PRODUCT

My problem lies in reconciling my gross habits with my net income.
—ERROL FLYNN

What product is the domestic record company licensing to the foreign distributor in these agreements? The domestic record company may license all its product, selected portions of its product, or, perhaps, just a specific recording. This, for obvious reasons, must be clearly spelled out. Generally, the foreign licensee is obtaining rights to the record company's entire catalogue. Sometimes, however, the record company does not have the rights to release a recording throughout the world, or there may be a restriction for a specific territory. (See all three examples at the end of this section.) The product of an artist who is signed only, for example, for the United States and Canada, cannot be licensed by the record company in South America, the United Kingdom, etc. Another artist might, for example, be signed for the entire world with the exception of France, and, accordingly, this artist's masters would have to be excluded from any sublicensing agreement for France.

It is very common for the license to be for all the product of the domestic record company, but conditional upon that product first having a commercial release in the United States (see Example 3). For reasons which will become clearer after reading two of the following sections—"Royalties, Advances, and Costs" and "Guaranteed Release"—the foreign distributor will certainly want some control over the release of product.

For ease of administration, maximum exploitation, and the fact that it is probably impractical to do otherwise, most record companies will license, to the extent they are able, their entire catalogue to one foreign licensee for each territory. The discussion of guaranteed release should be considered in connection with the scope of the product licensed.

SAMPLE CONTRACT PROVISIONS

EXAMPLE 1: All Product on Licensor's Three Labels
2. GRANT AND SCOPE OF RIGHTS. Licensor hereby grants to Licensee for the term specified herein an exclusive license to press and sell in those areas set forth on Schedule "A" attached hereto (hereinafter referred to as the "Leased Territory") phonograph records produced from tapes or matrices of all recordings:

(A) Released by Licensor on the "X" label, the "Y" label, and the "Z" label (herein collectively called the "Licensor label") in the United States of America prior to or during the term of this agreement;

(B) At the free disposal of Licensor for the Leased Territory; and

(C) Released by Licensee under the terms of this agreement.

(D) Nothing herein contained shall obligate Licensor to release any records whatsoever. Licensor shall not be obligated to secure the right to release recordings in the Leased Territory when securing licenses from foreign record companies authorizing Licensor to release records in the United States.

EXAMPLE 2: All Product Not Excluded from the Territory

1. During the term of this Agreement, Company grants to Licensee the right to manufacture and sell in the Territory phonograph records manufactured from each and every master recording which is presently owned by or which shall be owned by Company or otherwise acquired by Company, except all masters shall be excluded which Company does not now, or during the term of this Agreement control for use in the Territory.

EXAMPLE 3: All Product Released in the United States

1. LICENSE OF MASTER RECORDINGS:

Licensor hereby licenses to Licensee, and Licensee hereby accepts from Licensor for the term of this Agreement for the Territory only:

(a) Each and every master recording owned or controlled by Licensor (hereinafter referred to as the "Master" or "Masters" as appropriate), which:

(i) heretofore has been or which is during the term of this Agreement, released on a commercial phonograph record in the USA; or

(ii) which shall be acquired during the term of this Agreement by Licensor and which is released on a commercial phonograph record during the term hereof in the USA; (except such Masters which may be encumbered or otherwise restricted or prohibited for the Territory or in which Licensor has no rights for the Territory), for the purpose of manufacturing, distributing and selling phonograph records only in the Territory.

RIGHTS GRANTED TO LICENSEE

What rights are transferred to the foreign licensee by the record company? The most obvious is the right to manufacture and sell the recordings. Other rights, such as the right to use the name and likeness of the artists, the right to perform publicly and to broadcast, and the right to advertise are also usually transferred. Some rights, such as the right to use the record company's trademarks, the right to do commercial tie-ins (e.g., premium records), the right to distribute through record clubs, and the right to couple the recordings may or may not be transferred to the foreign licensee.

Some thought should be given to the issue of neighboring rights when granting rights to foreign licensees. For example, will the grant strip the record company of rights (and income) which would be due the company in connection with the exercise of neighboring rights? Or will the foreign licensee collect on behalf of, and remit to, the record company income from neighboring rights?

Keep in mind that these agreements are licensing agreements: The record company (the licensor) is licensing rights to the foreign distributor (the licensee) for a limited period of time. Generally, in this relationship the relative bargaining positions of the two parties are the opposite of the relative bargaining positions in an agreement between a domestic distributor and record company in that the record company will probably have more of an upper hand with the foreign distributor than it would have with a domestic distributor (see Example 1).

Also note that all the recommendations regarding the care that must be taken to retain copyrights and other ownership rights outlined in Chapter 12, "Foreign Subpublishing Agreements" (pages 353–354), should also be followed when licensing rights to a foreign distributor.

EXAMPLE 1: Grant of Rights

2. RIGHTS GRANTED TO LICENSEE

Licensor grants to Licensee the following rights, subject to the terms and conditions set forth herein:

(a) Except as otherwise expressly set forth herein, the right to manufacture, distribute, sell, advertise, publicly perform and broadcast in the Territory records containing the performances contained in the Masters.

(b) The right to use in the Territory the name, likeness and biography of each Artist whose performance is embodied in a Master only in connection with the advertising, publicizing or sale of records manufactured from the Masters; provided, however, that Licensee shall be bound by any restrictions imposed upon Licensor with respect thereto of which Licensee shall have been informed by Licensor.

(c) Except with the prior express written consent of Licensor, Licensee shall not release records embodying any of the performances contained in a Master:

(i) on any so-called "budget" or "low-priced" label;

(ii) on any so-called "premium" record;

(iii) in connection with any merchandising schemes or commercial tie-in arrangements; or

(iv) through any direct mail or mail order method of distribution, including, without limitation, record club distribution or other similar merchandising methods.

(d) Licensor has not granted and shall not grant to any third parties any rights in the Territory which are inconsistent with the rights granted to Licensee hereunder.

• • •

(e) Except as expressly provided for to the contrary in this Agreement, all rights of any nature whatsoever in the Masters are reserved by Licensor.

☛ Note the similarity to the grant-of-rights provisions previously reviewed, *except*, because of the different bargaining positions, the rights set forth in subparagraph 2(c), which in the grant-of-rights provisions would almost always favor the other party, are here subject to the licensor's complete control.

EXAMPLE 2: Export Provision and Limited Configuration

2. GRANT AND SCOPE OF RIGHTS. Licensor hereby grants to Licensee for the term specified herein an exclusive license to press and sell in those areas set forth on Schedule "A" attached hereto (hereinafter referred to as the "Leased Territory") phonograph records produced from tapes or matrices of all recordings:

• • •

(E) Licensee may also purchase records manufactured by Licensor in the United States and which Licensor will export to Licensee for sale in the Leased Territory . . .

(F) Insofar as it is permitted to do so, Licensor grants to Licensee the right to use and allow others to use the name, likeness and biography of each Artist whose performance is embodied in the records manufactured hereunder in connection with the advertising, publicizing or sale of such records . . . .

(H) It is expressly understood and agreed that the grant of rights contained herein authorizes Licensee to manufacture, distribute, sell and exploit conventional disc-type phonograph records from the master recordings covered by this agreement, and no other devices used in sound reproduction.

☛ This agreement provides for an alternative to the foreign distributor manufacturing the product—the right to buy finished product in the United States and to export to and import into the licensed territory. Subparagraph H contains an unusual restriction: The foreign distributor may only distribute records in the "conventional disc-type" configuration. At this time, the restrictions allow only CDs—no tapes, no DATs, and no downloads off the Internet.

ROYALTIES, ADVANCES, AND COSTS

Maybe this world is another planet's hell.
—ALDOUS HUXLEY

Always of interest, and of prime importance, is the money. In foreign distribution agreements, the payments made by the foreign distributor to the record company seem to fall into three categories: (1) royalties, (2) advances, and (3) costs. There is a tendency to mix these three categories together in the agreements. The examples below demonstrate a good cross section of provisions that deal with the payment obligations of the licensee.

As in artists' recording agreements, a starting point in calculating royalties is to determine whether the royalty is based upon the applicable wholesale price or the suggested retail price. There is, however, an added complication in those foreign territories where, by law, it is illegal to have an "applicable wholesale price" or a "suggested retail list price." This, of course, makes it impossible to use the normal royalty calculation formula (price x royalty rate = royalty), because there is no "price" to multiply by the royalty percentage.

As discussed in Chapter 3, in these territories the problem is solved by using a constructed price, or published price to distributors (PPD), an assigned price (as, indeed, is the "suggested retail list price") set by some local authority—usually a performance rights society—for the purpose of calculating not only record royalties, but also, in territories where the mechanical is based upon a percentage, mechanical license fees.

Presuming the domestic record company has any semblance of success, it is probable that the foreign distributor will pay an advance in connection with the foreign distribution agreement. More likely than not, the advance will be paid in increments (see Examples 1 and 2).

The treatment of royalties and advances is not very different from provisions in domestic recording agreements, but the cost provisions, whereby the foreign distributor reimburses or pays certain costs, are, generally, unusual enough to be surprising to someone reared on our homegrown variety of recording contract. (Look at Example 1, where the container charge for records manufactured in disc form is 6½%. Now you may or may not recall some of the provisions in the section on container charges in Chapter 3, where the record companies take a container deduction against an artist's royalties of 15%, 20%, or even 25%, two or three times higher than that which they will allow another company to take against them. These guys know what the real costs are.)

Also note how the issue of payments to the various union funds is handled. In both Examples

1 and 2, the foreign distributor must pay the record company any monies due the Music Performance Trust and Special Payment Funds. As discussed in Chapter 3, these costs are normally not charged back against an artist's royalties, yet here they are recouped against the foreign distributor.

All the delivery-element costs are also borne by the foreign distributor, for example, shipping costs, custom fees, costs of duplicate masters, artwork, promotional items, etc. (see paragraph 10 in Example 1 and paragraph 5 in Example 2).

In fact, as you review these provisions, it should become increasingly clear that virtually *all* costs are borne by the foreign distributor and not charged back to the record company. This of course means that the more product distributed by the foreign distributor, the more royalties are generated for the record company—even if the distributor's net profits shrink or disappear—and leads to a very interesting development with regard to guaranteed-release provisions (see the next section).

Note that Subparagraph 2(b) in Example 2 requires the foreign distributor to share income with the record company from the collection of public performance and broadcasting fees collected by the distributor under neighboring rights rules and regulations.

SAMPLE CONTRACT PROVISIONS

EXAMPLE 1: Costs Borne by Distributor

4. ROYALTIES PAYABLE TO LICENSOR. In consideration of the rights licensed hereunder, Licensee shall pay Licensor the following sums:

(a) A royalty equal to Sixteen (16%) Percent of the suggested retail list price in the country of sale of records manufactured from Masters licensed hereunder on 90% of net sales of such records.

(i) In addition, Licensee will pay Licensor 100% of the sums Licensor shall be obligated to pay pursuant to the Music Performance Trust Fund, Special Payments Fund, or similar Fund.

(ii) As used herein, the term "net sales" shall mean all records manufactured and sold hereunder less any returns and any credits for exchange, defective merchandise, errors in billing, errors in shipment and useable overstock.

(b) The royalty due hereunder shall be less:

(i) sums actually paid by Licensee to duly constituted governmental authorities for sales or excise taxes; and

(ii) an amount equal to Six and One-Half (6½%) Percent of the suggested retail list price for packaging costs of long-playing records and extended play records in disc form and an amount equal to Ten (10%) Percent of the suggested retail list price for packaging costs for long-playing records and extended play records in tape form.

(c) Licensee agrees that the suggested retail list price of records manufactured and sold hereunder shall not be less than the suggested retail list price of the top line records in comparable packaging manufactured and sold by Licensee under its own trademarks.

(d) Licensee shall notify Licensor of the suggested retail list prices for each country of the Territory, to the extent permitted by law, of the various types of records sold hereunder, the amount of deductible sales or excise taxes relating thereto, and the bases which shall be used to calculate royalties hereunder, within thirty (30) days of the date hereof, and shall notify Licensor of any changes therein within fourteen (14) days of any such change.

5. ADVANCES. Licensee shall pay to Licensor the following non-returnable advances to be recouped from royalties to be paid by Licensee to Licensor pursuant to Subparagraph 4.(a), above, not, however, including any sums of money due Licensor pursuant to Subparagraph 4.(a)(i), above:

(a) Ten Thousand ($10,000.00) Dollars concurrently with the execution of this Agreement;

(b) Ten Thousand ($10,000.00) Dollars upon the commencement of the second year of this Agreement; and

(c) Twenty Thousand ($20,000.00) Dollars upon the commencement of the third year of this Agreement.

• • •

10. PROMOTIONAL MATERIALS

• • •

(e) Licensor shall, upon request, supply to Licensee any such Materials in quantity, or plates for reproducing the Materials, at Licensor's cost price plus any actual expenses for packing, shipping and insurance. Licensee shall pay all customs fees, duties and other expenses relating to importation of the Materials. Licensee is hereby granted the right to reproduce any or all of the Materials for use as set forth above; provided, however, that Licensor itself has obtained the right to grant such right to Licensee without charge or liability to Licensor or any third party.

☛ Note that the only sure deductions from the record company's royalty in this example are containers (at a low charge) and taxes.

EXAMPLE 2: Advance As Guaranteed Minimum Royalty

2. Licensee agrees to pay to Company in United States dollars:

(a) A royalty of a sum equal to Eighteen (18%) Percent of the suggested retail list price of Ninety (90%) Percent of all records manufactured and sold hereunder (exclusive of taxes thereon), except that the rate of royalty shall be one-half (½) thereof for record club sales.

(b) A sum equal to Fifty (50%) Percent of all public performance and broadcasting fees, if any, received from broadcasters or others with respect to the performance or broadcasting of records manufactured from the Masters.

(c) Royalties or other sums, if any, which are payable pursuant to Company's agreements with the Trustee of the Music Performance Trust Fund, the Special Payments Fund, or any like fund.

(d) Licensee guarantees that the minimum royalties payable hereunder to Company shall be the sum of Sixty Thousand ($60,000.00) Dollars during the term of this Agreement. Said sum of money shall be deemed to be a non-returnable advance against the royalties due Company hereunder and shall be paid to Company as follows:

(i) On or before January 1, _____, the sum of Ten Thousand ($10,000.00) Dollars;

(ii) On or before July 1, _____, the sum of Ten Thousand ($10,000.00) Dollars;

(iii) On or before January 1, _____, the sum of Ten Thousand ($10,000.00) Dollars;

(iv) On or before July 1, _____, the sum of Ten Thousand ($10,000.00) Dollars;

(v) On or before January 1, _____, the sum of Ten Thousand ($10,000.00) Dollars; and

(vi) On or before July 1, _____, the sum of Ten Thousand ($10,000.00) Dollars.

(e) In the event that the royalties payable by Licensee to Company pursuant to Subparagraph 2.(a), above, exceed the minimum royalty provided for in Subparagraph 2.(d), above, the excess above such minimum royalty, if any, shall be payable at the time of the rendering of the royalty statement pursuant to Subparagraph 2.(f), below, for the quarterly period when the royalties exceed the minimum.

(f) Royalty statements setting forth in detail the royalties payable hereunder shall be rendered quarterly within forty-five (45) days following the end of each calendar quarter, together with payment of such royalties.

• • •

(i) All sums of money payable to Company pursuant to Subparagraphs 2.(b) and (c), above, shall be paid to Company by Licensee quarterly, as provided for in Subparagraph 2.(f), above.
3. Licensee agrees to pay, or cause to be paid, directly to the proprietors of the copyrighted musical or other material, or their duly authorized agents, and copyright royalties and license fees which may be or become due for the manufacture and sale of records hereunder which contain such copyrighted musical or other material.

• • •

5. Company agrees to deliver to Licensee the Masters by supplying to Licensee, at Company's cost for materials only plus any actual expenses incurred for packing and shipping, one or more duplicate tape recordings, acetate masters, or metal mothers (as selected by Licensee) of each Master . . . Subparagraph 2.(b) in Example 2 requires the foreign distributor to share income with the record company from the collection of public performance and broadcasting fees collected by the distributor under neighboring rights rules and regulations.

☛ The yearly advances are structured so that in each year the record company will receive at least the minimum payment. If, in any year, the royalty for that year exceeds the minimum guarantee, the record company also receives the excess for that year *whether or not* prior deficits have been recouped. In effect, this provision acts as if there is no cross-collateralization between yearly periods.

GUARANTEED RELEASE

STEPHANO:
This will prove a brave kingdom to me,
where I shall have my music for nothing.
—WILLIAM SHAKESPEARE
The Tempest, Act III, Scene 2

Depending on the size and importance of the domestic record company, there will usually be some form of guaranteed-release provision in the foreign distribution agreement. This guarantee can vary from an obligation to release each and every recording, or at least a substantial portion of all recordings, released by the record company to an obligation to release only those recordings which reach a certain level of success (see Examples 1 and 2). Some foreign distribution agreements have no guaranteed-release requirement and recordings are released, if at all, solely at the discretion of the foreign company.

As discussed in the previous section, it is generally to the advantage of the record company to have as much product as possible released in the territory. In addition, since virtually no recoupment is available to the foreign distributor, other than the recoupment of advances, each record sold results in some payment being due the domestic record company. In many ways, the position of the domestic record company is like (but better than) the position of an independent producer who receives an advance, is not responsible for any costs, and is paid from record one.

With so much at stake, it is little wonder that the issue of guaranteed release is one of the hotly negotiated points in this type of agreement. The domestic record company attempts to make the guaranteed-release commitment as extensive as possible; the foreign distributor wants to limit the guarantee as much as possible.

SAMPLE CONTRACT PROVISIONS

EXAMPLE 1: Guaranteed Release of All Top 100 Records

9. RELEASE OF RECORDS. Subject to there being no copyright or other legally binding restrictions which would prevent Licensee from doing so, Licensee shall commercially release in each country of the Territory each single record and Album released by Licensor in the USA during term hereof which shall reach the position of One Hundred (100) or higher in the Top single Record Chart and Top Album Chart of BILLBOARD, and each single record or album released by Licensor in the USA which Licensor is contractually required to release in the Territory (it being understood that Licensor shall advise Licensee in writing of any such contractual requirements) as well as any single record or Album released by Licensor embodying the performances of an artist as well as any single record or Album released by Licensor embodying the performances of an artists who is then currently engaged in or is preparing for a personal appearance tour in the Territory.

(a) The release of any such single record or Album by Licensee shall take place:

(i) within ninety (90) days after Licensee's receipt from Licensor of the master tapes or other parts and all necessary information referred to in Subparagraph 8. (b), above, and relevant packaging material for such single record or Album, as the case may be; or

(ii) within ninety (90) days after such single record or Album, as the case may be, shall have reached the aforesaid chart position; or

(iii) as quickly as possible following notification from Licensor of the proposed or then current personal appearance tour by the Artist whose performance is embodied on the record, whichever shall last occur. The foregoing shall in no way limit or derogate from the obligation of Licensee hereunder to use all reasonable efforts to exploit Licensor's Master in the Territory.

(b) In the event Licensee shall fail to release any such record in any country of the Territory in accordance with the foregoing, Licensor shall have the right, by written notice to Licensee, to cause all rights granted to Licensee hereunder for the Territory in the Master for such record to revert to Licensor. In addition, Licensee shall thereafter have no rights hereunder for the Territory in and to any other Master by the Artist(s) whose performances are embodied in the Masters which Licensee shall have failed to release in the Territory within said Territory; provided, however, that Licensee's rights in recordings previously released by Licensee which embody the performances of such Artist(s) shall continue pursuant to the terms of this Agreement. Notwithstanding anything to the contrary contained herein, Licensor shall thereupon have the sole and exclusive right, at Licensor's election, to exploit or to arrange for the exploitation of such Matters in such country of the Territory, provided that such Masters are not released by Licensor or Licensor's designee on any label used in the Territory by Licensee.

(c) Notwithstanding the foregoing, in the event that any such record subject to the provisions of this Paragraph 9 is unsuitable for release in any particular country of the Territory because of its political, moral or religious context, and Licensee so notifies Licensor in writing within fourteen (14) days after its receipt of a sample record or Master, Licensee shall not be required to release such record in the country of the Territory and all rights in and to the Master for such record with respect to such country of the Territory shall revert to Licensor, and notwithstanding anything contained to the contrary herein, Licensor shall thereupon have the sole and exclusive right, at Licensor's election, to exploit or to arrange for the exploitation for such Masters in such country of the Territory, provided that such Masters are not released by Licensor or Licensor's designee on any label used in the Territory by Licensee.

(d) Licensee agrees to comply with local law and register for copyright in each country of the Territory phonograph records derived from the Masters subject to this Agreement.

> ☛ The three required-release categories in this agreement are (1) recordings reaching a position in the top 100 on the charts, (2) product for which the record company has a commitment to release in the territory, and (3) any single or album of an artist who is to tour in the territory. Of more than passing interest is subparagraph 9(c), which exempts from the guaranteed-release requirements records "unsuitable" (for political, moral, or religious content) for release in a particular part of the territory. Also note that subparagraph 9(d) gives the licensee the right to register for copyright in each country of the territory, but the language *should* also read that the copyrights are to be registered in the name of the record company.

EXAMPLE 2: Top 100/Minimum of 20%/Soundtrack Albums
Limitation of Rights and Obligations to Exploit

(A) Licensee agrees to manufacture, distribute and sell the phonograph records described in Paragraph 2 of this agreement and it undertakes to use its best efforts consistent with Licensee's best business judgment with respect to market conditions in each country within the Leased Territory to exploit the market for Licensor's recordings in the Leased Territory so as to insure the widest possible sale of such records in the Leased Territory.

• • •

Licensee agrees to manufacture and distribute to the general public in the Leased Territory a minimum of twenty (20%) percent of the records released by Licensor in the United States during the term hereof. Licensee agrees to release in the Leased Territory all records which attain a position of at least number 100 in the "singles" and LP charts of BILLBOARD magazine and also soundtrack albums in each country of the Leased Territory where the picture is released. With regard to such Soundtrack Albums, Licensee undertakes to attempt to issue such albums to coincide with the release dates of the associated films according to such release dates in the various countries of the Leased Territory.

> ☛ Note the requirement for the release of soundtrack albums to coincide with the release of the film in the countries included in the territory. Soundtrack agreements usually contain a provision wherein the record company guarantees releases around the world that predate or coincide with the release of the film.

EXAMPLE 3: Top 100 Singles and Albums/Minimum of 50%/Soundtrack Albums

7. Licensee agrees that during the term of this Agreement:

(a) Licensee will release in the territory all of Company's singles and albums which appear in the top 100 of the national charts in Billboard.

(b) In addition to the singles and albums provided for in subparagraph 7 (a), above, and 7 (e) below, Licensee will release in the Territory not less than Fifty (50%) of all of Company's singles and albums.

• • •

(e) Licensee will release in the Territory motion picture soundtrack albums produced by Company at or before the release of each picture in the Territory.

• • •

(g) As used in this Paragraph 7, the term "release" means to manufacture or import and make reasonable efforts to market enough records to supply all key retail outlets in the Territory with enough records to expose the subject record to the public in the respective areas.

PAYMENT

> *That's the trouble with directors. Always biting*
> *the hand that lays the golden egg.*
>
> —SAMUEL GOLDWYN

As with foreign subpublishing agreements, and indeed any foreign agreement, payment and the method and machinery of payment must be addressed.

Since virtually any foreign subdistribution agreement will require the payments to be made in United States dollars, the time and method of converting the local currency into dollars must be dealt with in the agreement (see Example 2, where the record company has the option to name a different currency for any accounting period), as well as how and when money is to be transferred. The ever-present threat of blocked funds must be addressed. Provisions addressing tax issues, and tariffs and import fees for sending materials, etc., must also be included.

SAMPLE CONTRACT PROVISIONS

EXAMPLE 1: Paid in Dollars

9. With regard to the payment of Company's royalty, as provided for herein:

(a) All amounts payable under this Agreement shall be paid in United States dollars, unless Company specifies otherwise.

(b) Licensee shall make whatever currency conversion is necessary to pay Company hereunder. The costs of currency conversions, banking charges, permit fees, and transmittal costs, shall be the responsibility of Licensee.

(c) Licensee shall timely obtain all governmental permits necessary to make all payments to Company as and when required under this Agreement, including advances.

(d) If Licensee is in any manner prohibited or restricted from making payment of any monies hereunder as a result of any so-called "blocked funds" regulations, Licensee shall promptly so advise Company in writing. Licensee shall deposit any such blocked funds to the credit of Company in a bank or banks or other depository in the Territory designated in writing by Company.

EXAMPLE 2: All Taxes Paid by Distributor

11. With regard to statements hereunder:

(a) Distributor shall furnish to Company, on a quarterly basis within thirty (30) days after the close of the period for which such report is made, a detailed report regarding the earnings attributable to the Recordings in the Territory.

(b) Each report furnished to Company hereunder shall be in the English language. The report shall contain detailed cumulative and current periodic statements of the sales of the Recordings, the permitted deductions therefrom, all other expenses (regardless of whether deductible) incurred in connection with the sales or license of the Recordings.

(c) Distributor shall currently with the delivery of each report pay to Company any sums to which it is entitled.

12. In connection with all payments due Company hereunder, either as advance, royalty payment or reimbursement of costs and expenses, Distributor shall timely obtain all governmental permits necessary to make all payments to Company as and when required under this Agreement.

(a) Distributor shall also pay without limitation any tax, levy or charge, however denominated, imposed or levied by any jurisdiction in the Territory against Distributor, Company, or the Recordings (excluding only taxes based on Company's net income), including, without limitation, quotas, value added taxes, so-called "remittances" and similar taxes, licenses, contingents, turnover taxes, import permits and duties, and national, state, county, city or other taxes, however denominated, relating to or imposed upon the advance or any part thereof, any other amounts payable to Company, or other material, or the right or privilege to use the same in connection with the Recordings.

(b) Any amounts payable under this Agreement shall be paid in United States dollars. Distributor shall make whatever currency conversion is necessary to make such payments, and all costs of currency conversions including, without limitation, banking charges, permit fees, and transmittal costs, shall be borne solely by the Distributor and shall not reduce any amounts due Company in such bank or other depository as may be designated by Company, or promptly pay such funds to such persons or entities as Company may from time to time designate in writing.

(c) Company may, from time to time, designate any amount payable under this Agreement to be paid in the local currency of the Territory, or any other currency.

13. In the event that Distributor shall be prohibited or restricted from making payment of any monies at the time when same are due and payable to Company hereunder by reason of the laws or currency regulations within the Territory, Distributor shall promptly so advise Company in writing. Distributor shall, upon Company's request, deposit any such blocked funds to the credit of Company in a bank or banks or other depository in the Territory designated in writing by Company, or pay them promptly to such persons or entities as Company may designate in writing.

SUPPLYING OF MATERIALS AND PRODUCT

If you get up early, work late, and pay your taxes,
you will get ahead if you strike oil.
—J. PAUL GETTY

How does the foreign distributor learn what records have been released by the record company? How do they obtain copies of the recordings, advertising materials, and artwork which would allow them to fulfill their obligations under the agreement? Foreign distribution agreements contain provisions dealing with the logistics of the delivery of samples to the foreign distributor by the domestic record company. These provisions set forth the terms and conditions for the delivery of samples in sometimes exhaustive detail. See Example 1, which defines materials as "advertising, promotional, and packaging materials, including catalogues, supplements, release sheets, streamers, liners, photographs of artists, appropriate dealer accessories and other packaging materials" and goes on with "expenses for packing, shipping and insurance" and even names the number of samples of records (two) to be supplied to the foreign distributor.

SAMPLE CONTRACT PROVISIONS

EXAMPLE 1: Cost of Materials Borne by Distributor

10. PROMOTIONAL AND PACKAGING MATERIALS. With respect to the advertising, promotional, and packaging materials, including catalogues, supplements, release sheets, streamers, liners, photographs of artists, appropriate dealer accessories and other packaging materials, and the like (hereinafter referred to as the "Materials"), used by Licensor in connection with the records manufactured from Masters delivered to Licensee hereunder:

(a) Licensor shall supply to Licensee, free of charge, samples of its Materials, which shall be delivered to Licensee from time to time as prepared by Licensor for use in the USA. Licensee shall be required to pay all expenses for packing, shipping and insurance, along with custom fees, duties and other expenses relating to shipment of the Materials.

(b) Licensee shall have the right, insofar as Licensor possesses such right, to use any part or all of the Materials on or in connection with records produced hereunder.

(c) Unless otherwise agreed to in writing by Licensor, and subject to Paragraph 11, below, Licensee shall be required to reproduce such Materials, including all artwork contained therein, for use in the Territory in form and content substantially identical to such materials as are used by Licensor in the USA.

(d) Notwithstanding the provisions of Subparagraph 10.(c), above, in the event that the Materials for any such record are unsuitable for use in the Territory because of its political, moral, or religious context, Licensee shall notify Licensor in writing of such fact within fourteen (14) days after Licensee's receipt of a sample thereof. Subject to Licensor's prior written consent, Licensee shall use suitable alternative packaging prepared by Licensor or, at Licensor's election, prepared by Licensee and approved by Licensor in writing.

(e) Licensor shall, upon request, supply to Licensee any such Materials in quantity, or plates for reproducing the Materials, at Licensor's cost price plus any actual expenses for packing, shipping and insurance. Licensee shall pay all customs fees, duties and other expenses relating to importation of the Materials. Licensee is hereby granted the right to reproduce any or all of the Materials for use as set forth above; provided, however, that Licensor itself has obtained the right to grant such right to Licensee without charge or liability to Licensor or any third party.

(f) Licensee agrees to acknowledge, by suitable agreed legend, the ownership of any copyright in any Materials it may use. Licensor shall advise Licensee of any restrictions relating to the Materials prior to or concurrently with its delivery to Licensee.

(g) Licensee shall provide Licensor with two (2) free copies of each record released by Licensee hereunder in the form and packaging as released by Licensee, along with any Materials applicable thereto, promptly upon the completion of manufacture thereof.

(h) Any amounts due Licensor under this Paragraph 10 shall be paid within thirty (30) days of the receipt by Licensee of an invoice therefor.

TRADEMARKS

CLEOPATRA:

The merchandise which thou hast brought from Rome
Are all too dear for me: lie they upon thy hand,
And be undone by 'em.

—WILLIAM SHAKESPEARE
Antony and Cleopatra, Act II, Scene 5

The use, or nonuse, of the domestic record company's trademark or trademarks is usually expressly set forth in the foreign licensing agreement. Sometimes, for whatever reason, the record company does not want its trademark used in a specific foreign territory, or perhaps not outside of the United States at all. There are various reasons for a company to want its product released on a different label outside of the United States rather than on its own domestic label. The company may not, in fact, have the right to use its trademark in the foreign territory. For example, the RCA trademark of the dog listening to his master's voice belongs to EMI, Capitol's parent company, outside of the United States. Or, perhaps, the trademark is inappropriate in the language of the foreign territory or inappropriate for religious or moral reasons. Consider, for instance, how inappropriate the Buddah label (a 1970s label featuring a rotund Buddha on a pink background) may have been in some countries. Nonetheless, in December 1998 BMG announced the resurrection of the label name for catalogue reissues.

In most cases, however, foreign distribution agreements have provisions requiring that the domestic record company's trademark appear on the labels of its records released in the foreign territory. Trademarks have value and it is important for the record company to not only protect that value, but also to retain the rights to any increase in that value created by enhanced local name and product recognition. This requires that provisions be included in the agreement which license to the foreign distributor the right to use the trademark for the duration of the current distribution agreement. When the current distribution agreement is over, the record company may move to a different distributor, but will be able to take its value-enhanced trademark to the new relationship.

Trademark licenses require that the party licensing the use of trademark provide basic guidelines to the use of the trademark, including quality control. These guidelines are very important, not simply because of the intrinsic importance of maintaining quality control, but also because a company's failure to provide guidelines for a third party's use of its trademark may endanger the continuing legal existence of that trademark.

It should go without saying by now that just as the copyrights in songs should not be registered in the name of the foreign subpublisher or the copyrights in records registered in the name of the foreign distributor, it is extremely important for the record company to retain ownership of its trademark and not allow the foreign distributor any ownership interest in that trademark [see subparagraph l(a) in Example 2].

EXAMPLE 1: Trademark License

11. TRADEMARKS. For the term of this Agreement, Licensor grants to Licensee the sole and exclusive right to use Licensor's trademarks and logos (hereinafter referred to as the "Trademarks"), within the Territory for the purposes set forth herein solely on or in relation to records manufactured and/or marketed from Masters as provided for herein.

(a) Licensor shall indemnify and hold Licensee harmless against any adverse claim asserted against Licensee by any third party in the Territory as a result of Licensee's use of the Trademarks or any of them under this Agreement. In connection therewith:

(i) if any such adverse claim is asserted by any third party, Licensee shall have the right, in addition to any other rights which it may have, to manufacture, sell and advertise said records under any other trademark selected by Licensor with Licensee's approval, or, if no such trademark is selected by Licensor, under trademarks selected by Licensee with Licensor's approval, until such claim shall have been defeated or withdrawn or until Licensor shall have granted to Licensee the exclusive right to use under this Agreement another trademark upon the same terms and conditions as set forth in this Paragraph 11.

(ii) Licensor shall reimburse Licensee in respect of all costs and expenses incurred by Licensee in relation to any such adverse claim.

(b) Subject to the provisions of Subparagraph 11.(a), above, all records manufactured by Licensee under this Agreement shall be released only under the Trademarks and Licensee shall comply with Licensor's instructions with respect to the use thereof.

(c) All records manufactured by Licensee hereunder and all album covers, sleeves and other packaging and all Materials relating thereto, shall bear the Trademarks as the Trademarks appear on records, album covers, sleeves and other Materials supplied by Licensor hereunder. In connection therewith, Licensee shall comply with all label copy instructions received from Licensor. All label copy shall bear appropriate copyright notice.

(d) Any rights in and to the Trademarks which are not specifically granted to Licensee hereunder are expressly reserved by Licensor. Licensee agrees and acknowledges that it shall not acquire any rights of whatsoever nature in the Trademarks as a result of Licensee's use thereof and that uses thereof shall inure to the benefit of Licensor.

(e) Licensee shall not, directly or indirectly, during the term of this Agreement or thereafter, attack the ownership by Licensor of the Trademarks or the validity of the license herein granted to it. Licensee shall at no time use or authorize the use of any trademark, logo, trade name or other designation identical with or confusingly similar to any of the Trademarks used by Licensor and of which Licensee is aware.

(f) If Licensee is or becomes aware of any adverse use of a trademark or other designation similar to any of the Trademarks, Licensee shall notify Licensor thereof. Licensee shall not at any time apply for any registration of any copyright, trademark, or logo or other designation which includes any of the Trademarks used by Licensor, and Licensee acknowledges the knowledge of all such Trademarks, in whole or in part, and shall not file any document with any governmental authority or take over any other action which would affect the ownership of any of the Trademarks.

(g) At the expiration of the period during which Licensee has the right to sell records hereunder, Licensee shall execute and deliver to Licensor a document, in form and substance satisfactory to Licensor, assigning to Licensor all of Licensee's right, title and interest, if any, in and to the Trademarks. In the event Licensee fails to execute said documents, Licensor shall have the right to execute said documents as Licensee's attorney-in-fact and Licensee does hereby irrevocably constitute and appoint Licensor its true and lawful attorney-in-fact only for the purpose of executing such document.

EXAMPLE 2: Quality Control Essential for Trademark Protection

1. The records shall be advertised, distributed and sold, or otherwise used by Licensee only under the trademarks "X" and/or any other trademark Licensor may specify. Licensee agrees:

(a) Licensee acquires no right, title or interest in the trademark or in any trademark registration except the right to use said trademark in the country or countries of the Leased Territory.

(b) To limit its use of the trademark to goods substantially identical to and of quality and workmanship not inferior to goods manufactured by Licensor and in accordance with the specifications prescribed or approved from time to time by Licensor.

(c) To permit Licensor or its agents at any time to inspect the manufacture of said goods by Licensee to determine whether or not Licensee is maintaining the standards set by Licensor for the goods to which Licensee may affix said trademark.

(d) To send Licensor samples of the goods to which the trademark is affixed by Licensee whenever requested by Licensor.

(e) On the termination or expiration of this agreement or the term of this agreement (as the same may have been renewed or extended), immediately to discontinue the use of said trademark, or any colorable imitation thereof, by itself or in combination with any other words, letters, symbols or design.

(f) That the said trademark is not to be used by Licensee in combination with any other word, letter, symbol or designs.

(g) To execute any additional documents that may be necessary for the purpose of recording trademark licenses or any other document in any country or countries included in the Leased Territory; or any other document that may be necessary to protect Licensor's trademark during the term hereof; similarly, Licensor agrees to execute whatever additional documents may be necessary to permit Licensee to use the trademark during the term hereof.

(h) Licensee shall not have the right to include said trademark in its corporate or business name unless authorized to do so in writing by Licensor.

(i) Upon the termination of this agreement by either party for any reason whatsoever, Licensee hereby empowers Licensor or whomever it may appoint to take all necessary steps in the trademark office (or similar office) of the country or countries to which this license applies to cancel any trademark registration hereunder or portion thereof from the records of such office.

COVER RECORDS

When I die, I want people to play my music, go wild and freak out and do anything they want to do.
—JIMI HENDRIX

One step a domestic record company can take toward maximizing the chances of success when its records are released in a foreign territory is to specify that the company's own recordings do not have to compete against native versions of the same musical compositions, that is, cover records.

It is not unusual for a record to be a hit because of the material more than the artist—we all can dredge up the memory of some song which would have been a hit done by almost any artist with even a modicum of talent. It does not take a great stretch of the imagination to conjure up a situation where a foreign distributor hears such a no-fail recording made by the company it has entered into a foreign distribution agreement with and decides to record, release, and promote its own version instead of paying for the licensor's record. Imposing a restriction on the release of a cover record, at least by the record company's own licensee, may give the record company just the edge it needs to make sure *its* version will be the hit in that territory.

SAMPLE CONTRACT PROVISIONS

EXAMPLE 1: 2-Month Hold-Back on Cover Records

21. COVER RECORDS. Licensee, insofar as it is not otherwise contractually obligated, shall refrain from releasing in any country of the Territory any so-called "cover" record of any newly composed musical composition embodied on a master recording of a single record supplied hereunder by Licensor until a period of at least two (2) months has elapsed from the first day of release in that particular country of the Territory of records produced from Licensor's Masters.

EXAMPLE 2: 10-Week Hold-Back on Cover Records

17. Distributor shall not release any cover record in the Territory of any composition not previously recorded and released in the Territory included in a Recording until a period of at least ten (10) weeks after the initial release of records made from such Recording in the Territory.

RIGHTS ON TERMINATION

> *I'm always making a comeback but nobody ever
> tells me where I've been.*
>
> —BILLIE HOLIDAY

What happens to all these masters and records when the foreign distribution agreement terminates? Distribution agreements, foreign or domestic, are not like recording contracts, where upon termination the artist departs, leaving the masters behind, and continues to receive a royalty for records sold. At the end of foreign distribution agreements, the record company goes home, leaving behind a foreign distributor which may or may not be sadder and wiser for the experience.

In practice, of course there are numerous business details and paperwork to be taken care of, including the sometimes knotty problem of unsold product. In connection with inventory, there is usually some provision made for a sell-off, which gives the foreign distributor the right to sell remaining inventory for a period of time that is specified in the agreement and is subject to negotiation. At the end of the sell-off period, one of two things usually happens. There may be a transfer of the physical inventory left over, either at some determined price or at no charge, from the foreign company to the domestic company or the domestic company's designee. Alternatively, it may be specified that inventory remaining after sell-off must be destroyed. In the latter case, witnesses supplied by the domestic company may or may not be required to oversee the destruction of the inventory. Usually termination provisions specify a requirement that the foreign distributor provide some legal proof of destruction, for example, a certificate, signed under oath, stating that the goods have, in fact, been destroyed.

SAMPLE CONTRACT PROVISIONS

EXAMPLE 1: The Parties' Rights on Termination

15. OWNERSHIP OF LICENSED PROPERTY. All tapes, acetates, stampers, mothers or duplicates thereof, of Masters hereunder and all copyrights, ownerships and rights in and to such Masters, shall remain the sole and exclusive property of Licensor, subject, however, to the rights of Licensee under this Agreement.

16. RIGHTS OF TERMINATION OF LICENSOR. In the event of Licensee's Failure, as provided for in Subparagraphs 16.(a) and 16.(b), below, Licensor may, in addition to all of its other rights and remedies at law or otherwise, at its option, terminate this Agreement upon giving not less than ten (10) days' written notice to Licensee without prejudice to any rights or claims which Licensor may have.

(a) Licensee shall fail to account and make payments hereunder or shall fail to perform any other of its material obligations required of it hereunder, and Licensor shall have notified Licensee in writing of such failure and Licensee shall not have cured such failure within thirty (30) days after such written notification; or

(b) Licensee shall fail, in the sole judgment of Licensor reasonably exercised, to cause the standard of quality of the records manufactured hereunder in any country of the Territory to equal the standard of quality of records produced by or for Licensee of its own repertoires in such country of the Territory and shall fail to improve such quality to equal said standard within sixty (60) days after written notification from Licensor. If Licensor terminates this Agreement as aforesaid for the reasons set forth in this Subparagraph 16.(b), such termination shall only be in respect to such particular country of the Territory as to which Licensee breached the provisions of this Subparagraph 16.(b).

17. RIGHTS OF TERMINATION OF LICENSEE. In the event that Licensor shall fail to perform any of Licensor's material obligations hereunder, and Licensee shall have notified Licensor in writing of such failure within thirty (30) days after such written notification, then Licensee may, in addition to all of Licensee's other rights and remedies at law or otherwise, at Licensee's option, terminate this Agreement upon giving Licensor not less than ten (10) days' written notice. Such termination shall be without prejudice to any rights or claims which Licensee may have.

• • •

20. EFFECT OF EXPIRATION OR TERMINATION. Upon the expiration or termination of this Agreement:

(a) All pressing by Licensee shall cease, and Licensee shall not manufacture any further records from the Masters licensed hereunder.

(b) All Masters and all derivatives thereof and any other material in Licensee's possession or control used in the manufacture or records hereunder (including, but not limited to, tapes, mothers and stampers) shall promptly, at the option of Licensor and upon its written instructions, either:

(i) In the case only of material originally supplied by Licensor, that it be transferred by Licensee to Licensor or Licensor's designee, at Licensee's actual cost, plus shipment charges; or

(ii) Be destroyed by Licensee under the supervision of Licensor or Licensor's designee, or, at Licensor's written request, destroyed by Licensee without such supervision, provided Licensee provides Licensor with an affidavit of such fact, sworn to by a principal officer of Licensee.

(c) Licensee shall submit to Licensor not later than twenty eight (28) days after the expiration of this Agreement, a written inventory of all of then remaining copies of the records manufactured or imported hereunder.

(i) Licensor or its designee shall have the option, upon giving Licensee written notice of its election to do so not later than two (2) months after its receipt of such written inventory, to purchase such remaining copies which are unsold at the time Licensor makes such election, for an amount equal to Licensee's direct cost of manufacturing such records and the related packaging material and the amount of any sales taxes Licensee must pay in connection with such purchase.

(ii) If Licensor or its designee elects to purchase such remaining copies, Licensee shall promptly ship them, at Licensor's cost, to Licensor or its designee, or shall make them available at Licensee's place of business for Licensor or its designee to take possession thereof.

(d) Upon the expiration of this agreement, by reason of passage of time and not by reason of any termination by Licensor, and provided further that Licensee submits the aforesaid written inventory to Licensor within ten (10) days after such expiration, Licensee shall continue to have the right to sell then remaining copies of said records, on a non-exclusive basis only, until such time as Licensor or its designee notifies Licensee, in accordance with the foregoing provisions, that Licensor or its designee elects to purchase such remaining copies of said records.

(i) In the event Licensor or its designee does not so notify Licensee, Licensee's right to sell said remaining copies of said records shall terminate six (6) months after the expiration of this agreement.

(ii) If Licensor or its designee shall so notify Licensee, Licensee shall, promptly upon its receipt of such notification, cease any further selling of such remaining copies of said records and shall forthwith proceed in accordance with the provisions of Subparagraph 20.(c), above.

(iii) Licensee agrees that it shall not manufacture excessive quantities of records hereunder in anticipation of selling such records during said six (6) month period.

(e) All sales of records by Licensee subsequent to the expiration of this agreement shall, except as otherwise provided herein, be in accordance with the terms and provisions hereof. Without limiting the generality of the foregoing, such sales shall be in Licensee's normal course of business and at prices not less than the normal wholesale and retail prices of such records during the term hereof. Such sales shall be subject to the payment of royalties by Licensee under the terms of this agreement. Upon the expiration of the six (6) month period referred to in Subparagraph 20.(d)(i), above, Licensee shall destroy all then remaining records under the supervision of Licensor or Licensor's designee or, at Licensor's written request, Licensee shall destroy said records without such supervision provided that Licensee provides Licensor with an affidavit of such fact, sworn to by a principal officer of Licensee.

(f) Licensor undertakes that Licensee and Licensee's associates shall be under no liability whatsoever to any of the artists or to any third party in respect of or arising out of the sale by Licensor of the records purchased by Licensor under the provisions of this clause and Licensor hereby indemnifies Licensee and Licensee's associates against any costs, charges, claims, and expenses in respect of such sale.

☛ Of particular interest here is subparagraph 20(d)(iii), where the distributor agrees not to "manufacture excessive quantities of records" in anticipation of building up inventory for the sell-off period.

EXAMPLE 2: Product to Be Destroyed After 180 Days

15. Upon the termination or expiration of this Agreement, for any reason, Licensee agrees:

(a) To deliver to Company or its designated representatives, at Licensee's expense, all tangible property set forth in Paragraph 6 hereof [master tapes, matrices, mothers, stampers, artwork, etc.] and to execute and deliver to Company such documents as Company may require as evidence of the termination of Licensee's rights or interest to the possession, use or ownership of the tangible or intangible property set forth in Paragraph 6, above; or

(b) At Company's option, to destroy all such property and to deliver to Company such proof of destruction as Company may reasonably acquire.

16. Licensee further agrees, subject to Paragraph 17, below, upon termination or expiration, to destroy all records, pressings, advertising material and other material of every description not limited to the foregoing produced under or in connection with this Agreement. Licensee agrees to certify such destruction in such form as Company may reasonably require.

17. In connection with the termination or expiration of this Agreement for any cause, it is agreed that, upon termination or expiration:

(a) Licensee shall not have the right to thereafter add to its inventory acquired pursuant to this Agreement.

(b) Licensee shall immediately deliver to Company a certified inventory of records produced from the Masters and in possession at the date of termination or expiration.

(c) Licensee shall have the right to continue to sell such records in the regular course of business for a period of One Hundred and Eighty (180) Days after termination or expiration. Licensee shall pay to Company the same rate of royalty as is specified in Paragraphs 4 and 5, above, for all records sold by Licensee during said One Hundred and Eighty (180) Day period.

(d) At the end of the One Hundred and Eighty (180) Day period, Licensee shall deliver to Company a certified inventory of all such records not sold and all such records will be destroyed in the presence of a representative to be designated by Company.

CHAPTER 19

DIGITAL TRANSMISSION

ANTONY:
. . . the elements once out of it,
it transmigrates.

—WILLIAM SHAKESPEARE
Antony and Cleopatra, Act II, Scene 8

The ground rules for digital transmission are all set out in the 50-plus pages of the Digital Millennium Copyright Act, which was signed into law in October 1998. Chapter 21 discusses that act in detail. This chapter deals with the license agreements between the owners of recordings, usually record companies, and companies providing downloadable music to the general public. The aspects of these agreements that are similar or identical to other types of licensing agreements, such as foreign distribution agreements, are not reexamined here.

In the shakeout after the death and subsequent resurrection of Napster, the online music marketplace for downloading licensed music for pay has generally fallen into two distinct camps: subscription services, where the customer pays a monthly subscription fee, and so-called à la carte sites, where the user pays a set price for each download. Since life would be too easy if everything were black or white, some services combine subscription offers with à la carte services.

One major difference between the ways records have traditionally been sold and any of the download options is the buyers' ability to cherry-pick the product. No more do buyers have to accept a dozen lame cuts in order to possess the one or two they are really interested in. For no discernable reason, there seems to be a general consensus on à la carte pricing—99 cents per cut and around $10 for albums in the United States. Pricing in the United Kingdom is 79p per cut and £7.99 per album, which is roughly equivalent to U.S. prices when the exchange rate is factored in.

In an era where changes in the music industry are whipping past us with blinding speed and the ground is shifting so frequently that business on *terra firma* is more terror than firma, it is probably impossible to predict without crossed fingers what direction the digital revolution will take next. One thing is certain. There will be a rapid expansion of different services elbowing one another to dominate the online music marketplace followed in due course by the collapse and failure of many of them.

RIGHTS LICENSED

Every act of creation is first an act of destruction.
—PABLO PICASSO

Just what are rights licensed in these agreements? The basic right being licensed is, of course, the right to transmit recordings digitally, to make them available for download to buyers. The rights licensed are limited to digital transmission, with "hold back" provisions reserving other rights, such as traditional brick-and-mortar sales, to the licensor. Also, none of these agreements can give the licensee the right to use the musical compositions. That right can only be granted by the copyright owners of the compositions.

SAMPLE CONTRACT PROVISIONS

EXAMPLE 1: Rights Licensed

2.2 Licensed Rights. Label hereby grants to Company the non-exclusive right and license, but not obligation during the Term throughout the Territory, to make, cause or otherwise affect the "Digital Audio Transmission" and "Digital Phonorecord Delivery" of the Licensed Recordings. The Term "Digital Audio Transmission" shall mean a transmission that embodies a sound recording by any means now known or hereafter devised. The Term "Digital Phonorecord Delivery" shall mean each individual delivery of a phonorecord by digital transmission of a sound recording which results in a specifically identifiable reproduction by or for any transmission recipient of a phonorecord of that sound recording by any means now known or hereafter devised.

☞ Note that the rights granted are "nonexclusive." This appears to be the norm in these agreements.

EXAMPLE 2: Short Form

1. Rights Granted. You hereby grant us the non-exclusive license to those recordings set out in the schedule solely for distribution to our subscribers to enable them to share the files they have containing the recordings ("the Recordings"). You agree to deliver the Recordings to us upon our request in an agreed digital format preferably MP3 or WMA.

☞ This agreement is also nonexclusive. Note that this agreement permits file sharing. (For a discussion of file sharing, see Chapter 21, "Digital Millennium Copyright Act," page 541.)

EXAMPLE 3: Limitation of Rights Licensed

6. All rights and licenses not expressly granted to Licensee hereunder are reserved by Licensor. As between Licensee and Licensor, ownership of the Recordings shall remain with Licensor. Licensee shall have no right hereunder to modify or alter the Recordings, except that Licensee may employ audio-compression technology to encode the Recordings into digital audio files for purposes set forth herein. The rights granted by Licensor to Licensee hereunder do not include the right to perform, reproduce, or distribute those musical compositions embodied in the Recordings. Licensee agrees and acknowledges that nothing contained herein shall be construed as to permit Licensee's manufacture and/or distribution of Recordings in the form of phonorecords, such as pre-recorded compact discs, cassette tapes, or any other device now known or hereafter developed which would result in a physical copy of a Recording being made.

☞ The licensee's rights are limited to the right of digital transmission. The next-to-last sentence puts the licensee on notice that it must obtain licenses separately for the musical compositions. The last sentence prohibits the actual manufacture and/or distribution of recordings.

EXAMPLE 4: More Technical Terms Than I Need

2. Subject to and in accordance with the terms and conditions contained in this Agreement, and solely to the extent of the rights of Licensor or any of its Label Affiliates, Licensor grants to [Licensee], during the Term and in the Territory, a non-exclusive license to (i) copy, encode, store on servers or other electronic devices, and deliver an electronic digital file of each Master Recording of the Licensed Content ("Song File"), as both full-length copies and as Samples, to Customers by means of (a) transmission of the Song File from a [Licensee] Server through the Internet or (b) inclusion of the Song File on a Playback Device distributed to Customers and/or its Affiliates; (ii) reproduce, encode, store, and transmit the Meta Data from a [Licensee] Server through the Internet for the purpose of displaying such Meta Data on the Service and Customer's Playback Devices; (iii) permit Customers to Download and Stream the Licensed Content and Meta Data for use on their Playback Devices as part of the Service, including but not limited to in the form of Permanent Downloads; and (iv) otherwise reproduce, advertise, market, promote, distribute, sell, broadcast, and publicly perform and display the Licensed Content and Meta Data as part of the Service.

> ☛ One thing about Internet companies: They do love their technical terms, existing or created for the moment. Included in three fun-packed pages of definitions in the above agreement was the definition of "Meta Data," which translates into the photographs, cover art, text and liner notes, etc., that come with the actual CD.

TERRITORY

Fame is only good for one thing—they will cash your check in a small town.

—Truman Capote

Because of the nature of the digital beast, in these agreements the territory, if not legally or contractually, is, in reality, the entire world. Try as one might, it is virtually impossible with existing technology (and probably any new technology) to block someone in any given territory who has the requisite technical know-how (which is pretty minimal) from accessing a music-download site.

EXAMPLE 1: The World

2. The Term shall be for a period of twelve (12) months commencing on the date of this agreement. The Territory shall be the world.

EXAMPLE 2: The World, But. . . .

1.2 "Territory" for the purpose of this Agreement shall mean the World, subject to Section 2.4 below.

• • •

2.4 Restricted Regions and Reversions. Label promptly shall notify Company in writing if, and to the extent Label does not now have or shall at anytime during the Term no longer have the right to distribute a particular Licensed Recording within any or all countries of the Territory. Promptly following receipt of Label's aforementioned notice, Company shall discontinue distributing said Licensed Recording, or if applicable, use reasonable efforts to restrict end user access to said Licensed Recording in such country or countries.

☞ If the label loses the right to a recording within a country, the Company "shall discontinue" the distribution in that country or "use reasonable [but not necessarily successful] efforts" to restrict access.

EXAMPLE 3: Restricted Territory

(v) "Territory" means the United States, its territories and possessions, and Canada.

☞ Good luck.

COMPOSITIONS

What usually comes first is the contract.
— IRA GERSHWIN

Obtaining licenses and making payment for the use of musical compositions, both mechanical licenses and performance licenses, are (or should be) the responsibility of the licensee. Unfortunately, many licensees make this the responsibility of the party licensing the recordings. On behalf of licensor clients, I highly disapprove of this practice because of the distinct possibility that my client will be stuck with license fees while not receiving sufficient—or indeed any— payment from the licensee (see Examples 5 and 6). The licensee may attempt to incorporate existing mechanical licenses originally obtained by the owner of the recordings (see Example 1), but that raises issues of potential liability for payment for the licensor, especially considering that fact that the mortality rate among dot-com companies is high.

SAMPLE CONTRACT PROVISIONS

EXAMPLE 1: Licensee's Responsibility for Mechanicals and Performance Royalties

(d) except as may otherwise be provided herein, Company shall effect payment for any and all mechanical and public performance royalties with respect to any musical compositions embodied in the Recordings which become due with respect to the exercise of the rights and licenses herein by Company. Notwithstanding the forgoing, to the extent permissible under Label's mechanical licenses from publishers of musical compositions embodied in the Recordings, Company may rely upon said mechanical licenses for the Digital Phonorecord Delivery of Recordings hereunder until such time as Company has secured same in it's own right.

☞ This is the way it should be. The licensee pays all fees for sales and performances of recordings containing the compositions.

EXAMPLE 2: Licensor's Responsibility for Obtaining Licenses for Compositions

3. *Licensor's Obligations.* Throughout the Term, Licensor ... shall obtain all necessary performance right copyright licenses and mechanical licenses for Downloads from the applicable copyright proprietors of the musical compositions embodied in the Master Recordings.

EXAMPLE 3: Publishing Information

9. In connection with the delivery of Masters to [Company], [Licensor] shall furnish [Company] with the following information with respect to all compositions contained in each Master: (i) the name of songwriter(s); (ii) the name and ownership interest of each publisher, including the ad-

dress of each publisher and name of publisher's mechanical licensing agent; and (iii) identify any PD Composition, any Controlled Composition and/or a musical composition owned by one or more third party music publishers.

(a) As used herein, "PD Composition" for the purpose of this Agreement shall mean any musical composition in the public domain, subject to Label's pre-existing assignable license, or otherwise whereby Company may legally distribute recordings including such musical composition without obtaining a license from, or paying a royalty to the music publisher or copyright holder thereof.

(b) As used herein, "Controlled Composition" shall mean any composition owned or controlled, in whole or in part, directly or indirectly, by [Licensor] or [Licensor]'s music publishing designee and contained in a Master.

EXAMPLE 4: Controlled Composition

10. [Licensor], on behalf of its music publishing designee does hereby license to Company and its licensees the right to make Digital Phonorecord Deliveries of Controlled Compositions hereunder at a mechanical royalty per Controlled Composition equal to fifteen percent (15%) of "Adjusted Gross Revenue" (defined below) for each relevant accounting period of the Term, multiplied by a fraction, the numerator being the number of applicable Digital Phonorecord Deliveries of Controlled Compositions and the denominator being the number of applicable Digital Phonorecord Deliveries of all musical compositions (including Controlled Compositions) embodied on sound recordings licensed to Company. The term "Adjusted Gross Revenue" shall mean all sums received by Company derived from the Digital Audio Transmission and/or Digital Phonorecord Delivery of sound recordings, including Subscription Program Revenue for each relevant accounting period of the Term, less Allowed Expenses actually incurred by Company. Notwithstanding the forgoing, Company shall not deduct mechanical royalties when calculating Adjusted Gross Revenue for the purpose of determining the mechanical royalty for Controlled Compositions.

> ☛ This introduces you to the bane of these agreements for licensors: royalty payments based upon some proportionate share of revenue, a whole different method from traditional mechanical licenses for phonorecords. Just wait until you see the next section.

EXAMPLE 5: Licensor Responsible for Payments

(c) Licensor agrees that it shall obtain all necessary mechanical copyright licenses from the applicable copyright proprietors of the musical compositions embodied in the Licensed Content for the sale of Licensed Content in the form of Permanent Downloads. Licensor further agrees that it shall be solely responsible for all payments, if any, in connection with the proceeds of this Agreement or otherwise to copyright proprietors for such mechanical licenses, to Artists, producers, musicians, engineers and others whose performances and/or proceeds thereof are embodied on or incorporated in the Licensed Content and Meta Data, and for payments, if any, to the Musical Performance Trust Fund and the Administrator of the Special Payment Fund of the American Federation of Musicians, and to any similar fund established by a collective bargaining agreement with the entire recording industry, and agrees to hold Licensee harmless therefrom.

> ☛ This is another provision that scares the b'geebers out of me. I've got no problem with the licensor being responsible for paying the artists, producers, and the other parties

traditionally paid by a production company under a production agreement because this agreement is structured financially like a production agreement. But when it comes to mechanical licenses, MPTF, and the AFM Special Payments Fund, the royalty isn't there to cover these extra costs. Compare this to Example 6, below, where the royalty is higher to cover those costs.

EXAMPLE 6: Similar to a Traditional Distribution Agreement

2. (a) You shall obtain and pay for any necessary clearances and licenses for all uses of the Content authorized herein, including, without limitation: (i) any royalties and other monies due to artists, authors, copyright owners, producers and other third-party royalty participants from sales or other uses (including embodied sample usages) of the Content; (ii) all mechanical royalties payable to publishers and/or authors of copyrighted musical compositions embodied in Masters; (iii) all payments that may be required under collective bargaining agreements applicable to you or third parties other than Company; and (iv) any other royalties, fees and/ or sums payable with respect to the Content, metadata and other materials provided by you.

☞ This provision throws a wider net than Example 5 does. Nonetheless, the agreement itself lessens most of my qualms since the relationship between the parties in this agreement is structured very much like a traditional distribution agreement and results in a higher net return to the label—the licensee is taking the equivalent of a "distribution fee" of 9%.

ROYALTY

Royalty provisions in these agreements seem to fall into two categories: those specifying a percentage of some definition of profits (see Example 1, below) and those specifying a payment in dollars and (mostly) cents based upon downloads (see Example 2, below). There are, of course, services which combine subscription for sales and/or streaming and individual sales of downloads, and agreements with these services may have combinations of the two methods.

The royalty provisions that always drive me crazy are in the agreements where the royalty is based upon a percentage of profits. There's no way to get an idea up front what the earnings may be, except for a projection based upon absolutely no downloads or streaming whatsoever—which, of course, equals zip for earnings. Arguably, at the other end of the scale—you control 100% of all the downloads and streaming—there should be a basis for a valid projection of earnings, but, alas alack, it just ain't so. There are so many variables for costs to be deducted that even with two accounting periods having the same number of downloads, the actual dollar figures for those periods may be very different.

Boiled down to the simplest concepts, the royalty for subscription-based services is based upon a money pool collected from subscribers. The pool is then divided between recordings based upon the playing time of each recording relative to the total playing time of all recordings. After deducting a list of deductible costs and then multiplying the resulting amount by the percentage indicated in the agreement, the royalty is determined. For a nonsubscription download, it's the same formula without having to divvy up out of a common pool (or maybe you do have to divvy up; see Example 1). Simple? Yeah, yeah, sure. I haven't had as much fun sweating through a provision since I carefully (and needlessly, since there never were any profits) worked my way through a 700-plus-page definition of "net profits" for a film director. Example 1, below, pretty much gives you an idea of how convoluted most of the royalty sections of these agreements are. Example 2 provides for a set amount for each use.

SAMPLE CONTRACT PROVISIONS

EXAMPLE 1: Royalties: The Miniseries—A Percentage

5. ROYALTIES

5.1 Royalty Rate. Company shall pay Label a royalty equal to sixty percent (60%) of any and all "Net Revenue" including, without limitation, Label's proportionate share of "Subscription Program Revenue" (defined below). Notwithstanding the forgoing, Company shall adjust royalties payable hereunder based upon the length of playing time for each Licensed Recording in order to accommodate the higher statutory mechanical licensing rates applicable to Recordings with longer playing times. In so doing, Company shall nominally increase the royalty rate payable for downloads of Recordings with longer playing times and nominally reduce the royalty rate payable for downloads of Recordings with shorter playing times.

☛ The royalty rate is 60% of the "net," language which always means the devil is in the details. I also have a problem with the adjustment to "accommodate" longer playing times: "longer" (and "shorter") than what? The average? The median? Is it a set number? Or does it vary from accounting period to accounting period?

5.2 "Subscription Program Revenue" for the purpose of this Agreement shall mean amounts paid to Company for the right to receive Digital Phonorecord Deliveries of Recordings in general (as opposed to amounts paid with respect to a particular Licensed Recording) during a given accounting period. Label's share of Subscription Program Revenue shall be the total Subscription Program Revenue during each relevant accounting period of the Term, multiplied by a fraction, the numerator being the number of Digital Phonorecord Deliveries of Recordings during the applicable accounting period and the denominator being the number of Digital Phonorecord Deliveries of all sound recordings (including Recordings) during the applicable accounting period.

☛ Since the last line reads ". . . of all sound recordings," not ". . . of all sound recordings downloaded through subscription programs," I can't tell for sure whether or not the nonsubscription direct download is in the pool or not. A strict literal reading would indicate it is. Does this reduce the royalty payable for either subscription or nonsubscription, or perhaps both? Maybe. Language clarifying the intent would be in order for Label.

5.3 "Gross Revenue" for the purpose of this Agreement shall mean all sums received by Company derived from the Digital Audio Transmission and/or Digital Phonorecord Delivery of Recordings, including Label's share of Subscription Program Revenue; the term "Net Revenue" shall mean Gross Revenue less only "Allowed Expenses" (defined below) to the extent incurred by Company in connection with the receipt of Gross Revenue or the distribution of Recordings hereunder.

☛ Since the language provides that all Gross Revenue, notwithstanding the source, goes into the money pool and then all "Allowed Expenses" are deducted before determining "Label's share of Net Revenue," it sure sounds to me like Label is sharing expenses which may not ever be incurred by Label. For example: sales tax [5.4(b): what if Label's downloads never incurred any sales tax?]; customer credits [5.4(c): what if none of Label's downloads result in "customer credits"?]; mechanical royalties [(5.4(d), below: what if Label's recordings are all public domain compositions with no mechanical licenses?]; etc. You get the idea.

5.4 "Allowed Expenses" for the purpose of this Agreement shall mean:

(a) credit card transaction and other electronic commerce processing fees, including patent royalties payable to or retained by unaffiliated third parties in connection with effecting a transaction or transmission, if any;

(b) sales tax, if any;

(c) customer credits, including, but not limited to those on account of errors in billing and errors in transmission, if any;

(d) mechanical royalties, if any;

(e) public performance fees, if any;

(f) union, guild or other third party fees that may be required by contract or the Copyright Act, if any; and

(g) Internet referral fees payable to third parties who, through their web site, email or other means, refer to Company a source of Gross Revenue, if any, provided that such costs shall not exceed fifteen percent (15%) of Gross Revenue.

5.5 Royalty Exemptions. No fees or royalty shall be payable hereunder to Label for:

(a) a Digital Phonorecord Delivery made available on a "free" or "no charge" basis for the purpose of promoting Recordings;

(b) so-called "streaming" transmissions of Recordings made available on a "free" or "no charge" basis for the purpose of promoting Recordings;

(c) incomplete, aborted or non-functional Digital Phonorecord Deliveries; and

(d) more than one Digital Phonorecord Delivery of a particular Licensed Recording to a given end user.

EXAMPLE 2: Royalties: The Sequel Miniseries—Dollars and Cents

5. *Royalties.* Subject to the adjustment described below, and in full consideration of all rights granted and obligations undertaken by Licensor, Licensor shall be paid a royalty (the "Royalty") in the following amounts and manner:

(a) The amount of One Cent ($0.01) for each time that a Conditional Download is Played by a Customer for at least thirty-one (31) seconds during a calendar month (the "Accounting Period"). As used herein, the term "Played" shall mean a humanly detectable performance authorized by [Licensor] of a Master Recording that is rendered by a Playback Device in response to an action taken by a Customer to cause such performance to occur On-Demand.

☞ Under this agreement, a "Conditional Download" is a download that is limited to a short specified time, in other words, not a permanent download, which is addressed in subparagraph (b). I'm particularly interested in performances being "humanly detectable." By which human? Old Jake, the deaf night watchman? With or without the aid of machines? If one of my dogs (who can hear the smallest fragment of food hit the floor from across the county) is used ("doggy detectable"), would more royalties be paid?

(b) With respect to Permanent Downloads, (i) the "sale" of each Permanent Download (and its corresponding Master Recording(s)) shall occur when a license permitting the use of such Permanent Download is successfully downloaded by a Customer, which such Download was fulfilled by [Licensee]; (ii) with respect to the sale of a Permanent Download, payments shall accrue at the time that such Permanent Download is sold; and (iii) for each Permanent Download sold to a Customer during the Accounting Period, [Licensee] shall pay to Licensor the amounts set forth on Exhibit C.

(c) With respect to Streams, the amount of One Cent ($0.01) for each time that a Master Recording (other than Samples) was Streamed On-Demand for at least thirty-one (31) seconds in duration by Customers during the Accounting Period.

• • •

EXHIBIT C

Schedule of Royalties

Fifty Eight Cents ($0.58) for single Master Recordings classified by Licensor as frontline.

Forty Eight Cents ($0.48) for single Master Recordings classified by Licensor as mid-line.

Thirty Eight Cents ($0.38) for single Master Recordings classified by Licensor as budget.

$7.00 for multi-Master Recording configurations classified by Licensor as frontline, but in no event more than the aggregate price of the single Master Recordings contained in such configuration if sold separately.

$5.80 for multi-Master Recording configurations classified by Licensor as mid-line, but in no event more than the aggregate price of the single Master Recordings contained in such configuration if sold separately.

$4.65 for multi-Master Recording configurations classified by Licensor as budget, but in no event more than the aggregate price of the single Master Recordings contained in such configuration if sold separately.

For multiple CD sets, the royalty shall be $5.80 times the number of CDs contained in the set.

CHAPTER 20

COPYRIGHT

Writing about music is like dancing about architecture;
it's a really stupid thing to want to do.

—ELVIS COSTELLO

What is a copyright? The word can be used in various ways, for example, as a verb, "to copyright a work," and as a noun, "he bought the copyright." In either case, the compound noun *copyright* means exactly what its two parts together suggest: the *right to copy*.

In fact, a copyright is actually a bundle of rights, each of which can be copyrighted separately and sold, assigned, leased, and/or licensed separately. A copyright is like a telephone cable. The cable is made up of many individual strands of wire, each of which can carry a different message. A copyright is made up of many individual rights, and each right within that copyright is like an individual strand of the cable. In the same way that it is possible that only one of the many individual wires in a telephone is being used at a specific point in time, it is possible that only one right within a copyright is being used at a given time. It is also possible that each one of the individual strands in a telephone cable, or the individual rights in a copyright, may all be in use at once.

Copyright has been with us for many years. The first statutory recognition of copyright as a concept in our system was an English act (not to be confused with the Beatles or the Stones) known as the Statute of Anne of 1710 (more correctly referred to as "An Act for the Encouragement of Learning"—which is actually a pretty good description of the underlying concept of copyright). The "Anne" in this case was Queen Anne of England, the last of the Stuart monarchs.

The first paragraph of the Statute of Anne, after the introductory paragraph, declares:

> I. Whereas printers, booksellers, and other persons have of late frequently taken the liberty of printing, reprinting, and publishing, or causing to be printed, reprinted, and published, books and other writings, without the consent of the authors or proprietors of such books and writings, to their very great detriment, and too often to the ruin of them and their families: for preventing therefore such practices for the future, and for the encouragement of learned men to compose and write useful books; may it please your Majesty, that it may be enacted, and be it enacted by the Queen's most excellent majesty, by and with the advice and consent of the lords spiritual and temporal, and commons, in this present parliament assembled, and by the authority of the same; . . .

The complaints sound pretty current to me. Substitute "the public" for "printers, booksellers, and other persons" and "unauthorized downloading" for "printing, reprinting, and publishing" and you could be reading a complaint from the RIAA.

There have been a succession of copyright laws in England which have followed the Statute of Anne, but none has ever really replaced that act with a more homey-sounding title. The first actual use of the term copyright was probably in the early 1740s, in England.

In the late eighteenth century there was an altercation between England and her American colonies (you may have heard of it). When the dust finally settled, the United States of America found itself somewhat operational. The founding fathers, who must have loved "taking meetings," got together and worked up the legal document known as the United States Constitution to formalize the country's working status. These gentlemen included the following language in the Constitution in Article I, Section 8, Clause 8:

> The Congress shall have the power to promote the progress of science and useful arts, by securing for limited times to authors and inventors the exclusive right to their respective writings and discoveries.

Using the authority granted to them by the Constitution, the grand old men (and later women) of Congress have blessed us with several copyright acts over the years. The first copyright statute in the United States was enacted by the First Congress in its Copyright Act of May 31, 1790. Until Congress specified by statute that a particular form of expression was a "writing" and, as such, was protected, it was not protected by copyright law. In fact, music was not granted copyright protection in the United States until 1831, when Congress not only first included music as a "writing," but also specified that music was a "useful art," thereby fulfilling the requirements of Article I, Section 8, Clause 8.

At this time, there are only two copyright acts of any significance to us: the Copyright Act of 1976, Title 17 of the United States Code, as amended (under which we presently toil), and the Copyright Act of 1909 (only occasionally called out of retirement). Now that history is behind us (not necessarily a redundant statement), let's go back to discussing the copyright itself. Just what is the purpose of this bundle of rights, this thing called copyright?

In 1803 in England, Lord Ellenborough, in *Carey v. Kearsley*,[1] stated: ". . . while I shall think myself bound to secure every man in the enjoyment of his copy-right, one must not put manacles upon science." In 1975, the United States Supreme Court, in probably one of the best and most concise discussions of the purpose of copyright, said:[2]

> Creative work is to be encouraged and rewarded, but private motivation must ultimately serve the cause of promoting broad public availability of literature, music, and the other arts. The immediate effect of our copyright law is to secure a fair return for an "author's" creative labor. But the ultimate aim is, by this incentive, to stimulate artistic creativity for the general public good.

OK. Let's take a look at this bundle of rights.

COPYRIGHT DEFINITIONS

> *One forgets words as one forgets names. One's vocabulary needs constant fertilizing or it will die.*
>
> —EVELYN WAUGH

---

[1] 170 Eng.Rep. 681 (K.B. 1803).

[2] *Twentieth Century Music Corp. v. Aiken*, 422 U.S. 151, (1975) at 156.

The 1909 Copyright Act did not have a section containing definitions, and as a result, for many years we had to rely upon those old workhorses, the courts, to supply us with definitions of what various words and phrases actually meant. Anyone who has had any experience with courts and court decisions can well imagine how out of hand this got. A word might be defined as one thing in the federal courts in New York and as another thing in the federal courts in California.

If you had the misfortune (or good fortune) to be in a court somewhere between New York and California, say Kansas, you would choose the definition which was most beneficial to whatever position you were trying to foist on the court (unless, of course, it had adopted its own definition) and hope that the court had either the good sense and good taste or, perhaps, was gullible enough, to accept your choice of definitions. Of course, there was always the possibility that you would run into a word that had not had the privilege of being defined and you could take your own run at it. Ahhh—the free enterprise system!

One of the great delights of the 1976 Copyright Act is the inclusion of definitions. The following definitions are a representative sampling of those included in Section 101 of the Act and are the ones which seem to be of interest in our ongoing quest for information regarding the recording industry and the twists and turns involved in dealing with it. A close and careful examination of the words chosen for these definitions will be necessary for any proper appreciation of the joys of copyright and, incidentally, your rights in any given copyright:

A "collective work" is a work, such as a periodical issue, anthology, or encyclopedia, in which a number of contributions, constituting separate and independent works in themselves, are assembled into a collective whole.

A "compilation" is a work formed by the collection and assembling of preexisting materials or of data that are selected, coordinated, or arranged in such a way that the resulting work as a whole constitutes an original work of authorship. The term "compilation" includes collective works.

"Copies" are material objects, other than phonorecords, in which a work is fixed by any method now known or later developed, and from which the work can be perceived, reproduced, or otherwise communicated, either directly or with the aid of a machine or device. The term "copies" includes the material object, other than a phonorecord, in which the work is first fixed.

"Copyright owner," with respect to any of the exclusive rights comprised in a copyright, refers to the owner of that particular right.

A work is "created" when it is fixed in a copy or phonorecord for the first time; where a work is prepared over a period of time, the portion of it that has been fixed at any particular time constitutes the work as of that time, and where the work has been prepared in different versions, each version constitutes a separate work.

A "derivative work" is a work based upon one or more preexisting works, such as a translation, musical arrangement, dramatization, fictionalization, motion picture version, sound recording, art reproduction, abridgment, condensation, or any other form in which a work may be recast, transformed, or adapted. A work consisting of editorial revisions, annotations, elaborations, or other modifications which, as a whole, represent an original work of authorship, is a "derivative work."

A "device," "machine," or "process" is one now known or later developed.

A "digital transmission" is a transmission in whole or in part in a digital or other nonanalog format.

An "establishment" is a store, shop, or any similar place of business open to the general public for the primary purpose of selling goods or services in which the majority of the gross square feet of space that is nonresidential is used for that purpose, and in which nondramatic musical works are performed publicly.

A "food service or drinking establishment" is a restaurant, inn, bar, tavern, or any other similar place of business in which the public or patrons assemble for the primary purpose of being served food or drink, in which the majority of the gross square feet of space that is nonresidential is used for that purpose, and in which nondramatic musical works are performed publicly.

The term "financial gain" includes receipt, or expectation of receipt, of anything of value, including the receipt of other copyrighted works.

A work is "fixed" in a tangible medium of expression when its embodiment in a copy or phonorecord, by or under the authority of the author, is sufficiently permanent or stable to permit it to be perceived, reproduced, or otherwise communicated for a period of more than transitory duration. A work consisting of sounds, images, or both, that are being transmitted, is "fixed" for purposes of this title if a fixation of the work is being made simultaneously with its transmission.

An "international agreement" is

    (1) the Universal Copyright Convention;

    (2) the Geneva Phonograms Convention;

    (3) the Berne Convention;

    (4) the WTO Agreement;

    (5) the WIPO Copyright Treaty;

    (6) the WIPO Performances and Phonograms Treaty; and

    (7) any other copyright treaty to which the United States is a party.

A "joint work" is a work prepared by two or more authors with the intention that their contributions be merged into inseparable or interdependent parts of a unitary whole.

To "perform" a work means to recite, render, play, dance, or act it, either directly or by means of any device or process or, in the case of a motion picture or other audiovisual work, to show its images in any sequence or to make the sounds accompanying it audible.

A "performing rights society" is an association, corporation, or other entity that licenses the public performance of nondramatic musical works on behalf of copyright owners of such works, such as the American Society of Composers, Authors and Publishers (ASCAP), Broadcast Music, Inc. (BMI), and SESAC, Inc.

"Phonorecords" are material objects in which sounds, other than those accompanying a motion picture or other audiovisual work, are fixed by any method now known or later developed, and from which the sounds can be perceived, reproduced, or otherwise communicated, either directly or with the aid of a machine or device. The term "phonorecords" includes the material object in which the sounds are first fixed.

"Publication" is the distribution of copies or phonorecords of a work to the public by sale or other transfer of ownership, or by rental, lease, or lending. The offering to distribute copies or phonorecords to a group of persons for purposes of further distribution, public performance, or public display, constitutes publication. A public performance or display of a work does not of itself constitute publication.

To perform or display a work "publicly" means—

(1) to perform or display it at a place open to the public or at any place where a substantial number of persons outside of a normal circle of a family and its social acquaintances is gathered; or

(2) to transmit or otherwise communicate a performance or display of the work to a place specified by clause (1) or to the public, by means of any device or process, whether the members of the public capable of receiving the performance or display receive it in the same place or in separate places and at the same time or at different times.

"Sound recordings" are works that result from the fixation of a series of musical, spoken, or other sounds, but not including the sounds accompanying a motion picture or other audiovisual work, regardless of the nature of the material objects, such as disks, tapes, or other phonorecords, in which they are embodied.

A "transfer of copyright ownership" is an assignment, mortgage, exclusive license, or other conveyance, alienation, or hypothecation of a copyright or of any of the exclusive rights comprised in a copyright, whether or not it is limited in time or place of effect, but not including a nonexclusive license.

A "work for hire" is—

(1) a work prepared by an employee within the scope of his or her employment; or

(2) a work specially ordered or commissioned for use as a contribution to a collective work, as a part of a motion picture or other audiovisual work, as a translation, as a supplementary work, as a compilation, as an instructional text, as a test, as answer material for a test, or as an atlas, if the parties expressly agree in a written instrument signed by them that the work shall be considered a work made for hire. . . .

Phew! Are we still awake? Believe it or not, in the arcane world of copyright, those definitions were *hot* stuff! Well . . . maybe not hot, but essential.

Studying those definitions with care, sometimes right down to the placement of the commas, can explain away a lot of the mystery of copyright law and the decisions of the courts regarding the interpretation of copyright law. Take, for example, the definitions of "copies" and "phonorecords." Although the definitions are almost identical (or, more accurately, each is a mirror image of the other since each excludes the other), the fact that they are exclusive of each other makes a difference, since certain rights and restrictions apply only to "copies" or only to "phonorecords."

As to those definitions of "establishment" and "food service or drinking establishment," in 1998, to the dismay of performing rights societies, publishers, and composers, Congress added an amendment to the 1976 Act, the misnamed (from the music industry's viewpoint) Fairness in Music Licensing Act of 1998, which added these and other additional definitions to Section 101 of the 1976 Act.

COPYRIGHT INFRINGEMENT

Where there's a hit, there's a writ.

—SIR ROBIN JACOB, Judge of the High Court, England, clearing
singer/songwriter Bjork of copyright infringement, June 1995

Before dealing with the individual aspects of copyright, it is probably appropriate to discuss copyright infringement actions. Copyright infringement actions, which can be the bane of established artists (deep pockets and notoriety make them tempting targets), can also become mother lodes for unknown artists, leading to fame and fortune.

As always, one's view of infringement actions depend upon whether you are on the acting end or the receiving end. The outcome of any action for infringement hangs on two issues: first, the degree of similarity of the two works and, second, whether or not the alleged infringer had access to the allegedly infringed work. Similarity or, indeed, even being identical, does not in and of itself prove an infringement. Access has to be shown in order to sustain a successful copyright infringement action.

As a practical matter, similarity is undoubtedly the more important of the two issues. Without proof of access, a court may not sustain a claim of infringement; however, given enough similarity, courts will frequently do double back somersaults with a triple twist to find access. Proving access is an iffy business. Consider, for example, the following three cases in chronological order. Each ruling was made in the United States district court in New York City, and all were handed down within a one-year period.

Case 1: *Palmieri v. Estefan*[3]

In a motion, the court agreed to exclude certain evidence concerning possible access. The court stated that while wide dissemination of a song may be the proper basis for inferring that an alleged infringer may have had access, the "bare possibility" of access cannot be considered in combination to create any basis for the reasonable possibility of access. The evidence which was too insignificant to prove the reasonable possibility of access was (1) evidence of radio play; (2) BMI royalty statements; (3) the fact that two of defendant Gloria Estefan's business associates each possessed a copy of the plaintiff's recording of the song; and (4) videotape evidence of family reunions [plural] where plaintiff's recording of his song might have been played (plus testimony from Estefan's own brother-in-law that the song *had* been played at family gatherings—mind you, gatherings plural, not singular). Also excluded was evidence that the record had sold 40,000 copies, 2,000 of them in Miami where Estefan lived.

Case 2: *Spiegelman v. Reprise Records*[4]

The court rejected a songwriter's claim of infringement and granted a summary judgment for defendants. The court held that plaintiff could not show that the defendants had the "reasonable opportunity" to hear the songwriter's song prior to the creation of the alleged infringing work. The songwriter claimed he had performed the song in a restaurant in Haifa, Israel, in 1983 and, on two occasions, in New York City (editorial note: well, there

---

[3]35 U.S.P.Q. 2d 1382 (S.D.N.Y. 1995).
[4]35 U.S.P.Q. 2d 1732 (S.D.N.Y. 1995).

you are!). The court held, on page 1734, that these alleged performances did not "constitute such wide dissemination of the copyright work" that it raised any reasonable inference of access.

Case 3: *Santrayll v. Burrell*[5]

The court denied a motion for summary judgment on behalf of the defendant rapper against the plaintiff, who was an "unknown artist." While the plaintiff's song was not widely disseminated, tapes of the song were sent to acquaintances of the defendant and a local music video program aired plaintiff's song approximately eight times during a period when plaintiff *might have* visited New York. The court ruled that a reasonable jury hearing the evidence might find the two works to be "strikingly similar" so that copying and access are presumed. The court also held that even if the jury did not find the works "strikingly similar," a reasonable jury might find access in the case based upon what the court called a number of "somewhat attenuated" connections between the parties such as the mailings and the video broadcasts when the plaintiff might have been in New York.

Frankly, I don't see any significant differences between the facts in the *Santrayll* case, for which the court said a reasonable jury could find access, and the facts in the *Palmieri* case, where the court said that the evidence did not prove access.

I have noticed an apparent generosity and forgiveness on the part of the courts when the infringer is a famous artist. A prime example of such kindness on the part of a court is the case in which Bright Tunes Music Corp. sued George Harrison for copyright infringement on the grounds that "My Sweet Lord" was stolen from "He's So Fine."[6] Despite the fact that Harrison's tune had the same notes and chord progression as "He's So Fine," the court ruled that Harrison was guilty only of "subconscious plagiarism." Not, mind you, that I am saying or implying that it was not a subconscious infringement, but I am virtually certain that if I had been the infringer, the "subconscious" defense would not have worked.

Fair use is often used as a defense in infringement actions. Section 107 of the Copyright Act sets forth the guidelines for determining whether or not a "borrowing" of copyrighted material is a copyright infringement or an excused, fair use, of the material. (For a discussion of fair use, see below, pages 504–507).

SUBJECT MATTER OF COPYRIGHT

Just what can be copyrighted, or as the language is set forth in the Copyright Act, what is the "subject matter" of a copyright? As stated above, the foundation for all American copyright law is the Constitution, which granted Congress the power to grant authors the exclusive right to their writings. In order to qualify for a copyright, a work must (1) be a "writing," in other words, it must be fixed in some tangible form which allows it to be perceived, reproduced, or otherwise communicated, and (2) be the result or the product of creative originality.

Please do not be misled by the use of the word "creative." As distressing as this may sound, there is no legal requirement that the work in question have any artistic merit at all. If a work meets the criterion of "originality," which requires that it be an independent creation and not

---

[5] 539 U.S.P.Q. 2d 1052 (S.D.N.Y. March 25, 1996).

[6] *Bright Tunes Music Corp. v. Harrisongs Music, Ltd.*, 420 F.Supp. 177 (1976).

copied from a preexisting work, it will almost certainly meet the criterion of "creativity." Note that a work may be identical to an existing work, but that in and of itself does not prove that it is not original to the author. In order to prove that it was not original for purposes of copyright protection (and protection against a claim of infringement), there must also be a showing of access.

What this means is that if my parents had had the forethought to toss me into a locked attic at birth and, other than slipping food under the door in my formative years, keep me there, isolated me from all contact, and then furnished me with a typewriter—and I had then cranked out a little theatrical piece which I called *Hamlet* (hell of a story!—a father murdered, a ghost, revenge, even a funny gravedigger), I could get a separate copyright in that work, even if it was identical to the one written by that other guy. I could prove lack of access. Of course, no one would be going around naming festivals after me or bothering or needing to get my permission to perform *Hamlet*.

In connection with creative originality, in the *Santrayll* case, a United States district court in New York heard a motion for summary judgment on behalf of the defendant rapper, who claimed that although he had indeed copied the hook from plaintiff's song into his hit song, "Here Comes the Hammer," that hook (the syncopated quadruple repetition of term "uh-oh") did not contain sufficient originality to be capable of copyright protection. The court denied the motion, stating that "the repetition of the nonprotectible word 'uh-oh' in a distinctive rhythm comprises a sufficiently original composition to render it protectible by the copyright laws."[7] The court noted that Pepsi Cola licensed the defendant's song for use in television commercials and used the "uh-oh" hook. The court found the hook to be protected in its use, in spite of the otherwise unprotectible elements.

When it comes to derivative works, the most influential decision seems to be *L. Batlin & Son, Inc. v. Snyder*,[8] where the court held that for a work to be "derivative" it must contain "such new material as would entitle the creator to copyright on new material." The "originality" required was independent creation and distinguishable variation beyond merely trivial variation.

Section 102 of the 1976 Act deals, in the general sense, with the subject matter of copyright:

> (a) Copyright protection subsists, in accordance with this title, in original works of authorship fixed in any tangible medium of expression, now known or later developed, from which they can be perceived, reproduced, or otherwise communicated, either directly or with the aid of a machine or device. Works of authorship include the following categories:
>
>> (1) literary works;
>>
>> (2) musical works, including any accompanying words;
>>
>> (3) dramatic works, including any accompanying music;
>>
>> (4) pantomimes and choreographic works;
>>
>> (5) pictorial, graphic, and sculptural works;
>>
>> (6) motion pictures and other audiovisual works;
>>
>> (7) sound recordings; and
>>
>> (8) architectural works.
>
> (b) In no case does copyright protection for an original work of authorship extend to any idea, procedure, process, system, method of operation, concept, principle, or discovery, regardless of the form in which it is described, explained, illustrated, or embodied in such work.

---

[7]Op. cit., p. 1054.

[8]536 F.2d 486 (2d Cir.), *cert. denied*, 429 U.S. 857 (1976).

Subsection (b) of Section 102 is the bottom line as to what can be copyrighted. Copyright exists in the expression of an idea, and "in no case" does copyright protection exist for the idea itself. Ideas, in and of themselves, cannot be protected by copyright. It is what you do with the idea that determines whether it is protected under copyright law.

This concept, considered in light of the electronic revolution (or is that evolution?) brings up new and interesting problems in the area of copyright. In protecting the expression of an idea, copyright has traditionally protected the "packaging"—the book in which the expression is printed, the phonorecord containing the expression of the idea (the music), etc. Now, and certainly into the near and far future, the expression of the idea and the copyright may exist electronically, literally without material substance to be "packaged." With electronic transmissions, cyberspace, the Internet, and who knows what's next, the expression of an idea may exist without any packaging in the traditional sense. Certainly, this is the greatest revolution in communication since the invention of the printing press. Without the control of the packaging, how is the copyright owner going to be adequately protected by copyright? This is one of the reasons many record companies have backed away from the concept of the electronic transmission of phonorecords to the public. A partial answer to some of the questions raised by this electronic revolution was supplied by the passage of the Digital Millennium Copyright Act of 1998, which is discussed in the next chapter.

The eight categories set forth in subsection 102(a) are not meant to be exclusive; other types of "works of authorship" not mentioned could be included or afforded copyright protection. It is also presumed that some works will fall into more than one category.

Section 103 of the Act also deals with the subject matter of copyrights with respect to compilations and derivative works and is meant to be read in conjunction with Section 102. All the categories and ground rules set forth in Section 102 also apply to compilations and derivative works:

(a) The subject matter of copyright as specified by section 102 includes compilations and derivative works, but protection for a work employing preexisting material in which copyright subsists does not extend to any part of the work in which such material has been used unlawfully.

(b) The copyright in a compilation or derivative work extends only to the material contributed by the author of such work, as distinguished from the preexisting material employed in the work, and does not imply any exclusive right in the preexisting material. The copyright in such work is independent of, and does not affect or enlarge the scope, duration, ownership, or subsistence of, any copyright protection in the preexisting material.

Beyond the fact that compilations and derivative works are capable of obtaining a copyright, the important point to be made in connection with Section 103 is that the copyright in the new version applies only to the "new" material added by the "new" author. The additions have no effect, one way or another, on the existing copyright in the preexisting material.

Example

A, with permission, incorporates B's song in a book of songs. A also includes C's song, which is in the public domain. The book is published and copyrighted in the name of A. The copyright in the new book does not affect the preexisting copyright belonging to B, nor does it change the fact that C's song is in the public domain.

There is a distinction between compilations and derivative works. In order for a work to qualify as a compilation there has to be a bringing together or arranging of preexisting material, a collection, if you will, of stuff. It doesn't matter whether the stuff brought together is, was, or never was copyrighted material (but if it "is" under copyright, don't forget to get permission to use it). A derivative work also relies on preexisting materials, but for a work to qualify as a derivative work, the person or persons putting the material together have to do something with it other than just slap it together with other "stuff"—they must alter it, adapt it, rearrange it, or do something to it to change it.

Example: Compilation

I put together a greatest-hits album of a recording artist, featuring recordings made over a 30-year career. The resulting album is a compilation.

Example: Derivative Work

I put together a greatest-hits album of a recording artist, featuring recordings made over a 30-year career. I then bring in a number of artists and producers to overdub their performances onto the recordings and do remixes of the recordings. The resulting album is a derivative work.

The "new" copyright in a compilation does not replace the copyrights in the preexisting works. The copyright for the compilation protects both what is new in the compilation, for example, new introduction, comments, new artwork, etc., and the work as a whole. The individual preexisting works, if copyrighted, retain those "old" copyrights and the protection they afford.

The intent of Congress in using the word "unlawfully" in the second part of subsection (a) of Section 103 was to continue to protect the "legitimate" parts of a compilation or derived work if it turned out that part of the work was an infringement.

Example: Infringement

A's songbook, used in the above example, also contains a song by D which A thought was in the public domain, but is, in fact, protected by copyright. A's use of D's song is unlawful (an infringement). E now comes along and tries to pirate A's entire songbook. In spite of the fact that the songbook unlawfully contains D's song, A can protect the rest of the songbook. The one unlawful use does not invalidate the copyright on the rest of the book.

EXCLUSIVE RIGHTS IN THE COPYRIGHT

> *Whenever a copyright law is to be made or altered,*
> *then the idiots assemble.*
>
> —MARK TWAIN

Once you have a copyright, just what do you have? As the owner of the copyright, you have, subject to certain express exceptions, the exclusive right to exploit your copyrighted material. Section 106 of the Act sets forth the exclusive rights received by the copyright owner.

Section 106 reads as follows:

Subject to sections 107 through 118, the owner of copyright under this title has the exclusive rights to do and to authorize any of the following:

(1) to reproduce the copyrighted work in copies or phonorecords;

(2) to prepare derivative works based upon the copyrighted work;

(3) to distribute copies or phonorecords of the copyrighted work to the public by sale or other transfer of ownership, or by rental, lease, or lending;

(4) in the case of literary, musical, dramatic, and choreographic works, pantomimes, and motion pictures and other audiovisual works, to perform the copyrighted work publicly; and

(5) in the case of literary, musical, dramatic, and choreographic works, pantomimes, and pictorial, graphic, or sculptural works, including the individual images of a motion pictures and other audiovisual works, to display the copyrighted work publicly; and

(6) in the case of sound recordings, to perform the copyrighted work publicly by means of a digital audio transmission.

Since (4) and (6) (Subparagraph (6) was added to Section 106 in 1995) both deal with performance, we can say there are five basic rights of copyright under the 1976 Act:

1. The right to reproduce

2. The right to adapt

3. The right to publish

4. The right to perform

5. The right to display

The opening sentence of Section 106 specifies that the owner of a copyright has the "exclusive right to do and to authorize" the five basic rights in and to the copyright. "To do and to authorize" is not a redundant phrase. For example, a record company may sell you a copy of a CD (the "to do"), but that does not give you the right to burn copies and sell them (the "to authorize").

It is, of course, possible for these five cumulative rights to overlap so that any one act of infringement may violate two or more of the basic rights. In addition, each of them can be divided up into as many parts as the copyright owner desires and each of the "parts" may be owned and protected separately pursuant to Section 201 of the Act, which states in subsection (d):

(1) The ownership of a copyright may be transferred in whole or in part by any means of conveyance or by operation of law, and may be bequeathed by will or pass as personal property by the applicable laws of intestate succession.

(2) Any of the exclusive rights comprised in a copyright, including any subdivision of any rights specified by section 106, may be transferred as provided by clause (1) and owned separately. The owner of any particular exclusive right is entitled, to the extent of that right, to all of the protection and remedies accorded to the copyright owner by this title.

The principle of divisibility contained in subparagraph 201(d)(2) was new to our statutory copyright body of law. The 1976 Act was the first statutory recognition in America that copyrights can be divided into separate parts.

The passage of the Visual Artists Rights Act (VARA) in 1990 added new exclusive rights to the 1976 Act. VARA added a new section, 106A, which applies only to authors of works of "visual arts." VARA may be summarized as granting the author of a work of visual art the right to receive credit for the work in question, the right to prevent the artist's name from being used in connection with any work of visual art not created by the artist, and, using classic *droit moral* language, the right to prevent changes to a work of visual art "which would be prejudicial to his or her honor or reputation." Section 106A does, however, have an express exception to the right to transfer exclusive rights in a copyright provided for in Section 201(d)(2). In Section 106A(e)(1) the new section states that the author of a work of visual art may not transfer the right "to claim authorship of that work" which is granted in Section 106A(a)(1).

The exclusivity of these five basic rights is the foundation of copyright laws. After all, the Constitution, in Article I, Section 8, Clause 8, expressly uses the word "exclusive." Those of us who live in earthquake country, however, know that foundations are not always that secure.

In copyright legislation prior to the 1909 Act, the owner of any copyright had the sole and exclusive right to control the use or nonuse of the copyrighted material. In 1909 the first exception, and the first amendment to the 1909 Act, was the compulsory license. The Copyright Act of 1976 made additional exceptions to the copyright owner's exclusive right to control the copyright as set forth in Section 106. There are twelve sections in the 1976 Act which set forth and deal with those exceptions. Some of the exceptions are of no particular interest in terms of the music industry. Eight of them, however, are of great interest, and these are discussed individually below.

SECTION 107—FAIR USE

Prior to the enactment of the 1976 Act, one of the prime trouble areas in copyright law was the subject of *fair use* as a defense to a claim of copyright infringement. There were no statutory guidelines as to what was a fair, and therefore not infringing, use of copyrighted material. The courts would determine each case on the facts of that particular case, but in practice they frequently allowed the doctrine of fair use to be a successful defense to the infringement claim.

Back in 1845, Justice Story said:

> [I]n truth, in literature, in science and in art, there are, and can be, few, if any, things, which in the abstract sense, are strictly new and original throughout. Every book in literature, science and in art, borrows, and must necessarily borrow, and use much which was well known and used before.[9]

The new act recognizes this concept and provides statutory guidelines on the concept and for the courts. The language used by Congress is set forth in Section 107 and states as follows:

> Notwithstanding the provisions of section 106 and 106A, the fair use of a copyrighted work, including such use by reproduction in copies or phonorecords or by any other means specified in that section, for purposes such as criticism, comment, news reporting, teaching (including multiple copies for classroom use), scholarship, or research, is not an infringement of copyright. In determining whether the use made of any part of a work in any particular case is a fair use the factors to be considered shall include—
>
> (1) the purpose and character of the use, including whether such use is of a commercial nature or is for nonprofit educational purposes;

---

[9]*Emerson v. Davies*, 8 F.Cas. 615, 619 (CCD Mass. 1845).

(2) the nature of the copyrighted work;

(3) the amount and substantiality of the portion used in relation to the copyrighted work as a whole; and

(4) the effect of the use upon the potential market for or value of the copyrighted work. The fact that a work is unpublished shall not itself bar a finding of fair use if such finding is made upon consideration of all the above factors.

The above four factors are to be considered in determining whether a use is a fair use or an infringement, but they are not necessarily the sole criteria to be used by any court to make a determination. What has happened is that Congress has decided to set forth its understanding of the present state of the law in this area, but at the same time allow for growth and flexibility.

This, presumably, is the appropriate time and place to attempt to drive a stake through the heart of the great copyright "undead": the "4 bar," "8 bar," "16 bar," or whatever number you've heard, "rule." This "rule" states that as long as you are using only 4, 8, or whatever bars or even notes of copyrighted music it isn't a copyright infringement. Wrong, wrong, *wrong*! There ain't no such animal! Any alleged copyright infringement must be judged by and decided pursuant to the criteria set forth in Section 107.

On March 7, 1994, the United States Supreme Court issued a decision dealing directly with the question of fair use in a case brought by Acuff-Rose Music Inc. against Luther R. Campbell (a.k.a. Luke Skywalker), et al., a case commonly known as the "2 Live Crew case."[10] The group 2 Live Crew had recorded a parody (so they claimed) version of Roy Orbison's "Pretty Woman."

The publisher, Acuff-Rose, refused to grant permission for the release of the parody version, but 2 Live Crew proceeded to release the recording without the copyright owner's consent on the *As Clean As They Wanna Be* album. Acuff-Rose then sued for copyright infringement. The group claimed that their version, as a parody, was a fair use and, accordingly, not a copyright infringement. The case worked its way up through the federal courts (that's where copyright infringement cases are heard), starting with the district court, which found for 2 Live Crew. Acuff-Rose appealed, and the court of appeals reversed the district court's decision. From the court of appeals, the case progressed to the United States Supreme Court, which sent the case back down to the court of appeals for "further proceedings consistent with" the court's opinion, which was that 2 Live Crew's commercial parody may be a fair use within the meaning of Section 107. Justice Souter, in his opinion, wrote:

> Because we hold that a parody's commercial use is only one element to be weighed in a fair use enquiry, and that insufficient consideration was given to the nature of parody in weighing the degree of copying, we reverse and remand.[11]

Souter's opinion contains this analysis of the basis for the decision of the court of appeals: [12]

> The Court of Appeals thought the District Court had put too little emphasis on the fact that "every commercial use ... is presumptively ..., unfair," *Sony Corp. of America v. Universal City Studios, Inc.*, 464 U.S. 417, 451 (1984), and it held that "the admittedly commercial nature" of the parody "requires the conclusion" that the first of four factors rele-

---

[10]*Acuff-Rose Music, Inc. v. Campbell* 114 S.Ct. 1164 (1994).

[11]*Id.* at 1168.

[12]*Id.* at 1168–1169.

vant under the statute weighs against a finding of fair use. 972 E 2d, at 1435, 1437. Next, the Court of Appeals determined that, by "taking the heart of the original and making it the heart of a new work," 2 Live Crew had, qualitatively, taken too much. Id., at 1438. Finally, after noting that the effect on the potential market for the original (and the market for derivative works) is "undoubtedly the single most important element of fair use," *Harper & Row, Publishers, Inc. v. Nation Enterprises*, 471 U.S. 539, 566 (1985), the Court of Appeals faulted the District Court for "refus[ing] to indulge the presumption" that "harm for purposes of the fair use analysis has been established by the presumption attaching to commercial uses." 972 E 2d, at 1438–1439. In sum, the court concluded that its "blatantly commercial purpose . . ., prevents this parody from being a fair use." Id., at 1439.

In his opinion, Justice Souter discusses how Section 107 and fair use are to be applied to cases involving potential infringements. He states:[13]

> The text [of Section 107] employs the terms "including" and "such as" in the preamble paragraph to indicate the "illustrative and limitative" function of the example given. . . . Nor may the four statutory factors be treated in isolation, one from another. All are to be explored, and the results weighed together, in light of the purposes of copyright. . . .[14]
>
> The first factor in a fair use enquiry is "the purpose and character of the use, including whether such use is of a commercial nature or is for nonprofit educational purposes. . . ."[15]
>
> . . . the "fact that a publication was commercial as opposed to nonprofit is a separate factor that tends to weigh against a finding of fair use." [Citation omitted] But that is all, and the fact that even the force of that tendency will vary with the context is a further reason against elevating commerciality to hard presumptive significance. The use, for example, of a copyrighted work to advertise a product, even in a parody, will be entitled to less indulgence under the first factor of the fair use enquiry, than the sale of a parody for its own sake, let alone one performed a single time by students in a school. . . .[16]
>
> The second statutory factor, "the nature of the copyrighted work," . . . calls for recognition that some works are closer to the core of intended copyright protection than others, with the consequence that fair use is more difficult to establish when the former works are copied. . . .[17]
>
> The third factor asks whether "the amount and substantiality of the portion used in relation to the copyrighted work as a whole" . . . are reasonable in relationship to the purpose of the copying. . . . [W]e recognize that the extent of permissible copying varies with the purpose and character of the use. . . .
>
> The fourth fair use factor [Section 107(4)] is "the effect of the use upon the potential market for or value of the copyrighted work." It requires courts to consider not only the extent of market harm caused by the particular actions of the alleged infringer, but also "whether unrestricted and widespread conduct of the sort engaged in by the defendant . . ., would result in a substantially adverse impact on the potential market" for the original.[18]

---

[13]*Id.* at 1170.

[14]*Id.* at 1171.

[15]*Id.* at 1174.

[16]*Id.* at 1175.

[17]*Id.* at 1175.

[18]*Id.* at 1177.

A few months after the 2 Live Crew decision, on October 28, 1994, the Second Circuit court of appeals in New York handed down *American Geophysical Union v. Texaco Inc.*,[19] which dealt with photocopying for personal use as a fair use under the Copyright Act.

The court's ruling (two judges for the decision and one dissenting) upheld a federal district court opinion. The opinion simultaneously raised eyebrows and dropped jaws throughout the arcane world of copyright. A researcher employed by Texaco had copied eight articles from a scientific journal. Texaco had two separate subscriptions to the journal, and from one copy received through the subscription, the researcher made one copy of the articles for his own files for future reference. The court ruled against Texaco, holding that the copying was not a fair use, and was therefore not protected, because Texaco's employee, the researcher, was creating his own library at the expense of the journal. The journal belonged to a photocopying licensing agency, and the court held that if Texaco did not want to buy a photocopying license for its employees, then Texaco should buy a subscription for each employee who might need the articles.

SECTION 109—LIMITATIONS ON EXCLUSIVE USE: EFFECT OF TRANSFER OF PARTICULAR COPY OR PHONORECORD

> *This is one of those cases in which the imagination is baffled by the facts.*
>
> —WINSTON CHURCHILL

Section 109 of the Act deals with the right of an individual to sell or otherwise dispose of the physical copy of a copyrighted work. This is sometimes known as the "first sale doctrine." The rights do not extend to the copyright, just the physical copy. It may sound a bit silly today, but at one time it was a very serious question whether a record could be resold by a person who had bought it in the first place.

In the early days of the record business, there was a lawsuit over the resale by its buyer of a record by Fred Waring and the Pennsylvanians. The courts determined that transfer of the physical object itself did not affect the underlying copyright, a concept which was not challenged, but until passage of the 1976 Act, no statute specifically addressed the issue. In the 1976 Act, Congress decided to specify its desires with regard to the transfer of physical copies of copyrighted works. The result was Section 109.

Example

X buys a record which is copyrighted by the record company which produced, manufactured, and distributed the record. X turns around and sells the record to Y. This transfer from X to Y of the copyrighted record is not a copyright infringement.

A new subsection, Section 109(b)(1)(A), was added to the 1976 Act at the insistence of the recording industry. The clause for alarm was the pending invasion of the Japanese custom of record stores renting recordings to customers for the purpose of making their own copies. The recording industry reacted with all the aplomb of a chairman of the Joint Chiefs of Staff learning that aliens from outer space had landed on the lawn of the White House and were setting up huge barbecues. The new subsection provides that no one may "for direct or indirect commercial advantage" rent,

---

[19]1937 E3d 881 (2nd Cir. 1994) 32 U.S.P.Q. 2d 1545.

lease, or lend phonorecords. Interestingly, the recording industry tried to ally itself with the film industry to repel this alien invasion by also including video rentals. The film industry politely declined; for them, video rentals are a profit center.

Section 109 states:

> (a) Notwithstanding the provisions of section 106(3), the owner of a particular copy or phonorecord lawfully made under this title, or any person authorized by such owner, is entitled, without the authority of the copyright owner, to sell or otherwise dispose of the possession of that copy or phonorecord. . . .[20]

> (b)(1)(A) Notwithstanding the provisions of subsection (a), unless authorized by the owners of the copyright in the sound recording . . . and in the case of a sound recording in the musical works embodied therein, neither the owner of a particular phonorecord . . . may, for the purposes of direct or indirect commercial advantage, dispose of, or authorize the disposal of, the possession of that phonorecord, by rental, lease, or lending, or by any other act or practice in the nature of rental, lease, or lending. Nothing contained in the preceding sentence shall apply to the rental, lease, or lending of a phonorecord for nonprofit purposes by a nonprofit library or nonprofit educational institution. . . .

· · ·

> (c) Notwithstanding the provisions of section 106(5), the owner of a particular copy lawfully made under this title, or any person authorized by such owner, is entitled, without the authority of the copyright owner, to display that copy publicly, either directly or by the projection of no more than one image at a time, to viewers present at the place where the copy is located.

> (d) The privileges prescribed by subsections (a) and (b) do not, unless authorized by the copyright owner, extend to any person who has acquired possession of the copy or phonorecord from the copyright owner, by rental, lease, loan, or otherwise, without acquiring ownership of it.

The influence of Section 109 can be seen on promotional copies of albums given out by many record companies. These promotional albums, or freebies, are not transferred or sold. Ownership of the album does not transfer because the albums are not given away—they are loaned. Since they are loaned, the record company retains ownership of the copy of the album. The recipient of the promo album may have physical possession, but not ownership. Without ownership, the recipient cannot, by law, "sell or otherwise dispose of the possession of that . . . phonorecord." So much, legally and theoretically, for selling all your freebies to some record store for quick cash.

Of course when it comes to freebies, record companies have not been content to rely on statutory protection. In the past, records released as promos had white labels (and hence were sometimes known as "whites"), and packaging might be drilled with a hole or notched. Now, with the wonders of technology, record companies can use different bar codes for the freebies. Sometimes all three methods (counting drilled or notched as one method) are used. Why this high level of effort? To avoid having to give record stores a credit for returning product which was not purchased in the first place.

---

[20]Additional language, deleted here, was added in 1994, dealing with preexisting copies and phonorecords which had their copyrights restored.

The first-sale doctrine has, on occasion, been an issue in the consideration of various theories in connection with the legal consequences of digital downloading. (See Chapter 21, "Digital Millennium Copyright Act," the section "File Sharing," pages 541–543.)

SECTION 110—LIMITATIONS ON EXCLUSIVE USE: EXEMPTION OF CERTAIN PERFORMANCES AND DISPLAYS

Section 110 deals with exemption from copyright infringement for certain types of performance and displays (note that "performance" and "display" mean just that—this section does not apply to copying and distribution of materials), most of which are for not-for-profit and/or educational uses. Exempt are performance and display: in the course of teaching activities in a nonprofit educational institution; in the course of a public activity the net proceeds of which are to be used for educational, charitable, or religious purposes; for certain promotional purposes (e.g., a record being played in a store to promote sales of that record); and specifically for the blind or otherwise handicapped. Section 110 has multiple subsections, all going into much more detail than any casual reading requires. The Fairness in Music Licensing Act of 1998 added a considerable amount of new text and girth to Section 110. The important parts of that Act are discussed below, beginning on page 522.

SECTION 112—LIMITATIONS ON EXCLUSIVE USE: EPHEMERAL RECORDINGS

Section 112 sets forth in great detail the rules governing a type of copy, referred to as an "ephemeral recording," made for purposes of later transmission by a broadcasting organization legally entitled to transmit the work. Radio stations frequently make their own copies of recordings for broadcast; indeed, entire shows may be prerecorded (by copying) for later broadcast. Without this section of the act, the copying would be an infringement. (As discussed in Chapter 15, "Performance, Performing, and Neighboring Rights," in some countries copyright law does not give broadcasters the right to make "ephemeral recordings" without paying a broadcast mechanical fee.)

Section 112(a)(1) reads as follows:

> (1) Notwithstanding the provisions of section 106, and except in the case of a motion picture or other audiovisual work, it is not an infringement of copyright for a transmitting organization entitled to transmit to the public a performance or display of a work, under a license, including a statutory license under section 114(f),[21] or transfer of the copyright or under the limitations on exclusive rights in sound recordings specified by section 114(a),[22] or for a transmitting organization that is a broadcast radio or television station licensed as such by the Federal Communications Commission and that makes a broadcast transmission of a performance of a sound recording in a digital format on a nonsubscription basis, to make no more than one copy or phonorecord of a particular transmission program embodying the performance or display, if—
>
> (A) the copy or phonorecord is retained and used solely by the transmitting organization that made it, and no further copies or phonorecords are reproduced from it; and

---

[21]Licenses for Certain Nonexempt Transmissions under the Digital Performance Right in Sound Recordings Act of 1995.

[22]See the next section.

(B) the copy or phonorecord is used solely for the transmitting organization's own transmissions within its local service area, or for purposes of archival preservation or security; and

(C) unless preserved exclusively for archival purposes, the copy or phonorecord is destroyed within six months from the date the transmission program was first transmitted to the public.

Under this subsection a "transmitting organization" must first have the right or license to transmit a sound recording and then may make a *single* copy or phonorecord for its own transmissions within its own "local service area" which, after 6 months, must either be destroyed or preserved "exclusively for archival purposes."

The Digital Performance Right in Sound Recordings Act of 1995 (DPRSR), which deals with public performance by means of digital transmission, added new language to Section 112. The new language granted limited public performance rights in sound recordings to "transmitting organizations" broadcasting in a digital format. The DPRSR is discussed below, beginning on page 511.

SECTION 114—SCOPE OF EXCLUSIVE RIGHTS IN SOUND RECORDINGS

Section 114 of the Copyright Act of 1976 has carved out some exceptions to the rights that the copyright owners of sound recordings would otherwise have had pursuant to Section 106. [Recall that Section 106 specifies that the copyright holder has the exclusive right to (1) reproduce, (2) adapt, (3) publish, (4) perform, and (5) display the copyrighted work.] Subsection 114(a) specifically states:

(a) The exclusive rights of the owner of copyright in a sound recording are limited to the rights specified by clauses (1), (2), (3) and (6) of section 106, and do not include any right of performance under section 106(4).

The excluded right, subsection 106(4), is the right, "in the case of literary, musical, dramatic, and choreographic works, pantomimes, and pictorial, graphic, or sculptural works, including the individual images of a motion pictures and other audiovisual works, to perform the work publicly." The rights left to the owner of the copyright in sound recordings are the right to reproduce, to adapt, and to publish, as well as the right to perform the work publicly by means of digital audio transmission. Section 106(2), the right to prepare derivative works of copyrighted sound recordings, is in and of itself legal protection for copyright owners from the unauthorized use of recordings for sampling purposes.

Section 114(b) states, in part:

(b) The exclusive right of the owner of copyright in a sound recording under clause (1) of section 106 is limited to the right to duplicate the sound recordings in the form of phonorecords or copies that directly or indirectly capture the actual sounds fixed in the recording. The exclusive right of the owner of copyright in a sound recording under clause (2) of section 106 is limited to the right to prepare a derivative work in which the actual sounds fixed in the sound recording are rearranged, remixed, or otherwise altered in sequence or quality. The exclusive rights of the owner of the copyright in a sound

recording under clauses (1) and (2) of section 106 do not extend to the making or duplication of another sound recording which consists entirely of an independent fixation of
other sounds, even though such sounds imitate or simulate those in the copyrighted sound
recording. . . .

It is interesting that while the protection to the owner of the copyright in a sound recording extends to any portion of that recording if it is copied directly off of the protected recording, it does
not extend to soundalike recordings. A deliberate attempt to rerecord, as long as it is an imitation
and not an actual dubbed recording, is not an infringement. Even where the imitation is an effort
to match the original recording note for note, mix for mix, etc., it is not an infringement, even if it
impossible to tell the two apart.

In *Agee v. Paramount Communications*,[23] the court held that Paramount's televised program
Hard Copy's use of sound recordings as background music violated the plaintiff's exclusive right
to reproduce sound recordings under Section 114. The court stated that the right of reproduction
includes sync rights "even in situations where copies are not distributed to the public." Paramount
used the defense that the reproduction was incidental to a tape-delayed performance, which would
be excluded from plaintiff's exclusive rights under Section 114(a). The court rejected this defense,
stating that "Paramount's duplication and synchronization . . ., were designed to achieve more than
time shifted performance" since they allowed Paramount to more accurately synchronize the music
to the film and also allowed for the preservation of each such program for possible rebroadcast.
Paramount, the court held, had violated the plaintiff's right to reproduce the sound recording "at
the moment it put provisions of his recording on tape."

For, as Section 114(b) states, it is not a copyright infringement when the new recording "consists
entirely of an independent fixation of other sounds, even though such sounds imitate or simulate
those in the copyrighted sound recording." If Paramount had made soundalike copies, even if they
were indistinguishable from the originals, it would not have been held liable.

The DPRSR Act of 1995 also added new language to Section 114, creating a limited public performance right for sound recordings for digital transmissions on the Internet "to a particular member of the public as part of that transmission." The new language provides for a negotiated royalty
to be paid to the copyright owners of sound recordings. This performance right applies only to the
retransmission of sound recordings "by an interactive service licensed to publicly perform" the
sound recording, and the royalty goes only to the copyright owner of the sound recording—not to
artists or producers, unless, of course, they happen to be the copyright owner of the sound recording. At best, this very narrow performance right (compare this with the scope of the performance
rights granted, for example, by the terms of the Rome Convention, as discussed in Chapter 15)
barely affords record companies, producers, and performers the type of protection and compensation given to their equivalents in territories which are signatories to the Rome Convention. Only time
will tell if performance rights will be broadened to encompass other areas and provide performance
rights royalties to producers and performers.

---

[23]59 F.3d 317 (2d Cir. 1995).

SECTION 115—THE COMPULSORY LICENSE

BIONDELLO:

> I cannot tell; expect they are busied about a counterfeit assurance: take you assurance of her, "cum privilegio ad impremendum solum" to the church; take the priest, clerk and some sufficient honest witnesses:
>
> If this be not what you look for, I have no more to say. . . .
>
> —WILLIAM SHAKESPEARE
> *The Taming of the Shrew,* Act IV, Scene 4

cum privilegio ad impremendum solum [L.] With exclusive copyright

> —C. T. ONIONS, *A Shakespeare Glossary*

For the music industry, probably one of the most important sections of the new Act is Section 115, which deals with the compulsory license. Section 115 replaced—and expanded—Sections 1(e) and 10l(e) of the 1909 Copyright Act.

The compulsory license is the granddaddy exception to the copyright owner's complete control over the use of the copyrighted material. In effect, it puts a ceiling on what the publisher can charge record companies for the use of copyrighted music. The thinking behind the compulsory license is that music should be made available to the public. Without the compulsory license provisions, the copyright owner of a musical work could retain a monopoly on recordings of the musical work. With them, the copyright owner only has that monopoly until the work has been recorded and distributed. Once the work has been recorded and released, anyone may record the work, whether the copyright owner is willing or not, as long the party who wishes to record the work pays the requisite compulsory license fee.

In the 1909 Copyright Act, the compulsory license was the *only* exception to the copyright owner's right to control any and all uses of the copyrighted work. It was an outgrowth of the trust-busting activities of President Theodore Roosevelt, and was used to break up one company's monopoly in piano rolls. (Piano rolls are rolled-up strips of paper with perforations corresponding to a musical composition, which, when placed in a player piano and started, activate the keys of the piano. Piano rolls "mechanically" reproduce the music, and this was the origin of the terms "mechanical license" and "mechanical.")

When Congressional hearings were first held on the revision of the 1909 Copyright Act, there were some who wanted to do away with the compulsory license in its entirety. This movement never had much support, and the issue soon boiled down to a matter of dollars and cents. Everybody (after all, record companies were also music publishers) wanted to retain the compulsory license; it was just a matter of determining what the compulsory mechanical license rate would be. A 1967 House subcommittee report on copyright revision concluded that "a compulsory licensing system is still warranted as a condition for the rights of reproducing and distributing phonorecords of copyrighted music," but that "the present system is unfair and unnecessarily burdensome on copyright owners, and . . ., the present statutory rate is too low."

After a great deal of argument back and forth, Congress brought forth Section 115 of the new Act. The introductory clause of Section 115 reads as follows:

In the case of nondramatic musical works, the exclusive rights provided by clauses (1) and (3) of section 106, to make and to distribute phonorecords of such works, are subject to compulsory licensing under the conditions specified by this section.

"Nondramatic musical works" are individual songs or compositions not used as part of a dramatic story. Individual songs from a Broadway musical are nondramatic musical works for this purpose, but an entire musical is a dramatic musical work.

Before plunging ahead with "the conditions specified by this section," note that the compulsory license applies only to two of the six exclusive rights retained by the copyright owner as set forth in Section 106: first, the right to reproduce the copyrighted work in copies or phonorecords (clause 1 in Section 106), and second, the right to distribute copies or phonorecords of the copyrighted work to the public by sale or other transfer of ownership, or by rental, lease, or lending (clause 3 in Section 106).

Note the contrast between this provision and subsection 114(a). Subsection 114(a), which deals with sound recordings, makes reference to clauses (1), (2), and (3) of Section 106, while the introductory clause of Section 115, which deals with nondramatic musical works, applies only to clauses (1) and (3) of Section 106. The missing clause, clause (2), deals with the right to make derivative works. Section 115 does not give a right to create derivative works of musical compositions; it does, however, grant the right to make recordings and sell them. In the 2 Live Crew case discussed above, the group had applied for a mechanical license to record their version of "Pretty Woman," but were turned down. They never tried to obtain a compulsory license (arguably, their version was different enough to be a derivative work and would not have qualified for a compulsory license).

Note also that the introductory clause of Section 115 expressly states that the rights granted apply only to the right to make and distribute *phonorecords* of such works. The word "copies" is deliberately left out. If you will recall, the official definition of "copies" expressly excludes "phonorecords" and, of course, the definition of "phonorecords" excludes "copies."

The compulsory license provisions apply only to the right to make sound recordings of the copyrighted work and to sell and otherwise distribute them. The compulsory license cannot be used to justify either record or tape piracy. Nor can it be used to justify making and/or selling copies. Subsection (a) of Section 115, "Availability and Scope of Compulsory License," sets forth the scope of the compulsory license under the 1976 Act:

(1) When phonorecords of a nondramatic musical work have been distributed to the public in the United States under the authority of the copyright owner, any other person, including those who take phonorecords or digital phonorecord deliveries, may, by complying with the provisions of this section, obtain a compulsory license to make and distribute phonorecords of the work. A person may obtain a compulsory license only if his or her primary purpose in making phonorecords is to distribute them to the public for private use, including by means of a digital phonorecord delivery. A person may not obtain a compulsory license for use of the work in the making of phonorecords duplicating a sound recording fixed by another, unless: (i) such sound recording was fixed lawfully; and (ii) the making of the phonorecords was authorized by the owner of the copyright in the sound recording or, if the sound recording was fixed before February 15, 1972, by any

person who fixed the sound recording pursuant to an express license from the owner of the copyright in the musical work or pursuant to a valid compulsory license for use of such work in a sound recording.

The DPRSR Act of 1995 also updated the provisions of Section 115 to include "digital phonorecord deliveries," defining them as follows:

> As used in this section, the following term has the following meaning: A "digital phonorecord delivery" is each individual delivery of a phonorecord by digital transmission of a sound recording which results in a specifically identifiable reproduction by or for any transmission recipient of a phonorecord of that sound recording, regardless of whether the digital transmission is also a public performance of the sound recording or any nondramatic musical work embodied therein. A digital phonorecord delivery does not result from a real-time, non-interactive subscription transmission of a sound recording where no reproduction of the sound recording or the musical work embodied therein is made from the inception of the transmission through to its receipt by the transmission recipient in order to make the sound recording audible.

The provisions of subsection (a) of Section 115 of the 1976 Act are clear on several points that were ambiguous or nonexistent under the 1909 Act. A strict reading of that Act reveals that a third party could make use of the compulsory license provisions as *soon* as a recording of a work had been made. Technically, the 1909 Act did not require that the recording be distributed to the public.

Example

In the period before the 1976 Act, A hears world-famous author and composer B make a recording of his newest work, "Song." B has no intention of releasing "Song" himself, but intends to give the first shot at recording and releasing "Song" to C. On the basis that "Song" has been recorded, A obtains a compulsory license, records "Song," and is the first in the marketplace with "Song."

Under the 1909 Act, A's action, rushing A's version of "Song" into the marketplace before C's authorized version was perfectly legal and, as long as A followed the rules for compulsory licenses (e.g., filing for the compulsory license and paying on all records manufactured on a monthly basis), there was nothing either B or C could do to stop the release. The framers of the 1976 Act took care of this problem in the very first line of Section 115(a) (see page 513).

Accordingly, before a compulsory license can be obtained under the new 1976 Act, a work must have been released pursuant to a valid mechanical license issued by the copyright owner of the composition. The mere fact that the work has been recorded is no longer sufficient to qualify the work for a compulsory license. Also, the work need only be distributed, not necessarily *sold*, in order to qualify for a compulsory license for subsequent recordings. Since a compulsory license cannot be obtained until there has been an authorized recording distributed, the copyright owner of a composition has the right to control the first use of the composition. It is not uncommon for a publisher to put a hold on a song, promising an artist or producer that he or she will have the first commercial release of the song. Short of committing copyright infringement, there is nothing third parties can do to release their version until the first recording has been distributed.

The second sentence of the first clause ("A person may obtain a compulsory license only if his or her primary purpose in making phonorecords is to distribute them to the public for private use, including by means of a digital phonorecord delivery") is very interesting: What on earth, you may ask, can this mean? Congress decided that the compulsory license provisions were to apply only to records being made to sell to the public. The right of obtaining a compulsory license is withheld from broadcasters (with the exception of an addition to Section 112 by the DPRSR Act of 1995 granting a right to obtain a statutory license to a "transmitting organization" broadcasting in a digital format), jukebox operators, and background music services, unless the primary purpose of their recordings is to sell to the public. These businesses must obtain a negotiated license from the copyright owner. The last sentence in the first clause was placed in the new act so as not to get around the copyright protection granted to sound recordings by granting unauthorized duplicators the right to obtain compulsory licenses.

Clause (2) of Section 115(a) sets forth the extent to which a work can be arranged or altered without the consent of the copyright owner through the use of a compulsory license. The purpose of this clause is to allow the user of the copyrighted work the right to make arrangements of the work, but to limit those arrangements so that the work will not be "perverted, distorted, or travestied." The work can be arranged "to the extent necessary to conform it to the style or manner of interpretation of the performance involved. . . ." The right to arrange is limited by the condition that the arrangement cannot "change the basic melody or fundamental character of the work. . . ."

> (2) A compulsory license includes the privilege of making a musical arrangement of the work to the extent necessary to conform it to the style or manner of interpretation of the performance involved, but the arrangement shall not change the basic melody or fundamental character of the work, and shall not be subject to protection as a derivative work under this title, except with the express consent of the copyright owner.

Note that the right to protect a musical composition from an arrangement that changes "the basic melody or fundamental character of the work" is arguably a *droit moral*. As noted in Chapter 15, the only provisions in United States copyright law that could be said to pertain specifically to moral rights were added to the Copyright Act of 1976 on October 17, 1990, when the Visual Artists Rights Act became Section 106(A), subsection (a) of which is titled "Rights of Attribution and Integrity." Section 106A gives visual artists the right to protect their works from any intentional distortion, mutilation, or other modification that would be prejudicial to their reputations.

This whole issue of *droit moral* was a hot topic in the Congressional hearings on whether or not the United States would finally become a signatory to the Berne Convention, an international copyright treaty which does recognize moral rights. The government did not wish to include *droit moral*, which might prevent, among other unacceptable modifications of a work, the colorization of black-and-white films. Ultimately, the United States did become a signatory to Berne, claiming that our own copyright law provides protection for a work's "integrity."

The second clause of Section 115(a) also provides that, unless the copyright owner has given express consent, the arrangement cannot be protected as a derivative work under the act.

Section 115(b) deals with the mechanics of obtaining a compulsory license from the Copyright Office. The act requires an intended user to file a notice of intention with the copyright owner. Section (b), which is entitled "Notice of Intention to Obtain Compulsory License," reads as follows:

(1) Any person who wishes to obtain a compulsory license under this section shall, be-

fore or within thirty days after making, and before distributing any phonorecords of the work, serve notice of intention to do so on the copyright owner. If the registration or other public records of the Copyright Office do not identify the copyright owner and include an address at which notice can be served, it shall be sufficient to file the notice of intention in the Copyright Office. The notice shall comply, in form, content, and manner of service, with requirements that the Register of Copyrights shall prescribe by regulation.

(2) Failure to serve or file the notice required by clause (1) forecloses the possibility of a compulsory license and in the absence of a negotiated license, renders the making and distribution of phonorecords actionable as acts of infringement under Section 501 and fully subject to the remedies provided by Chapter 5 of the 1976 Act.

The provisions of Section 115(b) are straightforward. The intended user must notify the copyright owner of the intended user's intention to record the work. If the copyright owner cannot be found, it is sufficient to send notice to the Copyright Office itself. The notice must, however, be filed not later than 30 days after the making of the phonorecord, and in no case can it be filed after the distribution. Failure to file the proper notice, and to file it on time, makes the use of the copyrighted work an infringement. (This brings to mind an issue brought up way back in Chapter 3. It's all very well to state that the notice of intention shall be made not later than 30 days after making. But when, exactly, is a phonorecord "made"? More on this below.)

The meat and potatoes of the compulsory licensing section are included in subsection (c), "Royalty Payable Under Compulsory License." The first clause reads as follows:

(1) To be entitled to receive royalties under a compulsory license, the copyright owner must be identified in the registration or other public records of the Copyright Office. The owner is entitled to royalties for phonorecords made and distributed after being so identified, but is not entitled to recover for any phonorecords previously made and distributed.

If the copyright has not been registered, there can be no collection of compulsory license fees. Any sales prior to the proper registration are not subject to compulsory license fees. This provision replaces the old "Notice of Use" section of the 1909 Act, which specified that compulsory license fees were not due until a Notice of Use was filed with the Copyright Office.

Registration of the copyright is required both for compulsory license fees to be due and payable and also before any federal infringement action may be filed. The registration requirement brings up various issues. For example, the question of exactly what protection is provided to individual songs that are registered as part of a collection (a practice common to all impoverished songwriters to avoid registration fees on each song) has always lurked in the background. What happens if there is an infringement on one of the individual songs registered as a part of a collection? In a 1995 case, the court had to rule on the issue of individual protection versus registration of a collection as a whole. In *Szabo v. Errisson*,[24] the plaintiff (presumably an impoverished composer) had filed a collection of unpublished songs on tape, requesting a single copyright registration. A lower court had dismissed the plaintiff's case for infringement of one individual song on the grounds that plaintiff's registration did not specifically list the infringed song in the registration and, accordingly, had copyright protection only on the collection as a whole.

---

[24]68 F.3d 940 (5th Cir. 1995).

Not a particularly happy ruling for impoverished composers.

Szabo was appealed to the Fifth Circuit, where the court held that under appropriate circumstances the registration of multiple works is permitted and that the registration extends to "each copyrightable element in the collection." The court reversed the summary judgment which had been given to the defendant, holding that the copyright in a collection of unpublished works protected the individual songs included in the collection. The failure to specifically list the individual songs in the collection was irrelevant to the copyright status of those individual works.

The second clause of Section 115(c) states:

> (2) Except as provided by clause (1), the royalty under a compulsory license shall be payable for every phonorecord made and distributed in accordance with the license. For this purpose, and other than as provided for in paragraph (3), a phonorecord is considered "distributed" if the person exercising the compulsory license has voluntarily and permanently parted with its possession. With respect to each work embodied in the phonorecord, the royalty shall be either two and three-fourths cents, or one-half of one cent per minute of playing time or fraction thereof, whichever amount is larger.

The second clause contains several major departures from the 1909 Act. Pursuant to the older act, the user had to pay on each record manufactured, whether it was sold or sat in a warehouse, or even if it never left the manufacturer. The Copyright of 1976 Act recognizes that it is common in the record industry that more records will be manufactured by the record company than are sold to the public.

Before 1976 most negotiated licenses contained the language "manufactured and sold." Congress, however, chose to use the language "made and distributed." Just what is the difference between "made and distributed" and "manufactured and sold"? "Made"—a word with a broader meaning than "manufactured"—was used so that any process, now known or hereafter known, of reproducing a sound recording would be covered in the language of the act. "Distributed"—a word with a broader meanings than "sold"—was used to cover all contingencies, known and unknown. The clause also provides a definition of "distributed": It means the user has "voluntarily and permanently parted with [the record's] possession."

The choice of the words "voluntarily and permanently" was deliberate. Inclusion of the word "voluntarily" provided that the user would not be required to pay on records which were stolen, destroyed, or otherwise done away with without economic benefit to the user. By using "permanently," Congress was recognizing the concept and problem of returns: Theoretically, the user would not have to pay for records which were not permanently distributed, that is, returns. While recognizing the return of records as a possibility, Congress did not provide, as do recording agreements, for a reserve to be held back against returns.

Section 115(c)(3)(A) deals with compulsory licenses for digital transmission:

> (3)(A) A compulsory license under this section includes the right of the compulsory licensee to distribute or authorize the distribution of a phonorecord of a nondramatic musical work by means of a digital transmission which constitutes a digital phonorecord delivery, regardless of whether the digital transmission is also a public performance of the sound recording under section 106(6) of this title or of any nondramatic musical work embodied therein under section 106(4) of this title. . . .

Section 115(c)(3) continues on with some 24 subparagraphs detailing rules and procedures for the compulsory license for digital transmission. It also gives a definition of digital phonorecord delivery:

> ... A "digital phonorecord delivery" is each individual delivery of a phonorecord by digital transmission of a sound recording which results in a specifically identifiable reproduction by or for any transmission recipient of a phonorecord of that sound recording, regardless of whether the digital transmission is also a public performance of the sound recording or any nondramatic musical work embodied therein. A digital phonorecord delivery does not result from a real-time, non-interactive subscription transmission of a sound recording where no reproduction of the sound recording or the musical work embodied therein is made from the inception of the transmission through to its receipt by the transmission recipient in order to make the sound recording audible.

The fourth clause of Section 115(c) provides for an additional compulsory license royalty fee for recordings distributed "by rental, lease, or lending" on top of the existing fees:

> (4) A compulsory license under this section includes the right of the maker of a phonorecord of a nondramatic musical work under subsection (a)(1) to distribute or authorize distribution of such phonorecord by rental, lease, or lending (or by acts or practices in the nature of rental, lease, or lending). In addition to any royalty payable under clause (2) and chapter 8 of this title, a royalty shall be payable by the compulsory licensee for every act of distribution of a phonorecord by or in the nature of rental, lease, or lending, by or under the authority of the compulsory licensee. With respect to each nondramatic musical work embodied in the phonorecord, the royalty shall be a proportion of the revenue received by the compulsory licensee from every such act of distribution of the phonorecord under this clause equal to the proportion of the revenue received by the compulsory licensee from distribution of the phonorecord under clause (2) that is payable by a compulsory licensee under that clause and under chapter 8. The Register of Copyrights shall issue regulations to carry out the purpose of this clause.

Section 115(c)(5) specifies a timetable for making the required royalty payments:

> (5) Royalty payments shall be made on or before the twentieth day of each month and shall include all royalties for the month next preceding. Each monthly payment shall be made under oath and shall comply with requirements that the Register of Copyrights shall prescribe by regulation. The Register shall also prescribe regulations under which detailed cumulative annual statements of account, certified by a certified public accountant, shall be filed for every compulsory license under this section. The regulations covering both the monthly and the annual statements of account shall prescribe the form, content, and manner of certification with respect to the number of records made and the number of records distributed.

There is no provision for holding back a reserve, and credits for returned records must be taken in the future at the time they are returned—if there are sales to offset the returned records at that time.

For three years after passage of the Copyright Act of 1976, interim regulations were used by the Copyright Office for the process of collecting the monthly payments for compulsory license. In

1978 the Copyright Office began in earnest to research the accounting procedures in the music industry in an attempt to establish the final regulations for the reporting procedures for the compulsory mechanical license. It is not reported what the private thoughts of these governmental investigators were when they came into contact with music industry accounting procedures. (Probably there is no truth to the rumors that the sudden enormous increase in the national debt in the late 1970s can be traced to music industry accounting procedures falling into the hands of governmental officials.)

In November of 1980, the final regulations were published. The major question the Copyright Office had faced involved the meaning of "permanently distributed." In theory at least, the compulsory license fee is not due until the record is "permanently distributed." But when is that? How does a record company know whether or not a record will be returned or has been permanently distributed? In order to determine this, the Register of Copyrights set three basic rules:

1. The accounting procedures to be used by the record company must not be so complicated as to make use of the compulsory license impractical.

2. The accounting system used must insure full payment, but at the same time not cause overpayment. In order to accomplish this, an accounting system based upon a method known as FIFO (first in, first out) must be used, as opposed to FILO (first in, last out).

3. The accounting system must insure prompt payment.

If you have doubts that this really solves the accounting problems involving pinpointing when a record is permanently distributed, take heart in the fact that the Copyright Office viewed its own work with some skepticism, stating that "the parties remain divided on how to resolve this difficult question," that "the controversy over it is likely to continue," and that "the Office emphasizes that these final regulations should be considered experimental and subject to reconsideration in the light of experience." Even if the Copyright Office saw nothing contradictory in referring to a final, experimental regulation, the choice of words does not inspire confidence that this matter is, in fact, final.

Determination of the Statutory Rate

The major change from the 1909 Act set forth in clause (2) of Section 115(c) of the 1976 Act is the royalty rate specified by statute—usually referred to as the *statutory rate* or, sometimes, just *statutory*. This change carries great impact because this statutory rate, traditionally and actually, becomes the standard for not only the compulsory rates but also the negotiated rates. Under the old act, the statutory rate was 2 cents per part manufactured. Under the new act, as formulated originally, there was a sliding rate which was based upon records "made and distributed." The sliding rate which became effective January 1, 1978, was the greater of 2¾ cents or ½ cent per minute of playing time, or fraction thereof, for each record "made and distributed." In setting up the Copyright Act of 1976, Congress provided for what was known as the Copyright Royalty Tribunal. This group of stalwarts (most of whom were political appointments made in 1978, the year that the act was supposed to go into effect) was supposed to review and "make determinations concerning the adjustment of reasonable copyright royalty" rates as provided in sections 115 and 116 (jukebox fees), and to "make determinations as to the reasonable terms and rates of royalty payment as provided in section 118" (fees for noncommercial broadcasters).

In late December of 1980, the tribunal announced a raise in the compulsory license fee to 4 cents or ¾ cents per minute of playing time or fraction thereof. They also said that there would be yearly adjustments in the statutory rate on the basis of the cost of records to the public, which brought an immediate howl of protest from the record companies (not surprisingly, the very parties who would be raising record prices). Two lawsuits were immediately filed to block the plan—one by the Recording Industry Association of America (RIAA), with the U.S. court of appeals in Washington, D.C., and one by a group representing music publishers (who naturally had an entirely different view of what was going on), in the federal court of appeals in New York City.

Before either court could rule, some other ingredients were added to the stew. On March 4, 1981, Clarence James, Jr., then chairman of the Copyright Royalty Tribunal, appeared at an oversight hearing on the tribunal held by a House of Representatives Judiciary Subcommittee. The subcommittee, which happened to be chaired by Rep. Robert Kastenmeier, generally considered to be the main author of the Copyright Act of 1976, was shocked when James called for the various compulsory licenses to be done away with and for the tribunal itself to be abolished. The flavor of the whole moment seems best caught by the next day's edition of *Daily Variety*, which reported, on the first page, that "Panel members watched in rapture as the Tribunal member argued for deleting the body they created in the 1976 Copyright Act, with a startled Kastenmeier looking as if his first born had been flattened by a truck." Not too long after this historic meeting, Mr. James resigned as chairman of the Copyright Royalty Tribunal.

In 1982, the Washington, D.C. court of appeals upheld the new 4-cents rate but overturned the tribunal's plan for automatic raises, and a new plan, worked out by RIAA, ASCAP, CBS, the National Music Publishers Association, and the Nashville Songwriters' Association International, was submitted to the tribunal in late October of 1982. The tribunal seemed happy enough to adopt the work of these organizations, since they were, generally, representative of the parties on both sides of the fight over future rates, and approved the plan "in principle." The plan provided for automatic stepped-up increases in the statutory rate as follows:

• Effective January 1, 1983: 4¼ cents or .8 cent per minute of playing time or fraction thereof, whichever amount is larger

• Effective January 1, 1984: 4½ cents or .85 cent per minute of playing time or fraction thereof, whichever amount is larger; and

• Effective January 1, 1986: 5 cents or .95 cent per minute of playing time or fraction thereof, whichever amount is larger.

In 1987 the merry-go-round came around again and the Copyright Royalty Tribunal jumped on board and raised the rate to 5¼ cents or 1 cent per minute. In 1990 it was raised to 5.7 cents, and in 1992 to 6.2 cents or 1.1 cents per minute. The Copyright Royalty Tribunal is now defunct (for some fascinating details on its demise, see page 522), and the statutory rate is now set to increase every 2 years with prices set through the year 2006. For the period 1996 through 1997, the rate was set at 6.9 cents or 1.3 cents per minute. For the period 1998 through 1999 the rate cracked the 7 cents barrier, rising to 7.1 cents or 1.35 cents per minute. For the period 2000 through 2001, the rate was 7.55 cents or 1.55 cents per minute of playing time or fraction thereof, whichever was larger; in 2002 through 2003, the rate was 8 cents or 1.65 cents per minute of playing time or fraction thereof, whichever was larger; in 2004 through 2005, the rate is 8.5 cents or 1.65 cents per minute of playing time or fraction thereof, whichever is larger; and after 2006, the rate is 9.1 cents or 1.75 cents per minute of playing time or fraction thereof, whichever amount is larger.

Clause (6) of Section 115(c), the final clause, provides that if the copyright owner does not receive payments on time, according to regulations, the owner may given written notice to the licensee of the default, and if the licensee does not comply within 30 days, the compulsory license will be automatically terminated. Once the license is terminated, the making and/or distribution of all phonorecords for which the royalty has not been paid become actionable as acts of infringement.

SECTION 116—THE JUKEBOX EXEMPTION

When I was young I looked like Al Capone, but I lacked his compassion.
—OSCAR LEVANT

The question of how to treat jukeboxes under the copyright laws has always created quite an uproar. Under the 1909 Act, jukeboxes were exempt from making any payment for the use of the copyrighted works. A great deal of debate went into this subject, and the result was Section 116 of the Copyright Act of 1976. Basically, Section 116 provided that the operator of a jukebox may obtain a compulsory license to perform copyrighted works "publicly" by paying a royalty fee for each jukebox. The fee was originally set at $8 per year. The first review of jukebox fees was released in December of 1980. In it, the Copyright Royalty Tribunal changed the royalty fee for each jukebox from $8 to $30 for the period 1982 through 1983. The fee went to $60 in 1984. However, for small operators maintaining fewer than 60 jukeboxes, the rate was $25 in 1982–1983 and increased to $50 in 1984. After the demise of the tribunal, further increases in the jukebox fee were to be based upon increases in the consumer price index.

The collection and distribution of these fees had been fraught with problems from day one, both in collecting (the majority of jukeboxes were not licensed) and determining a fair division of the fees that are collected. In 1988 the Congress passed the Berne Convention Implementation Act of 1988 in recognition of the fact that the United States had finally gotten around to signing the Berne Convention. That act allowed jukebox operators to negotiate a license fee.

On behalf of music publishers, ASCAP, BMI, and SESAC negotiated with the trade organization representing jukebox operators, and what could be called an "all-in" licensing fee was worked out between the two groups. The Jukebox License Office was established, and the Jukebox License Agreement was created and signed.

The Jukebox License Agreement spells out the rules and regulations for jukebox operators' use of the copyrighted material (very much like the AFM Basic Agreement sets the rules for record companies using the services of union musicians). In 2004 the yearly rate for jukeboxes was $365 for the first jukebox, and for each additional jukebox operated, $83.

The Jukebox License Agreement also expressly disallows jukeboxes from using "transmissions, downloads and streaming of musical works" as a source for the recordings being played on the jukebox.

SECTION 118—NONCOMMERCIAL BROADCASTING

The opera is like a husband with a foreign title—expensive to support,
hard to understand and therefore a supreme social challenge.

—CLEVELAND AMORY

Under the 1909 Copyright Act, noncommercial broadcasters were free to play any music without having to pay licensing fees. Indeed, the copyright owner of musical compositions—for example, the score from a Broadway musical—might withdraw permission to perform the music publicly, and noncommercial stations could, sometimes gleefully, proceed to broadcast the music anyway.

Noncommercial broadcasters, under the provisions of Section 118 of the 1976 Act, are now required to pay for the use of copyrighted material in much the same manner as are commercial broadcasters. Congress initially attempted to set rates for noncommercial broadcasters, but, rightfully or wrongfully, lost its nerve and provided that the rates to be charged for use by noncommercial broadcasters could be negotiated by the parties (the owner of the copyright and the broadcasting entity) or, failing that, be set by the Copyright Royalty Tribunal. The tribunal, however, never a rock-solid body, was struck from the Copyright Act of 1976 by the Copyright Tribunal Reform Act of 1993, passed after hearings before the House of Representatives Copyright Subcommittee. (During the hearings, which offered more than a few amusing moments, the chairwoman of the tribunal accused one of the other members of running a cable television business out of the tribunal offices. The accused commissioner denied the allegation and, with the remaining commissioner's concurrence, stated that the tribunal should be abolished, saying: "This boat is a leaky vessel. It's time for the Tribunal to sail off into the sunset." Weeping, the chairwoman defended the tribunal's existence, claiming that the tribunal performed an important and much-needed essential service. When asked, however, she could not remember when the last meeting of the tribunal had taken place.) Section 118 now reads that in the absence of license agreements voluntarily negotiated by the parties, a "copyright royalty arbitration panel" shall be convened to set rates and terms, which shall be binding on all parties.

Section 253.5 of the Code of Federal Regulations, Title 37, Volume 1 deals with the "Performance of musical compositions by public broadcasting entities licensed to colleges and universities." It sets forth a royalty fee payable to ASCAP, BMI, and SESAC and provides for "voluntary license agreements," presumably at a lesser rate. The rates, as of July 1, 2002, are set forth as follows:

> (c) Royalty rate. A public broadcasting entity within the scope of this section may perform published nondramatic musical compositions subject to the following schedule of royalty rates:
>> (1) For all such compositions in the repertory of ASCAP, $244 annually.
>> (2) For all such compositions in the repertory of BMI, $244 annually.
>> (3) For all such compositions in the repertory of SESAC, $66 annually.
>> (4) For the performance of any other such compositions, $1.

FAIRNESS IN MUSIC LICENSING ACT

MERCUTIO:
You gave us the counterfeit fairly last night.

—WILLIAM SHAKESPEARE
Romeo and Juliet, Act II, Scene 4

In December 1998, much to the alarm of music publishers, composers, and the performing rights societies, the Fairness in Music Licensing Act of 1998 was passed and signed into law. The act is another example of congressional predilection for choosing names for legislation which imply one thing and enact the opposite (as, for example, the Clean Air Act).

Fairness to whom? one might ask. Certainly not to the members, composers, and publishers of ASCAP, BMI, and SESAC. The act exempted many "establishments" (small businesses and stores) and "food service and drinking establishments" (restaurants and bars) from having to pay royalties to the performing rights societies for the playing of music to the public.

This tug of war between businesses and the performing rights societies has been going on for years. The 1976 Act provided another "exception" dealing with the public performance of musical compositions by certain small businesses. Generally, the copyright owners of musical compositions license to performing rights societies (usually ASCAP or BMI domestically) the right to grant the right of public performance for profit to third parties. The 1976 Act exempted certain small businesses, as long as they followed the rules, from having to obtain licenses from the performing rights societies to "broadcast" music in their stores. The 1976 Act provided that the broadcast of music in a small business "on a small receiving apparatus of a kind commonly used in a private home" was not a copyright infringement. The general rule of thumb had been that if it was broadcast on a "regular" unit having no more than two speakers, it was an exempt use and the store did not have to obtain a license from the copyright owners through the performing rights societies.

In May 1992, the United States Supreme Court refused to hear appeals brought by BMI against adverse decisions relating to two chain stores, Edison Brothers Store and Claire's Boutiques, for playing radio music in their stores without a license. BMI tried, unsuccessfully, to argue that the size and number of the stores took them out of the "single receiving apparatus" exemption. The Court refused to hear the argument since it appeared that the stores were in fact using "small receiving apparatus of a kind commonly used in a private home."

There were subsequent attempts to exempt businesses from having to pay license fees for their use of music. The New York Arts and Cultural Affairs Law (which may be a prime example of what George Orwell called "doublespeak") attempted to overrule the Copyright Act of 1976 with a state statute in order to "protect small businesses" from, one presumes, the rapacious claims of the performing rights societies (such as ASCAP and BMI) and their equally rapacious members (music publishers and individual composers). The New York law required any such performing rights society using the music police (yes, they do exist) to investigate an establishment, say, a bar or restaurant, to notify the owner of the establishment within 72 hours that they were being investigated. If, for example, BMI sent investigators into a bar to see if the bar was playing music without the appropriate license, BMI was required by state law to inform the proprietor of the bar within 72 hours that the bar was under investigation. If BMI failed to do so, the bar proprietor could sue BMI for damages and attorney fees. Oh, yeah, and the bar owner could also get an injunction to stop BMI from investigating the bar's use of music.

The federal court took a dim view of this attempt by a state legislature to impose its own rules over the federal law and struck down the New York law, holding that the state law undermined the performing rights societies' ongoing investigations of copyright infringement; that it created a significant deterrent to enforcement of copyright; that the 72-hour notice requirement conflicted with federal statutes of limitation, which allowed 3 years (let's see, 72 hours versus 26,280 hours—not that much difference) and was not feasible; and that the provisions for damages, attorneys' fees, and injunctions would allow infringers to counterclaim under the New York statute and to offset damages if the performing rights society prevailed under the federal act.

While the music industry was congratulating itself on beating back the barbarians, the barbarians successfully breached the walls of an even bigger castle—the federal government. In 1998 the Fairness in Music Licensing Act became the law of the land, and a new, broader exception was incorporated into the 1976 Act under Section 110(5), subsection (B), which states:

> (B) communication by an establishment of a transmission or retransmission embodying a performance or display of a nondramatic musical work intended to be received by the general public, originated by a radio or television broadcast station licensed as such by the Federal Communications Commission, or if an audiovisual transmission, by a cable system or satellite carrier, if—
>
> (i) in the case of an establishment other than a food service or drinking establishment, either the establishment in which the communication occurs has less than 2,000 gross square feet of space (excluding space used for customer parking and for no other purpose), or the establishment in which the communication occurs has 2,000 or more gross square feet of space (excluding space used for customer parking and for no other purpose) and—
>
> (I) if the performance is by audio means only, the performance is communicated by means of a total of not more than 6 loudspeakers, of which not more than 4 loudspeakers are located in any 1 room or adjoining outdoor space; or
>
> (II) if the performance or display is by audiovisual means, any visual portion of the performance or display is communicated by means of a total of not more than 4 audiovisual devices, of which not more than 1 audiovisual device is located in any one room, and no such audiovisual device has a diagonal screen size greater than 55 inches, and any audio portion of the performance or display is communicated by means of a total of not more than 4 loudspeakers, of which not more than 4 loudspeakers are located in any one room or adjoining outdoor space;
>
> (ii) in the case of a food service or drinking establishment, either the establishment in which the communication occurs has less than 3,750 gross square feet of space (excluding space used for customer parking and for no other purpose), or the establishment in which the communication occurs has 3,750 or more gross square feet of space (excluding space used for customer parking and for no other purpose) and—
>
> (I) if the performance is by audio means only, the performance is communicated by means of a total of not more than 6 loudspeakers, of which not more than 4 loudspeakers are located in any 1 room or adjoining outdoor space; or
>
> (II) if the performance or display is by audiovisual means, any visual portion of the performance or display is communicated by means of a total of not more than 4 audiovisual devices, of which not more than 1 audiovisual device is located in any one room, and no such audiovisual device has a diagonal screen size greater than 55 inches, and any audio portion of the performance or display is communicated by means of a total of not more than 4 loudspeakers, of which not more than 4 loudspeakers are located in any one room or adjoining outdoor space;

(iii) no direct charge is made to see or hear the transmission or retransmission;

(iv) the transmission or retransmission is not further transmitted beyond the establishment where it is received; and

(v) the transmission or retransmission is licensed by the copyright owner of the work so publicly performed or displayed; . . .

This translates into a reduction of about 75% in fees paid to ASCAP and BMI. An establishment which uses music transmitted by radio, televisions, etc., which does not charge to hear or see the transmissions, and which does not "transmit beyond the establishment" does not have to pay licensing fees to ASCAP, BMI, or any other performance society if the establishment isn't a restaurant or bar and is under 2,000 square feet or if it *is* a restaurant or bar and is under 3,750 square feet.

If, however, either of these types of establishments exceeds the square footage limits, well, by golly, it can still avoid paying licensing fees if:

1. It has no more than 6 "loudspeakers" with no more than 4 speakers in one room; or

2. It has no more than 4 "audiovisual devices" (televisions or screens) with not more than 1 audio-visual device in any one room and no screen is bigger than 55 inches diagonally with no more than 4 speakers.

This is a considerable narrowing of the performing rights societies' ability to collect royalties on behalf of their members. As if the additions to Section 110(5) were not bad enough, consider a brand new section added to the 1976 Act, Section 512, Determination of Reasonable License Fees for Individual Proprietors. It provides that "an individual proprietor who owns or operates fewer than 7 nonpublicly traded establishments in which nondramatic musical works are performed publicly and who claims that any license agreement offered by [the] performing rights society is unreasonable" in the license rate or fee it sets for that proprietor is entitled to turn the matter over to a federal district court for a determination of what *is* a reasonable license rate or fee.

In my personal experience, I have never met a business owner who did not believe the license fees or rates charged by the performing rights societies were anything less than outrageous and unreasonable. And I have rarely seen a court of law adequately grasp the arcane workings of the music industry.

The Fairness in Music Licensing Act also added five new definitions to Section 101:

An "establishment" is a store, shop, or any similar place of business open to the general public for the primary purpose of selling goods or services in which the majority of the gross square feet of space that is nonresidential is used for that purpose, and in which nondramatic music works are performed publicly.

A "food service or drinking establishment" is a restaurant, inn, bar, tavern, or any similar place of business in which the public or patrons assemble for the primary purpose of being served food or drink, in which the majority of the gross square feet of space that is nonresidential is used for that purpose, and in which nondramatic music works are performed publicly.

The "gross square feet of space" of an establishment means the entire interior space of that establishment and any adjoining outdoor space used to serve patrons, whether on a seasonal basis or otherwise.

A "performing rights society" is an association, corporation, or other entity that licenses the public performance of nondramatic musical works on behalf of copyright owners of such works, such as the American Society of Composers, Authors and Publishers (ASCAP), Broadcast Music, Inc. (BMI), and SESAC, Inc.

A "proprietor" is an individual, corporation, partnership, or other entity, as the case may be, that owns an establishment or a food service or drinking establishment, except that no owner or operator of a radio or television station licensed by the Federal Communications Commission, cable system or satellite carrier, cable or satellite carrier service or programmer, provider of online services or network access or the operator of facilities therefor, telecommunications company, or any other such audio or audiovisual service or programmer now known or as may be developed in the future, commercial subscription music service, or owner or operator of any other transmission service, shall under any circumstances be deemed to be a proprietor.

TERM OF THE COPYRIGHT

Time is an illusion, lunchtime doubly so.
—DOUGLAS ADAMS

Under the Copyright Act of 1909, the term of copyright ran for an initial period of 28 years with one 28-year renewal. Originally, under Section 302 of the 1976 Act the term of copyright was as follows:

- Where the actual creator is known and deemed to be the author, the term is the life of the author and 50 years after the author's death (known as "life plus fifty" [Section 302(a)].

- Where there are two or more authors, the period runs for the life of the last surviving author plus 50 years [Section 302(b)].

- Where the author(s) were anonymous or chose to hide behind a pseudonym, or where the work was written as a work for hire, the term is the earlier of either 75 years from its first publication or 100 years from its creation [Section 302(c)].

- In the case of anonymous works and pseudonymous works, if at any time the name or names of the author(s) became known through registration with the Copyright Office, the period set forth in either Section 302(a) or 302(b) will apply to the copyright.

- After a period of 75 years from the year of first publication of a work or a period of 100 years from the year of creation, whichever expires first, if the Copyright Office provides a certified report that records disclose nothing to indicate that the author is living, or died less than 50 years before, anyone is entitled to the presumption that the author has been dead for at least 50 years [Section 302(e)].

On October 27, 1998, what is officially known as the Sonny Bono Copyright Term Extension Act was signed into law. This act tacked an additional 20 years onto each of the periods set forth in Section 302. The revised provisions of Section 302 read as follows:

(a) IN GENERAL.—Copyright in a work created on or after January 1, 1978, subsists from its creation and, except as provided by the following subsections, endures for a term consisting of the life of the author and 70 years after the author's death.

(b) JOINT WORKS.—In the case of a joint work prepared by two or more authors who did not work for hire, the copyright endures for a term consisting of the life of the last surviving author and 70 years after such last surviving author's death.

(c) ANONYMOUS WORKS, PSEUDONYMOUS WORKS, AND WORKS MADE FOR HIRE.—In the case of an anonymous work, a pseudonymous work, or a work made for hire, the copyright endures for a term of 95 years from the year of its first publication, or a term of 120 years from the year of its creation, whichever expires first. If, before the end of such term, the identity of one or more of the authors of an anonymous or pseudonymous work is revealed in the records of a registration made for that work under subsections (a) or (d) of section 408, or in the records provided by this subsection, the copyright in the work endures for the term specified by subsection (a) or (b), based on the life of the author or authors whose identity has been revealed. Any person having an interest in the copyright in an anonymous or pseudonymous work may at any time record, in records to be maintained by the Copyright Office for that purpose, a statement identifying one or more authors of the work; the statement shall also identify the person filing it, the nature of that person's interest, the source of the information recorded, and the particular work affected, and shall comply in form and content with requirements that the Register of Copyrights shall prescribe by regulation.

Because the initial period of copyright for so many works depends on the date of the author's death, U.S. copyright law is very specific on procedures to be followed in establishing that date. Section 302(d) states how any person with an interest in a copyright should go about recording with the Copyright Office evidence of an author's death (or continuing existence) on a particular date.

With regard to those musical compositions which were created prior to 1978, the maximum period of protection under the 1976 Act was 75 years. Many songs which might have slipped into the public domain under the 1909 Act were given extensions until the new act became effective and granted them continued protection. The 1976 Act granted these works an additional 19 years which, when added to the two 28-year terms, gave them a maximum of 75 years of copyright protection. In June of 1992 the Copyright Amendment Act of 1991, providing for an automatic copyright renewal term of 47 years for all copyrights originally copyrighted during the period 1963 through 1977 and still in their first 28-year period of protection under the 1909 Act, was signed into law. The 1998 amendment generally increased the period of protection of those recordings by an additional 20 years.

AUDIO HOME RECORDING ACT

> *It's nothing but rooms.*
>
> **—YOGI BERRA, on his new house**

In 1994 the Audio Home Recording Act was passed by Congress and signed into law. The purpose of the Act is, theoretically, to protect copyright owners from the duplication of their copyrighted works without compensation. Note that the Audio Home Recording Act has nothing to do with the compulsory licensing statutes, which deal with specific pieces of music being recorded. The Audio Home Recording Act deals with the home duplication of preexisting recordings.

With the advent of DAT technology it became possible for anyone with relatively inexpensive equipment to make digital reproductions of sound recordings that were of master quality. This technology opened the door to unrestricted duplication of recordings that could seriously cut into the earnings of performers, publishers, songwriters, record companies, producers, etc. Since it was practically and politically impossible to stop home duplication, another method was needed to provide compensation for lost sales. The answer was the Audio Home Recording Act, which was added to the Copyright Act as Chapter 10.

The Audio Home Recording Act requires manufacturers and importers to pay into a special fund a royalty on the sale of digital recorders and blank digital tapes, discs, or whatever. The royalty on the sale of digital recorders consists of 2% of "transfer price," or the value set for customs.

Section 1001 defines transfer price as follows:

> (12) The "transfer price" of a digital audio recording device or a digital audio recording medium—
>
> (A) is, subject to subparagraph (B)—
>
> (i) in the case of an imported product, the actual entered value at United States Customs (exclusive of any freight, insurance, and applicable duty), and
>
> (ii) in the case of a domestic product, the manufacturer's transfer price (FOB the manufacturer, and exclusive of any direct sales taxes or excise taxes incurred in connection with the sale); and
>
> (B) shall, in a case in which the transferor and transferee are related entities or within a single entity, not be less than a reasonable arms-length price under the principles of the regulations adopted pursuant to section 482 of the Internal Revenue Code of 1986, or any successor provision to such section.

The royalty is provided for in Section 1004(a)(3). There is a minimum $1 payment and maximum $8 payment per machine; if a machine has two or more digital recorders, the maximum royalty moves up to $12. The royalty for blank recording materials is 3% of the wholesale price. There is language included in Section 1004(a)(3) which allows for an increase in the royalty rate:

> ... During the 6th year after the effective date of this chapter, and not more than once each year thereafter, any interested copyright party may petition the Librarian of Congress[25] to increase the royalty maximum and, if more than 20 percent of the royalty payments are at the relevant royalty maximum, the Librarian of Congress shall prospectively increase such royalty maximum with the goal of having no more than 10 percent of such payments at the new royalty maximum; however the amount of any such increase as a percentage of the royalty maximum shall in no event exceed the percentage increase in the Consumer Price Index during the period under review.

The foregoing language is one of the most convoluted formulas squeezed into the fewest words it has been my misfortune to decipher. I know what it means, but I know if I try to explain it I will not only confuse you, but also confuse myself. Someday when I'm looking for some form of self-

---

[25]Miss Marion, the Librarian of Congress, has been substituted throughout the Copyright Act for the late lamented Copyright Royalty Tribunal, R.I.P.

punishment for some heinous act I've committed, I'm going to look up the committee report to try to figure out how in the hell Congress came up with this formula.

The monies collected from these sales of both hardware and software are to be collected by the Copyright Office and then to be distributed. The royalty payments once collected are put into two different funds: the Sound Recordings Fund and the Music Works Fund. The royalties collected are distributed to the two funds—two-thirds to the Sound Recording Fund and one-third to the Musical Works Fund. The royalties are allocated pursuant to Sections 1006(b) and (c) as follows:

(b) ALLOCATION OF ROYALTY PAYMENTS TO GROUPS.—The royalty payments shall be divided into 2 funds as follows:

(1) THE SOUND RECORDINGS FUND.—66 2/3 percent of the royalty payments shall be allocated to the Sound Recordings Fund. 2 5/8 percent of the royalty payments allocated to the Sound Recordings Fund shall be placed in an escrow account managed by an independent administrator jointly appointed by the interested copyright parties described in section 1001(7)(A) and the American Federation of Musicians (or any successor entity) to be distributed to nonfeatured musicians (whether or not members of the American Federation of Musicians or any successor entity) who have performed on sound recordings distributed in the United States. 1 3/8 percent of the royalty payments allocated to the Sound Recordings Fund shall be placed in an escrow account managed by an independent administrator jointly appointed by the interested copyright parties described in section 1001(7)(A) and the American Federation of Television and Radio Artists (or any successor entity) to be distributed to nonfeatured vocalists (whether or not members of the American Federation of Television and Radio Artists or any successor entity) who have performed on sound recordings distributed in the United States. 40 percent of the remaining royalty payments in the Sound Recordings Fund shall be distributed to the interested copyright parties described in section 1001(7)(C), and 60 percent of such remaining royalty payments shall be distributed to the interested copyright parties described in section 1001(7)(A).

(2) THE MUSICAL WORKS FUND.—

(A) 33 1/3 percent of the royalty payments shall be allocated to the Musical Works Fund for distribution to interested copyright parties described in section 1001(7)(B).

(B)(i) Music publishers shall be entitled to 50 percent of the royalty payments allocated to the Musical Works Fund.

(ii) Writers shall be entitled to the other 50 percent of the royalty payments allocated to the Musical Works Fund.

(c) ALLOCATION OF ROYALTY PAYMENTS WITHIN GROUPS.—If all interested copyright parties within a group specified in subsection (b) do not agree on a voluntary proposal for the distribution of the royalty payments within each group, the Librarian of Congress shall convene a copyright arbitration royalty panel which shall, pursuant to the procedures specified under section 1007(c), allocate royalty payments under this section based on the extent to which, during the relevant period—

(1) for the Sound Recordings Fund, each sound recording was distributed in the form of digital musical recordings or analog musical recordings; and

(2) for the Musical Works Fund, each musical work was distributed in the form of

digital musical recordings or analog musical recordings or disseminated to the public in transmissions.

Similar laws have existed for years in many foreign countries.

WORK FOR HIRE

Hard work is damn near as overrated as monogamy.

—HUEY LONG

The concept of a *work for hire* is very important in the music industry. As discussed in several earlier sections, most recording agreements contain an acknowledgment that the masters which are recorded pursuant to the agreement are works for hire. In addition, in an exclusive songwriter's agreement, the work created by the songwriter is a work for hire, whereby the employer (the music publisher) becomes the author for copyright purposes. Once an agreement has specified that a work is a work for hire, the employer/author owns the copyright. There is no right of reversion to the employee because, under copyright law, the employee was *never* the author. If the employee is ever granted ownership of the copyright, it must be done by assignment.

The status of a work as a work for hire also affects the term of the life of the copyright. A work having the artist as "author" has a term of copyright which extends from the moment of creation to 70 years after the death of the author. A work created by an employer as a work for hire has a term equal to the earlier of 120 years from creation or 95 years from first publication.

Unless a work is created by "an employee within the scope of his or her employment," which, in the case of the agreements we are interested in, is hardly ever the case, there must be a written agreement in order for the work to be considered a work for hire. Sections 201(b) and 101 are quite clear about this:

> (b). . . In the case of a work made for hire, the employer or other person for whom the work was prepared is considered the author for purposes of this title, and, unless the parties have expressly agreed otherwise in a written instrument signed by them, owns all of the rights comprised in the copyright.

I happen to believe that the condition of a written contract implicitly makes the execution of the written agreement a precondition of creating a work for hire. That is, since the copyright exists at the moment of creation of a work, anything signed after that is too late for the work to qualify as a work for hire. At best, it would be an implied assignment after the fact of creation.

Without a written agreement, the would-be employer has to rely on the work being created "within the scope of . . . employment." The 1976 Copyright Act does not define "scope of his or her employment," nor does it define "employee." This failure to define these terms has led to various interpretations of the concept by different courts. In 1989, the U.S. Supreme Court, in *Community for Creative Non-Violence v. Reid*,[26] decided that Congress had intended the 1976 Act references to "scope of employment" and "employee" to be read in the context of traditional legal concepts of agency. In other words, the same sort of checklist used to determine whether someone is an em-

---

[26]109 S.Ct. 2166 (1989).

ployee or an independent contractor is used to determine if the creator is an employee for copyright purposes.

At page 2178, the court stated it this way:

> In determining whether a hired party is an employee under the general common law of agency, we consider the hiring party's right to control the manner and means by which the product is accomplished. Among the other factors relevant to this inquiry are the skill required; the source of the instrumentalities and tools; the location of the work; the duration of the relationship between the parties; whether the hiring party has the right to assign additional projects to the hired party; the extent of the hired party's discretion over when and how to work; the method of payment; the hire party's role in hiring and paying assistants; whether the work is part of the regular business of the hiring party; whether the hiring party is in business; the provision of employee benefits; and the tax treatment of the hired party. . . . No one of these factors is determinative.

Accordingly, using the above determining factors, if the employee/author of a work is determined to be an "employee," the resulting work is a work for hire with the employer being the "author" pursuant to the first paragraph of the definition of work for hire in Section 101. If, on the other hand, the employee/author is not determined to be an "employee" the employer must rely on the second paragraph of the definition to establish that the work was a work for hire. Note that if the second paragraph is relied upon, it is necessary that "the parties expressly agree in a written instrument signed by them that the work shall be considered a work made for hire" in order for the work to qualify.

In *Hi-Tech Video Prods. v. Capital Cities/ABC*,[27] the court held that a video was not a work made for hire and invalidated the copyright which had been registered as a work made for hire because the plaintiff had no written agreement with the creators that the video would be a work for hire. Plaintiff was unable to prove that the individuals were employees rather than independent contractors and lost the copyright in the video.

Care should be taken in all instances where copyrights are being created that the intended author ends up as the registered author for copyright purposes.

Although it is of no particular importance to our review here, a case which deserves at least passing reference is *Urantia Foundation v. Maaherra*,[28] which dealt with the question of who, if anyone, was the author of a book created in the 1920s and 1930s. Supposedly the book was authored by "spiritual entities" speaking through a psychiatric patient who wrote answers to questions posed by a psychiatrist. (Is this a great country or is this a great country!) The psychiatrist formed a foundation and published the book in the 1950s with the foundation as the "author" and renewed the copyright in 1983 with the foundation as the "proprietor" of a work made for hire. The foundation argued that the book was a work for hire because the [loony] psychiatric patient was a "mere scribe" who contributed no copyrightable authorship to the work and that those who asked the questions were employees of the foundation. The court wasn't buying this and held the book could not be a work for hire as there was no employment relationship between the patient and the doctor.

---

[27]58 F.3d 1093 (6th Cir. 1995).

[28]895 F.Supp. 1347 (D. Ariz. 1995).

My thoughts, unfortunately, were not solicited by the court, which, I feel, missed the point entirely. The important question here is not the employment status between the patient and the doctor. Hey, guys! What about the spiritual entities? Who employed them? If this had been a post-1978 work authored by "spiritual entities," would one have to backdate the life-plus-50 or even 70 years for the term of the copyright? As a post-1978 work, do we not face the possibility that the copyright on this work had already expired before it was written?

There is more to this copyright stuff than is written in your books!

SAMPLING

The wages of sin aren't what they used to be.

—ORSON WELLES

Sampling, the process of "borrowing" sounds (including, frequently, copyrighted music, lyrics, and/or sound recordings), has been found to be a copyright infringement. In my opinion (and the opinion of many others, though not that of the people doing the borrowing who had the nerve to claim it *wasn't* an infringement), it took a damnably long time for sampling to be held to be an infringement.

The first case of any significance is *Grand Upright Music Limited v. Warner Brothers Records, Inc., Marcel Hall, professionally known as Biz Markie, Biz Markie Productions, Inc., Cool V Productions, Inc., Cold Chillin' Records, Inc., Biz Markie Music, Inc., Cold Chillin' Music Publishing, Inc., Tyrone Williams, and Benny Medina.*[29] In a Memorandum & Order granting an order for preliminary injunction, dated December 16, 1991, the judge was quite adamant that the use of *three words* of the Gilbert O'Sullivan recording and composition "Alone Again (Naturally)" was a copyright infringement.

On page 1 of his opening statement the judge said:

> "Thou shalt not steal" [footnoting Exodus, Chapter 20: Verse 15] has been an admonition followed since the dawn of civilization. Unfortunately, in the modern world of business this admonition is not always followed. Indeed, the defendants in this action for copyright infringement would have this court believe that stealing is rampant in the music business and, for that reason, their conduct here should be excused. The conduct of the defendants herein, however, violates not only the Seventh Commandment, but also the copyright laws of this country.

At page 7 (and including a footnote on that page) the judge pounded some more nails in that coffin lid:

> From all the evidence produced in the hearing, it is clear that the defendants knew they were violating the plaintiff's rights as well as the rights of others. Their only aim was to sell thousands upon thousands of records. [See below for the footnote which appears at this place.] This callous disregard for the law and the rights of others requires not only the preliminary injunction sought by the plaintiff but also sterner measures.

[29]U.S. District Court, Southern District of New York.

The footnote, pounding even more nails into that sucker, reads:

> [2]The argument suggested by the defendants that they should be excused because others in the "rap music" business are also engaged in illegal activity is totally specious. The mere statement of the argument is its own refutation.

If you haven't yet gotten the drift of the judge's opinion on this, let's forget pounding nails and just drive a stake through the culprit's heart with the judge's closing sentence, at pages 7 and 8:

> This matter is respectfully referred to the United States Attorney for the Southern District of New York for consideration of [criminal] prosecution. . . .

I think that about does it.

TRANSFER OF COPYRIGHT

We make a living by what we get, we make a life by what we give.
—WINSTON CHURCHILL

The Copyright Act of 1976 provides that ownership of a copyright shall vest in the author initially. In the case of a work made for hire, the copyright is owned by the person for whom the work was prepared. As discussed above, copyrights can be divided up into many parts, and each of those parts may be licensed or transferred separately. Generally, the transfer of a copyright will be done pursuant to an *assignment*. That assignment, in order to be valid, must be in writing. The requirements for a valid transfer of ownership in a copyright are set forth in Section 204 of the Act:

> (a) A transfer of copyright ownership, other than by operation of law, is not valid unless an instrument of conveyance, or a note or memorandum of the transfer, is in writing and signed by the owner of the rights conveyed or such owner's duly authorized agent.
> (b) A certificate of acknowledgment is not required for the validity of a transfer, but is prima facie evidence of the execution of the transfer if—
>> (1) in the case of a transfer executed in the United States, the certificate is issued by a person authorized to administer oaths within the United States; or
>> (2) in the case of a transfer executed by a foreign country, the certificate is issued by a diplomatic or consular officer of the United States, or by a person authorized to administer oaths whose authority is proved by a certificate of such an officer.

Getting the transfer notarized is a good idea. Getting it notarized is *prima facie*—self-evident— evidence of the validity of the transfer.

In a case dealing with the requirements for transfer of copyright ownership, *Papa's-June Music, Inc. v. McLean*,[30] the U.S. district court dismissed Harry Connick, Jr.'s complaint against his co-composer of songs on Connick's 1994 album *She*, in which Connick maintained that McLean was to receive only a 30% share of income. The court held that absent a specific written instrument to the contrary, McLean was entitled to a 50% share.

---

[30]921 F.Supp. 1154 (S.D.N.Y., 1996).

Connick had argued that there had been written agreements on two previous albums they had co-written which called for McLean to receive a 30% share. On the *She* album, McLean maintained that he had demanded a different royalty arrangement, and that there was no written agreement between the parties to the contrary. Connick argued that two royalty checks based on the 30% royalty calculation cashed by McLean constituted an appropriate "writing" to transfer the copyright interest because the royalty statements which accompanied the checks stated that the royalty calculation was based upon 30%.

The court rejected this argument, stating that there was a disagreement between the parties at the time the checks were endorsed and that the royalty notations on the accompanying statements indicated nothing more than a calculation of royalties. The court ruled that under Section 204 any writing purporting to transfer a copyright interest must show a clear and unambiguous transfer of the copyright interest.

In Section 205, the Act sets forth all of the requirements, effects, and results of the recording of transfers of copyrights:

> (a) . . . Any transfer of copyright ownership or other document pertaining to a copyright may be recorded in the Copyright Office if the document filed for recordation bears the actual signature of the person who executed it, or if it is accompanied by a sworn or official certification that it is a true copy of the original, signed document.

Frequently, it has been the habit of lawyers drafting transfers of copyrights to prepare an attached *short form* of assignment to the agreement, usually in the form of an exhibit or schedule. This short-form assignment avoids having to file a copy of the agreement with the Copyright Office, which would make the document a matter of public record. It has been suggested, however, that if the transfer takes place in the agreement and not in the short-form assignment, there may not be a proper recording of the transfer of copyright. To avoid this possible problem without publishing private documents for the world to see, it would appear sufficient to provide language in the agreement specifying that the transfer takes place in the short-form assignment itself, not in the agreement.

CHAPTER 21

THE DIGITAL MILLENNIUM COPYRIGHT ACT

There are two kinds of fool. One says, "This is old, and therefore good."
And one says, "This is new, and therefore better."

—JOHN BRUNNER

By all rights, this chapter should be folded into the chapter on copyright. After all, the Digital Millennium Copyright Act is a *copyright act* and is incorporated into the Copyright Act of 1976. It does, however, deserve its very own chapter as it is central to a major shift in the record business. The arrival of the digital download has changed the nature of the business more than any other single event in its relatively short history. Indeed, it has undoubtedly sounded the death knell of the preexisting business models for the recording portion of the music industry.

The question is, Is this change the equivalent of the meteor which struck the earth and wiped out the dinosaurs (bad for the dinosaurs, pretty good for small mammals) or the advent of the Gutenberg Bible (bad for monk illustrators, pretty good for readers)? Actually, both may be correct; it depends on who gets to play the roles of dinosaur/monk illustrators and who gets to play the roles of small mammal/readers.

Virtually from day one, the music business has been challenged by new technology: Mozart had to shift from harpsichords to those newfangled pianos; sheet music sales were threatened by player pianos (see page 512); the 33⅓-rpm album and the 45-rpm single were resisted by backers of 78-rpm records; etc. These changes seem pretty mundane today, but in their time this was major stuff. Sometimes these shifts were welcomed with mostly open arms: Switching from vinyl records to CDs saved the record industry from a major financial disaster. Labels were able to recycle their existing catalogues with relatively minor expenditures (digital remastering and shrinking the artwork for album covers), and the public almost overnight started to replace their existing vinyl or tape record collections with CDs. It was heaven on earth for record labels. Of course, every silver cloud has a dark lining. With the switch over to digital, every copy was a master. With every copy a master, copies could be made without being second-generation, or even first-generation copies. Then, of course, along came the Internet.

The Digital Millennium Copyright Act (DMCA) is, in its essentials, very copyright-owner–friendly. If it could be condensed into one short statement, that statement would be: "It's illegal to copy protected content unless you have permission." While this is not a startling revelation, nor does it stray from existing concepts of copyright, the details have given computer techies the heebie-jeebies from day one.

GETTING INTO THE ACT

*Only one thing is impossible for God: to find any sense
in any copyright law on the planet.*

—MARK TWAIN

The DMCA was signed into law in October, 1998. It's creation was spurred on by the necessity of dealing with the Internet and to bring American copyright law into alignment with the international treaty signed in 1996 at Geneva, the World Intellectual Property Organization (WIPO) Performances and Phonograms Treaty. On behalf of the signatory countries, WIPO administers international treaties dealing with intellectual property protection. Nearly 200 nations, including the United States, are signatories to WIPO.

With WIPO and other treaties, such as the Uruguay Round (which always sounded like some kind of fruit to me), the number of international intellectual property rights treaties reached some sort of critical mass, and the DMCA substitutes "international agreements" for preexisting references to individual treaties (e.g., the Berne Convention and the Universal Copyright Convention) and "treaty party" for any country, other than the United States, which is a signatory to any such treaty.

The DMCA was tacked onto the Copyright Act of 1976 as a new chapter, Chapter 12: Copyright Protection and Management Systems.

Section 1201: Circumvention of Copyright Protection Provisions

The DMCA prohibits "circumventing" software protection programs or, as they are quaintly known in the DMCA, "technological measures," in order to obtain access to copyrighted works. The dirty deed of getting around or past the firewall protecting a copyrighted work is, in and of itself, an illegal act, presumably whether or not the protected work is somehow accessed or copied. Further, no person shall "manufacture, import, offer to the public, provide, or otherwise traffic in any technology, product, service, device, or component, or part thereof, designed to circumvent protection programs."

The following sentence, the very first in a long section, is the key to this act. They might as well have called it: "Section Numero Uno!" This is it, baby! Don't pass through the protective shield. Don't steal protected copyrights.

> No person shall circumvent a technological measure that effectively controls access to a work protected under this title. . . . [Section 1201(a)(1)(A)]

The next sentence contains a reference to a 2-year waiting period—now long gone—before the provision was to take effect.

Subsequent provisions in Section 1201(a)(1) lay out exceptions to this prohibition that are, in concept, similar to the thinking behind the fair-use doctrine set forth in Section 107 of the Copyright Act, none of which have any particular bearing on our interests. These new provisions do not change any existing remedies for or defenses to copyright infringement. They do, however, set up new areas of potential liabilities where the traditional defenses against a claim of copyright infringement will not serve as a defense.

Subsection 1201(a)(3) offers two definitions that together elucidate what it means to "circumvent a technological measure" before laboriously working through details and exceptions to the prohibitions, none of which provide a safe harbor for the illegal downloading of recordings. The two definitions form a sort of yin and yang unitary whole: the negative—you may not access "without the authority of the copyright owner"—and the positive—you may access "with the authority of the copyright owner."

> (A) to "circumvent a technological measure" means to descramble a scrambled work, to decrypt an encrypted work, or otherwise to avoid, bypass, remove, deactivate, or impair a technological measure, without the authority of the copyright owner; and

> (B) a technological measure "effectively controls access to a work" if the measure, in the ordinary course of its operation, requires the application of information, or a process or a treatment, with the authority of the copyright owner, to gain access to the work.

Don't you just love "definitions" like these? Scramble/descramble. Encrypt/decrypt. What's next: do/undo, steal/desteal, jump/unjump? Then there's subsection (B); no sentence should have that many commas in it.

The DMCA does allow some "permitted" circumvention, including circumventing "cookies" to prevent "the collection or dissemination of personally identifying information about a natural person who seeks to gain access to the work protected, and is not in violation of any other law." [Section 1201(i)].

Section 1202: Integrity of Copyright Management Information

"Copyright management information" is a fancy way of saying the identification of the work, including copyright ownership, name of the "author," performers, etc. Section 1202 lays down the ground rules for what may and what need not be included when furnishing copyright management information. The "knowing" failure to list the information properly and/or to distribute misinformation for purposes of copyright infringement is a violation of the DMCA, whether or not there is an actual infringement. The first two subsections, Section 1202(a) and (b), are textbook examples of the classical definition of what elements make up a crime: first, the intent and, second, the physical act:

> (a) . . . No person shall knowingly and with the intent to induce, enable, facilitate, or conceal infringement—

> > (1) provide copyright management information that is false, or

> > (2) distribute or import for distribution copyright management information that is false.

> (b) . . . No person shall, without the authority of the copyright owner or the law—

> > (1) intentionally remove or alter any copyright management information,

> > (2) distribute or import for distribution copyright management information knowing that the copyright management information has been removed or altered without authority of the copyright owner or the law, or

> > (3) distribute, import for distribution, or publicly perform works, copies of works, or phonorecords, knowing that copyright management information has been removed or altered without authority of the copyright owner or the law, knowing, or, with respect to civil remedies under section 1203, having reasonable grounds to know, that it will induce, enable, facilitate, or conceal an infringement of any right under this title.

Subsection 1202(b), ending with the language "having reasonable grounds to know" for civil remedies under Section 1203 (discussed below), removes the requirement of "knowing intent" for civil actions. In other words, in order to be a crime, the "criminal" must have the actual intent to commit the act, whether or not the criminal knew it was an illegal act. If there was no intent, just dumb old negligence, there may be civil liability for the act (e.g., money damages), but not "criminal liability" (e.g., fines, the slammer, etc.).

As the excerpt below shows, the complete definition of "copyright management information" includes just about anything that gives identifying information about a work (title, ownership, author, etc.) other than "personally identifying information." "Personally identifying information" means "cookies" (see the reference to Section 1201(i), above) and the circumvention of cookies which collect and share personal information about online habits of the computer's users.

(c) ... As used in this section, the term "copyright management information" means any of the following information conveyed in connection with copies or phonorecords of a work or performances or displays of a work, including in digital form, except that such term does not include any personally identifying information about a user of a work or of a copy, phonorecord, performance, or display of a work:

(1) The title and other information identifying the work, including the information set forth on a notice of copyright.

(2) The name of, and other identifying information about, the author of a work.

(3) The name of, and other identifying information about, the copyright owner of the work, including the information set forth in a notice of copyright.

(4) With the exception of public performances of works by radio and television broadcast stations, the name of, and other identifying information about, a performer whose performance is fixed in a work other than an audiovisual work.

(5) With the exception of public performances of works by radio and television broadcast stations, in the case of an audiovisual work, the name of, and other identifying information about, a writer, performer, or director who is credited in the audiovisual work.

(6) Terms and conditions for use of the work.

(7) Identifying numbers or symbols referring to such information or links to such information.

(8) Such other information as the Register of Copyrights may prescribe by regulation, except that the Register of Copyrights may not require the provision of any information concerning the user of a copyrighted work.

On the face of it, the application of this provision seems rather problematic in that it doesn't appear that the copyright management information need be "conveyed," only that it should not be conveyed incorrectly. The fact is that the framers of the DMCA, using the same concepts that allow our forward-looking Congress to put off the responsibility for paying national debts to our great grandchildren who aren't even a gleam in the eyes of our yet-unborn grandchildren, shoved this matter off into an indeterminate future. This is revealed "downline" in subparagraphs 1201(e)(2)(A) and (B).

(A) *If* [emphasis added] a digital transmission standard for the placement of copyright management information for a category of works is set in a voluntary, consensus standard-setting process involving a representative cross-section of broadcast stations or cable systems and copyright owners of a category of works that are intended for public performance by such stations or systems. . . ."

(B) *Until* [emphasis added] a digital transmission standard has been set pursuant to subparagraph (A) with respect to the placement of copyright management information for a category or works. . . .

Until, and *if*, that standard is determined, who cares?

Section 1203: Civil Remedies

The DMCA does provide for civil remedies in Section 1203 ("stop that!" and/or pay damages) and criminal remedies in Section 1204 ("stop that!" and/or pay penalties and/or visit the slammer) for violations of the provisions of Sections 1201 and 1202. The possible civil remedies include:

- Injunctions, temporary or permanent [Section 1203(b)(1)]

- Impounding [Section 1203(b)(2)]

- Damages [Section 1203(b)(3); these are listed below]

- Recovery of costs [Section 1203(b)(4)]

- Reasonable attorney's fees [Section 1203(b)(5)]

- Destruction . . . "of any device or product involved in the violation" [Section 1203(b)(6)]

I don't know about you, but, for me, the last item conjures up the vision of superheroes in capes and leotards issuing forth from the Copyright Office destroying offending devices for the sake of democracy. For those of you silly enough to consider a career in the law, fantasizing about goofy scenarios like this is one of the ways to maintain your sanity when studying laws.

Following are excerpts from Section 1203.

(c) AWARD OF DAMAGES—

(1) IN GENERAL—Except as otherwise provided in this title, a person committing a violation of section 1201 or 1202 is liable for either—

(A) the actual damages and any additional profits of the violator, as provided in paragraph (2), *or* [emphasis added; one isn't liable for both]

(B) statutory damages, as provided in paragraph (3).

(2) ACTUAL DAMAGES—The court shall award to the complaining party the actual damages suffered by the party as a result of the violation, and any profits of the violator that are attributable to the violation and are not taken into account in computing the actual damages, if the complaining party elects such damages at any time before final judgment is entered.

(3) STATUTORY DAMAGES—

(A) At any time before final judgment is entered, a complaining party may elect to recover an award of statutory damages for each violation of section 1201 in the sum of not less than $200 or more than $2,500 per act of circumvention, device, product, component, offer, or performance of service, as the court considers just.

(B) At any time before final judgment is entered, a complaining party may elect to recover an award of statutory damages for each violation of section 1202 in the sum of not less than $2,500 or more than $25,000.

(4) REPEATED VIOLATIONS—In any case in which the injured party sustains the burden of proving, and the court finds, that a person has violated section 1201 or 1202 within 3 years after a final judgment was entered against the person for another such violation, the court may increase the award of damages up to triple the amount that would otherwise be awarded, as the court considers just.

(5) INNOCENT VIOLATIONS—

(A) IN GENERAL—The court in its discretion may reduce or remit the total award of damages in any case in which the violator sustains the burden of proving, and the court finds, that the violator was not aware and had no reason to believe that its acts constituted a violation.

(B) Nonprofit Library, Archives, Or Educational Institutions—In the case of a nonprofit library, archives, or educational institution, the court shall remit damages in any case in which the library, archives, or educational institution sustains the burden of proving, and the court finds, that the library, archives, or educational institution was not aware and had no reason to believe that its acts constituted a violation.

Two things about these provisions jump out at me. First, consider that *each* single violation under 1203(c)(3)(A) and (B) has a minimum award of $200 up to $2,500 for violating Section 1201 and a minimum award of $2,500 up to $25,000 for each violation of Section 1202. It sure wouldn't take long for those babies to add up! Second, the language in subparagraph (4) is a perfect example of fuzzy drafting. I can read it in about five different ways, more if I start running through the different combinations: (1) the violator violated rights of the same person more than once, or (2) any person, with the increase of the (3) old award, or (4) just the new award, or, perhaps, (5) both the old and the new award. At a possible $75,000 a pop, at the extreme, this can get very nasty for the habitual violator. That's why courts get called into the act to tell us what these laws mean.

For those dear readers of a criminal bent, be warned that any person who violates Section 1201 or Section 1202 for the willful "purposes of commercial advantage or private financial gain" may be whacked financially and may also do time.

Section 1204: Criminal Offenses and Penalties

As you read the provisions below, keep in mind that criminal masterminds caught with their hands in the digital cookie jar will probably also be hit with the top civil awards, $2,500 for violations of Section 1201 and $25,000 for violation of Section 1202—not to mention triple those awards for repeat offenders.

(a) IN GENERAL— Any person who violates section 1201 or 1202 willfully and for purposes of commercial advantage or private financial gain—

(1) shall be fined not more than $500,000 or imprisoned for not more than 5 years, or both, for the first offense; and

(2) shall be fined not more than $1,000,000 or imprisoned for not more than 10 years, or both, for any subsequent offense.

In September of 2003, the first person was found guilty by a jury of digital piracy under the DMCA for selling hardware to illegally tap into DirecTV satellite broadcasts. He was found guilty of one count of conspiracy, two counts of selling unlawful hardware designed to decrypt satellite broadcasts, and three counts of violating the DMCA. With the conviction he could have received a sentence of up to 30 years in the federal pokey and criminal fines of up to $2.75 million.

FILE SHARING

The issue in the DMCA with the most impact on the public is the downloading of music, whether with or without authority, and sharing those downloads. Certain existing defenses to claims of copyright infringement had to be "adjusted" in the DMCA to deal with file sharing. Section 109 of the Copyright Act of 1976 established by statute what is commonly known as the "first-sale doctrine" which can be summed up with the simple statement that when you buy a copy of a copyrighted work, say a CD, it is not a copyright infringement to resell the physical copy.

There are, however, ground rules for such sales. Sections 109(a), (b), and (c) all specify that the phonorecord or copy be a "particular" one—not just any old copy or one you burned, but the one you bought. Section 109 also reminds us that the phonorecord or copy must be "lawfully made"—you can't sell a copy that was "unlawfully made" and rely on the first-sale doctrine to protect you.

One of the aims of the DMCA was to develop a statutory first-sale doctrine specifically for digital downloads." Conceptually and traditionally, the first-sale doctrine always dealt with physical copies—CD, book, painting, etc. But what's a copyright owner to do when there isn't a physical copy? Since a digital download is nothing but a collection of 0s and 1s floating around in the ether (sounds like the beginning of a really bad blues song), there is no physical copy. That is, there is no physical copy until the download is copied onto a diskette or loaded on the hard drive of a computer. At this point, however, the downloader has passed beyond the realm of a first sale since the downloaded copy is a "reproduction" not the original copy. The first-sale doctrine has always been based on the concept that the particular original copy moves from one person to another, leaving the person who transferred the original copy without that copy. When sending a copy, even if the sender removed the file, the doctrine would not be a valid defense because the new copy would be exactly that: "new." A reproduction.

The question of fair use (see "Fair Use" in the previous chapter, pages 504–507) also comes into play in considering possible violations of the DMCA by file sharing. With the Internet crossing international borders (your online tech support may come from next door or from India, online gambling casinos are generally ensconced in friendly off-shore island nations, etc.), possible copyright infringements and the defense of fair use may have different ingredients in different jurisdictions. The DMCA was created to incorporate international treaties into the Copyright Act of 1976, but there are still important differences from country to country.

Indeed, file sharing and burning copies are actually much more common outside of the United States. For example, in terms of the percentage drop in sales of CDs because of downloading and burning copies, the drop in Germany has been almost double the drop here in the United States for the same period. The number of burned copies of CDs being sold commercially overseas is staggering. At last report, in China 9 out of every 10 CDs that are sold are pirated counterfeits. One friend of mine, visiting Thailand, was able to buy a DVD copy of a major motion picture for the equivalent of $2 from a street vender days before its first commercial release in the theaters anywhere in the world! In those countries lagging behind the United States in "illegal" downloading, the lag is not the result of greater moral turpitude but of scarcity of broadband access.

Peer-to-peer (know affectionately as "P2P") file sharing opens up (to mix a metaphor) a Pandora's box of worms in the ongoing battle to restrict illegal file sharing. P2P file sharing is a system where users can exchange files through the Internet either directly or through a server. If the server can control the content being shared by the users, the server can be held responsible for copyright infringement. If the server cannot control the content being shared, the server *probably* will escape responsibility for copyright infringement. I use the word "probably" because there is some fudge room on whether responsibility does or does not exist for the server.

Section 512 of the DMCA, which sets forth what are sometimes referred to as the safe-harbor provisions, provides the ground rules for determining whether or not the server will be caught with their hand in the cookie jar for copyright infringement if there is illegal file sharing. (I presume no one is going to use this book to set up a server system. If you've got the money and inclination to do that, go hire your own lawyer. I will spare you a long, detailed, and tedious discussion of Section 512. Unless you are a server, I don't think you care.)

After nailing Napster in its first go-round because it could control the content being shared, it got a little harder to nail servers with the coming of P2P sharing. With a wary eye on servers, the powers that be switched their gun sights to the individual users in order to staunch the flow of illegal file sharing. Under the No Electronic Theft Act (NETA), which became law at the end of 1997, reproducing and distributing copyrighted intellectual property (such as the sharing of music files) became not only a civil offense (which it already was) but also a criminal offense.

The NETA is one of those laws which was enacted to amend an existing law, our old friend the Copyright Act of 1976, and it has a lot of cross-referencing to sections in the existing law which are being amended. One of the changes was to amend subsection (a) of Section 506, "Criminal Offenses," to read as follows:

(a) CRIMINAL INFRINGEMENT—Any person who infringes a copyright willfully either—
(1) for purposes of commercial advantage or private financial gain, or
(2) by the reproduction or distribution, including by electronic means, during any 180-day period, of 1 or more copies or phonorecords of 1 or more copyrighted works, which have a total retail value of more than $1,000
shall be punished [as provided under Section 2319 of Title 18, United States Code, Criminal Infringement of a Copyright]. . . .

The No Electronic Theft Act defines "financial gain" as "receipt, or expectation of receipt, of anything of value, *including the receipt of other copyrighted works* [emphasis added]. If a user in any 180-day period (around 6 months) shares files of phonorecords with a retail value of $1,000.01 or more (that's approximately 56 albums at a suggested retail price of $18), the user can be charged with infringement.

In the spring of 2003, the RIAA began suing individual file sharers for copyright infringement. Since it was becoming increasingly difficult to hold servers responsible for illegal downloads, the logical way to put the fear of the RIAA in the end user was to sue the end user. This concept generated a great deal of ill will toward the record industry from end-user file sharers (along the lines of "how dare they sue me for stealing their music without paying for it"), but it also led to a decrease in the number of unauthorized file sharers. According to a study by the Pew Internet Project, the number of people pirating music did drop by half, from 35 million to 18 million. Many end users, figuring that the odds of being picked out individually for suit was somewhere between the odds of being struck by lightning and by a meteor, continued on their merry way down the infringement trail.

For the foreseeable future this battle between copyright owners and end users will continue. At the end of 2004 the motion picture industry followed the lead of the RIAA and began pursuing individuals who download films. The IFPI (see page 414) also promised to follow RIAA's lead by suing individual file sharers throughout Europe.

This war, and the fortunes of the warring parties, seem to ebb and flow, sometimes on a daily basis. And so it goes—on and on. The whole thing seems reminiscent of trench warfare in World War I. First one side makes a little progress. Then the other side recaptures the field. There's lots of bluster, noise, and casualties, and when the smoke clears, neither side has won the day.

Contrary to those who say that downloading will ultimately lead to the demise of the record industry, there are those who argue that it has given new life to a flagging business by providing exposure to new artists and product which otherwise would have disappeared into obscurity and sending buyers into the stores to snap up the recordings. It is a fact, however, that in every year since 1996, traditional record sales have dropped. Time, as it usually does, will tell whether downloading will gloriously reinvent the record business or pull down the handle on the toilet the business currently finds itself in.

CHAPTER 22

PERSONAL MANAGERS

Perhaps I'm old and tired, but I always think that the chances of finding out what really is going on are so absurdly remote that the only thing to do is to say hang the sense of it and just keep yourself occupied.

—Douglas Adams
The Hitchhiker's Guide to the Galaxy

In any discussion of personal managers, it is important to understand the terminology. *Manager* and *personal manager* are, in the music industry, used interchangeably and have the same meaning. They are not to be confused with *agents*. Personal managers and agents perform two different functions and, at least in some jurisdictions, California especially, for a manager to cross the line into an agent's territory can cause serious problems for the manager.

California law becomes particularly important in this regard inasmuch as so much music business takes place in, or at least flows through, California. Sooner or later if one party or the other wishes to obtain the jurisdiction of California law to settle a dispute, it will probably be able to do so, even if the agreement itself expressly states that the law of another jurisdiction applies to the contract. Because California law can play such an important part in the relationship between artist and personal manager, notwithstanding the fact that other state laws may not be as strict (or, indeed, may contradict California law), special attention must be paid to the ground rules in California.

Sections 1700 through 1700.46 of the California Labor Code describe and define what we lovingly refer to as "agents":

> A talent agency is hereby defined to be a person or corporation who engages in the occupation of procuring, offering, promising, or attempting to procure employment or engagements for an Artist or Artists. Talent agencies may, in addition, counsel or direct artists in the development of their professional careers.

For the purpose of distinguishing agents from managers, the critical words in the definition are "who engages in the occupation of procuring, offering, promising, or attempting to procure employment or engagements. . . ." When push comes to shove, the rule of thumb is that when it comes to finding employment for artists, agents *can* and managers *cannot*!

Prior to January 1, 1983, any offer, promise, or attempt to obtain employment was enough, in the eyes of California law, to turn a manager into an agent. After January 1, 1983, an offer, promise, or attempt to obtain employment may or may not be enough, in the eyes of California law, to turn a manager into an agent. Confused? It gets worse, but more on all that later. What, you may ask, is the big deal about whether a person is an agent or a manager? It can make a big difference.

First of all, a manager is not required to be licensed to function; indeed, there is no license for a personal manager in California. An agent, on the other hand, is required to have a license. Section 1700.5 of the California Labor Code states, in part, that "No person shall engage in or carry on the occupation of a talent agency without first procuring a license therefor from the Labor Commissioner...." How does one obtain such a license? Pursuant to California Labor Code Section 1700.6:

A written application for a license shall be made to the Labor Commissioner in the form prescribed by him and shall state:

(a) The name and address of applicant.

(b) The street and number of the building or place where the business of the talent agency is to be conducted.

(c) The business or occupation engaged in by the applicant for at least two years immediately preceding the date of application.

(d) The names and addresses of all persons, except bona fide employees on stated salaries, financially interested, either as partners, associates or profit sharers, in the operation of the talent agency in question, together with the amount of their respective interests.

If the applicant is a corporation, the application must state the corporate name; the names, residential addresses, and telephone numbers of all officers of the corporation; the names of all persons exercising managing responsibility in the applicant or licensee's office; and the names and addresses of all persons having a financial interest of 10 percent or more in the business and the percentage of financial interest owned by such persons.

The application must be accompanied by affidavits from at least two reputable persons who have known, or been associated with, the applicant for 2 years. These reputable persons must be residents of the city or county in which the business of the talent agency is to be conducted. The affidavits must assert that the applicant is a person of good moral character or, in the case of a corporation, has a reputation for fair dealing. (Of course if you believe the stereotype, you may assert that "fair-dealing agent" is an oxymoron.) Section 1700.7 states that "[T]he Labor Commission may cause an investigation to be made as to the character and responsibility of the applicant and the premises designated...." I suppose this in and of itself may be a problem for some individuals.

The application requirements are somewhat tedious, but shouldn't, by themselves, keep a personal manager who wants to become a talent agency from doing so. There is, however, another requirement, which is set forth in Section 1700.23:

Every talent agency shall submit to the Labor Commissioner a form or forms of contract to be utilized by such talent agency in entering into written contracts with artists for the employment of the services of such talent agency by such artists, and secure the approval of the Labor Commissioner thereof. Such approval shall not be withheld as to any proposed form of contract unless such proposed form of contract is unfair, unjust and oppressive to the artist. Each such form of contract, except under the conditions specified in Section 1700.45 of this code [arbitration], shall contain an agreement by the talent agency to refer any controversy between the artist and the talent agency relating to the terms of the contract to the Labor Commissioner for adjustment. There shall be printed on the face of the contract in prominent type the following: "This talent agency is licensed by the Labor Commissioner of the State of California."

The Labor Commissioner will not approve a form of contract that contains anything which is "unfair, unjust and oppressive to the artist." Since history has shown us that in the eyes of the California labor commissioner, most personal managers' commissions are unfair, unjust, and certainly oppressive, most personal managers do not care to submit themselves to the scrutiny of the labor commissioner.

There is another issue which attracts the attention of a manager when considering the possibility of being licensed as an agent. In approving the form of contract for representation, one of the matters which is scrutinized by the California Labor Commission is the amount of compensation due the agent for such representation. Although there are certain circumstances which allow agents to collect in excess of 10%, in most instances agents are limited to 10%. Managers, on the other hand, have no legal restriction on the commissions to be charged to clients, and managers generally charge more than agents for their services.

And that isn't all. There is also a requirement that the approved form must have a provision, or provisions, allowing the artist to terminate the agreement if a specified amount of work has not been obtained within a 90-day period. This, you must understand, would cause a lot of sleepless nights for most, if not all, managers—especially since it is sometimes in the artist's best interest for a manager representing the client's career to turn down employment rather than take whatever happens to be offered. (I think of it this way: It is a manager's obligation to say "no" while it is an agent's obligation to say "yes.")

One consequence of the strict limitations on the manager's function in California law has been, in the past, the relative ease with which artists have been able to break their contracts with managers who were deemed to be in violation of the law. Read on.

MANAGER ACTING AS AGENT

> *I was never ruined but twice; once when I lost a lawsuit,*
> *and once when I won one.*
>
> —VOLTAIRE

In California case law, *the* case dealing with the question of whether a personal manager is really an "artists' manager," as agents were called at that time, is *Buchwald v. Superior Court* [254 C.A.2d 347 (1967)] and its follow-up case, *Buchwald v. Katz* [8 Cal.3rd 493 (1972)], which are known generally as "the Jefferson Airplane case(s)." Buchwald (Marty Balin) was a member of the rock group Jefferson Airplane. Each member of Jefferson Airplane had entered into individual "personal management" agreements with Matthew Katz. The agreements provided for Katz to receive a percentage of each member's earnings. The agreements also stated that Katz would not obtain bookings or employment for the group and that any disputes would be arbitrated in accordance with the rules of the American Arbitration Association.

Within a year the inevitable dispute arose and Katz commenced arbitration proceedings. (Katz, it must be noted, has an extensive history of litigation, including similar lawsuits with other San Francisco–based artists, including Moby Grape and It's A Beautiful Day.) The group retaliated by filing a petition with the Labor Commission claiming that Katz was in violation of the California Labor Code. They contended that the Labor Commission had sole jurisdiction over the matter because Katz was an unlicensed artists' manager [agent]. Katz challenged the jurisdiction of the Labor

Commission under the premise that he was a personal manager, not an unlicensed artists' manager. At this point, the group filed an action in the courts seeking a ruling that the Labor Commission had sole jurisdiction and an order to enjoin the arbitration proceedings. The court ruled against Jefferson Airplane and ordered the group to submit to arbitration and to desist from proceedings before the Labor Commission. Disappointed but still game, Jefferson Airplane filed an appeal, the *Buchwald v. Superior Court* case. In *Buchwald v. Superior Court* the court stated, at page 367:

> Since the clear object of the Act is to prevent improper persons from becoming artists' managers and to regulate such activity for the protection of the public, a contract between an unlicensed artists' manager and an Artist is void.

The court went on (still at page 367) to discuss Katz's contention that the Artists' Managers Act does not give the Labor Commissioner jurisdiction over an artists' manager who is not licensed as such by the commissioner:

> Admittedly Katz was not licensed as an artists' manager.
>
> The Act, section 1700.3, defines "licensee" as an "artists' manager who holds a valid, unrevoked, and unforfeited license.... " Section 1700.4 defines "artists' manager."...
>
> Certain sections ..., refer to licensee in such context that the word can reasonably apply only to a licensed artists' manager. Other sections ..., refer to artists' managers in such manner that they apply reasonably to both licensed and unlicensed artists' managers. The Act thus refers to and covers two classes of persons, "licensees" who are artists' managers with valid licenses, and "artists' managers" who may or may not be licensed.
>
> It would be unreasonable to construe the Act as applying only to licensed artists' managers, thus allowing an artists' manager, by nonsubmission to the licensing provisions of the Act, to exclude himself from its restrictions and regulations enacted in the public interest....
>
> We conclude that artists' managers (as defined by the Act), whether they be licensed or unlicensed, are bound and regulated by the Artists' Managers Act.

Katz had another contention. This one was that he was not subject to the Artists' Managers Act because he had a written contract with the members of the group which stated he was not an artists' manager. The court had no trouble with this, stating, at page 355:

> The Act gives the Labor Commissioner jurisdiction over those who are artists' managers in fact. The petition filed with the Labor Commissioner alleges facts which if true indicate that the written contracts were but subterfuges and that Katz had agreed to, and did, act as an artists' manager. Clearly the Act may not be circumvented by allowing language of the written contract to control—if Katz had in fact agreed to, and had acted as an artists' manager. The form of the transaction, rather than its substance would control.
>
> It is a fundamental principle of law that, in determining rights and obligations, substance prevails over form.
>
> The court, or as here, the Labor Commissioner, is free to search out illegality lying behind the form in which a transaction has been cast for the purpose of concealing such illegality.... "The court will look through provisions, valid on their face, and with the aid of parol evidence, determine that the contract is actually illegal or is a part of an illegal transaction"[citation omitted].

A more reader-friendly way of stating this legal principle is: If it looks like a duck, walks like a duck, and is generally seen in the company of ducks—it's a duck.

Katz's next, and equally unsuccessful, contention was that the Superior Court had jurisdiction rather than the Labor Commissioner. The court replied, at page 361, after a rather uninteresting discussion:

> We hold as to the cases of controversies arising under the Artists' Managers Act that the Labor Commissioner has original jurisdiction to hear and determine the same to the exclusion of the superior court, subject to an appeal within 10 days after determination, to the superior court where the same shall be heard de *novo.*

Katz had yet another contention: Since the Artists' Managers Act allows private arbitration and the contracts called for arbitration, the order for arbitration was proper. Again, no cigar. The court stated, at page 360:

> This argument overlooks the basic contention of petitioners that their agreement with Katz is wholly invalid because of his noncompliance with the Act. If the agreement is void no rights, including the claimed right to private arbitration, can be derived from it. . . .
>
> It seems clear that the power of the arbitrator to determine the rights of the parties is dependent upon the existence of a valid contract under which the rights might arise.

The court ordered that the Labor Commissioner had the exclusive right to determine whether he had jurisdiction over the dispute. As reported in the second case, *Buchwald v. Katz*, at pages 496–497:

> The Labor Commissioner, following an evidentiary hearing, found and concluded that: (1) The members of The Jefferson Airplane were "artists"; (2) Katz had in fact obtained employment and bookings for The Jefferson Airplane; (3) the contract provisions to the contrary were a subterfuge; Katz was an unlicensed artists' manager; and (4) the Labor Commissioner had jurisdiction over the controversy. Upon the merits, the Labor Commissioner made the following award: "That the management contracts between petitioners . . . and respondent MATTHEW KATZ, are void for failure of respondent to comply with Sections 1700 to 1700.46 of the Labor Code; that the publishing contracts between petitioners and respondents . . ., are void for failure of respondent to comply with Sections 1700 to 1700.46 of the Labor Code; that petitioners are not liable to respondent for any sums spent by respondent in furtherance of petitioners' musical careers; and that respondent pay to petitioners the sum of $49,004.88 heretofore received as commissions."

This case continued upon its merry way. Katz appealed the order of the Labor Commissioner to the Superior Court, which agreed to hear the case conditional upon Katz posting a bond for $49,500. Katz did not post the bond, claiming that it was unnecessary to the appeal of the Labor Commissioner's ruling. The Superior Court refused to hear his appeal. Katz then appealed the decision of the Superior Court and was partially successful in the *Buchwald v. Katz* case. The California Supreme Court reversed the Superior Court's decision that the bond was necessary to proceed with the appeal of the decision of the Labor Commissioner. It did, however, state that the bond was necessary to stay the execution of the dollar award.

In June 1987, almost 21 years after the first suit (there were actually three separate suits) was filed, the Honorable Ollie Marie-Victoire (you've gotta love a judge with a name like that) dismissed all the suits. The basic legal concept was that these damn things have been sitting around here for nearly 21 years just gathering dust and cobwebs with no significant action being taken. Get 'em out of here!

The motion for the dismissal was not brought by any of the parties, but by BMG and BMG Music, Inc. (formerly the RCA Records Division of RCA Corporation, and RCA, Inc., who were apparently tired of sitting on publishing royalties which had been tied up for so many years. The Honorable Ollie Marie-Victoire ordered BMG and BMG Music, Inc., to disburse the royalties being held to the applicable parties. On the Jefferson Airplane side, the various publishing companies received $1,353,378.28 for the period up to November 30, 1987, and, for Canada, up to September 30, 1987. For the same periods, Katz received $65,210.10 for publishing and $65,614.94 for producer royalties.

This risk to the manager of losing everything if found to be an agent, and the fact that the Labor Code contained a provision (never used to my knowledge) which provided for criminal sanctions put a general damper on the enthusiasm of managers. I honestly believe that it was virtually impossible for a manager in California to adequately represent an artist without breaking the law—if you weren't breaking the law, you probably weren't doing your job as a manager. It was fundamentally a no-win situation for the manager.

Another, quite significant, negative effect of the confusion surrounding the "manager as agent" mess was managers' fears that the Labor Commissioner could require them to repay all the commissions which had been paid to them by artists. In the case of an artist-manager relationship that had survived for some period of time, and had even moderate levels of success, the repayment amount could have been an astronomical sum.

In the midst of all this tomfoolery, a new law was passed by the California legislature in the waning months of 1982. The new law, which became effective January 1, 1983, is known as AB997. After a great deal of lobbying back and forth by managers and agents (with a few incidental artists and politicians thrown in for good measure), AB997 was passed and signed into law. AB997 was passed for only a 2-year period and was to expire on December 31, 1985. It has been renewed on sort of an ongoing rolling basis, almost as if there were options being exercised for additional periods.

New York also has state statutes covering entertainment industry managers. New York's definition of a "theatrical employment agency," as set forth in Section 171.8 of New York General Business Law, is in many ways similar to the definition contained in Section 1700.4 of the California Labor Code. There is, however, one significant difference. The New York definition contains the following:

> . . . but such term does not include the business of managing entertainments, exhibitions or performances, or the artists or attractions constituting the same, where such business only *incidentally* [emphasis added] involves the seeking of employment therefor.

Because of this section of the New York General Business Law code, personal managers in New York have been allowed to do "incidental" booking without being a licensed agent.

Probably the most significant difference between the language of AB997 and the legislation which it supplanted is the legal right of personal managers to become involved in the procurement of employment. The new law allows managers to act with agents in the procurement of employment for clients *if* the agent requests the manager to act in conjunction with the agent. It also gives managers the legal right to negotiate recording contracts, and this may be done without an agent's request.

This negotiation of recording contracts by managers has certainly been going on for years. The difference is that before AB997 it was illegal. The manager not only ran the risk of having the management agreement voided but also ran the risk of criminal charges. There was always the possibility that a manager might be sent off to the pokey—a fate too good for them according to some disgruntled artists, but, nevertheless, a bit extreme. AB997 changes all this. Not only is the contract not voidable because of the "illegal" activities of the manager, but now the criminal sanctions have been removed.

The new law also provides for a 1-year statute of limitations: If an artist who believes that a manager has violated the law does not act within 1 year of the presumed violation, the right to act is waived. Under the old law, the artist could, and frequently did, wait a considerable time before attacking the manager.

AB997 also places restrictions on that portion of commissions that the manager would have to pay back in the case of an adverse judgment by the Labor Commissioner. Now only actual violations (procuring employment) are repayable, not all commissions collected. This provision, coupled with the 1-year statute of limitations, means there are fewer instances in which managers must repay large sums. Note, however, that even with the 1-year statute of limitations, a manager's liability may be substantial. In April of 1992, the Labor Commissioner ruled against Arsenio Hall's ex-managers (appropriately, the name of the management company was "X Management") and ordered the former managers to repay $2,148,445.78 in commissions collected during the 1-year period August 9, 1989 through August 8, 1990, the date Hall terminated his agreement with the managers.

In the Arsenio Hall case, the Labor Commissioner found that the management had "through its principals . . ., engaged in and carried on the occupation of a talent agency . . ., by either procuring or attempting to procure employment and engagements . . . without being licensed" and declared the agreement with the managers void as of September 1, 1987, the date the agreement began. The Labor Commissioner also stated that the managers "engaged in an act of self-dealing and overreaching while acting as an Artist's manager and talent agent," adding that they were "not entitled to compensation of any form."

The Labor Commissioner has gone to some rather bizarre lengths to find managers guilty of operating as agents without licenses. There have been several recent cases where the Labor Commissioner and, in at least one case, the court held that a manager was acting as an unlicensed agent because the manager aided in the selection of an agent and had the power "to engage" or "to terminate" the services of the agent. This right to assist, engage, and hire an agent was held to be "seeking employment" on behalf of the artist. Since the manager was not licensed as an agent—poof! No more contract.

Even though AB997 has mitigated somewhat the adverse legal consequences for managers of the statutory definitions of "agent" and "talent agency" contained in the California Labor Code, paranoia among managers continues to run wide and deep, for at least two good reasons.

First, the psychological consequences of the long-held belief that the manager's position is always hopeless, and the historical ease with which artists have been able to void personal management positions, are probably going to be around for a long time. Second, rulings made on the basis of these laws—both the pre-1983 laws and AB997—are often contradictory, and so part of the paranoia that is epidemic for personal managers is based upon the uncertainty of the whole thing. Now it is—now it ain't. For example, in one case prior to AB997, the Labor Commissioner held that the manager signing the artist to a recording contract and selling the masters to a record company was *not* in violation of the Labor Code, that the manager was *not* seeking employment as defined in the Labor Code, and the manager was able to maintain the contract. Beats the hell out of me. Personally, I think any manager who isn't paranoid just doesn't know what is going on.

PERSONAL MANAGEMENT AGREEMENTS

Most personal management contracts are quite similar. Examples of variations of the same provisions would be difficult to find and would ultimately be of little use or importance. Accordingly, in this chapter, each provision will be illustrated by a single example with accompanying text. In the following extracts "I," "me," "my," etc., refer to the artist, and the pronoun "you" refers to the personal manager.

COMMISSION

Probably the first question asked about any personal management relationship is, What's the percentage? In other words, what compensation is being taken by the personal manager for services rendered (or even not rendered, as the case may be)? There is no statutory limit on the percentage. After all, the personal manager is not licensed by the state and does not have to submit contract forms for approval. I have seen personal management contracts calling for a percentage as low as 5% and as high as 50%, and I am sure there are agreements in existence with percentages outside of this range. Most seem to fall in the 15% to 20% range, with 10% and 25% not unusual. The Conference of Personal Managers (an organization to which personal managers are not required to belong) has a rule for its members that commissions shall not exceed 15% for actors, writers, directors, and most others in show business, but it allows for commissions up to 20% for musicians and recording artists.

Provision is sometimes made for a change in percentage, usually starting low and getting higher.

Example

During each week, Personal Manager (PM) receives 10% of Artist's (A's) gross compensation up to $2,000.00. From $2,000.01 to $5,000.00, PM receives 15%. From $5,000.01 to $10,000.00, PM receives 20%. Anything over $10,000.00 per week, PM receives 25%.

Most commissions are based upon gross compensation, but sometimes certain areas either will be deleted from gross compensation or will be commissioned at a different rate.

Example

A pays PM a 20% commission on A's gross compensation, except PM's commission on songwriting and publishing will be only 10%.

Example

A pays PM a 20% commission, except for songwriting and publishing, where A pays PM 7½% up to a sum equal to the average songwriter and publisher royalties earned by A in the 2 years prior to signing with PM. Thereafter, on the excess, A pays PM 15% of song-writer and publisher royalties.

Example

A pays PM a 20% commission, but no commission is paid to PM for record royalties.

The provisions in personal management agreements dealing with compensation will usually be similar to the following:

> In compensation for your services I agree to pay you, as and when received by me, and during and throughout the term hereof, a sum equal to twenty (20%) percent, which per-centage figure shall be of any and all gross monies or other considerations which I may have as a result of my activities in and throughout the entertainment, amusement, music, recording, and publishing industries, including any and all sums resulting from the use of my artistic talents and the results and proceeds thereof and, without in any manner lim-iting the foregoing, the matters upon which your compensation shall be computed shall include any and all of my activities in connection with matters as follows: motion pic-tures, television, radio, music, literary, theatrical engagements, personal appearances, public appearances in places of amusement and entertainment, records and recording, publications, and the use of my name, likeness and talents for purposes of advertising and trade.

Note the scope of the language used in determining the personal manager's share of the artist's in-come from all areas of activity. We are talking *all-encompassing here*. Please also note that the per-centage is based upon the artist's *gross*, not net, income.

The provisions usually provide for ongoing compensation for the manager for income earned after the term of the agreement for those agreements entered into during the term of the agree-ment, including extensions, renewals, and modifications. For example, the personal manager would be entitled to continue to receive the agreed-upon share of record royalties even after the personal management agreement had expired.

> (a) I likewise agree to pay you a similar sum following the expiration of the term hereof upon and with respect to any and all engagements, contracts and agreements entered into during the term hereof relating to any of the foregoing, and upon any and all extensions, modifications, renewals and substitutions thereof and upon any resumptions of such en-gagements, contracts and agreements which may have been discontinued during the term hereof and resumed within a year thereafter.

Note that commissions are on gross. Additionally, note the all-encompassing nature of the areas for compensation to be commissioned by the manager, including, by implication, such payments made after the term of the agreement—even after the artist's death.

> (b) The term "gross monies or other considerations" shall include, without limitation, shares of stock, partnership interests, percentages and the total amount paid for a pack-age television or radio program (live or recorded), motion picture or any other entertain-ment packages, earned or received directly or indirectly by me or my heirs, executors, ad-ministrators or assigns, or by any other person, firm or corporation on my behalf.

The share of income is not limited to money; it may also be ownership of stock or a partnership interest. The manager is entitled to the manager's share of such "income," and, if a payment is required, for example, to acquire the stock, the manager pays a proportionate share.

(c) In the event that I receive, as all or part of my compensation for activities hereunder, stock or the right to buy stock in any corporation or that I become the packager or owner of all or part of an entertainment property, whether as individual proprietor, stockholder, partner, joint venturer or otherwise, your percentage shall apply to my said stock, right to buy stock, individual proprietorship, joint venture or other form of interest, and you shall be entitled to your percentage share thereof. Should I be required to make any payment for such interest, you will pay your percentage share of such payment, unless you do not want your percentage share thereof.

TERM OF THE AGREEMENT

The language used in the provisions in personal management agreements dealing with the term of the agreement are similar to those dealing with the term of artist recording agreements, including options, exercise of options, and conditions placed upon options. They are, however, more likely to have a longer initial period or to be for a flat period of time (e.g., 5 years) than are most recording agreements.

Although there is no rule or regulation which states that the initial period of the management agreement should be any particular length, managers would be advised to have the initial period at least 2 years in length. Personal managers are in the business of creating careers, and it usually takes at least a year to start putting all the right moves in place. A manager agreeing to an initial period of 1 year, especially if the artist has required some condition of exercise (e.g., a record contract, $100,000 in earnings, a multicity tour, or any one of a number of possible conditions) is taking a grave risk.

ESCAPE

> *Get rid of that devil, real simple,*
> *Put a bullet in his temple. . .*
>
> **—Lyric from Ice Cube's "No Vaseline"**
> **(making reference to his former manager)**

When representing the artist I try to include an *escape clause*. From the artist's standpoint this is very important because escape clauses provide a way out for the artist if, and more probably when, the relationship goes sour. These provisions should always be negotiated and must be customized to fit the circumstances. Do not expect to see an escape clause in a personal management agreement prepared on behalf of a personal manager. An artist has to request, or perhaps even demand, that it be included in the agreement.

Having an escape clause offers the artist an exit strategy from a relationship which may have become (at least in the artist's perception) untenable. The failure of the personal manager to perform some express "condition" for the exercise of the option to continue the agreement (the escape clause) is, under most circumstances, a cleaner and faster way to terminate the contractual relationship than to go through the time and expense (and risk) of a hearing before a Labor

Commissioner. Note, however, that determining just what measure of performance is to be used can be difficult. A common measure, and the easiest to apply, at least in theory, is earnings. If, for example, the artist does not earn $1 million the first year, the artist may terminate the manager's agreement. This, however, raises other problems. For example, is not the manager then guaranteeing employment to the artist?

Frequently, the personal manager will flatly refuse any such escape, and the artist must choose between either signing the agreement without an escape clause or not signing at all.

OBLIGATIONS OF THE MANAGER

Just what is it that the personal manager is supposed to be doing for his compensation? Most of the agreements provide something along the following lines:

2. As and when requested by me during and throughout the term hereof you agree to perform for me one or more of the services as follows:

(a) Advice and counsel in the selection of literary, artistic and musical material.

(b) Advice and counsel in any and all matters pertaining to publicity, public relations and advertising.

(c) Advice and counsel with regard to the adoption of proper format for presentation of my artistic talents and in the determination of proper style, mood, setting, business and characterization in keeping with my talents.

(d) Advice, counsel and direction in the selection of artistic talent to assist, accompany or embellish my artistic presentation.

(e) Advice and counsel relating to general practices in the entertainment and amusement industries and with respect to such matters of which you may have a knowledge concerning compensation and privileges extended for similar artistic values.

(f) Advice and counsel concerning the selection of theatrical agencies and persons, firms and corporations to counsel, advise, seek and procure employment and engagements for me.

3. You are authorized and empowered for me and in my behalf and in your discretion to do the following:

(a) Approve and permit any and all publicity and advertising.

(b) Approve and permit the use of my name, photograph, likeness, voice, sound effects, caricatures, literary, artistic and musical materials for purposes of advertising and publicity and in the promotion and advertising of any and all products and services.

(c) Execute for me in my name and/or in my behalf any and all agreements, documents and contracts for my services, talents, and/or artistic, literary and musical materials.

(d) Collect and receive sums due me as well as endorse my name upon and cash any and all checks payable to me for my services, talents and literary and artistic materials and retain therefrom all sums owing to you.

(e) Engage, as well as discharge and/or direct for me, and in my name theatrical agents and employment agencies as well as other persons, firms or corporations, who may be retained to obtain contracts, engagements or employment for me.

Notice the repeated references to "advice and counsel." That, basically and *legally*, is what personal managers do: They *advise and counsel*. As discussed above, generally speaking, in California personal managers cannot by law, unless they are licensed, do anything along the lines of "procuring, offering, promising, or attempting to procure employment or engagements for an artist or artists." This, of course, makes it somewhat hard to prove or disprove whether or not the manager is actually doing anything—good, bad, or indifferent. Artists, naturally, tend to believe it's either bad or indifferent. Managers, also naturally, believe they are doing "good."

Also, please note the language in subparagraph 3(c), which gives the manager a power of attorney to sign agreements for the artist. When I represent artists, I always add language to this sort of provision restricting the manager's right to execute agreements to those having a period of 2 weeks or less, such as, for example, a one-night concert or a week's gig at a club. Anything over 2 weeks and certainly anything *permanent*—such as signing away publishing rights or licensing the right to use the artist's name for some commercial item—should require the artist's own signature.

DISCLAIMER

Most personal management agreements have an express statement contained in them specifying that the manager is *not* an agent. This is to make sure that there is nothing in the agreement which may be used at a later date in a hearing with the Labor Commissioner to show that the personal manager was acting as an unlicensed talent agency. The language, of course, will not save a manager if the facts clearly show that the manager has, in fact, been acting in the capacity of an agent. There is also usually a provision whereby the artist states that the artist will, at all times, have an agent as further proof that the manager is not operating as an agent without a license. The following is typical.

It is clearly understood that you are not an employment agent or theatrical agent, that you have not offered or attempted or promised to obtain employment or engagements for me, and that you are not obligated, authorized or expected to do so. I shall be solely responsible for payment of all necessary commissions to booking or similar agencies. Employment of booking or theatrical agents on my behalf shall be arranged in consultation with you.

I shall at all times utilize proper theatrical or other employment agencies to obtain engagements and employment for me, but I shall not engage any theatrical or employment agency of which you may disapprove.

REVIEW OF EMPLOYMENT

Despite any disclaimer that the personal manager is not procuring employment for the artist, one of the manager's jobs, theoretically at least, is to review all offers of employment, such as bookings for concerts, nightclubs, television shows, motion pictures, commercials, etc., to "advise and counsel" whether or not the booking is a good career move. The following clause is typical:

I shall submit all offers of employment to you and will refer any inquiries concerning my services to you. I shall instruct any theatrical agency engaged by me to remit to you all monies that may become due me and may be received by it.

Note that although the language of the above provision in no way suggests that the personal manger will have anything to do with getting a job for the artist, labor commissioners have, in the past, been known to maintain that such a clause is proof that the manager is procuring employment and, accordingly, the personal management agreement is voidable. Current thinking is decidedly against such an interpretation, but I have no doubt that deep in the heart of many a labor commissioner this belief still lurks.

EXCLUSIVITY FOR ARTIST

Usually, in connection with the period of the agreement, there will be a statement, more or less like the following, dealing with exclusivity (the artist's promise not to have any other manager):

> I do hereby engage you as my sole and exclusive personal manager in the entertainment industry throughout the world for a period of. . . .

As an exercise, you might consider the concept of exclusivity in this context. Why, other than either jealousy or an excess of caution over conflicts, would a personal manager care if the artist has another personal manager or not? If the artist is willing to pay two or three or more personal managers it may be, in theory, to the benefit of the first personal manager to have the aid and assistance of the others. I imagine most arguments on either side would run roughly parallel to arguments for the pros and cons of bigamy, including the legitimacy of the offspring.

NONEXCLUSIVITY FOR PERSONAL MANAGER

Although personal manager agreements usually stipulate that the artist will not engage another personal manager, they also usually stipulate that the personal manager *will* have the opportunity to represent other artists, and will also have the right to bring in others to perform some or all of the personal manager's obligations.

> This agreement shall not be construed to create a partnership between us. It is specifically understood that you are acting hereunder as an independent contractor and you may appoint or engage any and all other persons, firms and corporations throughout the world in your discretion to perform any or all of the services which you have agreed to perform hereunder. I understand that you also represent or will represent and continue to represent other persons and performers and that your services hereunder are not exclusive and you shall at all times be free to perform the same or similar services for others as well as engage in any and all other business activities. You shall only be required to render reasonable services which are called for by this agreement as and when reasonably requested by me.

CLOSING THOUGHTS

> SERVANT:
>
> He hath songs for man or woman, of all sizes. . . .
> He has the prettiest love songs for maids; . . . he
> makes the maid to answer "Whoop, do me no harm,
> good man"; puts him off, slights him, with "Whoop,
> do me no harm, good man."

POLIXENES:

This is a brave fellow.

SERVANT:

He hath . . ., points more than all the lawyers in
Bohemia can learnedly handle, though they come to
him by the gross.

—WILLIAM SHAKESPEARE
The Winter's Tale, Act IV, Scene 4

I personally believe management is the most frustrating job in show business (I know, I've done it). The personal manager–artist relationship is probably the most tenuous of any long-term contractual relationship and is probably fraught with more tension and conflict than any other relationship between two human beings, including marriage. Like marriage, it should not be rushed into. Certainly, the divorce rate for manager-artist unions is even higher than the divorce rate for marriages.

CHAPTER 23

TURN OFF THE LIGHTS WHEN YOU LEAVE

Most music industry veterans know this much: When David Geffen is selling, it's probably not wise to be buying.

—JEFF LEEDS

Los Angeles Times, December 29, 2003

What can you say about an industry which over a period of 3 years (2000 through 2003) fell from a $40 billion a year industry to a $28 billion a year industry—a 30% drop! An industry that was already in economic free fall prior to 2000? Someone once said that the entertainment industry "eats its own young." The record industry has gone beyond that: It's like some mythical monster which chews up its own vital organs and limbs in a feeble attempt to stay alive.

There was a time, well within the memory of anyone over the age of 15, when the record industry was a thriving business. Cassettes, CDs, singles flew out of the bins at retail stores and people actually *paid* for them. Now retail stores and chains are, to quote a friend of mine, "dropping like pancakes." The major labels are involved in a dance of death, circling one another warily, waiting for an opportunity to leap forward to scoop up one (or two or three) of the others. Not so long ago it took the fingers on two hands to count the number of "majors"; now one hand will suffice, with a thumb left over.

Record companies, once profit centers for multinational corporate giants, are now moved about like chips on the table of a high-stakes poker game. The EMI Group has been trolling the waters for years to buy, partner with, or sell to another major; to date, EMI is still a bridesmaid and not a bride. BMG and Sony signed a prenuptial agreement and after finding that the wedding would be legal in the appropriate jurisdictions, moved in together. Universal Music Group is still looking for someone who can afford to take it off the hands of the French water company which bought it from Edgar Bronfman, Jr., who, missing the fun and games of the music business, bought the Warner Music Group. In the meantime, Universal led the movement to reduce the retail price of CDs—and found that no one was following.

Conventional wisdom had it that the downward spiral of the record business mainly could be laid at the feet of the Internet and free downloading. A vocal minority, however, argued that on the contrary, free downloading actually helped record sales. The reaction to that was, "What idiot would believe that?"

As it turns out, perhaps a smart idiot. Sales actually increased in the first quarter of 2004 over the same period in 2003 by well over 10%. Meanwhile, paid downloads were increasing at an impressive rate. Paid downloads in the first quarter of 2004 were 130% of the combined paid downloads in the preceding two quarters. That's over $25 million in the first three months of 2004, compared to slightly over $19 million for the entire period from July through December of 2003. Over the 12 months of 2004, there was an increase in paid downloads of over 150% over the previous year.

It's not easy to sort out the reason for this upswing. Proponents of conventional wisdom would probably argue that the increased sales are directly related to the RIAA's vigorous campaign of prosecuting individuals caught downloading illegally. A vocal minority might reply (probably with an introductory expletive related to animal husbandry) that the upswing is based upon good product finally hitting the marketplace—for the first time in nearly 4 years, during the first quarter of this upswing, albums by two artists sold over 1 million copies during the same 1-week period.

Like the proverbial silver lining, the upswing comes with a dark cloud. Most paid downloads are singles, not albums. SoundScan data indicate that the ratio of paid downloads of singles to paid downloads of albums is 25 to 1. Under present business models, record companies don't make money on sales of singles. If record companies shift back to having to rely on singles as a cash cow, the new days will be very grim indeed.

Upswing or plunging downward spiral, the record business just ain't what it used to be. Even the upswing didn't bring the industry within shouting distance of the old days. There is no question that the record business (not necessarily the music business as a whole) probably qualifies for some endangered species list.

It is easy for the record business to lay the blame for its woes on illegal downloading. While that is certainly part of the problem, some of the blame belongs to the record companies themselves. They didn't adjust their business models and thinking to the realities of the Internet until the genie was already out of the bottle. Now the record industry is faced with an entire generation that believes it is entitled to free music. That is all fine and dandy, except for one minor point: Where are the new artists going to come from if the record companies can't afford to sign, record, and support them?

The question is: Can the record companies survive long enough to develop a new working business model? If they don't, will there some be some other way for new artists to develop and flourish?

The Starbucks Connection

Ray Charles's last album, *Genius Loves Company*, which was finished just before his death in June of 2004, was partially financed and sold at the retail level by Starbucks. Starbucks had, in fact, the most sales of any retailer, including all the major retail record chains (and that includes Best Buy, now the largest single retailer based on volume). What was even more remarkable about this feat was that the price at Starbucks was full-bore, no discounts. Any Starbucks certainly has more daily foot traffic than almost any record store—a relatively captive audience with nothing much else to do than listen to the music being played and stare at the CDs for sale at the counter while waiting for their coffee. An interesting question is: How many of these would-be buyers might have wandered next door to a traditional record store to buy *Genius Loves Company* at a discount? Another is: Who can compete with Starbucks, which has a store every couple of blocks in thousands of cities and towns all over the world, when it comes to location? The answer: Nobody.

You can bet record labels are taking a close look at the partnership between Starbucks and Concord Records, the label releasing *Genius Loves Company*, and wondering what other multistore retailers they might hook up with to tap into this kind of market.

Going for the Gold

By 2005 the industry was in full swing with the ultimate in variable pricing, offering different versions of the same album. The lowest-priced version is the traditional album containing the tracks, cover, and booklet with liner notes. Higher-priced "deluxe" or "collector's" versions may contain everything in the traditional CD plus, for example, bonus tracks, a poster or longer booklet, and/or a DVD of a live performance, a T-shirt, etc. Some labels offer three versions of the same album. And, if you want to spend *really* big bucks, you can even buy gold-plated versions of some classic albums.

Digital-Only

At the end of 2004, Universal Music Group took a trial spin on a business model that may serve as the new paradigm for the record industry. Warner Bros. reportedly also has a similar model about to be tried out in the marketplace. The concept is cool and simple and will probably work. Universal's new label, Universal Music Enterprises Digital (UMED), is a digital-only label. Artists signed to the label receive no advances and, in fact, pay their own recording costs. The artist retains ownership of the masters and licenses them to UMED for a limited time. The label pays the artist a royalty on sales of around 25% of retail, without packaging or promotion deductions. The label provides some level of promotion and advertising to promote the product. If at some point during the licensed period, sales reach some predetermined level, reportedly as low as 5,000 units, the label has the option to pick up the artist and the product for traditional record sales.

The label's right to move the artist from digital-only license status to a traditional artist/record company relationship is reminiscent of the conversion clause discussed in Chapter 16, "Distribution" (see pages 440–443), with traces of exercise-of-option agreements discussed in Chapter 7, "Option Agreements" (see pages 246–254). The company lets someone else carry the load to prove the value of the artist and then exercises the right to commercially exploit the product.

I personally have an optimistic feeling about this new business model being able to ease the transition from the old business model, which is on a slippery slope to destruction, to a new one, which, like Mighty Mouse, may "save the day." Any way you look at what's going on, we are living in interesting times.

• • •

Finally, we must fall back on the observation of a major philosopher from the mid-20th century:

POGO POSSUM:
We have met the enemy and he is us.
— WALT KELLY

Glossary

I have studied it often, but I never could discover the plot.

—MARK TWAIN, on dictionaries

ab initio A Latin phrase used in legal documents (and hardly ever in polite conversation) meaning "from the beginning." For example, if a provision states that an agreement will be void *ab initio* if there is a breach of the terms, and then a breach occurs, the legal effect is that the agreement will be deemed never to have existed.

administering publisher The music publisher, usually in copublishing agreements, who has the right and authority to administer the copyright.

administration In music publishing agreements, managing or conducting the business of the exploitation of musical compositions. Generally, it includes not only the licensing of the various rights in the copyrights, but also bookkeeping, registering, payment of statements, and, last but not least, plugging the songs (getting them recorded and performed).

administration fee Fee paid to the publisher handling the administration of a musical composition, most frequently in copublishing agreements. Provisions for administration fees are sometimes also included in songwriters' agreements. They are usually based on a percentage of the gross sums received for the composition or the gross publisher's share of income.

advances Advances are prepayments of royalties which may become due. When the royalty payment becomes due, the advance is deducted from the payment and the excess, if any, is then paid.

AFM (AF of M) *See* American Federation of Musicians.

AFM Basic Agreement The labor agreement which sets forth the rules for the use of the services of AFM (American Federation of Musicians) members (everything from live performances through recordings for records, film soundtracks, television soundtracks, etc., including scale payments, pension payments, cartage, etc.) and the proceeds of their services (the sales of recordings, transmissions of music, etc., generating residual payments, MPTF, etc.).

AFTRA *See* American Federation of Television and Radio Artists.

agent The personal representative of an artist who is responsible for obtaining employment for the artist.

album A term used interchangeably with LP, which in the past referred to a 12-inch, $33^{1}/_{3}$-rpm vinyl disc, and CDs, usually containing more than one recording produced as a unit.

all-in production agreement A recording agreement where the party contracting with the record company (artist, producer, and/or production company) provides the record company with the services of the recording artist and the producer. All royalties are paid to the entity, which then pays artist and producer.

American Federation of Musicians (AFM) The labor organization to which musicians belong. It acts as the collective bargaining agent for its members, sets the rules and regulations for its members and the signatories of the AFM Basic Agreement, sets scale payments to members for performing at recording sessions, and provides pension and welfare plans for its members.

American Federation of Television and Radio Artists (AFTRA) The labor organization to which performers in the television (tape, not film), radio, and recording industries belong. Acts for and on behalf of its members in the same way as the AFM.

American Society of Composers, Authors and Publishers (ASCAP) One of the three performing rights societies in the United States. ASCAP collects and distributes music performance fees on behalf of composers, authors, and publishers.

A&R The initials refer to the Artists and Repertoire Department within a record company. In the past, A&R was responsible for producing records, but it is now likely to be responsible for finding new talent and independent producers. "A&R" is sometimes also used to designate record producers, for example, "He's A&R on the project. "

arm's length A term used in connection with dealings, negotiations, or contractual relationships between related parties where the parties treat each other without favoritism or as if they were not somehow related. Sometimes arm's-length requirements are included in agree-

ments; for example, a music publisher will reach an agreement with a composer not to give an affiliated record company a lower mechanical license rate.

ASCAP *See* American Society of Composers, Authors and Publishers.

at source Used in connection with the collection of royalties or fees directly from the entity owing the fees. For example, under such an arrangement, an American recording artist with an album being distributed by a foreign distributor would be paid directly by the foreign company; otherwise, the foreign distributor would pay the American company, which, in turn, would pay the artist.

audiovisual work Any work combining music and visual images which uses a machine and/or device (including without limitation: projectors, viewers, and electronic equipment). It may be on film, disc, or tape.

base royalty The term used to describe the percentage figure used in the computation of the royalty rate before reductions for certain types of sale. For example, a base royalty of 10% is reduced by one-half, to 5%, for record club sales. *Also see* Otherwise applicable royalty.

blocked currency (or funds) Monies, usually in the form of royalties, earned in a foreign country that will not let the money leave its borders. Since the money must be spent within the country, it is, in effect, blocked.

BMI *See* Broadcast Music, Inc.

bonus Often referred to as a *flat payment*, a nonreturnable, nonrecoupable payment made to, or on behalf of, a party in an agreement. It is neither an advance nor a royalty.

Broadcast Music, Inc. (BMI) One of the three performing rights societies in the United States. BMI collects and distributes music performance fees on behalf of composers, authors, and publishers.

budget A statement of the estimated cost of a recording session or a project.

budget record A recording sold at low cost, typically not more than 50% of a regular retail list price, to the consumer.

business affairs The department of a music company responsible for negotiating agreements. Sometimes responsible for overseeing the business of the company, it is usually staffed by lawyers.

chart (1) a written musical score containing arrangements; (2) a listing of singles and albums, in various genres (pop, country, R&B, etc.), with the most successful release at the top of the list; (3) when used as a verb ("to chart"), to reach a position on one of the charts. Chart activity refers to movement, usually upward, on one of the charts.

collection agent A person or company which collects claims for other parties. The most well-known collection agencies in the music business are The Harry Fox Agency, Inc., which collects mechanical license fees for many music publishers, and ASCAP, BMI, and SESAC, which collect music performance fees for music publishers and songwriters.

commercial tie-in A form of merchandising wherein, for instance, an artist's name and/or likeness is linked to a company's product in order to enhance the sales of the product—for example, Michael Jackson representing Pepsi Cola. It is usually distinguished from merchandising in that the product is preexisting and not named after the artist.

compact disc A 120-mm diameter disc-type digital record primarily reproducing sound (whether or not synchronized with or accompanied by visual images) by means of a laser.

compilation A collection of recordings by different artists on different tracks. *Also see* Coupling.

compulsory license A mechanical license granted pursuant to Section 115 of the Copyright Act of 1976. It is available to any party wishing to record and release a record containing a musical composition (subject to certain minor exceptions), whether or not the copyright owner wishes to grant the license. It is available once the musical composition has been recorded and distributed with the permission of the copyright owner.

computation price *See* Royalty computation price.

constructed price A fictitious price set for purposes of computing royalties in some foreign territories where, usually by law, there is no suggested retail list price or wholesale price for the sale of recordings. *Also see* PPD.

container Another term for the jacket or packaging of a recording, disc, or tape. Usually refers to the jacket on an album, but may also refer to the tape container or disc sleeve.

container charges Charges deducted from the royalty base ostensibly to cover the cost of the container in which a record is sold.

controlled composition A term used to indicate that the artist, producer, or production company in a record contract owns, or controls, a specified musical composition. Usually used to indicate that the musical composition is to be assigned, in whole or in part, to a designated publisher and/or that a reduced mechanical license rate is to be granted in connection with records manufactured and sold containing the composition.

copyright The exclusive rights in a work granted to the "author" of a work, either the creator of a work or the entity that has contracted for a work for hire, or to a subsequent assignee.

costs In the music industry, monies, for example, recording costs, expended on behalf of an artist, songwriter, or the like, which are charged back against subsequent royalties.

coterminous Agreements which terminate, or end, at the same time. For example, a recording agreement and songwriter's agreement which are coterminous will both terminate when either agreement ends for whatever reason.

coupling The joining together of recordings which were originally not recorded and released together on one record, usually an album. Most frequently, but not necessarily, *coupling* refers to an album containing performances, on different tracks, by different artists.

cover As a noun, (1) the jacket of a record, usually of an album, or (2) a short form for *cover record*, which is a recording of a musical composition which has already been recorded by another artist. Generally, cover records are made to exploit already successful recordings. Frequently, cover records are instrumental versions of hit recordings. (3) As a verb, "to cover" is to record a musical composition which someone else has already recorded, usually successfully.

credit (1) A printed acknowledgment of a contribution to a work. (2) As a verb, as in "to credit an account," an accounting function whereby sums are added to an account, usually a royalty account, either increasing the monies due or decreasing the amount of a deficit.

cross-collateralization The process of taking profits or income from one source (e.g., a songwriter's agreement or an album in a net profit position) and applying those profits or income to another source (e.g., a recording agreement or unrecouped recording costs from an album) to recover costs and/or advances.

cue sheets Information sheets indicating the length, title, composers, and publishers of musical selections included on soundtracks of films, television programs, and other like soundtrack performances. Performing rights societies rely on cue sheets to determine royalties for the public performances of the soundtracks.

demo costs Costs incurred in the production of a demonstration record or tape. In recording agreements these costs are usually included as a recording cost and are an advance against the artist's royalties. In songwriting agreements, these costs may be borne by the publisher, by the writer, or, more frequently, on a 50–50 basis.

demonstration record (or tape) Often referred to as a demo record (or tape), a recording made for the purpose of selling something—a song, an artist—by demonstrating the product being sold.

derivative work A work based on one or more preexisting works, such as a different musical arrangement of an existing song.

double album An album package containing two recordings in the same jacket.

droit moral A French phrase meaning "moral rights," which refers to the rights of an author of a work to maintain the artistic integrity of the work (protect it from distortion or misrepresentation) even after the right to publish the work has been granted.

employee for hire An individual employed to create a copyrighted work at the request of the employer. The employer becomes the owner of the copyright in the created work.

exercise The act by which a privilege (such as an option) is invoked by the party having the privilege. To exercise an option is to cause that option to become effective.

exhibition copy A copy of an audiovisual

work, usually a video, intended for nonhome use, including, without limitation, all video jukebox, television, and theatrical distribution.

fair use Use of a copyrighted work which is an exception to the copyright owner's exclusive right to exploit a copyrighted work. It applies only under certain circumstances and is a permitted use without the consent of the copyright owner. The principles of fair use are contained in Section 107 of the Copyright Act.

flat payment *See* Bonus.

flat period In an agreement, a fixed contract term, for example, 5 years, with no provisions for additional option periods.

flow-through provision A provision in an agreement which allows the terms, presumably more favorable, from another agreement to be incorporated into the current agreement. For example, an agreement between an artist and a production company may specify that no matter what that agreement provides, the artist will get the benefit of any more favorable royalty computation contained in the production company's agreement with the record company.

force majeure When used in a contract, a term referring to acts of a superior force, including, but not limited to, acts of God and labor unions, which result in an impossibility to perform under the contract.

Form I-9 The United States Immigration and Naturalization Service Employment Eligibility Certificate. Pursuant to the Simpson-Rodino Immigration Act of 1986, an employee is required to provide employers with proof that the employee is either a United States citizen or a legal resident alien who is authorized to become employed in the United States.

Fox Agency (Fox Office) *See* Harry Fox Agency, Inc.

freebies The term used to describe free goods given in connection with the sale of product. For example, records are frequently sold on a basis of "buy 10, get 3 free." The 3 records given away are freebies.

FSO (furnishing the services of) A term used in agreements in which an individual's services are "furnished" by a third party, for example, loan-out agreements in which a lending company furnishes the services of the recording artist to the record company.

generally accepted accounting procedures (GAAP) Guidelines setting procedures and rules for accounting and auditing.

grand performing rights The exclusive rights to perform a work dramatically, such as an opera, musical, etc. These are rights which belong to the owner of the copyright of a dramatic or musical work. The owner cannot be made to grant these rights to any third party (other than contractually).

Harry Fox Agency, Inc. The major collection agency in the United States for mechanical licenses. The Fox Agency, or Fox Office, issues mechanical licenses to record companies, collects mechanical license fees, and audits record companies, all on behalf of music publishers.

ips (inches per second) The measure of the speed of analog recording tape, for example, 15 ips, 30 ips. The term is usually, but not always, used in connection with the speed of a master tape.

indemnification An agreement to hold another party harmless from a loss or legal action, usually as a result of an incorrect warranty or representation.

inducement letter The document, usually in letter form, signed by an artist to acknowledge that a production company or loan-out company has the right to lend or furnish the artist's

services. The artist ratifies the agreement between the production company/loan-out company and the record company, publisher, film
company, or whatever institution to which the
artist is being contracted.

joint recording A recording made by two or
more different artists who join together to make
the recording. It is not to be confused with a
coupled recording.

key man clause A provision in an agreement
which provides that if a key man, such as, for
example, the president of the company or the
artist's producer, leaves the company, the agreement may be terminated.

K-Tel–type sales The selling of compilations directly to the consumer, using television
advertising. K-Tel was one of the first direct-
mail companies to sell records to consumers
using this method. Other companies that sell
compilations directly to the public are Ronco,
Sessions, and Pickwick.

lending agreement *See* Loan-out agreement.

less returns The language which allows the
record company to deduct returns from gross
sales in order to determine net sales.

letter of direction A letter directing a third
party (e.g., Record Company) to make a payment, usually in the form of a royalty, directly
to an artist or producer without the payment
being the responsibility of the company (e.g.,
Production Company) to whom the party receiving the payment is under contract.

licensee The party to whom a right is licensed. For example, a foreign record company
which is granted the right to release a domestic
company's recording in the foreign territory is
the licensee of the rights.

licensor The party who licenses a right. For
example, the domestic company licensing a

recording to a foreign record company for release in the foreign territory is the licensor of
the rights.

loan-out agreement An agreement whereby
a corporation lends, or furnishes, the services of
an individual to a record company, film company, etc. The lending company stands between
the individual and the company to whom the individual's services are being loaned. The lending company is responsible for the individual's
performance and for the individual's payment.

logo The symbol—type, graphic, or type and
graphic—used by a label, artist, or whatever to
distinguish that entity from all other entities.

mag Magnetic tape.

manager *See* Personal manager.

master The original recording of a musical
work, usually, but not always, on magnetic
tape. The term can be used to describe the original multitrack tape or a two-track stereo master tape which is either mixed from or recorded
from the original multitrack tape.

mechanical license Often simply called *mechanical*, the license granted to a record company by the music publisher/copyright proprietor which allows the record company to manufacture and distribute recordings containing a
musical composition or compositions controlled
by the publisher. *Also see* Compulsory license.

mechanical license fees The fees or royalties
payable pursuant to a mechanical license. The
fees may be determined by the statutory rate,
which is set by U. S. copyright law and is usually
payable for each record "made and distributed."

merchandising The right to market the
name, logo, characterization, etc., of, for example, an artist for commercial gain. Prime examples are T-shirts, posters, lunch pails, etc., with
the picture of an artist. In the music industry,

there is a distinction between merchandising, where the products are specifically made to exploit an artist's success, and commercial tie-ins, where an artist's name, logo, etc., is used to enhance the sales of preexisting product.

minimum number of masters The smallest number of masters an artist is obligated to deliver to the record company during a stated contract period if so requested by the record company.

morals clause A provision in a performer's agreement which allows the company to suspend or terminate the agreement if the performer commits or, sometimes, is even accused of, committing an immoral act.

most favored nation A term taken from diplomacy used in contracts to specify that the party promised "most favored nation" status will, if any other entity negotiates more favorable terms in their agreement, receive the same terms.

MPTF *See* Music Performance Trust Funds.

music performance fees Fees paid to the performing rights societies—e.g., ASCAP, BMI, and SESAC—for the privilege of performing music publicly for profit.

Music Performance Trust Funds (MPTF) Trust funds, to which record companies are required to contribute monies, which are used "to promote live music" by financing live concerts. The contributions are based upon a royalty due on the sale of recordings.

neighboring rights Rights of performers, producers, record companies, broadcast organizations, and others to royalties for the public performance of a preexisting work. Sometimes also referred to as *copyright-related rights*. Signatories to the Rome Convention of 1961 agreed to protect the neighboring rights of foreign nationals. The United States is not a party to the Rome Convention and, accordingly, does not grant neighboring rights as such.

net income The income remaining after the reduction of gross income by all deductible costs.

net royalties The royalty which remains after the deduction of costs. In recording agreements in connection with a sharing of royalties received from a third party, usually the licensing of rights to an outside party, net royalty is the sum remaining after deducting applicable costs, which may include MPTF payments, mechanical license fees, etc., and is shared, usually equally, between the record company and the artist or production company.

nondramatic musical works Individual musical works not used in conjunction with a dramatic performance. For example, a song from a musical recorded individually is a nondramatic musical work, but when the entire musical is recorded, it becomes a dramatic musical work. *Also see* Grand performing rights; Small performing rights.

nonreturnable advance Advance that is recoverable only from royalties earned. The artist, writer, or other entity (it could be a company) is not required to pay back the advance even if the royalties actually earned are less than the amount advanced.

normal-retail-channel distribution Distribution of full-priced recordings through standard distribution methods, as opposed, for example, to methods of distribution whereby recordings are sold at less than full price or through record clubs. The term is often found in recording agreements in provisions specifying that only full-priced record sales apply in determining sales plateaus for royalty accelerations and in determining base royalties.

open-ended agreement (or contract) A recording agreement having a term which is determined by the delivery dates of product, for example, one in which the initial period is one year and the four one-year option periods commence within a specified time (say, eight months) after delivery of the last album to be delivered in the prior period.

option A privilege which one party has which that party may or may not elect to exercise. In music agreements, it generally refers to the company's ability to continue the term of the agreement for an additional period.

option period The period or periods provided for in a contract that may or may not commence, depending on whether one or both of the signatories decides to exercise the option. A period or term of an agreement which exists after the initial period of the agreement.

otherwise applicable royalty A term referring to the reduction of the royalty rate, for example, "one-half of the otherwise applicable royalty." This may result in multiple reductions if the otherwise applicable royalty is already a reduced royalty; for example, the base royalty is reduced by half for record club royalties which are again reduced by half when applied to foreign royalties.

overcall Masters to be recorded by an artist in addition to the minimum number of masters contractually required to be recorded during a particular period. For example, if a contract calls for a minimum of two albums during the second year of the agreement and the record company then demands that the artist record a third album, the demand is an overcall.

override A royalty or other payment made to a third party that is in addition to the royalty terms specified in a given contract. For example, in a case in which a record company has all rights to masters and demos, the contract may specify that if the artist uses the demos to obtain a contract with another company, the other company must pay a royalty (the override) to the first company.

packaging *See* Container.

payola The common name for a violation of the Federal Communications Act in which recordings are broadcasted in return for a gift of something of value (e.g., money, drugs, a new car, or even a set of new tires), or services without public disclosure of the payment or gift.

performance rights society An association, corporation, or other entity that licenses neighboring rights, collects fees, and disburses royalties to performers for the use of preexisting copyrights.

performing rights society As defined in the Copyright Act of 1976, an association, corporation, or other entity that licenses the public performance of nondramatic musical works on behalf of copyright owners of such works, such as ASCAP, BMI, and SESAC.

personal manager Distinct from an agent, the personal representative of an artist who is responsible for advising and counseling the artist in the development of the artist's career.

phonorecords As defined in the Copyright Act of 1976, the material objects in which sounds, other than motion picture or audiovisual works, are fixed (including masters), and from which the sounds can be perceived, reproduced, or otherwise communicated, either directly or with the aid of a machine or device.

pipeline monies Royalties or other monies which have been collected but are not yet due for payment; in general, monies from foreign sources which have been collected by a licensee in the foreign territory but are not due to be paid to the licensor until some time in the future.

point Percentage. One point is 1 percent. Accordingly, an artist who says he has made a

10-point deal has entered into an agreement for a royalty of 10%.

point of attachment The connection or circumstance which allows something or someone, including a company, to qualify for inclusion within the terms of an international convention or treaty which would not otherwise apply.

PPD *See* Published price to dealers.

premium record A record given away or sold at a lesser rate in connection with some other product, for example, buy a tire and get a Christmas album for $1.

production company The entity which directly signs and produces a recording artist and then enters into an agreement with a record company and furnishes the services of the artist to the record company.

promo (promotional copy) A copy of a work, usually a record, which is given away free for promotional purposes. For example, records given to radio stations in order to obtain airplay are promos.

public domain work Work not protected by copyright, which may be used without restriction and without payment.

public performance The performance, display, or transmission of a work, either in person or by means of a device, to more than a normal circle of a family and its social acquaintances.

published price to dealers (PPD) Refers to the method of creating a fictitious price for royalty calculations in foreign territories, usually based on the equivalent of a wholesale price. *See* Constructed price.

rate A negotiated fee for mechanical licenses, usually lower than the statutory rate.

record club A direct-to-consumer method of selling records through the mail. Buyers usually become members and select purchases from a list mailed by the company.

record one The first record sold. The computation and payment of royalties goes back retroactively to record one.

recording advance A payment of royalties to a recording artist before any records have been sold, usually paid in connection with recording and delivery of the product.

recording fund A specific sum of money which is earmarked for all the costs of recording an album and which can be used contractually as a method of paying advances to a recording artist or production company. That is, if the record costs less to produce than the money in the recording fund, the artist or production company gets the difference after delivery. (Since all recording costs are usually recoupable, the entire recording fund is an advance.)

recoupable Recoverable. Advances are recoupable from royalties.

reserves The portion of royalties held back by a company against the subsequent return of product. Reserves are used by recording companies as a hedge against records being returned after royalties have been paid on those records.

retail price Price set for the sale of product to the consumer rather than sale to a distributor, one-stop, or dealer for purposes of resale.

return privilege The privilege, but not necessarily the right, of a distributor, one-stop, or store to return records which it is unable, or unwilling, to sell.

returns Those records which are shipped by a manufacturer or distributor which are then returned unsold. Returns are debited against the number of records sold. Royalties are not due on returns as these are not records sold.

reuse An additional use of musical material in a different medium. For example, a recording made originally for sale as a commercial recording is used on the soundtrack of a motion picture. The new use is a reuse.

reuse fee The fee that is payable for the reuse of musical material in a medium other than that for which it was originally recorded. For example, a recording was originally made for use as the soundtrack of a motion picture. A soundtrack album is released. Since this is a new medium, the musicians must be paid a second time, as if they had recorded the material again. The film is released on television. Another reuse fee is due the musicians.

rider The attachment to an agreement for a live performance setting forth the performers "special needs" (demands) for dressing rooms, food, equipment, etc.

right of first refusal A right which is given to one party to match an offer made to another party by a third party.

royalty A payment made for the use or sale of something to a party granting the right for such use or sale. For example, a royalty payable to an artist for the sale of records is a payment to the artist for the rights to the performances contained on the recording.

royalty acceleration A built-in increase in the rate of royalty, usually based upon sales and/or passage of time.

royalty-bearing product Any product for which a royalty is due when the product is sold. In the music industry, the term generally designates records and is frequently used in connection with formulas for advances or royalty acceleration, for example, "an increase of 1% upon the sale of 100,000 royalty-bearing albums."

royalty computation price The dollar amount of a recording, retail or wholesale, used to calcu-

late the royalty to be paid on sales of the recording. After all deductions (e.g., container charges) have been taken from the applicable wholesale or retail price of the recording, the royalty computation price is multiplied by the contractually agreed-upon royalty percentage, and the result is then multiplied by the applicable number of units sold to reach the royalty payable.

royalty-free product A product, usually a record, the transfer of which does not result in a royalty being due and payable, for example, freebies, promotional records, scrap, etc.

sampling Taking a preexisting sound recording or audio component, or portion thereof, to use in or to create a sound recording.

SESAC *See* Society of European Stage Authors & Composers, Inc.

signing advance An advance (prepayment of royalties) given at the time a contract is signed, usually to a recording artist or writer, but may also be given to producers, production companies, etc. It is an inducement to sign the contract. As an advance, it is recoverable from royalties.

single (1) A double-sided 7-inch 45-rpm vinyl recording, generally containing one musical composition on each side; (2) A CD with only one or two musical compositions.

single accounting unit When used in conjunction with royalties, a term which means that all agreements between the artist, writer, producer, production company, etc., and the record company, publisher, etc., are considered to be cross-collateralized. In other words, these separate agreements are lumped into one pot for royalty purposes, which allows the party doing the cross-collateralizing to offset the credits under agreement with the debits from another agreement. For example, unrecouped recording costs under a recording agreement could be recouped from the songwriter's royal-

ties under a songwriter's agreement with the publisher affiliated with the record company.

small performing rights The right to perform a musical work "publicly for profit," such as the right to broadcast a recording of a musical work over the radio.

Society of European Stage Authors & Composers, Inc. (SESAC) The third public performance society in the United States, along with ASCAP and BMI. It is much smaller than either ASCAP or BMI.

special payments funds These are trust funds to which record companies are required to contribute. The monies are distributed to members of the American Federation of Musicians based upon session work performed by such members.

statutory rate The mechanical license fee specified by the Copyright Act. *See also* Mechanical license fee.

sublicensee This is a licensee of a licensee. For example, artist A licenses a song to publisher B for the entire world, B turns around and licenses the song in the United Kingdom to publisher C. C is the sublicensee.

subpublisher A publisher, usually in another country, who is a sublicensee.

suggested retail list price The suggested selling price to the public set by the manufacturer of the product, for example, $15.95 for a CD. In the music industry, even though an album may sell for considerably less, the suggested retail list price is used by some record companies as the basis for computing royalties.

synchronization rights The right to synchronize visual images (e.g., film and video) with sound (a musical composition, e.g., a song on a film soundtrack). Such synchronization requires that the owner of the musical composition grant the user a synchronization license, for which a negotiated synchronization fee is paid.

term (1) A fixed period of time for which a contract is in force, as in "the term of the contract is 5 years." (2) A word or condition included in an agreement, as in "the terms of the agreement."

termination In the context of contracts in the music industry, the ending or stoppage of an agreement.

tour support The financial aid given to recording artists, usually by the record company, to assist the artist in making public appearances while on tour.

trademark A distinctive mark or logo used to identify a product, goods, or services.

TV/key outlet merchandising In the music industry, selling records, via television advertising, which may be obtained only at certain specific stores (the key outlets). Sometimes a type of premium sale.

unrecouped advance That portion of money paid in advance of sales and/or costs advanced to or on behalf of an artist (or other party) that is unrecovered because sales have not generated a sufficient sum of money to recover the entire advance. "Unrecouped" is sometimes used to describe an artist or writer whose royalty account indicates that advances and/or costs exceed earnings.

wholesale price The price of goods charged to the intermediary by the manufacturer so that the intermediary may sell to the public at a higher rate.

work for hire Under copyright law, (1) a work prepared by an employee within the scope of his or her employment or (2) a work specially ordered or commissioned if the parties expressly agree in writing that the work shall be a work made for hire.

Index

AB997, 549–551

Accounting, recording agreements and, 121–125

Accounting Department, 25

Accounting periods, royalty, 124–125

Acknowledgment, artist's inducement and, 204–205

Acuff-Rose Music, Inc. v. Campbell, 505n

Address, change of, 186

Administration agreements, 328–341
 compensation in, 337–339
 costs in, 339–340
 term of, 334–336
 territory of, 336–337

Administration fees, 318–322

Administration in copublishing agreements, 316–318

Administration income, 192

Administrators, duties of, 330–334

Advances, 103–104, 110
 conditional, 40
 on exercise of option, 38–39
 in foreign distribution agreements, 468–471
 in foreign subpublishing agreements, 345–347
 for injunction, 112
 in merchandising rights, 364
 nonshared, in songwriters' agreements, 298–299
 payable on delivery, 40
 payable when option period commences, 39
 production company and artist share, 113–114
 production fees as, 212
 recoupment of, in recording agreements, 103–116
 reduced by unrecouped balance, 111
 rolling, 346
 and royalties shared pro-rata, 121

signing, 104–105, 290
 in songwriters' agreements, 281–282
 songwriter's guaranteed, exclusive songwriters' agreements and, 281–287
 tied to record contract, 285–287

Advertising, 12
 approval over, 12
 in independent producer agreements, 219–221

Advertising content, control over, 12

Advertising Department, 23

AFM (American Federation of Musicians), 30, 228

AFTRA (American Federation of Television and Recording Artists), 30, 228

Agee v. Paramount Communications, 511

Agents, 544–546
 managers acting as, 546–551

Agreements, 3
 open-ended, 34–35
 preincorporation, 5

Albums
 multiple, 46
 soundtrack, 394–395

All-in agreements, *see* Production (all-in) agreements

Allowable returns, 71

Amenities, special, 17–19

American Federation of Musicians (AFM), 30, 228

American Federation of Television and Recording Artists (AFTRA), 30, 228

American performing rights societies, 407–411

American Society of Composers, Authors and Publishers (ASCAP), 289–291, 407–411

Analog tape copies, 91

Annual minimum compensation guaranteed, 144–145

APRA (Australasian Performance Rights Association), 414

A&R (Artist and Repertoire) Department,
    21–22
Arbuckle, Fatty, 163
Arm's-length relationship in copublishing
    agreements, 324–325
Art Department, 24
Artist and Repertoire (A&R) Department,
    21–22
Artist grants rights, 153
Artist indemnification for samples, 147
Artist/production company royalties in
    recording agreements, 119–121
Artist recording agreements, *see* Recording
    agreements
Artist Relations Department, 25
Artists
    conversion of, in distribution agreements,
        440–443
    exclusivity for, in personal management
        agreements, 556
    pro-rata royalties for, 235, 237–239
Artists' Managers Act, 547
Artwork in recording agreements, 181–184
ASCAP (American Society of Composers,
    Authors and Publishers), 289–291,
    407–411
Assignment, 533
    short-form, 534
Audio Home Recording Act, 527–530
Audiovisual works, 256
Audits, 122–123
Australasian Performance Rights Association
    (APRA), 414
Authorship, certificate of, 377
Automatic exercise of options, 42, 43-44
AV device, 257

Base royalties, 68
Berne Convention for the Protection of
    Literary and Artistic Works, 412
Billing, 11
Biographies, 183
Black Box, 355–357
Blocked funds, 84–85, 86, 87, 350, 353
BMI (Broadcast Music, Inc.), 289–291, 407–408,
    411
Bond, posting, 155
Box office, access to, 16–17
Box sets, 99
Bright Tunes Music Corp. v. Harrisongs Music,
    Ltd., 499n
Broadcast Music, Inc. (BMI), 289–291, 407–408,
    411
Broadcasting, noncommercial, 522
Broadcasting organizations, 422–423

Buchwald v. Katz, 546–549
Buchwald v. Superior Court, 546–547
Budget records in recording agreements, 94-97
BUMA (Vereniging Bureau voor Muziek
    Auteursrecht), 414
Business Affairs Department, 22
Business manager, 6
By-Laws Provision, 6

California Civil Code
    Section 990, 178
    Sections 986 and 987, 418
California Labor Code
    Section 2855, 28–29, 131
    Sections 1700 through 1700.46, 544–546
Canadian Musical Reproductions Rights
    Agency Limited (CMRRA), 414
Carey v. Kearsley, 494
CDs, *see* Compact discs
Change of address, 186
China, copyright protection in, 424
Civil remedies, 539–540
Claims, 154–155
CMRRA (Canadian Musical Reproductions
    Rights Agency Limited), 414
Coadministration, 333–334
Cohen v. Paramount Pictures Corp., 402–404
Collection agents, 319, 320
Collective publishing entity, 9–10
Collective work, 495
Commercial release, 137
Commercial tie-ins, 177
Commissions in personal management
    agreements, 551-553
Common-law trademark, 365
Community for Creative Non-Violence v. Reid,
    530–531
Compact discs, 87–90
    royalties on, 88–90
Company's obligations in distribution
    agreements, 435–438
Compensation guaranteed, annual minimum,
    144–145
Compensation in administration agreements,
    337–339
Compilation, 125, 495
Complimentary tickets, 17
Composers, duties of, 370–374
Compositions
    controlled, 196
    digital transmission and, 487–489
Compulsory license, 512–521
    royalties payable under, 516
Compulsory license fee, 287–288
Compulsory rate, 196

Concert, cancellation of, 12
Concert halls, 290
Concert riders, 10–11
Conditional advances, 40
Conditional downloads, 491
Conditional guaranteed release, 136
Conglomerates, 21
Consideration, 56
Constructed price, 64
  construction of, 83
  royalties on basis of, 65
Container charges in recording agreements,
      98–100
Contingent release, 137
Contract, standard, 28
Contributions, proportionate, 126
Controlled compositions, 196, 279
Conversion clause, 234, 440–441
Conversion of artists in distribution
      agreements, 440–443
Copies, 495, 513
Copublishing, 195
  in songwriters' agreements, 272
Copublishing agreements, 193, 310–327
  administration in, 316–318
  arm's-length relationship in, 324–325
  costs in, 318–322
  exclusive, 311
  nonexclusive, 311
  ownership in, 314–316
  performing rights in, 322–323
  right of first refusal in, 325–327
  term of, 312–313
  territory of, 313–314
Copyright, 192, 493–534
  defined, 493
  definitions in, 495–497
  exclusive rights in, 502–504
  international overview, 412–413
  joint ownership, 10
  management of, 328
  subject matter of, 499–502
  term of, 526–527
  transfer of, 533–534
    in master purchase agreements, 229–230
Copyright Act of 1909, 494
Copyright Act of 1976, U.S., 494–504
  Section 101 (definitions), 495–497, 525
  Section 102 (what is covered by copyright),
      500–501
  Section 103 (compilations and derivative
      works), 501–502
  Section 106 (exclusive rights), 502–503
  Section 107 (fair use), 499, 504–507
  Section 109 (first-sale doctrine), 507–509

Section 110 (performance and display), 509
Section 112 (ephemeral recordings), 509–510
Section 114 (exceptions to exclusive rights),
      510–511
Section 115 (compulsory license), 512–521
Section 116 (jukebox exemption), 521
Section 118 (noncommercial broadcasting),
      522
Section 201 (partial rights), 503
Section 512 (license fees), 525
  soundtrack agreements and, 401
Copyright Amendment Act of 1991, 527
Copyright infringement, 498–99
Copyright management information, integrity
      of, 537–539
Copyright owner, 495
  obtaining information from, 340–341
Copyright protection provisions, circumvention
      of, 536–537
Copyright Royalty Tribunal, 519–520
Corporate Resolution, 6
Corporations
  forming, 4–5
  informal agreement to form, 5
  intention to form, 5
Costs
  in administration agreements, 339–340
  in copublishing agreements, 318–322
  in foreign distribution agreements, 468–471
  in foreign subpublishing agreements,
      348–349
Coterminous arrangement, 270
Coterminous period, 272
Counterfeit tickets, 15
Coupling, 93
  in recording agreements, 125–129
Coupling clause, 215, 216
Courtesy copy, 185
Cover records in foreign distribution
      agreements, 479–480
Cowriters
  royalties to, 300
  in songwriters' agreements, 300–301
Credit in soundtrack agreements, 387–390
Credit obligations, detailed, 220–221
Criminal offenses and penalties, 540–541
Cross-collateralization, 215, 216
  in recording agreements, 101–103
  in video and DVD, 261
Cuts, number of, 45–46

DDC (digital compact cassette), 90
Decision making, 6
Delivery, 50–52
  in master purchase agreements, 226–227

Delivery requirements, 51–52
Demonstration costs in songwriters'
   agreements, 299–300
Denmark, copyright protection in, 427
Deposit, forfeiture of, 12
Derivative work, 495
Detailed indemnification, 157
Development agreements, *see* Option
   agreements
Digital compact cassette (DDC), 90
Digital Millennium Copyright Act (DMCA),
   501, 535–543
Digital Performance Right in Sound
   Recordings Act (DPRSR), 510, 511, 514
Digital transmission, 484–492
   compositions and, 487–489
   rights licensed in, 484–486
   royalties in, 489–492
   territory of, 486–487
Direct Consumer Plan, 81
Disclaimer in personal management
   agreements, 555
Distributed labels, 23
Distribution agreements, 429–455
   company's obligations in, 435–438
   conversion of artists in, 440–443
   distribution fees in, 446–447
   distributor's obligations in, 433–435
   exclusivity in, 438–439
   freebies in, 447–449
   inventory in, 451–453
   product in, 439–440
   reserves in, 449–451
   term of, 430–431
   termination in, 453–455
   territory of, 431–432
   warranties and representations in, 443–446
Distribution Department, 22–23
Distribution fees in distribution agreements,
   446–447
Distributor's obligations in distribution
   agreements, 433–435
DMCA (Digital Millennium Copyright Act),
   501, 535–543
Double dipping, 212
   pro-rata royalties with, 239–240
Double-pocket jackets, 99
Double recoupment, 238
Downloads
   conditional, 491
   of music, 541–543
   permanent, 491–492
DPRSR (Digital Performance Right in Sound
   Recordings Act), 510, 511, 514
Dramatic musical works, 513

Droit moral, 417–418, 515
DVD, *see* Video and DVD

Economy records, 94–97
Editorial Department, 24
Electronic transmission, 90–92
Emerson v. Davies, 504n
Employment, review of, in personal
   management agreements, 555–556
Employment status in soundtrack agreements,
   375–377
Enforceable life of recording agreements, 31
Equitable relief
   in recording agreements, 137–145
   in songwriters' agreements, 307–309
Equity, 138
Escalation, royalties with, 215
Escape clause in personal management
   agreements, 553–554
Establishment, 525
Excess recordings, 47
Exchange rates, 83–84
Exclusive copublishing agreements, 311
Exclusive rights in copyright, 502–504
Exclusive songwriters' agreements, 269–270
Exclusivity
   for artist in personal management
      agreements, 556
   in distribution agreements, 438–439
   in soundtrack agreements, 381
Exercise of options, 35–41
   advances on, 38–39
   advances payable on delivery, 40
   advances payable when option period
      commences, 39
   automatic, 42, 43–44
   negating, 44
   notice of, 40–41
   in option agreements, 248–249
   timely, 41–44
Exhibition copy, 257

Failure to deliver, 50–51
Fair use, 499, 504–507
Fairness in Music Licensing Act of 1998, 290,
   522–526
Federal trademark registration, 173
Fees in foreign subpublishing agreements,
   347–348
Felony, 165
File sharing, 541–543
Film producer, duties of, 374–375
Finland, copyright protection in, 427
First refusal, right of, 191
First-sale doctrine, 507–509

First-use issue, 169
Flat period, 31
Flow-through clause, 235, 240
Force majeur, 54, 59–62
Foreign distribution agreements, 463–483
  advances in, 468–471
  costs in, 468–471
  cover records in, 479–480
  guaranteed release in, 471–474
  payment in, 474–475
  product in, 465–466
  rights granted to licensee in, 466–468
  rights on termination in, 480–483
  royalties in, 468–471
  supplying of materials and product in,
      475–477
  territory of, 464–465
  trademarks in, 477–479
Foreign receipts, songwriter's share of, in
      songwriters' agreements, 296–298
Foreign royalties, one-half, 85–86
Foreign sales, 82–87
  record club, 82–85
Foreign societies, 413–416
Foreign subpublishers, 342
Foreign subpublishing agreements, 342–357
  advances in, 345–347
  costs in, 348–349
  fees in, 347–348
  payment in, 349–353
  term of, 343–344
  territory of, 344–345
Form "B," 54, 209
Form I-9, 54, 209
Founding member, 7
Foxx v. Williams, 139–140
France, copyright protection in, 424–425
Fraud, 169
Freebies, 75–77
  in distribution agreements, 447–449
  returns and, 76
FSO (furnishing the services of) company, 202
Full-royalty sales, 68
Funds, blocked, 84–85, 86, 87, 350, 353
Furnishing the services of (FSO) company, 202

Gatefold albums, 98–99
GEMA (Gesellschaft für musikalische
      Aufführungs und mechanische
      Vervielfältigungsrechte), 414
General partnership, 3–4
Germany, copyright protection in, 425–426
Gesellschaft für musikalische Aufführungs
      und mechanische Vervielfältigungsrechte
      (GEMA), 414

*Grand Upright Music Limited v. Warner
      Brothers Records [et al.]*, 532–533
Grant of rights
  in recording agreements, 148–153
  by songwriter in songwriters' agreements,
      304–307
  in soundtrack agreements, 381–385
Gross publishers' share, 318
Gross sums, 318
Group name, 7, 168, 170–172
Group provisions in recording agreements,
      188–191
Groups, formation and operation of, 3–19
Guaranteed advance, songwriter's, exclusive
      songwriters' agreements and, 281–287
Guaranteed annual minimum compensation,
      144–145
Guaranteed release
  conditional, 136
  in foreign distribution agreements, 471–474
Guaranteed video, 259–261

Hagar v. Capitol Records, Inc., 30
*Harper & Row, Publishers, Inc. v. Nation
      Enterprises*, 506
Harry Fox Agency, 198*n*
Headline billing, sole, 11
Hi-Tech Video Prods. v. Capital Cities/ABC, 531
Hold-harmless clauses, 154
Holograms, 99
Hotels, 290

Iceland, copyright protection in, 427
IFPI (International Federation of the
      Phonographic Industry), 414
Incorporation by reference
  in master purchase agreements, 225–226
  in option agreements, 250–251
Indemnification, 154–157
  artist, for samples, 147
  detailed, 157
  in songwriters' agreements, 302–304
Independent producer agreements, 206–221
  advertising in, 219–221
  producer's royalty in, 215–217
  production fee in, 211–213
  publicity in, 219–221
  record one in, 217–218
  recording costs in, 213–214
  term of, 210–211
Independents (indies), 23
Inducement
  artist's, 204–205
  in production (all-in) agreements, 234
  in recording agreements, 202–205

Inducement letter, 202
  sample, 203–204
Injunction, advances for, 112
Injunctive relief, 143
  in production (all-in) agreements, 243–245
Insurance, 5
  superstar, 142, 243, 244
International agreements, 496
International copyright overview, 412–413
International Department, 26
International Federation of the Phonographic
    Industry (IFPI), 414
Internet, 91
  singles on, 72
Inventory in distribution agreements, 451–453
Italy, copyright protection in, 426

Jacket charge, 98
Jackets, double-pocket, 99
Jackson, Michael, 164
Japan, copyright protection in, 426
Japanese Society for Rights of Authors,
    Composers and Publishers (JASRAC),
    414
JASRAC (Japanese Society for Rights of
    Authors, Composers and Publishers), 414
Joint recordings in recording agreements, 126,
    129–130
Joint work, 496
Jointly owned copyrights, 10
Jukebox license, 521

Key man clause in recording agreements,
    161–163

L. Batlin & Son, Inc. v. Snyder, 500
Label copy, 208
Label in recording agreements, 165–167
Latin America, copyright protection in, 426
Lease agreement, 230
Lease of masters in master purchase
    agreements, 230–232
Leaving member, 188
Legal Department, 22
License fees, mechanical, 196
Limited liability company (LLC), forming, 4–5
Liner notes, 208
List of rights granted, 150–151
List price, retail, *see* Retail list price
Live performances, 46
LLC (limited liability company), forming, 4–5
Loan-out agreements, 378–380
Losses, 8
Low-price records, 94–97
Lumley v. Wagner, 138

Major record companies, 275
Managers, 544–546
  acting as agents, 546–551
  obligations of, 554–555
Managing members, 4
Manufacturing agreements, 456–459
Manufacturing Department, 23
Master purchase agreements, 222–232
  delivery in, 226–227
  incorporation by reference in, 225–226
  lease of masters in, 230–232
  purchase price in, 223–224
  term in, 232
  transfer of copyright in, 229–230
  transfer of ownership in, 226
  warranties and representations in, 227–229
Master purchases, 108
Master use license in soundtrack agreements,
    398–399
Masters, 45, 210
  additional, limit on, 49
  costs in recording, 106–108
  lease of, in master purchase agreements,
    230–232
  overcall, 47
  reduce number of, 134
  studio, 49
  unrecorded, in recording agreements,
    130–134
Materials, supplying of, in foreign distribution
    agreements, 475–477
Maximum, negotiating, 47–48
MCA Records v. Newton-John, 140
MCPS (Mechanical Copyright Protection
    Society), 414
Mechanical Copyright Protection Society
    (MCPS), 414
Mechanical fees in soundtrack agreements,
    401–405
Mechanical license, 265
Mechanical license fees, 196, 265–266
  songwriter's share of, in songwriters'
    agreements, 287–288
Mechanical royalties, 199–200
Members, 4
  founding, 7
  leaving, 7, 188
  new, 7
Merchandise, promotional, 175–176
Merchandising, 13–14
Merchandising Department, 22–23
Merchandising rights, 358–366
  advances in, 364
  in recording agreements, 177–180
  rights licensed by, 361–362

royalties in, 362–364
term of, 358–360
territory of, 360–361
trademarks in, 365–366
Mid-line records in recording agreements, 95–97
Midler v. Ford Motor Co., 178*n*
Minimum commitment
adjusted, 49–50
in songwriters' agreements, 278
Minimum-commitment number, 47
Minimum compensation guaranteed, annual,
144–145
Minimum dollar amounts for promotion, 119
Minimum/maximum
after second album, 115–116
based on royalties, 114–115
Minimum-maximum provisions, 109
Miniseries, 490–492
Miscellaneous income
in songwriters' agreements, 296
in soundtrack agreements, 405
Morals clause in recording agreements,
163–165
Motown Record Corp. v. Brockert, 140–141
MPTF (Music Performance Trust Fund), 107,
116–117
Multiple albums, 46
Music, downloading of, 541–543
Music Performance Trust Fund (MPTF), 107,
116–117
Music rights for video and DVD, 265–268
Music supervisor, duties of, 368–370
Musical compositions, ownership of, in
recording agreements, 191–195

Name
group, 7, 168, 170–172
in recording agreements, 167–173
trade, 165
Napster, 542
National laws on neighboring rights, 423–428
Negotiating maximum, 47–48
Neighboring rights, 416–419
national laws on, 423–428
Net sales, 66, 67
NETA (No Electronic Theft Act), 542
New York Arts and Cultural Affairs Law, 523
Nightclubs, 290
No Electronic Theft Act (NETA), 542
Noncommercial broadcasting, 522
Nondelivery, 52
Nondramatic musical works, 513
Nonexclusive copublishing agreements, 311
Nonexclusive songwriters' agreements,
269–270

Nonexclusivity for personal manager in
personal management agreements, 556
Nonshared advances in songwriters'
agreements, 298–299
Norway, copyright protection in, 427
Notice provisions in recording agreements,
184–186

One-half foreign royalties, 85–86
One-half royalties, 80
One-stops, 429
Open-ended agreements, 34–35
Option agreements, 246–254
exercise of option in, 248–249
incorporation by reference in, 250–251
override in, 252–254
recording commitment in, 249–250
rights on nonexercise in, 251–254
term in, 247–248
Option-exercise letter, 29
Option periods, 36–38
Options, exercise of, *see* Exercise of options
Orphaned recordings, 251
Overcall, duration extended by, 49
Overcall masters, 47
Override in option agreements, 252–254
Ownership
of musical compositions in recording
agreements, 191–195
transfer of, in master purchase agreements,
226

Packaging charge, 98
Palmieri v. Estefan, 498
Papa's-June Music, Inc. v. McLean, 533–534
Participation agreement, 310
Partnership, general, 3–4
Payment
in foreign distribution agreements, 474–475
in foreign subpublishing agreements,
349–353
Percentage of sales, 65–67
Performance rights societies, performing
rights societies versus, 406
Performance society, term, 356
Performances
live, 46
public, 289
recording, 12–13
Performers' rights in Rome Convention of
1961, 420–421
Performing fees in soundtrack agreements,
399–400
Performing rights in copublishing agreements,
322–323

Performing rights societies, 496, 526
    American, 407–411
    performance rights societies versus, 406
Performing Rights Society (PRS), 415
Permanent downloads, 491–492
Personal management agreements, 551–557
    commissions in, 551–553
    disclaimer in, 555
    escape clause in, 553–554
    exclusivity for artist in, 556
    nonexclusivity for personal manager in, 556
    review of employment in, 555–556
    term of, 553
Personal managers, 544–546
    nonexclusivity for, in personal management
        agreements, 556
Personal Rights Protection Act of 1984,
        Tennessee's, 178–179
Personal service contracts, 29
Personality songbook, 304–305
Phonograph records, 62
Phonographic Performance Limited (PPL),
        414–415
Phonorecords, 496, 513
Photographs in recording agreements, 181–184
Picture disc, 89
Posting bond, 155
PPD (published price to dealers), 64
PPL (Phonographic Performance Limited),
        414–415
Preincorporation agreements, 5
Premium, definition of, 93
Premium records, 92–94
Price
    constructed, see Constructed price
    retail, see Retail price
    wholesale, see Wholesale price
Pricing, variable, 63
Print rights in songwriters' agreements,
        292–294
Print royalties, 293–294
Pro-rata royalties, 9
    for artist, 235, 237–239
    with double dipping, 239–240
Producer
    duties of, 206–210
    new, cap on royalties paid to, 242–243
    production (all-in) agreements and, 240–243
Producer agreements, independent, see
        Independent producer agreements
Producers' rights in Rome Convention of 1961,
        421–422
Producer's royalty in independent producer
        agreements, 215–217
Product

    in distribution agreements, 439–440
    in foreign distribution agreements, 465–466
    supplying of, 475–477
Production (all-in) agreements, 107, 233–245
    injunctive relief in, 243–245
    producer and, 240–243
    royalties in, 235–240
Production company, rate and, 201
Production costs
    recoupment in video, 261, 262
    in video and DVD, 261–262
Production fee
    as advance, 212
    in independent producer agreements,
        211–213
    recoupment of, 218
Profits, 8
Program, 256
Promotion, minimum dollar amounts for, 119
Promotion costs in recording agreements,
        117–119
Promotion Department, 24
Promotional merchandise, 175–176
Proportionate contributions, 126
Proprietor, 526
PRS (Performing Rights Society), 415
Public figure, 178
Public performance, 289
Public performance fees in songwriters'
        agreements, 288–292
Publication, 496–497
Publicity
    in independent producer agreements,
        219–221
    in recording agreements, 173–176
    right of, 173, 174, 178
Publicity Department, 25
Published price to dealers (PPD), 64
Publisher's share, 192
Publishing companies, 26
Publishing entity, collective, 9–10
Purchase price
    in master purchase agreements, 223–224
    in songwriters' agreements, 280–282

Radio stations, 290
Rate
    earlier date to determine, 200–201
    production company and, 201
    in recording agreements, 196–201
    variable, 198–199
Reasonable reserves, 73, 74–75
Record, 62, 257
    shop-worn, 452
Record agreement, see Recording agreements

Record club foreign sales, 82-85
Record club royalties, 66
Record clubs, 77–82
  specialty, 78
Record companies, 558
  major, 275
  setup of, 20–26
    Accounting Department, 25
    Advertising Department, 23
    A&R Department, 21–22
    Art Department, 24
    Artist Relations Department, 25
    Business Affairs, 22
    Distribution Department, 22–23
    Editorial Department, 24
    International Department, 26
    Legal Department, 22
    Manufacturing Department, 23
    Merchandising Department, 22–23
    Promotion Department, 24
    Publicity Department, 25
    publishing and, 26
    Sales Department, 22–23
    Special Products Department, 25–26
Record contract, *see* Recording agreements
Record one in independent producer
    agreements, 217–218
Recording, releasing versus, 47
Recording agreements, 27–205
  accounting and, 121–125
  advance tied to, 285–287
  artist/production company royalties in,
    119–121
  artwork in, 181–184
  budget records, 94–97
  compact discs, 87–90
  container charges, 98–100
  coupling in, 125–129
  cross-collateralization, 101–103
  defined, 27
  electronic transmission, 90–92
  enforceable life of, 31
  equitable relief in, 137–145
  force majeur, 54, 59–62
  foreign sales, 82–87
  freebies, 75–77
  grant-of-rights provisions in, 148–153
  group provisions in, 188–191
  inducement in, 202–205
  joint recordings in, 126, 129–130
  key man clause in, 161–163
  label in, 165–167
  merchandising rights in, 177–180
  mid-line records, 95–97
  morals clause in, 163–165

MPTF and special payments funds, 116–117
  name in, 167–173
  notice provisions in, 184–186
  ownership of musical compositions in,
    191–195
  percentage of sales, 65–67
  photographs in, 181–184
  premium records, 92–94
  promotion costs in, 117–119
  publicity in, 173–176
  rate in, 196–201
  record clubs, 77–82
  recording commitment, 44–54
  recoupment of advances in, 103–116
  release of recordings in, 135–137
  rerecording restrictions in, 158–161
  reserves, 72–73
  returns, 71–75
  royalties and, 62–63
  royalty acceleration, 68–71
  sampling in, 145–148
  sideman in, 186–188
  suspension, 54–59
  term of, 28–35
  termination, 54–59
  unrecorded masters in, 130–134
  warranties and representations in, 153–157
  wholesale or retail, 63–65
Recording artist, writer as, in songwriters'
    agreements, 274–277
Recording commitment, 44–54
  in option agreements, 249–250
Recording contract, *see* Recording agreements
Recording costs, 106–108
  definition of, 112
  in independent producer agreements,
    213–214
  shared by artist and production company,
    113
Recording fund, 108–110
  payment schedule, 111–112
Recording Industry Association of America
    (RIAA), 520, 542–543
Recording performances, 12–13
Recordings, 62
  excess, 47
  orphaned, 251
  release of, in recording agreements, 135–137
Recoupment
  of advances in recording agreements,
    103–116
  double, 238
  production cost, in video, 261, 262
  of production fee, 218
  royalties adjusted after, 224

Registration, federal trademark, 173
Release, 135
  commercial, 137
  conditional guaranteed, 136
  contingent, 137
  of recordings, in recording agreements,
    135–137
Releasing, recording versus, 47
Representations, warranties and, *see*
    Warranties and representations
Rerecording restrictions
  in recording agreements, 158–161
  reverse, 156–157
Reserves, 72–73
  in distribution agreements, 449–451
  reasonable, 73, 74–75
Retail list price, 63
  suggested, 64–65
Retail price
  changing wholesale price to, 64
  wholesale price or, 63–65
Retention of rights in soundtrack agreements,
    385–387
Retroactive royalties, 68
Return privilege, 71
Returned goods, royalties on, 72
Returns, 71–75
  allowable, 71
  freebies and, 76
Reverse rerecording restriction, 156–157
Review of employment in personal
    management agreements, 555–556
RIAA (Recording Industry Association of
    America), 520, 542–543
Right of first refusal, 191
  in copublishing agreements, 325–327
Right of publicity, 173, 174, 178
Rights
  granted to licensee in foreign distribution
    agreements, 466–468
  licensed by merchandising rights, 361–362
  licensed in digital transmission, 484–486
  on nonexercise in option agreements,
    251–254
  small performance, 289
  on termination in foreign distribution
    agreements, 480–483
Rolling advance, 346
Rome Convention of 1961, 419–422
  performers' rights in, 420–421
Royalties, 28
  accounting in recording agreements and,
    121–125
  adjusted after recoupment, 224
  and advances shared pro-rata, 121

artist/production company, in recording
    agreements, 119–121
base, 68
on basis of constructed price, 65
on budget records, 94–97
cap on, paid to new producer, 242–243
on compact discs, 88–90
and coupling, 125–129
to cowriters, 300
cross-collateralization and, 101–103
in digital transmission, 489–492
in electronic transmission, 90–92
with escalation, 215
in foreign distribution agreements, 468–471
in independent producer agreements, 217–218
joint recordings and, 129–130
mechanical, 199–200
in merchandising rights, 362–364
on mid-line records, 95–97
minimum/maximum based on, 114–115
not payable, 76–77
one-half, 80
one-half foreign, 85–86
payable under compulsory license, 516
on premium records, 92–94
print, 293–294
pro-rata, *see* Pro-rata royalties
producer's, in independent producer
    agreements, 215–217
in production (all-in) agreements, 235–240
and rate in recording agreements, 196–201
record club, 66
recording agreements and, 62–63
reduction of, 79–80
retroactive, 68
on returned goods, 72
split, 116–117
synchronization, 295
variable reduction by territory, 86–87
video, in video and DVD, 263–265
Royalty acceleration, 68–71
Royalty accounting periods, 124–125
Royalty rate, 62–63
  vinyl, 89
Russian Federation, copyright protection in,
    426–427

SABAM (Société Belge des Auteurs,
    Compositeurs et Editeurs), 415
SACEM (Société des Auteurs, Compositeurs et
    Editeurs de Musique), 415
Sales
  of Albums through Normal Retail Channels
    in the United States (USNRC Sales),
    70–71, 216

full-royalty, 68
net, 66, 67
percentage of, 65–67
Sales Department, 22-23
Sample clearance as delivery requirement, 147
Samplers, 127
Samples, artist indemnification for, 147
Sampling, 532–533
  in recording agreements, 145–148
Santrayll v. Burrell, 499
Scalping, 15
Schweizerische Gesellschaft fur die Rechte die
      Urheber Musikalischer Werke (SUISA),
      416
Scores, 368
  length of, 372
SDRM (Société pour l'Administration du Droit
      de Reproduction Mechanique), 415
Secondary meaning issue, 169–170
Security agreements, 459–462
Services, unique and extraordinary, 144
SESAC (Society of European Stage Authors
      and Composers), 289, 407, 412
Shareholders, 4
Sheet music, 292
Shop-worn records, 452
Short-form assignment, 534
SIAE (Società Italiana degli Autori ed Editori),
      415
Sideman in recording agreements, 186–188
Sides, 45
  unrecorded, union scale payment for, 133
Sight and sound device, 257
Signing advances, 104–105, 290
Sinatra v. Goodyear Tire and Rubber Co., 178*n*
Single-song agreement, 270, 271–272
Singles on Internet, 72
Small performance rights, 289
SOCAN (Society of Composers, Authors and
      Music Publishers of Canada), 416
Società Italiana degli Autori ed Editori (SIAE),
      415
Société Belge des Auteurs, Compositeurs et
      Editeurs (SABAM), 415
Société des Auteurs, Compositeurs et Editeurs
      de Musique (SACEM), 415
Société pour l'Administration du Droit de
      Reproduction Mechanique (SDRM), 415
Society of Composers, Authors and Music
      Publishers of Canada (SOCAN), 416
Society of European Stage Authors and
      Composers (SESAC), 289, 407, 412
Songs, 367–368
Songwriter compensation in songwriters'
      agreements, 280

Songwriters' agreements, 269–309
  advances in, 281–282
  cowriters in, 300–301
  demonstration costs in, 299–300
  equitable relief in, 307–309
  exclusive, 269–270
    songwriter's guaranteed advance and,
        281–287
  grant of rights by songwriter in, 304–307
  indemnification in, 302–304
  miscellaneous income in, 296
  nonexclusive, 269–270
  nonshared advances in, 298–299
  print rights in, 292–294
  public performance fees in, 288–292
  purchase price in, 280–282
  songwriter compensation in, 280
  songwriter's share of foreign receipts in,
      296–298
  songwriter's share of mechanical license fees
      in, 287–288
  songwriting commitment in, 277–280
  synchronization licenses in, 294–295
  term in, 270–274
  warranties and representations in, 301–304
  writer as recording artist in, 274–277
Songwriter's guaranteed advance, exclusive
      songwriters' agreements and, 281–287
Songwriter's share, 192
  of foreign receipts in songwriters'
      agreements, 296–298
  of mechanical license fees in songwriters'
      agreements, 287–288
Songwriting commitment in songwriters'
      agreements, 277–280
Sonny Bono Copyright Term Extension Act,
      526–527
*Sony Corp. of America v. Universal City
      Studios, Inc.*, 505-506
Sound recordings, 497
Soundtrack agreements, 367–405
  Copyright Act of 1976, U.S. and, 401
  credit in, 387–390
  employment status in, 375–377
  exclusivity in, 381
  grant of rights in, 381–385
  master use license in, 398–399
  mechanical fees in, 401–405
  miscellaneous income in, 405
  performing fees in, 399–400
  retention of rights in, 385–387
  sources of income in, 390–405
  synchronization licenses in, 396–398
Soundtrack albums, 394–395
Soundtracks, creating, 390

Source music, 368
Sources of income in soundtrack agreements, 390–405
Spain, copyright protection in, 427–428
Special amenities, 17–19
Special payments funds, 116–117
Special Products Department, 25–26
Specialty record clubs, 78
Spiegelman v. Reprise Records, 498–499
Split royalties, 116–117
Standard contract, 28
Star billing, sole, 11
Starbucks, 559
Statute of Anne, 493
Statutory rate, 196, 287–288
    determination of, 519–521
STEMRA (StichtingStemra), 416
StichtingStemra (STEMRA), 416
Stickers, 99
Stockpiling, 46
Studio masters, 49
Subpublishers, duties of, 353–355
Suggested retail list price, 64–65
Suing, 154–155
SUISA (Schweizerische Gesellschaft fur die Rechte die Urheber Musikalischer Werke), 416
Superstar insurance, 142, 243, 244
Superstar method, 144
Supplying of materials and product in foreign distribution agreements, 475–477
Support act, 11
Suspension
    alternatives to, 56
    with conditional limit on time, 58
    impact of, 55–56
    recording agreements, 54–59
Sweden, copyright protection in, 427
Synchronization license fees, 266-268
Synchronization licenses, 259
    in songwriters' agreements, 294–295
    in soundtrack agreements, 396–398
Synchronization royalties, 295
Szabo v. Errisson, 516–517

Tape copies, analog, 91
Tax relief, 5
Telemarketing, 80–81
Television, 397–398
Television Music License Committee, 408
Television networks, 290
Tennessee's Personal Rights Protection Act of 1984, 178–179
Term
    of administration agreements, 334–336

of copublishing agreements, 312–313
of copyright, 526–527
of distribution agreements, 430–431
examples of provisions for, 32–35
extension of, 57
flat period, 31
of foreign subpublishing agreements, 343–344
of independent producer agreements, 210–211
of master purchase agreements, 232
of merchandising rights, 358–360
of option agreements, 247–248
of personal management agreements, 553
of recording agreements, 28–35
of songwriters' agreements, 270–274
Termination
    in distribution agreements, 453–455
    in recording agreements, 54–59
    rights on, in foreign distribution agreements, 480–483
Territory
    of administration agreements, 336–337
    of copublishing agreements, 313–314
    of digital transmission, 486–487
    of distribution agreements, 431–432
    of foreign distribution agreements, 464–465
    of foreign subpublishing agreements, 344–345
    of merchandising rights, 360–361
    variable reduction by, 86–87
Tickets, 14–17
    approval of sales of, 16
    complimentary, 17
    counterfeit, 15
Timely exercise of options, 41–44
Timing, 55
Trade name, 165
Trade-Related Aspects of Intellectual Property Rights (TRIPS), 413
Trademark license, 478–479
Trademark registration, federal, 173
Trademarks
    common-law, 365
    in foreign distribution agreements, 477–479
    in merchandising rights, 364–366
Transfer of copyright, 533–534
    in master purchase agreements, 229–230
Transfer of ownership in master purchase agreements, 226
Transfer price, 528
TRIPS (Trade-Related Aspects of Intellectual Property Rights), 413
Twentieth Century Music Corp. v. Aiken, 494n

UCC (Universal Copyright Convention), 412-413

UMED (Universal Music Enterprises Digital), 560

Union costs limited to those based on payroll, 117

Union scale payment for unrecorded sides, 133

United Kingdom, copyright protection in, 428

Universal Copyright Convention (UCC), 412–413

Universal Music Enterprises Digital (UMED), 560

Unrecorded masters in recording agreements, 130–134

Unrecorded sides, union scale payment for, 133

Unrecouped balance, advances reduced by, 111

Urantia Foundation v. Maaherra, 531

USNRC Sales (Sales of Albums through Normal Retail Channels in the United States), 70–71, 216

VARA (Visual Artists Rights Act), 503–504

Variable pricing, 63

Variable rates, 198–199

Vereniging Bureau voor Muziek Auteursrecht (BUMA), 414

Video
  guaranteed, 259–261
  production cost recoupment in, 261, 262

Video and DVD, 255–268
  cross-collateralization in, 261
  definitions, 255–257
  music rights for, 265–268
  production costs in, 261–262
  video rights and, 257–259
  video royalties in, 263–265

Video clip, 256

Video device, 256

Video Performance Limited (VPL), 416

Video rights, video and DVD and, 257–259

Video royalties in video and DVD, 263–265

Video streaming, 398

Videogram, 256

Vinyl royalty rate, 89

Visual Artists Rights Act (VARA), 503–504

VPL (Video Performance Limited), 416

Waits v. Frito-Lay, Inc., 178n

Warranties and representations
  in distribution agreements, 443–446
  in master purchase agreements, 227–229
  in recording agreements, 153–157
  in songwriters' agreements, 301–304

White v. Samsung Electronics America, Inc., 179n

Wholesale price, 63
  calculation of, 64
  changing, to retail price, 64
  retail price or, 63–65

WIPO (World Intellectual Property Organization), 413

Work for hire, 497, 530–532

World Intellectual Property Organization (WIPO), 413

World Trade Organization (WTO), 413

Writer as recording artist in songwriters' agreements, 274–277

WTO (World Trade Organization), 413

Zacchini v. Scripps-Howard Broadcasting Co., 178n